W9-CAD-146

HOME REPAIR AND MAINTENANCE

by
Jack M. Landers
Chairperson
Department of Manufacturing and Construction
Central Missouri State University
Warrensburg, Missouri

Publisher
THE GOODHEART-WILLCOX COMPANY, INC.
Tinley Park, Illinois

Library of Congress Catalog Card Number 95-46732
International Standard Book Number 1-56637-273-9

4 5 6 7 8 9 10   96   00 99

Library of Congress Cataloging in Publication Data

Landers, Jack M.
  Home repair and maintenance / by Jack M. Landers.

    p.   cm.
  Includes index.
  ISBN 1-56637-273-9
  1. Dwellings--Maintenance and repair--
  Amateurs' manuals.
  I. Title.
  TH4817.3.L359   1996
  643'.7--dc20   95-46732
                                          CIP

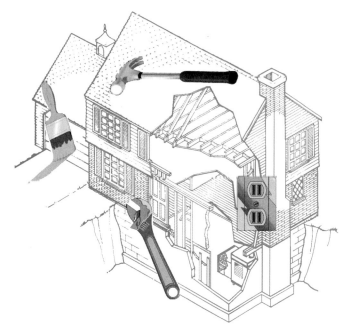

INTRODUCTION

HOME REPAIR AND MAINTENANCE provides you with all the basic information needed to understand and use hand tools, power tools, fasteners, and assorted building materials for the repair and maintenance of you home. You will gain knowledge of the structure and the various systems that need to be repaired or maintained.

HOME REPAIR AND MAINTENANCE teaches you the skills and techniques used in carpentry, masonry, plumbing, electricity, and other building trades. The book provides in-depth coverage of topics such as repair of roofs, gutters, walls, floors, concrete, furniture, water and waste systems, electrical wiring systems, heating and cooling systems, and insulation. Proper maintenance of all housing systems is stressed to prevent costly repairs in the future.

HOME REPAIR AND MAINTENANCE can improve your ability to repair and maintain a residential structure and its systems. Numerous illustrations and easy-to-read text make this book ideal for the home owner or the student.

HOME REPAIR AND MAINTENANCE can provide the basis for an exciting career path. Through the study and mastery of skills related to the technology of keeping an efficient home, you will find a sufficient number of trades and professions to develop a career path. Studying the skills and knowledge associated with home maintenance can be the basis for a career. At the end of a number of chapters, a list of related careers are provided. Those careers are discussed in further detail in Chapter 34 of this text. This chapter also discusses the process of a career search.

Jack M. Landers

CONTENTS

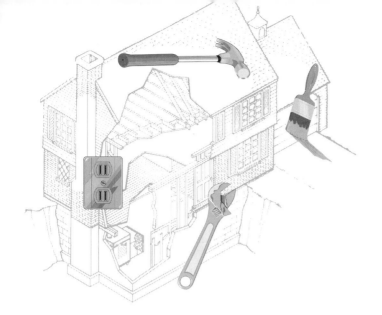

This chapter gives the reasons for doing your own home maintenance work.

After reading the chapter you will be able to:
  List the maintenance jobs needed most often.
  Describe the benefits of home maintenance.

Homes provide one of the basic physical needs called SHELTER. Most people are not very well adapted to earth's extreme climatic conditions. From the cold polar regions to the hot tropics, people have found life hostile without proper shelter. However, with adequate shelter people have flourished in all climates.

Primitive people found shelter in natural caves. Since the time of caves various natural materials have been used to make shelters. Early settlers built shelters of materials found locally. Log cabins were built of timbers from the surrounding forests. The sod house of the prairie and the igloo of the Eskimo were each made from the most common local resource. Each one served its owner well.

Much progress has been made in building materials and methods. Fig. 1-1 shows the use of

Fig. 1-1. This apartment complex uses building materials wisely. Economy is important in a world of limited resources. (Western Wood Products Assoc.)

7

efficient construction methods.

Today the ranch, split level, Cape Cod, apartment, townhouse and condominium each provide shelter in its own way, Fig. 1-2. The structures we use for shelter take many shapes. Generally, structures called HOUSES are made up of such components as walls, roofs, floors, windows, and doors. Houses are buildings, while HOMES are structures occupied by people who share activities.

The poet Edgar A. Guest once wrote ''. . . it takes a heap of living to make a house a home.''

The home means many things to many people. The home means much more than just shelter. To the typical family, the home is a place to:
- Prepare and eat meals.
- Sleep and rest.
- Pass idle and restful time.
- Store and display life's momentos.
- Receive and entertain friends and guests.
- Raise and educate a family.

The home serves as an expression of the occupant's likes. It often reveals a personality. Occupants generally take great pride in establishing a home. They carefully choose the interior wall color or texture, exterior structural design, and appointments and furnishings. Notice the harmony in Fig. 1-3. The home may allow occupants to create a special world. For example, a person who has a lifelong dream of being a sea captain may design and furnish a home with nautical appointments.

Fig. 1-3. Homemakers use a variety of geometric shapes, colors, textures, and styles to help create pleasing and desirable surroundings. The heating and lighting systems used here require periodic maintenance. (NMC/Focal Point)

Regardless of the design of the home, the primary purpose remains shelter. Most of the homes of today are products of 20th century technology. Today, almost every household in America is lighted electrically. Today, most houses have the comforts of piped fresh water, sewerage (drainage) systems, and environment controls.

Today, houses are designed and built to fit the personal preferences and needs of the owner. The owner's needs are a very large factor in housing design. For example, disabled individual have very different needs than others. See Fig. 1-4.

The accessibility to all aspects of the house must be one of the primary considerations of design. Family housing must not discriminate against people with disabilities. Care must be taken when designing such items as entrances, kitchens, and bathrooms. These items and many more are addressed in the Federal Fair Housing Act (FFHA) of 1988. These same items for public facilities are addressed in the American with Disabilities Act (ADA) of 1990.

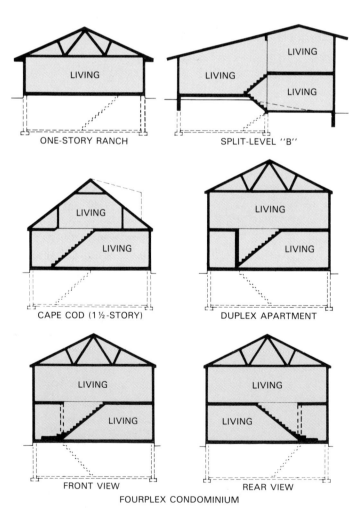

ONE-STORY RANCH

SPLIT-LEVEL ''B''

CAPE COD (1½-STORY)

DUPLEX APARTMENT

FRONT VIEW

REAR VIEW

FOURPLEX CONDOMINIUM

Fig. 1-2. There are many types of modern homes. Each provides shelter *if* maintained. Where can masonry skills be used in the homes shown here? Where can carpentry skills be used?

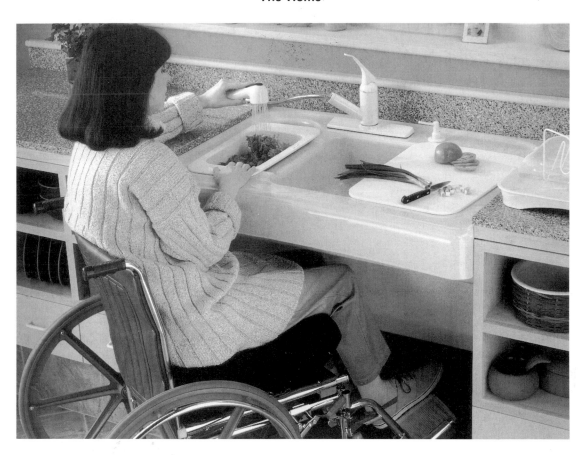

Fig. 1-4. Family housing must not discriminate against people with disabilities. The design of this kitchen sink allows for easy accessibility for people with disabilities. Refer to the Federal Fair Housing Act (FFHA) of 1988 for more information on such items.

Fig. 1-5. To make living easier, people use machines to do many household tasks. Several appliances used in this kitchen do such things as wash dishes, compact garbage, open cans, cook food and store food. (KitchenAid)

As a result of the many laborsaving appliances such as dishwashers, Fig. 1-5, garbage disposals, laundry appliances, and microwave ovens, the home uses many forms of energy. The home depends largely on energy in the form of electricity, gas, and/or oil. Energy is a natural resource which is rapidly dwindling. If the homemaker understands the energy use of the home, vast savings of this natural resource can be realized. Savings are helpful both to the family budget, and to the world supply of energy.

The home of today is a complex unit, Fig. 1-6. The structural, mechanical, and electrical parts need constant maintenance and repair. For the average homemaker this can become a major drain on the family income. The initial purchase of the home is probably the largest single investment the family will make. The maintenance and repair of this investment is the reason for this book. Succeeding chapters make it possible to avoid some professional labor costs. For example, furnace maintenance is easy if the step-by-step procedures of this book are followed. Understand that some maintenance details should be completed by qualified persons, experienced and trained in such areas. However, much of the maintenance required

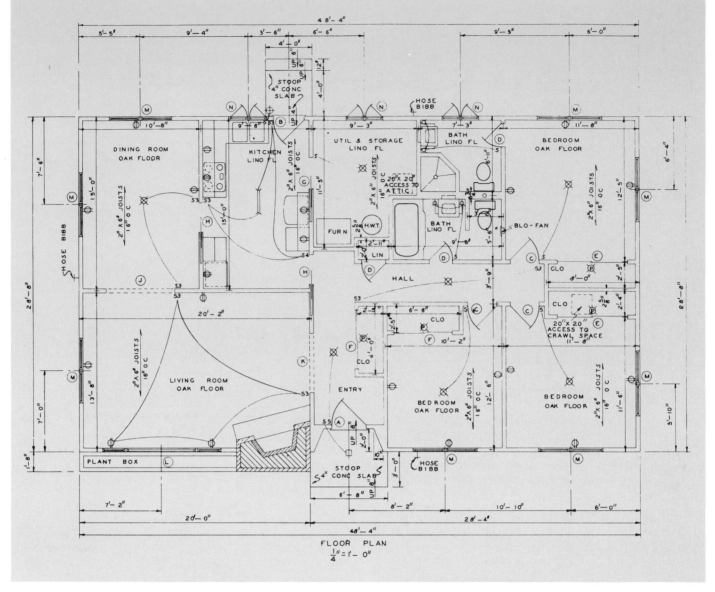

Fig. 1-6. There are many parts of the modern home. This floor plan shows a furnace, kitchen appliances, lavatory fixtures, walls, and floor materials. Repair of these items can often be done by the homeowner. (L.F. Garlinghouse Co.)

by the home can be done by the homeowner resulting in the saving of many dollars.

There are other reasons for learning to make home repairs. The job will be done just the way the occupant wants it done. The repairs can be scheduled for the most convenient times. Finally, learning how things work can help prevent expensive repairs. The homeowner will then know which home appliances need periodic cleaning and oiling to prevent breakdowns.

FUTURE HOMES

Future homes may include the integration of computer systems. Many of the mechanical, electrical, energy, and communication systems of the "smart homes" will be controlled from a single touch display screen, Fig. 1-7. Appliances may be operated from anywhere in the house with a simple wall switch, touch-tone phone, or remote con-

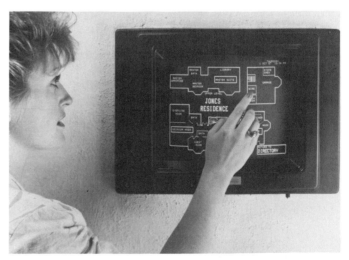

Fig. 1-7. Computers will help organize the future home. They will keep track of information needed to maintain the home. For example, an alarm may mean that it is time to clean the furnace filter. (Unity Systems)

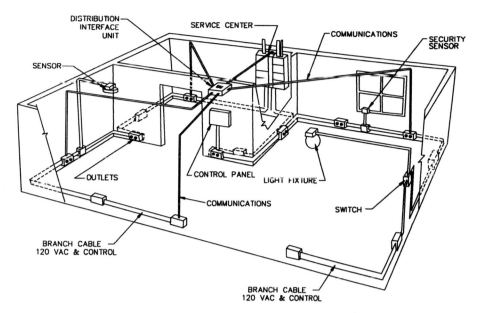

Fig. 1-8. "Smart homes" will revolutionize the current wiring systems of homes. (SMART HOUSE, L.P.)

trol. Some systems even allow the homeowner to operate the appliances through voice activation. The average homeowner will not be responsible for repair and maintenance of the computer-integrated system. However, information supplied by the computer may indicate repairs and maintenance that must be made to the mechanical, electrical, energy, or communication systems.

Systems of the "smart home" will also differ from systems that are presently installed. See Fig. 1-8. "Smart homes," such as those produced by SMART HOUSE, L.P., eliminate the need for the confusing network of wiring generally associated with current wiring systems. In many cases, sensors will be placed throughout the "smart home" to monitor the systems. The sensor then relays the information to a central service center where appropriate adjustments are made.

"Smart homes" may also be used to monitor security control systems. For example, doors and windows may be locked from remote locations in the home. In addition, "smart homes" may be adapted to fit the needs of everyone. A video recorder and playback unit may be plugged into almost any outlet in the house and the tape may be viewed in another room.

TEST YOUR KNOWLEDGE — CHAPTER 1

1. A home provides shelter only if it is:
   a. large.
   b. built of modern materials.
   c. maintained.
   d. facing south.

2. Appliances are often designed for easy _____ .

3. List three benefits of home repair when compared to professional services.

4. The easiest way to avoid major repairs is to follow the manufacturer's _____ _____ _____.

KNOW THESE TERMS

Maintenance, shelter, sewerage, fresh water, duplex, apartment, appliances.

SUGGESTED ACTIVITIES

Read the OWNER'S MANUAL for some of your home appliances. Make a chart showing the date the appliance was last cleaned or oiled. Then determine the next date when it should be checked. Put these dates on the chart. Keep the chart handy.

Write a brief paper on "What the Home Means to Me." Discuss your home with your parents, grandparents, friends and neighbors, to help you come to a conclusion about the home. List all the important aspects that will make up your home.

What are the basic requirements expected in a home for your future family? Define the requirements for sleeping, food preparation, dining, relaxing, entertainment, and business.

With a sketch pad, sketch a floor plan for your future home and the needs you have defined above.

2

HOME SAFETY

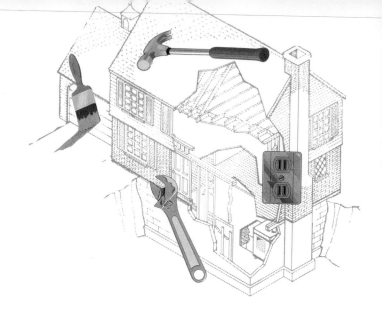

This chapter deals with the causes of accidents and tells how to prevent them.

After studying this chapter you will be able to:
- Describe a common myth about accidents.
- State what work habits promote safety.
- Explain the possible hazards of working with ladders and tools, electrical devices, and chemicals.
- List some safety aids everyone should have in their home.

When we look at types of accidents, the number of home accidents is surprisingly large. These can be minor, serious, and even fatal. Home accidents include those accidents that occur in the home and on the home premises to occupants, guests, and trespassers.

Accidents may occur during home maintenance due to careless procedures or an unsafe tool, Fig. 2-1. Trouble may be due to poor use of equipment or materials when making repairs. Accidents might injure the home mechanic or they might harm the bystander. Safety is worth practicing. It is the responsibility of the worker to understand the likely causes of home accidents and the general remedies for accident prevention.

The following are reasons for working safely:
1. To protect life.
2. To avoid injury.
3. To preserve one's professional talent.
4. To avoid costly material loss.
5. To avoid loss of time.
6. To avoid inconvenience.

The word "accident" must be more clearly defined. The only true accident is one caused by natural forces. Those involving human actions are not true accidents. All such mishaps are completely preventable. Accidents do not happen, they are made. It is a myth that they just happen. One hundred percent effort is needed at every step of a job to be certain of safety. To prevent surprises, simply do each tiny step 100% correct.

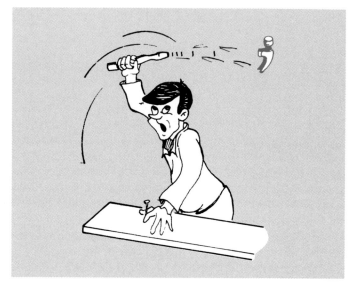

Fig. 2-1. Before using a tool, inspect it for hazards. Buy high quality tools. Keep them in good condition.
(Hand Tools Institute)

From this point, let's look at common accidents and identify some prevention procedures. For example, carpenters from time to time hit their fingers with the hammer. Accidents due to lack of skill cannot be avoided. Accidents due to lack of proper work attitude are avoidable. Poor work habits are obvious from a cluttered work area as in Fig. 2-2. A clean workplace saves effort and saves the worker and any bystanders from injury.

LIFTING

Lifting a heavy object improperly can injure your back. Keep your back upright when lifting objects. Let your legs do all the work.

STRAIGHT LADDERS

Ladder accidents are common to the home maintenance person. The following steps are

Fig. 2-2. Many accidents can be prevented simply by good housekeeping practices. Always store unused materials and tools properly.

necessary for safe use of straight ladders.

1. Only buy a ladder with non-skid footing, Fig. 2-3.
2. Inspect after buying and before using.
3. Never climb a damaged ladder.
4. Check working parts of extension type ladders for loose rivets, balls, rope, or cables before climbing.
5. Set straight or extension ladders at 75½ degrees, Fig. 2-4. Make the distance from base to top support four times the horizontal distance from ladder base to the support.
6. Raise and lower a ladder safely, as shown in Fig. 2-5.
7. Set ladder on firm level ground. Do not lean it sideways.
8. Never use ladder on snow or ice.
9. Keep rungs free from wet paint, mud, snow, grease, or other slippery materials.
10. Never "walk" or jog ladder while standing on it.
11. Never place the ladder in front of a door without locking the door.

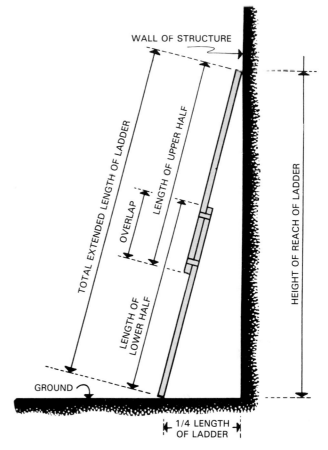

Fig. 2-4. The correct way to position a ladder is shown here. Arrange a ladder so that the distance between the ladder base and the wall foundation is 1/4 of the total extended length of the ladder.

Fig. 2-3. Look for ladder safety shoes like these when buying a ladder. If any ladders you already own do not have safety shoes, then be more careful using them.

Fig. 2-5. To raise a ladder, rest the base at the foundation. Then raise the top end and walk forward under the ladder. Reverse these steps to lower the ladder.

12. Always mount ladder from directly in front.
13. Never mount from side or step from one ladder to another.
14. Never stand above the third rung from the top.
15. Always remember to keep ladders away from overhead electrical power lines. This includes wooden ladders.
16. Do not overreach ladder, always keep belt buckle inside ladder side rails.
17. Never use ladder in high winds.
18. Never overload a ladder; ladders are designed for certain load-carrying capacities (weight ratings such as 200, 250, or 300 pounds).
19. Only one person on a ladder at a time.
20. Never use a ladder when in poor health or under medication.

STEPLADDERS

When work must be done inside the home, a stepladder is convenient. A stepladder is a portable self-supporting ladder which is not adjustable in length, Fig. 2-6. A stepladder has flat steps, a hinged back and a rack for pails. It also has a top plate. Never stand on the top plate or support any of your weight on the pail rack. Take care when opening and closing a ladder. Good quality stepladders are equipped with steel safety spreaders, designed so they will not injure the hands when opening and closing the ladder.

TOOLS

Tools are also involved in mechanically related accidents. Learn the proper way to use tools with sharp cutting edges, such as knives, chisels, and planes. Always respect the cutting edge tools for the potential hazard they are. Keep all cutting tools sharpened, as suggested in Fig. 2-7. A dull tool forces you to push harder, leading to slippage.

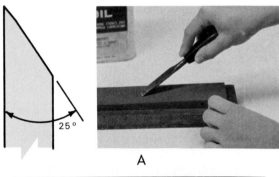

A

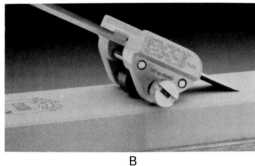

B

Fig. 2-7. A — Hone a wood chisel blade on an oilstone. If this is not enough, first grind the chisel to a 25° angle as shown. Then hone the tip at the same angle. Keep tools sharp to make work easier and safer. B — A honing jig helps produce a clean edge. (Woodcraft Supply Corp.)

When using any tool, cutting tool or not, always be prepared for the unexpected. This is especially true if you are using a power tool like that shown in Fig. 2-8. Be careful when a force other than your own is exerted. Improper use can channel this force in an unexpected direction. Never start cutting with a power saw until the blade is up to full speed. Do not remove the saw until the blade has stopped.

An extremely bad hazard of the power saw is that the saw continually changes position. A cut may begin without immediate harm, but then the worker

Fig. 2-6. Each leg of a stepladder should be set firmly in a level position before attempting to climb on the steps. Periodically check wooden stepladders for hairline cracks. It is best not to build your own stepladder.

Fig. 2-8. There is no reason to fear a power tool which is in good condition. Learn to use the portable power saw by making simple end cuts. Notice that the saw has a blade guard for safety of the operator and protection of the cutting edge. (Black and Decker)

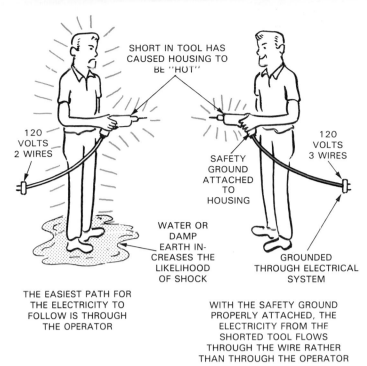

SHORT IN TOOL HAS CAUSED HOUSING TO BE "HOT"

120 VOLTS 2 WIRES

120 VOLTS 3 WIRES

SAFETY GROUND ATTACHED TO HOUSING

WATER OR DAMP EARTH INCREASES THE LIKELIHOOD OF SHOCK

GROUNDED THROUGH ELECTRICAL SYSTEM

THE EASIEST PATH FOR THE ELECTRICITY TO FOLLOW IS THROUGH THE OPERATOR

WITH THE SAFETY GROUND PROPERLY ATTACHED, THE ELECTRICITY FROM THE SHORTED TOOL FLOWS THROUGH THE WIRE RATHER THAN THROUGH THE OPERATOR

Fig. 2-10. Grounded tools provide safety for the operator.

can be surprised. NEVER place hands under the workpiece.

ELECTRICITY

Electricity is an unseen force which can be misdirected in many ways. The main hazards with electricity are electrocution and overheating. First the homeowner should understand thoroughly the basic principles of electricity and its function in household appliances. Know the electrical codes before attempting to alter or change the electrical system of your home.

Make periodic electrical inspections of all electrical appliances, Fig. 2-9. Check any power tool used for home maintenance. Look for unsafe electrical conditions, broken or exposed wires.

Never operate electrical tools near water or moist areas. If used outdoors, use only an outdoor exten-

sion cord. If a power tool is not DOUBLE-INSULATED, it must be properly GROUNDED, meaning it must have a three-prong plug. The correct use of the third prong is shown in Fig. 2-10. A Ground Fault Circuit Interrupter is also recommended. It will turn off the power at the first sign of trouble.

One caution deserves repeating. Keep the work area clean. A cluttered area is especially dangerous when electrical cords are used. Walking on them can make them unsafe. Be careful not to cut cords with power tools. Always know where the power cord is.

A very common mistake in using electricity is to add a branch plug to a duplex outlet for additional cords, as shown in Fig. 2-11. This overloads the branch. Overloaded electrical wires will overheat,

Fig. 2-9. Close inspection of electrical cords may prevent fire or electrical shock. Especially check the cord ends, since they get the most wear. Replace cords rather than splicing them.

Fig. 2-11. There are too many appliance cords at this outlet. A branch plug is designed chiefly for clocks and night lights. A large appliance easily overloads a circuit and could cause fire or damage to the appliance.

possibly causing fire. The branch plug also underfeeds the appliance which can damage it.

Electricity is a very useful and helpful item. Use it wisely and safely.

FIRE

When kept under control, fire is beneficial. Out of control, fire can be painful, even fatal and very costly. Fire can consume a home in just a matter of a very few minutes. It is the homeowner's challenge to prevent the uncontrolled disaster from happening.

Many sources of heat sufficient to kindle fire are found within the home. The kitchen range and oven, the heating system, domestic hot water system, and the fireplace must be maintained for safety. Laundry equipment, especially the clothes dryer, can overheat. The electrical system itself can be a fire hazard. These are only possibilities. It is more important to avoid improper storage of a variety of materials, solvents, paints, and cleaning and cooking oils. Also, piled waste and oily rags can spontaneously ignite and become open flame, Fig. 2-12. Do not store combustible materials close to an open flame, for example, the gas furnace and hot water heater. Also keep soldering equipment out of reach of small children.

Fire extinguishers should be kept in every home. They should be easy to reach as in Fig. 2-13. Some extinguishing agents for the home are cheap and easily contrived, for example, buckets of water and sand. Each extinguishing agent is best for one class of fires. Water is excellent for most fires except electrical fires or grease and oil fires. Most people are aware of the extinguishing qualities of baking soda. Baking soda can successfully put out small kitchen fires.

Fig. 2-13. A home fire extinguisher is inexpensive and readily available. Place it in a convenient area. Show each family member how to use the fire extinguisher.

The burning process is promoted by the addition of oxygen; when the proportion of oxygen in the air falls from a normal of 21 percent to less than 15 percent, the burning subsides. However, if the material remains hot, the fire may resume when the oxygen level rises to 21 percent again. Be sure that the area is completely cold before leaving it unwatched. It is always a good idea for the fire department to inspect the area even if you have put out the fire yourself.

Many portable fire extinguishers are available for purchase and use in the home. To be effective, portable fire extinguishers must be used on the intended class of fire. Fires are classified as follows:

Class A   Fires of ordinary combustible materials such as wood, paper, cloth, and rubber.

Class B   Fires of flammable liquids, gases, and grease.

Class C   Electrical fires.

Class D   Fires of combustible metals such as magnesium, titanium, zirconium, sodium, and potassium. (These are not likely to be found around the house.)

The correct class of fire for each fire extinguisher is on the label. Read the directions on each fire extinguisher. If you have more than one type, organize them for the quickest use.

CHEMICALS

Homeowners have a large number of chemical materials to use. Fig. 2-14 shows chemical materials to treat rose rust and kill weeds, poisons

Fig. 2-12. Spontaneous combustion does not need a spark of any kind. Suppose a spontaneous fire starts at night, long after work-related accidents "should" occur? Always store paint-soaked rags in fireproof containers.

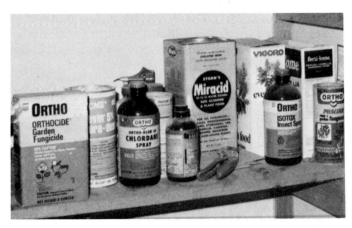

Fig. 2-14. Lawn and garden chemicals should be stored in one common space away from the reach of children. Never store chemicals in any kind of beverage containers.

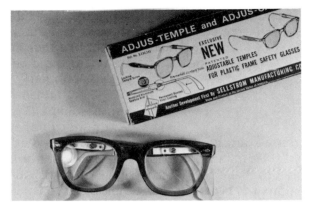

Fig. 2-15. Approved safety glasses are a minor cost to assure eye safety. Safety glasses are made of a shatterproof material such as plastic. Some styles fit easily over ordinary eyeglass frames.

to keep insects away from plants, and fertilizers to encourage plant growth.

Chemicals also serve as cleaning agents around the house. The home maintenance specialists may use many kinds of chemicals, paints, finishes, polishes, and waxes. Other chemicals, such as medicine and drugs, are as dangerous if misused as they are helpful when used as directed.

Chemicals of many descriptions are necessary around the home. It is the homeowner's responsiblity to properly store these items. Chemicals must be kept out of the hands of small children.

Fig. 2-16. Noise mufflers, such as earplugs, should be used when loud sound will be produced, such as when cutting with power saws. Don't assume you have avoided ear damage simply because you don't notice any change.

SAFE CLOTHING

Proper work clothes are important for safety. Be aware of the potential danger of each home maintenance job. All rings should be removed from fingers before working with power tools and with electricity. Never wear ties or torn clothing while working with power tools, and keep hair short or out of the way. Wear approved SAFETY GLASSES, Fig. 2-15, even if you already wear eyeglasses. Ordinary eyeglasses can shatter, causing loss of an eye. Gloves are a good idea if they are appropriate for the job. Industrial safety inspectors recommend ear plugs, Fig. 2-16, or ear muffs to prevent hearing loss. Without ear protection, there will be an almost unnoticeable decrease in hearing ability in loud areas.

SAFETY TIPS

Know your own limitations. Never try to do more than you can do safely. Asking for help is no disgrace compared to risking injury.

To prepare for the day an accident does occur, always have a First Aid Kit in a convenient, specified place in the home. Take the time to learn some of the simplest or most important first aid steps.

BUILDING CODES

Building codes are the common regulations for providing housing for human habitation. The codes address design, construction practices, and structural materials and their uses. The underlying purpose is to provide places of residence that are safe and healthful for its occupants. There is a wide range of building codes, which include not only housing, but also businesses, industries, sports complexes, transportation facilities, and all other types of structures. These codes are administered by some agency at the local level of government. The municipalities take considerable interest in maintaining a safe and healthful environment for the general population.

TEST YOUR KNOWLEDGE — CHAPTER 2

1. Accidents do not happen, they are _____ .
2. A good work habit to learn is to:
   a. Fear the dangers of working.
   b. Keep the workplace clean.
   c. Jump quickly.
   d. Find your own uses for tools.
3. When lifting heavy objects:
   a. Wait until daylight.
   b. Use your back as a lever.
   c. Keep your back upright.
   d. Wear eye protection.
4. Set up straight ladders so that the distance from the base to the top support is about _____ times as large as the horizontal distance from the ladder base to the building.
5. To get from one ladder to another nearby:
   a. Step across.
   b. Place a frame between them.
   c. Tilt the ladders closer together before crossing.
   d. Climb down and begin again.
6. A wooden ladder is safe to use near electrical power lines. True or False?
7. Explain how it is possible for a dull cutting tool to be more dangerous than a sharp tool.

8. _____ an electrical tool protects the operator if the tool has a short circuit.
9. Store oil rags in a _____ container.
10. An electrical fire should be put out only with an extinguisher intended for a _____ fire.
11. Do not store _____ in food or drink containers.
12. Which of these should be removed from fingers before working with power tools or electricity?
    a. Natural oils
    b. Rings
    c. Gloves
13. Keep a First Aid Kit in a:
    a. Cool, dry place.
    b. Convenient place.
    c. Specified place.
    d. Both b and c.

KNOW THESE TERMS

Hazards, mechanic, no-skid, honing, stepladder, spontaneous combustion, safety.

SUGGESTED ACTIVITY

Conduct a Safety Audit of your home. After reading Chapter 2, identify and list the possible safety hazards in your home.

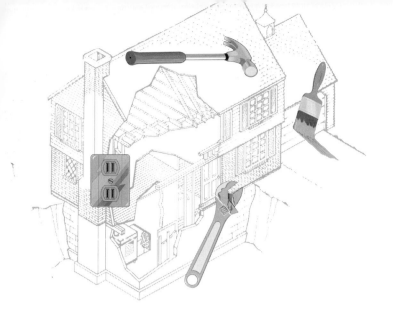

FIRST AID STEPS

BLEEDING

To Stop Severe Bleeding:

Apply direct pressure to the wound with pad or compresses. Use any clean cloth available. Don't remove pad to see if bleeding has stopped. Call paramedics or hospital.

JOHNSON & JOHNSON

Arm or Leg Wound:

Besides applying direct pressure, raise limb with pillows, a rolled-up coat, or a piece of furniture.

If pressure pad doesn't stop the bleeding, use your fingers or heel of your hand to press hard at pressure points shown here:

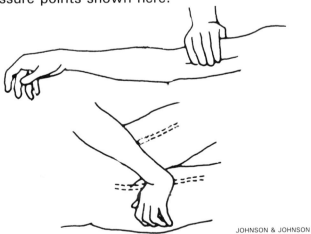

JOHNSON & JOHNSON

ELECTRIC SHOCK

Turn off electric power.

To remove victim from wire, use something absolutely dry—a broom handle, rope, a loop made from a dry shirt, or a looped belt.

If victim is not breathing, begin artificial breathing immediately. Don't stop until the victim is breathing well or help arrives. Call hospital or paramedics.

EYE INJURY CAUSED BY CHEMICAL

A DELAY EVEN OF SECONDS MAY GREATLY INCREASE AMOUNT OF INJURY.

Hold eyelids open and promptly rinse eyes with gentle stream of warm water for at least 15 minutes. Take victim to an eye specialist or to hospital.

Do not use eye cup.

Do not use eyedrops or drugs. They may increase injury.

SKIN INJURY FROM CHEMICAL

Flush skin with plenty of water. Follow with soap and water.

Cover area with loose, clean cloth.

Do not use ointments or grease (butter or margarine).

BURNS

If skin is broken, do not touch it. Wrap with loose sterile gauze and call paramedics or doctor.

Do not remove clothing if it is stuck to the skin.

Small burns can be immersed in cold water or cooled with ice. Wrap with sterile gauze.

Do not use grease or ointments.

Do not use cloth with loose fibers.

FRACTURES

For all kinds of bone fractures, keep the area from moving. Apply splints if the victim must be moved. Get professional medical help.

PUNCTURE WOUNDS

A puncture wound or dirty wound should be seen by a doctor immediately. An injection against tetanus may be needed.

FOREIGN OBJECTS IN EYE

If object is under upper lid, grasp eyelashes and pull upper eyelid forward and down over lower lid so object may stick to it.

If object is under lower lid, pull down lower lid and wipe off speck gently. Use **moistened** sterile gauze, **moistened** cotton-tipped applicator, or **moistened** tip of clean handkerchief.

Warning: If eye is scratched, or if object is in or on the pupil, tape gauze over eye. Consult a doctor.

POISONING

Call poison center or a physician immediately.

Do not induce vomiting if the poison is corrosive (acid or lye) or petroleum based. Give milk or water.

If the poison is not corrosive, induce vomiting if physician advises.

Save samples of poison and of vomitus for examination by physician.

FIRST AID EQUIPMENT

First Aid treatment can be given more quickly if a First Aid Kit is available, Fig. 3-1. This kit should contain the following items:

1. Several packages of sterile gauze squares 2 x 2 and 4 x 4 in. (50 x 50mm and 100 x 100mm).
2. A roll of 1 in. (25 mm) wide sterile gauze.
3. A roll of adhesive tape.
4. A box of adhesive bandages.
5. A pair of bandage scissors.
6. A package of sterile cotton applicators.
7. A pair of tweezers.
8. A bottle of mild antiseptic.
9. One 2 1/2 in. (62 mm) elastic bandage.
10. Several capsules of aromatic spirits of ammonia.
11. Instruction booklet.

Be able to recognize these items. Periodically renew the contents of the kit.

TEST YOUR KNOWLEDGE — CHAPTER 3

1. To stop severe bleeding, apply _____ to the wound.

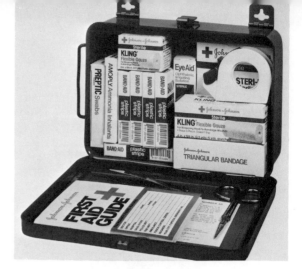

Fig. 3-1. A designated cabinet for the sanitary storage of First Aid supplies should be kept in every home. Do not use a common medicine cabinet for this purpose. (Johnson and Johnson)

2. Bleeding from an arm or leg wound is stopped by pressing hard on a _____ _____.
3. Which two of the following items could be used to remove a victim of electrical shock from the source of current?
   a. Garden hose.
   b. Dry cardboard box.
   c. Dry broom handle.
   d. Your foot.
4. In case of chemical injury to the eye, how _____ you do something is more important than how you do it.
5. Treat severe burns with grease or ointments. True or False?
6. It is important to keep a fractured bone from _____ .
7. The main problem with a puncture wound is:
   a. Staphylococcus infection.
   b. Pain.
   c. The difficulty in cleaning it.
   d. Tetanus infection.
8. If a corrosive substance like acid or lye is swallowed, do not _____ _____ .
9. An instruction booklet is the most important part of a _____ _____ _____ .

KNOW THESE TERMS

Pressure point, tetanus, corrosive, sanitary, paramedics, fractures, splints.

SUGGESTED ACTIVITY

Locate the First Aid kit in your home. Make a list of all the items in the kit and compare it to list of items in Chapter 3. Identify the items you need to obtain or replace.

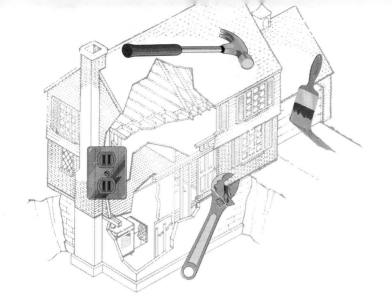

BASIC HAND TOOLS

A variety of tools are used by the home mechanic; many of them
are cutting or shaping tools.   (Stanley Tools)

This chapter describes the hand tools used by the homeowner and discusses some of their uses. Tool care steps are included.

After studying this chapter you will be able to:
- Recognize tools used for measuring, fastening, cutting, drilling, and other jobs.
- Choose the proper tool for an application.
- Decide on a program of tool storage, upkeep, and labeling.

BUYING AND RENTING TOOLS

Suppose you plan to use a tool only once. Consider renting the tool instead of buying it. Many hardware dealers rent individual tools or rent tool kits for the most common repair jobs.

If a tool will be used often, it is best to buy it, and when you purchase tools, buy the best. They cost less than the cheaper tools when you include a hidden expense. Poor tools need replacing again and again. But many firms that make good tools will replace any that are defective. Ask about guarantees before buying.

LEARNING ABOUT TOOLS

Almost everyone has noticed how quickly a professional carpenter, electrician, or plumber puts together a working structure. What we see is speed and economy of movement. But we do not appreciate each clever use of a tool. A clever idea is completely obvious while we are watching someone work, but would we think of it on our own? This chapter will include some of these helpful ideas whenever possible. Try to think of other ideas as each tool is introduced.

MEASURING AND LAYOUT TOOLS

A MEASURING TOOL is any device that determines height, width, length, or levelness. A LAYOUT TOOL is any instrument used to create circles, lines, angles, or to mark a workpiece. Tools the home mechanic will use include: rules, tapes, squares, levels, chalk lines, dividers, center punches, and awls.

The Rule

The folding wood rule, Fig. 4-1, is used to measure across a wide opening. One big advantage is that heights can be measured without needing two people and a ladder. The folding rule is the only rigid scale which can be put in your pocket.

When measuring horizontal distances with an unsupported rule, the numbers should not face the floor or ceiling. The folding rule can be extended farther if the numbers face to your right or left.

Avoid dropping the folding rule on its end. The joints may loosen enough to cause visible errors. Every joint offset adds up over several feet.

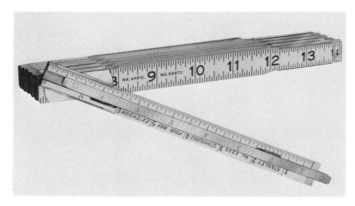

Fig. 4-1. This folding wood rule has a metal sliding extension. The slide can be used to take internal measurements. (Stanley Tools)

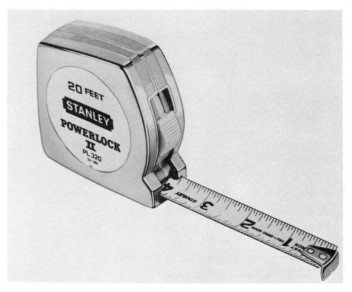

Fig. 4-2. This steel measuring tape will retract automatically for quick handling. The tape remains out until the lock button is raised. (Stanley Tools)

Dirt and rough joint surfaces will make it difficult to fold the rule. Keep the joints protected by applying graphite or silicone lubricant at regular intervals. Do not use common oil since it will attract dirt.

Tapes

The steel tape measure, Fig. 4-2, is the most compact general purpose length scale. Workers prefer the tape rule because it is accurate and it speeds up the measurement job. A spring inside the case rolls up the tape quickly.

On the end of the tape is a hook to catch the edge of the workpiece. Many tapes have a type of hook called a TRUE ZERO HOOK. The hook can slide a little on its mounting pins. This gives the accuracy of a true zero point whether the hook pulls on the workpiece or pushes on it. The purpose is to allow for the thickness of the hook tab for both ways of measuring.

Steel tape measures are available in different lengths and widths. Lengths ranging from 3 ft. (1 m) to 20 ft. (6 m) are sufficient for home maintenance work. Metric and conventional styles are widely sold. Tape widths range from 1/4 in. (6 mm) to 1 in. (25 mm). The wider tapes are more durable.

A special advantage of the tape measure is its flexibility. The tape can be used to measure along curved surfaces or twisting shapes. Curves as small as the roll in the tape case can be measured.

Care of Tapes

A measuring tape which will not retract with the use of one hand is even more bother than a common measuring stick. A tape must be kept clean, dry, and free of kinks if it is to work smoothly.

Substances the home mechanic must keep away from tapes include: paint, glue, caulking, tar, wall patching compound, and sanding debris. Recall that gritty compounds can travel through the air. This grit will wear away the numbers on the tape during rolling and unrolling.

Tape wear or breakage is often unavoidable. Some manufacturers of the better steel tape measures supply replacement tapes. No special tools will be needed to make the repair.

Squares

A square is used to lay out an accurate angle. A square is also a test gauge for checking an existing part.

The smallest square, the try square, is shown in Fig. 4-3. The try square is used to "try" the squareness of surfaces and edges and to lay out lines at right angles to an edge. Some can check a 45 ° angle. Try squares are available with blades 6 to 12 in. (15 to 31 cm) long. Handles are of metal or wood (usually brass-trimmed).

Fig. 4-3. A try square is small enough to carry in an apron or belt. This square will test a 90 or 45° angle. Both inside and outside corners can be checked. (Stanley Tools)

Another device for measuring 90 and 45° angles is the combination square, Fig. 4-4. There are two major advantages of the combination square. First, the square can be used when the piece to be checked is near the center of a gap in another surface. The scale of the combination square can extend across the opening after you center the measuring head. The scale of a try square may tip into the hole as you attempt to line up the head. Second, the sliding head of the combination square allows you to use it as a depth gauge.

A combination square is usually 12 in. (31 cm) long. Metric and conventional units are common.

Fig. 4-4. A combination square has a sliding head which is held in place with a thumbscrew. This square has a level vial in the measuring head. There is also a scribing point which is stored at the bottom of the head. (Stanley Tools)

The head of the square almost always has a level vial for easy layout of plumb lines and horizontal lines.

A third square is the carpenter's square, not shown. The carpenter's square is used to lay out roof rafters and stair framing. The home mechanic will need it only for projects involving large objects.

The squares require a little care. If a try square is dropped, it may not keep its accuracy. This is more pronounced than for the combination square, since the combination square relies on a wide sliding area.

Keep the combination square away from electrical sources or the parts may be welded together.

To maintain steel surfaces, some tool owners use a lemon oil furniture polish. The lemon oil protects and lubricates without attracting dirt.

The Level

A tool which greatly reduces labor is the level, Fig. 4-5. Many times a level can substitute for rules, tapes, and squares. For example, suppose you know your workbench surface is level. Then you can check the squareness of an entire assembly if you place it correctly on the workbench. A level will then show if each part is square in relation to the base being used.

The level also may be used in a similar way to lay out a new structure. The starting surface may be a floor or ceiling which is known to be level. With

Fig. 4-5. The aluminum level is light and easy to handle. This level has three vials for measuring in different positions. The tube of each vial is slightly curved at the center. (Stanley Tools)

some imagination, and some shims under the level, even angles can be laid out.

Levels are made of wood, aluminum, or magnesium. Wood levels will probably not scratch polished surfaces. If weight is important, magnesium levels are very light. The aluminum level is chosen for most jobs. Levels are available in lengths from 2 to 4 ft. (0.6 to 1.2m).

Levels are rugged and weatherproof, but there are some cautions. Keep oils and solvents away from plastic lenses and moisture seals. Avoid vibration from power saws, since the sound which resonates in the vials may break them. Store a level where it will not twist or bend. In case of breakage, replacement vials are available.

The Chalk Line

The best tool for laying out a long accurate line is a chalk line reel like that in Fig. 4-6. After locating the ends of the line, stretch it very tight, with the line touching the surface. Lift vertically at a point near you and snap the line against the surface. For very long lines, fasten the line at both ends or have someone hold the end down. Place your finger on the middle of the line and then snap each half separately.

Chalk lines are made in lengths from 50 to 100 ft. (15 to 30 m). Some chalk lines can be used as plumb bobs. Additional chalk is available, as is replacement line. Keep the chalk box and fresh chalk dry to prevent clumping.

Dividers

The divider, Fig. 4-7, is used to draw circles and arcs on a workpiece. The divider is usually steel with sharp points which will mark wood or metal. A divider is also used to transfer distances from a sample piece to a workpiece by direct marking. Or a line parallel to an edge can be marked if the divider is moved along that edge.

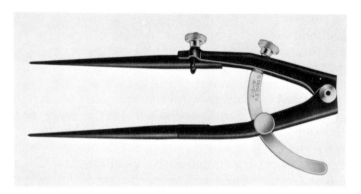

Fig. 4-7. A pair of wing dividers needs no scale. A length or radius is only copied from an original. Some dividers have a removable leg for adjustment and for inserting a pencil. (Stanley Tools)

Sometimes a sheet must fit an irregular edge. Fig. 4-8 shows how to match the edge using a divider which follows every bump.

Dividers are available with spans up to 7 in. (18 cm). Thus a circle with a diameter twice this amount can be drawn.

Trammel points are two steel points on a wood beam. They are used for larger circles.

Sometimes the divider points get dull. They can be sharpened on a grinding wheel. Remember that

Fig. 4-6. The chalk line reel coats the line as it is unwound. The top of the chalk box unscrews when chalk must be added. A locking handle converts this chalk line to a plumb bob. (Stanley Tools)

Fig. 4-8. An uneven surface can be copied onto a sheet with a divider. Cutting along the resulting scribe mark assures a perfect fit against the original.

the divider works best if the two legs are the same length. This is no problem for a divider with a removable leg. For a fixed divider, it will take some practice to control the sharpness and length at the same time. If the divider has flat sides on the inside, you may want to grind only the outside. This is for looks only, since the divider has no scale and will be set by point contact.

The Awl and Center Punch

Two tools used for marking are the awl, Fig. 4-9, and the center punch, Fig. 4-10. The major difference between them is that the awl is not designed for use with a hammer or mallet. Palm pressure alone is used on an awl.

The awl is used to form starter holes for wood screws or nails. It is helpful in leatherwork and upholstery. It is also used for scribing lines or patterns on wood, metal, or plastic. The awl will need very little maintenance.

The center punch locates center points for drilling. It is most often used on metal. The sharp point is placed on the desired location and the punch is struck with a ball peen hammer. A raised area around the center keeps a drill bit from wandering.

FASTENING AND DISASSEMBLY TOOLS

Home structures and appliances are held together with fasteners such as nails, screws, bolts, and staples. A large part of home maintenance involves

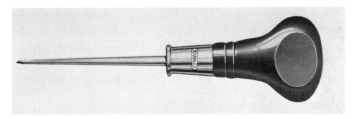

Fig. 4-9. This awl has flat sides to prevent rolling. Do not hit an awl with a hammer or mallet. Hand pressure is sufficient. (Stanley Tools)

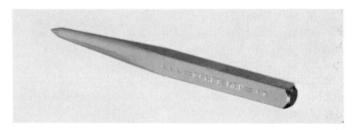

Fig. 4-10. A good center punch is made of tool steel. A center punch can mark on mild steel. (Sears, Craftsman Tools)

removing fasteners and inserting fasteners.

Fastening and disassembly tools are shown in Fig. 4-11. These tools include screwdrivers, hammers, pliers, and wrenches.

The Screwdriver

The screwdriver is the most frequently used tool around the home. Screwdrivers have a variety of

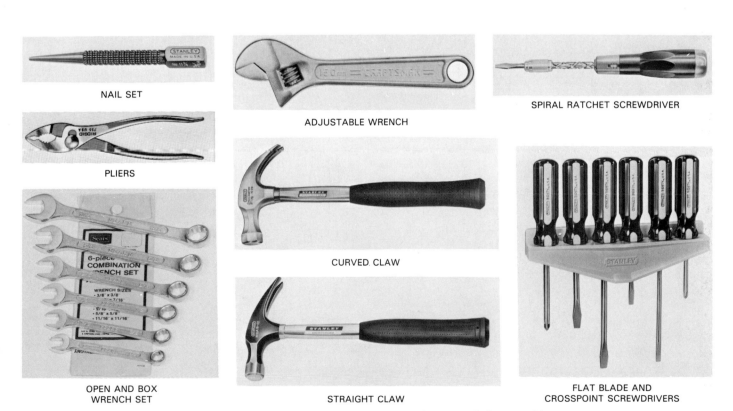

NAIL SET

ADJUSTABLE WRENCH

SPIRAL RATCHET SCREWDRIVER

PLIERS

CURVED CLAW

OPEN AND BOX WRENCH SET

STRAIGHT CLAW

FLAT BLADE AND CROSSPOINT SCREWDRIVERS

Fig. 4-11. The home mechanic uses many tools to fasten and disassemble structures.

different styles to match the screw head styles, Fig. 4-12. The straight blade style for the slotted head screw is most common. The Phillips or crosspoint head is frequently used for screws mounting various hardware items. For example, floor hardware is often installed with the use of the Phillips style screw. Screwdrivers are available in a variety of sizes, given by the length of the blade. Screwdrivers may be purchased in sizes ranging from 3 to 10 in. (7.6 to 25 cm) with the slant and blade size increasing proportionally to the length. Exceptions are the stubby and slender screwdrivers which are designed for difficult locations.

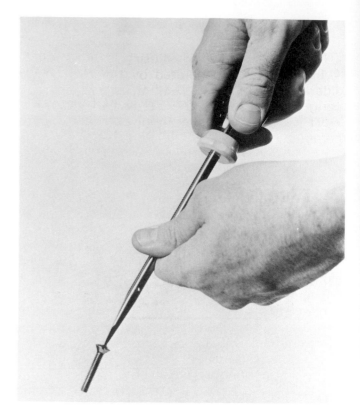

Fig. 4-13. The blade of this screwdriver has two parts. These parts expand or contract at the tip to hold a screw for easy placement. (Stanley Tools)

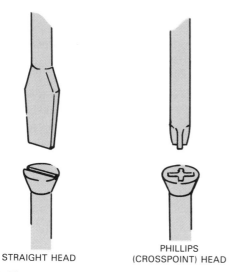

STRAIGHT HEAD   PHILLIPS (CROSSPOINT) HEAD

Fig. 4-12. Two screw head styles found in household items.

Screwdrivers should be matched to screw sizes and types. Screws driven with an undersized screwdriver are likely to receive slot and head damage. The screwdriver itself may also be damaged.

To drive repeated numbers of screws rapidly by hand, a spiral ratchet screwdriver may be your choice. By simply pushing down on the handle the spiral ratchet spins the driver blade. The ratchet can be reversed to remove screws or it can be locked for ordinary use. The ratchet comes with a variety of interchangeable blade sizes and styles.

There are offset screwdrivers for places out of reach. Screw-holding screwdrivers, Fig. 4-13, hold the screwhead to start the screw in difficult positions.

The Hammer

Hammers are available in many different sizes, shapes and for many different uses. For home use, the claw hammer is most practical. Types include either the curved claw or straight claw, which is sometimes called the ripping hammer. The curved claw is for general carpentry work while the straight claw is used for rough work and dismantling, hence the term ripping.

The claw hammer is available in a variety of face styles. The bell face, a slightly curved smooth face, is for general and finish carpentry. The checked face, which has a rough surface, is generally found on hammers for tough carpentry work.

Hammer weights are specified as the weight of the hammer head in ounces. The 7 oz. (200 g) hammer is for very light work while the 13, 16 and 20 oz. (370, 455 and 570 g) are for general carpentry and the 24, 28 and 32 oz. (680, 795 and 910 g) are for very heavy rough work. The 16 oz. (455 g) hammer is most suited to household maintenance jobs. Handles for these hammers are wood or rubber-coated steel. Hammers with handles of fiberglass with rubber grips are available.

The ball-peen hammer, Fig. 4-14, is generally considered the machinist's hammer and is used for metal work. It is used to start the spread of a rivet head.

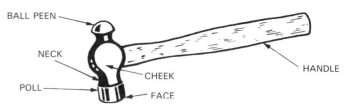

Fig. 4-14. The ball peen hammer is used for metalwork. The round end helps spread a rivet end.

Care must be taken when using any hammer, Fig. 4-15. The force generated by the blow is considerable. A chip shattered from any object can be dangerous. A good safety precaution is to always wear safety glasses or goggles while using a hammer.

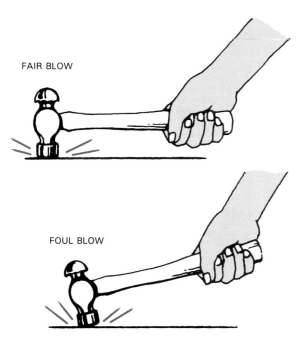

FAIR BLOW

FOUL BLOW

Fig. 4-15. To aim and strike a forceful blow, try to predict the final position of the hammer handle. (Hand Tools Institute)

Pliers

Aside from the screwdriver, a pair of pliers is probably the most frequently used tool. The familiar slip joint pliers is named for the two position pivot that provides a normal and a wide jaw opening. The slip joint pliers is available in many sizes (total length).

Other styles of pliers for special jobs have been designed:

1. The lineman's pliers for heavy-duty wire cutting and splicing.
2. The channel lock with a multi-position jaw that opens to a wide dimension.
3. The long nosed pliers which is used to shape electrical wire for screw terminal connections.

Wrenches

Many types of wrenches are available to tighten or remove nuts and threaded fasteners. The OPEN END WRENCH is used where a wrench of another type cannot be applied over the end of the work, for example on a flared tubing nut. A wrench having a fully enclosed end, called a BOX END WRENCH, is used where there is room to surround the end of the work, for example a nut. Metric sizes are available.

The adjustable wrench is like the open end wrench but adjusts to many sizes. The common openings used are 1/4 in. to 1 in. When using the adjustable wrench, turn it in the direction that the tip of the movable jaw points.

The Hex Key Wrench

The hex key wrench, Fig. 4-16, is sometimes called an Allen wrench. It fits the hexagonal recess in a setscrew.

A tool related to the wrench, the nut driver, is a screwdriver type device with a hexagon socket. It is convenient for small nuts on appliances.

The Nail Set and Punch

The nail set is used to drive the finishing nail head below the surface for later concealment. It is made to suit different size nailhead diameters. Common sizes are 1/32 to 5/32 in. (0.8 to 4 mm) in increments of 1/32 in. (0.8 mm). Nail sets are available in a square head or round head. Self-centering nail sets usually have round heads, while square headed nail sets have the advantage of not rolling when laid on a sloping surface.

Choose a nail set with a smaller tip than the head of the nail to be set. This assures that the resulting depression is no larger than the nail head itself. Putty or wood filling materials may be used to conceal the nail head.

The punch is shaped much like a nail set. The punch is used to knock out a rivet or bolt after drilling the head or flange away. In leatherwork, the punch is used to make holes or to add designs.

Fig. 4-16. The hex key or Allen type wrenches adjust settings or fasten hardware involving setscrews. (Stanley Tools)

CUTTING TOOLS

Many home repair jobs involve cutting out an old part or shaping a new one. Fig. 4-17 shows some of the cutting tools needed for repair work. These tools include saws, chisels, knives, planes, files, and shears.

The Saws

The wood cutting saws are the crosscut saw, ripsaw, backsaw, coping saw, and compass saw. Many plastics and other softer nonwood materials may also be cut with the wood cutting saws. Metals are cut with the hacksaw.

The Crosscut Saw and Ripsaw

The crosscut and ripsaw have the same shape and size. A close look at tooth styles is needed to see the difference between these saws.

The crosscut saw has a tooth style designed for the most efficient cutting of wood perpendicular to the grain, Fig. 4-18. In high quality crosscut saws, the saw blade has many tiny beveled points that cut sharply across the wood fibers. A less expensive saw has a flatter tooth.

For any saw, the quality of cut will depend on the number of the tiny points the saw has for each inch of blade, Fig. 4-19. The number of POINTS PER INCH is often stamped on the saw blade.

A common range for spacing of the points is 7 to 12 per inch (3 to 5 per cm). The saw with a larger number of points will give a much finer cut surface. For average cutting, the 7 or 8 (3 or 3.1) point saw is satisfactory.

To reduce saw friction and blade binding in the kerf (newly opened cut), the manufacturer gives set to the blade. Setting is the practice of alternately bending the points to the right and left of center. Set allows the kerf to be cut wider than the blade, thereby reducing friction. Setting may be needed again after many uses of the saw.

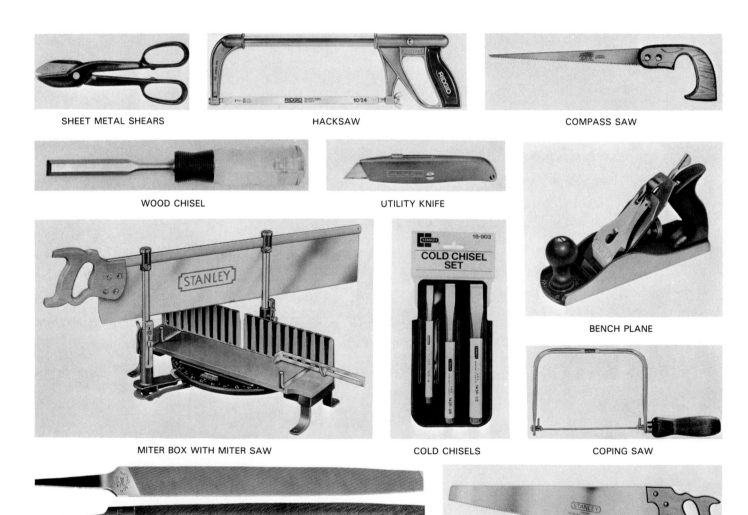

SHEET METAL SHEARS   HACKSAW   COMPASS SAW

WOOD CHISEL   UTILITY KNIFE

MITER BOX WITH MITER SAW   COLD CHISELS   BENCH PLANE   COPING SAW

FILES   CROSS-CUT SAW

Fig. 4-17. Cutting tools prepare home structures and components for fitting together.

(STANLEY TOOLS, RIDGE TOOL CO., SEARS ROEBUCK & CO., AMERICAN SAW AND MFG CO.)

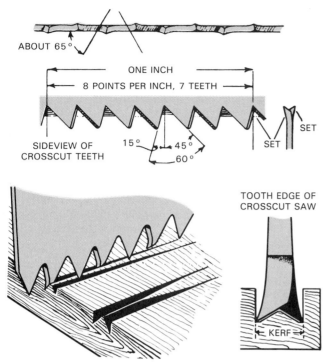

Fig. 4-18. The included angle of the crosscut saw tooth is 60°. Note the bevel ground on each tooth.

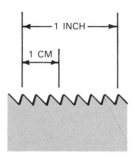

Fig. 4-19. The quality of cut depends on the number and size of teeth a saw blade has. The blade with 8 per in. (3 per cm) is used for most cross-cutting.

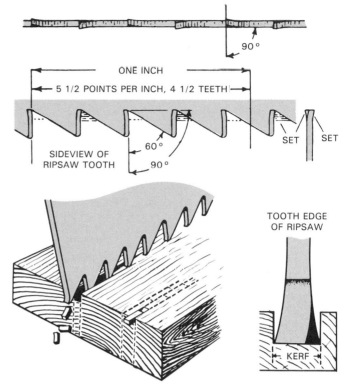

Fig. 4-20. The included angle of the ripsaw is 60°, just as for the crosscut saw. However, the tooth direction is different. Also, no side bevel is ground in the rip tooth.

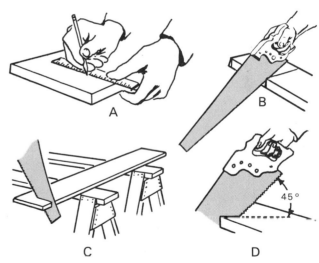

Fig. 4-21. Correct position for cross-cutting. A — Mark desired cut line. B — Place board across two sawhorses and cut outside the area they occupy. C — Start cut near butt of saw. After starting the cut, the saw stroke should use nearly the whole length of saw blade. D — Cutting strokes should be made with saw blades held at 45° to the material surface. (Disston)

The ripsaw, in contrast to the crosscut saw, is designed to cut parallel to the grain, lengthwise on the board. The tooth style is shown in Fig. 4-20.

The ripsaw is usually a little longer than the crosscut saw and has 2¼ to 7 points per inch (1 to 3.6 points per cm). The common point count is 5½ per in. (2.2) for general ripping of the crosscut saw.

Using the Crosscut Saw and Ripsaw

When starting a cut with a crosscut saw, place teeth at the waste side of the measurement mark to assure proper length of cut piece, Fig. 4-21. Start near the butt of saw, using a short draw stroke (upward stroke), repeat slowly a few times until a slight groove is started. Then cut straight with full length strokes. It is best to maintain an angle of 45° between the saw blade and the face of the work.

To cut using the ripsaw, start with a draw stroke,

Fig. 4-22. Put very little pressure on the blade until the kerf is well established. Then take long, easy strokes using nearly the entire length of the blade. Get well above your work so the eye is on the same line with the saw blade and work. Hold the ripsaw blade at a 60° angle to the work surface. If the

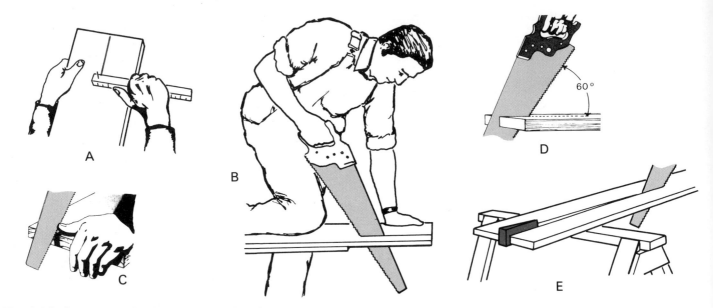

Fig. 4-22. Correct position for ripsawing. A — Mark the entire length of the rip cut. B — Place work at knee height across saw horses. C — Start the cut at the end of the blade with a draw stroke (upward motion). Put very little pressure on the saw until kerf is well established. Then take long, easy strokes. D — The proper angle for ripping is 60° between tooth edge and board surface. If board is thin, lessen the angle to 45°. E — When ripping a long board, after the cut has extended several feet the kerf may close and pinch the blade. To avoid this, insert a small wedge at start of cut. (Disston)

stock being ripped is thin, the angle should be reduced to about 45°.

The Backsaw and Miter Saw

The backsaw and miter saw are identical except for length. Designed for cutting joints, the backsaw is usually made in lengths from 10 to 16 in. (25 to 40 cm) with the 12 to 14 in. (30 to 35 cm) length being commonly used. The tooth style is of the crosscut variety and very fine, 12 to 13 teeth per in. (30 to 33 teeth per cm). Small teeth give the user a much smoother and precise cut.

The miter box saw is a longer version of the back saw, up to 26 in. (66 cm) in length with 11 teeth per in. (4.3 per cm). A miter is used to aid with the precision cutting of the miter saw. The miter box usually has guides for cutting 90° and 45° cross cuts.

The Coping Saw

The coping saw is designed to cut curved, delicate ornamental and filigree work. It is also used to start holes for larger saws. The coping saw consists of a frame which supports a removable and replaceable blade. The blade length is from 6 to 6 5/8 in. (15 to 17 cm), with varying blade thickness, as narrow as .007 in. (0.02 cm). The cutting tooth design is of the crosscut style. The saw has approximately 10 to 20 teeth per in. (4 to 8 per cm). Different blade types are available for cutting wood, plastics, and thin metal. The blade may be rotated in the frame to allow a variety of cutting angles. Saw frame depths are 8 to 12 in. (20 to 30 cm).

Saw types include scroll, fret, and deep throated coping saws.

The Compass Saws

The compass saw is sometimes called the keyhole saw because of its ability to enlarge a small hole. While there is a difference between the two saws, the major variation is the blade length. The compass saw has a blade 12 to 14 in. (30 to 35 cm) long and 8 to 10 teeth per in. (3.6 to 4 per cm). The keyhole saw has a blade usually 10 to 12 in. (25 to 30 cm) long with 10 teeth per in. (4 teeth per cm). Both have a pistol grip type of handle. The blades of both have a taper starting from a narrow tip and widening at the handle. Both saws will make either straight or curved cuts from a bored hole.

The Hacksaw

The hacksaw has a rigid frame with a removable and replaceable blade. With the proper blade, the hacksaw is capable of cutting almost any common metal. To avoid breakage of the blade, the proper tension must be drawn on the blade with adjustment of the frame, Fig. 4-23. The blades are available in a large variety of styles and numbers of teeth per inch. Selecting the proper blade for each job is important. Fig. 4-24 lists types of sawblades needed to cut different materials.

A general rule of thumb for the tooth selection is: when cutting any metal at least two teeth should contact the material at all times, Fig. 4-25. Use a coarse toothed blade for thick metals and a progressively finer blade for the thinner metals.

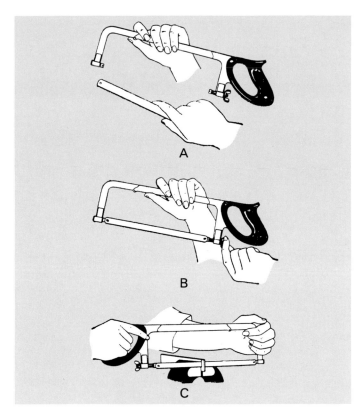

Fig. 4-23. Replacing hacksaw blade. A — Make sure teeth are pointing away from hand grip and place holes in blade over both pins. B — Put tension on blade using wing nut. C — Method of grasping hacksaw for use.

Set for the hacksaw also reduces friction of the blade for a free motion and finer cut. Hacksaw blades are available with the regular set, each alternate tooth bent in opposite directions, and the wavy set, used for the very fine toothed blades.

HACKSAW BLADE SELECTION

Teeth Per cm	Teeth Per inches	Material to be cut
5.5	14	bronze, aluminum, copper, brass, cast iron, and machine steel more than 1 in. (2.54 cm) thick.
7.0	18	copper, aluminum, high speed steel, and annealed steel 1/4 to 1 in. (0.6 to 2.54 cm) thick.
9.5	24	1/8 to 1/4 in. (0.3 to 0.6 cm) iron, steel, wrought iron pipe, brass and copper tubing and electrical conduit.
12.5	32	for materials above if walls are less than 1/8 in. (0.3 cm)

Fig. 4-24. Choose hacksaw blade based on material being cut and on thickness of workpiece.

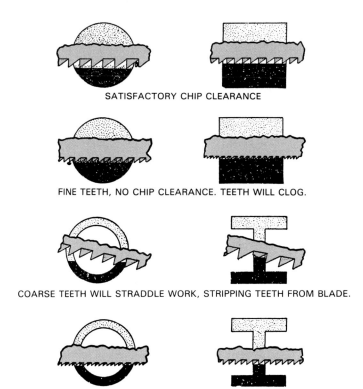

SATISFACTORY CHIP CLEARANCE

FINE TEETH, NO CHIP CLEARANCE. TEETH WILL CLOG.

COARSE TEETH WILL STRADDLE WORK, STRIPPING TEETH FROM BLADE.

TWO TEETH AND MORE ON EACH SECTION.

Fig. 4-25. Effects of various choices of hacksaw blades.

The Utility Knife

The utility knife has a sharp blade for cutting anything from poster matting to roofing shingles. It has a removable and disposable blade. The cutting edge is retractable for safety when not in use.

Chisels

Chisels are designed and manufactured for cutting metal and wood. Home upkeep will probably require both wood and metal cutting chisels. The cold chisel is used to cut metal which is not case-hardened. A brick chisel, Fig. 4-26, may be used to cut masonry block tile or brick by grooving deep enough for a fracture of the unit. The cold chisels are available in a variety of sizes according to length and shank diameters. For best performance, grind the cutting edges as shown in Fig. 4-27. The tip of each chisel should have a 65° included angle.

The wood cutting chisels have wood or plastic handles which may be struck with the hand or with

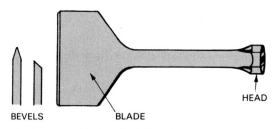

BEVELS   BLADE   HEAD

Fig. 4-26. The wide blade of a brick chisel helps direct the path of breakage.

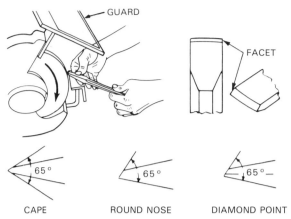

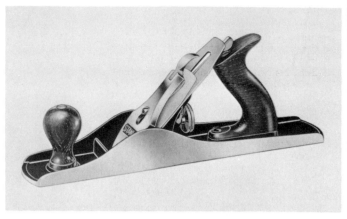

Fig. 4-27. Top — Desired surface shape when sharpening a cold chisel. Bottom — Sharpening angles of cold chisels. Note recommended upward tilt of chisel for the grinding wheel direction.

a soft-faced mallet. A hammer may be used only if a metal shank extends completely through the handle. The commonly used wood chisels are from 9 to 10 1/2 in. (23 to 27 cm) long and have a variety of widths from 1/4 to 1 1/2 in. (0.6 to 3.8 cm). The cutting edge is ground to 30°.

The Planes

Planes are used to trim wood to a smooth and finished size or to straighten irregular edges. They are available in many sizes and styles for specialized jobs. Planes used for special jobs are shown in Fig. 4-28. The jack plane, photograph A in Fig. 4-28, is used for work on home structures that may remain visible or may require a close fit. Sizes of the jack plane range from 12 to 15 in. (30 to 38 cm) in bed length. The PLANE IRON (cutting edge) is 2 3/8 in. (6 cm) in width. The plane iron is set to the bed at a 45° angle, making it ideal to plane the edge and face grains of wood. The cutting edge is adjustable both in depth of cut and alignment from side to side. The lateral adjustment lever aligns the blade with the bed.

The junior jack plane, not shown, was designed for easy use by junior high school students. It is 11 1/2 in. (29 cm) long with a 1 3/4 in. (5 cm) wide cutting edge. Adjustment and use are similar to that for the jack plane.

The Bench Plane

Refer again to Fig. 4-17. The bench plane is a shorter version of the jack plane. The bed is identical with the exception of the 9 in. (23 cm) length. The size will allow closer planing of confined spaces. However, the shorter bed will give a slightly more wavy surface.

The Block Plane

The block plane, photograph B in Fig. 4-28, is designed for planing the end grain of wood. The

Fig. 4-28. Types of planes for skilled homeowner. Top — Jack plane. Bottom — Block plane. (Stanley Tools)

plane is approximately 6 in. (15 cm) long. The blade is set at a much lower angle to provide a shearing type of cut. The blade is also upside down compared to other planes.

The block plane is designed to be held in one hand, leaving the other hand free to help support or hold the work. In addition to cutting on end grain, the block plane is also a valuable tool to do a variety of other trimming and planing jobs.

The File

The file is used to finish metal surfaces and to remove small amounts of material when fitting parts together. Types of files include flat, half-round, or round. Files have lengths from 6 to 12 in. (15 to 31 cm).

Files are also classified by coarseness: coarse, bastard, second-cut, smooth, and dead-smooth. For most home maintenance jobs, the smoother files are used.

To prevent injury, avoid using any file without a handle. Broken files are also unsafe.

Files should be cleaned regularly using a file card. The steel bristles of a file card are very short and stiff. Even caked aluminum and solder can be removed from a file with a few strokes along the grain of the file.

Utility Shears

The utility shears has many advantages. Heavy sheet metal and sheet plastic are best cut by the hand shear if any curved cuts are needed. For curved cuts, a hand shear can do what a machine shop shear cannot.

DRILLING AND BORING TOOLS

Some work requires holes for mounting hardware or for inserting pieces into framework. The drilling and boring tools shown in Fig. 4-29 are used to make starter holes and deep circular cuts.

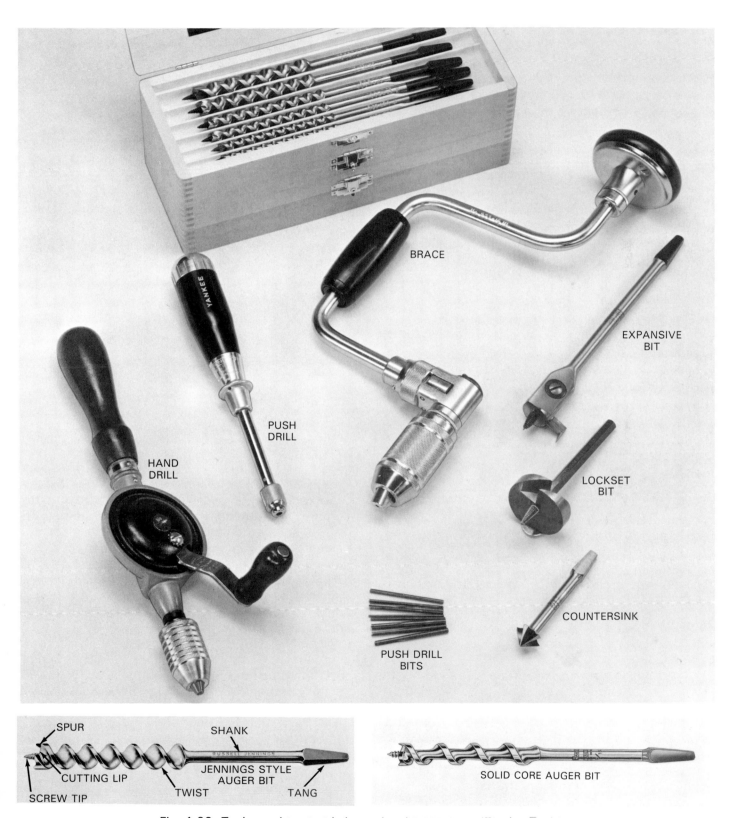

Fig. 4-29. Tools used to start holes and make openings. (Stanley Tools)

The Brace and Bit

The BRACE is the holding device by which force is applied to the BIT. The brace and bit can be used to bore a hole in any material a power drill can, but is able to bore holes up to 3 in. in diameter.

The Auger Bit

The auger bit is a spiral shaped wood cutting tool for boring holes 1/4 to 1 in. (6 to 25 mm). Bit sizes increase in steps of 1/16 in. (1.6 mm). Usually the bits are 7 to 10 in. (17 to 25 cm) long with extensions available for deeper boring. An electrician's auger bit is made for the very deep boring jobs. The auger bit is characterized by:

1. The square taper tang for a firm grip by the jaws.
2. The screw tip.
3. The cutting spur for smooth cutting of wood fibers.

The most widely used form of the auger bit is the Jennings type, sometimes called the double twist. Another type is the solid center bit. The solid center bit is a stiffer bit, which is useful for wavy grain woods and extremely hard woods. For a hole diameter greater than 1 in. (2.5 cm) and up to 3 in. (7.5 cm), the expansive bit was developed, Fig. 4-30. The expansive bit has one adjustable cutting edge which can be expanded to increase the diameter.

A special bit available for use with the hand brace is the forstner bit. It is used for boring flat bottom holes.

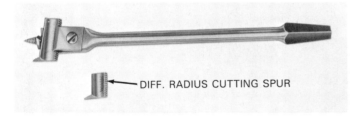

DIFF. RADIUS CUTTING SPUR

Fig. 4-30. The expansive bit. A small cutting spur (left) is needed for holes too small for the unused end of a large spur to clear. (Stanley Tools)

The Brace

A turning force for the brace depends on the sweep of the brace. Sweep is equal to the diameter of the circle traced by crank motion. Braces are available in sizes 8 to 14 in. (20 to 35 cm) with sweeps of 10 in. (25 cm) being common. An important part of a good quality brace is the ratchet, which may be set to transform a back and forth motion to a full turning movement of the chuck. This enables the operator to bore a hole close to an obstruction.

Sharpening an Auger

The auger bit is sharpened with a special auger bit file. The process is shown in Fig. 4-31. The cutting surfaces running outward from the long axis of the bit are sharpened only on the side nearest to the square tang end. Do not file on the side nearest to the feed screw end.

To sharpen the two side spurs, file only on the inside surface. Also, the spurs must be the same length when finished.

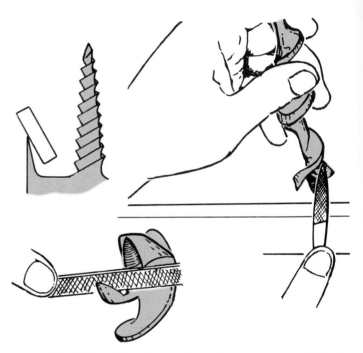

Fig. 4-31. Right. Filing the cutting edge of an auger bit. Left and bottom. Filing the spur. File on inside surface only.

Hand Drill and Push Drill

Sometimes it is inconvenient to extend a power cord to a work area. This is especially true for work on yard and garden structures. For these cases, the hand drill and push drill substitute for the power drill.

The hand drill uses the same bits as for the power drill. The chuck holds bits up to 1/4 in. (6 mm) in diameter. Some hand drills have a 3/8 in. (10 mm) chuck. The handle is turned clockwise for drilling and counterclockwise to back out the drill bit.

The push drill is preferred for starting accurate screw holes since the bit wanders less than the bit for a power drill. Fig. 4-32 suggests how the bit design improves accuracy. A symmetrical point is more likely to stay centered when pressure is applied. Push drills use bits ranging in size from 1/16 to about 3/16 in. (2 to 5 mm).

GENERAL PURPOSE TOOLS

Some tools aid in the use of other tools or are needed for routine maintenance. General purpose

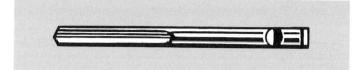

Fig. 4-32. Drill point for push drill. The symmetrical point helps avoid wandering of the bit when starting holes in precise locations. (Stanley Tools)

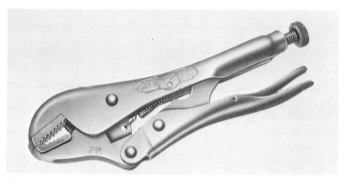

Fig. 4-34. Adjustable grip locking pliers conforms to parts of all sizes. (Petersen Manufacturing)

tools include the vise, the locking pliers, C-clamps, and oil cans.

For holding work while performing some operations, a vise is a necessary tool. Many kinds of vises are available: the woodworking vise with soft faces for marproof holding, Fig. 4-33, the machinist's vise for holding work securely, generally for metals and pipe, and the bench vise which is best suited for home maintenance.

The locking pliers, Fig. 4-34, is used for temporary holding of parts to allow free use of both hands. Although it is intended to hold metal plates during welding, it has many uses in home maintenance. The high gripping force helps to pull or turn odd-shaped hardware. Lower force allows wood or plastic items to be held or supported if the risk of damage is low. Tool length ranges from 5 to 9 in. (13 to 23 cm).

The C-clamp, not shown, holds parts larger than 1/2 in. (1 cm) long or wide. The clamp can extend where other clamping devices will not reach. Care is needed with some materials to be clamped. For wood gluing jobs, shims or pads are recommended to avoid denting the surface.

The oil can is one of the most important tools for home maintenance. Timely oiling of machinery can prevent major repairs. The oil can with a long tube is especially useful for oiling parts in small spaces.

CARE OF TOOLS

For efficient work, the home mechanic should have a designated storage place for all tools. Whether that place is a toolbox, tool cart, wall panel, or shelf, the convenience of organization is worth the effort of proper storage, Fig. 4-35.

Fig. 4-33. The carpenter's vise is one of many vise styles. (Stanley Tools)

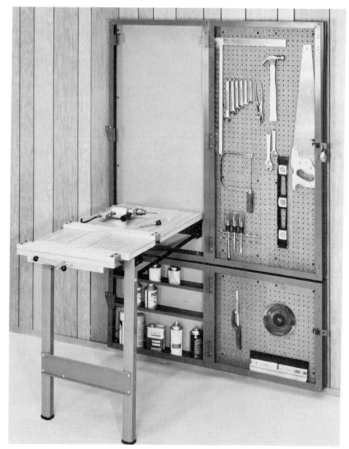

Fig. 4-35. The efficient worker has a complete storage section for home tools. (Hirsch Co.)

Upon completion of a home repair job, the tools should be cleaned of all dust, dirt, and material wastes. Wipe the tool with a small spot of oil, or rust preventive solution. Any cutting edge tools should be resharpened if needed and protected from damage in storage. For example, the plane iron (the cutting edge) should be retracted to a position above the plane bed. This procedure prevents cutting edge damage should the plane be improperly stored. If rust begins to accumulate due to high humidity, oil and fine abrasive cloth may be used to remove it. Also commercial rust removers are available through a tool and hardware supplier.

VINYL DIPPING

For winter use, handles of pliers, shears, wrenches, and other metal handled tools are often more comfortable for the user if they have vinyl coated grips. You may have tools which are not coated, but which you would like to coat. It is a comparatively simple process to dip the tool handle, Fig. 4-36. Any totally metal tool handle may be dip coated: pliers, combination wrenches, etc. A liquid

Fig. 4-36. Applying a vinyl cushion grip to metal tool handles. The tool is heated before dipping.

coating called a Plastisol, or called a vinyl dispersion, is obtainable from most plastic supply companies in a variety of colors. The following is the simple procedure:

1. Clean the tool thoroughly. It should be free from dirt, oil, and old paint.
2. Heat the tool in a pre-heated oven 400 °F for 20-30 minutes.

3. Use a pliers to grip the tool. Dip to the level of the grip needed. The cross section thickness will be determined by the following:
   a. The size of the form and its temperature.
   b. The length of time left in the vinyl plastic — about 90 seconds.
4. With a steady motion, withdraw the tool from the liquid vinyl plastic. Be careful not to touch the sides of the container.
5. Heat the vinyl dipped tool in the oven for curing for 20 minutes at a temperature of 350 °F. Again take all precautions not to touch the freshly dipped tool.
6. Cure the tool by placing in cold water for 2-5 minutes.

TOOL IDENTIFICATION

It is always a good idea to have your tools marked for positive identification. Several methods are available. A simple method uses color codes. Select a color and on each tool apply a patch of durable paint. Make sure this patch is located in an out-of-the-way place, away from tool wear and free from any normal operation of the tool.

The vibrating engraver makes a lasting mark for tool identification, Fig. 4-37. By engraving your name or initials, each tool is easily recognized. To expand this idea, the local law enforcement agencies often keep a list of code numbers or symbols used by residents. Consistency of coding is one advantage. Visit your local agency to obtain your code number. This number may also be applied to all household appliances and possessions. In many instances the local agencies will loan you a marking tool. The owner may wish to use a personal identification number such as a drivers license number or a social security number.

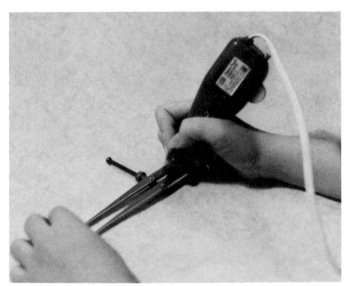

Fig. 4-37. Using the vibrating pencil to mark a tool for identification.

SOME HINTS ON HAND TOOL USE

For each tool, there are special features that affect its use. For example, the width of a standard screwdriver blade must be very close to the slot width of the screw. Damage to the tool and screw can occur if the width is wrong. The blade of a Phillips screwdriver also must fit properly in a Phillips head screw. If the blade is the wrong size, or held at an angle, the screw slot may be marred, Fig. 4-38A.

When removing a long nail from a piece of wood, you should slip a small block of scrap wood under the hammer head. This will increase your leverage, relieve strain on the handle, and prevent damaging the wood, Fig. 4-38B.

Many tools are used for purposes that are not safe. Choose the right tool for your work and do not substitute.

VOLT-OHM-METER

A very useful tool for repairing modern electrical and electronic appliances is the volt-ohm-milliammeter (VOM). It detects electrical current. A correct reading often is given on the appliance. The meter reading can be compared to it. Most problems are diagnosed this way. See Fig. 4-39.

Most hand-held meters read voltages in the following ranges: 0 to 600 volts DC, 0 to 300 volts DC, 0 to 600 volts AC, and 0 to 250 volts AC. Often, one scale is used for both AC and DC. Most of these meters will measure in multiples of 300, such as 300, 600, and 1200 volts. Start with the

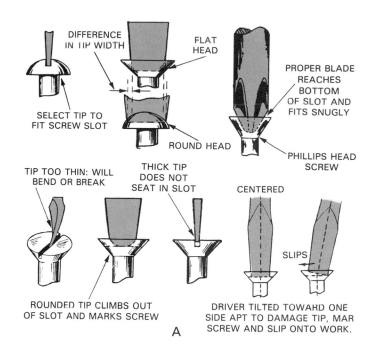

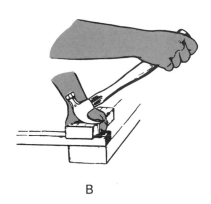

Fig. 4-38. Hints when using hand tools. A—Correct use of a screwdriver insures the screw is not damaged. B—Use a piece of scrap wood when removing long nails.

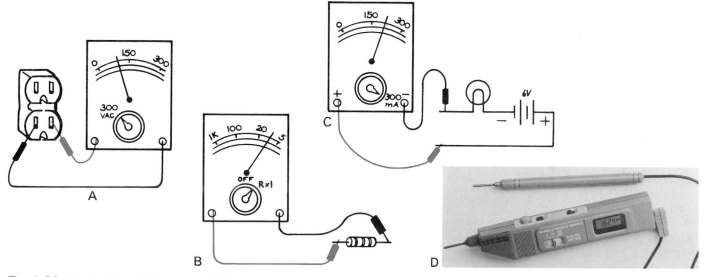

Fig. 4-39. A volt-ohm-milliammeter (VOM) tests many electrical parts of appliances. A — To measure voltage, set pointer to 300 volts or higher. While measuring, turn pointer to the lower scales a step at a time. B — Set pointer to Rx1 to check resistance of most appliance components. Never use ohmmeter setting if any circuit voltage is present. C — Learn to measure current by connecting a simple lamp circuit. Set pointer to highest possible scale first. Scale reads in milliamperes (mA). Put red probe on terminal nearest to positive source point. D — Digital meter sets its own range. (Beckman Industrial Corp.)

highest possible range when measuring an unknown voltage.

Resistance to current flow is measured in ohms. The dial pointer can be set to one of the following: Rx1, Rx100, Rx1K, or Rx100K. Each setting describes how you convert a scale reading to a resistance value. For example, with pointer at Rx1, the scale reading is identical to the actual resistance value in ohms. As another example, with the pointer at Rx1K, you multiply every scale reading by 1000 ("1K") to get the actual resistance of the part being tested.

Test most small appliances with pointer at Rx1. For example, a 1200 watt toaster should have a resistance of about 12Ω.

Be careful when making resistance measurements on a circuit which may contain batteries or may not be isolated from a power source. A voltage can damage the meter movement or bend the needle. Always test for any voltages present by first using the meter as a voltmeter.

The amount of DC current in a circuit can be measured with an ammeter. Hand-held meters measure current in 1/1000 units of current called milliamps. (The meter is not useful for house wiring current tests.)

To measure current, simply break into the circuit in a convenient place. Set the pointer at its highest setting, usually 250mA or 600mA. Touch the red probe at the nearest positive point. Note that reverse polarity will not harm the meter.

TEST YOUR KNOWLEDGE — CHAPTER 4

1. A folding wood rule allows a _____ to be measured without needing two people and a ladder.
2. To transfer the pattern of an irregular surface onto another surface, use a:
   a. Level.
   b. Square.
   c. Divider.
   d. Chalk line.
3. The most commonly used hammer is the _____ claw hammer.
4. An adjustable wrench is turned in the direction in which the tip of the _____ (fixed, movable) jaw points.
5. To reduce saw friction and blade binding, _____ is given to the blade.
6. When cutting any metal with a hacksaw, at least _____ teeth contact the material at all times.
7. The blade of the _____ plane is upside down compared to other planes.
8. Sharpen the two side spurs of an auger on the _____ (outside, inside) surface.
9. The purpose of a tool identification mark is to:
   a. Prevent theft.
   b. Help recover stolen items.
   c. Discourage theft.
   d. (a) and (b).
   e. (b) and (c).
10. A meter used as an ohmmeter can be damaged if it is used on a circuit that has any _____ present.

KNOW THESE TERMS

Home mechanics, measuring, cutting, drilling, leveling, fastening, filing.

SUGGESTED ACTIVITIES

Make a list of common tools which you do not have. Visit a hardware store to examine closely some of these that interest you. Compare any tools which exist in more than one style. Make a note of any new fact you discover. Summarize this information for your class.

As a class project, bring samples of scraps of materials from home. These may be of metal, wood, plastic, brick, or rubber. Learn to use some of the hand tools by making layout patterns, holes, cuts, and planed surfaces, or by fastening materials together.

Also gain skills by disassembling and reassembling broken appliances brought from home. See if you can identify the problem. Ask your instructor for guidance, tools, and additional supplies.

Obtain liquid polyvinyl dipping plastic. Following the manufacturers suggested procedure add plastic insulating grips to the metal household tools, such as pliers.

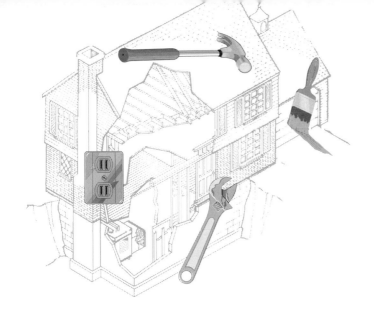

POWER TOOLS

This chapter discusses some power tools used for home maintenance. The tools include the power drill, circular saw, saber saw, router, belt sander, table saw, radial arm saw, and grinder. The chapter includes suggestions for purchase and use of these tools.

After studying this chapter you will be able to:
- List the main parts of each power tool.
- Describe what materials can and cannot be worked by each tool.
- Choose a tool with the correct speed, size, and power for the job.
- Adjust and position the tool for desired result.
- Work safely.

Power tools speed the completion of laborious tasks. Therefore, they give you the ability to do jobs which you probably would not otherwise attempt. They do, however, require a greater investment than that for hand tools.

Many small power tools are manufactured and sold for home use. These include the portable electric drill, circular saw, saber saw, router, and power sander.

THE PORTABLE ELECTRIC DRILL

The portable electric drill is probably the power tool most frequently used by the home mechanic, Fig. 5-1. With the proper bit, almost any material can be drilled. The tool's versatility makes it ideal not only as a drill, but as a paint mixer, grinder, polisher, or power source for many other attachments. With the availability of the cordless-rechargeable drill, use is no longer limited to the length of the power cord.

The electric drill is available with many chuck sizes. Size is determined by the largest bit shank the chuck will accept. Sizes are 1/4 in. (6 mm), 3/8 in. (10 mm), 1/2 in. (13 mm), or 3/4 in. (19 mm).

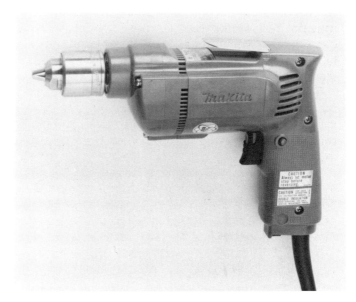

Fig. 5-1. The 1/4 in. (6 mm) portable electric drill is the most commonly used power tool. (Makita U.S.A., Inc.)

The power of the drill varies with the size. Generally the 1/4 inch drill has about 1/5 horsepower while the 3/4 inch has about 1 1/2 horsepower. Speed of the electric drill usually decreases as size increases. Speeds range from about 1000 revolutions per minute (rpm) for the 3/4 inch drill to about 3500 rpm for the 1/4 inch drill. While the speed is decreasing among the drill sizes, the torque (or turning power) increases for drills that hold larger bits.

The lower speed and higher torque of the heavy-duty drill provide an advantage over the light-duty home use models. There is often less heating or burning of metal and wood because of the slower rotation of the bit. But a higher torque gives about the same cutting speed as for the small home model. Cost should be balanced against usage when choosing heavy or light duty.

Variable speed electric drills are available. They provide any speed from zero to full depending on trigger pressure. This allows close control of the cutting rate. The common full speed is 2000 rpm for a 1/4 in. (6 mm) drill.

Some drills have reversing switches which allow the drill to rotate in the opposite direction. The device is useful for backing a drill bit out of the hole if it binds.

The most common bit for the electric drill is the twist drill, Fig. 5-2. There are specialized drill bits for high-speed electric drills. Fig. 5-3 shows a power bit for making clean holes in wood, and a flat spade bit for rapid drilling of wood when ragged edges are acceptable. There are tools which make power drill use easier. When holes must be in a precise location or run true to a surface, a drilling jig is used, Fig. 5-4. The jig is a metal block or disc with holes of different sizes. The jig is clamped in the desired position on the work. The holes keep the drill bit at the proper angle and location.

Another drilling aid is a depth stop. It is a ring which is held onto the drill bit spiral with a setscrew. Many holes of the same depth can be quickly drilled using the depth stop.

SAFE USE OF POWER DRILLS

Before changing drill bits, unplug the tool. Be sure to remove the chuck key after use. The keyless chuck drill provides the home mechanic an alternate to the keyed chuck. See Fig. 5-5. This drill chuck provides a quick and safe means of changing drill bits. Drill bits are secured in this chuck by simply rotating the chuck head. Manufacturers of household power drills have eliminated the need for a key to secure the bit within the chuck.

It is imperative that electrical shock protection be an integral part of the drill design. Two methods of assurance are:

1. The wire grounding cord (a three prong plug protects the user from shock in case of internal shorting).
2. The double insulated housing, usually a plastic case with a two wire electrical system.

When buying a drill always look for the Underwriter's Laboratory seal of approval. This assures that the model design has been tested by an independent group and found to be safe.

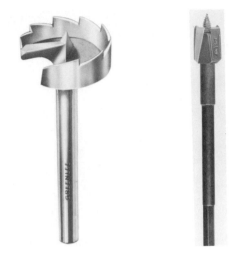

Fig. 5-3. These specialized bits are used with the power drill when drilling wood. (Greenlee Tool Division, Vermont American Tool Company)

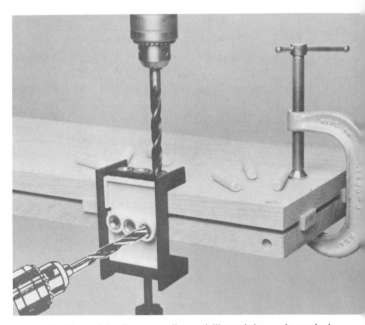

Fig. 5-4. Use a bit alignment jig to drill straight and true holes with a power drill. These holes are being drilled for dowels. (American Intertool, Inc.)

Fig. 5-5. This keyless chuck drill provides a quick and safe means of changing drill bits. (Black and Decker)

Fig. 5-2. Twist drill bit is used in power drills and hand drills to pierce metal. (Vermont American Tool Company)

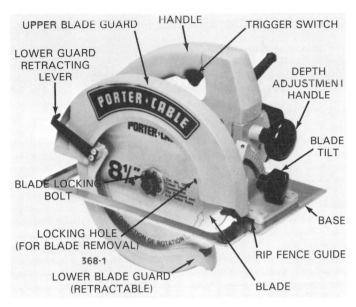

UPPER BLADE GUARD
HANDLE
TRIGGER SWITCH
LOWER GUARD RETRACTING LEVER
DEPTH ADJUSTMENT HANDLE
BLADE TILT
BLADE LOCKING BOLT
LOCKING HOLE (FOR BLADE REMOVAL)
368-1
LOWER BLADE GUARD (RETRACTABLE)
BLADE
RIP FENCE GUIDE
BASE

Fig. 5-6. Parts of the portable power saw. (Porter-Cable)

THE PORTABLE CIRCULAR SAW

If you expect to do a good deal of sawing, decide if your time is worth more than the cost of a portable circular saw. Also consider the cost of rental. Before deciding, learn the parts of the circular saw, Fig. 5-6, and know the function of each.

Portable circular saws are available in a variety of sizes. Saw size is listed by the diameter of the saw blade it will accept: 5 1/2 in. (14 cm), 6 1/2 in. (16 cm), 7 1/4 in. (18 cm), and 8 in. (20 cm). Power of the circular saw varies according to size. The 7 1/4 inch saw may range in power from 1 to 2 horsepower (hp). The 5 1/2 inch, which is ade-quate for home use, is available from about .5 to .8 hp. Speed of the saws usually decreases with the size. For the 7 1/4 inch saw, it is about 5300 rpm and for the 5 1/2 inch, it is about 4000 rpm.

The weight of the saw, a critical factor when selecting a saw, also varies with size. While the 7 1/4 inch saw may weigh between 12 and 12 1/2 lb. (26 and 27 kg), the 5 1/2 inch only weighs about 5 1/2 lb. (12 kg). When choosing the saw, it should be capable of cutting a 2x4 on a 45° angle. Saw guide equipment and use of the saw are shown in Fig. 5-7.

Each circular saw is slightly different from another. Learn the special procedures needed to use each saw. Most steps are the same for all portable circular saws.

The circular saw is not intended to cut with a side-to-side deviation less than about 1/16 in. If cutting without a jig, do not attempt to force the blade into a desired path. This will cause some binding and overheating of the blade.

SAFETY PRACTICES WITH THE PORTABLE SAW

Always observe the following rules of safety when using a portable circular saw:
1. Use grounded 3 wire electrical receptacle or the double insulated saw.
2. Know where your power cord is in relation to your intended cut.
3. Unplug the saw when making adjustments or when changing blades. Do not yank the cord to unplug.
4. Keep both hands on saw grips and handles while cutting.

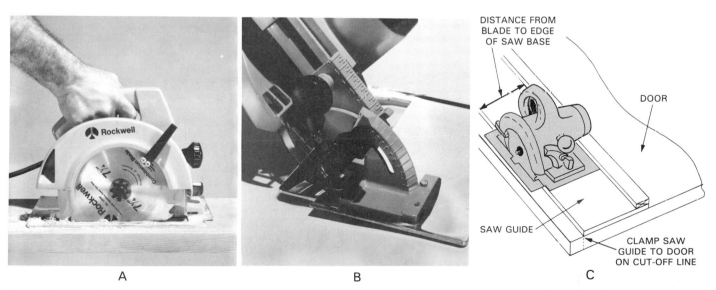

DISTANCE FROM BLADE TO EDGE OF SAW BASE
DOOR
SAW GUIDE
CLAMP SAW GUIDE TO DOOR ON CUT-OFF LINE

A
B
C

Fig. 5-7. A — Ripping a board with a portable power saw. To prevent binding, adjust blade depth so that blade extends no more than about 1/8 in. beneath the board. A support column slides to set the depth. Note how retractable blade guard ensures the operator's safety. B — The saw blade can be tilted at any angle for bevel cuts. Find the desired angle on the protractor (degree scale). Loosen knob to set pointer. C — Use jig when cutting off a door or other item. Jig uses factory-cut edge on furring strip. A two-piece guide strip is not needed if splintering is acceptable. (Emmet Osgood)

5. Check the lower retractable blade guard to prevent lodging.
6. Start the saw before entering the cut.
7. Maintain a sharp blade.
8. Have the workpiece secured properly on sawhorses or a firm support.

SUGGESTIONS FOR USING THE POWER SAW

There are ways to save work when using the portable circular saw. Some suggestions are as follows:
1. To avoid splinters when cutting paneling or other sheet products, put masking tape on the cut line. It is best used on the upper side.
2. To cut straight edges on a door bottom or other visible area, make a jig. Refer again to Fig. 5-7. Use two pieces of plywood. One should have a factory cut edge. The other will be cut while the factory edge is used. This second piece then serves as a visual guide to be placed on all future cutting lines.

THE BAYONET SAW

The bayonet saw, Fig. 5-8, is sometimes called the saber saw or portable jigsaw. This saw is useful for making curved cuts as well as straight cuts. With the proper style of blade the bayonet saw can cut wood, plastic, metal, linoleum, and even glass. It is versatile such as during paneling when cutting for outlets, switches, and other openings. Use the

least forward pressure needed to cut, since the blade is easily broken.

Bayonet saws are sized generally by their horsepower rating in the range of 1/5 to 1/3 hp. Speed is given as the number of strokes per minute (SPM). Normally speed is 3200 SPM. Some saws have two speeds. The second speed is approximately 2500 SPM. Some models provide a variable speed from 0 to 3200 SPM. Weight generally ranges from about 3 to 4 1/2 lb. (6.5 to 9.9 kg).

An attachment for the saber saw is the edge guide. This helps to make straight cuts. When using a saw of any kind at all, a strip of adhesive tape helps prevent splinters.

ROUTERS

The router, Fig. 5-9, is a power tool needed for decorative edge work and certain joints in woodworking. The cutting bits have a wide variety of

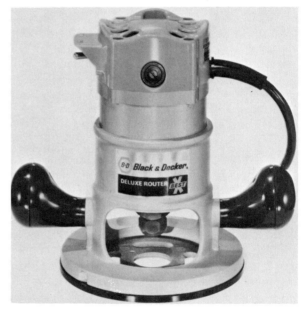

Fig. 5-9. The power hand router gives the home mechanic professional quality joining capability. (Black and Decker)

Fig. 5-8. The bayonet or saber saw makes cuts which are straight or curved. Work can begin from an edge or from an inside point. The saw cuts a variety of material. Do not force the saw when cutting.   (Makita U.S.A., Inc.)

shapes and designs, Fig. 5-10. They are available in either tool steel or with a carbide edge for long service.

The router has a high-speed motor (24,000 rpm) with its shaft held vertically. The shaft has a chuck for holding the bits on the end. The router size is indicated by the horsepower of the motor. Motor power ranges from 1/2 to 1 1/2 hp. The 1/2-3/4 hp router is common for work at home.

Safety procedures for router usage are:
1. Make sure the collet nut of the chuck is tight to hold the bit securely.

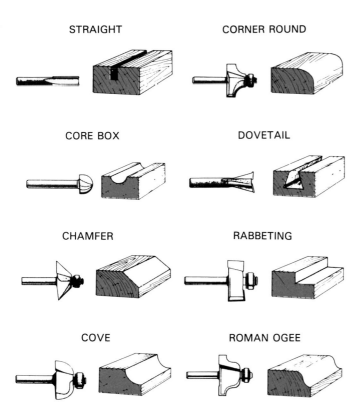

STRAIGHT   CORNER ROUND

CORE BOX   DOVETAIL

CHAMFER   RABBETING

COVE   ROMAN OGEE

Fig. 5-10. Router bits usually have two cutting edges and are available to the home mechanic in many sizes.   (Bosch)

Fig. 5-11. Belt sanders reduce labor by one half or more. This particular sander has a dust collecting bag which helps keep the work area clean. (Black and Decker)

2. Never set the router down while the bit is turning.
3. Always remember that the router bit protrudes below the router base.
4. Never change cutter bits or make adjustments without disconnecting the power cord.
5. Hold the router firmly with both hands and work from left to right.
6. Feed the router into the work at the proper speed. Moving too slowly will cause overheating of the bit and will burn the wood. Moving too fast will cause overheating of the motor and possible splitting of the work. Practice on a piece of waste material and carefully watch the performance.

POWER SANDERS

Two types of electric sanders are the belt style and pad style. Both types are portable.

Belt sanders, Fig. 5-11, are suited for rapid removal of excess material from flat surfaces. Belt sanders are listed by the size of belts they require. Common belt sizes are 3 x 24 inch, 4 x 24 inch, or 3 x 27 inch. The actual sanding surface is the size of the base shoe given in square inches or square centimeters.

The speed of the sanding belt is rated in surface feet per minute (SFPM). Speed is normally about

1200 SFPM. Power ratings of belt sanders range from 1 to 1 1/2 hp.

Some belt sanders are equipped with internal dust collecting systems. A dust collector is important when working indoors.

Several types of pad sanders may be purchased:
1. The orbital sander, Fig. 5-12, which has a pad that travels in an elliptical pattern.
2. The straight line sander which moves in a straight back and forth motion much like normal hand sanding.
3. Dual action sanders, which are capable of giving both the orbit motion and the straight line motion.

Fig. 5-12. The finish sander, or orbital sander, produces a surface with few sanding streaks. The sanding pad moves in an oval (orbital) pattern. This sander has a dust extraction attachment.   (Black and Decker)

Speed of the orbital sander ranges from 4000 to 10,000 orbits per minute (OPM). The faster speed gives a smoother surface.

The pad sanders are generally lighter in weight than most belt sanders. Pad sander weights range from 3 to 5 lb. (6.6 to 11 kg).

There is a third type of sander, the portable power contour sander. It is sometimes called a "flap wheel." The contour sander is different from the belt or pad sander because it will sand curved surfaces. The revolving head holds several stiff brushlike pads. Each supports a flap of sandpaper. Revolving at a rapid rate (approximately 3200 rpm), the flexible brush and abrasive will adjust to almost any contour. Uses include removing old wood finishes or removing rust from metal furniture.

THE TABLE SAW

The table saw, Fig. 5-13, is used for fast and accurate cutting of pieces thinner than about 2 in. The table saw is also called a bench saw or circular saw. A table saw is sized by the diameter of the largest blade it will accept. Blade sizes range from 6 to 12 in. (15 to 30 cm) on home models. A saw with an 8 to 10 in. (20 to 25 cm) blade is most popular. You should select one which will cut a 2 x 4 at a 45° angle.

Motors for the table saw will vary in horsepower. A saw for larger blades will have a larger motor. The 10 inch saw will normally be powered by a 1 to 1 1/2 hp motor.

Table saws are especially well suited for crosscutting and ripping, Fig. 5-14. Ripping can be done very accurately because work is guided along an edge called a rip fence. The table saw also makes a variety of specialty cuts like the bevel cut and miter cut. The saw is used for cutting various joints, grooves, rabbets, and dados when equipped with a dado head, Fig. 5-15.

The table saw is not generally used for crosscutting pieces longer than 4 ft. To crosscut pieces shorter than about 4 ft., use a miter gage. The gage is usually a 6 in. long guide edge. It can be set at a right angle to the blade or as much as 45°

Fig. 5-14. When using the table saw always remember to use safety shields and wear appropriate eye protection. Note anti-kickback device with jagged points. (Rockwell)

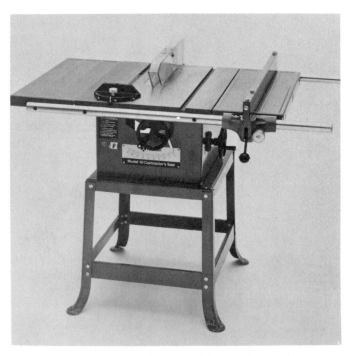

Fig. 5-13. The table saw has a rip fence and cutoff gauge for accurate and safe crosscutting and ripping operation. The saw accepts a 10 in. blade. (Rockwell)

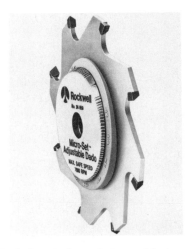

Fig. 5-15. Dado heads form dados, rabbets, and other joints used in cabinet construction. The blade of this dado head "wobbles" to form the groove. (Rockwell International)

44

from a right angle. Crosscutting pieces larger than 4 ft. is difficult even with the miter gage.

Safety is very important when using the table saw. Take the following precautions:

1. Never wear loose clothing while operating the table saw.
2. All guards should be in place during operation.
3. Always stand to one side, never directly in front of the blade. Pieces may be thrown toward the front.
4. Wear eye protectors while operating the table saw.
5. Always feed the saw from the front (end at which blade rotates downward).
6. Disconnect the power while changing blades or making adjustments.
7. Never make a cut until the saw has reached full power.
8. Use a push stick when cutting pieces less than a foot on a side.

THE RADIAL ARM SAW

The radial arm saw, Fig. 5-16, does much the same work as the table saw but the nature of its operation is different. The radial arm saw cuts from above the work instead of from beneath. In crosscutting pieces longer than four feet, the radial arm saw has a great advantage. The work is stationary and the saw motor unit moves across the work. It is difficult to stabilize a long piece on a table saw when crosscutting.

For ripping, the motor and blade unit of the radial arm saw is locked parallel to the guide fence (rip fence) and the work is pushed beneath and through the saw. For angle cuts, the support arm (overarm) and motor blade unit can be rotated to the sides (right or left of center) and locked in position. The blade is moved outward through the piece as in crosscutting.

Angles in other directions can be cut. The motor blade can be tilted at any angle up to 45° for miter cuts.

The maximum cutting depth is almost the radius of the blade. Cutting depth is adjusted by raising or lowering the overarm on the rear column.

Because of the complex design, the radial arm saw is usually higher priced then the table saw. Sizing of the saw is again done by the largest diameter blade which can be mounted on the arbor. The 10

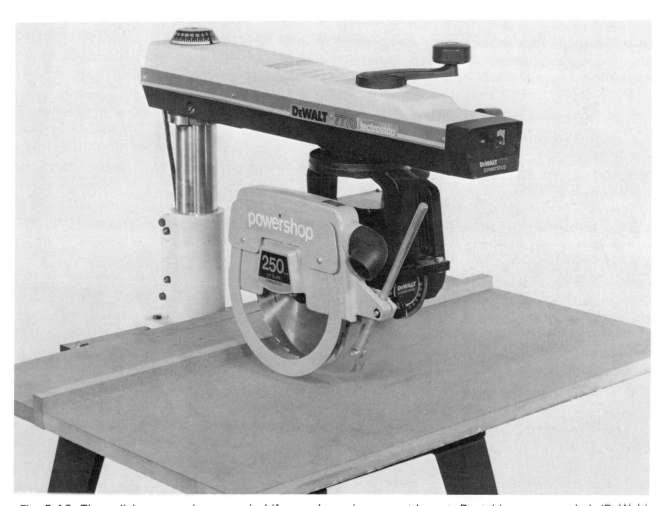

Fig. 5-16. The radial arm saw is economical if many long pieces must be cut. Rental is recommended. (DeWalt)

in. (25 cm) is the most frequently used radial arm saw. The 10 inch saw will usually rip a maximum of 24 in. (60 cm) in width. However, since the overarm length determines the cut width, do not choose a saw only by blade size.

The radial arm saw table and rip fence are always made of wood which with continued use must be replaced. Since the saw cuts from above, the blade must cut into the top slightly and cut through the rip fence. Replacement is done easily with like material.

Follow the same safety precautions as for the table saw. There is one specific precaution for ripping with the radial saw. Always push the work into the saw from the direction that is indicated on the saw guard, never from the rear. Proper direction is opposite to the rotation direction at the bottom of the blade.

THE GRINDER

Bench or pedestal grinders differ very little. The name only refers to the method of mounting, Fig. 5-17. The grinder consists of a motor with the shaft extending from both ends and with abrasive wheels attached. Explosion protection guards cover most of the wheel. Eye shields provide eye safety while allowing the worker clear vision of the work.

The grinder is sized according to the diameter of the abrasive wheel it accepts. The 6 in. (15 cm) wheel is most suited for home use. Power of the 6 inch bench grinder is generally .50 hp. Speed for the 6 inch grinder will range from 3200 rpm to 3600 rpm.

The grinder may be used for many jobs from sharpening a lawn mower blade to the sharpening of your cutting edge tools. Cloth and fiber wheels are available for polishing and buffing. Cleaning is done with wire brush wheels.

Wheel coarseness is important for fast work and for safety. Always select the right abrasive wheel for jobs to be performed and materials being worked. Choose wheels and brushes as follows:

Coarse	For soft materials, rapid removal of material
Medium	For an intermediate step to the smooth finish
Fine	To produce a smooth finish
Wire Brush	To remove rust, paint, etc.
Fiber Brush	To remove corrosion and thin oxides
Cloth Buffer	To give a high polish for nonferrous materials

Check the condition of a grinding wheel before use. A crack may be difficult to see. Tap the wheel lightly on the side with a non-metal object. A dull or dead sound indicates a bad wheel. Discard it.

When replacing grinding wheels, always check to match the rpm rating of the wheel to the grinder's rpm. Always follow safe procedures for grinding:

1. Adjust tool rest properly, level and about 1/8 in. (3 mm) from the grinding wheel.
2. Position eye shield correctly.
3. Wear eye protectors.

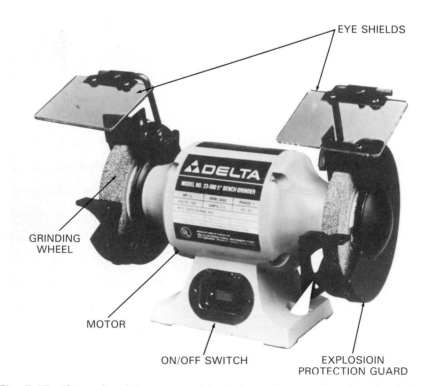

Fig. 5-17. General maintenance and tool sharpening require a bench grinder. (Delta International Machinery Corp.)

4. To grind a part, hold it flat on the tool rest.
5. Disconnect electrical power when making adjustments or changing abrasive wheels.
6. Wear leather gloves when grinding.

When grinding, take precautions to prevent overheating the workpiece. Overheating can damage the temper of metal. Have a container of water nearby. Plunge the workpiece into it for rapid cooling. Some grinders have a water tray mounted on the frame.

TEST YOUR KNOWLEDGE — CHAPTER 5

1. Because of a slower bit speed, the heavy-duty drill cuts slower than does the light-duty drill. True or False?
2. When cutting with a portable circular saw, the blade should extend no more than _____ in. beneath the board.
3. The _____ of the bayonet saw is easily broken.
4. A router cut proceeds:
   a. From left to right.
   b. From right to left.
5. The table saw gains its accuracy from a guide called a _____ _____ .
6. Use a _____ _____ when cutting small pieces with a table saw.
7. Which of the following is preferred for crosscutting a long, narrow board?
   a. The table saw.
   b. The radial arm saw.
8. The width of a rip cut on a radial arm saw is set by sliding the motor unit along the _____ .
9. The tool rest of a grinder should be about _____ in. away from the grinding wheel.
10. A _____ saw blade will bind if you try to maintain too much accuracy in the cut.
11. Use a _____ when cutting off a door with a portable circular saw.

KNOW THESE TERMS

Portable saw, motor, tool rest, grinding wheel, plunge, eye protectors.

SUGGESTED ACTIVITIES

Visit a local building site, millwork shop, or hardware store. Be sure to get permission from the supervisor at any building site or millwork shop. Watch closely to learn how each power tool is adjusted and used. Pay special attention to the jigs and fixtures used to align workpieces. Make a list of the jig applications. Include sketches and give an oral report to your class.

Practice at school and at home using some of the power tools. Perhaps an item at home needs work. Bring the smaller pieces to class for advice.

Cordless, rechargeable drills are not limited by the length of the cord. (Panasonic Industrial Co.)

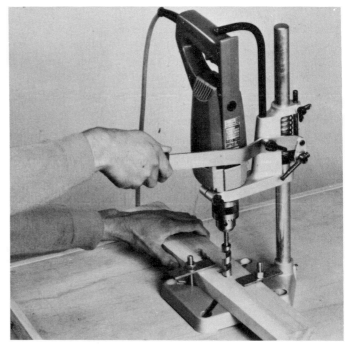

Drilling holes which are parallel to each other requires a steady drill support. This device converts a portable electric drill into a drill press. (Makita Power Tools)

6

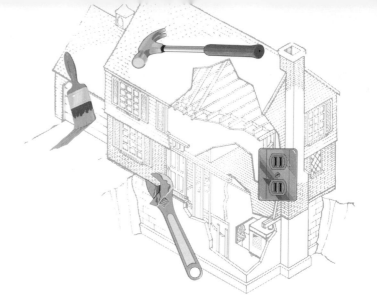

FASTENERS

This chapter describes the types and uses of fasteners. It introduces nails, threaded fasteners, special purpose fasteners, related hardware, and adhesives.

After studying this chapter, you will be able to:
Name some common fasteners.
Choose proper hardware for a job.
Produce strong joints between materials.
Show knowledge of safe work methods.

Fasteners for the home mechanic may be divided into two categories: mechanical and chemical. The mechanical fasteners include nails, threaded fasteners, staples, and plastic inserts. The chemical fasteners include a vast assortment of adhesives, mastics, and glues.

Mechanical fastening is very common for home repair jobs. Nails traditionally have been accepted and are practical. Easy to install, nails have excellent holding power. Screws and staples are equally valuable for holding multiple pieces together.

NAILS

Nail sizes are indicated by the term "penny" and abbreviated "d", after an old English system based on the price of 100 nails. Sizes range from 2 penny (2d) to 60 penny (60d). Today the term indicates the length of the nail and also the diameter, Fig. 6-1. For example, the 2d common is 1 in. (2.54 cm) in length with diameter equal to 15 1/2 wire gauge. Weight is 876 nails per pound or 1930 nails per kilogram.

Common nails have relatively thick heads and are larger in diameter than other styles of nails, Fig. 6-2. Common nails are the most frequently used for general construction purposes, Fig. 6-3. They have greater holding power than most other nails because of their larger diameter.

Box nails are smaller in diameter then the common and have a thinner head. They were originally designed for fastening wooden shipping boxes, hence the name. Today they are used frequently in the construction industry in place of common nails. The smaller size is less expensive per individual unit. The box nail is less likely to split the wood than the larger common nail.

Casing nails have a head shaped somewhat like a cone. The cone allows the nail to be set below the wood surface and still give sufficient holding power. These nails are used to install window and door casings in residential type construction. Putty or wood filler covers the nail head.

Finishing nails have small barrel shaped heads smaller than the casing nail. The smaller head makes it much easier to set below the surface without splitting the wood. However, they do not have the holding power of other nails. Finishing nails are used primarily for installing window, door, and other finish trim in house construction.

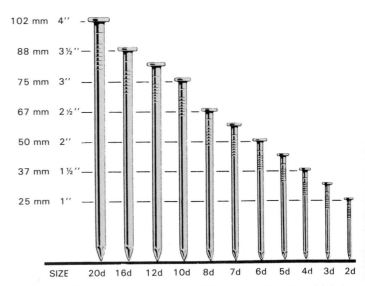

Fig. 6-1. Nail sizes start at 1 in. (25 mm) in length which is called 2d. They range up to 60d which is 6 in. (152 mm). A nail should be 3 times as long as the thickness of the item being held.

Brads are shaped like finishing nails and are used when small finishing nails are needed. Brads are 1 in. (2.54 cm) or shorter in length.

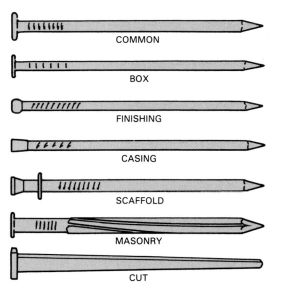

Fig. 6-2. There are many styles of nails used for wood and masonry.

Wire nails are the shorter version of the box nail. They are less than 1 in. long. The wire nail has a small flat head to distinguish it from the wire brad.

There are many special purpose nails:
1. The ring shank nail (also called pole barn nail).
2. The colored nail.
3. The roofing nail.

The pole barn nail has a series of rings stamped around the shaft, and along approximately 2/3 of its length. The rings greatly increase the nail's holding power. Colored nails are used to install wall paneling and are self-concealing because of their color match. Roofing nails have large heads for application of roofing materials. Other nail types include galvanized nails, which have a special zinc coating to prevent rusting.

Masonry nails are made round, square, fluted, and spiraled, of hardened and tempered steel. They are used to fasten furring strips, and door or metal framing parts to masonry and concrete.

Drywall nails are specially designed to prevent "popping." (Popping occurs when wood shrinkage causes nail withdrawal.) The shank of the nail has

JOINING	SIZE & TYPE	PLACEMENT
Wall framing:	16d common or box	
Wall sheathing:		
3/4'' (19mm) boards	8d common or box	6'' (15cm) o.c.
plywood 5/16 to 1/2'' (8 to 13 mm)	6d common or box	6'' (15 cm) o.c.
plywood 5/8'' to 3/4'' (15 to 19 mm)	8d common or box	6'' (15 cm) o.c.
subflooring	8d common or box	12'' (30 cm) o.c.
underlayment	1 1/4x14 ga. ringshank	12'' (30 cm) o.c.
Roof sheathing:	6d to 8d common or box	
Roofing, asphalt:		
new construction	7/8'' to 1 1/2'' (22 to 38 mm) galv.	4 per shingle
reroofing	1 3/4'' to 2'' (44 to 50 mm) galv.	4 per shingle
Roofing, wood:		
new construction	3d or 4d galv. shingle	2-3 per shingle
reroofing	5d or 6d galv. shingle	2-3 per shingle
Soffit:		
3/8'' (9 mm) plywood	6d or 8d galv. common or box	12'' (30 cm) o.c.
Siding:		
Bevel-lapped	9d galv. common or box	1 per stud
drop or shiplap	8d galv. common or box	1 per stud
shingles or shakes	3d-6d galv. shake	2-3 per unit
plywood	2x14 ga. galv.	
Trim:		
door/window	4d-12d casing or finishing	
molding	4d-12d casing or finishing	
Furring:		
wood to wood	8d common or box	
wood to masonry	1 1/2'' to 1 3/4'' (37 to 44 mm) concrete nail	

Fig. 6-3. Nail use chart shows size, type, and placement of nails for some home structures.

angular rings which bite into the wood wall stud. The head is dish shaped and drives to just below the surface of the gypsum. The depression in the gypsum surface holds the drywall compound.

Nails are sold by the pound or kilogram. Any quantity may be packaged by your supplier from bulk stock. The local supplier also has in stock prepackaged units of 1 lb. (.5 kg) and 5 lb. (2.5 kg). If you expect to use enough, the 50 lb. (25 kg) box of nails is probably the most economical quantity.

Nail Removal and Replacement

Nail removal is an important part of home maintenance. The homeowner may need to remove old nails, nails in temporary structures, or nails which begin to go crooked.

A claw hammer or nail puller acts as a lever to remove nails. However, care must be taken if the surface holding the nail is soft or is decorative. To avoid damaging the surface, use a block or putty knife under the hammer or nail puller.

Nail placement depends on the material the nail will penetrate. Household nailing involves masonry, hardwood, softwood, and combinations of these.

Masonry nails can be 3 in. apart in mortar, but no closer than the next core in hollow core cement blocks. The very sharp driving blow harms the granular cement more than it does the mortar.

Wood nails cannot be used in thin pieces of hardwood unless holes are drilled. The wood will crack. Nails can be placed in thick pieces of hardwood.

All nails can be used in softwood. Pilot holes are not needed. However, two or more nails near the end of a plank cannot be put in the same run of grain. A crack may not appear immediately, but will form later. Choose a different grain run for each nail.

THREADED FASTENERS

The family of threaded fasteners includes screws, bolts, and a great variety of special threaded items. The Greek inventor, Archimedes, in approximately 250 B.C., put the principle of the spiral to practical use in the threaded fastener. The spiral is used to exert great pressure with a small turning force.

Screws that make their own threads are of two basic types:
1. Thread-forming, Fig. 6-4.
2. Thread-cutting, Fig. 6-5.

Thread-forming screws are popular today because they save time. They are used extensively for sheet metal jobs. Thread-cutting screws are used for metal, plastic, and sometimes wood.

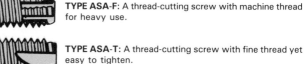

TYPE ASA 17: Thread-cutting screw with coarse thread for wood.

TYPE ASA-D: Thread-cutting screw with general use.

TYPE ASA-F: A thread-cutting screw with machine thread for heavy use.

TYPE ASA-T: A thread-cutting screw with fine thread yet easy to tighten.

TYPE ASA-BT: A thread-cutting screw similar to the above but with coarse thread.

Fig. 6-5. Thread-cutting screws form clean threads in drilled holes.

The driving recesses of screw heads are varied, Fig. 6-6. However, the slotted and phillips are most frequently used around the house. The underside of the screw head is important for proper seat and stress distribution, Fig. 6-7. Plastics may be split by a head with a steep cone.

There are special purpose screw heads. Tamperproof screws provide protection wherever pilferage or vandalism might occur. Fig. 6-8 shows one type

TYPE ASA-A: Thread-forming screw for use in thin metal .015 to .050 thick.

TYPE ASA-B: Thread-forming screw for use in heavier metal .050 to .200 thick.

TYPE ASA-AB: Thread-forming screw with a locating point which acts as a ramp.

TYPE ASA-BP: Thread-forming screw has a cone point for use where holes are slightly misaligned.

TYPE ASA-U: Thread-forming screw with steep helical thread is driven or hammered into hole.

Fig. 6-4. Thread-forming screws fasten quickly.

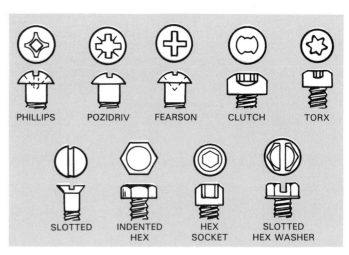

PHILLIPS   POZIDRIV   FEARSON   CLUTCH   TORX

SLOTTED   INDENTED HEX   HEX SOCKET   SLOTTED HEX WASHER

Fig. 6-6. Screws having these driving recesses are used both in home structures and in appliances.

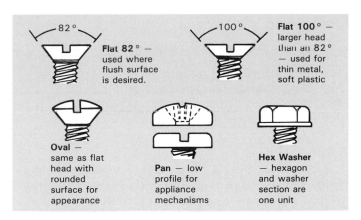

Fig. 6-7. Consider surface fit, appearance, convenience, and hole coverage when choosing a screw head style.

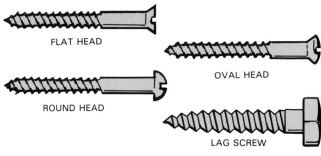

Fig. 6-9. Types of screws used for wood. The first three screws are for light duty. They have low profile heads for visible locations. The lag screw is used in framework for heavy loads.

One-way Screw
Installs with ordinary screwdriver. Has no bearing surface for removal. To be removed, it must be drilled and a screw extractor used.

Spanner Head Screw
Driven and removed with special spanner. Provides moderate security, with advantage of being able to remove it if desired.

Break-Off Head Screw
This screw installs with hex socket head wrench. Hex head is then sawed or broken off, leaving low rounded head that cannot be removed.

Fig. 6-8. Tamperproof screw heads provide low cost security.

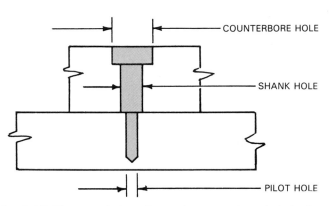

Fig. 6-10. To properly install wood screws, form hole in three sections.

of screw head used to discourage removal. Such screws are ideal for securing items used on home security equipment. The screws are safeguards in public places such as hallways, cafeterias, and rest rooms. The tamperproof screw heads cannot be removed by conventional tools.

Wood Screws

Wood screws, shown in Fig. 6-9, are tapered to easily form new threads in wood. Select the wood screw length so that at least two-thirds of its length is in the base material to which you are fastening. This rule does not apply when the base material is no thicker than the attached piece. To help when placing screws, you must drill a pilot hole, Fig. 6-10. Pilot holes in hardwood must be closely sized to the screw. Check a drill size chart, Fig. 6-11. Choose drill sizes for pilot holes in hardwood 1/64 in. larger than those for softwood.

The shank size of a wood screw is determined

SCREW NUMBER	PILOT HOLE SOFTWOOD		PILOT HOLE HARDWOOD		SHANK CLEARANCE HOLE SOFTWOOD AND HARDWOOD		COUNTERSINK HOLE	
	in.	mm	in.	mm	In.	mm	in.	mm
0	1/64	.4	1/32	.8	1/16	1.6	3/16	4.8
1	1/32	.8	1/32	.8	5/64	2.0	3/16	4.8
2	1/32	.8	3/64	1.2	3/32	2.4	3/16	4.8
3	3/64	1.2	1/16	1.6	7/64	2.8	1/4	6.4
4	3/64	1.2	1/16	1.6	7/64	2.8	1/4	6.4
5	1/16	1.6	5/64	2.0	1/8	3.1	1/4	6.4
6	1/16	1.6	5/64	2.0	9/64	3.6	5/16	8.0
7	5/64	2.0	3/32	2.4	5/32	4.0	5/16	8.0
8	5/64	2.0	3/32	2.4	11/64	4.4	3/8	9.5
9	3/32	2.4	7/64	2.8	3/16	4.8	3/8	9.5
10	3/32	2.4	7/64	2.8	3/16	4.8	3/8	9.5
11	7/64	2.8	1/8	3.1	13/64	5.2	7/16	11.0
12	7/64	2.8	1/8	3.1	7/32	5.6	7/16	11.0
14	9/64	3.6	9/64	3.6	1/4	6.4	1/2	12.8
16	9/64	3.6	5/32	4.0	17/32	13.5	9/16	14.2

Fig. 6-11. Wood screw pilot-hole and shank clearance-hole sizes. Note that pilot holes for hardwood are 1/64 larger than for the same screw in softwood.

by the diameter of the screw measured at the un-threaded part just below the head and is designated by a wire gauge number. This part of the screw is known as the body or shank. Shank diameters range from number 0, 1/16 in. (1.5 mm), up to number 24, 3/8 in. (9.5 mm). Holes for shank clearance are the same for screws in softwood and hardwood.

Lag screws are used to support heavy items or mount metal brackets designed to withstand strong forces. They are usually made with either a square or horizontal head for driving with a wrench. Lag screws are sized according to diameter and by length. Lengths range from 2 to 8 in. (5 to 20 cm).

Sometimes screws driven near an end or edge of a board will crack it. You may want to take special steps to avoid this. One solution is shown in Fig. 6-12. Drill a hole for a dowel to run across the wood grain. The center of the hole should be below the surface by about the thickness of the board.

After inserting the dowel, proceed as you would for any wood screw. The screw will grip the cross grain of the dowel. No crack is likely to occur.

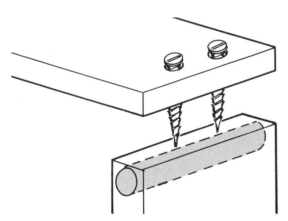

Fig. 6-12. To help avoid splitting at an edge, insert dowel across existing grain.

Machine Screws

Machine screws are available in a variety of head styles. Styles and some sizing rules for both machine screws and wood screws are shown in Fig. 6-13. Machine screws are sized by gauge numbers from 0 to 12 (1/16 to 7/32 in.) for small screws, and by diameter measurement for larger screws. The range of the diameter listing method is 1/4 in. (6 mm) to 1/2 in. (12 mm). The lengths range from 1/8 to 3 in. (3 to 76 mm).

Bolts

In contrast to a machine screw, a bolt is generally defined as a fastener used with a nut and tightened by turning the nut. To further define the terms, note that if it has a slot or recess in the head, it is not a bolt. A machine bolt is illustrated in Fig. 6-14. Sizes are determined by the number of threads per unit of length. Two systems currently prevail:
1. The inch (conventional) system.
2. The International system of metric units (SI).

Fig. 6-14. A machine bolt has a gap above threads. Bolt is not designed for tight fit in hole.

The inch system lists screws by number of threads per inch. For example: 1/2 x 20 means a screw with 1/2 inch diameter and with 20 threads per inch. Some smaller machine bolts have diameters given by gauge number. For example: 6-32 means diameter is wire size 6 and screw has 32 threads per inch.

Metric threads are listed in a simmilar way to that of the inch method, but with some variations. Metric threads are designated with an "M" prefix followed by the diameter given in millimeters. Instead of the number of threads per inch, the metric designation is given in pitch (spiral advance) of the thread. For example: the M8 x 1.0 is 8 mm in diameter and the pitch is 1 mm per revolution. The coarse metric threads are seldom designated but commonly understood. For example, M8 means 8 mm, and a pitch of 1.25 mm is understood.

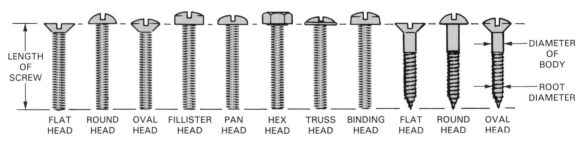

Fig. 6-13. Screw size is measured not by the overall length, but by the part which is not above the surface. Method uses final position the screw has when snug. The three wood screws included are measured in the same way. Note head styles of machine screws.

Carriage bolts, Fig. 6-15, have coarse threads. Screw head styles include a countersunk flat topped head in addition to the round head. Large square shoulders keep the head from turning when the nut is tightened. Normally, a square nut and washer is used with the carriage bolt.

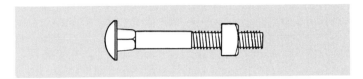

Fig. 6-15. Carriage bolt is used to join wood pieces such as planks.

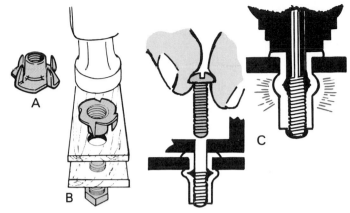

Fig. 6-17. Several types of devices provide threads in wood, metal, or plastic. A—Tee nut. B—Use hammer to embed tee nut. C—A threaded blind rivet provides threads in thin materials.

Nuts and Washers

Fig. 6-16 shows some styles of nuts and washers. Nuts allow quick changes in framework using bolts. Washers protect soft surfaces. Nut styles include square, hexagonal, and wing types. Square nuts are turned with an open end wrench. The hexagonal nut is normally tightened by an open end wrench or by a closed (box) wrench for high torque. The winged nut is for temporary structures and removable items. These uses require low turning torque and only the thumb and forefinger are needed for tightening.

Several types of threaded inserts provide threads in soft or thin materials. See Fig. 6-17.

A barbed tee nut provides steel threads in wood. It makes wood-to-metal application possible. It is used for knockdown work or when old screw holes have become useless. It mounts flush without countersinking. To attach, first drill a hole in wood to fit the barrel of the tee nut. Then insert and hammer the barbs into the surface. Screw or bolt is inserted from opposite direction.

Refer again to Fig. 6-17. A threaded blind rivet is used in thin metal or in plastic that is not brittle. Rivet is set with special tool or can sometimes be set when screw is used the first time. A third type of insert is the E-Z Lok. This cuts into wood without crushing the fibers.

The flat washer is designed to prevent the nut from burying itself into the wood and destroying the

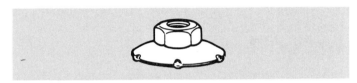

Fig. 6-18. Preassembled bolts, nuts, and washers save time and hold tight.

material. Locking washers are used for metal applications where vibrations might dislodge the nut. The preassembled nut and washer is made as a unit, but the parts are free to rotate independent of each other, Fig. 6-18.

Drywall Anchors

There are several types of fasteners which attach to wall materials. Types for light walls include the toggle bolt and plastic flaring anchor, Fig. 6-19.

Toggle bolts are used when fastening to hollow walls. A hole is drilled large enough to pass the spring-loaded toggle wing through the hollow center. The wings spread out and bear against the wall as the head of the bolt is secured.

The plastic flaring anchor mounts in walls of any thickness. It is designed to flare behind a thin wall, wedge inside a thick wall, or adjust for an intermediate thickness. The flaring anchor is available

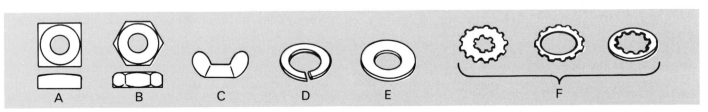

Fig. 6-16. Common nuts and washers. A — Square nut. B — Hexagonal nut. C — Wing nut. D — Spring lock washer. E — Flat washer. F — Locking washers.

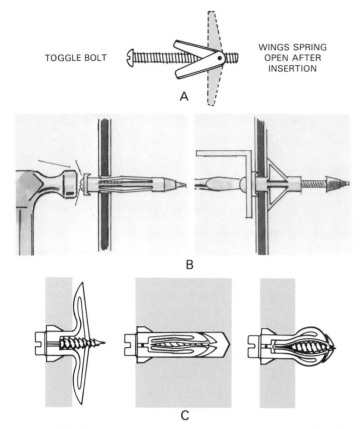

Fig. 6-19. Light loads can be supported on hollow walls with wall anchors. A—Spring wing toggle bolt. B—How to install an expandable anchor. C—Plastic anchors hold 100 lbs. (Rawl Plug)

U-bolts and eye bolts are special purpose fasteners and clamps. They are used to mount round or tubular stock. For example, the U-bolt mounts a T.V. antenna to a post. The eye bolt often supports a rope or cable.

Turnbuckles consist of a steel sleeve and two screw eyes. Half of the sleeve and one screw eye have right-hand threads while the other half has a left-hand thread. Turning the sleeve left or right will either lengthen or shorten the distance between the eyes. The turnbuckle is used, for example, to tighten the guide wires on a T.V. antenna.

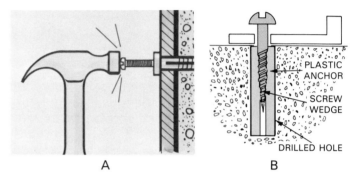

Fig. 6-20. A—Type of masonry anchor for quick installation. B—Cutaway view shows how one masonry anchor works. (Rawl Plug)

for wall thicknesses of 3/16, 1/4, 3/8, 1/2, and 5/8 in. (5, 6, 9, 12, and 15 mm).

Masonry Anchors

When hanging objects to a masonry wall, a fastener is needed which will not loosen with vibration. Plastic plugs inserted into predrilled holes provide the gripping base for screws, Fig. 6-20. Screws cause the plastic plug to expand and grip the sides of the hole. Plastic plugs are available in several sizes. Sizes are 1/4 to 1/2 in. (6 to 12 mm) in diameter and 1 to 2 in. (25 to 50 mm) in length.

To install a 1/4 inch anchor, drill a 1/4 inch hole with a carbide masonry drill and drive the plastic gently in place, flush with the surface of the wall. Insert the proper gauge size thread-forming screw and tighten it supporting the desired bracket or unit to be hung.

The wall anchors will not support large or heavy objects. However, they will support pictures, curtain rods and towel bars. Additional systems must be used for the heavier accessories like mirrors, bookcases, cabinets, and closet rods.

Hook and Loop Fasteners

Some fasteners are forged or bent into a loop to encircle an object being held. See Fig. 6-21. Looped fasteners include the eye bolt, U-bolt, and turnbuckle.

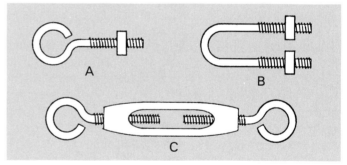

Fig. 6-21. Special fasteners: A — Eye bolt. B — U-bolt. C — Turnbuckle.

STAPLES

Staples permit rapid and efficient fastening of light materials. The staple is a ''U'' shaped fastener available in many sizes, Fig. 6-22. Lengths range from 1/4 to 9/16 in. (6 to 14 mm).

Staples are applied with an electric or air operated gun, a hand operated gun, or with a hammer tacker, Fig. 6-23. For safety, always point staple guns away from others.

Staples attach screen wire to frames, ceiling tile to furring strips, or insulation batts to studs, Fig. 6-24. They are especially useful when work involves reaching or when one hand must be free to hold the material.

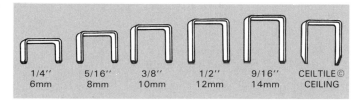

Fig. 6-22. Common sizes of staples for light use.

Fig. 6-24. The stapler saves effort when work position leads to fatigue. Nails and screws are more difficult to hold when placing in ceiling. (Arrow)

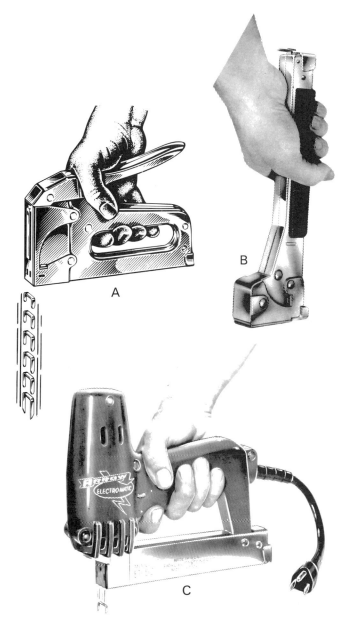

Fig. 6-23. Staplers for general use: A — Hand operated stapler (Arrow Stapler). B — Hammer tacker — impact operated (Arrow Stapler). C — Electric operated (Duo-Fast).

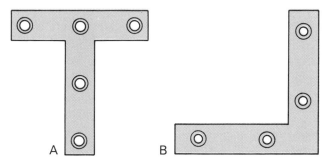

Fig. 6-25. Types of flat reinforcing plates. A — T-plate. B — L shaped plate.

BRACES AND MENDING PLATES

Hardware items are available for repairing, mending, or reinforcing almost any kind of wood joint. Metal plates come in a variety of shapes for use in strengthening chair legs, table tops and legs, and door frames. They vary in length, width, and weight as well as in types of metal and finishes.

There are four types of mending plates: straight, T, L, and inside corner. There are also other bracing devices.

The simplest mending plate is the straight plate. It is a flat piece of metal with screw holes drilled and countersunk to accept flat headed screws. The straight plate is used to reinforce an end-to-end or edge-to-end joint. Where a plate detracts from the appearance of a piece of furniture, it may be recessed into a mortise or covered with another material.

Fig. 6-25 shows a T-plate and an L-plate. The T-plate reinforces an intersection of two pieces that form a T or a cross. The L-plate strengthens a corner of a screen or a wood frame.

Fig. 6-26 shows both a corner mending plate and a related bracing device called a corner bracket. The inside corner plate is a narrow strip of metal bent at a 90° angle. The legs are equal or different lengths. The corner plate reinforces an inside corner against motion that would bend the 90° angle, but not against a twisting motion.

The corner bracket, B in Fig. 6-26, is more stable than the corner mending plate. The sides and curved shape reduce twisting. A corner bracket matches furniture design better than a mending plate.

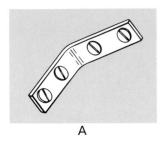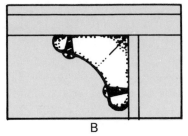

Fig. 6-26. Corner reinforcement. A — Corner mending plate. B — Corner bracket. A corner mending plate and a corner bracket mount on the same kind of inside corner.

Fig. 6-27. Epoxy adhesive consists of two parts: resin and hardener. Epoxy will bond dissimilar materials.

ADHESIVE	PACKAGE COMPONENTS	METHOD OF APPLICATION	MATERIALS BONDABLE	POT LIFE	SHELF LIFE	SETTING TIME	CLAMP TIME	CLEAN-UP SOLVENT
acrylic	two part, liquid and powder mix as needed	brush, paddle, or spatula	wood or metal, high water resistance, not affected by gasoline, or oil	3 to 20 minutes	indefinite at room temp.	3 to 20 min.	low pressure 5-30 min.	acetone
acrylonitrile	one part, ready to use	brush	textiles, fabrics —carpet, tents, boat sails, etc.	N.A.	indefinite	quick	none	acetone or Ketone
aliphatic	one part, liquid	brush, paddle or spatula/easy to work with	wood, furniture, cabinets	N.A.	indefinite if stored above 32°F	15 min.	2 hrs. moderate pressure	warm water
cellulose	one part, ready to use	apply directly from tube	model work, small repairs on china, wood, glass	N.A.	indefinite	60% Strength 90% Strength 2 hrs. 100% Strength overnight	5 min. low pressure	acetone
contact cement	one part, liquid	brush, roller	high pressure plastic laminates, hardboard and plywood	N.A. if covered	12 month at 60-80°F	20-25 min.	contact pressure	acetone
cyano-acrylate	one part, liquid	direct from squeeze tube Note: Read directions on pkg.	china, glassware, porcelain, metal, plastic etc.	N.A.	indefinite	few seconds	low pressure	water prior to setting, difficult to clean
Epoxy	two part, liquids	brush, paddle, spatula	almost anything	N.A.	indefinite	5 min. to overnight	low pressure	acetone; Difficult to clean
Polyvinyl Chloride	one part liquids ready to use	directly from tube	china, marble, glass, porcelain, wood, or metal, high water resistance	N.A.	indefinite if stored above 32°F	20 to 30 min.	8 hr. at 70°F moderate pressure	water
Resorcinol	two part, liquid and powder	brush, spatula	wood, excellent for boat and aircraft use	3-4 hrs.	indefinite	10 hrs. —70°F 6 hrs. —80°F	10 hrs. —70°F 6 hrs. —80°F high pressure	cold water before setting
Styrene Butadiene	one part, thick paste	trowel	bonds ceramic tile	N.A.	indefinite if stored above freezing	48 hrs.	hand pressure	mineral spirits, turpentine
Urea Formaldehyde	one part powder, mixed with water	brush, roller, spatula	wood, high pressure plastic laminates—water resistance	3 to 5 hrs.	indefinite if kept dry	9 to 13 hrs. at 70°F	9 to 13 hrs. at 70°F high pressure	cold water

Fig. 6-28. Table of adhesive types and guidelines for use.

Corner brackets are available with many attractive metal finishes. Some mending plates also have finishes. One finish simulates wrought iron.

ADHESIVES

Often the best way to fasten two or more pieces together is with an adhesive. Adhesives include glue, epoxy resins, and cements.

The space age has brought many new ways to bond different materials to each other. Knowledge of these materials and skill in using them are important for repairing modern home equipment.

Household adhesives, Fig. 6-27, have made home repair jobs much easier. However, choosing among the many adhesives available has become more difficult. The chart in Fig. 6-28 provides information to help you choose the correct adhesive.

Joint preparations for adhesives will determine the success or failure of the glue repair. Most adhesive joints rely on surface-to-surface contact. Tight fitting joints are critical. Make sure that the bonding area is clean, free from dirt, oil, and old glue, Fig. 6-29. For bonding metal, glass, and other

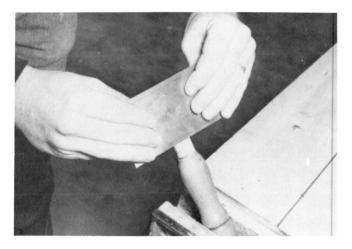

Fig. 6-29. Clean the surface of the piece to be bonded. Old adhesive, paint, and dirt will interfere with the strength of the joint.

nonporous materials, wipe the surface with a degreasing agent. Select the appropriate adhesive and follow the manufacturer's instructions completely.

DRY WALL SCREWS

The dry wall screw was designed to secure dry wall gypsum board to metal studs with the aid of power screw drivers. The process allows rapid installation of the wall finishing materials with the speed and efficiency necessary in the semi-automatic installation of wallboard. Although

designed for use with dry wall, the metal must resist the corrosive action of gypsum and the torque forces of a power screw driver. The wedge-headed screws may be of a variety of coatings; zinc, chromate, and bronze. The dry wall screw is used for other applications, because of these characteristics. This style of screw may be used for attaching subfloor decks along with any construction applications. The advantage of the dry wall screw is that it offers superior holding power over conventional fasteners.

TEST YOUR KNOWLEDGE—CHAPTER 6

1. A _____ nail has a zinc coating to resist rust.
2. A _____ or putty knife protects a soft surface when removing a nail.
3. A nail should be _____ times as long as the thickness of the item being held.
4. When driving two or more nails near the end of a plank, do not place them in the same _____ .
5. Sheet metal fastening is done with _____-forming and cutting screws.
6. Pilot holes for wood screws in hardwood require drill sizes _____ larger than that needed for the same screw in softwood.
7. To reduce cracking at the end of a board due to wood screws, install a _____ across the grain.
8. A _____ _____ provides steel threads in wood.
9. Fasten insulation batts to studs with _____ .
10. For reinforcing a corner of a piece of furniture, the _____ _____ is preferred.
11. A common adhesive for bonding unlike materials is _____ .
12. Old glue _____ (will, will not) form a bond with new glue.

KNOW THESE TERMS

Penny, gauge, common, box, casing, ring shank, threaded fasteners, break-off, pilot hole, countersink, root diameter, spring lock, washer, staples, adhesive, dry wall screw.

SUGGESTED ACTIVITIES

Convince yourself of the strength of modern adhesives by testing some of them. Apply the adhesive to some items that are wood, metal, or glass. Follow the application instructions closely. When cured, try to pull the objects apart. Demonstrate the results to your class.

7

LUMBER AND BUILDING MATERIALS

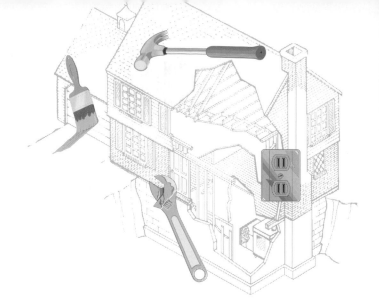

This chapter introduces the types of wood used in lumber and plywood. The chapter defines hardwood and softwood and lists the species of trees which supply the wood types. The terms "nominal size" and "dressed size" are defined. The chapter explains the meaning of lumber and plywood grade markings. Wood composites and metal materials are mentioned.

After studying this chapter, you will be able to:
- List the common softwood and hardwood species.
- Describe several ways boards are cut from a log.
- List the dressed sizes for the most common lumber used.
- Read and decode the grade markings on lumber and plywood.
- Choose proper wood types and grades for interior and exterior use.
- Request woodwork items by name.
- Choose wood products by cost and quality.

To select the correct kind of lumber for home repair jobs, you need to know about the different kinds of wood, what they are used for, what are their specific characteristics, and how they differ. One of the largest questions the home mechanic has is the understanding of the nominal versus actual size concept. Other questions involve finished lumber compared with dimension lumber, hardwood and softwood, and whether to use boards or plywood sheets for a job.

Lumber and plywood are both used for general construction repair and to make furniture and cabinets. In residential construction, lumber is used for framing. Frame uses include floor joists, studs, ceiling joists, and rafters. See Fig. 7-1. Plywood may be used for floor underlayments, boxing, and roof sheathing. Other wood products are flooring shingles, moldings, and finish trim.

Fig. 7-1. Residential construction lumber is usually derived from the more abundant and less attractive species. (Weyerhaeuser)

FOREST REGIONS OF THE UNITED STATES

The 50 states have 10 different forest regions. Forest region borders are defined by the most common species growing in that area. Even though a particular species may grow in more than one region, groupings are taken by average species population.

The Continental forests are divided into six regions, Fig. 7-2. Each region will yield lumber for a different use by the home mechanic.

The West Coast forest yields the giant redwood, ponderosa pine, Douglas fir, spruce, and many others. The construction industry receives a large percentage of its fir plywood and redwood siding boards from this region.

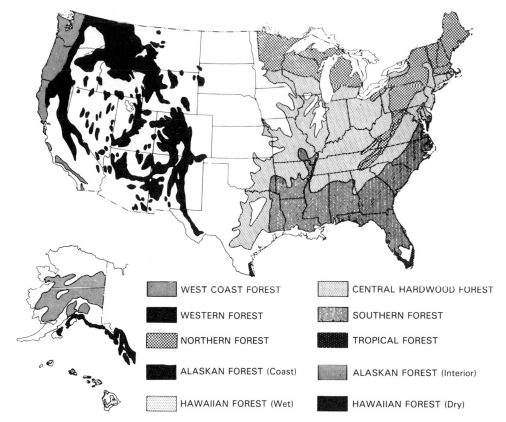

Fig. 7-2. Forest regions of the United States.

WEST COAST FOREST

WESTERN FOREST

NORTHERN FOREST

ALASKAN FOREST (Coast)

HAWAIIAN FOREST (Wet)

CENTRAL HARDWOOD FOREST

SOUTHERN FOREST

TROPICAL FOREST

ALASKAN FOREST (Interior)

HAWAIIAN FOREST (Dry)

The Western forest lies in the western one-third of the nation. It produces nearly one-fourth of the lumber used in residential and light frame construction. The six major lumber-producing species of this region are: ponderosa pine, Idaho white pine, Engleman spruce, Douglas fir, western red cedar, and western birch. Most of the bevel siding and cedar shingles are produced from this region. Aspen is the predominant hardwood.

The Southern forest, noted for long and short leaf yellow pine, produces also loblolly pines and slash pines. The Southern forest produces many hardwoods such as red and black gum, oaks of several species as well as cottonwood, ash, and pecan.

The Central hardwood forest produces a large amount of the hardwood lumber for furniture and cabinetmaking. Among the many species in this forest are walnut, oak, beech, hickory, maple, elm, ash, eastern red cedar, and some pines.

The Northern forest, known for pulpwood production, provides hard maple, cherry, birch, and basswood. These are used for furniture and cabinets. Softwoods such as pines, spruce, and fir yield framing lumber.

The tropical forest has a limited production. However, the species found in this area are bay, mangrove, eucalyptus, and mahogany.

SOFTWOOD

Softwood is lumber produced from the coniferous trees. Coniferous trees have cones and needles.

They include evergreen species of trees. Spruce, redwood, pine, fir, and hemlock are examples of the softwood species.

Spruce, pine, and fir are the main sources for lumber products. Lumber is sawed from the tree and remains rough until it is planed to a finish dimension. There are two sizes listed for lumber. These are the nominal size and the actual (dressed) size. Refer to Fig. 7-3.

Because of shrinkage due to drying in a kiln and planing to finished dimension, lumber is actually smaller than the nominal size by which it is sold. For example, 1 x 6 in. (2.5 x 15 cm) as sold would

NOMINAL SIZE		DRESSED SIZE	
in.	cm.	in.	cm.
1 x 2	2.5 x 5.0	3/4 x 1 1/2	2.0 x 4.0
1 x 3	2.5 x 7.5	3/4 x 2 1/2	2.0 x 6.0
1 x 4	2.5 x 10.0	3/4 x 3 1/2	2.0 x 9.0
1 x 5	2.5 x 13.0	3/4 x 5 1/2	2.0 x 14.0
1 x 8	2.5 x 20.0	3/4 x 7 1/4	2.0 x 18.0
1 x 10	2.5 x 25.0	3/4 x 9 1/4	2.0 x 24.0
1 x 12	2.5 x 30.0	3/4 x 11 1/4	2.0 x 29.0
2 x 4	5.0 x 10.0	1 1/2 x 3 1/2	4.0 x 9.0
2 x 4	5.0 x 15.0	1 1/2 x 5 1/2	4.0 x 14.0
2 x 8	5.0 x 20.0	1 1/2 x 7 1/4	4.0 x 18.0
2 x 10	5.0 x 25.0	1 1/2 x 9 1/4	4.0 x 24.0
2 x 12	5.0 x 30.0	1 1/2 x 11 1/4	4.0 x 29.0
4 x 4	10.0 x 10.0	3 1/2 x 3 1/2	9.0 x 9.0
4 x 6	10.0 x 15.0	3 1/2 x 5 1/2	9.0 x 14.0

Fig. 7-3. Lumber sizes. Actual or "dressed" size is not the same as the nominal size.

actually measure only 3/4 in. x 5 1/2 in. (2 x 14 cm). Plan the repair project according to the actual dimension.

Softwood Species

Softwood species vary in their resistance to weather and decay. Select the lumber by species for the particular job at hand. See Fig. 7-4. Common framing for structural members not exposed

SPECIES	CHARACTERISTICS	USES
Pine	uniform smooth texture, works well finishes beautifully, resists warping	House construction, cabinet/furniture making, millwork, molding
Hemlock	Lightweight, machines well, low resistance to decay	framing lumber, sub-flooring, doors, paneling, boxes and crates
Fir	easily worked, finishes moderate resistance moisture and decay	door and window frames, plywood veneer, general millwork, and interior trim
Redwood	lightweight, easy to work, low structural strength, high resistance to decay	outdoor furniture, fencing, deck surfaces, siding, paneling
Spruce	strong, harder, low resistance to decay	boxes and crates, ladders, general millwork
Cedar, western	lightweight, high decay resistance uniform texture, straight grain easy to work	siding, shingles, shakes, outdoor patios, decks, boxes
Cedar, eastern	color variations, pungent odor, high decay resistance, small boards	furniture, chests, posts, novelties, closet linings

Fig. 7-4. Softwood species and general uses. The group number is a shorthand for identification.

to the elements could be sawn from pine, hemlock, fir, and spruce. If the members are to be exposed to weather, such as in porches, decks, and fences, then select western cedar, redwood, and to a lesser degree fir.

Treated Softwood

Softwood for parts which are to be set into the earth, or lumber for exposure to the weather and high decay conditions, is often treated chemically to protect against decay and insect damage, Fig. 7-5. Wood which is naturally decay resistant can be pressure treated to resist other causes of damage like rodents. The treatment increases the already high lifetime as an outdoor use material.

Fig. 7-5. Chemical treatment of wood provides resistance to decay or insects. Certain chemicals increase the flame resistance. The treatment is done in a huge pressure vessel like this one. (Koppers)

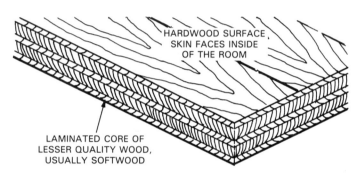

Fig. 7-6. Hardwood plywood has the look of real wood paneling and the convenience of a thick sheet. The surface skin was sliced from a log's circumference by an unrolling process.

HARDWOOD

Hardwood is lumber produced from the deciduous trees. These trees have leaves instead of needles. Deciduous trees lose their leaves each fall. Of course not all deciduous trees produce hardwood.

Wood of the group consists mainly of oak, walnut, maple, and birch. Hardwood lumbers generally cost more than softwood and are usually stronger and harder. Hardwood lumbers are normally used for furniture and cabinet making, decorative trim, and paneling.

Hardwoods are as easy to work as softwoods if the cutting tools are kept sharp. Hardwoods have good color and detailed grain patterns. This makes them highly desirable for decorative effects that add warmth.

Their scarcity, high cost, and beauty, place these woods at a premium, so they are used for interior purposes only. Cost is reduced if a veneer is used instead of a solid piece. Look at Fig. 7-6. Hardwood veneers are bonded onto a softwood core. These provide the home mechanic with a sound and economical panel.

Hardwood Species

Many different kinds of hardwood, some native to the United States and some imported from various parts of the world, are used in fine furniture and for interior wall paneling. Refer to Fig. 7-7.

Many hardwoods are prized for special marking. Irregularity in the growth and also defects in the wood may provide this variation.

The names hardwood and softwood are misleading. Some softwoods have more strength and hardness than some hardwoods.

SPECIES	CHARACTERISTICS	USES
Cherry	close grained, resist warpage, ages to a deep red color works well	furniture, cases, fine tables
Oak	strong, deep grained, resists moisture absorption, finishes well	furniture, flooring, barrels, structural support members
Maple	strong, machines well, shock resistant, fine texture, close grained	furniture, bowling alley floors, bowling pins, industrial application
Walnut	moderately strong, fine-textured superior color and grain configuration works easy, finish well	furniture, gunstocks, wall paneling, picture frames, veneering
Mahogany (imported)	fine grained, easy to work, reddish color, resists warping	furniture/cabinets
Teak (imported)	hard-durable, resistant to moisture, resist decay	boat building, furniture, construction, flooring, trim
Ash	tough, light colored, highly elastic, finishes well	furniture, paneling
Hickory	strong, light colored, susceptible to decay and insects	tool handles, industrial application, some furniture

Fig. 7-7. Hardwood species, general uses, grain type, and strength.

LUMBER GRADES

A lumber grading system is a result of combined efforts of the U.S. Department of Commerce and the American Lumber Standards Committee. Detailed rules are developed and applied by regional trade associations of lumber producers. For example, for softwood, the Western Wood Products Association; southern pine, Inspection Bureau; and for redwood, the California Redwood Association. There are others. The hardwood grades are established by the National Hardwood Lumber Association.

When lumber is cut from the log in different ways, the pieces are very different in appearance and strength. See Fig. 7-8. Much depends on the

FACE

END

PLAIN SAWED   QUARTER SAWED   RIFT SAWED

Fig. 7-8. Wood grain patterns revealed by three methods of sawing boards. Plain sawed wood is found in planking. Quarter sawed is found in wall and ceiling framing. Rift sawed is used for furniture surfaces.

number and size of the imperfections. Grades are based on:

1. The number, size, and location of these defects.
2. The structural load which the piece is capable of supporting.

Softwood Grades

The American Lumber Standards for softwood divide softwood lumber into these groups:

1. Yard
2. Structural
3. Factory and shop

Subgroups are shown in Fig. 7-9. The number of defects and their place in each piece determine the grade it will be.

Softwood lumber which is sold retail or without special ordering is classified as yard lumber. Yard is lumber generally stocked by the local lumber dealer. Each board will display an approved grade mark, Fig. 7-10.

Softwoods are graded on the condition of the whole board. A simple standard has been made to simplify the grading rules for thickness, width, and length.

CLASSI-FICATION	USAGE NAME	GRADE	DESCRIPTION
Yard	Finish	A Select	(free of nearly all defects)
		B Select	(very few defects)
		C Select	(increasingly more defects)
		D Select	(increasingly more defects)
	Common	1 Common (Construction)	(some defects, does not affect strength)
		2 Common (Standard)	(some defects, begins to affect strength)
		3 Common (Utility)	(lesser strength)
		Economy (Economy)	(many defects, affects strength)
	Dimension (structural)	1 Dimension	(will support greater load)
		2 Dimension	(will support lesser load)
		3 Dimension	(will support lesser load)
Structural		Joist and planks	2 to 4 in (5 to 10 cm)
		Beams and stringers	5 in and over (13 cm and over)
		Post and timbers	6 in x 6 in (15.0 cm x 15.0) any length
Factory And Shop	Factory Plank	1 Clear Factory	nearly free from any visible defects
		2 Clear Factory	increasingly more defects
		3 Clear Factory	more defects
	Shop Lumber	Select Shop Tank and boat 1. shop box 2. shop box	manufacturing grades (re-cut to make item)

Fig. 7-9. Choose softwood lumber grades by strength and appearance.

Yard lumber grades are:
1. Select boards: materials used for finish work and usually less than 2 in. thick, rated as A, B, C, or D. Grade A has supreme appearance and then progressively more imperfections will appear.
2. Common Lumber: light framing material 2 to 4 in. (50 to 100 mm) and 2 to 6 in. (50 to 150 mm) wide. Rated as 1, 2, 3, and economy. Number 1 is the superior quality for

Fig. 7-10. Example of grade mark found on softwood yard lumber. A — Identifies the grading association, in this case the Western Wood Products Association. B — Is a number assigned to each mill. C — Is a grade name abbreviation. D — Identifies the wood species. E — States moisture content of lumber when unseasoned or "green."

strength requirements, then progressively lesser in quality.
3. Dimension Lumber: structural framing material 2 to 4 in. thick and 6 in. wide. Rated as 1, 2, 3 dimension. Number 1 dimension stands to support a greater load followed by those of lesser strength.

The home mechanic must understand that quality construction does not require that all lumber be of the best grade. Today lumber is graded for specific uses. In a given structure several grades may be appropriate.

Hardwood Grades

Hardwood grades are based on the amount of usable lumber in each piece of a given width and length. The percentage of the board free of defects determines the grade. See Fig. 7-11. This percentage is called "clear face cutting". Four standard grades of hardwood lumber are: firsts and seconds — combined into FAS, Selects, No. 1 Common, and No. 2 Common.

SOFTWOOD PLYWOOD

A plywood panel is made from a number of thin sheets of wood called veneers. See Fig. 7-12. Layers of select logs are peeled in giant lathes to form the veneers. Each layer is the same thickness. Then the veneers are bonded under pressure as shown in Fig. 7-13. This material is bonded with the grain of each ply running at about a right angle to the grain of an adjacent ply. Cross bonding produces high strength in both directions. The result is a lightweight panel product suited for hundreds of uses around the house. There is an advantage from the structure of plywood. Cutting is easy because of the alternating grain from layer to layer.

Softwood plywood is manufactured in two types: exterior type with a 100 percent waterproof glue line and interior type with highly moisture resistant glue. Veneers for inner plys in interior types of plywood may be of lower grade than those in exterior type.

GRADE	QUALITY
First	91 2/3% clear face cutting 8 to 16 ft. long — 6 in. wide or wider (2.5 to 5 m long — 15 cm wide or wider)
Seconds	83 1/2% clear face cutting 8 to 16 ft. long — 6 in. wide or wider (2.5 to 5 m long — 15 cm wide or wider)
Selects	91 2/3% clear face cutting 6 to 16 ft. long — 4 in. wide or wider (1.7 to 5 m long — 10 cm wide or wider)
No. 1 Common	66 2/3% clear face cutting 4 to 16 ft. long — 3 in. wide or wider (1.2 to 5 m long — 7.8 cm wide or wider)
No. 2 Common	50% clear face cutting 4 to 16 ft. long — 3 in. wide or wider (1.2 to 5 m long — 7.8 cm wide or wider)

Fig. 7-11. Choose hardwood grades by the minimum percentage of pieces having a defect.

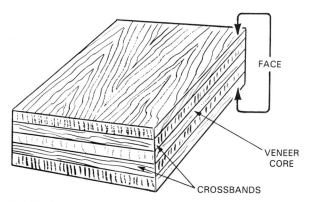

Fig. 7-12. Plywood is a sheet product made from thin veneers. The grain of alternating veneer layers in plywood runs in different directions. This gives plywood its strength. (Frank Paxton Lumber Co.)

Specify exterior type plywood for all exposed applications, for example, soffits and sidings. Interior type plywood is highly moisture resistant but the bond is not permanently waterproof. It may be used anywhere it will not be subjected to continuing moisture conditions or extreme humidity. For example, interior grade is enough for roof sheathing and subflooring.

Grades of Softwood Plywood

Within each type of plywood there is a variety of grades based on appearance and strength. They are listed in part by the grade of the veneer (N, A, B, C, or D) used for the face and back of the panel. Grade N is the highest. It allows no more than six repaired defects on a 4 x 8 sheet.

See Figs. 7-14 and 7-15. Panel grades are designated by type of glue and by veneer grade on the face and back. For example, "A-C, EXT" means "A" face veneer, "C" back veneer with exterior type glues. (Refer to Appendix B.)

Refer again to Fig. 7-15 for an explanation of grading symbol codes. "Exposure 1" means recommended for protected areas, but withstands weather during long delays in construction. "Exposure 2" withstands shorter construction delays. These examples are taken from "performance rated" plywood. The homeowner need not purchase this top grade for most projects.

OTHER WOOD PRODUCTS

There are many sheet materials which are made from leftover wood products such as chips,

Fig. 7-13. Plywood veneer production. Pressure roller not only bonds layers, but also improves the finish on the surfaces.

TYPICAL TRADEMARK

APA
RATED SHEATHING
32/16 15/32 INCH
SIZED FOR SPACING
EXPOSURE 1
000
NER-QA397 PRP-108

Specially designed for subflooring and wall and roof sheathing. Also good for a broad range of other construction and industrial applications. Can be manufactured as conventional veneered plywood, as a composite, or as a nonveneer panel. For special engineered applications, veneered panels conforming to PS 1 may be required. EXPOSURE DURABILITY CLASSIFICATIONS: Exterior, Exposure 1, Exposure 2. COMMON THICKNESSES: 5/16, 3/8, 7/16, 15/32, 1/2, 19/32, 5/8, 23/32, 3/4.

(1) Specific grades, thicknesses and exposure durability classifications may be in limited supply in some areas. Check with your supplier before specifying.

(2) Specify Performance-Rated Panels by thickness and Span Rating. Span Ratings are based on panel strength

TYPICAL TRADEMARK

APA
RATED STURD-I-FLOOR
24 oc 23/32 INCH
SIZED FOR SPACING
T&G NET WIDTH 47-1/2
EXPOSURE 1
000
NER-QA397 PRP-108

Specially designed as combination subfloor-underlayment. Provides smooth surface for application of carpet and pad and possesses high concentrated and impact load resistance. Can be manufactured as conventional veneered plywood, as a composite, or as a nonveneer panel. 1-1/8″ plywood panels marked PS 1 may be used for heavy timber roof construction. Available square edge or tongue-and-groove. EXPOSURE DURABILITY CLASSIFICATIONS: Exterior, Exposure 1, Exposure 2. COMMON THICKNESSES: 19/32, 5/8, 23/32, 3/4, 1-1/8.

and stiffness. Since these properties are a function of panel composition and configuration as well as thickness, the same Span Rating may appear on panels of different thickness. Conversely, panels of the same thickness may be marked with different Span Ratings.

A

TYPICAL TRADEMARK

| A-A · G-1 · EXPOSURE1-APA · 000 · PS1-83 |

Use where appearance of both sides is important for interior applications such as built-ins, cabinets, furniture, partitions; and exterior applications such as fences, signs, boats, shipping containers, tanks, ducts, etc. Smooth surfaces suitable for painting. EXPOSURE DURABILITY CLASSIFICATION: Interior, Exposure 1, Exterior. COMMON THICKNESSES: 1/4, 11/32, 3/8, 15/32, 1/2, 19/32, 5/8, 23/32, 3/4.

TYPICAL TRADEMARK

APA
A-D GROUP 1
EXPOSURE 1
000
PS 1-83

For use where appearance of only one side is important in interior applications, such as paneling, built-ins, shelving, partitions, flow racks, etc. EXPOSURE DURABILITY CLASSIFICATION: Interior, Exposure 1. COMMON THICKNESSES: 1/4, 11/32, 3/8, 15/32, 1/2, 19/32, 5/8, 23/32, 3/4.

TYPICAL TRADEMARK

APA
C-C PLUGGED
GROUP 2
EXTERIOR
000
PS 1-83

For use as an underlayment over structural subfloor, refrigerated or controlled atmosphere storage rooms, pallet fruit bins, tanks, boxcar and truck floors and linings, open soffits, and other similar applications where continuous or severe moisture may be present. Provides smooth surface for application of carpet and pad and possesses high concentrated and impact load resistance. EXPOSURE DURABILITY CLASSIFICATION: Exterior. COMMON THICKNESSES[4]: 11/32, 3/8, 1/2, 19/32, 5/8, 23/32, 3/4.

TYPICAL TRADEMARK

APA
A-C GROUP 1
EXTERIOR
000
PS 1-83

For use where appearance of only one side is important in exterior applications, such as soffits, fences, structural uses, boxcar and truck linings, farm buildings, tanks, trays, commercial refrigerators, etc. EXPOSURE DURABILITY CLASSIFICATION: Exterior. COMMON THICKNESSES: 1/4, 11/32, 3/8, 15/32, 1/2, 19/32, 5/8, 23/32, 3/4.

TYPICAL TRADEMARK

APA
UNDERLAYMENT
GROUP 1
EXPOSURE 1
000
PS 1-83

For application over structural subfloor. Provides smooth surface for application of carpet and possesses high concentrated and impact load resistance. EXPOSURE DURABILITY CLASSIFICATION: Interior, Exposure 1. COMMON THICKNESSES[4]: 3/8, 1/2, 19/32, 5/8, 23/32, 3/4.

(1) Specific grades and thicknesses may be in limited supply in some areas.

(2) Exterior sanded panels, C-C Plugged, C-D Plugged and Underlayment grades can also be manufactured in Structural I (all plies limited to Group 1 species) and Structural II (all plies limited to Group 1, 2 or 3 species).

(3) Some manufacturers also produce panels with premium N-grade veneer on one or both faces. Available only by special order. Check with the manufacturer.

B

TYPICAL TRADEMARK

APA
RATED SIDING
303-18-S/W
24 oc 15/32 INCH
GROUP 1
SIZED FOR SPACING
EXTERIOR
000
PS 1-83 FHA-UM-64
NER-QA397 PRP-108

Proprietary plywood products for exterior siding, fencing, etc. Special surface treatment such as V-groove, channel groove, striated, brushed, rough-sawn and texture-embossed (MDO). Stud spacing (Span Rating) and face grade classification indicated in trademark. TYPE: Exterior. COMMON THICKNESSES: 11/32, 3/8, 15/32, 1/2, 19/32, 5/8.

TYPICAL TRADEMARK

APA
DECORATIVE
GROUP 2
INTERIOR
000
PS 1-83

Rough-sawn, brushed, grooved, or striated faces. For paneling, interior accent walls, built-ins, counter facing, exhibit displays. Can also be made by some manufacturers in Exterior for exterior siding, gable ends, fences and other exterior applications. Use recommendations for Exterior panels vary with the particular product. Check with the manufacturer. EXPOSURE DURABILITY CLASSIFICATION: Interior, Exposure 1, Exterior. COMMON THICKNESSES: 5/16, 3/8, 1/2, 5/8.

C

Fig. 7-14. Selected list defines grades of softwood plywood panels. A — Panels designed to rigid specifications (performance rated). B — Sanded and touch-sanded panels. C — Specialty panels.   (American Plywood Assoc.)

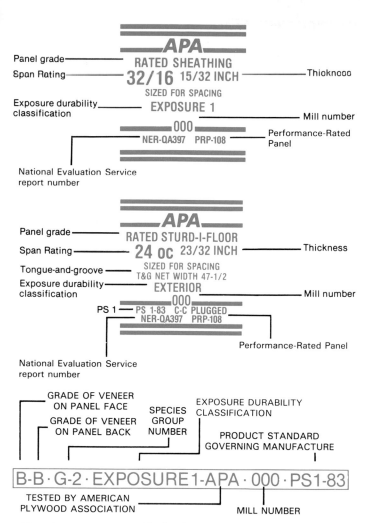

Fig. 7-15. Explanation of some grade symbol codes for softwood plywood. (American Plywood Assoc.)

sawdust, and shavings. These sheet materials include hardboard, particle board, waferboard, and oriented strand board. The following is a list of some of the colors, properties, and uses of these sheets:

1. Hardboard: hair-thin fibers, resin-filled, brown tint, one or both sides smooth, used for cabinets and built-ins.
2. Particle board: 1 in. shavings bonded with resin or adhesive, tan in color, resists warping, used for cabinets, room dividers, and doors.
3. Waferboard: 3 in. flakes bonded with waterproof resin, wood color unchanged, used as backing for cabinet surfaces, in wet areas (kitchen, bath).
4. Oriented strand board: wood fibers arranged at right angles, bond is resin or glue, used for sheathing, subflooring, or interior wall finish.

TRIMS AND MOLDING

Many makers of wood building materials have a complete line of millwork, Fig. 7-16. Some molding types are: base, brick casings, bed molding, quarter rounds, and corner guards. These moldings are usually made of good clear grade ponderosa pine. Often, moldings are stocked by the local dealer in random lengths from 6 to 16 ft. (200 to 500 cm).

Another source of moldings is a manufacturer of prefinished paneling. These companies often supply hardwood moldings and trims that match the panels in finish and in contour. These accessory products let the home mechanic finish edges around doors, windows, and other openings with complete confidence. These prefinished molding products are easy to cut and install and look like professional work when completed. Most moldings are installed using 2d finishing nails.

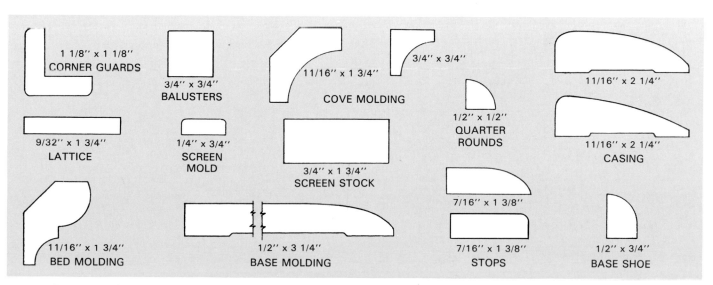

Fig. 7-16. Standard molding shapes and sizes. Most moldings are made of ponderosa pine. (Weyerhaeuser)

TEST YOUR KNOWLEDGE — CHAPTER 7

1. Redwood is a _____ (softwood, hardwood).
2. Fir is a _____ (softwood, hardwood).
3. The dressed dimension of a 2 x 4 (5 x 10 cm) is _____. (   ).
4. Hardwood is produced from trees having _____ (leaves, needles).
5. The "COMMON" grade of lumber is classified as: _____ lumber.
   a. FINISH
   b. YARD
   c. STRUCTURAL
   d. FACTORY
   e. SHOP
6. Wood for furniture surfaces is often cut with the _____-sawing process.
7. Which of the following is NOT found in a grade mark for softwood yard lumber?
   a. Wood species.
   b. Mill number.
   c. Percent clear-cutting.
   d. Mark of grading association.
8. Hardwood giving 83 1/2% clear face cutting is graded as _____ .
9. "FAS" is an abbreviation for _____ .
10. Cutting of plywood is easy because the layers have alternating _____ .
11. Softwood plywood graded N has less than _____ defects per 4 x 8 sheet.
12. The plywood mark A-C refers to the grade of the _____ veneer and the back veneer.
13. Plywood which can resist the weather a long time during construction, but must then remain protected, is rated "Exposure _____."
14. Cabinet surfaces for wet areas have a support made of _____ .
    a. Hardboard.
    b. Particle board.
    c. Waferboard.
    d. Oriented strand board.
15. It is possible to get ponderosa pine moldings as long as _____ ft. (cm).
16. Most moldings are installed with 2d _____ nails.

KNOW THESE TERMS

Forest regions, softwood, hardwood, nominal size, Douglas fir, grades, plywood, molding, APA.

SUGGESTED ACTIVITIES

Get samples of 1 in. boards with different grain directions. These can be of softwood or hardwood, and may have been weathered. Note if the pieces are warped and note the direction of the curve. Try to break the various samples. What effect does grain direction have on ease of cracking? Repeat these steps with plywood. Which would you choose for a bath tile area or for floor underlayment? Discuss the findings of each person in class.

CAREERS

Lumber retail (wholesale) salesperson, building supply owner (operator), delivery worker, carpenter, forester, building developer, contractor, lumber manufacturer.

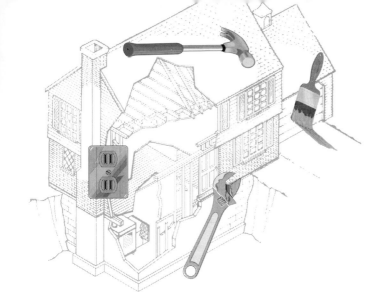

8

STRUCTURAL PARTS OF THE HOUSE

This chapter describes the major structures of a house. The structures include the foundation, floor framing, exterior wall framing, ceiling and roof framing, and interior wall framing. The chapter does not attempt to teach how to maintain major home structures. Only a description of each structure is given.

After studying this chapter, you will be able to:
■ Define terms used for the materials, masonry units, and wood framing members found in each of the major house structures.
■ Locate studs and other frame components when you need to mount items or do remodeling.
■ Recognize a job which is beyond your abilities.

There are many parts of the home. Some involve the structure of the building. Others involve the electrical system, plumbing system, heating system, and also the many appliances and furnishings in the home.

The structural parts of the home are more important than the utility systems and appliances. One reason is that knowledge of home structures is needed for work on any other system or appliance. This chapter discusses only the structural parts. Other parts or systems are described as needed.

There are many types of houses. However, each relies on four major structures for stability:
1. Foundation.
2. Floor framing.
3. Exterior wall framing.
4. Ceiling and roof framing.

The purpose of the foundation is to provide a base which is not moved by freezing and thawing. The foundation extends at least 4 ft. into the earth in northern climates.

The purpose of floor framing is to support vertical loads and to tie the floor platform together horizontally. It prevents the base of exterior walls from slipping inward or outward.

Exterior wall framing provides:
1. Support for the roof.
2. Support for insulation materials.
3. Space for plumbing and electrical service.
4. Load-free areas for windows and doors.
5. A nailing base for interior and exterior coverings.

Walls can be of masonry or wood. Only wood framing will be discussed in detail.

Ceiling and roof framing supports both vertical and horizontal loads. Sloping roof members (rafters) give the angle needed for water drainage while supporting roof materials and other weight. Ceiling members (joists) prevent the rafters from splaying outward.

A fifth major house structure is the framing of interior partitions. Some partitions provide support for ceiling and roof. A detailed discussion of all types of interior framing is beyond the scope of this book.

The following units will discuss the four major structural parts of the house. Visual inspection steps for maintenance are provided. Rules for fastening to these structures are also included. The structure of a typical house is illustrated in Fig. 8-1.

FOUNDATION

Although the wood frame house is noted for its strength and resilience, adequate and properly installed footings and foundations are essential to support the frame structure. Fig. 8-2 shows the arrangement of parts for a foundation. In a basement, the footing is found partly under the floor.

Foundations extend far enough below grade to be free from frost action during winter months. Today, many foundation walls are poured-in-place concrete. Homes built a few years ago may have masonry unit (block) or even stone foundations. A foundation can also consist of treated wood. All serve to support the frame.

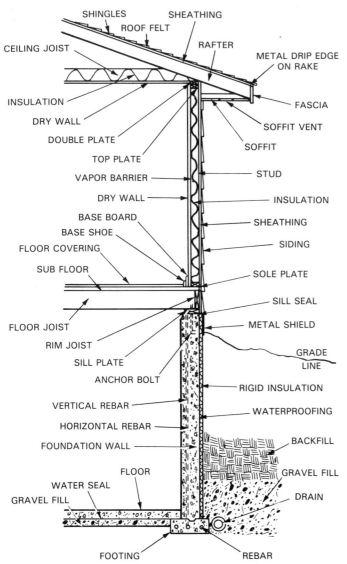

Fig. 8-1. The many individual components of a wood frame structure from foundation through the roof. Work on the home often begins with inside and outside surface coverings.

The foundation is the most important part of a house. A solid foundation keeps other structures in good condition. The homeowner can avoid massive repairs by correcting any foundation problems early.

Proper maintenance of the foundation of a house begins with a visual inspection. If your house has a basement, and if it is of masonry, examine any cracks in the wall. Decide if any cracks are getting wider. A change means that the ground is shifting or that masonry materials are crumbling.

Look for lime deposits at cracks. Lime indicates the presence of water at some time. Erosion from water may be removing the earth support or may be forcing earth against the walls. Minor defects can be repaired with mortar.

If the foundation is of treated wood, uncover some of it. Look for mold damage and termite trails. Poke the wood with an awl or screwdriver to test

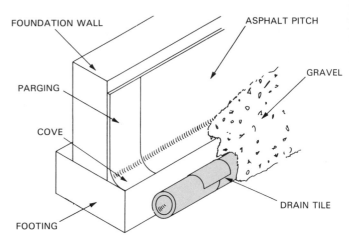

Fig. 8-2. For regions of high ground moisture, the foundation is equipped with a footing drain for the removal of excessive ground moisture. (National Forest Products Assoc.)

for rot. A preservative is sufficient for minor damage.

Major trouble with any type of foundation requires immediate attention. It is best to call for professional help.

FLOOR FRAMING

Floor framing consists of sills, beams, headers, joists, and subflooring. All members are tied together to support the loads expected on the floor, Fig. 8-3. Joists give lateral support to exterior walls.

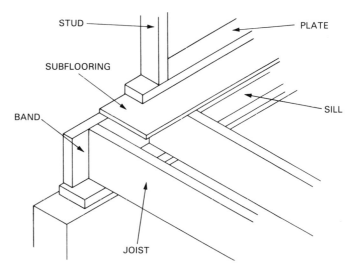

Fig. 8-3. First floor framing at exterior wall. Framing style is called platform construction. (National Forest Products Assoc.)

Sills which rest on continuous foundation walls usually consist of one thickness of 2 in. lumber set on the walls in such a way that it will provide full and even bearing, Fig. 8-4. Two inches is the NOMINAL or labeled thickness. Actual thickness is

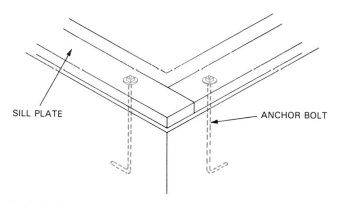

Fig. 8-4. Most common method for anchoring the wood frame to the concrete foundation. (National Forest Products Assoc.)

less. Sills are anchored to the foundation with 1/2 in. bolts spaced approximately 8 ft. apart. Some floor joists rest on suitably spaced beams to carry the loads between supports, Fig. 8-5.

Floor joists are the framing members which support the floor deck, usually 2 x 10 in. wood spaced on 16 in. centers. Joists are placed so that the top edge provides an even plane for installation of the subfloor and finish floor. Joists are seldom of sufficient length to span the entire width of the house and are usually supported at the given point by a beam either of steel or built up of wood.

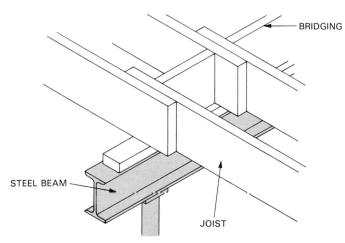

Fig. 8-5. For a long span, floor joist rests on center beam of steel. Sometimes an adjustable post supports the steel beam. (National Forest Products Assoc.)

EXTERIOR WALL FRAMING

Common types of exterior wall framing are strong and stiff enough to support the vertical loads from floors and roofs, Fig. 8-6. Walls of 2 x 4s are designed to resist the lateral loads resulting from earthquakes and, in some areas, from hurricanes.

Recent wall frame designs save energy. Fig. 8-7 shows a special type of corner framing which allows

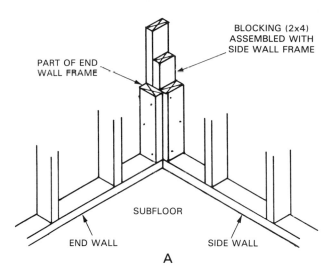

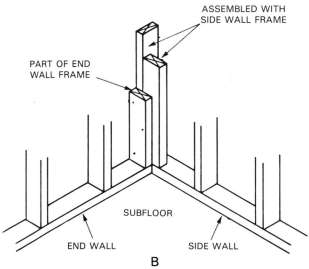

Fig. 8-6. Exterior corner framing. Inside corner is needed for wall surface. A — Blocking is used to align inside corner. B — No blocking is needed when one stud is turned 90° from studs on its plate.

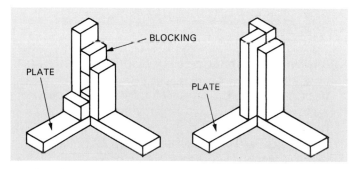

Fig. 8-7. Special exterior corner framing provides space for insulation. Metal clips hold drywall material. The clips maintain a space between studs and drywall. (National Forest Products Assoc.)

space for two thicknesses of insulation. Metal spacers are used. Gaps between insulation sections are eliminated. The insulation sections do not end at each stud as for the older method.

For all types of exterior framing, top plates are doubled and lap joined (overlapped) in certain places. These places include exterior wall corners and intersections of partitions with exterior walls. This ties the building together into a strong unit. Windows and door openings have additional reinforcing to be structurally sound when the exterior wall is complete, as shown in Fig. 8-8. Where these openings occur, a header is used. Size of the header depends on the width of the opening. Ends of most headers are supported on trimmer ends.

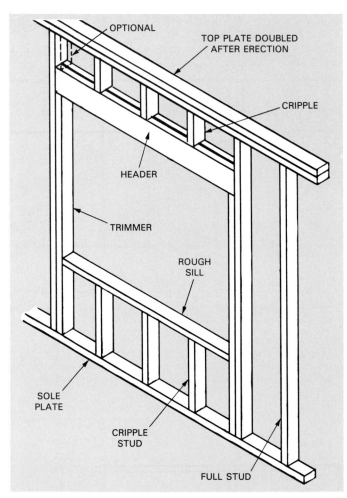

Fig. 8-8. Window framing provides opening which puts little stress on window. Headers and trimmers support the weight.

INTERIOR PARTITION FRAMING

There are two types of interior partition:
1. Bearing partitions which support floors, ceilings, or roofs.
2. Nonbearing partitions which carry only the weight of the partition. Never modify bearing partitions without consulting a skilled carpenter or an inspector.

Vertical members for both interior and exterior walls are called studs. Studs are at least nominal

2 x 4s spaced on 16 in. centers, occasionally 24 in. centers. Corners created by intersecting walls interrupt the mounting pattern for wall materials. Wall materials are usually held at such corners with nails placed in a nailer (wood strip to hold nails), as shown in Fig. 8-9.

The homeowner who wants to mount a shelf or cabinet on a wall can use wall anchors or nails. When wall anchors are too light for the job, nail into a wall stud. To find a hidden wall stud, a stud locating tool is used. See Fig. 8-10. A stud locating tool contains a movable magnet. The magnet is attracted to the nail heads present at each stud. (The nails hold gypsum and panel materials.) Move the tool across the area near the desired mount location. Magnet motion shows where the stud is.

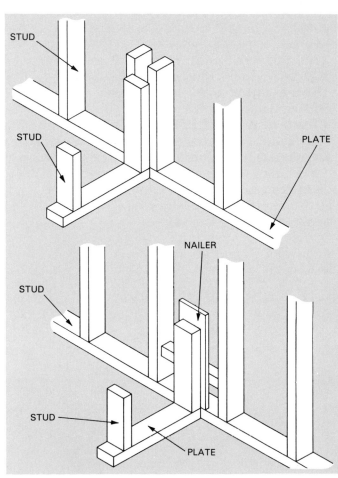

Fig. 8-9. Two methods of joining interior partition with an exterior wall. Each method forms corner for wallboard.

ROOF AND CEILING FRAMING

There are many styles of roof framing. Fig. 8-11 illustrated one type of roof frame.

A roof is designed to withstand the maximum anticipated snow and wind loads. Each member has a function. Ceiling joists are nailed to exterior

Fig. 8-10. A stud locating tool indicates the presence of a nail. Nails are present in studs to fasten wall paneling or gypsum board. (Zircon Corporation)

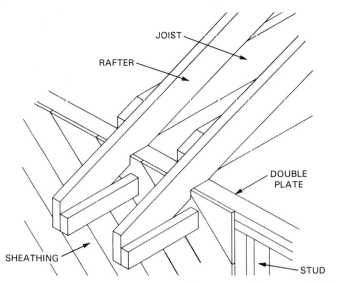

Fig. 8-12. Ceiling framing and roof framing at the eave. Each ceiling joist is nailed to a rafter.

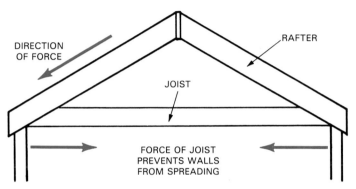

Fig. 8-13. A triangular structure is very strong. Forces are balanced among joists and rafters.

walls and to the ends of rafters. Refer to Fig. 8-12. The principle of roof and ceiling structure is illustrated in Fig. 8-13. Note how a triangle shape provides strength.

Metal reinforced roof framing is sometimes used. See Fig. 8-14. Where ceiling joists are at right angles to rafters, short joists are nailed to ends of the rafters and to the top plate. The short joists are tied to the ceiling joists by metal straps or framing anchors. Subflooring is necessary to provide a tie across the entire building.

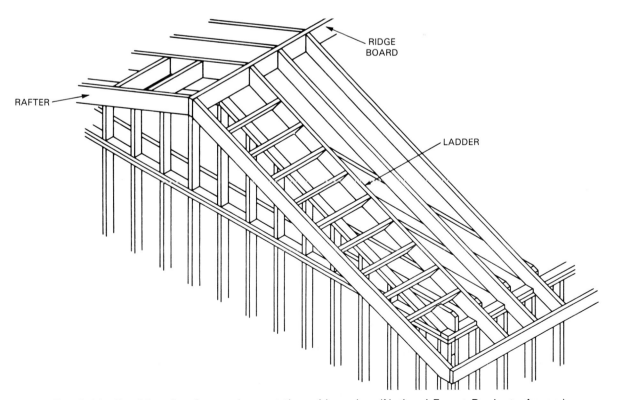

Fig. 8-11. Roof framing for overhang at the gable end. (National Forest Products Assoc.)

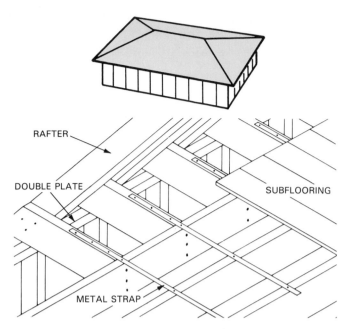

RAFTER

DOUBLE PLATE

SUBFLOORING

METAL STRAP

Fig. 8-14. Special roof framing with ceiling joists at right angles to rafters. Inset — Typical roof that may use this type of framing. Roof style is called a hip roof.
(National Forest Products Assoc.)

PLANNING THE WORK

The installation of various objects, like heavy pictures or closet rods, requires that a solid stud be located. Remodeling of the frame structure will require the location of frame members and the knowledge of what to expect behind the cover of siding or drywall.

Before starting any work on surfaces or the interior of home structures, it is a good idea to try your ideas on paper. Get a house plan such as shown in Fig. 8-15. Determine the SCALE of the drawing (size relative to actual size). For example, if a notation on the drawing gives the scale as ''1/4'', this means that each 1/4 in. on the drawing represents 1 ft. on the real object.

Use paper cutouts to represent large objects you wish to move or alter. Make them to the same scale as that of the house plan. Test all desired changes on the cutouts. Also find out how much material you need for a job by measuring distances on paper. Then convert each distance (number) to the actual size. For example, if the scale is 1/4, multiply the

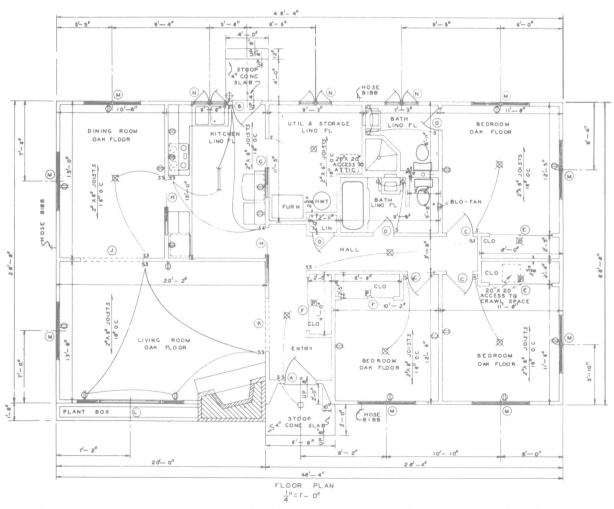

Fig. 8-15. A house floor plan is drawn to scale: Objects are shown with their true shapes. Note label which says that 1/4 in. represents 1 ft. Test your design and repair ideas on paper before starting work. (L.F. Garlinghouse)

drawing measurements by 4. The result is the number of feet for the actual length.

BUILDING CODES

Before any home project is commenced which may require a structural change of exterior design, including roof or foundation change, inquire with the local building authority. The municipal or other governmental authority may require a building permit. A paper application, fee, and identification of the project is necessary before work and progress.

TEST YOUR KNOWLEDGE — CHAPTER 8

1. A foundation is built to be free from the effects of _____ .
2. To spot foundation trouble, look for _____ _____ .
3. Horizontal ceiling and floor timbers are called _____ .
4. For long spans, floor joists are supported on a _____ .
5. Vertical timbers for interior and exterior walls are called _____ .
6. A _____ supports the weight over a door or window.
7. A header is supported by:
   a. The sill.
   b. Trimmer studs.
   c. Studs of the same length as room height.
   d. Ceiling joists.
8. Exterior wall top _____ are doubled and overlapped at partition intersections.
9. An inexperienced person is allowed to modify:
   a. A nonbearing partition.
   b. A foundation.
   c. A bearing partition.
10. To use a house plan, first determine the _____ of the drawing.

KNOW THESE TERMS

Stud, rafter, joists, footing, foundation, waterproofing, subfloor, anchor bolt, scale.

SUGGESTED ACTIVITY

Sketch an area of your house. Make the sketch 1/4 in. = 1 ft. scale. Locate and list all the significant structural parts in this area.

CAREERS

Builder, carpenter, form designer, form setter, general contractor, subcontractor, structural engineer, architect, architectural engineer.

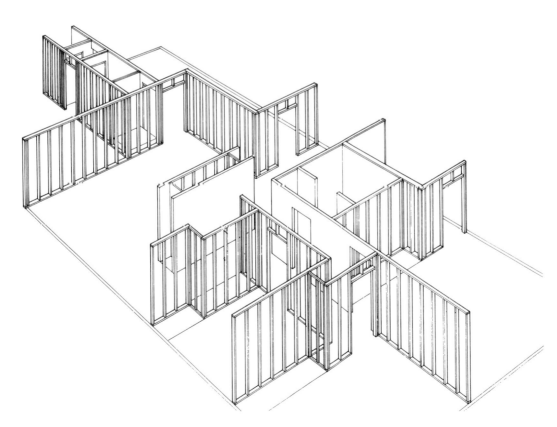

Partitions in a house follow a consistent pattern. The homemaker with a knowledge of what is inside of walls will have little difficulty in making minor repairs.

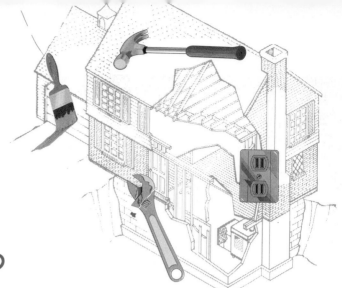

9

EXTERIOR WALL COVERINGS

This chapter tells how to maintain siding, brick, and other coverings on exterior walls. Major wall frame repair is not discussed.

After studying this chapter you will be able to:
- List the types of siding and facing used on exterior walls.
- Explain how to fix split or decayed wood siding.
- Describe how to repair brick and stone facing.
- Do simple repair jobs.

Siding is used on exterior walls to protect the house from heat and cold and against penetration of rain and moisture. To remain watertight, there must be no unprotected openings in the wall. Joints at window and door frame openings must be sealed with a good caulking material, and damaged areas repaired immediately, Fig. 9-1. Since most exterior walls are accessible, repair is comparatively easy to make. Materials for repair are readily available. Most homeowners will be able to repair or replace damaged areas of the structure's siding.

TYPES OF SIDING

All types of siding are affected to a greater or lesser degree by the sun, expansion and contraction from moisture, temperature changes, and wind. Wood siding must be protected from these elements by paint, stain, wood preservatives, or oils. Masonry siding will last longer if sealed against moisture with a waterproofing solution. Whether the siding is of wood or masonry, all joints must be sealed at junctures of porches, roof edges, and window or door frames. Damaged siding should be repaired or replaced as soon as possible to prevent additional damage to the interior frame.

Although wood siding is cut and milled in many shapes and sizes, individual styles generally fall

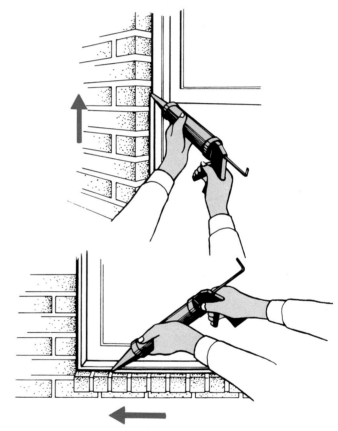

Fig. 9-1. Because of the uneven expansion between siding and window units, they often separate, letting moisture in at this point. Periodic inspection and recaulking prevents future repair problems. Best bead is produced if gun points upward when you move gun upward. Point downward when you move downward. (Illinois Dept. of Energy and Natural Resources)

into one of the following groups:
1. Beveled siding or clapboard, Fig. 9-2.
2. Shingles and shakes, Fig. 9-3.
3. Tongue-and-groove, or shiplap generally referred to as horizontal installation materials.

Fig. 9-2. Clapboard siding is made from an extremely straight, fine grained, and highly decay resistant wood such as redwood and western red cedar. (Western Red Cedar Assoc.)

Fig. 9-3. Wood shingle siding adds beauty to the structure and gives all the advantages of vertical wood grains. (Merry, Calvo, Lone and Baker Inc.)

4. Board and batten or vertical installation, Fig. 9-4.
5. Plywood or composition sheet products which have a variety of textures and designs.
6. Masonry siding usually made of brick or stone.
7. Stucco materials applied over a wire mesh for strength.

There are other products such as cement, asbestos shingles, vinyl siding, and metal siding. Metal siding is most common.

Fig. 9-4. The appearance of a home is enhanced with vertical siding. Here a tongue-and-groove joint is used. (California Redwood Assoc.)

BEVELED SIDING

Beveled siding has been used for many years as an exterior wall covering. It is made from either red cedar or redwood, both of which are decay resistant woods. Beveled siding is overlapped to prevent water from entering between the lap. The nails along the lower edge penetrate the next row below, Fig. 9-5.

Nails used to fasten bevel siding and any other exterior siding material should be galvanized. Galvanized nails do not oxidize (rust) with moisture. Rusted metal nails stain the wood, and leave an unsightly streak below the nail. Even paint or other sealers become discolored in time.

Repairing Beveled Siding

Clapboard siding sometimes splits in a horizontal direction. To repair a split clapboard, remove any

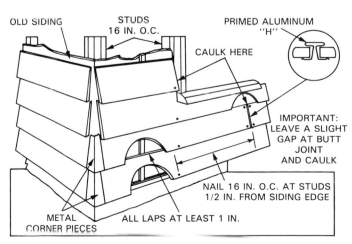

Fig. 9-5. Detail view of horizontal lap siding. (Georgia Pacific)

75

paint or resin from the split. Pry the section below the split away from the wall. Use a flat pry bar or flat nail puller. Prepare to coat the split edge with a waterproof adhesive. See Fig. 9-6. To hold the piece while the adhesive sets, clamp the split edge together by driving a few nails into the siding below the split edge. Force the edge upward against the nails. Leave it until the adhesive has set. Remove the temporary nails, and nail the bevel siding to the sheathing or stud. Caulk the holes made in the siding by the temporary nails.

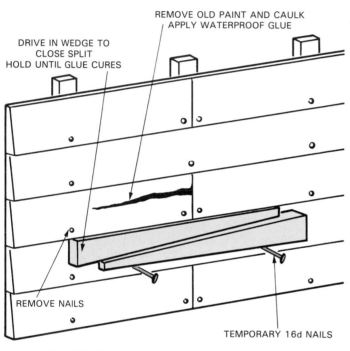

DRIVE IN WEDGE TO
CLOSE SPLIT
HOLD UNTIL GLUE CURES

REMOVE OLD PAINT AND CAULK
APPLY WATERPROOF GLUE

REMOVE NAILS

TEMPORARY 16d NAILS

Fig. 9-6. Method for repairing split clapboard.

The most difficult task is replacing a damaged section of bevel siding. See Fig. 9-7. Ends of the section must be cut at stud locations.

First remove the nails from the clapboard above the damaged section. Lay out the cut lines centered over the studs. Drive small wooden wedges under the loosened clapboard beyond the cut lines. Using the compass saw, Fig. 9-8, cut the bevel siding and remove the damaged section. Patch and seal the building paper if necessary to make it weathertight. Cut the replacement clapboard to correct size and slide it under the overlapping clapboard. Drill pilot holes if siding is hardwood, Fig. 9-9. Nail the lower edge, fill the nail holes, and caulk the joints with a good caulk.

WOOD SHAKES AND SHINGLES

Wood shingles and shakes overlap like beveled clapboard siding. They are tapered so they may be laid in rows. Use a similar procedure to repair

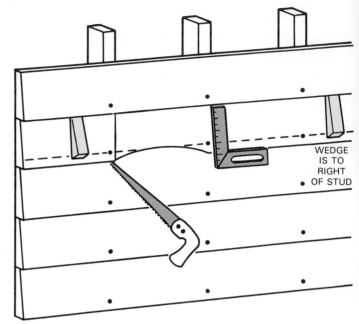

WEDGE
IS TO
RIGHT
OF STUD

Fig. 9-7. Three steps to follow for removing damaged clapboard. 1. To lift clapboard clear of damaged piece, drive wooden wedges under after nails have been removed. 2. With small try square mark cut lines. 3. Cut out damaged clapboard with compass saw.

Fig. 9-8. Compass saw. (Stanley Tools)

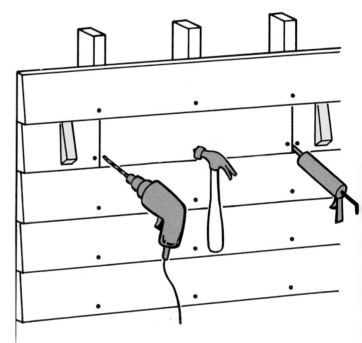

Fig. 9-9. Wooden wedges remain in place for easy fitting of replacement clapboard. After drilling pilot holes, fasten new piece with nails into studs. Then caulk joints and nail heads.

shingles as used for bevel siding. Remove the individual shingle and replace with a new shingle. No cutting is generally required.

The nails of shingles are not exposed on the lower edge, Fig. 9-10. Removal of nails may be difficult. A special hacksaw device, however, may be slipped up under the shingle to cut the nail. The tool is shown in Fig. 9-11. Then the shingle is pulled downward and out. The new shingle may be slipped up under the row above. It is held by placing nail through shingle above or by using construction adhesive.

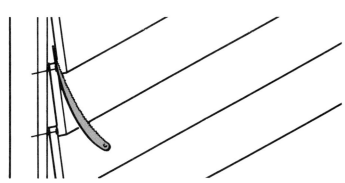

Fig. 9-10. Shingle and shake arrangement covers all nails. Nails must be cut from below.

Fig. 9-11. Mini hack saw handle supports blade for removal of nail under shingles. (Stanley Tools)

ASBESTOS SHINGLES

The cement-asbestos siding shingle is a very brittle, easily broken unit. These shingles are usually fastened only from the lower edge with aluminum or galvanized nails. Sometimes the shingles will have a nail in each upper corner.

The damaged shingle can be broken away from the lower (exposed) nails with a chisel if done carefully. The upper nails must be removed with a hacksaw blade slipped under the shingle.

Then remove the old shingle by sliding down and out. Repair the building paper if it is necessary. Replace the new shingle by sliding it under the top shingle. Nail the lower edge. Normally there are three pre-punched holes in the lower edge.

Warning: The removal and disposal of asbestos shingles require a plan to be filed with the proper

authorities. These materials are considered a health hazard, proper disposal is important for the future environmental protection.

TONGUE-AND-GROOVE AND SHIPLAP

Tongue-and-groove and shiplap siding boards are milled to have interlocking joints, Fig. 9-12. Because of the interlocking joints, these siding boards are more difficult to remove for replacement. They should be cut with a portable power saw set slightly shallower than the depth of the boards. Make a cut parallel to the joint. With a small pry bar, split the board at the joint and remove it.

The replacement shiplap board may be slipped up under the one above, then nailed in place. The interlocking ends do not need to be cut away. However, the replacement tongue-and-groove

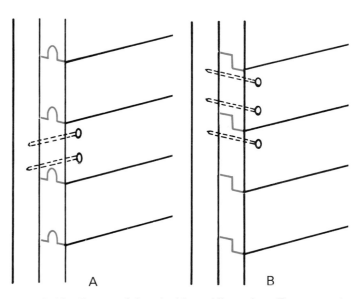

Fig. 9-12. Types of interlocking siding. A — Tongue-and-groove siding. B — Shiplap siding.

board will need the inner lip trimmed off, Fig. 9-13, to allow it to fit over the tongue of the board below. Face-nail the boards to hold in place. Caulk the nail holes and end joints.

BOARD AND BATTEN

Board and batten siding is shown in Fig. 9-14. Loose battens may be face-nailed to secure the tight seal necessary. Wind blowing on loose batten boards makes noise within the house.

Cracks and other small defects cause openings in the boards. They are usually easy to repair. Caulk with a good, flexible caulk.

Replacement is comparatively easy. Remove batten boards by using a small pry bar working from the edges. Loosen and remove the nails holding the

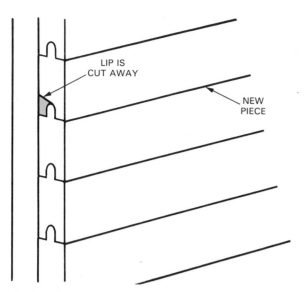

Fig. 9-13. To insert a new section of tongue-and-groove siding, cut off the inner lip of the piece, as shown here. Face-nail the new piece.

board. Replace battens and replace boards underneath if needed.

PLYWOOD SHEETS

Many houses have plywood sheets which simulate the various horizontal and vertical siding materials. Some composition materials are also used.

Sheet siding materials are fitted together with several types of joint. The simplest joint is the butt joint, which is used with many of the composition materials. Plywood siding materials are strong enough to hold with the shiplap type of joint.

Sheets are comparatively easy to remove and replace. If the nails can be raised and pulled, the sheet may be pulled free. If nails and construction adhesives have been used, it becomes more difficult to remove. A chisel may be needed to remove adhesive and fragments of the siding.

It is best to remove the entire sheet for replacement. However, if the damaged area is small, it should be marked and cut with a portable power circular saw and the section pried out. The replacement piece should be cut to size with attention to

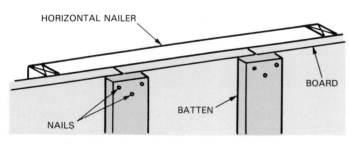

Fig. 9-14. Board and batten siding terms.

pattern match. Then nail in place. Caulk the joint and apply a matching finish.

BRICKFACE

A typical siding structure using brickface is illustrated in Fig. 9-15. Maintenance of brickface is usually limited to mortar repair.

Cracked and crumbling mortar can be repaired by cleaning out the joints and filling or tuck-pointing with fresh mortar. Use a cold chisel to remove the soft mortar to a depth of one inch. Brush or clean out thoroughly. Mix a mortar from masonry cement and sand or use a mortar premix obtainable from a local supplier. Dampen the opening to be filled with water and work the mortar into the joint with a trowel. Let set a few minutes and remove the excess mortar. Point (fill by pushing with trowel point) the joint to compact the mortar and set it against the brick. Finishing the joints by striking with a small round rod will give a smooth joint and a slight concave appearance. Refer again to Fig. 9-15.

Damaged brick, or stone which is chipped, cracked, or softened should be removed. Brick is easier to repair than stone.

To replace brick, use a cold chisel to remove the mortar from all sides of the piece. Remove the unit and clean the mortar from the adjacent surfaces. Apply a layer of mortar to the new piece on the lower side of the opening. Set the new brick in the opening on the fresh mortar and settle into position. Fill the remaining joints with fresh mortar and proceed to finish the mortar joint. Repair of stone facing is similar.

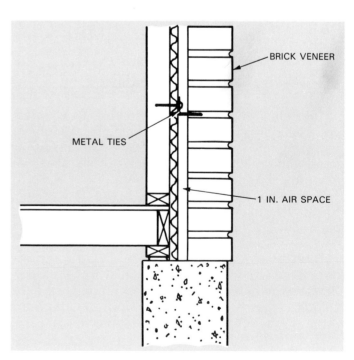

Fig. 9-15. Brick veneer siding structure.

Cracks which develop between masonry siding and the brick mold (wood molding on frame) of the window or door opening should be sealed to prevent moisture from entering behind the masonry siding. Mortar should not be used for this. However, a good flexible caulk will expand or contract with changes in spacing between the brick and wood molding.

METAL AND VINYL SIDING

Most metal and plastic sidings are installed with a system unique to each manufacturer. Both materials may bend or buckle under expansion and contraction conditions if improperly installed. In addition, vinyl siding will crack and metal will dent. Since special tools are used to install these types of siding, repairs and replacement may require the help of a local installer-contractor. If you attempt to make these repairs, read very carefully the manufacturer's installation procedures.

TEST YOUR KNOWLEDGE — CHAPTER 9

1. Clapboard is a type of _____ siding.
2. A _____ closes a horizontal split in beveled siding while the adhesive sets.
3. Drill _____ _____ before renailing hardwood siding.
4. With overlapping board, shingles, or shakes, remove a broken piece by:
   a. First removing the shingle above it.
   b. Removing hidden nails with an end-cutting pliers.
   c. Cutting hidden nails with a hacksaw blade.
   d. Cutting the old piece with a power circular saw.
5. A new piece of _____ siding must be trimmed before it can be inserted.
6. A joint in board and batten siding is covered:
   a. By an interlocking structure.
   b. With a metal strip.
   c. By the next higher board.
   d. By a batten strip.
7. It _____ (is, is not) necessary to replace an entire sheet of plywood siding if the damaged area is small.
8. To repair mortar if the brick or stone is still solid, clean out the old mortar to a depth of _____ in.
9. To _____ a mortar joint means to compact the mortar with the trowel point.
10. To seal masonry siding to window and door moldings, use:
    a. Mortar.
    b. Caulking.
    c. Glue.
    d. Resin.

KNOW THESE TERMS

Beveled siding, batten, caulking, tongue and groove.

SUGGESTED ACTIVITIES

Obtain samples of siding materials. Samples can be found at building supply centers that cut pieces for customers. A building site may be a source. Make a model of a section of wall with siding. Include studs, plywood sheathing, and the siding. Note any discoveries you make about the workability of materials and list any problems you had. Discuss the model in class.

Inspect the outside walls of your home. Look for splits, insect and mold damage, loose nails, and problems with mortar. Make a list of steps needed for repair. Discuss your ideas in your class. Do not make repairs unless authorized to do so.

CAREERS

Siding specialist, retail (wholesale) salesperson, contractor, installation specialist, mason.

10

ROOF COVERING AND GUTTER REPAIR

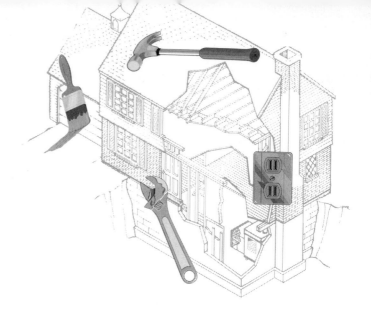

This chapter tells how to repair roof surfaces and gutters. Methods for estimating material quantities are discussed. The chapter shows accepted practices for replacing an entire roof covering. Materials and devices for gutter protection are described.

After studying this chapter, you will be able to:
■ List the many types of roof covering materials.
■ State which roof types can only be repaired by an experienced roofer.
■ Describe how to begin applying a row of shingles for each type of roof.
■ Calculate shingle amounts required.
■ Plan shingle and flashing work.
■ Recall rules for cleaning and painting gutters.

ROOF COVERINGS

The type of roof covering will depend on the style of roof and the locality. Tile roofs are used in the west and southwest United States. Steep sloped roofs are common in areas with large amounts of snow. Slate and wood shingles are found on the more expensive houses, Fig. 10-1.

Probably the most common roof material is the asphalt shingle. Wood, slate, metal, and fiberglass are also frequently used roof coverings.

Many homeowners are not aware of roof trouble until long after the roof begins to leak. Hard to notice leaks develop in a roof and unseen structural damages often follow. In addition, some types of insulation absorb moisture. Water from a leak or from condensation destroys its insulating quality for the same reason that using a wet pot holder to hold a hot pan can burn the hand.

A new roof surface is probably needed if recent water stains are visible on ceilings and walls, or if, in the attic, there are water stains on the underside of the sheathing or rafters. Other signs of age are roof shingles that have lost their color, or are cracked, blistered, or curled.

A new roof, properly applied, may last 15 to 25 years. It should be impervious to rain, snow, and sleet, and it should be attractive. It should resist the destructive ultraviolet rays of the sun (the worst enemy of the roof), and withstand high winds. A roof must be fire resistant since chimneys release flying sparks. Asphalt roof shingles fit these requirements and as a result are used on more than 80 percent of homes in the United States.

TYPES OF ROOF COVER

Asphalt roof shingles are tough, durable, and come in a wide variety of attractive colors. The selection lets you match the roof color to the color of the rest of the house, siding, and trim. Usually a new asphalt roof can be applied directly over the old roof. Only asphalt roof repair will be discussed at length in this chapter. Asphalt shingle and flat asphalt roofs are discussed.

Asphalt shingles are generally made in 12 x 36 in. sections with notches cut into the lower edge to resemble several smaller units. The shingle is made of a felt base saturated with waterproof asphalt. It is coated with mineral granules for protection, durability, and color.

A recent variation of the asphalt shingle is the addition of fiberglass fibers added to the base shingle material. These fibers allow a reduced weight of the roof covering while increasing the strength of the shingle. The resulting advantage is a greater weather resisting covering, longer life and easier installation. Other qualities remain identical to the original asphalt shingle.

Wood shingles and shakes are 16 to 18 in. long. A random width unit is also available. The shingles are cut thin and uniform. Shingles taper from 3/8 in. at the butt-end to paper thin at the top edge. Shakes are split thick and are irregular with little or no taper. Shakes form a waterproof roof with a rustic look. Repair of wood shakes is similar to that for wood shake siding. Refer to Chapter 9. A method for wood shingles is discussed in the present chapter.

Slate shingles are cut in rectangular shapes from thin sheets of natural slate. Repair involves cutting nails from under the next shingle as is done with tile wall siding. Nails, adhesive, or epoxy can be used to fasten a new tile.

Fig. 10-1. Roofs are designed to shed water away from the house. This one is made of treated wood shingles, called shakes. (Koppers)

Clay roofing tile are made of fired clay material. Fired tiles are waterproof. Two styles of clay tile are made: curved tiles which are manufactured and used in concave and convex rows, and flat tiles which are made to overlap like other roof tiles and shingles. Repair of a curved clay tile roof is best left to an experienced roofing contractor. Repair of a flat tile roof is similar to repair of a slate roof or the types of tile wall siding.

The flat or built-up roof is generally covered with several layers of asphalt. Pea gravel or sand is spread over the top layer and embedded in the asphalt to protect against sun damage. Repair is described later in this chapter.

LOCATING LEAKS

Sometimes the most difficult task of repairing a roof which is leaking is locating the source of the leak. Refer to Fig. 10-2. Water, after coming through the roof, may run down the underside of the sheathing or rafter. It can drip onto the ceiling joist and maybe run along the joist before reaching the ceiling. Finally it penetrates the ceiling and leaves a telltale stain.

Insulation above the ceiling area may disguise the location of the leak by absorbing and retaining the moisture. Insulation also may delay the detection of a leak because it absorbs water.

Inspection of a roof for leaks may be done from both above and from the attic. Check closely the areas where chimneys or plumbing vents come through the roof. Another common problem area is the valley where two or more roof surfaces meet.

If outside inspection is not conclusive, check in the attic. Look for fresh water stains on the rafters or sheathing. It may help to inspect during a storm to pinpoint the trouble area.

You may need to make temporary repairs to prevent leaking until more permanent repairs can be made. Use a roof caulking compound to seal the leak and work it well into and around the area of the leak.

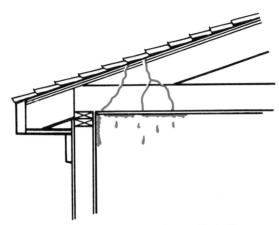

Fig. 10-2. A roof leak can be difficult to find. The appearance of water on the ceiling does not mean that the leaking roof is directly above the water spot.

At this point, you should review the safety procedures with the ladder. Most roof repairs will require the use of a ladder. Before using the ladder, check it for loose rungs and cracked side rails. Place it in the area where it is to be used. Adjust the height to about 2 feet above the roof edge. Set the bottom leg firmly on the ground and approximately 1/4 the ladder's length from the base of the house. When reaching out, keep your hips between the side rails. Keep one hand on the ladder while working with the other hand.

REPAIR OF ASPHALT SHINGLES

Damaged and missing asphalt shingles can be replaced without reroofing. Shingles with self-sealing tabs are more difficult. Shingles are applied from the lower edge of the roof working upward to the top in an overlapping pattern.

Remove each damaged shingle by lifting the one above it. Then remove the nail holding the old shingle. Normally there are three tabs per shingle unit. Slide the unit downward and out. Repair any damage to the roofing felt layer. Slip the replacement shingle into place. Lift the shingle above very gently and nail replacement shingle.

As a precaution, caulk and seal the lifted shingle to the new one. If the damaged area was small and a replacement shingle is not available, slip a piece of aluminum or copper under the leaking tab and caulk in place.

WOOD SHINGLE REPAIR

Repair of wood shingles (thin and tapered) is similar to the repair of wood shakes (thick and non-tapered). Also refer to Chapter 9 on siding repair. Recall that the nail must be cut to remove. First it is helpful to split the old wood shingle. This lets you work up under the overlapping shingle. When replaced, nail down the four corners of the exposed section of the shingle and cover the nailheads with asphalt cement.

FLAT ROOF REPAIR

Flat roofs are repaired by patching them with asphalt, saturated felt, and asphalt cement. Surface blisters should be cut with a utility knife and repaired in the same way as for other small cracks and holes. Asphalt cement is worked into the edges of the cracks and the material is pressed down. Over the opening apply a layer of asphalt cement that extends on either side of the crack. Next press a patch of suitable size down onto the cement. Nail the edge of the patch down with roofing nails. Cover both the patch and nailheads with asphalt cement. If desired, a second and larger patch can be applied over the first patch in the same manner.

ESTIMATING TAB SHINGLE QUANTITY

When the problem is too extensive to be corrected by a simple repair, it probably is best to replace the entire roof.

Estimate the amount of shingles needed to cover the roof area. Multiply the length of the roof times the distance from the eave to the ridge of the roof in feet, and convert this to "squares."

$$\text{Squares of shingles} = \frac{\text{area in feet}}{100}$$

A square is the area equal to 100 square feet or an area 10 feet by 10 feet. This unit of measure takes into account that the overlapping areas of shingles use a double amount of material.

The areas of simple surfaces, rectangular in shape, or made up of rectangular elements, can be computed easily. The area of the simple shed roof, Fig. 10-3, is the product of the eave line and the rake line, A x B. The area of the common gable roof, Fig. 10-4, equals the sum of the two rakes, B and C, multiplied by eave line A. Likewise, the gambrel roof style, Fig. 10-5, is estimated by multiplying the sum of the rake lines A, B, C, and D by the eave line E.

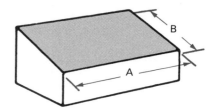

Fig. 10-3. How to find the shingle area of a simple shed roof. Multiply the two lengths labeled A and B.

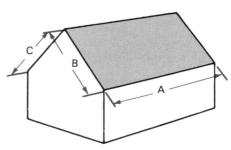

Fig. 10-4. Finding shingle area of the common gable roof. Add the lengths B and C. Then multiply the sum by length A.

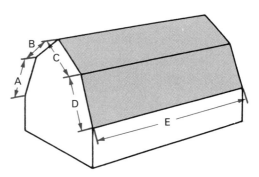

Fig. 10-5. Shingle area for the gambrel roof. Add A, B, C, and D. Then multiply by E.

When ells and gables or dormers enter the computation, the estimate becomes more difficult. The simple methods described cannot be followed without climbing over the roof to measure the required lengths.

A method has been worked out to let the worker estimate the areas to be roofed without climbing on the roof. The method requires that:
1. The pitch be known or determined.
2. The horizontal area in square feet covered by the roof be computed.

Pitch

The span, rise, and run of a simple gable roof are shown in Fig. 10-6. The pitch of the roof is most often stated as the relation between the rise and the span. If the span is 24'-0" and the rise is 8'-0", the pitch is said to be 8/24 or 1/3. If rise were 6'-0", then the pitch would be 6/24 or 1/4. The 1/3 pitch roof rises 8" per foot of horizontal run, and the 1/4 pitch roof rises 6" per foot of run.

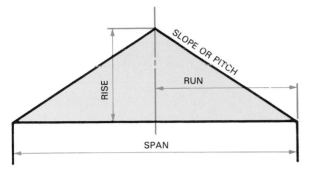

Fig. 10-6. Roof pitch terms and their relation to each other.

It is possible to determine the pitch of any roof without leaving the ground by using a carpenter's folding rule in the following way.

Stand across the street or road from the building. Form a triangle with the rule. Hold the rule at arm's length, and take a sighting of the house through the triangle, as shown in Fig. 10-7. Align the roof slope with the sides of the rule, being sure that the base of the triangle is held horizontal. Take a reading on the base section of the rule. Then locate, using the chart in Fig. 10-7, the corresponding rule reading line. Use the number nearest the actual rule reading. In the vertical column below the rule reading, the pitch and the rise per foot of run are given. In the case illustrated, the reading is 22. Under the number

22 the pitch is listed as 1/3, and the rise is 8 inches per foot of horizontal run.

Horizontal Area

A typical house has a roof complicated by valleys, dormers, and variable height ridges. To estimate the amount of roofing material needed, a house plan is helpful. See Fig. 10-8. A projection below a

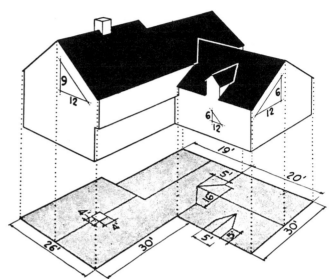

Fig. 10-8. Typical house roof shown in perspective and in plan view. (Asphalt Roofing Manufacturers Assoc.)

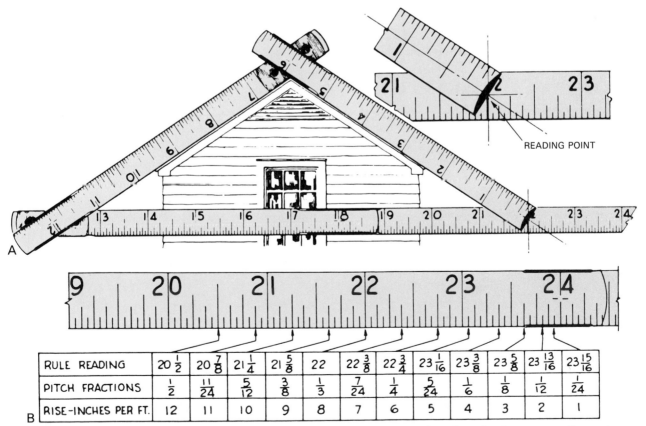

RULE READING	$20\frac{1}{2}$	$20\frac{7}{8}$	$21\frac{1}{4}$	$21\frac{5}{8}$	22	$22\frac{3}{8}$	$22\frac{3}{4}$	$23\frac{1}{16}$	$23\frac{3}{8}$	$23\frac{5}{8}$	$23\frac{13}{16}$	$23\frac{15}{16}$
PITCH FRACTIONS	$\frac{1}{2}$	$\frac{11}{24}$	$\frac{5}{12}$	$\frac{3}{8}$	$\frac{1}{3}$	$\frac{7}{24}$	$\frac{1}{4}$	$\frac{5}{24}$	$\frac{1}{6}$	$\frac{1}{8}$	$\frac{1}{12}$	$\frac{1}{24}$
RISE-INCHES PER FT.	12	11	10	9	8	7	6	5	4	3	2	1

Fig. 10-7. Use of carpenter's rule to find roof pitch. A—Sight along roof outline. B Convert reading point to pitch. (Asphalt Roofing Manufacturers Assoc.)

perspective view shows the total ground area (horizontal area) covered by the roof. If you can determine the total horizontal area, a conversion chart can tell you how much roof area (called slope area) is involved. A chart is provided in this chapter. Some computation is needed before using the chart.

Most of the measurements needed to determine the horizontal area and roof pitch can be made on the ground or taken from the floor plan. Very little climbing on the roof is required.

As an example of how to compute the horizontal area, use the numbers from Fig. 10-8. The rise of the main roof is 9 inches per foot, while that of the ell and dormers is 6 inches per foot. All of the areas covered by a roof part with a 9 inch per foot slope are estimated and totaled. The areas involved with the 6 inch per foot slope are totaled.

The horizontal area under the 9 inch slope roof will be:

$$26 \times 30 = 780 \text{ sq. ft.}$$
$$19 \times 30 = 570 \text{ sq. ft.}$$
$$\text{Total} = 1350 \text{ sq. ft.}$$

Less $8 \times 5 = 40$ (triangular area under ell roof)
$4 \times 4 = 16$ (chimney)
56

Adjusted Total $= 1294$ sq. ft.

The area under the 6 inch rise roof will be:
$20 \times 30 = 600$ sq. ft.
$8 \times 5 = 40$ (triangular area projecting over the main house)

Total $= 640$ sq.ft.

Slope Area

After calculating the horizontal areas below a house roof, use the chart in Fig. 10-9 to find how much the slope area (roof area) is. Continue to use the previous example.

First check if the numbers 1294 or 640 appear in the column labeled "HORIZONTAL." Since they do not, a direct reading does not appear in the chart. Instead, use the row labeled "CONVERSION FACTOR" for these cases.

For the 9 inch per foot slope, the conversion factor appears in the top box (with 9" heading). The factor is 1.250.

The slope area is:
$1294 \times 1.250 = 1618$ sq. ft.
For the 6 inch per foot slope:
$640 \times 1.118 = 716$ sq. ft.
Therefore, the total shingle area to be covered is:
$1618 + 716 = 2334$ sq. ft.
You should order 24 squares of shingles.

RISE (Inches per ft. of horizontal run.)	1"	2"	3"	4"	5"	6"	7"	8"	9"	10"	11"	12"
PITCH (Fractions)	1/24	1/12	1/8	1/6	5/24	1/4	7/24	1/3	3/8	5/12	11/24	1/2
CONVERSION FACTOR	1.004	1.014	1.031	1.054	1.083	1.118	1.157	1.202	1.250	1.302	1.356	1.414
HORIZONTAL (Area in Sq. Ft. or Length in Feet)												
1	1.0	1.0	1.0	1.1	1.1	1.1	1.2	1.2	1.3	1.3	1.4	1.4
2	2.0	2.0	2.1	2.1	2.2	2.2	3.2	2.4	2.5	2.6	2.7	2.8
3	3.0	3.0	3.1	3.2	3.2	3.2	3.5	3.6	3.8	3.9	4.1	4.2
4	4.0	4.1	4.1	4.2	4.3	4.5	4.6	4.8	5.0	5.2	5.4	5.7
5	5.0	5.1	5.2	5.3	5.4	5.6	5.8	6.0	6.3	6.5	6.8	7.1
6	6.0	6.1	6.2	6.3	6.5	6.7	6.9	7.2	7.5	7.8	8.1	8.5
7	7.0	7.1	7.2	7.4	7.6	7.8	8.1	8.4	8.8	9.1	9.5	9.9
8	8.0	8.1	8.3	8.4	8.7	8.9	9.3	9.6	10.0	10.4	10.8	11.3
9	9.0	9.1	9.3	9.5	9.7	10.1	10.4	10.8	11.3	11.7	12.2	12.7
0	10.0	10.1	10.3	10.5	10.8	11.2	11.6	12.0	12.5	13.0	13.6	14.1
20	20.1	20.3	20.6	21.1	21.7	22.4	23.1	24.0	25.0	26.0	27.1	28.3
30	30.1	30.4	31.0	31.6	32.5	33.5	34.7	36.1	37.5	39.1	40.7	42.4
40	40.2	40.6	41.2	42.2	43.3	44.7	46.3	48.1	50.0	52.1	54.2	56.6
50	50.2	50.7	51.6	52.7	54.2	55.9	57.8	60.1	62.5	65.1	67.8	70.7
60	60.2	60.8	61.9	63.2	65.0	67.1	69.4	72.1	75.0	78.1	81.4	84.8
70	70.3	71.0	72.2	73.8	75.8	78.3	81.0	84.1	87.5	91.1	94.9	99.0
80	80.3	81.1	82.5	84.3	86.6	89.4	92.6	96.2	100.0	104.2	108.5	113.1
90	90.4	91.3	92.8	94.9	97.5	100.6	104.1	108.2	112.5	117.2	122.0	127.3
100	100.4	101.4	103.1	105.4	108.3	111.8	115.7	120.2	125.0	130.2	135.6	141.4
200	200.8	202.8	206.2	210.8	216.6	223.6	231.4	240.4	250.0	260.4	271.2	282.8
300	301.2	304.2	309.3	316.2	324.9	335.4	347.1	360.6	375.0	390.6	406.8	424.2
400	401.6	405.6	412.4	421.6	433.2	447.2	462.8	480.8	500.0	520.8	542.4	565.6
500	502.0	507.0	515.5	527.0	541.5	559.0	578.5	601.0	625.0	651.0	678.0	707.0
600	602.4	608.4	618.6	632.4	649.8	670.8	694.2	721.2	750.0	781.2	813.6	848.4
700	702.8	709.8	721.7	737.8	758.1	782.6	809.9	841.4	875.0	911.4	949.2	989.8
800	803.2	811.2	824.8	843.2	864.4	894.4	925.6	961.6	1000.0	1041.6	1084.8	1131.2
900	903.6	912.6	927.9	948.6	974.7	1006.2	1041.3	1081.8	1125.0	1171.8	1220.4	1272.6
1000	1004.0	1014.0	1031.0	1054.0	1083.0	1118.0	1157.0	1202.0	1250.0	1302.0	1356.0	1414.0

Fig. 10-9. Use this table to convert horizontal distances to slope distances and to convert horizontal areas to slope areas. (Asphalt Roofing Manufacturer's Assoc.)

REROOFING WITH TAB SHINGLES

Tab shingles can be applied over wood shakes, wood shingles, or tab shingles. When reroofing, it is a general practice to add a second layer of tab shingles over the old ones. However, instead of adding a third roof layer, totally remove all layers, and then add the tab shingles.

If the application is over an old wood roof, prepare the roof as follows:

1. Remove all loose or protruding nails and renail loose shingles.
2. Split or badly warped shingles should be removed and replaced with new shingles.

When the shingles and trim at eaves and rakes are badly weathered, they should be cut back far enough to allow for the application of 4 in. to 6 in. (10 cm to 15 cm) of nominal 1 in. thick wood strip. Nail firmly in place allowing the outside edges to project beyond the edges of the roof deck. It is recommended that beveled wood "feather strips" be used along the butts of each course of old shingle to level out the new shingles, Fig. 10-10.

Most reroofing is done over an old roof. If old tab shingles are to be covered and remain in place, nail down or cut away all loose, curled, or lifted shingles. Sweep all debris from the roof.

If old tab shingles are square butt strip shingles which are to be covered with new self-sealing butt strip shingles, it is suggested that a starter course be installed. Refer to Fig. 10-11. Cut off tabs of new

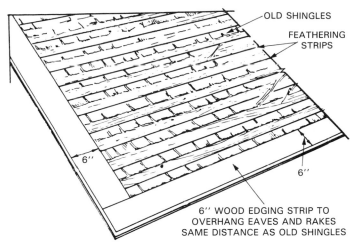

Fig. 10-10. How to prepare for reroofing with wood shakes. Place wood edging strips at rakes and eaves. (Asphalt Roofing Manufacturer's Assoc.)

shingle. It is best if the head portion is equal in depth to the visible depth of the old shingle. Depth is normally 5 in. for the starter shingle.

For the first course, cut 2 in. from the top edge of a full width new shingle. Align this cut edge with the lower (butt) edge of old shingle. On the second course use full width shingle. Align top edge with the butt edge of old shingle in next course. For the third and succeeding courses, use full width shingles. Nail each shingle unit with a minimum of four nails, one at each end and one each at the top of each notch.

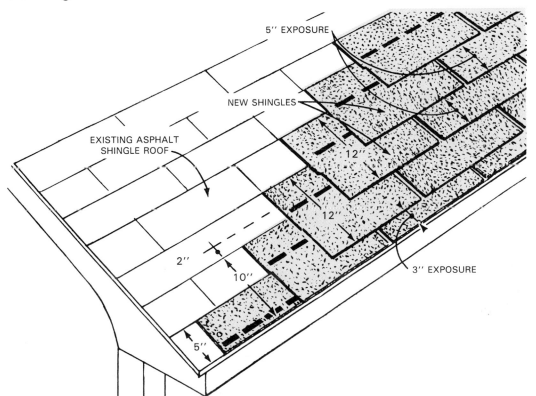

Fig. 10-11. Align the top of the new tab shingles with the butt edges of the old for smoother reroofing. (GAF Corporation)

VALLEY TREATMENTS

Valleys exist where two sloping roofs join at an angle causing runoff water to be diverted toward and along the joint. Because drainage concentrates at the joint, it is especially vulnerable to leakage. A smooth unobstructed drainage way must be provided with enough capacity to carry away the water rapidly. Two procedures are commonly used with the square butt tab shingle:

1. The open valley, Fig. 10-12.
2. The woven valley, Fig. 10-13.

For the open valley, use a mineral surfaced asphalt roll roofing of a color to match, or use metal flashing. Lay it down the center of the valley. Bring each course of shingles to a chalk line as shown in Fig. 10-12. Cut at the chalk line.

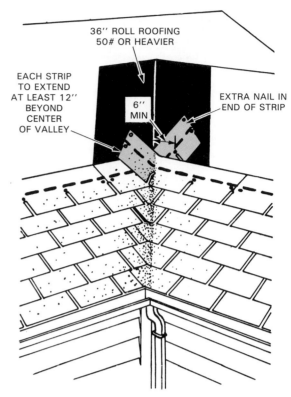

Fig. 10-13. The woven valley.
(Asphalt Roofing Manufacturer's Assoc.)

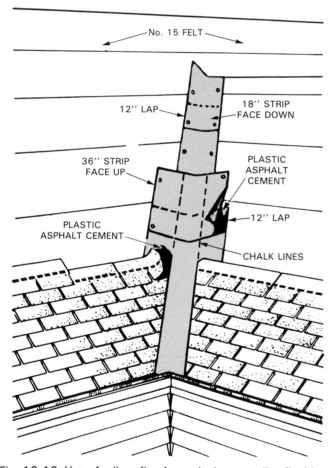

Fig. 10-12. Use of roll roofing for typical open valley flashing.
(Asphalt Roofing Manufacturer's Assoc.)

For the woven valley, lay shingles over the valley by applying them on both roof areas at the same time. Weave each course in turn over the valley.

Estimate the required amount of valley roll roofing or metal shingles in a way similar to the method for slope areas. Fig. 10-14 is a table and illustration used for converting a horizontal length to the actual length. Pitch or rise is taken as the average of the numbers for the two intersecting roofs.

FLASHING AGAINST A VERTICAL WALL

When the rake of a roof (triangle end for example) abuts a vertical wall, the best method of sealing the joint is to use metal flashing shingles applied over the end of each course. See Fig. 10-15. The method is called step flashing.

Metal shingles are rectangular in shape. Lengths range from 5 in. to 6 in. (12 cm to 15 cm). Width is 2 in. more than the exposed face of the roofing shingle.

When used with strip shingles laid 5 in. (12 cm) to the weather, they are 6 in. by 7 in. (15 to 18 cm). They are bent to extend 2 in. over the roof deck and the remainder extends up the wall surface. The finished siding is brought down over the flashing to serve as a cap.

To install simple flashing against a vertical wall when reroofing, place a strip of roll roofing 6 in. to 8 in. (15 cm to 20 cm) wide over the old shingles, abutting the wall surface. Use a row of nails along each edge. Place the nails 4 in. (10 cm) apart.

As each course of asphalt shingles is brought to the abutting wall, cover the strip with asphalt cement. Secure the shingle firmly by imbedding into the cement. For improved appearance and a water-tight joint, use a caulking gun to apply a bead of

RISE { Inches per foot of horizontal run	4″	5″	6″	7″	8″	9″	10″	11″	12″	14″	16″	18″
PITCH { Degrees	18° 26′	22° 37′	26° 34′	30° 16′	33° 41′	36° 52′	39° 48′	42° 31′	45°	49° 24′	53° 8′	56° 19′
PITCH { Fractions	1/6	5/24	1/4	7/24	1/3	3/8	5/12	11/24	1/2	7/12	2/3	3/4
CONVERSION FACTOR	1.452	1.474	1.500	1.524	1.564	1.600	1.642	1.684	1.732	1.814	1.944	2.062
HORIZONTAL (Length in Feet)												
1	1.5	1.5	1.5	1.5	1.6	1.6	1.6	1.7	1.7	1.8	1.9	2.1
2	2.9	2.9	3.0	3.0	3.1	3.2	3.3	3.4	3.5	3.6	3.9	4.1
3	4.4	4.4	4.5	4.6	4.7	4.8	4.9	5.1	5.2	5.4	5.8	6.2
4	5.8	5.9	6.0	6.1	6.3	6.4	6.6	6.7	6.9	7.3	7.8	8.2
5	7.3	7.4	7.5	7.6	7.8	8.0	8.2	8.4	8.7	9.1	9.7	10.3
6	8.7	8.8	9.0	9.1	9.4	9.6	9.9	10.1	10.4	10.9	11.7	12.4
7	10.2	10.3	10.5	10.7	10.9	11.2	11.5	11.8	12.1	12.7	13.6	14.4
8	11.6	11.8	12.0	12.2	12.5	12.8	13.1	13.5	13.9	14.5	15.6	16.5
9	13.1	13.3	13.5	13.7	14.1	14.4	14.8	15.2	15.6	16.3	17.5	18.6
10	14.5	14.7	15.0	15.2	15.6	16.0	16.4	16.8	17.3	18.1	19.4	20.6
20	29.0	29.5	30.0	30.5	31.3	32.0	32.8	33.7	34.6	36.3	38.9	41.2
30	43.6	44.2	45.0	45.7	46.9	48.0	49.3	50.5	52.0	54.4	58.3	61.9
40	58.1	59.0	60.0	61.0	62.6	64.0	65.7	67.4	69.3	72.6	77.8	82.5
50	72.6	73.7	75.0	76.2	78.2	80.0	82.1	84.2	86.6	90.7	97.2	103.1
60	87.1	88.4	90.0	91.4	93.8	96.0	98.5	101.0	103.9	108.8	116.6	123.7
70	101.6	103.2	105.0	106.7	109.5	112.0	114.9	117.9	121.2	127.0	136.1	144.3
80	116.2	117.9	120.0	121.9	125.1	128.0	131.4	134.7	138.6	145.1	155.5	165.0
90	130.7	132.7	135.0	137.2	140.8	144.0	147.8	151.6	155.9	163.3	175.0	185.6
100	145.2	147.4	150.0	152.4	156.4	160.0	164.2	168.4	173.2	181.4	194.4	206.2

A   B

Fig. 10-14. A — Use this table to determine length of flashing needed at valleys and hips. Take pitch or rise as the average of those for the two intersecting roofs. B — For horizontal length, take half the horizontal width of the smaller roof section as shown. (Asphalt Roofing Manufacturer's Assoc.)

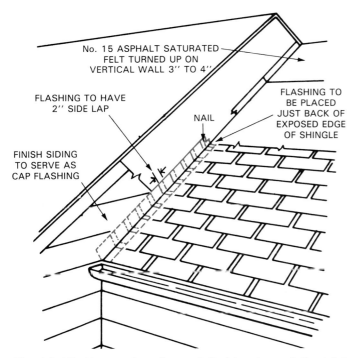

Fig. 10-15. How to install metal flashing to seal the joint between sloping roof and vertical wall. (Asphalt Roofing Manufacturer's Assoc.)

asphalt cement caulk between the ends of the shingles and the siding.

CHIMNEY FLASHING

A chimney projecting through a sloping deck which is being reroofed with asphalt shingles re-

quires special care. If old metal flashing is good, it should be left in place and reused, but if badly decayed, it should be removed and replaced.

Apply a strip of roll surface at the front and sides of the chimney as shown in Fig. 10-16. It should be laid so that it abuts the chimney on all sides. It should be secured to the old roof with a row of nails along each edge at the junction where it meets the chimney. Cover nail heads with a heavy coating of asphalt cement. Coat the strip itself with asphalt cement.

The end shingles of each new course as applied along the chimney should be cut to allow about a 1/4 in. (6 mm) space from the brickwork. Embed each end shingle in asphalt cement. The cement should be squeezed through the joint at the point where the shingle abuts the chimney.

GUTTERS

Gutters and downspouts are used to control roof drainage. The gutters catch and carry water to the downspouts. The downspout delivers the water from the gutter to the grade level. At grade level, drainage pipes or splash blocks are used to divert the water away from the foundation. A splash block is shown in Fig. 10-17.

Some gutter systems have concealed drainage tubes to move water far from the foundation as shown in Fig. 10-18. Where gutters are missing, fail to work properly, or where tubing is blocked, water may damage the exterior and interior walls and the foundation of the house. Water draining

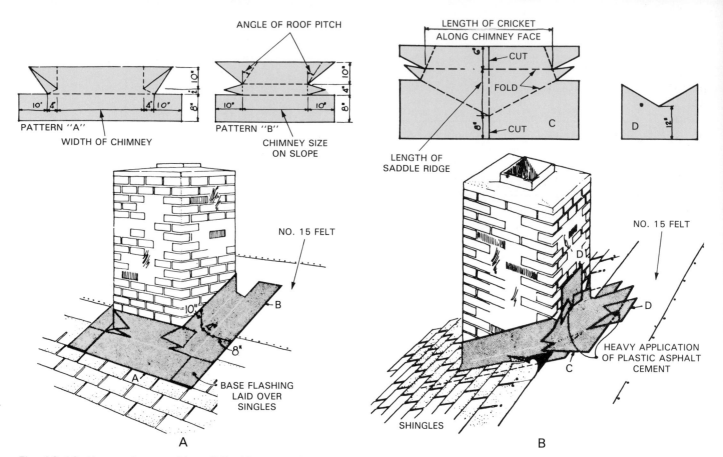

Fig. 10-16. How to form and install flashing at a chimney. A — Base flashings cut and applied. B — Flashing over cricket in rear of chimney.

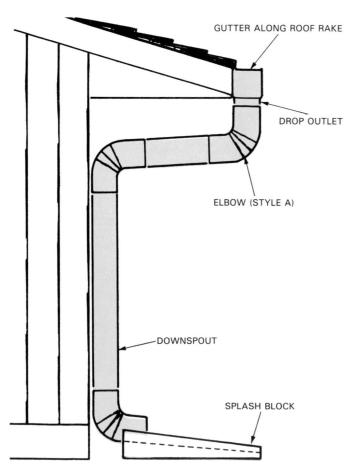

Fig. 10-17. The simple gutter system consists of a rake catch trough and a downspout.

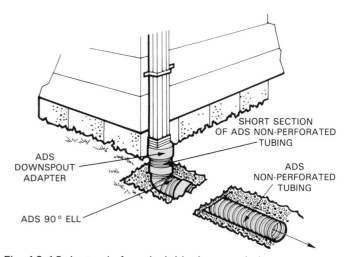

Fig. 10-18. Instead of a splash block many drainage systems use downspout runoff tubing to carry water farther from the basement wall before releasing. (Advanced Drainage System)

down the frame wall above grade level may cause the exterior paint to crack, blister, and peel. When wood becomes saturated it begins to rot. Excessive water concentration in the soil around the basement foundation may seep into the basement.

Gutters and other parts of the roof drainage system may be made of metal, vinyl, or in some rare cases wood. Metal, aluminum, galvanized steel, and vinyl are used most extensively today.

Maintenance of a gutter system begins with periodic inspection for debris, Fig. 10-19. Remove accumulated leaves and sticks.

Special strainers are made to fit into the mouth of the drop outlets, Fig. 10-20. If wet leaves accumulate in a gutter, not only will they block the drainage, but their weight may pull the hangers loose and cause the gutter to sag. Prolonged dampness in the metal gutter speeds the decay of metal gutters, causing rust-out and leakage.

Painting Gutters

Sometimes paint will prevent most gutter trouble. Many gutter systems, of vinyl or aluminum, can be left unpainted. However, the galvanized steel gutter will corrode once the galvanized surface

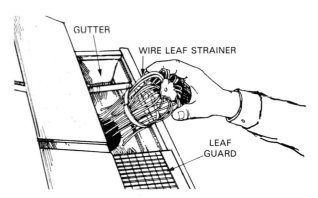

Fig. 10-20. Leaf guards and the wire leaf strainer will help prevent blockage of the downspout inlet. (GAF Corporation)

wears off. Paint the inside of the gutter with an asphalt paint. The outside should be primed with a primer paint suitable for galvanized steel. Finish with two compatible top coats of paint. New gutters should be allowed to weather six months or one year before paint will adhere.

Stopping Gutter Leaks

Leaks appear from two sources.
1. A loose joint.
2. A hole or crack in the gutter.

Steel gutters may be reparied by soldering, or with asphalt cements or epoxy cements. Vinyl gutters may be repaired with fiberglass and epoxy resin cements.

Repairing All or Part of Gutter

Planning is the first step in gutter work. You may need to remove more than the damaged section to fit a new piece in. Learn which pieces allow for bending or for sliding past other parts. Refer to Fig. 10-21. If you change hanger styles, inspect your

Fig. 10-19. Gutters trap leaves and other debris. Twice a year, clean the gutter system. (GAF Corporation)

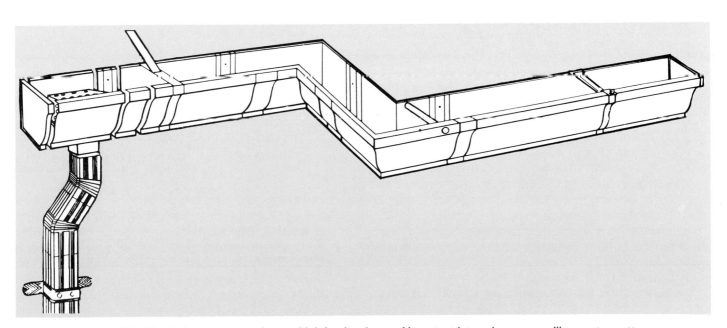

Fig. 10-21. Typical gutter mounting and joining hardware. You must know how you will mount a gutter before choosing a trough style. (Crown Aluminum Industries)

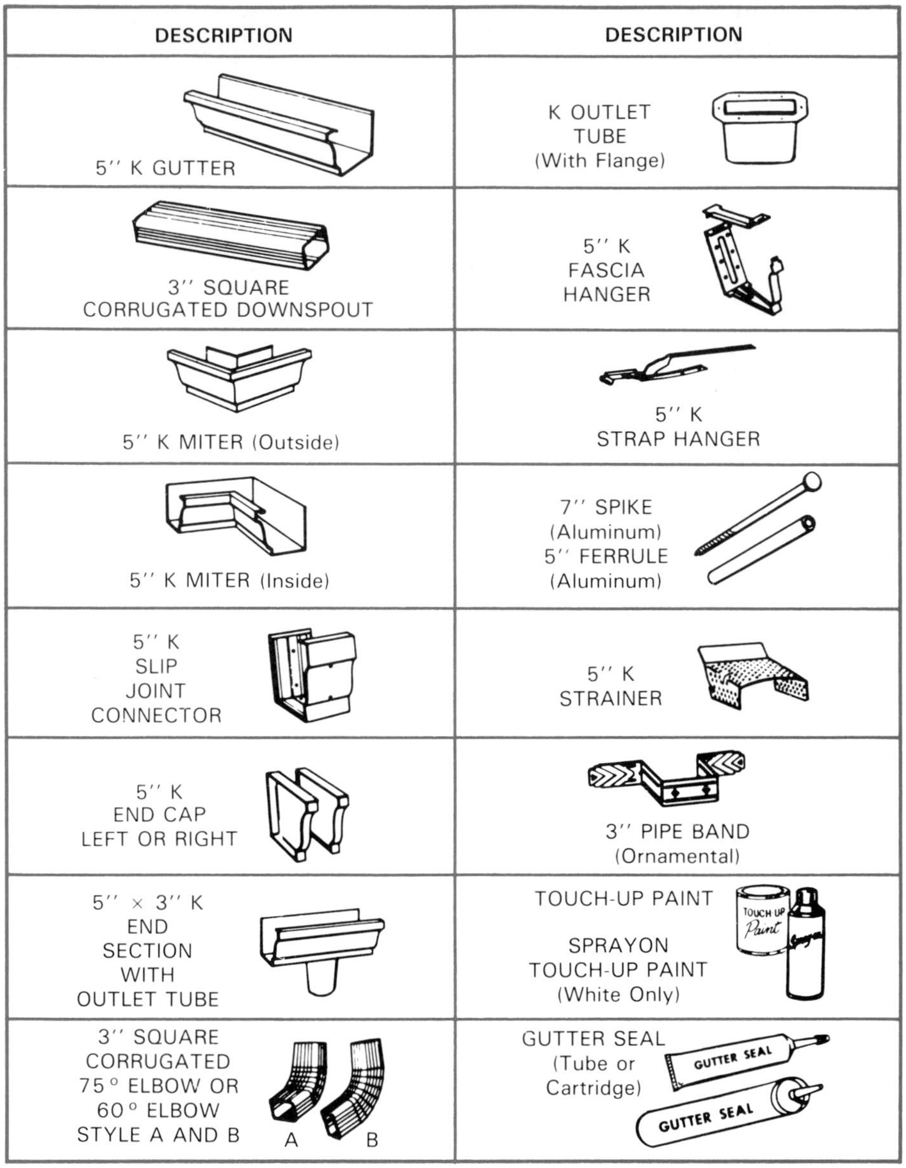

DESCRIPTION	DESCRIPTION
5″ K GUTTER	K OUTLET TUBE (With Flange)
3″ SQUARE CORRUGATED DOWNSPOUT	5″ K FASCIA HANGER
5″ K MITER (Outside)	5″ K STRAP HANGER
5″ K MITER (Inside)	7″ SPIKE (Aluminum) 5″ FERRULE (Aluminum)
5″ K SLIP JOINT CONNECTOR	5″ K STRAINER
5″ K END CAP LEFT OR RIGHT	3″ PIPE BAND (Ornamental)
5″ × 3″ K END SECTION WITH OUTLET TUBE	TOUCH-UP PAINT SPRAYON TOUCH-UP PAINT (White Only)
3″ SQUARE CORRUGATED 75° ELBOW OR 60° ELBOW STYLE A AND B A B	GUTTER SEAL (Tube or Cartridge)

Fig. 10-22. Metal parts and some equipment needed for gutter installation. Consider plastic gutter parts if fitting between two existing sections. (Crown Aluminum Industries)

roof and eave construction closely. Look for decay, but also look for mounting clearance and water seal points at brackets.

A partial list of parts you may need is shown in Fig. 10-22. Some gutter systems require soldering. Others fit very tight without special joint work. Consult the manufacturer for directions.

You may decide to replace the gutter on one wall at a time. Be sure to follow building codes. The slope is the most important property of a gutter system. It controls how clean a gutter stays and affects winter ice buildup. Mount gutters with a slope of 1 in. for each 16 ft. of length.

TEST YOUR KNOWLEDGE — CHAPTER 10

1. _____ can hide a roof leak by absorbing water.

2. Wood shakes have irregular shapes with little or no _____ .
3. An adhesive can be used to fasten new slate shingles or _____ roof tile.
4. Before removing a wood shingle, it helps to _____ it.
5. The first step in flat roof repair is to cut any _____ .
6. The area of which type of roof equals the sum of the two rakes multiplied by the eave line?
   a. Gambrel roof.
   b. Gable roof.
   c. Shed roof.
7. Roof pitch is measured from the ground with a carpenter's _____ .
8. Use _____ strips when putting asphalt shingles over any wood shingle roof.
9. The exposure for a starter strip of asphalt

shingles is _____ in.

10. Nail each asphalt shingle with a minimum of _____ nails.

11. The first course to receive a full width shingle is the _____ (first, second, third, fourth).

12. The _____ valley consists of alternate overlapping shingles.

13. When a roof abuts a vertical wall, seal the joint with _____ _____ shingles.

14. Nailheads near a chimney flashing joint must be covered with _____ _____ .

15. Use a _____ in. wide edge strip at each rake or eave when preparing to reroof with wood shakes.

16. The usual exposure for middle courses of asphalt shingles is _____ in.

17. Roll roofing in an open valley should overlap _____ in.

18. Asphalt felt under metal flashing shingles at a vertical wall should extend upward _____ or _____ in.

19. Galvanized gutters must weather at least _____ months before paint will bond.

20. A _____ _____ is a long flat strip which keeps a gutter clean.

KNOW THESE TERMS

Tab shingles, pitch, slope, guttering, valley, ridge, flashing, square.

SUGGESTED ACTIVITIES

Study types and package sizes for asphalt shingles. Get manufacturer's literature from a local building supply center. Prepare a report with information about kinds, color, quality, weight, and cost. Also collect literature on (or samples of) metal flashing shingles, roofing felt, asphalt cement, and feather strips. Present your findings to your class.

Get a carpenter's rule. Try the method of measuring roof pitch described in this chapter. Do this for a roof of known pitch suggested by your instructor.

CAREERS

Roofing subcontractor, roofing installer, salesperson, repair/maintenance specialist, construction manager, estimator.

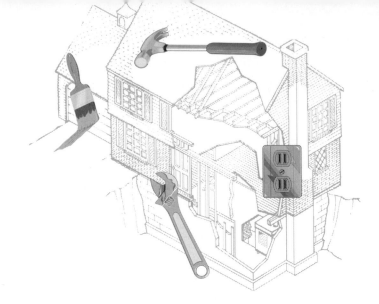

DOORS AND WINDOWS

This chapter covers the types of interior and exterior doors, their mounting structures, and steps for repairing or replacing doors. The chapter describes styles of windows, opening and closing mechanisms, and maintenance steps for wood and metal parts.

After studying this chapter, you will be able to:
Identify solid and hollow core doors.
Decide which door hinge is causing each binding problem.
Describe how to hang a new door.
Explain how a lock is installed.
List some types of windows.
State the procedures for reglazing or for replacing glass.
Discuss screen repair steps.

Doors, because of their frequent use, wear out quicker than other house components do. Interior doors, called passage doors, are opened and closed several times a day. Closet, bathroom, and bedroom doors each are operated several times a day. Exterior doors are not only operated frequently, but must when closed provide a weather seal restricting the loss or gain of heat energy. The hinges, tracks, and latching or locking devices wear and break down on occasion. Most repairs are simple and easy.

Exterior doors are often made of solid wood. Today many exterior doors are built with metal skins over a wood frame. See Fig. 11-1. They are filled with plastic foam for energy conservation. Interior doors are most likely to be wood with hollow cores. They are lighter in weight than exterior doors. See Fig. 11-2. Some styles have solid wood panels.

There are folding, Fig. 11-3, sliding, swinging, and pocket doors, Fig. 11-4. These move on some sort of hardware devices.

Overhead garage doors use some sort of specialized track system for support and for a guide

A

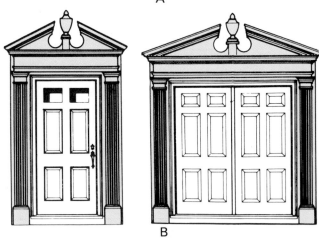

B

Fig. 11-1. An exterior door can be of wood or can have a metal skin. A — A double width wood door. B — Inside and outside metal skins of these doors do not contact each other. This reduces heat flow. Foamed core provides insulation. (Pease Industries Inc.)

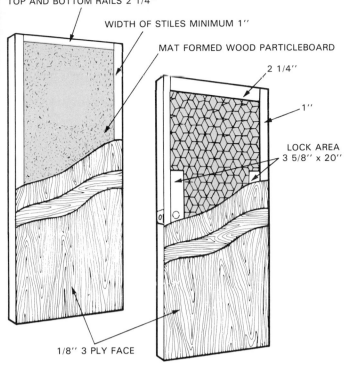

TOP AND BOTTOM RAILS 2 1/4''

WIDTH OF STILES MINIMUM 1''

MAT FORMED WOOD PARTICLEBOARD

2 1/4''

1''

LOCK AREA
3 5/8'' x 20''

1/8'' 3 PLY FACE

Fig. 11-2. Left. This solid core door is made rigid with a particleboard slab. Right. Hollow core door resists stresses, yet is light. (Midwest Doors)

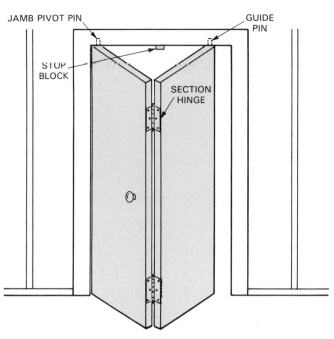

JAMB PIVOT PIN

GUIDE PIN

STOP BLOCK

SECTION HINGE

Fig. 11-3. The folding door saves about one half of the space needed for a door which swings. Repair involves keeping all brackets tight. Note: The stop block keeps door from bending inward when closed.

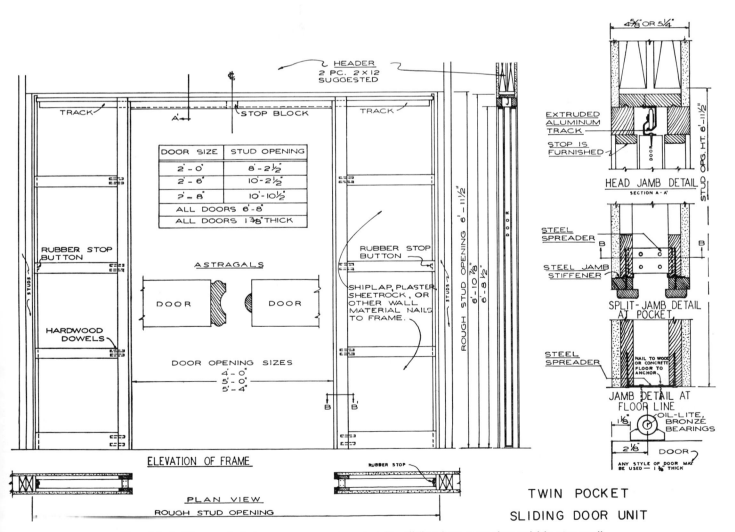

DOOR SIZE	STUD OPENING
2'-0"	8'-2½"
2'-6"	10'-2½"
2'-8"	10'-10½"
ALL DOORS 6'-8"	
ALL DOORS 1⅜" THICK	

Fig. 11-4. The pocket door saves much space by sliding into a pocket within the wall.

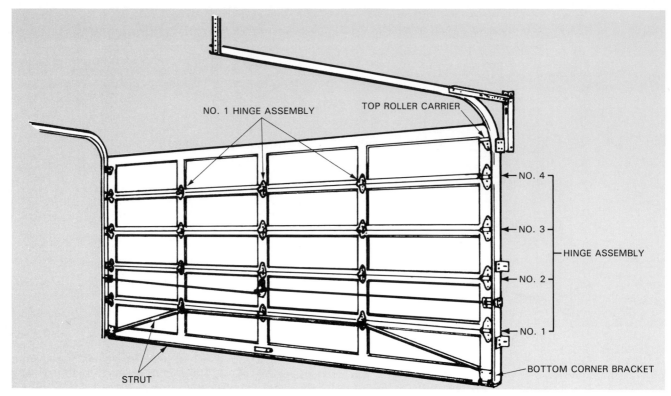

Fig. 11-5. Mechanism for the overhead garage door.

during opening and closing, Fig. 11-5. Garage doors may have automatic door opening devices, Fig. 11-6. Units are often radio controlled from the car. This is convenient for bad weather or night operation.

The home mechanic can repair many of the more common problems with doors. The home owner can install new doors, correct sticking problems, and replace lock and hinge hardware. With persistence, one can make openings for new doors.

STICKING DOORS

Hinged doors can sag. This may due to changing environmental conditions, settling of the foundation or improper installation. The door hinge then causes binding problems.

Suppose the door has symptoms of binding at the top latch side. Note the problem site in Fig. 11-7. There are two causes:

1. The top hinge.
2. The door jamb.

The top hinge problem is as follows. Screws may be loose allowing the door to drop. The door pivots downward on the lower hinge. If this is the case, tighten the hinge screws, Fig. 11-8.

The door jamb may have shifted. The door may need to be planed. Using a jack plane, remove some of the wood in area of binding. Door will need to be removed from opening. Pull the hinge pivot pins and separate the hinge, Fig. 11-9. Set door on edge with binding edge upward and proceed to plane the

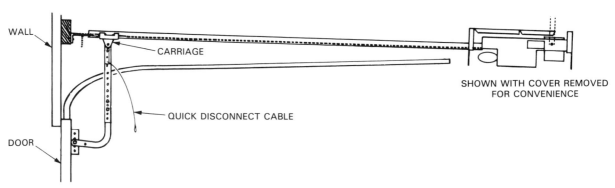

Fig. 11-6. Structure of the automatic garage door opener/closer. Maintenance begins with steps suggested by the manufacturer. Note: balance devices are needed just as for manual operation.

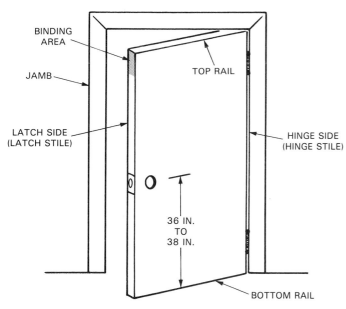

Fig. 11-7. Parts of a door. Note position of most common binding area.

Fig. 11-8. The hinge of an interior door requires periodic maintenance. Check and tighten hinge screws.

Fig. 11-9. To remove a hinged door, lift the pivot pin of both top and bottom hinge. This frees the door.

edge, Fig. 11-10. After planing, sand lightly and stain to original color and finish. Remount door in opening.

Suppose the door binds against the jamb near the bottom on the latch side. Tighten the bottom hinge or shim the top hinge outward, Fig. 11-11. Each door should have enough clearance to pass a stiff piece of cardboard through all the gaps around the closed door without binding.

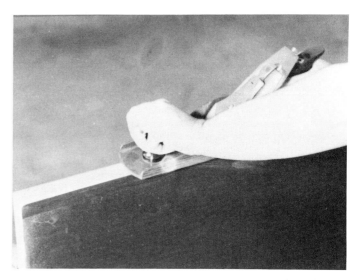

Fig. 11-10. Sometimes settling of the house structure causes binding of the door with the door jamb. Carefully plane the edge. Refinish the edge to original color after planing.

Fig. 11-11. Settling of the structure may require shifting the door angle. A cardboard shim placed behind the hinge will adjust the fit.

If the door does not latch properly, check the strike plate, Fig. 11-12. Take these related steps:
1. Check its vertical position.
2. Check its lateral position.
3. Check the latch bolt assembly for possible sticking.

Fig. 11-12. A reliable latch plate or strike plate depends on proper depth and vertical height.

When the door moves freely and the latch is lined up but will not reach the strike plate, place a shim under the strike plate to move it out close enough to catch. If this is not enough, the latch plate may be moved by placing a shim under it.

If loose screws at the hinge cannot be tightened, try replacing the old wood with a dowel as shown in Fig. 11-13. Drill the hole with a 1/4 in. (6 or 8 mm) or larger drill. Glue a dowel pin in the hole. When the glue cures, redrill a pilot hole for the screw and replace the hinge.

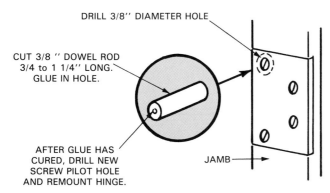

DRILL 3/8'' DIAMETER HOLE

CUT 3/8 '' DOWEL ROD 3/4 to 1 1/4'' LONG. GLUE IN HOLE.

AFTER GLUE HAS CURED, DRILL NEW SCREW PILOT HOLE AND REMOUNT HINGE.

JAMB

Fig. 11-13. Repair of stripped hinge screw area.

HOW TO HANG A NEW DOOR

To hang a new door, start by sawing off the protective ends, or remove the metal protector caps that project from the stiles (vertical edges). Measure and mark the door width and height, then cut it to size. Use a plane to trim the hinge and latch stiles. Round and shape the edges slightly. Next square the top and bottom rail.

Place the door in opening. Use small tapered wedges to lift and position door with about 1/8 in. (3 mm) space at top, Fig. 11-14. Allow clearance at bottom for carpet. Leave a space of 1/2 in. For an exterior door, allow for threshold height.

Install hinges next. Recommended position of hinges is 6 in. (about 15 cm) from the top and 10 in. (25 cm) from the bottom. If the door is a solid core door, a third hinge centered between the top and bottom should be used. Mark their position on the jamb and door with a fine pencil mark. Recall that wedges under the door determine the alignment.

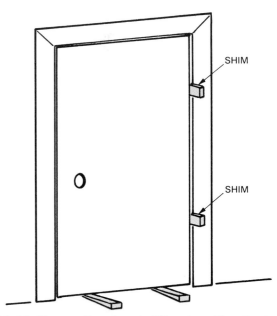

SHIM

SHIM

Fig. 11-14. Use small wedges to lift and position the door for installation. Wedges align the door during installation of hinge and latch hardware.

Cut a shallow depression called a gain for the hinge on both the door and jamb, Fig. 11-15. Install the hinges on the door. Remove pivot pins and separate the two leaves. Install a second leaf on jamb. Set door in opening. Insert pivot pin to hinge leaves. Make final adjustment.

INSTALLING LOCK

Before installing a lock, learn about its parts. See Fig. 11-16.

Installing a cylindrical or tubular lock in place of an existing lock is not a complicated operation. See Fig. 11-17 and Fig. 11-18. It does demand close attention to detail if the lock is to work properly. Follow the manufacturer's instructions.

Installation of a lock in a new door requires the drilling of two holes. One is a large hole in the face of latch stile. Its size is stated by the manufacturer.

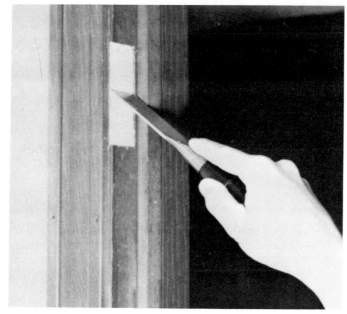

Fig. 11-15. To install a new hinge, cut a gain (inset for hinge) in door or jamb or both. Use a wood chisel to cut the hinge gain.

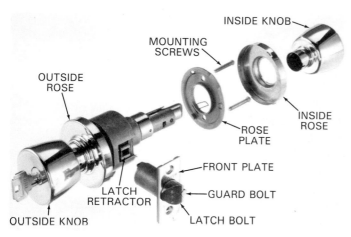

Fig. 11-16. Cylindrical (tube shaped) lock. Learn its parts before installing. (Dexter Lock)

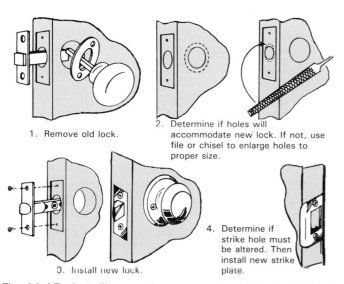

1. Remove old lock.

2. Determine if holes will accommodate new lock. If not, use file or chisel to enlarge holes to proper size.

3. Install new lock.

4. Determine if strike hole must be altered. Then install new strike plate.

Fig. 11-17. Installing a replacement cylindrical lock. (Weiser)

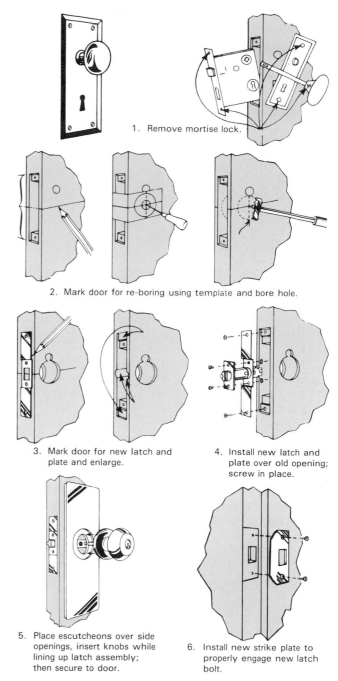

1. Remove mortise lock.

2. Mark door for re-boring using template and bore hole.

3. Mark door for new latch and plate and enlarge.

4. Install new latch and plate over old opening; screw in place.

5. Place escutcheons over side openings, insert knobs while lining up latch assembly; then secure to door.

6. Install new strike plate to properly engage new latch bolt.

Fig. 11-18. Replacement of a mortise lock with a cylindrical lock. (Weiser)

The hole is for the cylindrical case or spindle and stem.

Second, drill a smaller hole in the center of the edge of the latch stile intersecting the cylindrical hole. This will house the latch bolt.

Mortising is necessary to set the latch plate flush with the door. A clean edge on the hole can be made with a device called a mortise marker. Use of one is shown in Fig. 11-19. Mortising is also required for the strike plate on the jamb side.

DOOR SEALS

The homeowner can save heating energy by sealing spaces around doors. There are many types of

Fig. 11-19. Using a mortise marker to help install a door lock. The tool cuts the outline of the mortise gain (shallow area). After creating the clean outer edge, remove the wood inside with a chisel. (Dexter Lock)

seals for side and bottom edges of doors. The easiest to install are made of flexible material. Fig. 11-20 shows one style of lower door seal which flexes to adjust to door pressure. A bevel planed on the bottom of the door allows for any mismatch in the fit.

DOOR SWINGS AND SIZES

The most common door is the hinged door. The door is called either right-hand or left-hand, depending on which side the hinge is located. If you are confused about reference to the swing, there is a simple rule of reference. Suppose you are standing on the outside and facing the exterior door, standing in a corridor facing an interior door, or in a room facing a closet door. If the hinges are on the left-hand side of the door, this is a left-hand door. See Fig. 11-21. If the hinge is on the right-hand side,

the door is a right-hand door. Note that the views are taken from outside of each building, room, or closet.

Often, a door may be defined by a term called bevel. For the door to swing freely in the jamb opening, its vertical edge opposite the hinges must be beveled slightly. Hence a correct reference may be ''left-hand bevel'' door. An exterior door which swings to the left away from the viewer into the room is called the left-hand regular bevel. If the door swings left outward toward the viewer, it is a left-hand reverse bevel.

Interior doors which swing both ways through an opening are called double-acting doors. A Dutch door is cut and hinged to allow the top and bottom portions to open and close independent of each other.

Doors are produced in a variety of sizes for almost any application. Interior doors have standard widths. Common widths are 2'-0'' (61 cm), 2'-6'' (76 cm), 2'-8'' (81 cm). Exterior doors for a double-door entrance may be 2'-6''. Other sizes are 2'-8'' for a secondary passage (inside garage) and 3'-0'' (91 cm) for a single-door entrance.

The standard height for residential doors is 6'-8'' (about 203 cm), although doors of 7'-0'' (213 cm) are available. Interior doors are commonly 1 3/8'' thick and exterior doors are usually 1 3/4'' thick.

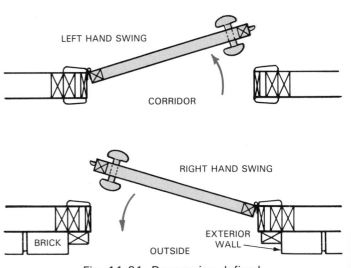

Fig. 11-21. Door swing defined.

WINDOWS

Repair of windows, with the exception of replacing broken glass, is generally limited to maintenance of the opening and closing devices. Those with a more ambitious desire can consider replacing entire units or remodeling where the installation of new windows is required. You will need advice from the supplier and manufacturer on this procedure.

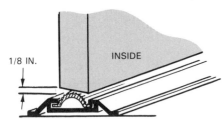

Fig. 11-20. The efficiency of an exterior door can be brought up to modern standards with a threshold seal called a bulb. Most seal bulbs are vinyl. Plane a 1/8 in. bevel on the bottom of the door.

TYPES OF WINDOWS

Windows differ by how they open and close and by the methods of fastening. Double-hung windows are probably the most used type of window. They have been used since early colonial days. Today casement windows, sliding windows, and special windows like jalousie, awning, and picture windows are used in residential construction in the United States.

A double-hung window consists of an upper and lower sash and a frame in which the sashes can operate vertically, Fig. 11-22. Both sashes are held in their channels by strips of wood and metal called stops. The lower sash moves in the inside channel while the upper sash moves in the outside channel. The two sashes are designed to seal when the upper sash is raised and the bottom sash is lowered. The frame which houses the sashes is called the jamb. It is made up of the side jambs, head jamb, and sill. Any raising and lowering mechanisms are housed between the side jambs and wall framing trimmer. The devices are concealed by the inside and outside casings.

Fig. 11-23. Casement window units. (Andersen)

Fig. 11-22. Double-hung window unit. (Andersen)

Casement windows are windows which consist of one or more sashes that are hinged on one side and mounted to the jamb. See Fig. 11-23. Sashes open outward. They are held open with a mechanical arm. A crank and worm gear mechanism moves the arm.

Sliding or gliding windows work similar to the double-hung window, but in a horizontal position, Fig. 11-24. The guide channels are on the head jamb and sill of the frame. Some sashes have rollers built into the lower edge to reduce friction.

Fig. 11-24. Horizontal operated sliding window unit. (Andersen)

Jalousie windows consist of a series of horizontal glass louvers which overlap when closed. They are mounted in a frame. The frame is usually metal. A cranking mechanism pivots to open and close the louvers. Since jalousie windows cannot be completely airtight, they should be used only in the more moderate climates.

The term "picture window" means a large non-movable sash permanently fixed into its frame. Picture windows often butt against one or more side windows. A side window is operable to provide ventilation.

Awning windows have sashes which are hinged at the top. See Fig. 11-25. An awning window is opened by swinging the bottom outward to provide ventilation. The advantage of this window is that it may remain open during rainy weather. Awning windows are often stacked and are used in combination with picture windows to provide a window wall.

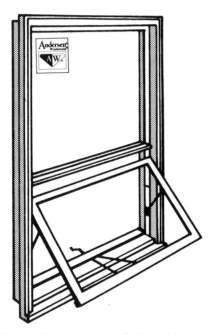

Fig. 11-25. Awning type window. (Andersen)

WINDOW REPAIRS

There are several window repairs the home mechanic can do with simple tools. These repairs include:
1. Reglazing windows.
2. Replacing glass panes.
3. Freeing stuck sashes.
4. Replacing sash cords.

Reglazing windows

Glazing is the putty-like substance used to seal the glass to the sash frame. Weather causes it to age and crack. Note the consistency (when new) of one type of glazing material shown in Fig. 11-26. Repair as follows:
1. Remove all old glazing material with putty knife. Stubborn putty may be heated to loosen. Clean with paint scraper, wire brush, or other tool.
2. Inspect the metal glazing points. Replace or relocate to hold the glass firmly in place.
3. Coat the surface of wood sashes with linseed oil. Otherwise, wood absorbs oil from new glazing material.
4. With your fingers, place a ribbon of glazing material around the edge of the glass. Glazing compound will remain more elastic than putty, however either is acceptable. Apply putty with a knife as shown in Fig. 11-26.
5. With a putty knife, press the material into a triangular shape by sliding the knife forcefully along the ribbon.
6. When the glazing material has dried a few days, it should be painted to seal out the moisture and keep it from cracking.

Fig. 11-26. Reglazing a window. Pressure of putty knife forms smooth surface. (Cooks Paint)

Replacing Broken Glass Panes
1. Remove broken glass, putty, and glazing points.
2. Obtain double strength glass about 1/8 in. (3 mm) thick.
3. Cut or buy glass 1/8 in. (3 mm) smaller than the opening.

    Cutting requires scribing a line with the wheel of a glass cutter, Fig. 11-27. Then lay glass over a table edge or a sharp edge with the marked side up. Tap the glass under the

Fig. 11-27. Cutting glass. Once you start, keep moving. Use oil on the cutter.

line with the glass cutter, Fig. 11-28. Sometimes an even downward pressure helps to break glass on the line.

4. Line the glass recess with a bedding of glazing material and press the glass into it.
5. Push or gently tap the glazing point into the wood to hold the glass tight against the sash. (Spring clips are used on metal sashes).
6. Proceed with the reglazing procedure listed under the heading REGLAZING WINDOWS.

Freeing Stuck Sashes:

Sashes of double-hung windows often become stuck when fresh paint dries between the sash and the sides of the frame. Sides of the frame in the form of channels are called stops. Moisture also affects window movement. Periods of high humidity cause wood frames and sashes to swell and stick.

To free painted sashes, use a utility knife. Gently work blade around the sash to cut the paint seal. Second, get some two, three, or four inch hardwood tapered blocks. Wedge them under the double-hung sash from the outside above the sill. Tap gently until the sash begins to move.

Paint sticking can be prevented if certain steps are taken before painting:

1. Raise the sash and clean the channels (the stops).
2. Coat channel edge with a hard wax.
3. Paint the window with window raised about 1/2 in.
4. Close window after 24 hour curing period.

These simple precautions will reduce the chance of sticking.

Replacing Sash Cords:

Older double-hung windows have cords or chains attached to sash weights. Weights and cords help raise and lower a sash and insure the hold position. To correct a broken or tangled cord, remove the access pocket cover located in the lower side of the inside channel. This gives you access to the weight. Remove the inside sash stop (vertical channel) and swing the sash inside. Remove the old cord. It is fastened on the upper edge of the sash. With new length of cord, thread over pulley at top of the side

jamb. Tie to weight through access pocket and knot the sash end. Slip the knot into sash cord pocket. The parting stop (between inside and outside sash tracks) may be removed for repair of the upper sash. Replace stops and sashes.

Some window frames do not have the access pocket. It is necessary to remove the window casing to gain access to window weights.

Routine Window Maintenance

Frozen pulleys often are freed and then maintained by applying a small amount of oil containing a penetrating solvent. Work can be done without removing the sash or the stops.

Maintenance of a casement, awning, sliding, or other mechanically operated window begins with cleaning. Be sure the channels are free from paint and dirt. Problems with opening mechanisms involve dirt, rust, and wear. Plastic parts wear more than metal parts. Rollers of sliding windows should be lubricated periodically with a silicone lubricant or graphite. Clean the tracks often to avoid fast wear of the rollers due to grit.

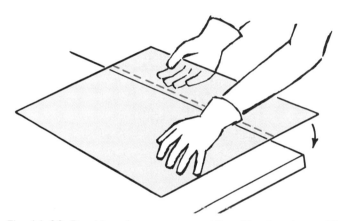

Fig. 11-28. Breaking glass on a scored line. Tap the glass with an end of the cutter. Wear thick gloves.

SCREENS

A screen for a window opening is sometimes torn or rusted. Repair small holes with a piece of screen. For non-metal screens, use a needle and strong thread to darn the patch in place. For metal screens, use a strand of wire instead of thread.

Plastic screens can be finished with a light coat of screen paint. Coat the entire screen. Strands which are separated but not broken can be held down with the paint. Metal screen strands may be repositioned with an awl. A coating of clear nail polish will help hold metal strands and painted plastic strands in place.

Screening is available in plastic, fiberglass, aluminum, copper, and steel. Plastic, fiberglass, and aluminum require the least care and are economical.

Rescreening requires careful removal of the old screen. The wood molding on a wood frame must be removed gently to avoid reducing the holding power for the new screen. A flat tool, such as a putty knife, can be worked under the center of each section of molding to pry it up. Working toward both ends, remove molding brads and screen staples. Attach new screen at one end of frame and stretch screen evenly across length of frame. Several ways of stretching the screen are practical. One way is to attach a clamp made of two pieces of 1 x 2 in. wood. Hold the screen mesh with the clamp. Wedge the screen frame away from clamp. This draws the screen taut and holds it securely while the screen is stapled to frame. Cut the screen from roll and replace molding.

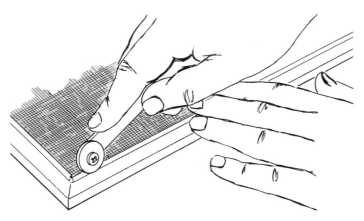

Fig. 11-29. Tighten a screen by rolling it into the edge track. The screen will be held by a spline.

A second way to install a screen is shown in Fig. 11-29. Plastic screen material is held in an aluminum track with a rope-shaped bead called a spline. The spline is most often pushed into the tracks with a roller.

Aluminum frames hold the screen with a flexible plastic spline (rope or band) which forces the screen into a narrow groove in the metal frame. Damaged screen can be removed by prying loose the spline and lifting spline and screen from frame. Special tools designed to force the screen into the groove are available and should be used to repair screens with aluminum frames. Align the screen so that it fits squarely. Fasten one side by inserting the spline. Be sure to keep the aluminum frame square. At the corner, bend the spline around and continue fastening the screen, holding it taut and square. When completely around the screen, trim the excess.

Another way to produce a tight screen is to warp the frame with clamps during the mounting step. When the frame is released, the screen becomes very tight.

TEST YOUR KNOWLEDGE — CHAPTER 11

1. A loose top hinge on a door can cause binding at the _____ (top, bottom) of the latch stile.
2. To hang a new door, position it using _____ .
3. A hinge or strike plate is set in a shallow depression called a:
   a. Slot.
   b. Gain.
   c. Bevel.
   d. Notch.
4. _____ the bottom rail of an exterior door to seal against a vinyl bulb threshold.
5. Use a dowel _____ in. in diameter to repair a ruined hinge screw hole.
6. Glazing is:
   a. A glass plate.
   b. A putty-like material.
   c. A term meaning to replace a glass pane.
7. After painting sashes, let dry at least _____ hours before closing them.
8. Only a _____ lubricant or graphite should be used on the rollers of sliding windows.
9. Methods for making new screen mesh tight within a frame often use _____ .
10. Screen mesh is held in most aluminum frames with a plastic rope called a _____ .

KNOW THESE TERMS

Solid core, folding door, jamb, threshold, hinges, cylinder lock, mortise lock, right-hand swing, left-hand swing.

SUGGESTED ACTIVITIES

Check a building supply center to see a model of a hollow-core door. If one is not displayed, get literature instead. Try to get the most modern information. Also consult your instructor for any model views. Note how much room is given for inner hardware. This information is useful if you intend to work on doors. Discuss your findings in class.

With your instructor's help, practice cutting glass. Begin with small pieces. Try to achieve straight lines. Wear heavy gloves. Be careful with any glass fragments. Be aware of others near you.

CAREERS

Interior designer, installer, sales, manufacturer, maintenance/repair.

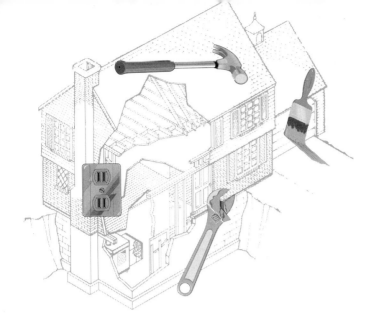

12

INTERIOR WALLS AND CEILINGS

This chapter describes interior wall and ceiling materials. It tells how to patch plaster, patch gypsum, and install gypsum. The chapter suggests ways to maintain ceramic tile and install new tile. It tells in detail how to panel a wall. Suspended ceilings are discussed.

After studying this chapter you will be able to:
■ Recognize types of wall and ceiling materials.
■ List repair steps for holes and cracks in walls.
■ Tell how to solve ceramic tile problems.
■ List ways to fasten wood paneling or gypsum board.
■ Describe hanging devices for suspended ceilings.

Often, walls and ceilings have cracks, dents, open joints, exposed nails, holes, bulges, and other defects due to normal use or accidental damage. Minor problems like cracks or exposed nails can be repaired by simple corrective techniques. Major problems, such as bulging or loose plaster, or water damaged gypsum board require removing and replacing sections of the ceiling or wall.

PATCHING PLASTERED WALLS

Most cracks in plaster walls are caused by settlement, vibration, or humidity. Some may be due to faulty construction. This chapter discusses how to cover cracks and small holes.

It takes careful inspection to find hairline cracks that could become larger. Whatever their size, all cracks must be repaired before redecoration can begin.

Hairline cracks are repaired by first removing all loose particles along the length of the crack. Brush out dust. With a putty knife, spread SPACKLING COMPOUND across the crack, forcing it into crack as deep as possible. Spackling compound is a paste with glue in it.

Smooth out the repair material and let dry thoroughly. Then sand lightly. Prime the repaired area with shellac or vinyl paint sealer to prevent future absorption of paint.

To fill a large area in a plastered wall, it is best to use plaster as the patching material. First check to see if the laths are still in place. Laths are wood strips attached over the studs for the plaster to adhere. If the laths are broken, attach wire mesh backing material behind the hole. Cut the wire narrow enough to insert through the hole, but larger than the opening. Fasten the mesh to the broken laths with wire, Fig. 12-1.

Once the backing material is secured, brush or spray water over the damaged area. Moisture prevents the plaster from drying too quickly. Apply the first plaster coat. It should penetrate the wire mesh and cover the edges of the hole. Let it cure and apply a second coat. Strike the second coat smooth while it is still wet. When dry, sand the patch smooth and seal with shellac or vinyl sealer.

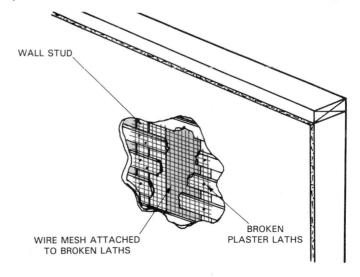

Fig. 12-1. When plaster laths are broken, attach wire mesh or hardware cloth to the laths to provide support for the plaster.

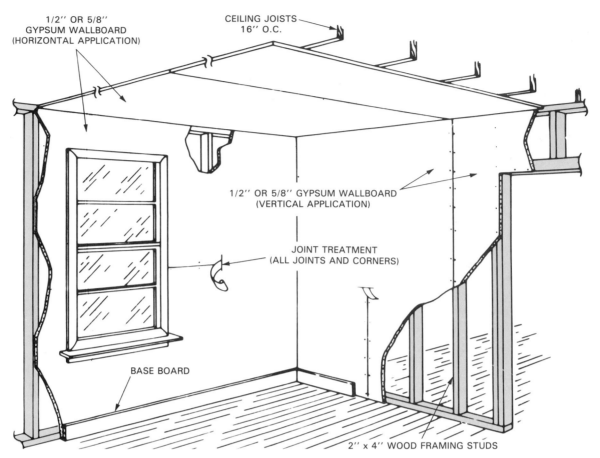

1/2'' OR 5/8''
GYPSUM WALLBOARD
(HORIZONTAL APPLICATION)

CEILING JOISTS
16'' O.C.

1/2'' OR 5/8'' GYPSUM WALLBOARD
(VERTICAL APPLICATION)

JOINT TREATMENT
(ALL JOINTS AND CORNERS)

BASE BOARD

2'' x 4'' WOOD FRAMING STUDS

Fig. 12-2. Wood stud framing provides a firm, level, and even base for single-ply gypsum board application. All joints are taped and hidden with compound. (Gypsum Assoc.)

WALLBOARD

Wallboard has largely replaced plaster for interior construction, Fig. 12-2. Better known as gypsum board, the thin lightweight panels enable fast installation. This reduces cost for interior walls and ceilings. Gypsum board today meets the requirements for modern building design. It is common in residential, commercial, and institutional construction.

Gypsum boards consist of a fire resistant gypsum core covered on both sides with a tough layer of paper. Gypsum boards are available in 1/4, 3/8, 1/2, and 5/8 in. thicknesses (about 6, 8, 12, and 15 mm). Panels are 4 ft. wide and have various lengths from 8 to 16 ft. Panels longer than 8 ft. are used as shown in Fig. 12-3.

Panels are tapered on the face side. This allows for application of wallboard joint compound and joint tape. Panels may be tapered for special decorative architectural purposes. Panel styles are shown in Fig. 12-4.

Cutting Gypsum Board

To cut gypsum board, check measurements carefully to make sure panel will be supported at

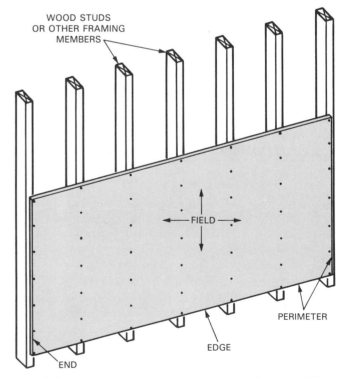

WOOD STUDS
OR OTHER FRAMING
MEMBERS

FIELD

PERIMETER

EDGE

END

Fig. 12-3. Large sheets have fewer joints to be treated later. Horizontally applied wallboard has its paper bound edges at right angles to studs. Note the terms used for the areas. (Gypsum Assoc.)

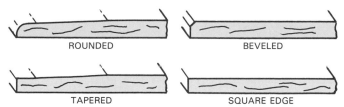

Fig. 12-4. Four standard edges used on gypsum board.

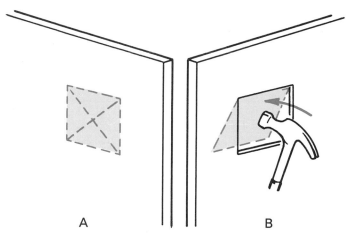

Fig. 12-6. Holes in gypsum wallboard can be opened with hammer if backside is scored. A—Shape of score pattern. B—Loosen piece with hammer.

the edges. Make a straight cut on the face side of the full length or width. Using a utility knife and straightedge or square, draw the knife along the edge scoring the paper layer. Break the gypsum core by snapping or bending away from the scored line. With the partially separated portion folded back about 90°, cut the exposed backing paper with utility knife from the reverse side, Fig. 12-5.

Holes for electrical outlets and other objects should be carefully measured and marked by pencil. Drill holes at corners of openings. Use the utility knife to score the outline of the outlet. On the reverse side, score diagonal lines across the opening outlet, Fig. 12-6. With a hammer, strike a sharp blow to the face of panel. The opening will break into four triangular pieces. Cut the remaining paper backing and trim opening.

There is another way to make a mid panel opening. It may be sawn with a coarse tooth compass saw after drilling the corners.

Repairing Gypsum Board Walls

Locate stud to the right and left of the repair area. With pencil or chalk line, mark a line over the center of studs. Finish outlining defect by drawing lines at top and bottom of it. See Fig. 12-7. Remove the nails within the area. Cut the gypsum board with utility knife or saw and remove outline area. Trim edges.

Prepare two replacement gypsum board panels. Cut a back-up plate of gypsum board to fit between the studs. Its vertical size should be 3 to 4 in. greater than the opening. Or use a 5 in. strip as

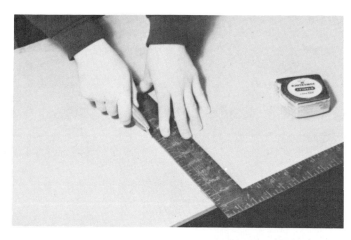

Fig. 12-5. With sharp knife, score through the paper cover. Fracture on the cut side. With second pass of the knife, cut along the inside angle. Then reverse the break direction.

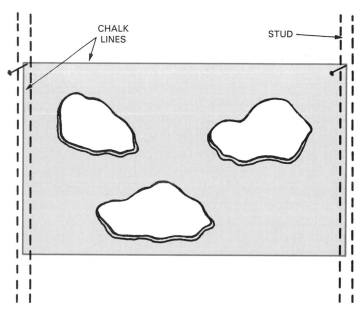

Fig. 12-7. With chalk line, measure and lay out the section to be removed. Be sure side edges end on studs.

shown in Fig. 12-8A. For the full size panel, apply two beads of construction adhesive to it at the top and the bottom. Insert the top edge into the hole, raising it high enough to swing the bottom edge through the opening. Lower the back-up plate until the bottom bead of adhesive contacts the inside of the existing gypsum wall. Hold until adhesive holds back-up plate to wall. Wait 15 to 20 minutes.

To the already cut patch panel, apply construction adhesive to the back side. Cover the middle to about 1 in. (25 mm) from the edge around its perimeter. Insert patch into opening. Press adhesive against back-up plate and nail edges to exposed studs. Let dry for about one hour. Conceal the edge joints according to the procedure labeled ''Taping a Gypsum Board Joint.'' To fix a hole in wallboard which is less than 6 in. wide, fasten a wood strip

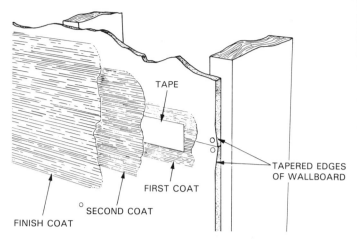

Fig. 12-9. Several layers of drywall compound are needed to conceal the joint. Note how tapered edges of wallboard allow proper feathering. Tape helps prevent cracks.

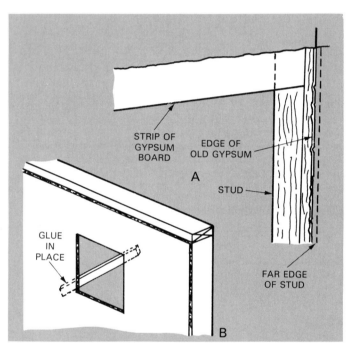

Fig. 12-8. Repair for a large hole (A) and small hole (B) in a gypsum wall. A—To back up the top and bottom of a large hole in gypsum wall, put drywall material between studs. Note piece exposed at top of hole. Four backup pieces are needed for hole involving three studs. B—To patch a small hole in gypsum board, use a back support strip. Attach the patch to the strip. Fill the joints and finish the surface.

1 in. by 1/4 in. by about 9 in. to the back side of the gypsum board with adhesive as shown in Fig. 12-8B. Fasten the gypsum board patch to the strip. Allow to dry, fill large joints with spackling compound, and conceal the edge joints according to the following procedure.

Taping a Gypsum Board Joint

If a joint in gypsum is properly taped, it will blend into the surrounding wall. Apply compound and tape in several steps to obtain good results, Fig. 12-9.

Gypsum board joint compound may be purchased in ready-mixed pails or in a powder form to be mixed on the job with water. Use very little water or the compound will crack or shrink when it dries. Follow the manufacturer's directions.

Joint tape is a special 2 in. (50 mm) wide paper strip. It is perforated and has tapered edges to give additional strength to the joint. The paper is available in 75, 250, and 500 ft. (22m, 75m, and 150m) rolls. See Fig. 12-10. The paper tape is applied with the compound that fills the joint between

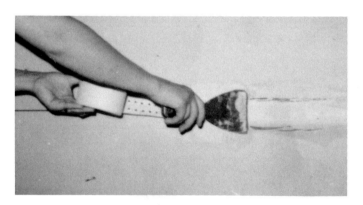

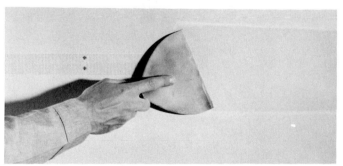

Fig. 12-10. Top. The tape and the first coat of compound are applied at the same time. Bottom. One style of joint tape. The mesh allows good penetration of the compound.
(National Gypsum)

two panels. The compound is forced through the perforations of the tape. This strengthens the bond.

Allow the embedded paper tape and joint compound to dry. Most workers wait overnight. Apply a second coat of joint compound directly over the first coat. Extend the edges to a width of 6 to 8 in. (15 cm to 20 cm). Feather the edges. Let dry again then add a third coat. This third and final ap-

Fig. 12-11. To save effort, use a screen-back abrasive sheet to sand the joint. Add a second application of joint compound if needed. Then resand. Repeat for desired finish.

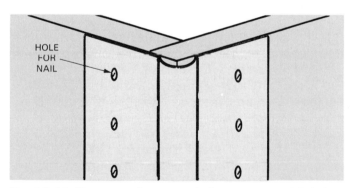

Fig. 12-12. Use a metal corner strip for a neat, straight edge. Compound fills the low areas of strip.

plication should be feathered out to a width of from 12 to 14 in. (30 cm to 35 cm). When the final coat has dried thoroughly, sand lightly with medium grade sand paper wrapped around a block. A grit size of 80 to 100 is best. Sand until no edge or mark is seen, Fig. 12-11. Seal with shellac or vinyl sealer. When dry, apply the wall cover or paint. If the repair involves an outside corner, use a special metal corner strip, Fig. 12-12.

CERAMIC TILE

Ceramic tile is the most permanent and maintenance-free of all surfacing materials. It requires no special surface treatment other than washing with a mild detergent and water, whether it is used on floors or walls. Tile has to be washed less often than other surfaces that receive the same amount of wear or the same kind of soiling. Even when ceramic tile is poorly maintained for a long time, a good washing brings back the shine.

KINDS OF CERAMIC TILE

There are three types of ceramic tile—glazed wall tile, ceramic mosaic tile, and quarry tile. The following describes these types:

1. Glazed wall tile is used for wall surfaces, although modern extra-duty glazes are used for countertops and light-duty floors. The face of this tile is a glass-like substance that is fused to the body by firing at temperatures of about 2000°F in ovens called kilns.
2. Ceramic mosaic tile is made in small shapes less than 6 x 6 in. (15 x 15 cm) square in face area and 1/4 in. (6 mm) thick. A 6 x 6 in. square is in turn made of 1 in. square colored blocks. Early mosaic tile was unglazed, but glazed ceramic mosaics are popular.

   Ceramic mosaics are extremely durable and were once known as "floor tile" because of their principal use. Today, they are also used for countertops, building exteriors, window sills, fireplaces, swimming pools, and for decorative effects on walls.
3. Quarry tile is a heavy duty tile used on floors. Most are earthy-red 6 in. (15 cm) squares. More shapes, colors, and sizes are available today than ever before. Quarry tile withstands hard use, since wear reveals a fresh surface.

TILE GROUT

Tile grout is the hard white or gray material filling the joints between the tiles to form a continuous surface. It is as hard, long lasting, and chemically inert as portland cement. Grouts are substantially more stain resistant than hardened portland cement.

TILE MAINTENANCE

Glazed Wall Tile and Extra-Duty Glazed Floor Tile
Wipe glazed tile with a damp sponge or cloth to maintain the luster. However, routine cleaning can be done on wall tile with commercial window cleaners, all-purpose cleaners, or spray type cleaners. Routine cleaning of glazed floors is best done with a dilute solution of a soapless detergent.

Shower Areas

Shower areas present a slightly more difficult maintenance problem. Soap scum, body oils, and hard water deposits build up in proportion to shower use. Therefore, periodic cleaning should be scheduled to avoid the extra work of major cleaning. Shower walls can be cleaned by spraying an all-purpose cleaner on the tiles. In areas where hard water is a problem, a solution of white vinegar and water should remove the deposits. Commercial tile cleaners, available from ceramic tile distributors, will also work and will avoid the vinegar smell. Follow the same cleaning methods for glazed shower floors.

Heavy-Duty Cleaning

Heavy-duty cleaning is needed for neglected glazed tile installations. For walls, use a household scouring powder on a sponge, a commercial tile cleaner, or an all-purpose cleaner used with a household cleaning pad. Avoid steel wool pads to prevent rust stains. Rinse and wipe dry.

Glazed floors can be cleaned with a commercial tile cleaner or a strong solution of a soapless detergent and a scrub brush. Rinse and dry.

UNGLAZED CERAMIC MOSAIC FLOORS AND WALLS

Routine Cleaning

Wiping with a damp sponge or mop is usually the only maintenance required. More complete cleaning can be done on floors and walls with a dilute solution of a soapless detergent. As unglazed floor tiles age, maintenance becomes easier because with time, the surface wears. The result is a soft sheen. This helps keep the floor looking fresh.

Shower Areas

Unglazed tiles in shower areas with soap stains should be cleaned with an all-purpose cleaner. Apply and allow to stand for at least five minutes before scrubbing lightly with a sponge (on walls) or a brush (on floors). Hard water deposits can be removed with a commercial tile cleaner or with a solution of white vinegar and water.

Heavy-Duty Cleaning

For heavy-duty cleaning on unglazed ceramic tile walls, use household scouring powder on a wet sponge or an all-purpose cleaner on a household cleaning pad. Avoid steel wool pads due to rust stains. Rinse and wipe dry.

For unglazed tile floors, mix a household scouring powder with water to form a thick paste. Mop this over the floors. Allow the paste to set for at least five minutes and scrub vigorously with a scrubbing brush. Rinse and wipe dry.

QUARRY TILE FLOORS

Routine Cleaning

Occasional mopping with a dilute solution of soapless detergent is all that is needed to keep quarry tile floors in good condition.

Heavy-Duty Cleaning

For heavy-duty cleaning of quarry tile, a thorough scrubbing with an all-purpose cleaner or a scouring powder paste is recommended.

PREVENTIVE CLEANING

Mildew on any tile type can be eliminated by scrubbing the tile with commercial tile cleaner or a fungicide such as ammonia. If discoloration remains after this treatment, a bleaching agent wiped over the area should remove it. Rinse and wipe dry.

Mildew in showers can best be avoided by allowing the shower curtain or door to remain open when not in use. This will allow more light into the area and also speed drying after use. Some silicone treatments that help prevent mildew are available.

If hard water stains are a continuing problem, the repair or installation of a water softener is suggested.

An application of a silicone sealer after you have cleaned the tile and grout will help prevent staining of the grout joint and keep it white longer.

When water solutions are used, the hotter the water the more effective the cleaning action.

JOINTS BETWEEN TUB AND TILED WALL

A joint between wall and tub is sometimes troublesome because of cracked and crumbling grout. This is caused by flexing or settling of the tub. Corner joints may also crack in new construction as the house settles. To repair, it is best to completely remove the old grout with a pointed instrument. Take care not to chip the tile or the tub. Dry the joint thoroughly and fill it with a white flexible caulking compound. Silicone rubber type caulks are especially good for this repair. They are packaged in toothpaste-size tubes and are widely available.

LOOSE OR BROKEN TILE

Loose or broken tiles can be easily replaced by the owner with organic adhesives (mastics) designed for use with ceramic tile. All the old bonding material and grout should be scraped from the backs and sides of old tiles before applying the fresh mastic. Allow the tile adhesive to cure for 24 hours before grouting. Many loose tiles usually indicate a serious bonding problem that should be checked by a competent tile mechanic.

TILING A NEW WALL

New ceramic tile can be installed over gypsum or over plywood. Begin by measuring to end the cut tiles at convenient places. Set up plumb lines and level lines. See Fig. 12-13.

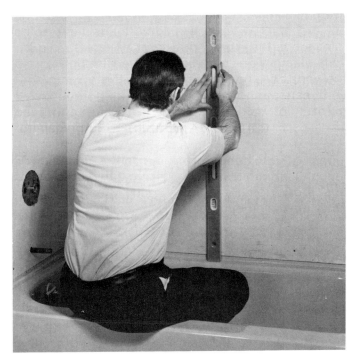

Fig. 12-13. Preparing to install new ceramic tiles on shower wall. Start by drawing a plumb line using a carpenter's level. (American Olean Co.)

Adhesive must have a specified thickness. A special trowel is used to apply the mastic, Fig. 12-14. The trowel has a serrated (notched) edge to remove most of the adhesive. This avoids an excess.

Place the tiles carefully. Tiles must be set down while you hold them parallel to the wall. Do not slide the tile or the mastic will collect at the edge.

Maintain an even spacing between tiles for the grout. Apply the grout in a thick coating over everything. This may be done with a rubber-coated grout float. Wipe the excess off with a cloth.

Some tile installers apply grout only to the joints. This method requires quick work to avoid grout which drys out before all sections are finished.

CERAMIC TILE COUNTERTOPS CLEANING AND MAINTENANCE

Countertops and vanity tops are exposed to some of the worst household staining agents. The grouted joints between the tiles are the most easily stained. It is important, therefore, to keep these joints in good repair. Any loose, cracked, or powdery joints should be scraped out and refilled with a good grout. (Small units of grout can be purchased at any tile distributor or most hardware stores.) Silicone rubber tub caulks are also good for repairing these joints.

Cleaning Countertop Grout

To clean stained countertop grout joints, cover the tiles and joints with a thick solution of a foaming scouring powder and hot water. Allow this solution to stand for five to ten minutes. Scrub with a stiff bristled brush and rinse. Additional treatments may be necessary for badly soiled counters. If stains still remain, apply undiluted household bleach for at least five minutes, rinse well, and dry.

Once the counter is cleaned and dried, the grout joints should be treated with a silicone sealer to help keep them clean longer. This treatment should be repeated every three to four months.

STAIN REMOVAL

Occasionally ceramic tile installations are misused or abused. The result is a stain that requires

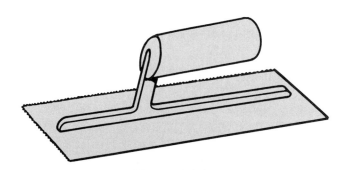

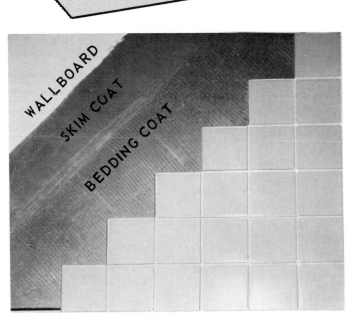

Fig. 12-14. Top. Thickness of mastic for ceramic tile is controlled through use of notched trowel. Bottom. Tiles are put in place without sliding them over the formed mastic ridges. Note how spacing is left for joint grout. (Gypsum Assoc.)

corrective procedures other than the routine measures already outlined.

There are two different types of surfaces in a ceramic tile installation, the tile face and the surface of the grouted joint. Cleaning must be tailored to tile or tailored to grout.

Broadly speaking, there are two cleaning methods:

1. Physical separation of the stain or foreign substances from the surface.
2. Chemical reaction of the stain or foreign substance. Chemical reaction either bleaches the stain or dissolves it.

Physical Method

This may involve simply the use of a soap or detergent. A detergent can get under the stain to lift it out by displacing it. Or the physical method may involve a fine abrasive cleaner that wears the stain from the surface.

Chemical Method

This involves chemical reaction between the cleaning and the staining substance. Ideally then, the cleaner is chosen after learning the chemical identity of the staining substance. See the STAIN REMOVAL GUIDE given in this chapter.

With glazed tile, strong acids may not be used since some glazes are damaged by acid. With unglazed tile having relatively porous bodies, a cleaning agent that is itself colored may not be used.

When the nature of the staining compound is not known, and cannot be determined, a "blind" approach must be taken. A sequence of treatments should use compounds that cover a broad chemical front. Rinse completely between treatments.

Repetition of a treatment is often effective. Hot chemical solutions also help. As with many chemical reactions, heat often increases the rate of action. Hot solutions will sometimes remove the more stubborn stains.

If continued staining is a problem, apply a sealer after the surface is thoroughly cleaned and dried.

STAIN REMOVAL GUIDE	
Type Of Stain	**Stain Removal Agent**
Grease and Fats	Sal Soda and Water
Inks and Colored Dyes	Household Bleaches
Iodine	Ammonia
Mercurochrome	Liquid Household Bleach
Blood	Hydrogen Peroxide or Household Bleach
Coffee, Tea, Food and Fruit Juices, Lipstick	Soapless Detergent in hot water followed by Hydrogen Peroxide or Household Bleach

Fig. 12-15. When planning the layout or when estimating materials for a paneled room, make sketches of your ideas. Confirm all sizes on the plan. (Masonite Corp.)

A slurry of a household scouring powder and water is not only excellent for cleaning and removing stains from ceramic tile countertops but is a good all-purpose stain remover. Allow the slurry to stand for 30 minutes and scrub.

PANELING A WALL

Labor costs for home remodeling are rising along with new housing costs. The homeowner can save more money than ever today with do-it-yourself projects. For example, you can convert a basement or bare attic into a warm family room or extra bedroom. All you need are the proper tools, the prefinished paneling of your choice, and panel adhesive or color-coordinated nails. The following photos show how to do it.

Measure the length, width, and height of the wall areas to be paneled, then draw an outline plan showing overall dimensions, Fig. 12-15. Include measurements and locations of windows, doors, stairways, pipes, ducts, and beams. Then take the plan to your local home center or lumber dealer. A dealer will help you determine the number of panels and other materials you'll need. Most paneling comes in 4 x 8 ft. (about 1 200 mm x 2 400 mm) sheets.

Paneling can be installed over masonry, plaster, or drywall. To install paneling over masonry or concrete, as in the typical basement, first apply a vapor barrier of foil or plastic over the walls. Then, using concrete nails, install 1 x 2 in. (about 25 x 50 mm) furring strips horizontally at top and bottom of wall and vertically along the wall on 16 in. centers. (For additional stability, you may want to add horizontal furring strips between the vertical strips.) Place extra furring on each side and under all window openings.

When building a wall to section off a portion of your room, use 2 x 4 in. (about 50 x 100 mm) construction.

If you're paneling over an existing smooth plaster or drywall surface, mount the panels directly to the wall.

After the first nail is driven into a furring strip, use a level to check plumb, Fig. 12-16. Shim if necessary with a strip of wood or piece of cedar shingle. Then complete nailing the furring strips into place.

Unwrap panels after delivery and stand them on the long edge in the area to be paneled. See Fig. 12-17. Let panels stand for at least 48 hours before installation so they can adjust to room temperature and humidity.

Fig. 12-17. Lay new paneling on its side to adjust to room air. Note that commercially available prefinished paneling has a random set of grooves. Two panels are identical, while a third adds variety. Also note simulated plank joints. (Masonite)

Match grain and color before installation by standing the panels around the walls. This will show the most pleasing pattern for the room.

When cutting panels with a circular saw, cut from the back side of the panel, Fig. 12-18. If using a hand saw, mark and saw on the front surface. This will insure that the rough edge of the cut is on the back side of the panel. When cutting for height, deduct 1/2 in. (12 mm) from your wall height measurement. The installed panel should be 1/4 in. (6 mm) above the floor and 1/4 in. (6 mm) below the ceiling.

Fig. 12-16. When using sheet products like paneling, be sure furring strips are plumb. This allows joints to be made over the strip. (Masonite)

Fig. 12-18. Using a portable power saw to cut paneling. Work from the back side to avoid splintering the finished surface. (Masonite)

To cut openings for electrical outlets, use as a pattern a junction box which matches the one in the wall. Refer to Fig. 12-19. Drill holes in each corner of the pattern, keeping the holes inside your drawn pattern if an overcut would be seen. Then cut out the opening with a jigsaw or keyhole saw.

Panels can be mounted with nails or panel adhesive. For nail installation, set the panel in place 1/4 in. (6 mm) below the ceiling and tack with one nail to hold in place while checking plumb.

Place level on the edge of the panel to check true plumb. This is important because the first panel establishes vertical alignment for all panels to follow.

Using color-coordinated nails, tack the panel at the top corner to hold in place. Then place nails 4 in. (100 mm) (vertically) apart along the panel edges. Fig. 12-20 shows nail angle.

Nails in middle of panel (into studs) should be 8 in. (about 200 mm) apart, Fig. 12-21.

Fig. 12-20. Toenail along the edge (nail at an angle). Use nail set to finish driving the nail. (Masonite)

Fig. 12-19. The portable jig saw may be used to cut outlines like those for electrical outlets or switches. (Masonite)

Fig. 12-21. Nail the middle of the sheet on studs or furring strips. Fewer nails are needed than for edges. Use enough to prevent bulging. (Masonite)

Installing With Adhesives

For adhesive installation, first clean all studs with a wire brush to assure a good adhesive bond. Adhesive consistency is suggested in Fig. 12-22. Trim the applicator end of your adhesive cartridge to lay a bead about 1/8 in. (3 mm) wide. Apply a continuous strip of adhesive at panel joints and to top and bottom panel edges. Place 3 in. (70 mm) beads of adhesive 6 in. (150 mm) apart on the studs. Do not skimp — beads must be at least 3 in. long.

Fig. 12-23. Set panel into bed of adhesive gently and press to make contact with entire adhesive bed. Pressure also spreads the material. (Masonite)

Fig. 12-22. The use of construction adhesives reduces the need for nailing of mid-sheet areas. (Masonite)

Fig. 12-24. Remove paneling sheet from adhesive bed briefly. Check contact areas for shortage of adhesive. (Masonite)

Set panel into place 1/4 in. (6 mm) from ceiling and tack at the top with one nail to hold the panel in place. Check plumb and adjust as needed. Then press the panel into place with a firm, uniform pressure, Fig. 12-23. This will spread the adhesive bead evenly between studs and panel.

Soon after, grasp the bottom of the panel at the edges and slowly pull the panel out and away from the studs, Fig. 12-24. This allows trapped solvent to escape easily. It also forces more adhesive into surface pits.

After two minutes, repress the panel at all stud points. After 20 minutes, check the panel for bulges. Apply pressure at all edges and intermediate stud points to assure firm adhesion and an even panel surface.

Install successive panels. Apply a 1/8 in. (3 mm) continuous bead of adhesive at panel joints, Fig. 12-25. Apply beads at top and bottom edges as before.

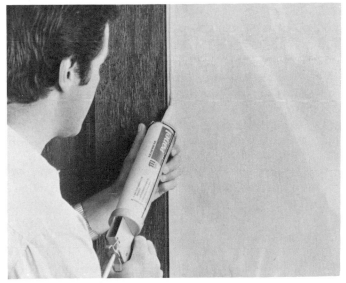

Fig. 12-25. Apply adhesive carefully in the joint area. If there is too much adhesive, it could squeeze out to the surface. (Masonite)

When paneling job is complete, you're ready to finish the room with ceiling and floor materials. If desired, add matching moldings and furnish to taste.

It is likely that the insulation value of the wall has been improved enough to notice. You may want to test it, Fig. 12-26.

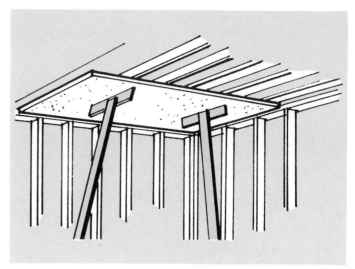

Fig. 12-27. When mounting gypsum wallboard on ceiling joists, use T-braces to hold the panels while you nail. (Georgia-Pacific)

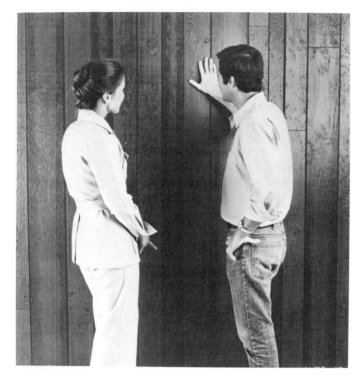

Fig. 12-26. How the completed paneling should look. You may want to test the improved insulation value the paneling has added. (Masonite)

CEILINGS

Ceilings can be done with gypsum wallboard if you plan to paint the ceiling or texture the ceiling surface later. If you want to install a new gypsum board ceiling, remove old ceiling to give a smooth, uniform and stable nailing surface. New or replacement drywall panels may be either adhered and/or nailed to the ceiling. Fig. 12-27 shows a way to save effort. Fasteners for application of dry wall materials should be long enough to reach through any of the original ceiling material and reach deeply into the framing members. Some styles of fasteners for gypsum are shown in Fig. 12-28.

The gypsum system offers a method of lowering a ceiling. For heat energy conservation, it is practical to consider the lowering of any high ceiling to the popular 8 ft. (about 2.4 m) ceiling. In suspended gypsum board ceilings, drywall channels are clipped to suspended cold rolled channels rather than to framing members. See Fig. 12-29. Hangers are suspended by steel wires to the new height.

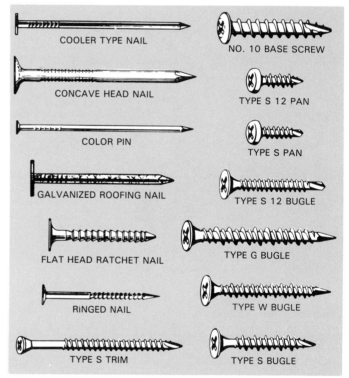

Fig. 12-28. Fasteners for gypsum materials. (Gypsum Assoc.)

Acoustical Tile Ceiling

Acoustical tiles attach to 1 x 3 in. (about 25 x 75 mm) furring strips which are nailed at right angle to joists, Fig. 12-30. Center-to-center spacing of strips depends on the size of the ceiling tile. Acoustical tile offers the benefit of beautiful, textured and designed tiles plus energy effectiveness, and soundproofing. If joists are fairly uniform, tiles can be attached to furring strips that are nailed to the joists. If the levelness of the joists is a problem or if there are projections below the joist line such

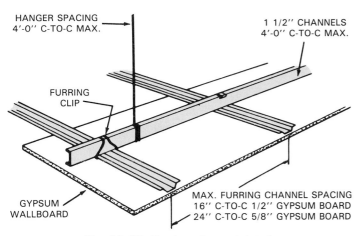

Fig. 12-29. Furring channel details.

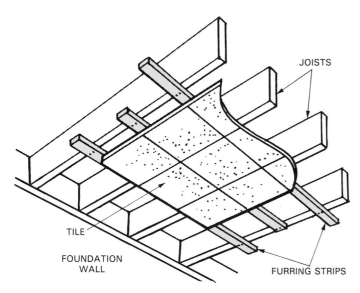

Fig. 12-30. In this acoustical tile system, the tiles are mounted on wood furring strips using staples. Place staples in edge tongues. (Georgia-Pacific)

Fig. 12-32. Installing simulated wood ceiling tile onto existing ceiling. Top. Mounting clips with instructions. Bottom. Panels are held with clips that snap onto the track side walls. Tongue and groove joints provide additional strength. (Armstrong World Industries, Inc.)

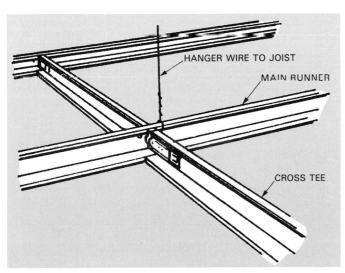

Fig. 12-31. A suspended ceiling provides a way to lower a ceiling. Tiles are tilted and slid into space. The average room system can be installed in a half day. (Celotex)

ac pipes and heating ducts, then a suspended ceiling might be the answer to the problem.

The suspended acoustical ceiling is a gridwork of t-channel metal bars or of wood strips that hang from wires attached to the joist or ceiling above. See Fig. 12-31. The gridwork edges in turn support the acoustical tiles. No fasteners are needed to hold the tiles. Tiles can be removed to work in the space above.

Sizes of the tiles are 2 x 2 ft. (about 50 x 50 cm) or 2 x 4 ft. (50 x 100 cm).

Ceiling tiles that look like wood are available. A printing process provides many styles of wood grain. See Fig. 12-32. Lightweight tracks annd clips mount on both old and new construction.

Tracks mount with small drywall nails. Small nail sizes reduce damage when driving nails into an existing ceiling.

TEST YOUR KNOWLEDGE — CHAPTER 12

1. Small cracks in a plaster wall are repaired with _____ _____.
2. Use _____ _____ to support a large patch in a plaster wall.
3. The edges of gypsum wallboard are _____ to allow for filling joints to level.
4. To make a small hole in gypsum for inserting an object, cut diagonal lines on the back side so you can use a _____ .
5. Drywall joint tape is applied _____ (before, after, at same time as) the first coat of compound.
6. Fasten a back-up plate behind a hole in gypsum using:
   a. Nails.
   b. Wallboard compound.
   c. Screws.
   d. Construction adhesive.
7. _____ _____ is a substance much like portland cement used to fill joints between ceramic tiles.
8. After cleaning tile and tile grout, apply a _____ sealer to keep the joint clean.
9. To speed up any type of chemical cleaning, mix solutions using _____ water.
10. Paneling can be fastened directly over plaster or drywall. True or False?
11. Install a vapor barrier _____ (before, after) placing furring strips.
12. Panel adhesive beads must be at least _____ long.
13. Before the adhesive sets, pull paneling away from wall a little to:
    a. Add more adhesive.
    b. Improve drying and bonding.
    c. Correct the panel alignment.
    d. Remove excess adhesive.
14. A drywall ceiling may be lowered to save _____ .
15. One advantage of a suspended acoustical ceiling is that one or more _____ can be removed to work above.

KNOW THESE TERMS

Gypsum board, plaster, spackling, suspended ceiling, drywall.

SUGGESTED ACTIVITIES

Learn to recognize plaster walls and gypsum walls. Inspect walls or ceilings in your house. Check visually or tap on the surface. Your instructor may have other samples. The information is important for proper repair.

Practice taping wallboard joints. This can be done at home or school. If time permits, make a display showing the result at each step of the process. Give a report in class.

Experiment with some of the chemical cleaning agents for ceramic tile and for tile grout. Do this only on approval of your instructor.

CAREERS

Plastering, drywaller, tile installer, finish carpenter.

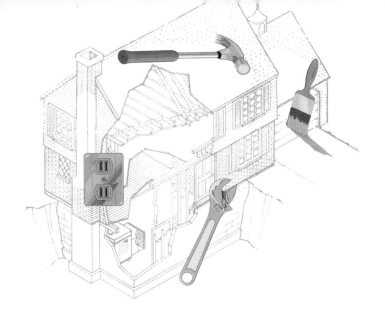

13

FLOOR COVERINGS

This chapter describes sheet floor materials, ceramic floor tile, wood floors, and carpeting. It includes repair and installation steps for floor materials.

After studying this chapter you will be able to:
■ List the layers of underlayment required for each type of floor.
■ Describe the precision of smoothness needed under a floor material.
■ Lay out guidelines to place resilient tile.
■ List common ways to stop floor squeaks.
■ Recall a method to fix a sagging floor.

Many types of floor coverings are installed over structural concrete slabs, steel decks, or wood subfloors. They may be thin membranes that add little to the structural strength of the building. Thin floor coverings are sheet materials such as linoleum, plastic, rubber, cork, and asphalt. Pre-cut materials include wood veneer tiles. All but wood tiles are referred to as resilient coverings. Rigid floor coverings, like ceramic and quarry tile, slate, and stone are also nonstructural.

Carpeting is another type of floor covering. Carpets provide insulation for heat and sound. With developments in technology, carpeting today is one of the most economical floor coverings.

In time, any floor covering will need to be refinished or replaced. There are several ways to improve the appearance of floors. Good wood floors wear down slowly, but stain and show scratches. They can be sanded and refinished, restoring them to nearly the original state. Carpeting and resilient flooring also wear down and show marks with use. Stone and quarry or slate tile withstand heavy use better than any other type of floor coverings.

RESILIENT FLOORS

Resilient flooring materials are available in both sheet and tile form. Although the standard tile size

is now 12 x 12 in. (30 x 30 cm), some styles and patterns are still made in the older 9 x 9 in. (22 x 22 cm) size. Sheets of resilient materials are available in rolls or cut from rolls 6, 9, or 12 ft. (about 180, 280, or 370 cm) wide.

Resilient flooring must be installed over a smooth surface, Fig. 13-1. Resilient flooring in time will conform to the shape of the floor beneath it. Wood floors that are in good condition, level and smooth, can be covered directly with a resilient material. Wood floors made up of tongue and groove boards tend to cup in time and should be sanded evenly. Set any nails below the surface and fill gaps. Paint on any floor should be roughened by sanding, so the adhesive will bond.

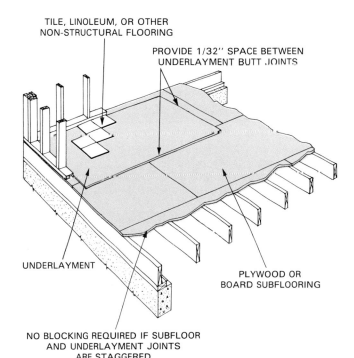

TILE, LINOLEUM, OR OTHER NON-STRUCTURAL FLOORING

PROVIDE 1/32" SPACE BETWEEN UNDERLAYMENT BUTT JOINTS

UNDERLAYMENT

PLYWOOD OR BOARD SUBFLOORING

NO BLOCKING REQUIRED IF SUBFLOOR AND UNDERLAYMENT JOINTS ARE STAGGERED

Fig. 13-1. Resilient floor covering installation details. Resilient floor coverings must be applied over a smooth surface. (American Plywood Assoc.)

An underlayment of 1/4 in. (6 mm) hardboard, particle board, or plywood should be installed over a wood floor which is in poor condition. Glue underlayment material with construction adhesive and nail every 4 in. (about 10 cm). Remove the base shoe and base board. Lay the underlayment in staggered rows to avoid four corners coming together at the same point.

Installing Resilient Tiles

Tiles may be laid in any number of patterns and arrays. Unfortunately, most rooms are not exactly square. To avoid problems, three methods are generally followed:

1. The pyramid method.
2. The partial width way.
3. The diagonal pattern method.

The pyramid method is illustrated in Fig. 13-2. Chalk one line centered on the width and one on the length of the area. These lines must meet at a right angle. Check them with a square or by measur-

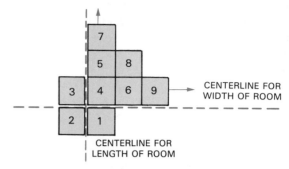

Fig. 13-2. Using the pyramid pattern method to lay tile, start in the center of the room and proceed outward.

ing distances. (See Fig. 13-4.) Lay four tiles around the center and proceed in an outward pyramid motion. Edge tile around the perimeter of the room will have to be cut.

Fig. 13-3 shows how to begin the partial width method. Starting in one corner use full width tile. Lay the length and width of the room, matching the

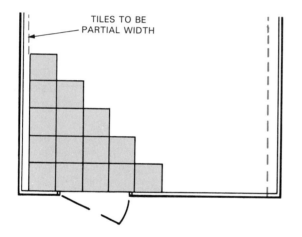

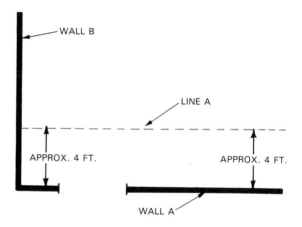

Fig. 13-3. Layout for partial width method. Left. Desired edge result. Pattern avoids pieces narrower than about 4 in. Right. From entranceway wall, measure and mark approximately 4 ft. at two points. Snap a temporary guide chalkline. Check doorway edge location by laying loose blocks from doorway to chalkline. Move points as needed to adjust. Snap a final chalk line (line A) across these points. Then lay tiles.

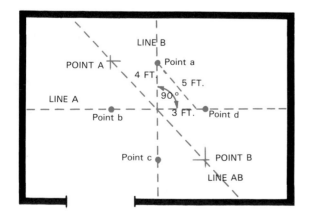

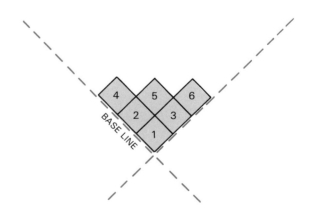

Fig. 13-4. Diagonal pattern of floor tile placement. Left. Layout procedure. Right. How to begin placing tile.

corners of four tiles. The last course of tiles along the wall width and length will be of partial length and width.

For the diagonal pattern method, refer to Fig. 13-4.

The diagonal pattern method requires careful planning. Layout involves the use of geometry techniques. The procedure is as follows (refer to Fig. 13-4, top):

1. Find the center of the room by snapping chalk lines. Snap each line from the center of a wall to the center of the opposite wall (Lines A and B).
2. Prepare to adjust the angles of intersection to 90°. Measure 3 ft. from the center along Line A and 4 ft. along Line B. Measure the diagonal distance between. This distance should be 5 ft. If it is not, adjust by moving lines A and B as needed. Divide the adjustment equally.
3. From the center, measure 4 ft. along each line toward all walls and mark the points as a, b, c, and d.
4. Using a radius of 4 ft., scribe intersecting arcs to the right and left or top and bottom of points a, b, c, and d.
5. Snap a chalk line (Line AB) through points A and B and extend to nearest walls. You may want to snap the other chalk line at 90° to the one just drawn if you feel it will help in placing tile.

Refer again to Fig. 13-4, right, to see the order of tile replacement.

Using Tile Adhesive

Choose the mastic or adhesive carefully to meet the manufacturer's specifications. Use either brush-on adhesive or one which is applied with a notched trowel. A notched trowel is shown in Fig. 13-5. The adhesive must have the proper degree of tackiness before tiles are applied. Read the manufacturer's directions before starting.

Where tiles meet a doorway or passage, use a protective metal strip to cover the exposed edge.

Repairing a Tile Floor

Damaged tile can be removed and replaced in a few simple steps. Remove tile with putty knife, working from the center of the broken tile outward to the edge. Take care not to damage surrounding tile or the job may become larger and larger. Tile which seem to have a very strong bond may be loosened with heat. An electric iron, propane torch, or heat lamp can be used to soften and loosen the bond.

The old adhesive should be scraped from the subfloor and a new tile adhesive applied before replacing tile. Be sure you have the suggested solvent available for tool clean-up when finished.

WOOD FLOORS

Wood floors are generally assembled with tongue-and-groove boards of either soft or hardwood species laid over a subfloor. Fig. 13-6 shows layers involved. Also refer to Fig. 13-7. Damaged tongue-and-groove floor boards are difficult to remove.

To prepare a section of damaged board for removal, mark cross cuts with pencil and square. Drill a series of holes across the width of the board only through the floor board, not through the subfloor. Keep holes to the inside of marked lines.

To remove the section, set a portable circular saw to the depth of the floor board and make two cuts lengthwise parallel to the tongue edge and groove edge. These cuts can be nearly to the middle of the strip to avoid damaging other boards and avoid nails. With a sharp chisel, trim the cross cut and lift out the damaged section. With the chisel, finish trimming the cross cut, give it a slight undercut.

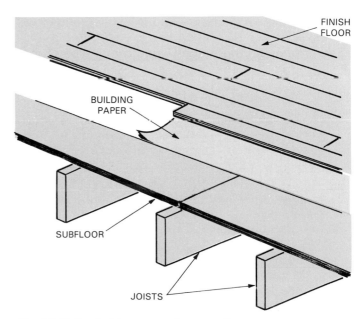

Fig. 13-6. Typical tongue-and-groove floor system over wood joists.

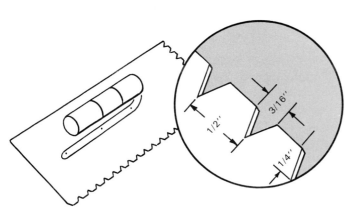

Fig. 13-5. A notched trowel is used to spread adhesive.

Fig. 13-7. Tongue and groove wood flooring is commonly end-matched for neat appearance and fast installation. Toenail the pieces to the subfloor using 2d finishing nails. (Weyerhaeuser)

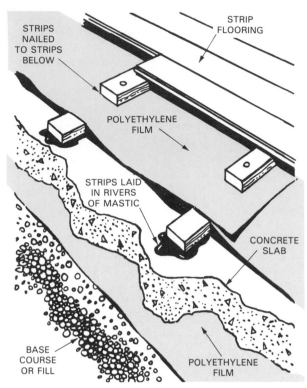

Fig. 13-8. Typical wood floor over concrete slab.

To replace the piece, measure and cut to length the replacement board and cut off the lower part of the groove. Insert the tongue side first and drop into opening. A mallet and block may be needed to drive board into place. Nail and set the nail heads. Fill with a good wood filler and sand smooth.

Wood floors can be assembled over concrete if proper steps are taken. See Fig. 13-8. The Flooring Manufacturers Association has developed a method of laying strip wood flooring over a concrete slab that is designed to meet Federal Housing Administration requirements. Strips of wood called sleepers are fastened to the slab with construction adhesive and supplementary concrete nails. Strips are nominal 1 x 2 in. (25 x 50 mm).

Put a layer of 4 mil polyethylene plastic film over these sleepers as a moisture barrier. Then nail a second set of 1 x 2 in. wood strips directly over the first set. Fasten the tongue-and-groove wood flooring directly to this sleeper arrangement.

STOP WOOD FLOOR SQUEAKS

Floors that creak and squeak can usually be fixed if the subfloor and floor joists are accessible from below. Floors have a greater tendency to squeak during the less humid periods of the year.

Possible causes for squeaking are:
1. Nails holding the subfloor have pulled loose.
2. Improper spacing of subflooring causing edges to rub together.
3. Floor joists have warped and twisted away from the floor.
4. Floor board may have pulled loose from subfloor.

To locate the boards where squeaking occurs, have someone walk on the floor above while you watch and listen from underneath. Look for any movement. Mark with chalk each different problem until all are located.

If subfloor has pulled loose from floor joist, drive cedar shims between pieces to tighten them, Fig. 13-9. A metal angle or cleat may be nailed alongside the floor joist while subfloor is weighted down against the joist. Construction adhesive applied to subfloor and joist before applying cleat will also help.

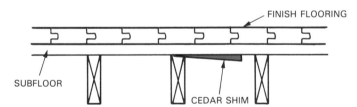

Fig. 13-9. Stop floor squeaks by closing gap under subflooring with wedge.

To correct a twisted joist, add bridging between surrounding joists and twisted joist.

Separation of floor boards and subfloor may be corrected by using wood screws through the subfloor into the floor boards. Also use adhesive when adding screws. See Fig. 13-10. Drill holes about 1/4 or 5/16 inch in diameter through the subfloor. By injecting construction adhesive before application of screw you may greatly increase the effects of the screws.

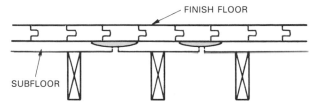

Fig. 13-10. To stop squeaks, first drill small hole for applying construction adhesive. Insert tip of tube to force glue between subfloor and finish floor.

SAGGING FLOORS

A sagging floor may indicate structural problems: joist too small, too long of span, or joists too far apart for the load they are expected to carry. More often it is the result of a warped joist or of weakened wood. If the problem is not getting worse, simple repairs are enough.

The sagging floor may be raised and straightened by using a basement post jack or house jack. Add a cross beam under the joists. Its size may vary according to the span distance. A 4 x 6 in. (10 x 15 cm) or 4 x 8 in. (10 x 20 cm) beam should be large enough. With jack raise the cross beam until joist and floor are level. Fix permanent post under cross beam and remove jacks. Steel or wood post can be installed. Regardless of the type of post used, it should rest on a concrete pad 18 to 25 in. (45 to 65 cm) deep and about 24 in. (60 cm) square.

CARPETING

Carpeting requires only a smooth surface and can be installed over almost any kind of existing flooring: old wood floors, resilient tile, plywood, concrete, and many others. Carpeting can help insulate against drafty floors and add some soundproofing. For the home decorator, carpeting allows designs with many colors, textures, and pattern arrangements.

All carpeting consists of two basic components, the backing and the surface pile. See Figs. 13-11 and 13-12. Woven-back carpets are generally installed over a pad, while cushion or foam-backed carpets are installed directly on the floor layer. Indoor-outdoor carpets and many foam-backed carpets are mildew resistant and unaffected by

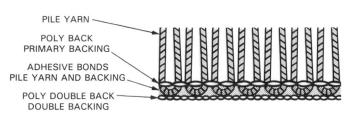

Fig. 13-11. Parts of carpeting. (Sears, Roebuck and Co.)

moisture. These are suitable for basements or other below grade areas. The woven-back carpets have heavy, stiff backs. The back is generally woven from jute fibers which are highly susceptible to moisture.

Surface pile fibers may be either natural or synthetic. Natural piles consist of cotton or wool. Synthetic piles are probably most familiar to the homeowner. They consist of nylon, polyester, polypropylene, acrylic, and other plastic compounds. See your dealer for information on which fiber to choose for a given area. Each has its advantages and disadvantages.

INSTALLING CARPET

The method used to install a carpet depends on the type of backing and on whether or not the carpet will be wall-to-wall. A woven-backed wall-to-wall carpet must be stretched tight with special tools and then brought over a "tackless strip." The job is not recommended for most homeowners. However, the home mechanic will have little trouble with rubber-backed or indoor-outdoor carpets and small woven carpets. This chapter does not discuss the more complex jobs.

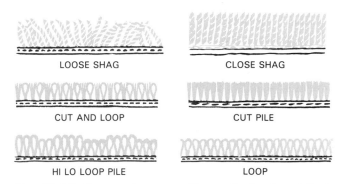

Fig. 13-12. Carpet pile types. (Sears, Roebuck and Co.)

Choosing the pad for a woven-backed carpet is essential to the comfort of the carpet. Padding can prolong the life and increase the sound-proofing capacity of carpeting. Most pads are latex rubber foams, vinyl foams, or fitted cushions made either of animal hair or of a combination of hair and jute fibers. Today, the latex and vinyl foams are considered most practical. Some have waffled surfaces which tend to hold the carpet in place.

Floor surface preparation for carpeting is comparatively simple. Rid the surface of any unevenness, drive protruding nails down in wood floors, and fill any voids of wood or concrete floor with wood putty or patching mortar. Shim or remove some of the old floor at edges as needed, especially at door openings.

Use double-face or seaming tape to fasten rubber-backed and indoor-outdoor carpeting. Installation of woven-backed wall-to-wall carpet is best left to a professional. Place doubleface tape at edges and 2 ft. apart in other areas. A paper cover on the upper side of the tape keeps it from sticking until needed.

Unroll the carpet to extend upward a few inches on each wall. Then fasten it with the tape before cutting the carpet at the base moldings. Cut carpet at moldings as shown in Fig. 13-13. The cutting action tends to force the carpet under the molding. This saves one step of the job. Finish at door openings with metal or plastic strips.

Install strips of rubber-backed carpet with seaming tape under the joint. You may need to coat the tape yourself. Use a similar method for every edge and joint of indoor-outdoor carpet.

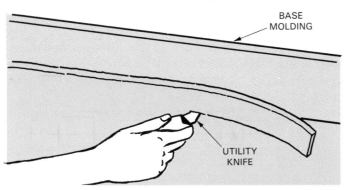

Fig. 13-13. Cutting rubber-backed carpeting at base molding. The cutting action helps insert the carpet into the crack.

Estimating Carpet Coverage

All types of carpeting are available in several widths which vary with the manufacturer. Rolls are made in 6, 9, 12, and 15 ft. (180, 280, 370, and 460 cm) widths. Runners, strips of carpet for stairs and halls, are available in 3 ft. (about 100 cm) widths. Most wall-to-wall carpeting is priced by the square yard. To determine how many square yards (square meters) will be needed to cover a given room, multiply the length by the width of the room in feet and divide by 9 (in cm and divide by 10 000). (One square yard is equal to 9 square feet and one m² equals 10 000 cm².)

TEST YOUR KNOWLEDGE — CHAPTER 13

1. Sheet flooring materials such as linoleum,
plastic, rubber, cork, and asphalt are called _____ coverings.
2. Put an _____ of 1/4 in. plywood under resilient flooring to cover an uneven floor.
3. To help remove damaged asphalt tiles, use _____ .
   a. Solvent.
   b. ''Dry ice.''
   c. Heat.
   d. A vacuum.
4. To fit a new piece of tongue and groove wood flooring, cut off the _____ (upper, lower) part of the groove.
5. Wood floors over concrete are installed on _____ .
6. List four items used to stop floor squeaks.
7. Use a type of _____ to raise a sagging floor.
8. Any type of support post must rest on a concrete pad about 25 in. deep and _____ in. square.
9. Install a _____ before placing a woven-backed carpet.
10. Use _____ or seaming tape to fasten rubber-backed or indoor-outdoor carpet to floor surface.

KNOW THESE TERMS

Resilient floor, notched trowel, underlayment, carpet.

SUGGESTED ACTIVITIES

Make models of floor systems. These may involve wood, tile, resilient materials, and carpeting. Show the layers that make up the installation. Use samples of flooring or adhesive. Use thin craft supplies to scale down the thicknesses.

Practice drawing centerlines inside of rectangular outlines. This skill is needed if tiles are to come out straight. Work on both paper and large models or real rooms. Ask your instructor about the mathematical basis of a ''3, 4, 5-right triangle.'' This information may become your rule of thumb if you forget the directions given in a particular book.

CAREERS

Carpet layer, carpet cleaner, salesperson, subcontractor, materials distribution, finish carpenter.

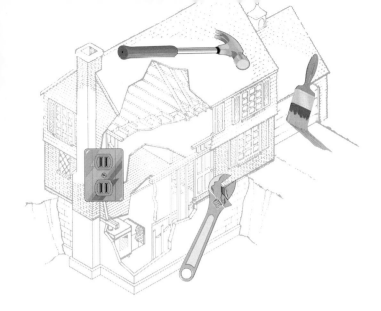

14

CABINETS

This chapter describes cabinet types and kitchen arrangements. It discusses cabinet surfaces and metal hardware. The chapter covers cabinet adjustment and simple repairs.

After studying this chapter, you will be able to:
- Recognize cabinet styles.
- List features of wood, metal, and plastic surfaces or shaped items.
- Tell how to install plastic laminate.
- List purposes of the many hinges and catches.
- State some ways to adjust hinges, catches, and drawer guides.
- Recall steps for wood frame repair of cabinets.
- Make designs for efficient kitchens.

Cabinets are used in the bathroom, laundry and other types of storage areas. Maintenance of all cabinets is similar. This chapter discusses cabinets in kitchen storage and kitchen service areas as examples.

Kitchen cabinets provide storage and counter top work space. They hide appliances or match their surfaces. Cabinets often have lighting and ventilation systems.

CABINET TYPES AND SIZES

Cabinets in a Grouping

To learn about cabinets, you must first know how they are related to kitchen design. A cabinet type depends on how it is used with other cabinets in a grouping. The number of cabinets will depend on the kitchen design used. Sometimes the construction of the cabinet frame depends on the kitchen layout.

With years of development, four basic kitchen shapes have emerged. Refer to Fig. 14-1. The four kitchen shapes are:
1. The I shape. All wood areas are located along one wall.

2. The L shape. Cabinets and appliances are arranged along two walls meeting at the corner.
3. The U shape. All areas are located along three walls joined at two corners.
4. The corridor shape, sometimes called the galley kitchen. Cabinets are located on two opposing parallel walls.

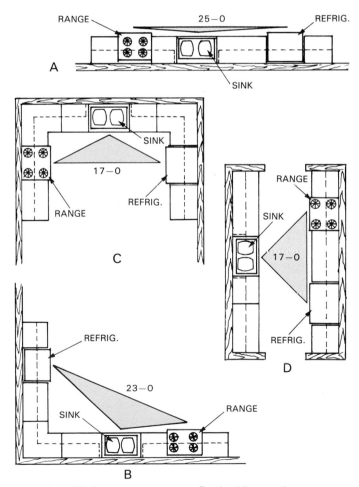

Fig. 14-1. Kitchen arrangements. Dashed lines refer to upper cabinets. A—I shaped kitchen. B—L shaped. C—U shaped. D—Corridor. Make distance around each triangle less than 24 ft.

A

B

Fig. 14-2. Kitchen arrangements that break up space. A—The peninsula kitchen. B—The island kitchen, which gets its name from the table usage. (St. Charles Manufacturing)

A

B

C

There are other shapes or adaptations. These include the peninsula, and the island, Fig. 14-2. For an overview of kitchen types, see the collection presented in Fig. 14-3.

In any kitchen arrangement, cabinet function and maintenance depend on nearby objects. The direction of door swing is one example. Other examples include rate of surface wear or even decay. More important, access for service depends on layout. Learn what to expect when servicing a cabinet.

Cabinet Sizes

Kitchen cabinets are limited to a set of standard sizes. This makes certain dimensions uniform from

Fig. 14-3. Ceiling and base cabinet styles. A—All surfaces are flush. Ceiling cabinet provides light toward ceiling and for counter. B—This kitchen is designed for economy. Ceiling cabinets are inexpensive and system is compact. C—No ceiling cabinets are used here. Arrangement hides shape of range unit. (St. Charles Manufacturing)

one house to another. Both commercial producers and custom manufacturers use the standard size for the basic units. Fig. 14-4 gives the dimensions which are used throughout the industry. Most standard base cabinets are 34 1/2 in. (90 cm) high with an additional 1 1/2 in. (5 cm) for the counter to make the work surface height 36 in. (95 cm) from the floor. The depth of the base cabinet from wall into room is 24 in. (60 cm). The counter top overhangs the base front 1 in. (2 cm) bringing the total depth of the base cabinet to 25 in. (62 cm).

Most base cabinets have storage compartments containing one drawer and one shelf below. However, drawer stacks are often used. The stack will contain 3 or 4 drawers of various heights. Each drawer is from 15 to 36 in. (40 to 90 cm) wide. Sink or appliance fronts do not have drawers but a false drawer front is installed to match the design.

Wall or upper cabinets are usually 12 to 13 in. (30 to 33 cm) deep. A vertical length of 30 in. (76 cm) is maximum. This allows a work space of 18 in. between the counter surface and the bottom of the wall section of cabinet. Height of cabinet located over the range is either 15 or 18 in. The 15 in. height results from a vented hood installed over the range. Cabinet heights located over the refrigerator, based on height of refrigerator, may be 12 or 15 in.

Sizes of Related Structures

Wall cabinets are not often located over the sink area due to a window. If the sink is on an interior wall, a 12 or 15 in. soffit may be installed. A cabinet soffit is generally framed in above the cabinet to act as a filler. It is furred down 12 in. (30 cm) if the ceiling is 8'-0'' (182 cm) high. Soffit may be adjusted for other ceiling height.

The depth of the soffit varies from 13 in. (33 cm) minimum depth for upper cabinets to 24 in. (60 cm). Deeper soffit may contain lighting for the work surface.

Eating bars, if designed into the cabinet unit, have standard cabinet height with the bar stool seating or have height reduced to 30 in. with chair seating. Writing desk and household record storage are often a part of the kitchen cabinet plan. They are usually 30 in. high and from 18 to 24 in. deep.

CABINET SURFACES

Counter Top Surfaces

Cabinet tops for kitchen cabinets must be durable. The material must withstand knife cuts, severe blows, and hot dishes. The material must also resist stains from foods and drinks, and must be nonporous. In addition to these needs, color and pattern are important.

Ceramic tile often is used for a durable counter surface. It does however have the disadvantage of being an uneven surface. The grouted joints may be difficult to clean.

Resilient tiles, vinyl, asphalt, rubber, and others are sometimes used. Wood surfaces are often used but are difficult to clean and remove food stains. Wood surfaces can be expensive to install and maintain. Stainless steel and porcelain and steel have been used. The stainless will scratch and porcelain will chip.

The most common counter top is the high-pressure plastic laminate, Fig. 14-5. Plastic laminates are surfacing products that combine colors and patterns with durability. These materials are composed of many layers of kraft paper sealed with special phenolic resins. The layers are then covered by a melamine resin. This is a patterned sheet saturated with melamine plastic topped with a clear protective sheet of the same plastic. These built-up materials are placed in a large hydraulic press between stainless plates. The piece is subjected to extreme heat and pressure to form a hard-surface sheet. When installed over wood or particle board, it provides a cabinet top which resists wear. Stains and low temperature burns are easy to clean with soap and water.

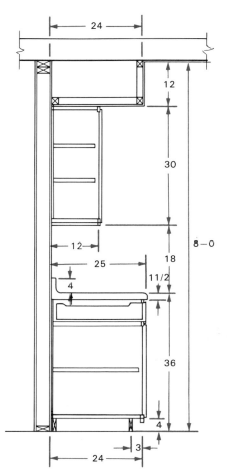

Fig. 14-4. Typical kitchen cabinet sizes. Dimensions are standardized for cabinets. Therefore, a cabinet can be replaced by another without major framing work.

Fig. 14-5. Plastic laminate counter top. (Scheirich Cabinetry)

Grades and Classes of Plastic Laminates

The general purpose or standard grade is 1/16 in. (1.6 mm) thick and is available in a wide range of widths and lengths. The standard grade can be applied on both horizontal and vertical surfaces.

Formable (post-forming) grade is approximately 1/20 in. thick. It is designed to permit re-heating to form curves. It is applied around door and sill ledges and rolled or contoured counter top surfaces.

The vertical grade is about 1/32 in. (0.8 mm) thick and is designed only for vertical surfaces. It is used on furniture and cabinet fronts.

A flame retardant grade is 1/16 in. (1.6 mm). This grade is designed for wall paneling and other vertical uses as in restaurants, hotels, and public buildings.

Installation of Plastic Laminates on Old Counter Top

Plastic laminate can be applied by the home mechanic with a few tools and persistence. The needed tools are: hand saw, block plane (with a jig), paint brush, and a kitchen rolling pin.

First remove all existing counter top material and scrape off any old adhesive. Repair any defects or voids and sand entire surface lightly.

Cut plastic with fine tooth hand saw about 1/4 in. larger than needed to fit the counter top. Set it aside. If plastic laminate is going to be placed on the trim front edge, that strip should be cut and installed first.

Select the correct adhesive, usually recommended by the manufacturer. Most adhesives are of the contact cement type. Brush a coat evenly onto the plastic laminate and the cabinet top. Allow some curing time (approx. 15 minutes).

Place the 1 1/2 in. edge strip on first. Plane and sand the top edge flush with the top of substrate, Fig. 14-6. Set top surface sheet in place.

A note of warning: contact cement bonds instantly and gives no degree of adjustment after contact. However to gain a little working time, spread wax paper, kraft paper, or wood dowels between the adhesive coated surfaces. Strips should be separate but overlapping. Position plastic laminate, and gently remove the waxed paper strips or other items one at a time.

Once the plastic laminate is in position, press out all air bubbles with rolling pin.

Prepare or rent a jig to hold a block plane or a small router at 45° to the counter edge. Refer again to Fig. 14-6. Trim the excess flush with outside edge. Most jigs can follow the flat surfaces to maintain angle and depth. Sand and polish the edge.

CABINET HARDWARE

Cabinet hardware refers to the metal or plastic units which aid in drawer and door operation. Hardware is different for flush-mounted doors compared

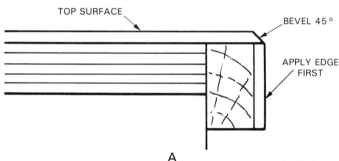

TOP SURFACE

BEVEL 45°

APPLY EDGE FIRST

A

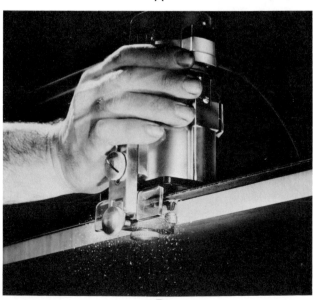

B

Fig. 14-6. How to apply plastic laminate counter surface. A — Desired result. B — Use a router and jig to get an accurate bevel. (Delta)

to doors which cover all or part of the cabinet front. Most cabinet doors cover the front (called the offset door). The overlap is about 3/8 in. (10 mm) on each edge. This allows full coverage of the opening so very little dust can enter the cabinet while the door is in closed position. Hinges are available in three styles:

1. Invisible, Fig. 14-7.
2. Semiconcealed, Fig. 14-8.
3. Exposed, Fig. 14-9.

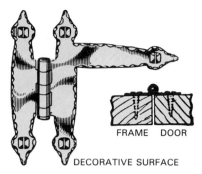

Fig. 14-9. Exposed type of hinge.

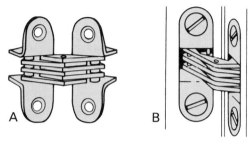

Fig. 14-7. A —The invisible link hinge is concealed when cabinet door is closed. This hinge is sometimes called a Soss hinge. B — Drill bit inside of a square cutter is used to make the mortise (hole) for the hinge mechanism.

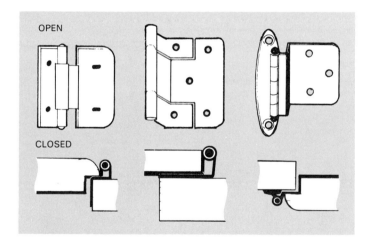

Fig. 14-8 Semi-concealed cabinet hinges. Most require a mortise.

The offset door has the semiconcealed or has the exposed hinge. The invisible hinge has a pivot pin nearly hidden in darkness when the door is closed. The semi-concealed has the barrel of pivot pin exposed to the front when door is closed. Some styles of semi-concealed hinges expose the styled mounting tab and mounting screws. The exposed type of hinge is in full view from the front when the door is closed and all mounting screws are displayed.

Flush mounted doors require the invisible hinge. Make mortise (hole) with special drill press bit.

Hinges are available in many accent styles and metal finishes. These include polished chrome, polished brass, and antique brass and copper.

Door Catches

Door catches hold the door in a closed position. There are several common types:

1. Magnetic catch.
2. Elbow catch.
3. Double roller catch.

The magnet catch is a small magnet often housed in a plastic case mounted on the door, Fig. 14-10. By magnet attraction, the door is held in a closed position. The elbow catch, shown in Fig. 14-11, is opened with a lever held with a spring. This catch is used with either wood or metal cabinets. Fig. 14-12 shows a double roller catch with spring. It consists of two nylon rollers held together by a spring mount. The rollers are located on the cabinet side and a tongue is mounted on the door. When forced between the rollers, the tongue is held tight.

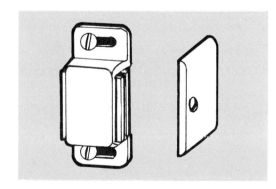

Fig. 14-10. Magnet door catch.

Fig. 14-11. An elbow catch. It is only used with double door. Access is through the second door.

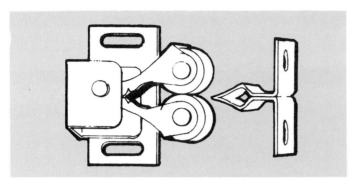

Fig. 14-12. Double roller catch is designed for quiet operation. (Door is held out from cabinet by a small amount.)

Cabinet Pulls

Cabinet pulls are used as much for appearance as for function. They generally match the design theme for the entire house. Pulls will correspond to

the hinge finish and are usually sold in sets. Some styles are shown in Fig. 14-13. They are easily removed for repair or refinishing of the drawer or door.

Drawer Slides

Drawer slides or guides are used to:
1. Reduce friction between the drawer and cabinet frame.
2. To guide the drawer into its closed position.
3. Provide a stopping mechanism to keep drawer from opening too far.

Some inexpensive drawer slides for lightweight drawers consist of three separate pieces of nylon which slide against a hardwood slot or track. Others have three metal brackets with rubber or plastic rollers.

A heavy duty drawer guide consists of side or bottom mounted tracks with nylon rollers and steel ball

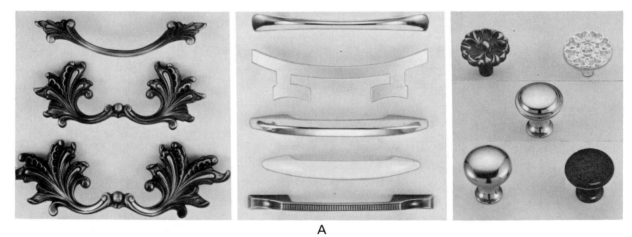

A

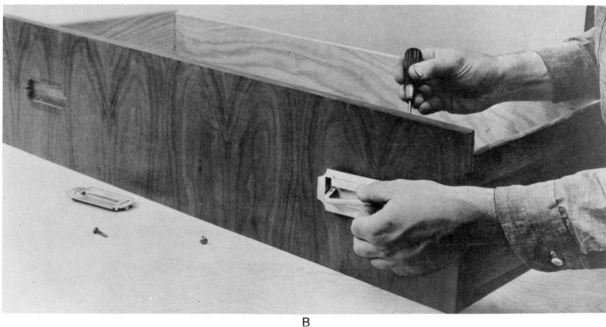

B

Fig. 14-13. A—Drawer and door hardware. Pulls with 3 in. centers, knobs. (Amerock Corp.) B—To provide strength, fasteners for most drawer pulls attach from the rear.

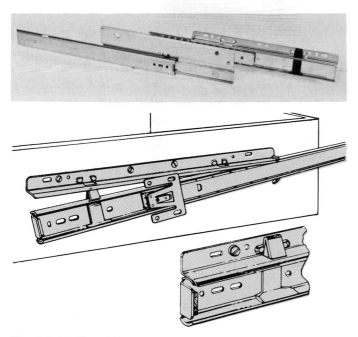

Fig. 14-14. Top. Metal drawer glide. Bottom. Mounting holes for screws are usually elongated. Glide problems can often be solved by adjusting the mount position. (Accuride Co.)

bearings, Fig. 14-14. Some types of these will support at least 100 pound (45 kg.) loads within the drawers.

REPAIR OF HARDWARE

Repair of rollers or wheels is not practical. Replacement of entire assemblies is best. However, the homeowner will not often need to replace parts. It is more likely that some kind of adjustment is the only step needed.

CABINET ADJUSTMENT

Cabinet problems may stem from age, misuse, or effects of a shifting structure. Drawers or doors may stick, drag, or bind.

Wood tracks that stick can be renewed with candle wax. For a worn wood track, build it up with thumbtacks. See Fig. 14-15. Other correction procedures are limited to repairs involving the cabinet hardware. (Severely worn wood parts cannot be easily repaired. Maintenance of wood glides and similar structures often requires replacement or requires professional help.)

Cabinet doors may usually be adjusted at either the point of the hinge or the catch. The catch, if used, will have slotted screw holes. Refer once more to Fig. 14-12. Loosen the mounting screws one-half to one turn to move the catch inward or outward to the correct position. If operations have improved, re-tighten the screws.

Many cabinet hinges are manufactured with mounting screw holes which do not allow further

adjustment after mounting. Refer back to Figs. 14-7 and 14-8.

Suppose the gap between door and cabinet for an invisible style hinge is wrong. You need to adjust the door by moving the door right or left in relation to the cabinet. Remove the mounting screws from the cabinet, place a cardboard shim behind the hinge, and replace the screws. Trim excess exposed shim material from around the hinge.

For other types of hinges with non-slotted screw holes, first try cardboard shims. If this is not enough, consider forming screw holes in a new location. The steps are described next (as a solution to a similar problem).

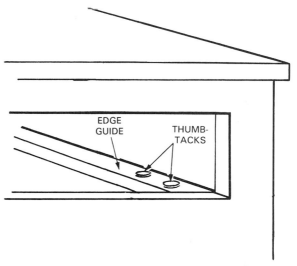

Fig. 14-15. To repair a badly worn drawer guide track, build it up with thumbtacks.

Worn Screw Holes

Older designs or much-used cabinet doors will sometimes have loose hinge mounting screws. This is especially true of cabinets made of the softer wood species.

To correct this, remove the hinge to expose the worn screw holes. Cut or fashion wood slivers to fit the screw hole. Coat with carpenters glue and set into screw hole by tapping lightly with mallet or hammer. Allow glue to set. Trim excess glue and wood of plug, leaving plug flush with surface of cabinet face and door stile. Remount the hinge by redrilling the pilot hole, (appropriate size for the screw), and replace the screws. The procedure often leaves the door nearly as solid as new.

Drawer Guide Adjustment

Cabinet drawers suffer two major ailments:
1. Maladjusted or worn slide, glides, or guides.
2. Loose wood joint fits.

Hardware devices can be adjusted without special tools. Wood joints require more care.

The drawer glides are attached to the drawer back, drawer sides, or underneath the drawer. Drawer hardware items are attached by screws. The screws pass through holes in the hardware which are slotted or elongated. Slightly loosening these screws, making the appropriate adjustment for smooth operation, and re-tightening the screws are usually sufficient.

CABINET REBUILDING

Cabinet drawer joints will often loosen and separate. To re-glue the drawer, carefully disassemble the various components of the drawer; bottom, front, back, and right and left sides. Take extreme care not to chip, split, or splinter the various parts.

Scrape the old glue from the joint areas. Use carpenter's glue to re-glue the components. Spread a thin coating of glue on both surfaces of each joint. Use small wire nails to hold the parts while the glue sets. Clamps may be an alternative to the nails. Carpenters use wood clamps from 6 in. to 2 ft. in span. For any clamping or holding method, always check the drawer for squareness while assembling the drawer, Fig. 14-16.

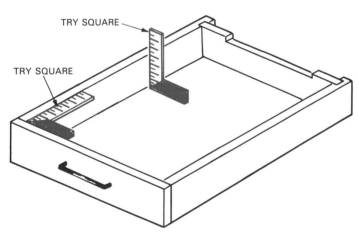

Fig. 14-16. While re-gluing and re-assembling the drawer, test for squareness at several places.

Broken Drawer Bottom

If the bottom of a drawer has a large hole or is badly cracked or warped, first remove it by cutting into pieces. There are two ways to replace the bottom. The bottom can be fit back into an existing groove, called a dado. Refer to Fig. 14-17. Support strips can sometimes be fastened inside the drawer to hold it.

Warped Door

If a warped door is part of an antique or non-replaceable cabinet, consider having the door straightened professionally. The professional has

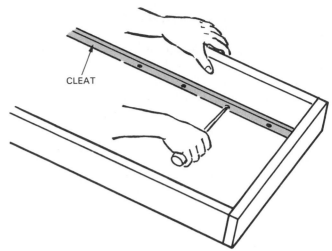

Fig. 14-17. A new drawer bottom can be mounted to wood strips or it can be held in the original dado (groove). Strip size is about 1/2 x 1/2 in. Glue the new bottom to top surface of strips. Set strip height to match original height of bottom.

equipment to soften the wood (very dry ammonia gas is used under pressure). A press is used to straighten it.

The home mechanic can reduce the amount of warpage with a brace. See Fig. 14-18. Mount a strip of hardwood such as oak to the warped area with screws. If this is not sufficient, plane a curve on the strip and remount it. Repeat the procedure until the warp is removed. However, be careful with a severely warped door. Soak it for a few hours first. Then tighten the screws a little at a time so the door does not crack.

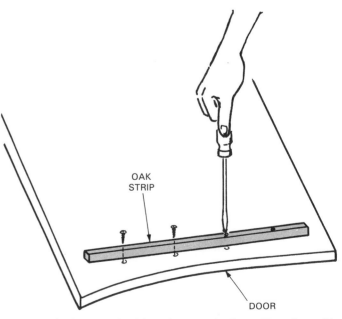

Fig. 14-18. A warped cabinet door can be forced into line with a straight or curved strip of hardwood. Increase the curve as needed with a plane. Soak the door first to help prevent cracking.

REMODELING

The ambitious homeowner may redesign and remodel the kitchen service area to add new and improved appliances. Efficient kitchen planning involves proper placement of appliances, and requires thought to provide enough storage space, room for food preparation, and a clean-up area. Good planning will reduce the amount of walking to perform kitchen duties.

A general rule of the "kitchen triangle" should test each kitchen design. Glance once again at Fig. 14-1. Draw a triangle line from the front center of the refrigerator to sink, then to the range and back to the refrigerator to produce the triangle. On a scale drawing, add the lengths of all three lines. If the total exceeds 24 ft. (7.3 m) then the efficiency of the plan will probably be low.

Individual distances greater than 8 ft. (2.4 m) require more walking. If the triangle distance is less than 12 ft. (3.6 m), the counter top will probably be too small for easy work. When planning, explore several plans and choose the most efficient one.

TEST YOUR KNOWLEDGE — CHAPTER 14

1. Cabinets placed on two opposing parallel walls form what kind of kitchen?
   a. I shape.
   b. Peninsula.
   c. Sunken.
   d. Galley.
2. An inexpensive cabinet surface material which resists wear and low-temperature burns is _____ _____ .
3. When putting new plastic laminate on a countertop, install the _____ (top, edge trim) first.
4. Flush-mounted doors require the _____ type of hinge.
5. Before starting major repairs on a wood drawer that sticks, first lubricate it with _____ _____ .
   a. Graphite.
   b. Candle wax.
   c. Silicone.
   d. Fine oil.
6. A badly worn wood guide track can be built up with _____ .
7. Door catch location can be adjusted if the screw holes are:
   a. Countersunk.
   b. Slotted.
   c. Re-drilled.
   d. Angled.
8. To hold a drawer together while glue dries, use wood clamps or wire _____ .
9. When straightening a warped door with a brace, _____ the door first to help avoid cracking it in the process.
10. When adding the three lengths of a "kitchen triangle," the result should not be more than _____ ft. for good efficiency.

KNOW THESE TERMS

Cabinets, sink, corridor, counter top, base cabinet, invisible hinge, drawer.

SUGGESTED ACTIVITIES

Inspect two types of cabinets you have access to. These cabinets may or may not be broken. For both of them, imagine that you must:
   a. Fix a broken drawer bottom.
   b. Install a plastic laminate countertop.
Make detailed plans of every step you would take to do this job. Include sizes of wood pieces to be used. Show how you would place the plastic laminate without a mistake with contact cement by listing your preparation for it. Can you devise a jig for beveling the 45° edge? Check into rentals at a hardware center.

CAREERS

Cabinetmaker, architect, interior designer, salesperson.

15

CONCRETE, MASONRY, AND FIREPLACE MAINTENANCE

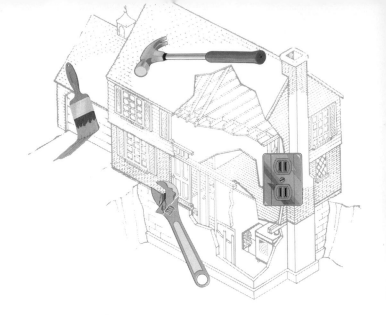

This chapter covers concrete and masonry bonding materials. It includes building principles for concrete, brick, and stone. The chapter tells how to maintain masonry structures.

After studying this chapter, you will be able to:
- State the components of concrete.
- Describe how to mix concrete or mortar for common uses.
- Compute amounts of concrete needed.
- Tell how to pour and finish concrete.
- Give the steps for repairing holes and cracks in concrete and masonry.
- List steps for laying brick.
- Describe chemical or physical cleaning methods.
- Tell how to maintain metal fireplace and chimney units.
- Prepare for working with stone.

Concrete can be prepared in several ways. You can:
1. Purchase it as a dry premixed and bagged product at your local supply dealer.
2. Get it ready-mixed by the truck load, Fig. 15-1. Usually one cubic yard is a minimum amount.
3. Mix the ingredients from start.

Regardless of how you obtain it, concrete contains standard ingredients. These are portland cement, sand, and coarse aggregate. Concrete requires water to promote the chemical process of hydration. The chemical process creates the hardened concrete. Concrete is as durable as limestone.

CONCRETE MIX PREPARATION

Concrete is not a simple material. To get the right products for the right job, one must understand the mix. The water-to-cement ratio will determine the

Fig. 15-1. It is best to get concrete ready-mixed for a large home maintenance project. Plan the use of ready-mixed concrete thoroughly.

strength of the concrete paste that binds the aggregate together.

Too much water will make the paste thin. The aggregate will settle out. This results in a powdery and weak concrete. A mix with too little water will yield a concrete too stiff to be placed and worked properly. The result is "honey-combing", marked by large uncontrolled air spaces within the concrete. The following table will aid in the proper mix (expand the amounts in proportion):

For basement floor, driveways, and walls.
1 cu. ft. portland cement, type II (1 bag)
2 1/2 cu. ft. sand
3 1/2 cu. ft. aggregate
5 to 5 1/2 gal. water (if aggregate are extremely wet 4 1/2 gal. water)
(this mix will yield a concrete with a strength of 3500 PSI at 28 days)

For foundation walls, retaining walls, and footings.
1 cu. ft. portland cement, type II (1 bag)
3 cu. ft. sand
4 cu. ft. aggregate
5 1/2 to 6 gal. water (if aggregate are extremely
    wet 4 1/2 to 5 gal. water)
(this mix should yield a concrete with 3000 PSI
    at 28 days).
Note: Use air-entrained cement where concrete will be subjected to freezing and thawing, and where de-icing chemicals are to be used.

Coarse aggregates of gravel or crushed rock should not exceed 1 1/2 inches (3.8 cm) size. Where slab pours are being made, the aggregate should not be greater than one third the thickness of slab. Said another way, the slab must not be thinner than three times the aggregate size.

PLACING AND FINISHING CONCRETE

Anytime concrete is being worked, plan the project well in advance. Timing is important. Before placing concrete:
1. Have forms in place, Fig. 15-2.
2. Prepare surface by cleaning to remove any debris.
3. Moisten the surface.
4. Have tools at hand: shovels, rakes, floats, trowels, and edgers.
5. Have additional help available if a large amount of concrete is to be placed.

Regardless of method of getting concrete, such as mixing by hand or buying ready mixed, always place as near its final position as possible. Do not dump concrete in widely separate piles and rake them together. The aggregate may separate from the cement paste. Dump each succeeding load against the previous one. Never place concrete on frozen ground or allow the mix to freeze during the first 48 hours. Do not pour concrete onto muddy ground. Do not allow concrete mix to fall distances in excess of 4 or 5 ft. (120 to 150 cm).

When pouring slabs, immediately after pouring, scrape off (strike off) or screed the surface, Fig. 15-3. Place a strike-off board across the form edges. With a sawing stroke, remove the excess concrete and fill in the low area.

Some workers follow with a process called "jitterbugging." The process embeds the coarser aggregates into the concrete and leaves a thin layer of water, cement, and sand on top for the finish.

Float after striking off. Floating further smooths the surface by removing the marks created by the back and forth motion of the strike-off board. See Fig. 15-4.

Fig. 15-3. After pouring concrete, tamp into place, and level with a straight edge board or screed. Rest screed on form edges and move in sawing motion across form to remove excess concrete fill.

Fig. 15-2. This form will support concrete against slumping although the angle is steep. Sidewalls are completed before pouring the steps.

Fig. 15-4. Soon after screed work, use a wood float to help work larger aggregates downward. This brings a layer of sand and cement to the surface to provide the finish. About 30 minutes after cement begins to set, use a steel trowel to get a smooth finish.

Finishing cannot begin until the water sheen leaves the surface and the concrete is well into the curing cycle. This waiting period is essential if you are to get a durable surface. This requires skill to determine at which stage the concrete is ready for finishing. On hot days the waiting time is shortened, on cool days the waiting time can be several hours. Additives can be included to shorten the waiting time.

Edging

Immediately after floating, but before finishing, run a trowel between the concrete and side form to a depth of about 1 in. (2.5 cm). Then wait for sheen to disappear. Plan to do edge and surface finishing at the same time. After the surface finish is complete, use an edging trowel and gently run between the side form giving the new concrete slab a radius edge, Fig. 15-5.

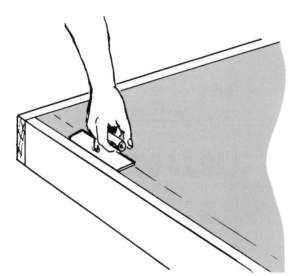

Fig. 15-5. Edging gives the concrete a small radius. This improves the edge strength and the appearance.

Joint after edging. Use a jointing trowel to mark in cross joints. Control joints are spaced 4 to 5 ft. (1.2 to 1.5 m) apart in sidewalks and 10 to 15 ft. (3 to 4.5 m) in floors, driveways, and patios. These control joints form the location of future cracks in a controlled fashion. In summary, the steps are done in this order: screed, float, poke trowel in edge, wait, finish surface, finish edge, joint.

Curing

Curing is the chemical process which seals aggregate and sand in a permanent position. Slow curing promotes concrete with a greater strength and durability. Generally curing means to extend the chemical process period by keeping the moisture in the concrete for a long time. This period normally lasts 6 days. Curing can be accomplished by one

of the following:
1. Cover the surface with sheets of polyethylene plastic or waterproof paper, sealing the edges and ends.
2. Cover the concrete with burlap, canvas, or straw and soak with water.
3. Keep concrete moist with a sprinkler system.
4. Build a dam around the slab and floor to hold a layer of water.
5. Spray a pigmented curing compound on the damp concrete.

REPAIRING DAMAGED CONCRETE

If damage is not extensive, you can use any number of commercial patching compounds. These may be latex, vinyl, or epoxy. Follow the instructions on the container.

For major patching jobs, plastic patch compounds may be too expensive and too rapid curing. Instead, use a mixture of one part portland cement, 2 parts sand, and 2 parts fine aggregate (pea gravel). Add water until paste just starts to slump.

Chisel out any loose or broken fragments of the concrete to a depth of 1 in. (2.5 cm). Undercut the edge to allow the patching material to anchor itself, Fig. 15-6. Prepare large holes or holes needing finished edges using a power saw with an abrasive

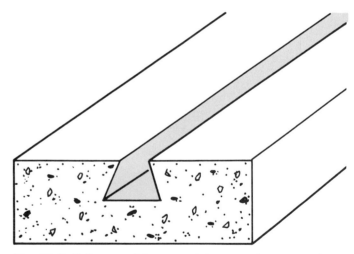

Fig. 15-6. Before repairing a crack in concrete, remove loose pieces and undercut the opening.

blade like that shown in Fig. 15-7. A power saw can be set to cut the bevel for the undercut.

Moisten the patch surface. It should not be too wet. Water should not be standing free. Pour patch mixture into void. Strike and finish. Keep traffic off the patch area for at least 6 days.

Patching of small cracks can be done in the same manner. If a crack is too small or narrow to take the gravel, mix a grout of 1 part portland cement and

Fig. 15-7. Use an abrasive blade to save work on all kinds of masonry cutting jobs. Saw frame can be set to cut bevels on edges of slabs, tiles, clay pipe, and other ceramic objects. (Makita Power Tools)

3 parts sand. Mix with water until material has a stiff paste consistency. Work this into the crack. Strike and finish.

COMPUTING VOLUMES OF CONCRETE

The first step in estimating how much concrete you will need is to calculate the area in square feet that the structure will cover. Measure the dimensions of the area and determine how many square feet (square meters) there are. Second, multiply the area times the desired thickness of the concrete in feet (meters). This gives you cu. ft. (cu. m).

to convert cubic feet to cubic yards:
divide by 27
(27 is the number of cu. ft. in a cu. yd.)

The volume conversion is not needed in the SI (metric) system of units. It is easier to calculate if dimensions are already in meters.

Here is an example (later add waste):

A 4 in. (10 cm) thick slab 25 ft. by 15 ft. (7.5 m by 4.5 m) would require 4.6 yd³ (3.4 m³). For a quick reference, use the chart in Fig. 15-8. As an example of using the chart, suppose the area is 13.2 ft. by 13.2 ft. (4.03 m by 4.03 m), and the desired depth is 4 in. (10.1 cm). The area is 175 sq. ft. (16.25 m²). Read across from 175 to the 4 in. diagonal line. Then move down from the crossing point to the quantity. The quantity is 57.5 ft.³. This quantity is also 2.1 cu. yd. or 1.62 m³.

MASONRY MORTARS

For the small repair job or for use by an amateur bricklayer, the dry mix mortar available at the local supplier is probably most common. The choice of mortar depends upon the size of the job.

Mortars are mixed in small batches using a garden hoe and mortar box or a clean metal wheelbarrow.

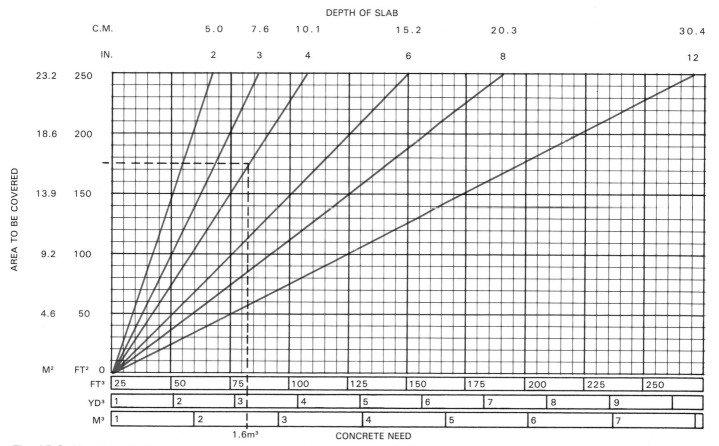

Fig. 15-8. Use this chart to calculate the amount of concrete needed. Read across from the slab area side on the left. Stop at the diagonal line for the thickness of the concrete. Then project the crossing point down to the quantity scale to get the volume in units of ft³, yd³, or m³ required.

Add enough water to the dry mix to make a smooth mortar. Mortar that is of correct consistency will slide readily from the trowel. It will be stiff enough to not sag but will keep its shape when piled. Mix only the amount of mortar which can be used in about one hour.

It is less expensive for larger jobs to mix your own ingredients. The key to good masonry mortars is the use of masonry cement. This cement has lime added in proper amounts to keep the mortar pliable and workable. The following mix is recommended for general home repair work:

Retaining wall and general home repair.

1 part masonry cement

3 parts sand

Mortar is colored by adding up to 10 percent by weight a powder or paste colorant to the cement. Ask the masonry supplier about colorants. Colored mortars may be used to emphasize or conceal a mortar joint.

Several masonry tools are needed for the bricklaying job. Besides the garden hoe and wheelbarrow, these tools include a pointed trowel, hammer, wide chisel, spirit level, jointing tool, a mason line, and a tape measure.

LAYING BRICK

Handling the pointed trowel is the key to laying bricks correctly and quickly. A strong even bond requires that the mortar be properly placed before bricks are laid. Only careful attention to trowel techniques will make this possible. The following are some suggestions:

1. To pick up mortar, slice off a section of mortar from a spot board and draw free from remaining mortar. Form into a roll.
2. Lift mortar by sweeping motion to place onto trowel evenly.
3. Hold above course of brick, pull trowel back, and roll mortar off in one smooth motion.
4. Use point of trowel to make a furrow. Level the mortar edges to form a bed about 1/2 in. (12 mm) thick.
5. "Butter" brick: hold brick in hand and with brick form a wedge-shaped mortar bed, Fig. 15-9. When the buttered end is placed against preceeding brick, butter forms vertical joint.
6. Level brick, Fig. 15-10.
7. Strike excess mortar from joint, Fig. 15-11.
8. Like concrete finishing, the mortar joint needs curing time before the joint can be finished. At the proper time, use the jointing trowel to seal the edges smooth and shape the joint. See Fig. 15-12.

Using the Line

To lay a course of bricks level, plumb, and aligned, use a line. After the first course is completed,

Fig. 15-10. Set brick unit into mortar bed by tapping gently with heel of trowel. Then check accuracy using a spirit level.

Fig. 15-9. Butter brick while holding in hand. Brick is too small to cover when in place.

Fig. 15-11. Strike off excess mortar with edge of trowel. Check plumb of outside face of brick.

Fig. 15-12. Finish mortar joint with jointing tool when mortar begins to set. About a week later, scrub surface of brick with a solution of muriatic acid to remove spots of mortar on brick.

less and hammer. Proceed as shown in Fig. 15-14. Regrout with general purpose mortar mix.

To repair the firebox area, it is important to note that the brick and the mortar of this area is entirely different from the brickwork of other masonry areas. Firebrick and fireclay mortar are designed to resist the high temperatures of the open fire. Before attempting the repair job, contact the local supplier for these materials. Common face brick and cement mortars will not withstand high heat.

Cleaning New Masonry

New masonry work often needs cleaning to remove mortar from brick surface. This is accomplished by brushing with a stiff wire brush. If mortar stains persist, apply a commercial masonry cleaning compound or a dilute solution of muriatic acid. Mix 1 part acid with 9 parts water. (Caution: when mixing this solution, always add acid to water. Never add water to acid. Wear rubber gloves and protective clothing.) Use a long-handled stiff

build up columns of several courses (leads) at the corners. See Fig. 15-13. Fasten a taut line by blocks, pins, or nails to the leads and align all brick of that course to the line.

Place each brick without touching the line with the brick. This is done by cupping the hand downward with the fingers extended over the line. Brick is held with all of the fingers. After each course, move the line up for next course.

FIREPLACE MAINTENANCE

Crumbling mortar and loose bricks in a fireplace, chimney, or flue are fire hazards and should be repaired as soon as possible. Remove loose mortar with the aid of a small chisel 3/8 in. (9.5 mm) or

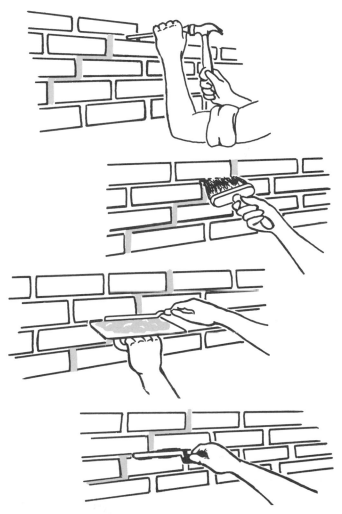

Fig. 15-14. Clean out loose or cracked mortar with a cold chisel. Clean by brushing with stiff brush and water. While joint is still damp, fill with mortar grout. Press firmly to be sure no holes remain. Scrape off excess mortar and finish joint.

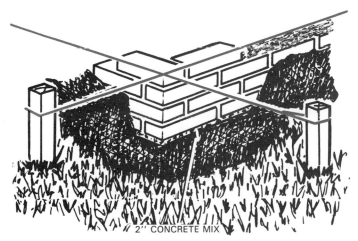

Fig. 15-13. Use taut line to keep the brick straight. To use line, cup your hand over the brick and the line without touching the line.

bristle brush. Apply the solution to damp brick and scrub. Follow by flushing the masonry thoroughly with fresh water.

Until just recently, it was believed that dirt, grime, and other pollutants on outside masonry walls gradually corroded the brick surface. New research now suggests that it may build a protective barrier. Cleaning may be harmful.

If cleaning of brick siding is desired, several methods are possible:

1. Flushing of the wall with water. The ordinary garden hose works well for easily dissolved materials.
2. High pressure water spray or water jet.

Fig. 15-15. Remove soot stains with stiff bristle brush and detergent.

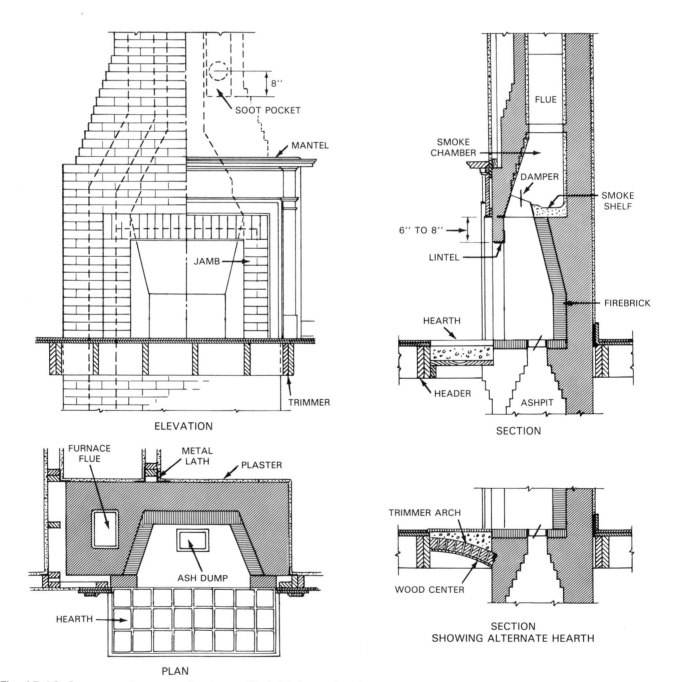

Fig. 15-16. Structure of masonry fireplaces. Firebrick is required in all heated areas. Note other type of support for hearth on lower right.

Pressure is between 600 and 1000 pounds per square inch (4150 and 6900 kilopascals). The rental service companies supply machines which blast off the dirt. Some machines have reservoirs to hold and meter detergents and other chemicals. There are also machines that generate steam for cleaning purposes. If the job demands this extreme measure, always choose the machine that produces the lowest pressure and weakest chemical for the job.

3. The acid solution if pressure system fails.
4. As a last resort, try sandblasting. This system however seriously damages the surface by wearing the face of the brick or stone. Silicone spray films or other waterproofing compounds are needed following the sandblasting.

Efflorescence is a fairly common problem that affects masonry. It especially affects new masonry. Efflorescence is caused by mineral salts bleeding from the masonry material. The salts appear if there has been excessive moisture. Deposits remain on brick and joint surfaces. New masonry is affected by the moisture of the mixture. Old masonry is affected by moisture from outside.

Before the problem can be eliminated in old masonry, the leak must be found and stopped. For old and new masonry, remove the efflorescence from brick with a wire brush. Apply one or two coats of neutralizer purchased at the local supply store.

Smoke stains above and around fireplace openings are often difficult to remove. Scrub with stiff brush and a household detergent, Fig. 15-15. If stain persists, the dilute acid solution may be needed. Always protect yourself and the surrounding area when using the acid solution.

FIREPLACE STRUCTURE AND REMODELING

Before repairing or remodeling a fireplace area, you must know how some typical fireplaces are constructed. Fig. 15-16 provides elevation and section views of different types of fireplaces. Repair any cracks, holes, or weak mortar as described earlier in this chapter. Remember that special fire resistant brick and fireclay mortar must be used.

Not all fireplaces and chimneys are built with masonry. See Fig. 15-17. Modern chimneys consist of triple-walled metal pipes.

Triple-wall pipes may become corroded. The pipes cannot be repaired, but must be replaced.

A more common problem is leakage at the roof or at the raincap. Replacement raincaps are available.

For a roof area leak, check the metal flashing for holes, rust, or bare nail heads. If problem is minor, recoat with roofing cement. Lift shingles if needed to apply new cement.

Refer again to Fig. 15-17. A prefabricated fireplace requires little maintenance. Problems are limited to damper function and door supports. Only routine maintenance is needed.

Most homeowners are able to do some remodeling on a fireplace. The front surface of an existing fireplace can be changed. For example, stones which are nearly flat can be gathered and then

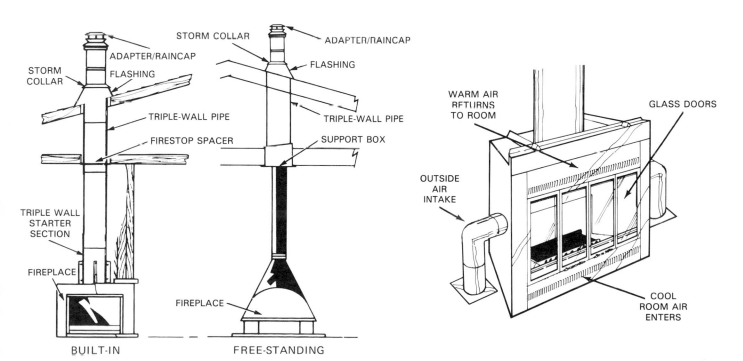

Fig. 15-17. Left. Structure of modern chimneys using no masonry. Right. Structure of prefabricated fireplace. It has metal parts and some firebrick parts. Outside air intake provides air for burning. (Preway Inc.)

A

B

C

Fig. 15-18. Installing fieldstone facing on a fireplace. A — Firebrick and special mortar is required. Note steel lintel (arrow). B — Hold stones in place with copper wires and nails driven into wall. Remove wires later. Wooden form (arrow) and second lintel are used. C — Typical appearance of facing when finished. To get proper finish, clean with mild muriatic acid and coat with silica solution.

mounted on the face. The procedure is shown in Fig. 15-18. The stones must be held tight until the mortar sets. Use wires to hold them. Copper wire is recommended to avoid stains and contaminated mortar. Many wires should be fastened to the wall with galvanized nails.

Place stones and tie them in. Apply mortar and finish to desired joint depth and shape. After the joints have partially set, rake out some of the mortar. Remove the exposed parts of the wires. Fill the holes with mortar and refinish the joints.

After a week, clean the face stones with a mild solution of muriatic (hydrochloric) acid. If you want a slightly yellow aged look, coat the stones with a solution of "water glass" (dissolved silicate compounds). The material may be obtained at a local hardware store.

If glass doors are to be installed, plan how to match the edges. You may need to fit the doors before finishing the stonework. The timing depends on the type of door mount used. Consult the glass door manufacturer.

TEST YOUR KNOWLEDGE — CHAPTER 15

1. Name the three dry materials in concrete.
2. A concrete slab must not be thinner than _____ times the aggregate size.
3. Wait until the water sheen leaves the surface before _____ the concrete.
4. Arrange in the correct sequence the following steps for working on wet concrete:
   a. Screed.
   b. Poke trowel in edge.
   c. Float.
   d. Finish surface.
   e. Finish edge.
   f. Wait.
   g. Joint.
5. Concrete is _____ by keeping it moist for a few days.
6. To patch a crack in masonry, you must first _____ the walls of the hole.
7. Mix most mortar as follows: 1 part masonry cement to _____ parts sand.
8. To convert cubic feet to cubic yards, divide by _____ (9, 3, 27, 12).
9. To pick up mortar on a trowel, you need to form it into a _____ .
10. To set brick following a mason's line, hold the brick with thumb and _____ (one, two, three, four) other fingers while sensing the line position.
11. Use _____ mortar for any firebox repair.
12. When is cleaning of brick harmful to it?
13. After sandblasting brick, _____ it with silicone spray or other films which seal porous surfaces.

14. If a triple-walled metal chimney pipe is corroded:
    a. Solder it.
    b. Mount a sheet metal patch on it.
    c. Route the smoke through another shell section.
    d. Replace it.
15. To fasten odd-shaped stones to a wall with mortar, first hold them in place with _____.

KNOW THESE TERMS

Concrete, aggregate, sand, float, screed, forms, troweling, edging, mortar, brick, damper.

SUGGESTED ACTIVITIES

Estimate the concrete needed for a patio, sidewalk, yard wall, or an interior remodeling job. Choose a project from home, work, or your school. Use the chart in this chapter or calculate the volume yourself. Get price quotes for this amount of concrete. Identify any special technique you need to learn or develop. Compare your results with others in your class.

Compare the instructions given on the packages for fireclay mortar and for cement mortar. Also compare the list of raw materials used in these types if possible. Your instructor may suggest building a small class project or separate items with 5 to 10 bricks maximum. This is best if left in place where you build it. Break the structure apart later for inspection or for re-use.

CAREERS

Concrete technician, concrete inspector, concrete finisher, mason, form carpenter.

The final block or brick in any course must be buttered on both ends. Set block by tapping with the handle of the trowel.

16

LANDSCAPE MAINTENANCE

This chapter introduces landscaping tools, equipment and supplies, and landscaping methods. It discusses tool sharpening, lawnmower maintenance, making landscape plans, and proper tree spacing. The chapter gives advice in choosing shrubs and provides hints for doing common landscape work.

After studying this chapter, you will be able to:
- List some items needed to sharpen tools.
- Describe steps for sharpening a lawnmower blade.
- Recall when and how to change lawnmower engine oil.
- Tell how to store gasoline powered equipment over winter.
- Give a method for sharpening a pair of shears.
- Describe rust removal methods.
- State spacing rules for wide and narrow trees.
- List quick ways to plant grass seed or fix a garden hose.

Every home maintenance shop usually has a variety of lawn care tools and equipment. Lawn tools need occasional cleaning and sharpening to stay in good operating condition. Trimming shears, lawn mower blades, garden hoses, and shovels need maintenance to give the service that is expected. The homeowners who do not generally get involved with many of the home repair jobs usually take great pride in the lawn and landscape care of the home. They keep to a regular schedule of weeding and fertilizing. Also, those who do well in landscaping have paid a great deal of attention to the proper maintenance and storage of their equipment.

SHARPENING LAWN TOOLS

The following tools and supplies are needed to sharpen most cutting edge tools used in landscape care and improvement.

1. Combination oilstone 1 x 2 x 8 in. (25 x 50 x 200mm). (Coarse one side and fine the other side).
2. Oil dispensing can with light machine oil.
3. Electric grinder, one coarse aluminum oxide wheel and one medium or fine wheel.
4. Container of water for cooling while grinding.
5. One mill file 10 or 12 in. (25 or 30 cm).

Sharpening the Lawn Mower Blade

Remove the blade from the lawn mower. See Fig. 16-1. Note: for safety, remove the spark plug wire or with an electric mower, be certain the power cord is disconnected to prevent accidental starting of mower, Fig. 16-2.

Clean the grass and debris from the mower blade by scraping with a putty knife. Sharpen, using a mill file or a grinder, Fig. 16-3. Adjust tool rest on power grinder to get the proper angle on the blade. Maintain the existing angle. Do not start grinding operation until the eye protection shield is in correct position. Goggles are recommended.

Begin grinding with the coarse wheel until the bevel edge is tapered to a fine edge. Remove all nicks. Do not round back the outer corner of the blade. Grind equal portion from each edge to keep blade in balance. Finish the grinding operation by using the medium or fine grade wheel.

Check the balance of blade by putting a screwdriver blade, Fig. 16-4, or other rod-like object, through the bolt hole of lawn mower blade. Turn to several positions. If blade tends to gravitate from stopped position, this means the downward end needs more material removed by grinding. Continue until there is no movement from the checked position.

Finish the sharpening operation by honing the finished edge. Pass the oilstone over the blade a few times to remove any grinding burr. Remount the blade on the lawn mower.

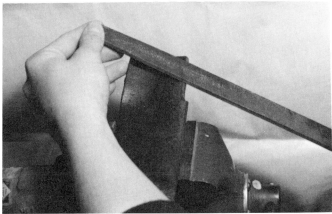

Fig. 16-1. The lawnmower blade requires periodic sharpening. A hand file keeps the blade edge sharp. Disconnect spark plug wire or 120 volt power supply cord before working on blade.

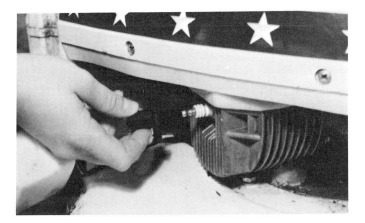

Fig. 16-2. To prevent an accidental start of the power lawn mower, remove the spark plug wire before doing any work.

Fig. 16-3. A grinder like this can be used instead of a mill file to sharpen a lawn mower blade. Adjust tool rest to desired angle. Use safety shields. (Rockwell)

Fig. 16-4. Check the balance a few times while sharpening the mower blade. Spin the blade slowly on the shank of a screwdriver. If it shows no pattern where it stops, the blade is balanced.

filing stroke which consists of pushing the file lengthwise—straight ahead or slightly diagonally—across the cutting edge. Mill files are designed to cut on the forward stroke. Observe the angle of the bevel edge. Do not alter this angle in the sharpening process. Continue the forward strokes until the cutting edge has been covered from the top to the throat of the shear. Turn the trimmer over and sharpen the second cutting edge in the same manner. Hone the beveled edge with an oilstone to remove the file burr and produce an unmarked cutting edge.

MOWER ENGINE UPKEEP

The lawn mower engine needs regular care to prevent rapid wear and frequent breakdown. Items to

Sharpening Trimming Shears

Place the trimming shears in the open position in a holding vise. See Fig. 16-5. Place the shears with the beveled cutting edge slanting upward and to the rear. Begin with a good sharp mill file. Use a straight

Fig. 16-5. Hand style trimming shears may be sharpened with a smooth cut file. File the bevel (the sides with rivet heads) from tip to throat of the shear. Sharpen until the bevel cross section forms a corner edge. Repeat on opposite side. Do not file on the inside surfaces (those which contact each other).

check include oil, the air cleaner, dirt and grass buildup, the muffler, and the spark plug. Winter storage requires special steps.

The most important job is to maintain the proper amount and quality of oil in the crankcase. The oil should be checked before each use or when fuel is added.

For a two stroke engine, oil is mixed with the fuel as specified. For a four stroke engine, the oil level is checked visually. A plug in the crankcase filler hole is common. See Fig. 16-6. For the type of filler having a plug, the oil should be to the top of the filler hole ring or notch, or to a similar mark inside the hole.

Generally, oil in a new engine should be changed after two hours of running. The next oil change can wait for 10 to 50 hours. Consult the engine manufacturer for the exact length of time between oil changes.

To drain the oil, it should be warm. Run the engine to warm it and to stir up the contaminants. Disconnect the spark plug before proceeding. Oil can be drained from a plug in the bottom of the crankcase or sometimes poured from the filler plug hole.

Refill with oil of the recommended type and weight. Do not overfill as this leads to oil foaming and fouled spark plugs. For safety, dispose of oily rags or clean them right away.

There are service steps which affect performance more than engine life. Some routine maintenance steps for good performance are as follows:

1. Clean or replace the air cleaner before you can see the dirt, or at stated intervals. Do not run engine without one, or grit may damage the cylinder wall, piston, and rings.

2. Remove dirt or grass from engine cooling fins.
3. Replace corroded muffler parts to avoid poor engine efficiency. The unit is balanced for good valve operation.
4. Inspect spark plug at least twice a season. If spark plug gap will not stay clean or keeps burning away, consult owner's manual or a service shop.

An engine must be prepared for winter storage. Drain the fuel from the tank and run the engine until it stops. This avoids varnish buildup. Remove the spark plug and squirt a few drops of oil into the cylinder. With the plug out, rotate crankshaft to spread the oil over the cylinder and piston. Next spring, before using the mower, change the crankcase oil.

RUST REMOVAL

Ironwork or sheet metal items need constant cleaning to avoid staining or holes. Some iron items are unpainted. These include shovels, other yard tools, and saws. Care of saw blades is used as an example of cleaning steps to take.

Tools that have not properly been cared for can be restored in most cases. Cleaning, sharpening, and perhaps installing new handles or painting will put them back into working condition. The first step is removal of accumulated rust and dirt. Rust can be removed with chemical rust removers and rust can be prevented with oil coatings. See Fig. 16-7. Choose a remover for thick or thin rust based on labels on the products. Other rust removers include naval jelly and penetrating oils. Heavy duty coatings include Cosmoline® and plastic coatings.

For all rust removers, follow the directions on the container. Never mix different rust removers.

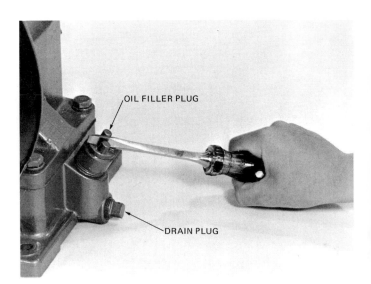

OIL FILLER PLUG

DRAIN PLUG

Fig. 16-6. Removing an oil filler plug from a mower engine crankcase. (Briggs and Stratton Corp.)

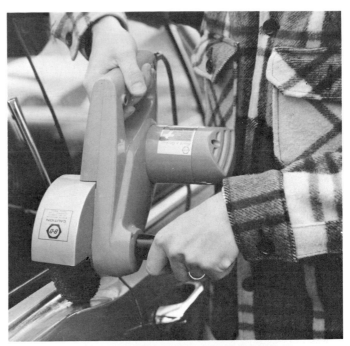

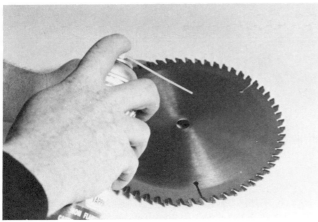

Fig. 16-7. Materials for cleaning and protecting. Top. A rust remover. The label tells how long to leave the paste on before scrubbing. Consult label when removing very thick rust. Bottom. Putting a light protective lubricant on a tool after use.

Fig. 16-8. Rust removal by power tool. Top. Abrasive pad conforms to curves and takes off paint and rust. (Black and Decker). Bottom. Wire wheel wears out more slowly than a pad does. (Makita Power Tools)

These solutions are brushed or wiped on the rust surface, left for the specified length of time, then removed. The rust which is loosened comes off with the chemical. An old toothbrush helps get the chemical solution into the hard-to-reach areas.

There are other ways to remove thin rust from metal. Use steel wool or fine abrasive cloth and some light oil or turpentine. The lubricant on the abrasive helps loosen the dirt and grease, and washes off the loose material giving a clean surface.

Power tools make rust removal easy. Attachments include wire brushes or polishing pads, Fig. 16-8. An electric drill with a grinding or wire brush attachment will help loosen the tough, deep set dirt and rust. Wear safety glasses or goggles when using revolving power driven tools. Sometimes rust and pieces of the abrasive wheel break off and could cause injury.

STORING TOOLS

Proper tool storage is important:
1. For safety.
2. To protect cutting edges and smooth surfaces.
3. To reduce tool replacement.

Tools should be cleaned and put away properly after use. Clean any residual dirt and debris thoroughly. Garden tools will rust even after dirt has dried. Wipe with a clean cloth saturated with a light oil or spray a light coating of oil from a pressurized aerosol can. Refer again to Fig. 16-7. Hang tools on a board, a rack, or some designated space where they will remain dry, ready for the next use.

LANDSCAPE PLANNING

Landscape planning means:
1. The locating of the house and other structures in relation to the lot boundaries.
2. The location of present plantings and proposed future plantings.

Landscape architects may give the homeowner suggestions about designing the yard. Many

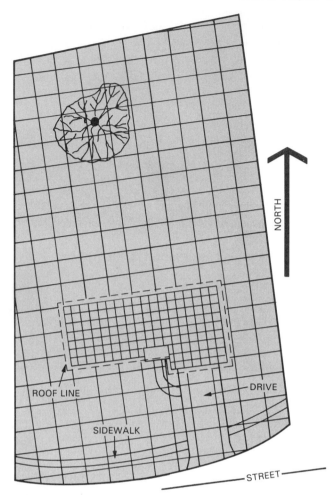

Fig. 16-9. Use a plot plan to prepare for creation of the land-scaping plan.

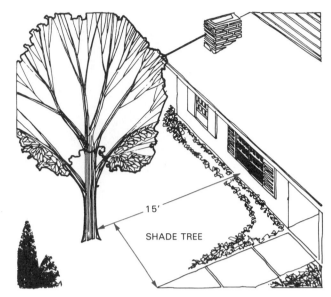

Fig. 16-10. Always know the mature size of any tree to be planted near the house.

nurseries offer free landscaping services, sample plan drawings, and advice to their customers. This help enables most persons to plan the landscape that will surround the house.

The home mechanic, with some background information, can create a landscape plan from start to finish. After understanding a few basic concepts, you can prepare a landscape plan as useful as one provided by an architect.

To start the landscape plan, make a scale drawing of the lot boundaries. From information given in the surveyor's description, draw in the structural features such as the house, the driveway, sidewalk, and fence. Prepare a grid system of lines representing intervals of every 10 ft. (3 m), see Fig. 16-9. Position all existing trees, shrubs, and bushes currently found on the lot. Draw to size those which you intend to keep as a part of the future landscape system. Mark other ones for removal. Correct location will be easily completed with the grid pattern.

Know the amount of space taken by each future planting when it is mature. Consider this first to avoid disappointment when the plants are full grown. Carefully measure the distance from planting site to the house and to other plants, Fig. 16-10.

Consider all roof overhangs.

A tree that will have a height of 20 ft. (6 m) or more should be planted at least 15 ft. (4.5 m) from any structure. This spacing is needed to keep the roots away from the foundation of the house. Avoid root damage to pavement by planting large trees at least 10 ft. (3 m) from sidewalks or drives.

Large trees with spreading branches such as locusts need a distance of 65 ft. (20 m) between their trunks, Fig. 16-11. Note that the distance is more than double that needed near a building. When trees are set closer, branches intertwine, shut out light to grass and lower shrubs underneath, and spoil the shape of the trees. Also be careful that a tall tree will not shade a low tree.

Often, you need to match a wide tree with a narrow one, Fig. 16-12. Trees with a pyramidal or oval shape grow well within 45 ft. (14 m) of a large tree.

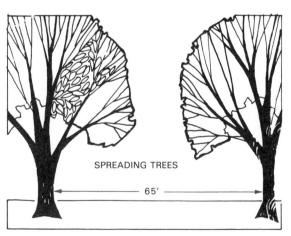

Fig. 16-11. Spacing for large spreading shade trees.

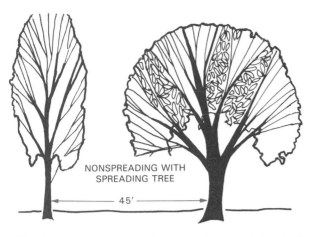

Fig. 16-12. Space trees at least 45 ft. apart if planting spreading shade trees with nonspreading ones.

Nonspreading trees under 35 ft. (10 m) in height need about 35 ft. (10 m) spacing for ample room to show their form, Fig. 16-13.

Plot the Shading Effect

Before any shade tree is located, determine the overall character of your property. Then decide which type of trees will look best. On the landscape grid, sketch the shade pattern produced by the summer sun at varying times of the day with a particular tree placement, Fig. 16-14.

One way to determine the direction of a shadow and also its length on the ground is to use a pole. You must wait until summer to do the test.

Another way is to calculate the maximum summer sun height (angle) on paper and then make some estimates from this. First know the latitude angle of your state. For example, the tip of Florida is at 25° north, and Canada begins at about 49° north. To find the maximum sun angle, subtract the latitude from the number 113.45. (Therefore, the

sun will be 88.45° high at the tip of Florida.)

Now perform a viewing test outside:
1. Image how high the sum will be.
2. Place yourself at or near the desired shade position (whether at ground level or window levels).
3. Estimate if the predicted tree height will shade your view of the sun.
4. Draw the shaded point in the landscape grid.
5. You may adjust for areas at other times of day.

Graph the shade tree plantings in this way to plan maximum shade when you want or need it, or avoid it if you desire. For the most afternoon shade, plant a shade tree 10 ft. (3 m) south and 20 ft. (6 m) west of the corner of the house.

Landscaping With Small Plants

Dwarf-type fruit trees are very popular on small lots. These trees need only about 10 ft. (3 m) between plantings, Fig. 16-15.

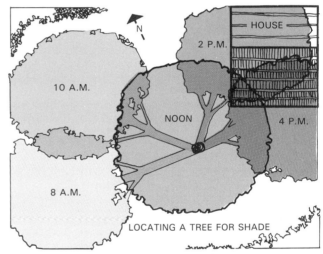

Fig. 16-14. To locate a tree for shade, note the shadow path from movement of the sun.

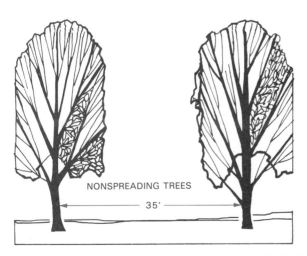

Fig. 16-13. Nonspreading trees can be as close as 35 ft. Note that since they can be close to a house, their form should match the house style better than for wider trees.

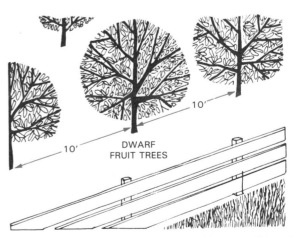

Fig. 16-15. Dwarf fruit trees can be used in a small lot. Only 10 ft. on each side is needed for proper growth.

Trees such as small ornamentals like the redbud or flowering crab can be placed within 8 ft. (2.5 m) of a structure. See Fig. 16-16. Keep the house-side branches trimmed. Roots from these species do not present a problem to foundations or drains. Note: do not prune a flowering tree in warm weather. They are best pruned in the dead of winter.

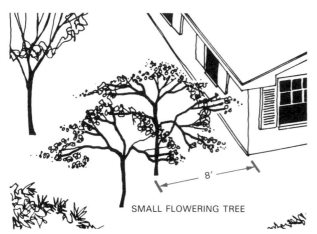

Fig. 16-16. Flowering trees provide a view nearly at window level.

For the plantings close to foundations, select some of the evergreens, spreading junipers, or yews, Fig. 16-17. Allow at least 3 ft. (1 m) between the house and the trunks of these foundation plantings for good air circulation and penetration of light.

The arbor vitae is an evergreen reaching 20 ft. high. In winter, evergreens reduce wind speed, add color, and provide shelter for birds.

Don't make the most common mistake of many new homeowners who overplant trees and shrubs, just because they are small, to take away a barren look. Crowding plants only will mean having to cut them out later. Not only money but also time will be wasted. Give very careful thought to the location and spacing before you do any landscape planting on your lot. Consider locations of gutters, swimming pools, and roofs with a low slope. Leaves can be messy or can cause roof damage.

LANDSCAPING HINTS

There are too many different types of work involved with landscaping and outdoor equipment to cover them in an organized way. Instead, a collection of useful hints and tips is given. Figs. 16-18 through 16-21 show tips for:
1. Choosing a fence design.
2. Planting grass seed.
3. Transplanting a tree.
4. Repairing a garden hose.

Fig. 16-18. A fence with slats (boards) on alternating sides lets a breeze pass through while blocking most lines of sight.

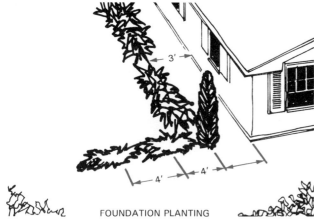

Fig. 16-17. Foundation plantings normally are evergreen for a year-round border or patch.

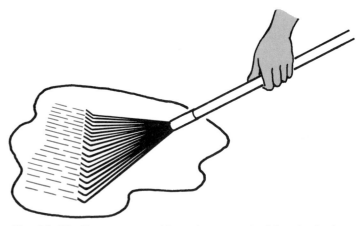

Fig. 16-19. Set grass seed into the ground with a leaf rake turned upside down. Add straw to keep seeds moist and hidden from birds.

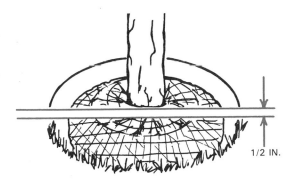

Fig. 16-20. Transplanting or making new planting. To avoid killing the tree, leave the top of the root ball exposed 1/2 in. Provide a light 8 to 10 in. diameter ring of fertilizer about 2 in. under the surface.

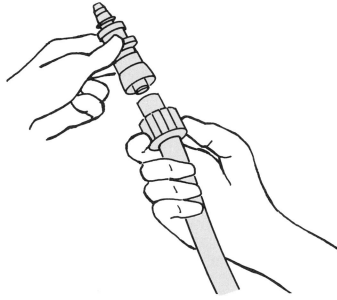

Fig. 16-21. Use of mending kit to splice a leaky section of garden hose. Another simple joint uses a 1 1/2 in. long pipe nipple and two hose clamps.

TEST YOUR KNOWLEDGE — CHAPTER 16

1. Before working on a gasoline or electric lawnmower, disconnect the spark plug wire or _____ cord.
2. To sharpen the bevel on a lawnmower blade, begin grinding with a _____ (coarse, fine) wheel.
3. The crankcase oil in a new lawnmower or snowblower engine should be _____ after several hours of running.
4. To sharpen a pair of shears, file:
   a. On the inside cutting surface with a forward stroke.
   b. On the bevel side with a forward stroke.
   c. On the bevel side with a backward stroke.
   d. On the inside cutting surface with a backward stroke.

5. Never _____ different kinds of rust removers.
6. Which of these least affects a tool in storage?
   a. Oil coatings bleeding into wood handles.
   b. Wet dirt or compounds.
   c. Rattling against other tools in a collection.
   d. Dry dirt.
7. A landscape plan, or any job plan, begins with a reduced _____ drawing.
8. Space a 20 ft. (6 m) tree at least _____ ft. (m) from any structure.
9. It is common to plant a shade tree south and _____ of a house corner.
10. The spacing for two trees is at least _____ (equal to, 2, 3 times) that between a tree and building.
11. To reduce winter wind, a(n) _____ (deciduous, evergreen) plant is recommended.
12. Push _____ into the soil with a leaf rake turned upside down.
13. Staggered _____ boards provide both privacy and air circulation.
14. When planting a tree, leave the top of the root ball or clump exposed about _____ in.
15. Flowering trees are best pruned in _____ (fall, spring, mid-winter).

KNOW THESE TERMS

Mill file, sharpening, homeowner, rust, transplanting, landscape plan.

SUGGESTED ACTIVITIES

Bring out a copy of the owner's manual for a lawnmower. Look up the maintenance schedule for oil changes, and for the air cleaner and other systems. Recall when service was last done. If you are a student, bring the booklet to class. Compare and discuss some service requirements in class.

Prepare several scale drawings. Include a landscape plan of the entire yard, a detail of a small section, and a shade direction plan. Draw grids and objects and add notes as required by your instructor. Arrange trees with proper spacing for each type.

Find out about types of grass seed at the library or at a garden center. Make a chart showing the names, the grass color, planting method, planting season, watering required, and most common growing area of the country. Decide which type you would use for your climate. Consider cost and the expected traffic or shade in a given area. Discuss in class which would be good or poor choices.

CAREERS

Landscape architect, landscaper, horticulturists.

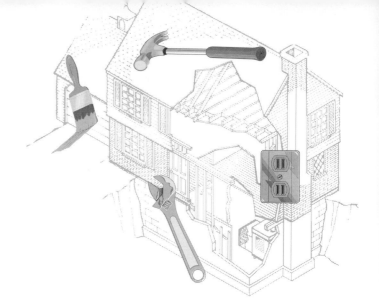

PAINTS AND DECORATING

This chapter introduces the tools and equipment used for painting. The equipment includes rollers, brushes, pads, spray cans, and spray guns. The chapter tells how to prepare a surface for painting and how to apply paint evenly. Paint problems and their solutions are discussed.

After studying this chapter, you will be able to:
■ Give the purpose of flagging on a brush.
■ Choose a brush for latex paint or for oil paint.
■ Choose rollers by thickness and type of covering material.
■ List the order for painting parts of a house.
■ Tell how to thin paint or remix it.
■ Describe the patterns used for spray painting.
■ Plan both trim work and work on large surfaces.
■ Describe how hot, cold, or foggy weather cause paint problems.
■ Prepare or prime metal for painting.

If the home mechanic has never painted a house before, the project may seem very complex. There is little need for concern. By following some basic guidelines, one step at a time, the job can be completed with few visible marks, with little trouble, and with a sense of accomplishment.

Should there be special problems with the particular job at hand, consult a local paint supply dealer. They are usually very helpful. Their experiences provide background for good advice. It is likely they have seen a similar problem before.

HISTORY OF PAINT

Paints date back to the cave period. They have been used through the years to decorate surfaces and protect them from the weather. Paint is also used to improve lighting and heating effects for better working conditions. It promotes safety and adds to cleanliness and sanitation.

Water-thinned paints, made from casein and egg whites or glue, were used by the Egyptians as early as 3000 to 2000 B.C. Very little progress was made in paint for centuries. In the early colonial days in America, lime and water made a whitewash mixture that was used as paint. In the early part of the twentieth century, animal glue and whiting (chalk from the White Cliffs of Dover, England) were mixed to make a binder for pigment. This calcimine paint was not highly washable or durable.

Casein paint was developed about the same time as calcimine paint. It was composed of casein, whiting, preservatives, and a hiding pigment (coloring substance). This type of paint was widely used at the 1933-1934 Chicago World's Fair.

Vegetable oils made possible the oil-resin and latex emulsion paints. "Latex" once referred only to a substance extracted from the rubber plant, but it now refers to a variety of synthetic resins.

Oil Base Paints

Oil base paints are extremely popular. They consist mainly of either white or colored pigments and certain vehicles, or liquids. These paints are used for both exterior and interior work. A good house paint should contain at least 65% pigment, the remaining 35% or less being composed of the flax seed.

Drying oil is an oily liquid which, applied as a thin film dries or hardens within 48 hours when exposed to normal weather. This oil should compose 80 to 90 percent of the vehicle, with thinners (turpentine and mixed spirits) and driers making up the remainder. Castor, tung, fish, perilla (Asiatic mints), poppy, hemp seed, and soya oils are other drying oils which give different strengths or stability to a particular paint.

Carbonate or sulfate of lead (white lead) was once recommended as a hiding pigment, with vegetable, animal, or mineral color pigments added. White lead is considered hazardous today.

Extender pigments do little in covering a surface, but they are necessary to prevent the other pigments from settling into a hard mass.

Some other pigments used are zinc oxide, titanium dioxide, titanium magnesium, titanium barium, and titanium oxide.

Various formulas are derived for different paints. Materials are added to prevent such common paint failures as chalking, checking, cracking, scaling, mildew, blistering, and discoloration.

PAINT DEVELOPMENT

Materials for paints from animal, vegetable, and mineral products have been obtained from every part of the world. Linseed oil from the flax fields, varnish gums from buried prehistoric forests, and tung oil from China and later from the southern United States are some of the ingredients used to manufacture paint.

Manganese, cobalt, zinc, chalk, and iron oxides contribute mineral pigments for paints. Oil and gas fields produce some mineral spirits, carbon and lamp blacks, and benzene (naphtha).

Beeswax, shellac gum, and some lime from oyster shells are used in paints.

Agricultural implements, mechanical and electrical products, modern buildings, steel structures, and thousands of other products owe their usefulness to paint. Paint provides permanence, stability, safety, and beauty. Uses can involve items in modern science, engineering, and products for living.

PREPARING THE SURFACE

To prepare for painting, remove all loose paint with a scraper or wire brush down to the bare wood, Fig. 17-1. Sand the rough surface smooth with abrasive paper. Countersink protruding nailheads. Spot prime the nailheads to seal against rusting. Fill nail holes, cracks, and large imperfections with appropriate filler and sand thoroughly, Fig. 17-2.

EQUIPMENT NEEDED

The equipment for painting is not difficult to get nor is it very costly. The most important items are scrapers, brushes, rollers, ladders, containers, and drop cloths, Fig. 17-3. Ventilation equipment is suggested for enclosed areas.

Brushes

Select brushes carefully. See Fig. 17-4. It is suggested that a better grade brush be chosen. The low cost brush will not give the results that most homeowners expect. A well crafted brush is firmly constructed with bristles clamped tightly in the metal ferrule. Cheaper kinds tend to shed bristles as the paint is being spread, spoiling the finish.

Quality bristles are springy and resilient for easier brushing. Lesser grade bristles will become limp and finger (bunch together in clumps) while you paint, making it difficult to apply a smooth coat. See Fig. 17-5. Better bristles are shaped to a tapered edge. This lets the painter feather the paint at the end of each stroke to lessen the chance of lapmarks.

Fig. 17-1. For proper paint adhesion, remove all loose paint down to the bare wood. (Cooks Paint)

Fig. 17-2. Sand the repaired surface lightly before applying primer paint. (Cooks Paint)

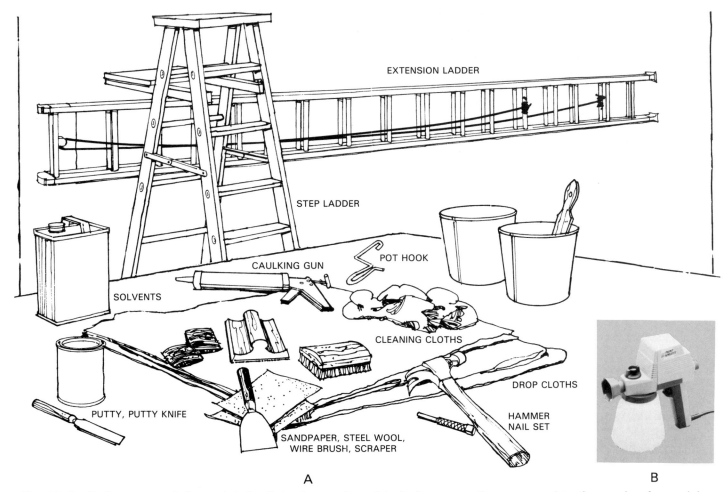

EXTENSION LADDER

STEP LADDER

POT HOOK

CAULKING GUN

SOLVENTS

CLEANING CLOTHS

PUTTY, PUTTY KNIFE

SANDPAPER, STEEL WOOL,
WIRE BRUSH, SCRAPER

DROP CLOTHS

HAMMER
NAIL SET

A

B

Fig. 17-3. Equipment needed to paint. A—Note the number of tools for preparation compared to the number for applying paint. (Benjamin Moore   B—A power spray painter.   (Power-Flo Products Corporation)

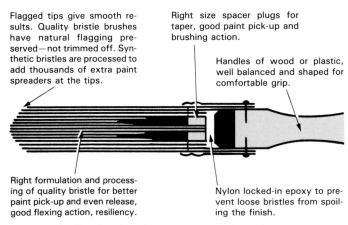

Flagged tips give smooth results. Quality bristle brushes have natural flagging preserved—not trimmed off. Synthetic bristles are processed to add thousands of extra paint spreaders at the tips.

Right size spacer plugs for taper, good paint pick-up and brushing action.

Handles of wood or plastic, well balanced and shaped for comfortable grip.

Right formulation and processing of quality bristle for better paint pick-up and even release, good flexing action, resiliency.

Nylon locked-in epoxy to prevent loose bristles from spoiling the finish.

Fig. 17-4. Quality brushes save rework and save money. (Wooster)

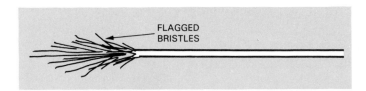

Fig. 17-5. Finger separation of brush filaments occurs in poor quality brush.

FLAGGED BRISTLES

Fig. 17-6. Enlarged view of an individual bristle showing the flagged end. (Sherwin-Williams)

Types of Brushes

Brushes are available in two types:

1. Natural bristle.
3. Synthetic filament.

Natural bristle brushes are made with animal fibers. Better quality varieties, such as hog bristles, have flagged ends which fan out in a branched pat-

tern. See Fig. 17-6. Flagged bristles carry more paint to give large coverage with fewer dips of the brush.

Synthetic brushes are made of nylon polyester, polypropylene, styrene, or vinyl filaments. Better synthetic types are artificially flagged for greater paint capacity. While synthetic brushes may be used with solvent-thinned paints, they are especially suited for latex paints.

It is important to note that water will cause natural bristles to swell and distort, ruining their performance. For this reason, do not use natural bristle brushes for water base paint products.

Size and Shape

Brushes are available in a wide variety of shapes and sizes. Many painters prefer a 3 1/2 in. (90 mm) or 4 in. (100 mm) wide brush, Fig. 17-7, for exterior wood siding. For trim areas a 2 1/2 in. (60 mm) angular brush, Fig. 17-8, makes precise edging much easier, and a round sash brush will take care of narrow window moldings. For masonry surfaces, a stiff fibered 6 in. (150 mm) brush provides the best results.

Fig. 17-7. Wide brush for interior walls or exterior coverings. (Wooster)

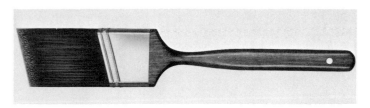

Fig. 17-8. Angular sash brush. (Wooster)

Rollers

Rollers, Fig. 17-9, also vary in quality, and the better grade varieties will serve longer and give a more consistent job. A bargain roller sleeve will not carry as much paint and the pile will mat quickly to create a blotchy appearance on the surface. During the period of use, the core to which the pile is attached may be softened by water or solvents, making the roller virtually useless. Some roller tubes can be filled with paint and/or attached to a paint supply pump.

Roller types differ in fabric composition and length of pile, sometimes called the nap. Choose a roller fabric that is compatible with the type of paint to be used. Lambswool works well with oil-based paints but will not spread easily with water-based paints. Mohair or synthetic fabrics are better for latex products. Choose a nap length for the surface being painted. For stucco, a 1/2 in. (10 mm) pile roller will work well. Rougher surfaces such as concrete blocks, textured ceilings, brick, or poured concrete will need the extra penetration of a 3/4 in. (20 mm) pile roller.

Pad Applicator

Pad applicators are one recent innovation to paint application. See Fig. 17-10. Flat, rectangular shaped pad applicators are available for easy painting on shake and shingle surfaces. They have a rug-like texture to provide fast, neat coverage by forcing paint into the surface grooves with one or two

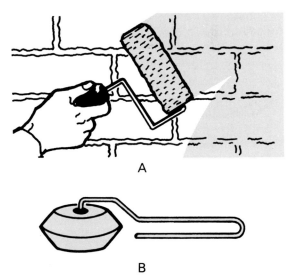

A

B

Fig. 17-9. A — A roller quickly paints flat surfaces, but will not fit into inside corners and will deposit too much paint on edges and outer corners. Trim the areas first with a brush or pad. B — Edge roller can fill in corners. (Sherwin-Williams)

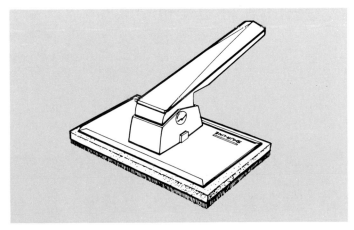

Fig. 17-10. A pad applicator holds more paint than a roller and creates less spatter. (Shur Line)

strokes. Pad applicators reduce spatter, and the painter will be able to paint right up to trim surfaces. A special pad applicator is sold with guiding devices. The unit lets the painter "cut in" trim or ceiling lines as simply as running it along the edge. When using a pad applicator, be sure to load with the correct amount of paint, not too little and not too much. A few trial strokes in an unseen area lets you learn the techniques. Your supply dealer will offer helpful advice on selecting a pad applicator and type of dispensing tray.

Spray Tools and Application

Recent improvements have made spray equipment easier to operate and versatile enough for all types of paint on most exterior surfaces. The benefits of spray equipment are speed of application and a smooth, uniform result. Due to the nature of spray equipment, it is expensive to purchase. Rental is suggested at an hourly or daily rate.

Aerosol spray containers give the home mechanic the ability to spray paint without the added expense of the equipment. While aerosol spray containers are simple and easy to use, a few general steps should be followed to assure the best possible results:

1. Thorough mixing is vital before applying any paint or coating. This is especially true of aerosol paint, Fig. 17-11. Shake the can vigorously for at least one minute after rattle of the steel agitator ball is heard. Repeat frequently during use.

2. Mask areas not to be sprayed to prevent overspray. Press spray head down to spray. Hold container vertically 12 to 16 in. (30 to 40 cm) from object to be coated and move evenly across work using a side-to-side motion. See Fig. 17-12 and 17-13 for patterns to use with any spray painter. For canned paint, lap each pass about one-third over the previous pass. Several thin coats applied in successive passes are better than one heavy coat which will tend to sag and run.

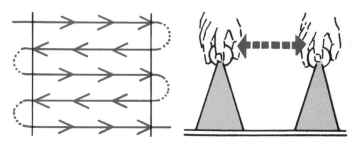

Fig. 17-12.   Spraying pattern.   (Rust-Oleum)

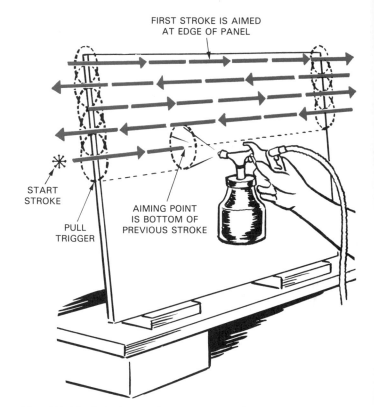

Fig. 17-13. Painting with a spray gun. Start the stroke with a dry gun, pull trigger when gun is opposite the edge of work, and release at end of stroke.

3. Immediately after spraying, turn can upside down and press the spray head for 2-3 seconds to blow out any material remaining in the nozzle, Fig. 17-14. Wipe spray head clean. If spray head is clogged, pull from can and rinse in paint thinner. Run fingernail through slit at end of stem to remove coating. Carefully replace spray head on can. To make sure you use all the coating material in the can, turn spray head nozzle so it lines up with black dot printed on rim of the container. This will assure that spray can stem inside the container is positioned to draw out all the paint.

EXTERIOR APPLICATION

It is important that paint be thoroughly stirred before, and occasionally during, application. The

Fig. 17-11.   Aerosol spray containers have one or two steel balls which mix the coating when the can is shaken. (Rust-Oleum)

Fig. 17-14. Proper cleaning of the nozzle with propellant gas only.

Fig. 17-15. Always start painting the highest points and move downward. (Wagner Spray Tech Corporation)

paint supply dealer will put the paint in a mechanical shaker before leaving the store. However, if there is much delay before using, it will need a vigorous stirring at the beginning.

Generally paint is ready to apply right from the container. No thinning is necessary. In most cases, thinning will reduce the protective ability of the paint and cause it to run or sag in vertical surfaces.

However, after painting in hot, dry, or breezy weather, the paint (particularly latex varieties) may lose some of its easy spreading qualities through rapid evaporation. To improve the paint consistency, thin sparingly with the appropriate thinner, usually stated on the label. Add a little at a time, being careful not to over thin. Stir thoroughly.

Latex paints should be thinned only with clean water. For solvent-thinned or oil base paints, add solvent only when necessary and in moderation.

Temperature of Painting

Always avoid painting when the air or surface temperatures are lower than 50 °F (10 °C). It is also best not to paint if the weather is threatening. A shower can ruin a freshly applied paint job.

Solvent-thinned paints should never be applied over damp surfaces, in foggy weather, or before dew has evaporated. This moisture will be trapped by the paint and eventually cause blistering and peeling. Latex paint may safely be applied over damp surfaces.

Weather Conditions

While scheduling the job, begin with a side of the house that will remain in the shade until that side is finished. Do this with each succeeding side until completed. Painting in the shade is important, both for your personal comfort and since direct rays of the sun and a hot surface will accelerate the normal drying rate of the paint you apply. Premature drying interferes with the leveling qualities of the paint and produces lapmarks. This is especially true with latex paints. With oil base paints, particularly deep colors, dry blisters will develop on the surface.

If a strong wind is blowing, paint will dry too fast. For best results, reschedule painting for a calmer day.

Painting Method

Begin painting at the peak or eave-line of the house, Fig. 17-15, and steadily move down and across the face in sections. Paint cornice and overhang areas at the same time, if they are to be the same color as the siding. On bevel or clapboard siding, the first surface to paint is the area where two boards overlap. Use a narrow side of the brush and force paint up under the lap, as shown in Fig. 17-16. Then turn the wider portion of the brush and

Fig. 17-16. Turn brush on its narrow side and brush the lower edge of clapboard siding. Force paint up to seal the joint. (Cooks Paint)

coat the face of the board, Fig. 17-17. Paint down four or five boards, then move the ladder horizontally to a new position a comfortable arm's length away. Continue painting across the house until the entire side of the house is completed at that level.

For a better appearance on clapboard siding, do not try to paint one section of house completely from top to bottom. By the time a new column is started the edge of the preceding column has already begun to dry and will resist any additional brushing. Blending attempts will be impossible. Lap marks form if the wet and dry paint layers overlap, and they disturb the horizontal lines of the clapboard surface.

Top-to-bottom painting is proper for shingle surfaces or vertical board and batten siding. The individual vertical breaks provide natural breaking points, so paint is conveniently in vertical sections.

Try to schedule lunch and rest breaks or end of day's work when you reach a natural breaking point or inconspicuous spot on the surface of the house.

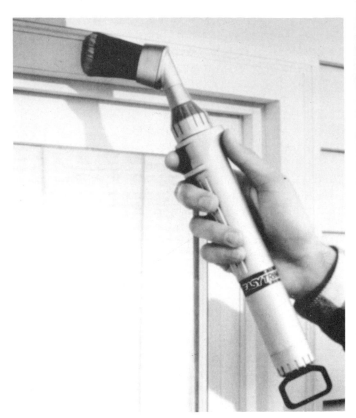

Fig. 17-18. Paint the trim areas last.
(Power-Flo Products Corporation)

Fig. 17-17. Use horizontal brush strokes when painting bevel siding. (Benjamin Moore)

can. This will rob the brush of one half of its paint. Put holes in the cupped area of the container rim to drain excess paint.

Brush Strokes

When applying with a brush, use long smooth strokes. Oil base house paint should be brushed

Trim Out

Paint trim areas last. Coat window sash and door paneling areas first. Then do the remainder of the window frames, sills, and door trim, Fig. 17-18. Do not worry about getting paint on the window glass along the putty line. This will help protect the puttied surface from water seeping through and onto the sash. Scrape off excess paint, after it has dried, with a razor blade scraper to create a neat edge.

Loading the Brush

To load your brush with paint, immerse the first 1/3 of the bristles in the paint and tap the brush lightly side-to-side against the inside of the can, Fig. 17-19. Do not drag the bristles across the lip of the

Fig. 17-19. Dip the brush about 1/3 to 1/2 the depth of the bristles. Allow drips to fall off while over the container. (Benjamin Moore)

back and forth several times to produce a well-spread, even coat. If paint tends to gather along the horizontal edge of the bevel siding, this is a sign that it is being applied too heavily or not being brushed out enough.

Latex paints do not require as much brushing. These paints dry quickly and excessive brushing will cut deep brush marks into the paint film. Latex paints should be applied generously. Give it one or two back and forth strokes and leave it alone. If applied generously, you will not need to brush it much.

After prolonged brushing, paint will accumulate in the heel of the brush where the bristles meet the ferrule. To eliminate this build-up, occasionally drag the heel of the brush over the lip of the can. Repeat as needed to clear away excess paint.

Roller Application

Roller application works well on the porous surfaces of masonry and stucco, Fig. 17-20. Begin by dipping roller in paint and rolling it back and forth over the grill in the roller tray to remove excess paint. If paint drips from the roller when it is picked up, it is overloaded. A roller is ideal for flat surfaces, but will not fit into inside corners and will deposit too much paint on edges of outer corners. Plan to trim these areas with a brush or pad applicator first to assure good paint coverage. With the roller, apply paint using long, even strokes in different directions to coat the surface. For a neat appearance, finish off with strokes in one direction. To avoid spattering yourself or a nearby surface, roll no faster than about 1 ft. in 4 seconds.

Fig. 17-20. A coarse textured surface requires a long nap roller pad. (Benjamin Moore)

Using Colored Paint

If a color other than white is being used, it is recommended that about three-fourths of the way through the container, stop painting and stir up a fresh container. Pour a portion of the new container into the paint that is presently being used, stir well, then pour them back and forth several times, Fig.

17-21. This procedure called "boxing" will minimize the chance of a noticeable color variation.

Stopping and Re-starting

While painting, periodic interruptions stop the job of painting, like lunch or rest breaks. To keep the paint in the applicators from hardening, wrap each tool separately in a plastic bag, Fig. 17-22. Protect

Fig. 17-21. Paint color is never identical from one container to another. Boxing the paint helps produce a uniform color between containers.

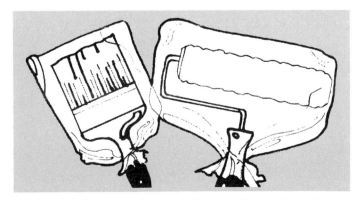

Fig. 17-22. Paint can dry out during a coffee or lunch break. To store paint equipment for less than 1 hour, seal the items in a plastic bag. Note that some paints can dissolve polyethylene bags. The storage method cannot be used.

partially used containers or trays of paint from developing a skin on top by draping a water dampened rag over the latex paint or a dry rag over solvent-thinned paint.

CLEAN-UP PROCEDURES

The sign of a good home mechanic is the method for and thoroughness of clean-up procedures. Use of drop cloths before, during, and after the painting process will greatly reduce the clean-up job.

Paint storage is also important. Store cans upside down to avoid a paint skim on top.

Clean-up for Tools Used in Oil Paint

Brushes: First, remove as much excess paint as possible from the brush with a paint paddle or putty knife. Then pour some mineral spirits or other solvent brush cleaner into a can or bucket. It is a good idea to wear rubber gloves. Dip the brush several times to dispense most of the paint.

While the bristles are still wet, brush out heavy collections of pigment with a fine wire brush. Pay special attention to paint that accumulates in the heel of the brush.

Squeeze the brush free of residue and drop it in a fresh can of mineral spirits. With your fingers, work the bristles back and forth and dip several times. Change to clean mineral spirits and dip the brush until no trace of the pigment remains. It may be necessary to do this two or three times.

Shake or spin the brush free of mineral spirits, Fig. 17-23. Comb through the bristles with your wire brush to straighten them out.

Carefully wrap the brush in a piece of newspaper or make a jacket of cardboard to protect and preserve the shape of the bristles. Store it flat or hang it up. Most brushes are sold with a bristle jacket — keep this. You can use it as a permanent storage wrapper.

Do not leave brushes in a container of mineral spirits. The open liquid is a fire hazard. The practice will also shorten the life of the brush. The bristles can become misshapen and the bottom of the brush clogged with settling paint.

For rollers, scrape out the excess paint with your paint paddle and immerse the roller in mineral spirits. Work paint out of the roller fabric by hand. Wear rubber gloves. Change to a container of fresh mineral spirits and work the fabric. Repeat if necessary until all traces of pigment is gone. Squeeze out excess solvent and wash with soap and water. Wipe the roller with a rag and store in a plastic bag. Hang the roller sleeve to prevent flat spots in the nap. Clean the roller frame in mineral spirits too. (Hardened paint may prevent it from turning.)

Cleaning Tools Used in Latex Paint

Follow the same procedure for brushes and rollers used in both oil base and latex paint. However, for latex paint, substitute warm, soapy water for mineral spirits. Be sure to rinse everything thoroughly. It may be convenient to clean brushes, roller, and pans under running water in the basement laundry tube. See Fig. 17-24. Again, hang rollers up to dry (do not lay them flat). Store brushes

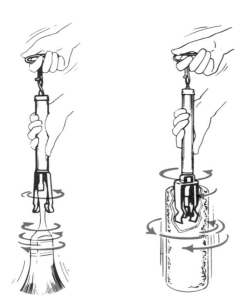

Fig. 17-23. A special device spins paint out of a brush or roller. (Shur Line)

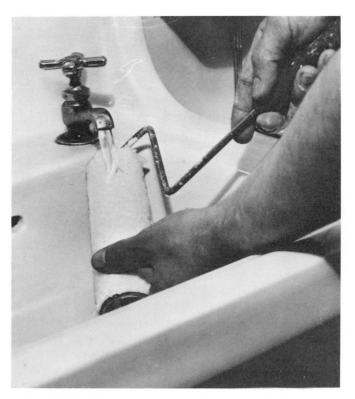

Fig. 17-24. Water base paints clean up easily in water.

in jackets so they will be in good condition when needed next time.

INTERIOR APPLICATION

With the room in order, equipment at hand, and surfaces prepared, the painter may begin. Always start with the ceiling. Then move to the walls, and finish with the wood trim and doors. Interior wall and ceiling paint are usually latex base paints.

Understand the Paint

Read the label on the paint container, Fig. 17-25. This is especially important today when there is such a wide range of improved paint products. These may call for special surface preparation and application. For best results, always follow directions exactly.

Stir thoroughly, even if it has been mechanically shaken by the store operator. Paint and enamel should be well mixed just before using. Stir rapidly, working pigment up from bottom of can.

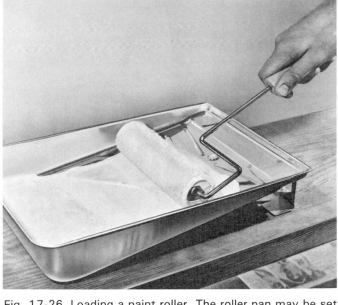

Fig. 17-26. Loading a paint roller. The roller pan may be set on a board or table, or clipped onto a stepladder. (Benjamin Moore)

Fig. 17-25. Follow the directions on the paint container. The label has information about mixing, workability, application, coverage, recoating procedures, and clean-up.

Choosing a Roller or Brush

Most people find a roller easier and faster than the brush for interior ceilings and walls. However a brush or pad is necessary for getting into corners between ceiling and walls. Load the roller as shown in Fig. 17-26.

Paint the Ceiling First

Start by painting a two or three foot strip across the shortest length of the room, Fig. 17-27. This will allow the painter to cover the next strip before the last edge is dry. Painting into a dry edge sometimes leaves a lapmark when dry. Lapping problems can be avoided if two people coordinate their efforts on large surfaces. Light strokes help to eliminate lapmarks.

Fig. 17-27. Move the roller in a long stroke without stopping. This spreads the paint evenly. (Benjamin Moore)

Using a Brush with Interior Paint for Walls

A brush is seldom used on ceilings due to dripping. A brush is better for walls.

Dip bristles only one-third their length into the paint. Tap the brush gently against the inside edge of can to avoid dripping paint. Note that this procedure is different than for oil paints as was shown in Fig. 17-19.

Starting at the ceiling line, paint down in three foot wide strips, brushing from the painted into the unpainted area, Fig. 17-28. Flat paint should be applied in wide overlapping arcs. When a few square feet have been covered, lay off lightly (feather) with parallel upward strokes.

Fig. 17-29. Masking tape placed on an edge makes cleanup easier and gives a sharp finish line. (Benjamin Moore)

Fig. 17-28. Applying latex flat enamel. Brush in long, sweeping strokes. Speed is more important to an even coating than getting the first coat thick. (Benjamin Moore)

Using a Roller for Walls

Move the roller across the wall in slow, smooth strokes, working first in one direction, then in another. Quick short strokes and heavy, uneven pressure may cause bubbles or spatters. Apply paint from top to bottom as recommended for brushing.

Teamwork is a good idea when painting walls. Two people working together will speed up and simplify any painting job. While one person "cuts in" edges by painting a narrow strip at the ceiling line, around doors and windows, and along baseboards, the other can fill in the large surface areas. Finish an entire unit, one wall, before proceeding to another.

Protecting Window Glass

Painting window sashes calls for patience and a steady hand. Fig. 17-29 shows how to make the job easier by stretching masking tape along edges of window panes before painting. When paint is dry, tape can be pulled off leaving a clean, sharp edge. Spatters on glass can be wiped off when wet, or removed with razor blade when dry.

Painting a Window

Adjust a window so the lower part of upper sash may be painted first, Fig. 17-30. Then raise the up-

Fig. 17-30. To paint a double hung window, move the upper sash below the lower sash and paint this edge first. (Benjamin Moore)

per sash almost to the top to finish painting it. The lower sash comes next. With the window open slightly at top and bottom, it can be finished easily.

Paint the window frame next (out to or beyond wall). Do the recessed part of frame first, then the frame. Finish window sill last.

Painting a Door

Paint the door frame first, covering wall area as needed. Then paint the door on the top, back, and front edge. If the door is paneled, paint panels and panel molding first, starting at the top. Keep a clean cloth handy to wipe off any paint that gets on the area around the panels. Paint the rest of the door last, starting at the top.

Paint Baseboard Last

A cardboard, plastic, or sheet metal guard held flush against the bottom edge of the baseboard will protect the floor covering and prevent picking up dirt in the brush, Fig. 17-31. Do not let paper or drop cloth touch baseboard before paint is dry.

Fig. 17-31. A paint shield helps when painting base trim. The shield is a must when carpeting extends to the board. (Benjamin Moore)

Painting with Enamels

High gloss enamels and semigloss paints are flowed on more generously and with less pressure than flat paints, Fig. 17-32. (Be generous, just as with latex paint.) Complete a small area at a time. Brush on the paint with horizontal strokes, then level off with even vertical strokes. Work quickly and never try to go back and touch up a spot that has started to set. Wait until the coating dries.

DIAGNOSING PAINT PROBLEMS

Paint does not fail without cause. To successfully prevent house paint problems, you must be able to recognize the factors that contribute to paint failure.

Moisture

Some moisture is present in most materials. Moisture may be excessive in the structure under a coat of paint. Excess moisture is a common cause of paint failure. It causes blistering and peeling. It can produce staining and mildew on painted surfaces. Unless the source of moisture is located and eliminated, more serious trouble will develop.

Fig. 17-32. Painting with gloss or semigloss enamels usually requires less pressure than for latex paints. A little more stroking is needed for a finish without ridges.

Surface Preparation

Many homeowners do not realize the need for careful surface preparation. Poor results follow a paint job where there was little or no preparation.

The home painter is encouraged to follow the detailed surface preparation information offered here. It may result in some extra initial effort, but it should save hours of labor and unnecessary expense in the future. The result will be a paint job giving long lasting protection.

Under Eave Peeling

Peeling under eaves is a condition that originates between paint layers. Top coats of paint peel away in paper thin layers from previously painted coats underneath, Fig. 17-33. It generally appears on surfaces protected from normal exposure to weather under eaves, overhangs, and porches.

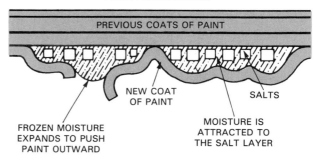

Fig. 17-33. How peeling begins. The problem can occur even in a protected area. Chemical compounds from the paint or from the air attract water. When the water freezes, it lifts the paint.

The problem can usually be traced to chemicals in the environment. The air contains chemical substances which, in the presence of moisture from fog or dew condensation, combine with pigments in paint to form chemical salt deposits. On vertical unprotected surfaces these deposits are normally washed away by rain. But, protected surfaces never get a heavy rain shower, and salt deposits accumulate here. The salts attract moisture even after new coats of paint are added to the surface. At low enough temperatures, moisture in the salt layer freezes and expands, forcing the top coat of paint outward. Then the top layer peels away from the rest of the paint.

Scaling under eaves may also be seen in protected areas where gloss paints have been applied. Lack of weathering leaves these surfaces hard and glossy. A new coat of paint will not bond properly to the slick surface. This condition is sometimes referred to as intercoat peeling.

Corrective procedures for this condition are:
1. Scrape the troubled areas.
2. Wash with a detergent solution.
3. Rinse with strong stream from a garden hose.
4. Sand glossy surfaces to assure proper bond with new coats of paint.

Blistering and Peeling

Blistering and peeling can develop with gloss house paint on a wood surface. Usually there is also excessive moisture in the wood. See Fig. 17-34. The moisture migrates to the surface as temperature changes, causing the paint to blister and eventually peel.

If there is a blistering and peeling problem, excess moisture lingering in the wood surface is the cause. There are various ways that moisture can accumulate in the surface. Water can enter from:
1. Uncaulked cracks and joints that allow moisture to seep into adjoining wood surfaces.
2. Worn out caulking that crumbles and falls out, no longer protecting the wood surfaces beneath.
3. Leaking roofs, damp basements or crawl spaces, loose siding, and other structural defects that provide a place for moisture to enter a structure.
4. Ice or trash-choked gutters that force water up under shingles which eventually migrates to the wood of nearby walls.
5. Moisture buildup inside the house, especially during the winter months, that condenses on the inside of cold exterior sidewalls.

To correct this condition, first eliminate the source of moisture buildup. Carefully inspect the outside of your home and also judge interior conditions which could be the source of humidity and dampness. If necessary, make repairs on gutters,

roofs, and siding.

Thoroughly inspect all windows and trim areas for gaps or for joints which leak.

If there is evidence of blistering and peeling near the masonry foundation, moisture is probably migrating from the ground through the masonry and into the adjoining wood. Waterproofing the foundation area will help prevent this from recurring.

Excess humidity can build up in kitchen, bath, and laundry areas. It may cause blistering and peeling on nearby exterior windows and walls. In this case, you may need to vent these areas to relieve moisture buildup.

To prepare for painting, remove all loose paint with a scraper or wire brush down to the bare wood. Sand the surface smooth. Prime-seal all bare wood with a good primer tinted toward the finish color, Fig. 17-35. Allow primer to dry one or two days before applying finish coats.

Non-moisture Blistering

The problem is a blistered surface where there is no evidence of moisture accumulation. This condition usually occurs when deep color solvent-thinned house paints and enamels are applied in the direct rays of a hot summer sun. Dark colors retain heat which causes the paint surface to dry rapidly. The solvents are trapped before they have a chance to evaporate. These solvents later vaporize and raise the outer layer in a pattern of blisters.

To correct the problem, scrape off the loose and usually brittle scale. Generally the primer is not affected, and it is not necessary to prime before painting.

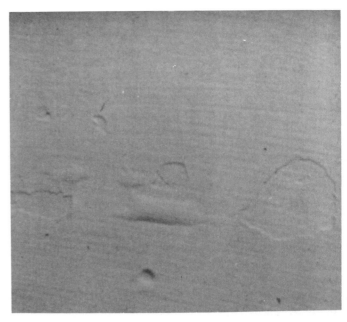

Fig. 17-34. There are two main causes of blistering. One cause is painting in very hot weather. Another is moisture forced from inside in winter. (National Decorating Products Assoc.)

Fig. 17-35. Prime all exposed wood areas with a good primer-sealer before applying finish coats. Consult label to choose oil base or latex type primers. (Cooks Paint)

Checking and Cracking

Checking, also called alligatoring, is characterized by a pattern of short narrow breaks confined to the top layer of paint. See Fig. 17-36. Cracking is a problem that appears later. In this case the split reaches the wood surface. The crack allows moisture in. The water will eventually loosen the paint from the surface in sections.

Checking or cracking usually develops as paint begins to lose its elasticity. Newly applied paint can

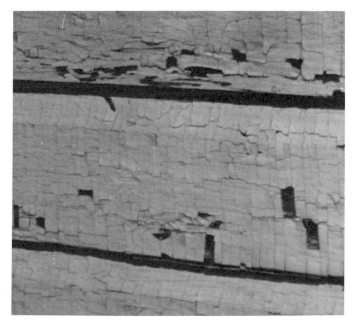

Fig. 17-36. Alligator pattern may be the result of a very glossy undercoat or due to wood expansion and contraction. (National Decorating Products Assoc.)

stretch by five percent. This enables it to expand and contract with the wood surface in response to changes in temperature and humidity.

Older homes have often received many coats of paint. The underlying paint layers become brittle with age and no longer expand and contract with the wood surface. As the wood swells, stress breaks the bond between layers to form checks. More motion widens the breaks to form cracks. Because wood expands to a greater extent between the grain lines, more force is exerted across the grain. As a result cracks are likely to form in the grain direction.

Corrective procedures for checking and cracking are as follows:
1. Remove as much loose paint as possible with a scraper and wire brush.
2. Smooth rough surface and bare wood with abrasive paper.
3. Repair voids, splits, and nail holes.
4. Prime with a good grade primer.
5. Add finish coats.

Excessive Chalking

The sign of chalking is a powdery residue on the surface. Chalking is the normal result of weathering and occurs in time with all paint. On most surfaces moderate chalking is helpful, particularly with white. When it rains, dirt and dust are washed away with the chalky residue. This keeps the painted surface relatively clean. Chalking also prepares the surface for repainting by reducing the thickness of the outer paint layers. This lessens paint buildup and the possibility of future checking and cracking. Normal chalking will usually leave traces of paint dust on the fingertips.

To test for excessive chalking, wipe a gloved hand over the surface. If paint dust covers the entire hand, it is wise to repaint. Do not paint over a heavily chalked surface without removing the chalk residue. The paint cannot bond firmly to the undersurface and will soon start to peel.

Corrective steps for chalking are:
1. Use a stiff fiber brush to remove the powder.
2. Spray with a strong stream of water from garden hose to wash away the dust.
3. When the surface is thoroughly dry, apply a good prime coat.
4. Apply a coat of finish paint.

Wrinkling

Solvent-thinned paints may develop a random pattern of bumps in the painted surface. See Fig. 17-37. This wrinkled effect usually occurs when conditions interfere with the normal drying time of the paint. To form a smooth surface, a coat of paint must dry at a regular rate all the way through.

If paint is applied too heavily and not brushed out

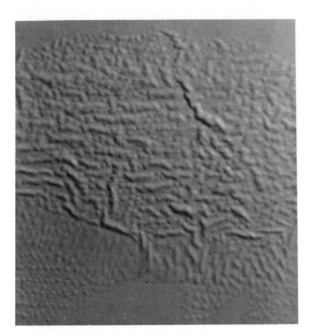

Fig. 17-37. One cause for wrinkling is that a second coat was put on before the first was dry. Other causes include painting in the hot sun or over a glossy finish. (National Decorating Products Assoc.)

thoroughly, the surface will dry while layers beneath remain wet. This allows the dry film to move about and form wrinkles. Applying a coat too thick may be an attempt to cover the surface with extra paint for more protection.

Wrinkling may also occur in colder weather when paint from cans stored in the garage or basement thickens. To avoid overly thick application in cold weather, immerse the can in a pail of warm water. Do not thin the paint.

Wrinkling also occurs when the temperature is very high. Excessive heat dries the surface at a much faster rate than normal and seals a wet layer of paint underneath.

Hints to correct and prevent wrinkling are:
1. Remove the wrinkled layers of paint by scraping or sanding.
2. For difficult to remove paint, use a paint remover to soften the paint and make scraping easier.
3. If wrinkling has occurred in isolated areas, be sure to feather-sand edges of spots where you have removed the paint. This smooths the transition into good paint surfaces.
4. Prime the areas of bare wood. Allow to dry completely. Apply one or two coats of good grade finish paint.

Mildew

Mildew is a fungus growth that can damage painted surfaces in almost any climate. Where humidity and temperature are high, mildew is likely. Homes in the southern and coastal regions are most vulnerable to mildew growth. Often thick shrubbery and trees close to the house can block out the sun. The cover allows dampness to increase. Mildew spores will thrive.

It is sometimes difficult to distinguish mildew from dirt accumulation. One way to be certain is to soak a piece of cloth with household bleach and dab it on the surface without wiping. If it is mildew, the spots will bleach out in a few minutes. If it is ordinary dirt, it will be unaffected by the bleach.

Mildew must be completely removed or the spores will continue to grow through the new paint.

Some corrective procedures for mildew are:
1. Prepare a solution of 1 cup trisodium phosphate, 1 quart 5% sodium hypochlorite (household bleach) and 3 quarts of warm water. Safety Precautions: When using any washing solution, you should protect your hands with rubber gloves and protect your eyes with work goggles. Wash hands, arms, and face thoroughly when finished.
2. Scrub the solution into the surface, Fig. 17-38, and allow it to remain there three to five minutes. Then thoroughly hose the surface with clean water.
3. When completely dry, apply a good mildew-resistant primer.
4. Finish with a mildew-resistant paint.

PAINTING GUTTERS AND DOWNSPOUTS

New gutters and downspouts are coated with a fabricating oil that must be removed prior to painting. The oil will interfere with the paint bond, and peeling can result.

Preventive action is needed on new galvanized gutters and downspouts. If you intend to paint

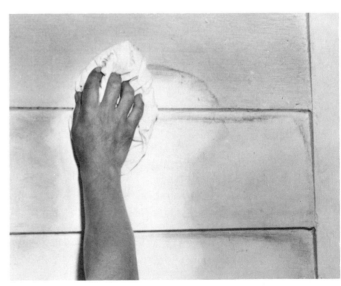

Fig. 17-38. Mildew is a growing organic substance and must be chemically destroyed before repainting. (Benjamin Moore)

galvanized surfaces immediately, it is necessary to remove all traces of surface oil. Moisten a rag with mineral spirits and wipe all surfaces to be painted. Change to fresh rags frequently to remove all oily residue. Prime with a metal priming paint and allow to dry one or two days, Fig. 17-39. Finish with one or two coats of finish paint.

Just a tip about painting galvanized surfaces: If the surface is allowed to weather naturally for six months to one year, the oil will evaporate and the air will etch the surface. This helps give a "tooth" for the paint to grip.

ESTIMATING PAINT COVERAGE

To calculate the amount of paint needed, you must determine the number of square feet of surface to be painted. Three of the following steps provide a simple formula for determining square footage:
1. Figure the largest areas to be painted.
2. Figure the accessory items to be painted.
3. Total the figures.
4. Find gallons needed.
Proceed as follows:
1. Figure the general area to be painted. Look ahead to Fig. 17-40. A simple formula for an entire house:
   A. (Length of house + width) × 2 = total distance.
   B. Total distance × height of house = total side wall area.
   C. (1/2 gable height × width of gable base) × 2 = total gable area.
   D. Total sidewall + total gable area = total surface to be painted.
Note: the home mechanic does not need to subtract window and door area from the total surface figure if each opening is less than 100 sq. ft. (9m²).

Example, See Fig. 17-40:
   A. (50' + 42') × 2 = 184 ft.
      (15.24 + 12.8m) × 2 = 56.08m
   B. 184' × 14' − 2576 sq. ft.
      56 × 4.26m = 238.56m²
   C. 1/2(14') × 42 × 2 = 588 sq. ft.
      .5(4.26) × 12.8 × 2 = 54.52m²
   D. 2576 sq. ft. + 588 sq. ft. = 3164 sq. ft.
      238.56m² + 54.52m² = 293.08m²
2. Figure special areas:
   These simple formulas will help estimate paint requirements for the following special areas. Add the figures for each area together with the total area above:
   A. Balustrades
      Measure the front area and multiply by 4
   B. Lattice Work
      Measure the front area and multiply by 2
   C. Cornices
      Measure the front area and multiply by 2
   D. Gutters and Downspouts
      Measure the front area and multiply by 2
   E. Stairs
      Count the risers and multiply by 8
   F. Porches
      Multiply the length by the width
   G. Eaves
      Measure the underside area and multiply by 2
   H. Eaves with Exposed Rafters
      Measure the area and multiply by 3
3. Total the surface figures.
4. Use the surface total to determine gallons of paint required.
To do this, divide the total area by the spreading rate. The spreading rate is the area covered by a gallon of the paint selected. Spreading rates are usually listed with the directions located on the can. Figure primer and finish coat needs separately.

MATCHING OR APPLYING METAL COATINGS

Any surface that needs paint may have special protection problems. With metal surfaces, Fig. 17-41, the problems are rust and corrosion. There

Fig. 17-39. Choose the correct metal primer for galvanized guttering. Check with the painting supply dealer before starting the job. (Benjamin Moore)

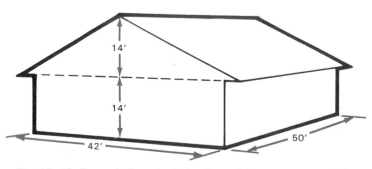

Fig. 17-40. Example for calculating the paint coverage needed.

Fig. 17-41. Metal surfaces for outdoor use may be subject to heat or mild acid rain. Before recoating, be sure to remove all loose rust. (Rust Oleum)

metal fixtures on boats, and lawn furniture.

Epoxies, discussed in the masonry section of this chapter, can also be used on metal surfaces. One clear finish designed for brass and chrome shows the beauty of the metal and inhibits corrosion as well. Such a coating works on exterior metals and indoors on door knobs, door push plates, appliances, and light switch plates. Epoxy is useful in any other place that needs protection against finger marks and corrosion.

Some paints give extra protection for metal surfaces. Aluminum paints provide moisture or thermal barriers. These paints can have colors or the normal silvery tint. They resist rust and moisture when properly primed. Aluminum paints dry fast, often within five minutes.

The even finish that results from aerosol spray painting protects metal with few weak points or streaks. For repairing nicks and scratches and doing any small job, aerosols will match a glossy or a flat finish. You can get clear, rust-preventive finishes for bumpers and chrome on cars, and heat-resistant paint for engines, barbecues, furnaces, and boilers. There are also metal-flake enamels for bicycles, fuse boxes, cabinets, and signs.

In homes that have oil heat, the tank is often drab or may develop rust easily. You can give it a bright, functional finish by applying a coat of two-part epoxy. Used by industry for coating tanks, epoxies chemically fuse to the surface and are as tough as baked-on coatings.

MASONRY COATINGS

The two kinds of masonry paint problems are alkali and surface moisture. There are several new coatings which help solve these problems.

One new latex masonry paint can be used on any surface above or below grade. This paint resists water and alkali. It also works on properly primed metals. This latex paint is a good coating for foundations, interior or exterior basement walls, concrete block retaining walls, worn tile roofs, stone, stucco, and brick. See Fig. 17-42.

Epoxy enamels have an appearance which is good enough for indoor uses. The older epoxies come in two-part kits that have to be mixed. They allow the homeowner to control how fresh the mix is. A one-part epoxy that can be tinted is new on the markets. For all epoxy products, use eye protection and respirator as stated by the manufacturer.

The wet basement is another problem for homeowners. Paint manufacturers are testing a coat of silicone applied to the exterior of concrete or block foundation walls. The coating helps solve the problem of dampness downstairs. If applied before backfilling, the silicone should resist leaks from the hydrostatic pressure against a basement wall. One

are, however, new paints and coatings that will protect metal and give it an attractive finish.

One of the biggest problems for homeowners is making paint stick to gutters and downspouts. For this job, you may need a special primer that adheres to the galvanized surface. Such paints, available in a dull gray color, have a compound of zinc dust that sticks to the galvanizing better than ordinary primers would. When the primer is dry, you can use any exterior house paint.

Shed roofs, mesh fencing, garage doors, and water pipes have similar paint-adhesion problems. Until recently, you needed to wait six months to a year before painting galvanized surfaces. (The weathering would etch the surface, making it easier for the paint to adhere.) With some new primers, you no longer wait for weathering. Exterior latex paints can sometimes be used on galvanized metal without a primer.

Steel mesh fencing and fence posts can be painted much the same way. Often a roller works much faster than a brush. After the primer is dry, you can paint with epoxy enamel or latex.

Enamel is the most popular top coat for metal. With proper priming, this paint gives metal the same tough, glossy finish it provides for wood surfaces. Use enamels for metal window frames, touch-up jobs on cars, radiators, register vents, bicycles, toys, various implements, signs, house trailers,

coating (called "Drylok") is applied to the inside surface instead of the outside.

Masonry requires careful surface preparation before painting. If you are covering an old coat of paint with new latex, make sure the surface is clean and the old paint is in good condition. With bare masonry, you may need to apply a surface conditioner or a factory-recommended primer to insure adhesion. (But some latex needs no primer.) Before applying any epoxy, you must completely remove any previous finish. The strong solvents in the epoxies can penetrate old paint and cause it to wrinkle or lift.

ROOF AND FLOOR SILICONE

The new silicone coatings and caulks are extremely versatile. Many contractors are using a coat of urethane foam topped with silicone roof coating to make a sound, tight new roof. This system can also be used to repair a gravel-asphalt or tile roof. The foam and silicone are sprayed over the present roofing. They add only 1/4 pound per square foot to the roof load. Their insulating qualities can increase the efficiency of an air conditioner.

You can buy one silicone coating especially designed for traffic areas. This product has been combined with an aggregate that produces a nonslip finish. Use around pool aprons, steps, and porches.

The one drawback to silicone is the expense. When building contractors use silicone coatings,

Fig. 17-42. A new acrylic water base coating becomes water-resistant when dry. However, the paint can be cleaned up with only soap and water soon after painting. (Rust Oleum)

they quote prices $50 to $100 more than a normal job. But the long life (silicones have a life expectancy of about 20 years) and the low maintenance of the finish often make the cost worthwhile.

ALUMINUM ROOF PAINT

Another good roof coating is aluminum paint. It forms a film that resists temperature extremes, smoke, and weathering. Aluminum paints also have good heat reflecting ability. Some of them now come in colors in addition to the conventional silvery sheen.

LIQUID FLOOR MATERIALS

For an attractive floor in a kitchen, bedroom, or basement playroom, try one of the new seamless flooring products. These products are used to form a floor about 1/4 in. thick. The material is simply applied by pouring out of the can. There are several types: acrylic, urethane, epoxy, and polyester. Each has drawbacks as well as advantages. The acrylic system is good for exterior use and retains color well, but can be easily scratched. Urethanes, on the other hand, are flexible and resist abrasion. However, they yellow if used outside unless an ultra-violet shielding ingredient is added.

With any seamless floor, you must use only one system from one manufacturer. Follow the directions exactly. Each part of a kit, which usually contains a base coat, decorating chips, and a glaze coat, is compatible with the other parts. Mixing two kits may cause adverse chemical reactions. Unlike other finishes, seamless flooring becomes a permanent part of the surface to which it is applied.

While working with solvents, paints, and other chemical materials, work in a well-ventilated space and respect the manufacturers recommendations for handling these materials.

TEST YOUR KNOWLEDGE — CHAPTER 17

1. Bristles of a high quality brush have ends which are _____ .
2. Do not use natural bristle brushes for _____ base paint.
3. The shape of a sash brush used for narrow moldings is:
   a. Angled 1/2 in. thick.
   b. Round.
   c. Angled 1/4 in. thick.
   d. Cut straight 1/4 in. thick.
   e. Wedge-shaped.
4. The recommended paint roller material for oil base paint is _____ .

5. To paint masonry, the nap length of a roller should be _____ in. (mm).
6. A pad applicator with a guiding device lets the painter "_____" trim.
7. Which is not recommended when a person is spray painting?
   a. Shake container very well.
   b. Allow a strip to dry out before you get back to it.
   c. Paint a strip and return with paint on that strip.
   d. Shake the can from time to time.
8. Latex paints should be thinned only with clean _____ .
9. _____-thinned paints should not be applied in foggy weather.
10. Try to work on the side of the house which is in _____ .
11. Begin painting at the _____ (corner, eave-line) of the house.
12. To avoid lap marks on clapboard siding, paint in sections which are long in the _____ (vertical, horizontal) direction.
13. When loading a brush with paint, avoid drips by scraping the bristles on the lip of the can. True or False?
14. Which paint should be applied generously to save brushing?
   a. Latex.
   b. Enamel.
   c. a and b.
   d. Oil base.
   e. b and d.
   f. None of the above.
15. Use a pad applicator or brush to trim the wall or ceiling areas that a _____ will not reach easily or will not provide good coverage for.
16. For long storage, put brushes in:
   a. A clean can.
   b. Mineral spirits.
   c. A paper or cardboard jacket.
   d. Plastic wrap.
17. After brushing paint onto wall area of a few square feet, finish lightly with parallel _____ strokes.
18. Non-moisture paint blisters can result from painting when the weather is too _____ (hot, cold).
19. The strong solvents in enamel and _____ paints for masonry prevent painting over existing paint.
20. A two-part epoxy for oil tanks is nearly as durable as a _____ finish.

KNOW THESE TERMS

Oil base protection, chalking, mildew, bristles, synthetic, spray, aerosol, pigment.

SUGGESTED ACTIVITIES

Describe in a short report the kinds of drying oils (Japan drier, tung oil) and their properties. For each, list some advantages, disadvantages, and some uses. Include drying times and resistance to moisture and chemicals. Then consider sources and costs. Your instructor may provide samples for testing. Compare your reports in class.

Make test patches for paint types. Begin with bare wood and metal or begin with previously painted items. Test latex paints, oil paints, enamels, epoxies, metal primers, aluminum paints, and also flooring compounds. Note if any of the paint types ruin the old paint. You will begin to learn how much brushing each type of paint requires.

CAREERS

Painter, biochemist, salesperson.

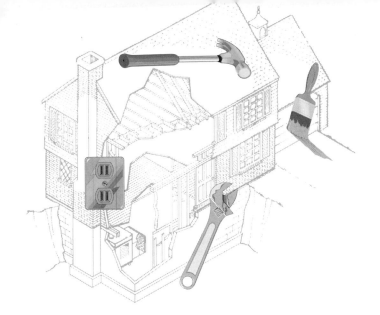

18

WOOD, METAL, AND FURNITURE FINISHES

This chapter describes some methods for removing and re-applying furniture finishes. Topics include sanding, staining, filling, sealing, and coating of wood. The chapter also discusses removing and applying colored metal coatings.

After studying this chapter, you will be able to:
- Describe types and grades of abrasive products.
- Decide whether a wood species can be easily stained or bleached.
- List some ingredients used in a bleaching process.
- Discuss steps for wood filling.
- Describe types of wood coatings.
- Be familiar with some wood and metal finishing schedules.
- Recall some steps for making antique glaze finishes.
- List components of a furniture cleaning mixture.
- List steps for fixing spots, stains, and scratches.
- List some colors possible with metal coatings.

Finishes are applied to a wood surface for protection or for decoration. Protection of the surface is needed to ward off decay or to extend the wearing life. Wood finishes for furniture and cabinets are usually clear, and they enhance the grain pattern and color of the natural wood. The home mechanic may not intend to remove or redo furniture finishes. However, the care of finishes is important to the homeowner.

CHARACTERISTICS OF A GOOD FURNITURE FINISH

Furniture should have certain features when it has been successfully refinished. First, it should have a smoother surface than before. This means it was sanded very smooth before recoating, and all pores and holes in the wood were filled. The finish will have no drips, dust specks, bubbles, or blisters.

Most furniture is more attractive with a satin finish than a high gloss. The finish should be dry and hard without any sticky spots. The color of your finish should be characteristic for the type of wood as well as a color that will blend (not necessarily match) with the other furnishings in the room.

HISTORY OF FINISHES

History of Varnish

The word "varnish" is derived from the Latin word vernix. A translucent fossilized resin which we know as amber was transported from the North Sea to Egypt.

These fossilized resins and copals (fossilized tree resins) were once used in the manufacture of varnish. Copals were dug from the earth in the upper African Congo and in India. Chemists have now, however, developed synthetic resins which are more durable than the original fossil gums.

History of Shellac

Natives of India were using shellac to protect surfaces in homes and temples before the time of Julius Caesar (100-44 B.C.). Europe did not use this substance until just before 1600, although Marco Polo had introduced it several hundred years before.

Once a year, tiny insects swarm on the lac trees in India. During this time, the female lays about 1,000 eggs at a time. The sap of the tree is secreted as a gum which covers both the bugs and the eggs. This liquid hardens and several months later is broken as the eggs hatch and the young move to other trees. The crust is harvested from the tree twigs, put through purifying processes, and made into a gum which is the basis of commercial shellac.

Shellac is used in drafting inks, lead pencils, as an electrical wire coating, as a hat stiffener, and as a base coat for other finishes. It is also used to guard against dust, dirt, and wear.

History of Lacquer

Lacquer is a quick-drying product that plays a very important role in wood finishing. It is constantly being changed and improved.

Records show that the Japanese and Chinese were using lacquer over 2,000 years ago. Plain wooden pieces were often covered with several hundred layers of lacquer until the coating was thick enough to carve. These objects often required years of labor to complete. The oriental lacquer needed moisture to cause it to harden properly.

Chinese lacquer was obtained from the sap of a tree. The tree was tapped and the sap emerged as a grayish-white liquid that darkened to black when exposed to air. It was eventually pounded, heated, and stirred to evaporate excess moisture and then stored in airtight containers.

After World War I, explosives manufacturers had a surplus of gun cotton (nitrocellulose) and other chemicals. From these surplus materials, chemists developed a synthetic lacquer which dried very rapidly. Rapid drying was a valuable characteristic, especially for use in new automobile and furniture finishes. Lacquer also became a valuable finish for shoes and leather products. It is often used in hair spray, fingernail polish, and many other product finishes.

Finishes used today are developed to be environmentally friendly. However, care must be taken when using and disposing these materials. Refer to the manufacturer's instructions and any local ordinances when disposing of any finishing materials or chemicals. This will prevent the materials from chemically creating any unwanted compounds that would be a hazard to the user and inhabitants of the home.

Fig. 18-1. Removing old finish with portable power contour sander. The wheel consists off layers of sandpaper strips combined with bristles. (Black and Decker Co.)

ABRASIVE MATERIALS

Abrasive: A substance used to grind, polish or wear away a softer material.

Sanding: The process that controls how wood fibers are cut with an abrasive. Sanding is done after all edge tool work has been completed.

Source of Abrasives

1. Natural — Mined or quarried.
2. Manufactured — Formed in electric furnaces at temperatures over 4000°F.

Kinds of Abrasives

1. Aluminum Oxide Paper — This is a purple-brown colored paper. It cuts faster, lasts longer, and is tougher than other abrasives. It is especially good for use on hard woods.
2. Garnet Paper — A tawny-red colored paper. Also a very good abrasive, it will smooth soft wood as effectively as aluminum oxide but requires more effort on hard woods. In some areas, it is more generally available than aluminum oxide.
3. Silicon Carbide — A shiny steel gray or black paper. This paper comes in fine grits for finishing work. It is used mainly for removing the "hair grain" on fibrous woods such as some mahoganies and for smoothing between coats of finish. For the latter use, it should be wet with mild soapy water. This is the hardest of the finishing papers.

Power sanding tools are available. Fig. 18-1 shows a "flap wheel" used on curved surfaces.

Grit Size

The grit of finishing paper to use depends on the condition of the wood. See Fig. 18-2. Unless the wood is very smooth before you begin sanding, it is necessary to start with a coarser (80 or 100) grit and then use finer (120 to 180) grits. Usually at least two or three different grits should be used in smoothing a piece of wood.

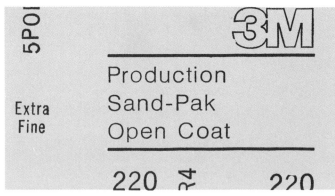

Fig. 18-2. The back side of abrasive has information about the type and grit size of abrasive paper.

Steel Wool Grade

Steel wool is used for final smoothing before the finish is applied and for smoothing between coats of finish. It should always be used for final smoothing of bare wood after an abrasive paper has been used. It is safe to use on curves, turning, and edges. It gives a satin-like smoothness and brings out the grain. Number 000 is most commonly used.

Abrasive Coatings and Backings

Backing materials are first printed with a trademark, grade size, weight of paper, and other markings, then given glue sizing. They are finally electrostatically coated with the abrasive.

Abrasive Papers

There are four kinds of abrasive papers in common use for refinishing furniture at home. One of these, sandpaper, has several disadvantages and is not generally recommended if the other papers are available. The sand grains dislodge while you are working and could easily scratch the wood. It "fills up" with sawdust quickly and must be replaced often. It is less expensive per sheet than the other papers but much more of it is needed for the same amount of surface. This makes it as expensive to use as the other paper. The following summary of letter names will help you choose an abrasive. There are two things to consider:
1. Backing
   Type "A" — Waterproof Paper
   Type "B" — Cloth Backing
2. Weights of Backings
   Type "A" — Finishing Paper (100 to 200 grit)
   Type "C" — Cabinet Paper (100 to 200 grit)
   Type "D" — Cabinet Paper (40 to 80 grit)
   (Waterproof, 120 to 600 grit, A or C paper)
   Type "E" — Belts, discs, drums for machines
   Type "J" — Light, flexible work on small machines (cloth)
   Type "X" — Large production machines (cloth)

Abrasive Coats

1. Open Coating
   Space between the grains so that only about 70 percent of the surface is covered. Prevents "loading up," especially on soft materials.
2. Closed Coating
   Grains are packed closely together, covers surface completely. Used for heavy sanding operations, especially on power machines.

BLEACHING, COLORING, FILLING, AND SEALING OF WOODS

There are too many developments in finishes and finishing to cover in one chapter. There are a number of books on the many products and procedures.

However, some of the more popular treatments of wood are presented here.

Bleaching

Dark spots, streaks, and natural wood coloring are removed by bleaching. However, it is sometimes difficult to remove the color without damaging the wood fibers. Bleaches are often composed of strong chemicals. They require protection of the skin and utmost safety in use. Bleaching should be done only when necessary to obtain a uniformly light color.

Choose light-colored wood if bleaching is necessary or desired. Darker woods are more difficult to lighten. Because of their structure and coloring, ash, birch, oak, maple, mahogany, and walnut are easier to bleach than gum, pine, and poplar.

The use of oxalic acid and sodium hypochlorite as bleaching agents is widely accepted. These are followed by borax. Borax acts as an alkalizing agent, neutralizing or counteracting the acid.

Oxalic acid can be obtained in white crystal form. Approximately 3 ounces dissolved in 1 quart of hot water forms a mild bleaching agent. Oxalic acid is very toxic. Keep children away.

The application of the oxalic acid solution is followed by application of sodium hypochlorite (ordinary household laundry bleach). It bleaches most woods several shades lighter. After the bleach has been applied and has dried, it should be neutralized. Wash it off with a borax solution of about 1 ounce of borax per quart of water. All solutions are made with hot water, but they are cooled before they are put into use.

Commercial two-solution bleaches are usually the most satisfactory. There are several brands on the market, but only two are discussed briefly here. The manufacturer's instructions should be followed exactly.

A common two-solution bleach is oxalic acid and sodium bisulfite. Each is mixed separately in a 5 to 10 percent solution of water. The acid is applied by spray or brush and allowed to dry. The sodium bisulfite is then applied. Mixture of these two chemicals creates the bleach, sulfur dioxide.

Potassium permanganate is the second two-solution bleaching process. It is applied in a 2 to 10 percent solution with one or several coats, depending on the effect desired. A brown color appears and is cleared with a 5 to 10 percent solution of sodium bisulfite. To remove the salts of this chemical reaction, the wood is partially neutralized by sponging with clear water.

Most two-solution bleaches are alkaline. They have to be neutralized with a 5 to 15 percent acetic acid (vinegar) solution and then sponged with clear water. If the caustic salts are left on any part of the project, they will injure the finish when it is applied.

Allow at least 48 hours for final drying. The grain of the wood has been raised and must be smoothed. Sand it lightly to avoid cutting through the thin layer of bleached wood. Woods can be finished by any of the accepted methods after sanding.

Blonding

Blond finish mixes are obtained by adding white lacquer to clear lacquer. A uniform light coat sprayed on wood as a sealer produces a blond color that does not hide the wood grain. This technique works very well on light woods, such as maple and birch.

Staining

A stain is used to change the color of a surface, and it often emphasizes the beauty and grain of the wood. It is the first step in the finishing operation after finishing in the white.

Stain is used to match lighter wood with the predominant color of a piece and to change the color of the entire object, Fig. 18-3. The lighter sap streaks in wood such as walnut can be stained to match the darker heartwood. Inexpensive woods can be stained to resemble walnut or other more expensive woods. Walnut, cedar, and cherry have sufficient natural color that they do not require stain.

Some furniture is stained to give the popular colonial maple color. There is no fixed tone for this maple furniture, however. The orange-brown antique color is most frequently used. A touch of orange to any medium-brown stain gives a close copy of the antique maple color.

The object is stained and sealed with a wash coat of orange shellac. A second coat of wiping stain is applied and then wiped, leaving the antique effect. Other finish coats are added to build up the finish.

Many special stains are available in numerous colors. They are divided into four groups: water, oil, spirit, and non-grain-raising (NGR).

Water stain comes in concentrated powder form. Water-soluble colors (usually aniline dyes) are dissolved in hot water. Use a glass or enamel container to mix this stain. Water stain penetrates deeply, gives greater transparency than oil, has less tendency to fade, and does not bleed into coats of finish. However, it does raise the grain, and it is hard to apply with a brush or by wiping without streaking.

Spraying is the best method of application. Raise the grain one or more times and sand. You can apply a shellac wash coat before application of the stain. These steps help eliminate the necessity for resanding.

These powders can be made into non-grain-raising stain. Use less hot water, and then bring the mixture to proper strength by adding alcohol or special solvents.

Fig. 18-3. A stain to look like mahogany. Water clean-up stains are popular for ease of use. (Deft, Inc.)

Oil stains are usually classified as:
1. Pigmented or wiping (ground or mixed in oil).
2. Penetrating (soluble in benzol, naphtha, or turpentine).

They can be purchased in ready-mixed forms, Fig. 18-4. Additional colors can be obtained by mixing some of these prepared products.

Penetrating oil stains are often used to color wood filler. A thin solution of this filler-stain mixture is sometimes rubbed into the wood to stain and fill simultaneously. For the best quality work, this dual operation is not recommended, especially because oil stain normally penetrates wood less effectively than the many other stains.

Oil stains do not raise wood grain and they are relatively easy to apply to a uniform color. Any excess stain should be removed because it bleeds. Pigmented (wiping) stains are better than the penetrating stains because they fade less.

Apply a coat of boiled linseed oil to all exposed end grain before staining. This produces a uniform color when the stain is put on.

Spirit stains are mostly aniline dyes that are soluble in alcohol. They are difficult to apply evenly, they fade quickly in sunlight, they bleed, and they cut through most finishes. However, because they penetrate easily, they are popular for use in refinishing old furniture.

Staining for Refinishing

1. Remove the old finish with a prepared remover and steel wool. A wood file, emery cloth, and steel wool are used to remove finish and clean in tight places.
2. Sand all areas with wet-dry sandpaper.
3. Mix a penetrating stain. Test for the desired color on scrap wood or on the bottom of the project.
4. Apply the stain with a brush to all parts of the object.
5. Remove all excess stain before it dries.

Shading and Highlighting

Shading is done by spraying or wiping shading materials on the finished work and wiping them off to give a highlighted or aged (antique) appearance. Wiping or shading stains, tinting colors, and shading lacquers are common materials. Dye is often added to clear lacquer or varnish for use over sealer coats to give a uniform transparent color. Spray shading is used to give a uniform overall tone to make different species of woods look the same.

When pigment instead of dye is added to varnish or lacquer, the finish becomes opaque. Opaque enamels cover the grain giving a painted effect.

Bone white is a typical shaded finish. When the white color is dry, spray on a coat of wiping stain. Wipe off before the stain reaches the tacky (sticky) stage. This leaves highlights. Highlighting is also done by one or more of the following:

1. Sanding certain spots with steel wool or abrasive paper.
2. Blending wiping stain with a brush.
3. Detail shading with a special spray gun.

Filling

After thorough sanding, and also after staining when desired, the most important operation in obtaining an excellent built-up finish on open-grain woods is the application of a good filler. Filler is not a coat of finish; it is a material that fills the pores of the wood.

Wood filler is a product made from silex, with a drier, a solvent (thinner), and a vehicle. Silex is ground quartz or silica. Silex and boiled linseed oil were the main ingredients of the older fillers. Small amounts of Japan drier and turpentine were added. Sometimes wood flour replaced silex.

Two types of filler for wood pores are paste and liquid. Paste filler dries slowly because of the linseed oil it contains. It can be thinned as desired with linseed oil and turpentine. It requires from 12 to 48 hours drying time, depending on the oil content, before a sealer should be applied. The oil has a tendency to expand. The oil seals by expanding, provides a good lubricant in filler application, and it helps enrich the natural color of the wood.

A shellac sealer coat is the best kind to use over this type of oil-paste filler because lacquer-type sealers tend to check and have an "orange-peel"

Fig. 18-4. A—A type of stain called color-in-oil. Several can be mixed together to get a desired color. (Benjamin Moore) B—Typical three-part finish. Color-in-oil may be added to part #1. If desired, skip #2 and 3 to use an armor coat instead. (General Finishes Sales & Services Co.)

texture if the filler is not perfectly dry. Some wood finishers prefer to apply a wash coat of shellac (1 part shellac to 6 or 7 parts alcohol) before filling wood that has exceptionally large pores, such as mahogany and ash.

Newer paste fillers are very fast drying because of their synthetic resin-base vehicles. A good general-purpose thinner for most of these fillers is a varnish makers' and painters' naphtha (VM & P naphtha). A minimum drying time of 2 hours is suggested, depending on the driers and reducers (thinners) used to thin the paste or liquid.

Liquid filler is usually made from cheap varnish and a small amount of silex. It is often used on inexpensive work in medium close-grain woods. A thin paste filler is more satisfactory for all work, however.

The following procedure is useful in properly filling the pores for natural colors or toned effects.

1. Apply a wash coat of shellac over stain, or over natural-colored wood with large pores (ash, oak, mahogany), before filling.
2. Thin the filler to a workable consistency. Color or tint it as necessary. For example, a white-tinted filler accents the grains of oak and ash.
3. Apply filler with the grain to 1 or 2 ft.² (0.3 m²) or to one piece of a project at a time. Use a cloth or a brush.
4. Let the filler dry until it has a dull appearance. Do not allow thick filler to dry on top of wood surfaces. It will harden and often require scraping and sanding to remove.
5. Rub the filler across the grain using burlap, coarse rags, or the palm of your hand. Apply ample pressure to push the filler to the bottom of the pore holes. Filler that catches only in the top portion of the pores may drop or wash out when dry, especially during brush finishing. Air that is trapped in pores that are not completely filled may break through the finish, causing bubbles and blisters in the surface finish coats.
6. Rub flat surfaces across the grain with clean burlap or excelsior (wood wool). This both removes most of the surplus filler and works it more deeply into the pores.
7. Remove surplus filler from all corners using a cloth, a stick, or a putty knife.
8. Using cheesecloth or any other soft fabric, wipe with the grain to remove streaks and all remaining filler on the surface.
9. Allow the filler in the pores to dry thoroughly before completing the remaining finishing operations.

Sealing

Close-grain woods do not require fillers. They do, however, need a sealer coat on which to build finish.

Open-grain woods require a sealer after filler has been rubbed in.

One or more sealing coats are used. They prevent bleeding of the stains or fillers and they seal (close) pores and fibers, making a good base for later finish coats. As the first coat of the finish, sealers prevent moisture absorption as well as absorption of other finish coats.

Lacquer sealers and shellac are common sealing materials. Both can be brushed or sprayed. Shellac is available in cuts (mixtures) ranging from 2 to 12 lb. (4.4 to 26kg). A common grade is termed four pound cut. This means that 4 lb. of lac resin are dissolved in 1 gallon of alcohol. One part of four pound cut shellac to three parts alcohol or a mixture of half alcohol and half shellac (two pound cut) can be easily brushed or sprayed.

Because oil-base materials tend to bleed, a shellac-type sealer should be used over all oil base stains and fillers. This sealer coat should dry at least 2 hours. Varnish sealers should dry overnight before they are sanded.

COATING MATERIALS

Rapidly expanding chemical technology has given the consumer a large number of liquid finishes. New products are fast replacing the older forms of paint, shellac, varnish, and lacquer.

Protective Wood Coatings

If the surface receives extreme abrasive wear, for instance a boat hull or deck, and yet it demands an attractive coating, try any of the one or two-part epoxies. The newer one-part epoxy combines the durability of the two-part epoxy with the convenience of a regular enamel. Two-part epoxies come in a kit of equal-volume cans (two pints, two quarts, etc.) and the contents must be mixed to form the coating. The one-part epoxy is complete in one can and, unlike the two-part epoxy, it can be tinted.

These epoxy coatings adhere well to most surfaces and resist detergent, oil, and alkali. However, even though they are weather resistant and hold up under heavy use, epoxies tend to lose gloss upon exposure to a combination of sunlight and weather.

If you need an exterior gloss, use an implement or industrial enamel. These enamels, which double as marine finishes, are designed for almost any heavily-used wood or metal surface.

In the past, exterior wood that was to be stained had to be treated with a preservative first and then stained to the color desired. Now there are many exterior stains with the preservative added. This greatly reduces the time necessary to finish fences and decks.

One simple finish for furniture is paint. It covers wood grain which may not match other furniture.

Some paints for wood do not require a primer, Fig. 18-5. These paints are thick enough to fill in a rough surface.

One recent development has brought new safety for wood interiors: fire retardant paint. Upon heating, the fire retardant paint will swell and create an insulating layer between the fire and the combustible material. Available in attractive colors, it can be applied to walls, panels, or ceilings. Fire retardant paint comes in easy-to-apply latex. It is also available in a two-coat finish system.

Woodwork and cabinets must stand up under kicks, bumps, and scratches and still look clean. You need tough, flexible coatings that will take a detergent washing. Latex and oil-based enamels work well here, but the one-part epoxy enamels provide the ideal finish for any heavily used interior surfaces.

If you need a clear finish for your woodwork or cabinets, try the urethane or polyurethane varnishes. For other uses such as wood floors, no ordinary varnish matches their toughness, and they will last a long time depending on the traffic they have to bear. Some non-urethane finishes provide a tough surface, Fig. 18-6.

SPECIAL COATING INFORMATION

There is a large variety of finishes you can put on wood furniture. If you have an old damaged piece you'd like to reclaim, try antiquing it. Simply patch any cracked veneer and apply the undercoat and glazing compound according to the manufacturer's directions. These kits are intended for putting color on an otherwise unusable piece of furniture. With practice, you can also get some startling effects by using the color and glaze on wall paneling, plywood, woodwork, and doors.

Try any of the older forms of lacquer, shellac, or varnish on your wood furniture, but never apply urethane varnishes or epoxy enamels directly to an older finish. The powerful solvents may cause the previous finish to wrinkle.

Versatility in finishing products is increased since many are available in aerosol cans. Practically anything applied with a brush can now be sprayed from a container. Varnish, lacquer, latex, enamels, silicones — all are available in aerosols.

When you refinish furniture, an aerosol will spray an even coat of varnish onto intricately carved wood (a brush would ruin the job). For touch-ups, you can even have aerosol paint tinted to match any color swatch or sample.

Finishing Schedules

The finishing schedule is somewhat like a cooking recipe. It lists the ingredients and steps for completing a particular finish on a certain material. If the home mechanic is familiar with the materials to be worked with, then one has some notion of what

Fig. 18-5. Painting a storage bench to black out the natural grain of the wood. A gloss finish will result. (Rust-Oleum)

Fig. 18-6. Clear finishes for home furniture are available in three "sheens" or degree of shine: gloss, semi gloss, and satin or flat. (Deft)

the results will be. Our finishing materials have different results if used in different combinations. Varying the procedure (schedule) will give the finish a different result. Even the same schedule used on different materials will have varying end results.

A finishing schedule also may serve as the printed record of the finish procedure and will preserve the techniques for future duplication. It provides a record of steps taken and materials used. Following are examples of simple finishing schedules:

Finishing schedule for built-up finish on open grain woods (oak, pecan, ash, etc.):

1. Prepare the surface (sand until all defects are removed).
2. Wash coat end grain (prevents excessive absorption of stains to darken end grain).
3. Stain.
4. Seal (to prevent further absorption of finishing materials).
5. Fill with paste wood filler (let dry, according to instructions).
6. Seal (to lock in filler) (variation of coloring procedure may be done at this point such as: distressing, highlighting, or splattering).
7. First coat top protective finish.
8. Rub (with 400 or 600 grit wet or dry abrasive paper).
9. Repeat steps 7 and 8 until satisfactory buildup is obtained.
10. Polish (with power abrasive and lubricant).

Finish schedule for built-up finish on closed grain woods (cherry, maple, pine, etc.):

1. Prepare surface.
2. Wash coat end grain.
3. Stain.
4. Seal (variation of coloring procedures).
5. First coat top protective finish.
6. Rub.
7. Repeat steps 5 and 6.
8. Polish.

Finishing schedule for penetrating finish (should be used on wood which has good natural grain and coloring, like walnut, teak, rosewood, etc.)

1. Surface preparation.
2. Apply first coat of penetrating finish (home mix preparation* or commercial preparation).
3. Let stand wet for 30 minutes, wipe dry.
4. Allow 8 hour drying time before second coat.
5. Apply second coat, sand while wet with 600 grit wet or dry abrasive paper, wipe dry.
6. Allow 8 hours drying time.
7. Repeat steps 5 and 6 until satisfactory finish is achieved.
8. Polish dry with coarse clean cloth.
* Home prepared penetrating finish:
   1/3 part boiled linseed oil
   1/3 part spar varnish
   1/3 part mineral spirits

Finish schedule for metal finish (sheet metal or wrought iron):

1. Remove rust or mill scale.
2. Degrease by wiping surface with thinner or degreasing agent.
3. Apply primer coat.
4. For sheet metal, rub lightly with 400 grit abrasive paper to smooth surface.
5. First coat protective finish.
6. Repeat step 5 until satisfactory coating is obtained.

Antique Glaze

This is a two-tone blended finish that gives the effect of age. It is produced by keeping a color coating translucent. A color (often black) is used over a base coat and then wiped off. A glaze is usually used on painted wood, but can also be used on stained surfaces. Prepared glazing liquids can be purchased or a glaze can be mixed at home, Fig. 18-7.

For an opaque base coat, use enamel undercoat or a good semigloss enamel. This coat need not be completely smooth as irregularities in the paint hold the glaze. Apply two coats.

If a previously enameled surface is to be glazed, buff it with steel wool and clean it with turpentine or mineral spirits. All old wax must be removed.

A commercial glazing liquid is available in many communities. It should be thinned with turpentine or mineral spirits to the consistency of thick cream. Color to the desired shade with burnt umber color-in-oil, similar to that for black, Fig. 18-7. If this is not available, a glazing liquid can be made by mixing one part varnish with three parts turpentine and coloring as above.

Fig. 18-7. Commercial antique glosses are available. Many colors can be created using the standard tinting colors. (Benjamin Moore)

A base coat should dry 48 hours before the glaze is applied. For small areas, brush the glazing liquid over the entire surface. On large areas, apply to only part of the surface so that glaze will not dry before it can be wiped.

With a pad of cheesecloth, wipe away most of the glaze. Leave the glaze thicker in crevices and inside corners. Blend to give the effect of highlights. Leave it lighter where wear and handling would wear the finish with age.

If lighter areas are needed for contrast, wipe some areas with a cloth dampened in turpentine. This is often done on a raised carving or designs of mirrors or picture frames. It is possible to clean off all the glaze with turpentine and start over again.

On picture frames, no protective coat is needed over the glaze. On furniture that will receive hard use, apply low gloss varnish after the glaze has dried for several days.

Waxes

A hard coat of paste wax, Fig. 18-8, should be given to furniture as soon as the final finish is dry and should always be kept on the furniture to protect it. Liquid self-polishing wax should never be used on furniture. It has a water base which could raise the grain of the wood.

Furniture Polishes

Furniture may be cleaned and maintained with commercial furniture polishes. However, certain precautions should be taken. One is in using the newer silicone polishes.

Silicone Polishes

It has been found that furniture on which silicone polish has been used must have special precautions taken before it is refinished. Any residue of silicone polish left on the surface will cause cracks to develop in varnish, paint, or lacquer applied over it. Even a complete removal of the previous finish by sanding or with paint and varnish remover may not prevent this condition from occurring.

If old finish is not to be removed:
1. Before the surface is sanded, wash thoroughly with turpentine allowing it to stand.
2. Wipe dry with a clean cloth.
3. Repeat using fresh cloths for both washing and drying.
4. Sand lightly.
5. Apply a special barrier coat.
6. Let the barrier coat dry overnight, sand lightly, and apply the new finish.

FURNITURE THAT NEEDS ONLY CLEANING

If furniture has a smooth, hard finish, it may need only cleaning instead of refinishing.

General Cleaning

A good, general cleaner for furniture may be made at home by mixing together the following ingredients:
1 tablespoon turpentine
3 tablespoons boiled linseed oil
1 quart hot water

The turpentine and boiled linseed oil can be purchased at most paint or hardware stores. The mixture must be kept hot as you use it. Using a clean cloth, wet it in the solution and rub it on one section of the furniture at a time. Then polish with a dry clean cloth. In this mixture, the turpentine serves to cut the dirt while the oil lubricates and polishes the wood.

The mixture should not be used on a shellac finish as the water may cause it to spot or turn white. A worn shellac finish should usually be removed, and the article refinished. To determine whether or not the finish is shellac, rub a small area on the underside of the piece with denatured alcohol. If the finish is shellac, it will soften.

When your furniture has been thoroughly cleaned, protect it with a good polish or wax.

White Spots

If your furniture is badly soiled and shows white spots, rub ffff grade rottenstone into the surface with a pad of 000 steel wool that has been kept wet with lightweight mineral oil or paraffin oil. Always rub with the grain of the wood and rub lightly to avoid damaging the finish. Wipe off the mixture with a soft, dry cloth.

FURNITURE CARE

Normal care of furniture consists of the daily "dusting." However, periodic renewing of the finish can be done with little effort. Once yearly is

Fig. 18-8. Waxes are applied to a completed finish to increase its wearability. Wax may be applied in paste or liquid form.

generally enough to renew and bring new life to a finish. Renewing consists of simply removing the accumulation of grime which does not wipe off with the dusting operation.

Lemon oil polish does an excellent job of renewing an old finish. Saturate a clean soft rag with the lemon oil and wipe on a film of oil over the entire finished surface. Let set a few minutes and with a second clean, dry, soft cloth wipe off excess oil. A very thin film will remain.

If the finish has noticeable fine scratches in it but they do not go through the finish coating, these may be removed by mixing a small amount of rottenstone (very fine abrasive) with the lemon oil. Mix a few sprinkles of rottenstone with a few drops of lemon oil and use a cloth pad to buff out the fine scratches. Finally wipe clean with a second cloth, Fig. 18-9. Continue until desired shine is reached.

Fig. 18-10. To renew wood paneling, dip a soft sponge in paint cleaner. Clean by working with a vertical motion.

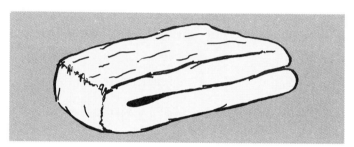
Fig. 18-9. A clean soft rag can be used as a rubbing pad. Avoid a tight weave like denim, since large grits can project out far enough to scratch. Some wood finishers prefer cheesecloth.

For those deep scratches that penetrate the wood through the finish, the home mechanic may dip a cotton swab in a wood stain of a matching color and swab into the scratch. Finally use a little lemon oil to clean the applied stain from the surrounding surface.

Cleaning Wood Paneling

Beautiful wood paneling will also need cleaning from time to time. Sponging with a good paint cleaner will probably succeed, Fig. 18-10. If stubborn stains or dirt persist, a 000 steel wool dipped in the paint cleaner might be used. However, be careful not to rub through the finish.

CHEMICAL COATING FOR METALS

During the furniture renewing process, certain metal ornaments may also need renewing. For copper and brass, two results are possible:
1. Complete removal of the surface.
2. Surface coloring.

Brass polish removes the entire surface. Listed next are a few chemical solutions used to achieve various colors, especially on copper or brass.

Coloring Solutions for Copper and Brass

1. Brown on copper
   1 part barium sulphide
   25 parts hot water
   (Rub on or dip)
2. Brown to Black on copper
   1 quart water
   1/3 oz. nitrate of iron
   (Rub on or dip)
3. Brown to black on copper
   1 part potassium sulphide (liver of sulphur, lump)
   25 parts warm water (vary as desired)
   (Dip and allow to dry)
4. Dappled effect on copper
   1 part household ammonia
   1 part water
   a pinch of sulphur
   (Rub on or dip — color takes place upon drying)
5. Silver on copper
   11 grams silver nitrate
   6 grams salt
   7 grams cream of tartar (Rochelle salts, Potassium tartrate)
   (Rub on with a rag)
6. Verde Green on copper and brass
   4 oz. salt
   1 oz. chloride of iron crystals
   3 oz. verdigris
   5 oz. ammonium chloride (sal ammoniac)
   2 oz. cream of tartar
   1 pint water
   (Dip and allow to dry)
7. Olive Green on copper and brass
   1 part perchloride of iron
   2 parts water
   (Immerse desired time, allow to dry)
8. Antique Green on copper and brass
   1 1/2 oz. cream of tartar

1/2 oz. ammonium chloride (sal ammoniac)
1 1/2 oz. salt
6 oz. boiling water
4 oz. copper nitrate
(Apply with brush, allow to dry)

Note: Dipping generally produces a more uniform color than rubbing on of the solution. However, it is not practical to dip large projects. However, the brushing or rub-on method may be improved by first wetting the article.

9. Bright Green on brass only
   2 oz. ammonium chloride
   2 oz. copper sulphate
   1 pint boiling water
   (Apply with stiff brush, allow to dry)

10. Antique brass
    Butter of antimony
    (Rub on, allow to dry)

11. Dull Green on brass
    4 oz. copper sulphate
    2 quarts boiling water
    (Immerse, allow to dry)

12. Red-brown on brass
    8 oz. nitrate of iron (432 grains-one oz.)
    8 oz. hyposulphate of soda (28.35 grams — one oz.)
    2 quarts water (1 pint — 16 oz.)
    (Immerse, allow to dry)

TEST YOUR KNOWLEDGE — CHAPTER 18

1. When using silicon carbide abrasive paper on fibrous wood, wet it with _____ _____ .
2. Generally, begin sanding wood using _____ grit paper.
3. Abrasive coatings which are ''_____'' help prevent ''loading up'' of the abrasive spaces while sanding.
4. Which of the following wood species are easy to bleach?
   a. Pine.
   b. Oak.
   c. Poplar.
   d. Mahogany.
   e. Maple.
5. A common bleaching process requires the use of _____ acid followed by sodium hypochlorite and borax.
6. Blond finish mixes are obtained by adding _____ _____ to clear lacquer.
7. Dissolve most water-soluble color stain crystals in _____ _____ .
8. Stains that are soluble in _____ (oil, water) do not raise the wood grain.
9. Two types of filler for wood pores are _____ and _____ .
10. Apply wood filler _____ (with, across) the grain and later rub it _____ (with, across) the grain.
11. Lacquer sealers and _____ are common sealing materials.
12. A _____ -part (one, two) epoxy can be tinted.
13. A urethane or polyurethane varnish is often used for a _____ finish on woodwork or cabinets.
14. Urethane varnish or epoxy enamel may cause an older finish to _____ .
15. Finishing schedules can provide a record of a successful finish effect in case you want to _____ it.
16. For antique glazing, the base coat should dry _____ hours before the glaze is applied.
17. Turpentine, linseed oil, and _____ (hot, warm, cold) water make a good furniture cleaning mixture.
18. Buff out very fine scratches in furniture using _____ mixed with lemon oil.
19. To clean wood paneling, use a sponge dipped in _____ _____ .
20. To form antique green on copper or brass, _____ produces a more even color than that produced by brushing.

KNOW THESE TERMS

Varnish, grit size, steel wool, bleaching, stain, wax, polish.

SUGGESTED ACTIVITIES

Your instructor may suggest that you practice some bleaching methods. You may then learn about the special steps and special hazards for each in a controlled classroom situation. For those bleaching solutions used, try them on at least two types of wood. If time is short, try the other bleaches on just one wood type such as oak.

On a wood sample, make test patches using several staining, sealing, and glazing processes. Also test the effects of base coats on the later finishes by following some steps chosen from this chapter. Note any advantages or disadvantages related to appearance and ease of application. Report this to the class.

Choose at least one of the metal coloring processes for brass or copper. Carry out the procedure on both flat and curved surfaces. For steps that allow either dipping or brushing, compare the results. Keep a record of the time involved for some of the drying steps. Use your notes for future references.

CAREERS

Furniture repair, furniture refinishing, furniture salesperson, interior designer.

19

REPAIRING AND REFURBISHING FURNITURE

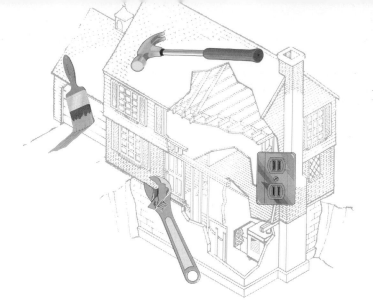

This chapter tells how to repair loose joints or dented surfaces of furniture. It discusses some types of glue used in furniture repair. It includes directions for using paint and varnish removers.

After studying this chapter, you will be able to:
■ Tell how to remove finishes without causing damage.
■ Tell how to use removers on curved or bumpy items.
■ List some methods of repairing or regluing dowel joints.
■ Choose a glue for a project.
■ Explain steps for fixing dents or holes in furniture.
■ List types of repairs using wood blocks, wedges, and also metal brackets.
■ Tell how to conceal metal reinforcements.

The home mechanic can do many simple repairs of old furniture. This can save a large amount of money. However, there are certain cases where it may be wiser not to repair a piece.

FURNITURE WORTH REPAIRING

Furniture is valuable if it is well constructed of good wood, not merely if it is old. Repairing and refurbishing furniture, whether it is an old article or a modern piece, requires time, energy, patience, and some expense. A piece of furniture worth reclaiming is made of good wood, is well designed, well constructed, and serves a special use in the home. If the piece has these essentials, the final results will be worth the time and effort required for repair, Fig. 19-1. If not, it might be wiser to use other furniture rather than trying to repair the piece that does not meet these standards.

Furniture Woods and How They Affect Refinishing
Some surface refinishing is often needed following structural repairs.

It is important to know what the wood is and whether it is solid or veneer before you begin refinishing.

Decide first whether your furniture is of solid or veneered construction. If it is veneered, take great care with sanding. Heavy sanding may cut through the top layer of wood and spoil the piece. It is best to use only steel wool for smoothing veneered woods. If the furniture is solid construction, any amount of sanding can be done that is necessary to give a smooth finish.

Some woods are "open-grained". That is, they have many small pores on the surface. Open-grained woods include oak, walnut, mahogany, ash, chestnut, and elm. To have a very smooth surface on open-grained woods, a paste wood filler may be used to fill these pores. A filler will also prevent clogging of these pores with dust and make the furniture easier to clean. Other woods (cherry, birch, pine, maple) are called closed-grained and do not have these surface pores. On these woods, a paste wood filler is not needed.

REMOVING THE OLD FINISH

All finish should be carefully removed before a new finish is applied. Taking off layers of old paint or varnish is not difficult, but it does often require patience and time. If the finish goes deep into the wood, you may want to use both a remover and sanding to make sure the old finish is completely removed.

If the surface is contoured or curved, a belt sander cannot be used. A special sanding wheel is needed. Refer again to Fig. 18-1. For information on abrasive papers to use in sanding, see the preceeding chapter.

REMOVERS

A good commercial paint and varnish remover is best for taking off the old finish. However, one

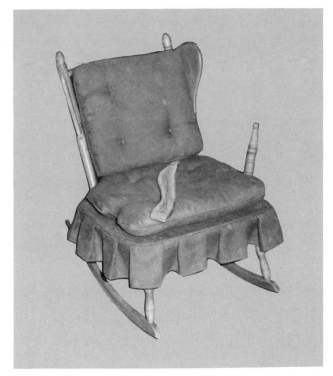

Fig. 19-1. Before rebuilding a piece of furniture, decide if it is worth the effort.

The most generally available type of remover is a liquid that can be applied with a brush, cloth, or piece of steel wool. Removing the finish will be much easier if you allow enough time for the remover to reach the wood before you scrape it off. Follow the directions on the label carefully.

Different brands must be taken off at different stages. If the remover is scraped off sooner than it should be, much of the finish is left intact and a second application is needed.

With this type of remover, the finish is scraped off with a paint scraper or putty knife after it has softened. (Always scrape in the direction of the grain.) The number of applications needed will depend on the number of layers of finish and how old it is.

Most commercial removers in the past have required a special afterwash of denatured alcohol. Others may have required a water wash. Many of the newer ones do not require this special wash and will save time.

CAUTION — Use removers outdoors whenever possible, or in a well-ventilated place. They are flammable and the fumes of some may be poisonous if the ventilation is not good. Never use removers near a fire, and destroy at once all cloths and papers used with them.

When you have selected your remover, place the furniture in a horizontal position on a thick layer of old newspapers. Work at a comfortable height. If necessary set the article on a table or sawhorse.

Shake the remover thoroughly and pour a small amount into a can or jar. Keep the original container tightly covered. Apply the remover to one section at a time with a brush and stroke in one direction only, Fig. 19-3.

disadvantage is that a paint remover will raise the grain.

There are many good commercial removers on the market, Fig. 19-2. If you are refinishing many pieces of furniture, you may like to experiment with different brands to find the ones you like best. A thicker or "paste" type remover may be easier to use on vertical surfaces such as woodwork or wall paneling.

Fig. 19-2. Paint and varnish removers are available from the local supplier. Read the label carefully before buying.

Fig. 19-3. Apply paint and varnish remover in one direction. Wait a few minutes and remove with a scraper, putty knife, or other smooth-edged tool. (Benjamin Moore)

Let the article stand until the finish blisters (usually 10 to 20 minutes). However, the finish must be kept moist. If it starts to dry before it softens, apply another coat of remover.

Scrape with a putty knife and take care not to scratch the wood. Repeat until all traces of the old finish are gone. If the furniture has curved surfaces, use a toothbrush dipped into the remover, Fig. 19-4. An orangewood stick is good to use in cleaning out carvings. For turnings or other circular shapes, a cord drawn back and forth across the depression will remove the excess material, Fig. 19-5.

Fig. 19-5. Pull a cloth or small twine through a curved depression to help clean the crevasse. (Benjamin Moore)

Fig. 19-4. Use an old toothbrush to pick the dissolved finish from a bumpy surface such as this carving. Another suggestion is to sprinkle sawdust after the surface has dissolved. With light brushing, the surface will clean easily.
(Benjamin Moore)

BLEACHING DARKER SPOTS

You may discover stains or dark spots in the wood when the finish is off. You may not always be able to remove these completely, but you can usually lessen them greatly by bleaching. Oxalic acid is the most common bleach for this purpose.

The solution should be used hot. Apply with a dish mop or brush. To prevent rings or light spots, apply the bleach to the entire surface.

When the surface has bleached, wipe with clear water and then wash with a solution of 1 part household ammonia in 10 parts water. Then rinse again with clear water.

REPAIRING FURNITURE

Any loose or weak parts, dents, or small holes should be repaired at this stage. If a part is weak, it should be replaced. If warped pieces can be soaked, they can be straightened with clamped blocks or with weights. Badly warped pieces should be repaired by a cabinet maker. All loose parts should be glued.

Fig. 19-6 shows types of wood joints. Joints using blocks or dowels can often be repaired by the home mechanic.

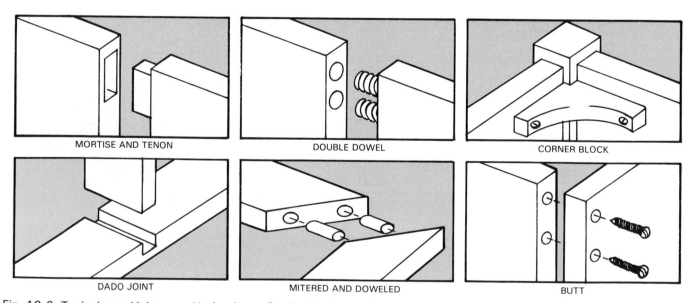

MORTISE AND TENON

DOUBLE DOWEL

CORNER BLOCK

DADO JOINT

MITERED AND DOWELED

BUTT

Fig. 19-6. Typical wood joints used in furniture. Quality furniture often uses two dowels in a joint. The butt joint is weak. Note the spiral on the dowel to release trapped glue.

Glues

There are two types of glue that are good to use at home for repairing furniture: plastic resin and polyvinyl glue.

Plastic resin is a powder to be mixed with water. It must be used within four hours after mixing. It is strong, waterproof, and does not stain or dry out. However, it must be used with pressure and is not good for poorly fitting joints. It should remain clamped for at least 16 hours. Apply a thin coat to both surfaces. Some brand names are Weldwood and Cascamite.

Polyvinyl glue is a very fast drying glue that comes ready to use. It is of adequate strength, fairly water resistant, and fills well. It is not good for outdoor furniture or any metal parts. It only needs to be applied to one surface. Clamp at once.

Some brands of polyvinyl glue are Franklin's Evertite, Elmer's Glue-All, Weldwood Presto-Set, Dunlap Quick Set, and LePages Sure-Grip. These are synthetic glues that replace the glues made from animal products.

Other types of glue include yellow glue and resorcinol glue. These types are not often used for home repairs.

Repairing Loose Joints

Loose joints using dowels can be repaired by:
1. Replacing the dowel with a larger size.
2. Regluing the dowel joint.

To replace a dowel, you must have clear access to all holes used. In the simplest case, the dowel can be drilled out from the side of the joint. Insert any dowel using a leather mallet, Fig. 19-7. For the greatest strength, the dowel diameter should be no greater than 1/3 the thickness of the frame piece. Drill carefully using a drilling jig, or use a smaller dowel wrapped once in cloth. Soak the cloth and dowel in glue.

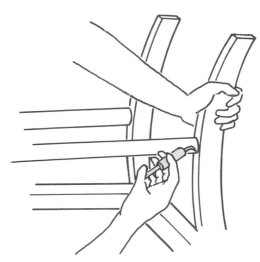

Fig. 19-8. Regluing a loose dowel joint. Inject glue through small hole drilled in convenient place. Then clamp the joint together.

The original dowel and joint can be reglued. See Fig. 19-8. Pull the joint apart a little. Make a hole in the side of the frame just large enough for a syringe needle or tube.

Inject glue to fill the joint. Continue until glue appears at two or more places around the joint on the inside of the frame. Drill a second needle hole if needed. Put glue on the exposed parts of the dowel.

Force the joint together. Hold it with clamps or with a tight band. Let dry for 16 hours. Cover hole with wood filler and sand the area.

Before gluing, scrape off all old glue. If the surfaces are smooth, roughen them with coarse garnet paper. If parts do not fit tight, fill the extra space with plastic wood.

When the glue is applied, use pressure with clamps if you have them. If not, make a tourniquet of a band of strong cloth and use a stick to tighten it. See Fig. 19-9. Protect the wood by using pads of wax paper between the clamps or tourniquet and the furniture.

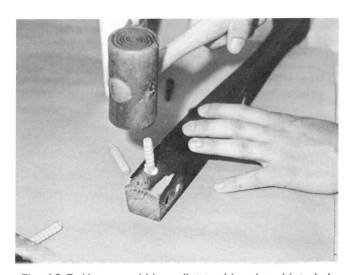

Fig. 19-7. Use a rawhide mallet to drive dowel into hole.

Fig. 19-9. A rope and tourniquet holds a joint together during regluing, and is economical.

Small Dents

In softwoods such as pine, maple, or fir, a dent can be raised with water. Put a few drops of water on the dent and allow it to stand. As the water is absorbed, keep adding more until the surface of the dent is higher than the wood around it. As it dries, the wood will shrink back a little.

If the dents are in a hardwood, heat must be used. Adjust an iron for a moderate temperature. Lay a clean, damp cloth on the dent and hold the iron barely above (not touching) the cloth, Fig. 19-10. Allow 24 hours for the surface to dry. If the woolen cloth used is not white, test to make sure it is colorfast, or use a paper towel.

Fig. 19-11. Many defect-filling products are available from local paint stores. Follow directions on the container. (Benjamin Moore)

Fig. 19-10. Dents having bruised and compressed wood fibers may be lifted by steaming. Place a hot iron just above a moist pad for a few seconds. Repeat as needed. Keep iron at low heat.

Small Holes

Four methods may be used for filling small holes. Plastic wood or wood putty are two products which may be used, Fig. 19-11 and Fig. 19-12. Glued sawdust and, fourth, shellac are other materials.

A method which works well in large holes is to use a sawdust glue mixture. Mix glue with sawdust of the same kind of wood as the piece of furniture.

Stick shellac is possibly the best but also the most difficult of the methods. See Fig. 19-12. Buy a stick that matches the color of your wood. Heat the end of the stick over a flame or use a household iron until the stick is ready to drip. At the same time heat a screwdriver or other slender metal tool. Press the stick shellac into the hole and level it off with the heated tool. Remove excess stick shellac and let it stand until the filling is thoroughly hard. Smooth by sanding.

PREPARING FOR AND APPLYING THE NEW FINISH

A beautiful finish depends on the fine, smooth condition of the wood before the finish is applied.

Fig. 19-12. Repairing a wood surface. Top. Melting stick shellac into the defect with a burn-in knife. Middle. Wood putty is easy to mix and use. Bottom. Adding color to natural shade of plastic wood.

Thorough sanding is essential to a smooth finish. Sanding should always be done in the direction of the grain of the wood.

An abrasive paper is easier to use if it is held over a block. Sanding blocks with handles are available at most hardware stores for a low cost. If these are not available, a small block of wood may be used.

Sanding is probably the most important step in getting a beautiful finish. Do too much rather than too little. After sanding thoroughly, remove any sanding dust. Vacuuming is best, Fig. 19-13.

Applying Stains

In many cases stain is not needed. But when the wood has no natural beauty or if a piece of furniture is made of a combination of woods (such as rungs of chairs of a different wood), then stain is used to blend the light woods with the dark woods.

One stain which is not available commercially and is becoming very popular for pine paneling and furniture is the "Old Pine Finish." To get this finish requires a type of tobacco stain.

Break up one plug of chewing tobacco in a jar. Add 1 pint (0.15 L) of household ammonia. Place lid on jar and soak for about one day. Strain through clean nylon hose, dip lintless cloth into satin, and apply several coats to get the desired color. This stain will dry lighter but it shows up darker again when the finish is applied. Allow to dry 24 hours.

Although there are several types of stains, oil stains are the best to use at home. Varnish stains should be avoided — it is very difficult to apply them evenly and to avoid streaks.

Varnish

Varnish is available for a satin finish or a gloss finish. The satin finish is preferred, since the surface does not show small scratches. Varnish can be used on wood that has a material already applied to the surface such as paste wood filler or the enamel for a "pickled finish."

Shellac

A shellac finish scratches very easily and is not water resistant. Water may cause spots or turn the finish white. Thus, it is not recommended for use on furniture.

Lacquer

Lacquer is a durable surface finish but it is difficult to apply at home because it dries so rapidly. If a spray gun is available, lacquer is easier to apply.

Wiped-Off Finish

Enamel may be wiped on open-grained woods with a soft cloth to produce a "pickled" finish. The enamel stays in the pores of the open-grained wood while most of it is wiped off the surface. White, ivory, or light gray are the most common colors to use, although any color may be used. Dip a soft cloth in the enamel and wipe on the wood until the surface is dry. If more color is desired, repeat the process. Let dry at least 24 hours. Satin-finish varnish is good to use as the finish over the enamel. This is an especially good finish for oak.

REPAIRING WITH REINFORCEMENTS

Weak joints can often be built up to provide strength. Materials to build them up include wood blocks, triangles, wedges, or metal brackets, plates, and pins. It is best to use hardwood for the wood reinforcements.

Fig. 19-14 shows some joint types used on tables. To attach wood blocks of any shape, clean

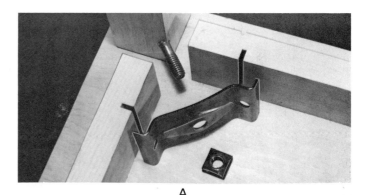

A

B

Fig. 19-14. A—Sometimes a glued wood joint can be made strong with a corner bracket and hanger bolt. Use a wood chisel to form slots for bracket. Some brackets attach to rails with screws. B—Suggested joint result for high strength. Table leg is attached with screws and glue blocks. (Drexel Furniture Co.)

Fig. 19-13. Vacuum the piece free of any sanding dust. Use a household cleaner or a shop vacuum cleaner. (Benjamin Moore)

the furniture joint of all old glue and varnish. Cut and sand, or chisel and grind the wood reinforcement to fit tightly.

Drill any screw pilot holes needed. Test the fit of the screw mounting.

Apply polyvinyl carpenters' glue or use a hot glue gun. Clamp the piece in place or use the screw mount to apply pressure. Let the work set up. Let it dry one hour for hot glue and 24 hours for liquid glue.

To attach metal brackets as was suggested in Fig. 19-4, cut one or more slots in the furniture frame rails to receive the ends or side edges of a metal bracket. Slots can be cut with a table saw or a dado head if the rail is removable, or using a wood chisel if the rail is not removable. Another method may use small glue blocks to hold back the metal bracket.

Sometimes a chair back or a furniture rail is cracked. A crack repair procedure is shown in Fig. 19-15. To pull together two sides of a crack, cut a shallow slot, called a gain, to receive a mending

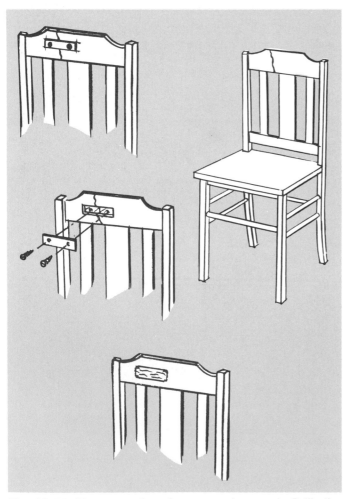

Fig. 19-15. Use a mending plate to repair a crack. Drill pilot holes farther apart than holes in plate. Soak or steam the wood to let screws pull crack together when tightened. Fill the area, sand, and stain to blend edges.

plate. The slot should be twice as deep as the thickness of the mending plate. Drill the screw pilot holes farther apart than the holes in the mending plate. The extra pilot hole distance should be about as much as the width of the crack. When the screws are tightened, they will pull the crack together if the wood has been soaked or steamed.

Cover the plate and screws with wood filler and sand the area smooth. The wood filler may contain a color or it may be colored after sanding. Blend all edges following the methods given in Chapter 18.

TEST YOUR KNOWLEDGE — CHAPTER 19

1. Oak, walnut, mahogany, and ash are called _____ (open, closed)-grained woods.
2. A paint remover can _____ the grain of wood.
3. To remove softened paint, scrape _____ (with, across) the grain.
4. To prevent rings or light spots when bleaching with oxalic acid, apply it to the _____ surface.
5. If warped wood can be _____ , it can be straightened.
6. A fast-drying glue which is somewhat water-resistant is:
   a. Contact cement.
   b. Plastic resin glue.
   c. Polyurethane glue.
   d. Polyvinyl glue.
7. Fit an undersize dowel by wrapping it once in _____ and soak in glue.
8. An inexpensive substitute for a band clamp is a _____ tightened with a stick.
9. A household iron is used to:
   a. Melt glue.
   b. Lift a wood dent.
   c. Apply stick shellac.
   d. a and b.
   e. b and c.
10. The coloring substance in the ''Old Pine Finish'' for wood is _____ _____ .
11. Because it dries fast, _____ is best applied with a spray gun.
12. A compatible finish over enamel is satin-finish _____ .
13. The time required for hot glue to set up is _____ hour(s).
14. If a table rail cannot be removed, cut slots for any metal brackets by using a _____ _____ .
15. To conceal a mending plate, put it within a shallow slot called a _____ .
16. To pull a crack together with a mending plate, drill the wood pilot holes _____ (closer together, farther apart) than the plate hole centers.

KNOW THESE TERMS

Paint remover, scraper, ventilation, lacquer, water putty, corner brace.

SUGGESTED ACTIVITIES

With your instructor's help, try patching some holes in wood using stick shellac. Your instructor may recommend using a flame, hot metal blade, or a hot iron. Determine how much pressure will seat down the shellac without pulling too much out again. Note any unusual effects. Compare your project with others in your class.

In your library, look up the following types of glue:
1. Yellow glue, also called aliphatic resin.
2. Resorcinol glue.

Find out how resistant each is to water for use on outdoor furniture. Try to learn how long each much be clamped to set it. Also investigate the total drying time, in hours, before the item can bear weight. Check if ventilation is required. Make a report to your class.

CAREERS

Furniture restorer, cabinetmaker, interior designer, materials salesperson.

Attaching wood corner blocks with glue and screws. The adjustable band clamp holds all four corner joints at one time.

20

WALLPAPER

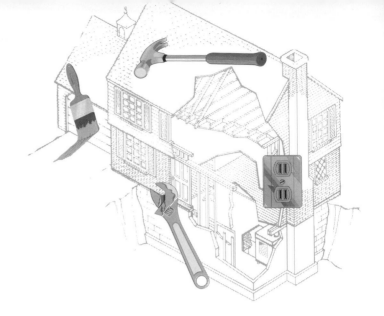

This chapter describes how to hang wallcoverings on ceilings and walls. It lists steps to prepare for paperhanging. The chapter gives methods for cleaning wall coverings.

After studying this chapter, you will be able to:
- Prepare walls and ceilings for coverings.
- Match three different pattern styles.
- Know how to fold wallpaper for easy handling.
- Describe how to hang coverings in corners.
- Compare hanging methods for prepasted and unpasted paper.
- Explain how to avoid trouble at doors and windows.
- Estimate the number of rolls needed.

Today's wallcovering is a product that is beautiful, durable, and economical. You can choose from many patterns to suit your decorating needs. Designs include traditional living room or contemporary dining room, a child's bedroom, or modern bath.

You enjoy how it looks when completed, but you expect the job to be hard work. However, while advances in styling and scrubbability of new wallcoverings were being made, some improvements in hanging were developed. Whether you choose prepasted or fabric-backed vinyl, hanging is not difficult. Prepasted paper saves times, and vinyl coverings are stiff enough to avoid kinks. Some wall coverings are made for easy removal. These strippable coverings can be changed as often as desired without leaving much residue.

HANG CEILING FIRST

To avoid getting paste on walls, do the ceiling first. Then paper the walls. However, this chapter discusses these two steps in the reverse order.

Also remember that any painting on ceilings or walls must be done before papering.

PREPARING TO HANG WALLPAPER

Before starting, take a few minutes to read the manufacturer's instructions for both the wallpaper paste and the wallcovering. The short time this takes will save a lot of time in the end. Some types of wallcoverings have slightly different hanging techniques. Reading the instructions will make that particular wallcovering job easier and more professional.

Before hanging, inspect your wallcovering closely. Is it the right color and pattern? Check the rolls and find a run number. Make sure that the number is the same on all your rolls. That way you can be sure the color is uniform. Now unfold each roll and check for flaws. Sometimes there are streaks or missing colors. You do not want to get halfway through the job and have to return what is left. It is best to check and make sure that everything looks just right before you begin.

Once you have selected your wallcovering, purchase your ceiling and matching trim paints. Wallpapering is easier if paint is applied prior to hanging.

TOOLS TO HANG WALLPAPER

You probably have most of the tools you need around the house. The special professional tools that will make your job easy can be purchased at a decorating supply store.

Some of the most often used tools are shown in Fig. 20-1. Wallcovering tool kits are available from the supplier. Kits usually include everything which will be needed to hang wallpaper at a modest cost. Some choices for tools are:
1. A paste bucket with an application grid, Fig. 20-2, or a roller tray.
2. A 7 in. (18 cm) roller frame.
3. A 7 in. roller with a 3/8 in. (9 mm) nap for rolling the paste onto the wallcovering. This is

Fig. 20-1. Equipment needed for hanging wallpaper. (Sherwin-Williams Co.)

Fig. 20-2. A roller grid helps remove excess paste. (Glidden)

Fig. 20-3. The chalkline can also act as a plumb bob. It gives the paperhanger a vertical line to start the project. (Stanley Tools)

6. A wallpaper knife. See Fig. 20-4. This one is good for rough cutting. It's sharper, easier, and faster to use than a razor and it is much safer.
7. A drop cloth. You will need this to cover your floor and carpet. Newspapers will not do. They leave ink stains on your carpet and furniture.
8. A seam roller. Use this to seat down the seam edges. Some paperhangers prefer not to use a seam roller, but to allow shrinkage to take up the deliberate excess seam paper.

Fig. 20-4. A sharp knife is convenient for trimming the paper. (Hyde Tools)

Some of the things you can find around the house include:

1. A yardstick (meter stick), 6 in. (150 mm) putty knife, scissors, and a pencil for measuring, marking, or cutting your wallcoverings.
2. A large plastic bucket and sponge to help clean up after each strip is hung.
3. A screwdriver for removing plates from switches and outlets.
4. A stepladder and large flat table from which to work.

If you choose a prepasted wallcovering, be sure to use a handy water tray. It is an inexpensive time saver that makes the job much easier.

more efficient than using a brush. However, a brush may be used effectively.

4. A chalk line for making sure that the wallcovering is hanging straight, Fig. 20-3. More about this important tool later.
5. A smoother. This is a plastic squeegee that is used to brush the wallcovering onto the wall. It is excellent for getting out bubbles that may be trapped behind the wallcovering.

WALL PREPARATION

Proper wall preparation is the most important part of any wallcovering project. Make sure that all walls are clean, smooth, and dry. Wallcoverings will not bond to dirt, grease, or to soapy residue. Remove any loose wallpaper with one of the following:

1. A rented wallpaper steamer.
2. Warm water and vinegar.
3. A wallpaper remover concentrate.

Follow these steps by using a wallpaper scraping blade.

Remove any loose plaster from holes and cracks and fill with a patching material. Then sand to a smooth finish. Spot prime these areas with a good latex wallcovering primer-sealer, Fig. 20-5. Latex primer is an excellent product for sealing porous surfaces such as new gypsum board or plaster, simulated plaster, porous or chalking paints, or wood and composition board. Also consider a wall sizing compound.

Fig. 20-5. A vapor barrier latex primer-sealer will give the home protection against moisture problems and heat loss if used before papering exterior walls. (Glidden)

A primer is usually a fast-drying compound which allows wallcoverings to be applied only two hours after priming. When you decide to change your walls, a primer allows the wallcovering to be stripped off without damaging the surface.

Be sure to dull the surface of all gloss paints with sandpaper or a commercial cleaner. After sanding or cleaning, rinse well and let the surface dry completely. It is a good idea to apply latex primer to the entire wall if you are not sure about the quality of the paint or if it is a very glossy surface. This will insure a good bond for your wallcovering.

To insure maximum adhesion over special areas like glass tile, or an old vinyl paper that is impossible to remove, prime with a good latex primer.

If you have old wallcovering, it should be removed along with the paste residue underneath. Wash walls with soapy water. Fabric-backed and most other wallcoverings sold in the last few years can be dry-stripped. Test a small section to see if it will come off easily. If not, score the paper surface and use a wallpaper remover solution. Mix with water and roll it onto the walls. Be sure to follow the manufacturer's instructions. Scrape the covering off with a blade while peeling large sections outward.

Mildew grows in moist, dark environments, particularly in bathrooms, basements, and closets. If your walls have been exposed to moisture or if you notice discolored areas, eliminate any possibility of mildew before applying your wallcovering. Wash your walls with a cleaner such as a mildewcide or equal parts of household bleach and water. Scrub to remove any stains and rinse thoroughly.

WALLPAPER ADHESIVES

Wallpaper paste is a nonstaining adhesive that dries clear. Most allow excellent slippage so you can position your wallcovering on the wall. Paste is easy to mix in cold water and is recommended when hanging paper wallcoverings or fabrics that are not backed. One pound of dry mix is usually enough to hang six to eight rolls of wallcovering.

Vinyl wallcovering adhesive is made for lightweight fabric and paper-backed vinyl wallcoverings. It mixes easily in cold water and dries slowly enough for positioning.

Vinyl ready-mixed wallcovering adhesive is excellent for hanging cloth or fabric-backed, light or medium weight vinyl wallcoverings as well as foils and mylars. It forms a tight bond that penetrates surfaces and is premixed for your convenience. One gallon is usually enough for two to four rolls of paper.

STARTING THE JOB

Look around your room and find the most inconspicuous corner or edge. Start from there. See Fig. 20-6. Measure from your starting place to a point that is one half inch less than your wallcovering strip. So, if your wallcovering is 28 inches, measure out 27 1/2 inches.

Since ceilings and floors may not be level, it is important to make sure that the first strip of wallcovering is hung absolutely vertically. To do this, you will need a plumb line. Tack the plumb line to the wall at the point you measured. Be sure to tack it near the ceiling. When the weight stops swinging, hold it snugly against the wall and snap the chalked string, Fig. 20-7. This leaves a vertical line on your wall — a plumb line.

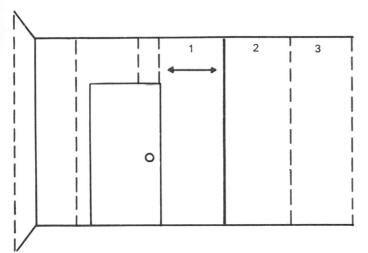

Fig. 20-6. Start hanging the strips at a window or door. This makes the edge less visible. (Sherwin-Williams Co.)

CUTTING AND MATCHING

Measure and cut a strip that is equal to the height of your wall plus an extra four inches for trimming (2 in. (50 mm) at the top and 2 in. at the bottom.) Now unroll the second strip, matching the patterns side to side with your first strip, Fig. 20-8. The second strip and all succeeding ones will probably be a little bit longer than the first because of the pattern repeat.

Now is a good time to mention the different ways that various wallcovering designs match at the seams. Refer to Fig. 20-9. First, there are patterns with no match. These are the easiest to hang and include plain paper and vertical stripes. The next

Fig. 20-8. Before cutting any paper to length, note how the pattern repeats. (Sherwin-Williams Co.)

type is the straight across match. A plaid covering would be a good example of this match. The horizontal stripe continues straight across the room.

The third type of match is the drop match. This pattern shows how the match drops down with succeeding strips. This type of match is not any more difficult to hang but you have to be careful when cutting to allow for matching. A drop match also requires a little bit more wallcovering as there is more waste involved.

In addition, seam types are:
1. Not overlapped (meaning butted).
2. Overlapped 1/16 in. (wire edge).
3. Overlapped 1/2 in. (lapped).

Lapped seams are used in corners. Butt seams are used elsewhere.

APPLYING THE PASTE

After mixing your paste (the ready-mixed is ready to use out of the container), dip your roller or brush

Fig. 20-7. Snap a straight line from ceiling to floor to give a "plumb" mark as a starting place. (Sherwin-Williams Co.)

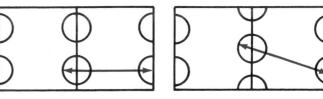

STRAIGHT ACROSS MATCH   DROP MATCH

Fig. 20-9. Besides straight match and drop match, a third random match means that each strip is hung as desired. There is no consistent element in the design to place opposite the next strip. Most textured strips are of this type.

into the paste and then cover the back of the strip, Fig. 20-10, starting at the center and working outward. If you are working on a small table only put paste on 1/2 of the length. The rest will be done later.

Be sure to apply the paste evenly and liberally. Missed areas will create bubbles on the strip when you hang it.

Fig. 20-10. Spread paste from the center outward and toward the bottom. Apply paste to each strip just before hanging it. (Sherwin-Williams Co.)

Now fold the top of the strip down to the middle, paste to paste, Fig. 20-11. Be careful (especially with mylars and foil) not to crease the wallcovering. Fold the bottom upward to the middle in the same way.

If using a small table, finish applying the paste to the bottom half of the wallcovering and then fold the bottom edge to the middle, paste to paste.

The preceding folding procedure is called "booking" and will keep the adhesive moist while you get ready to hang this strip. It also makes it much easier to handle.

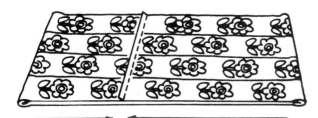

Fig. 20-11. Fold the paper to touch paste side to paste side. This step makes hanging easier. Some papers must set at this stage a few minutes before hanging. (Sherwin-Williams Co.)

HANGING THE FIRST STRIP

Take the first strip and open the top fold. Slide the strip into position against your plumb line. If you are starting in a corner, let the edge lap around the corner about 1/2 in. (12 mm). Leave about 2 in. (50 mm) at the top and 2 in. at the bottom for trimming.

Use an edge of a smoother or use a smoothing brush to force the wallcovering into the ceiling line. See Fig. 20-12. Follow down with a few strokes to help the wallcovering adhere lightly. Unfold the bottom half and slide it carefully into position next to the plumb line, Fig. 20-13.

A

B

Fig. 20-12. A — Use a smoother to push the paper into the corner at the ceiling line. (Glidden) B — Another kind of fit at ceiling line. (Sherwin-Williams Co.)

Fig. 20-13. Unfold the bottom half and adjust edge parallel to plumb line. (Glidden)

Fig. 20-15. Trim the floor edge, wall edge, or ceiling edge. Use a six inch wallscraper or putty knife to guide the knife blade. (Sherwin-Williams Co.)

Fig. 20-14. Use a smoothing brush or board to set the paper in place. To remove air bubbles, work from the center toward the edge. (Sherwin-Williams Co.)

The second or other strip should be hung in exactly the same manner, but be sure the seams match. Do not overlap the seams. Butt them together gently so that they just meet.

After trimming the second strip, use a seam roller, unless the pattern is flocked, to firm up the seams, Fig. 20-16. Do not apply more than about 5 lbs. of pressure.

When the entire strip is even with the plumb line, smooth it out carefully, Fig. 20-14. Work out any bubbles by coaxing them from the center to the top and to the sides.

Take your wallpaper knife and carefully trim the excess paper at the ceiling, floor, or other edge. See Fig. 20-15. Use your putty knife as a guide between the wallpaper and the knife.

Fig. 20-16. After the piece has been fully smoothed, roll the seams to assure a good bond. (Sherwin-Williams Co.)

Rinse off the strips as you go with a clean damp sponge to remove excess paste, Fig. 20-17. Also, be sure to remove any paste from the ceiling, baseboard, and trim. This is very important.

INSPECT THE WORK

Now is the time to step back and take a good look at your wallcovering. If everything looks good, then keep on going around the walls. Do not skip any areas above, below, or even placed over doors or windows as you go.

Fig. 20-17. Before starting next piece, wipe surface to remove excess paste. (Sherwin-Williams Co.)

HANGING THE CORNER

Corners need not cause trouble. They are not difficult to do. They just take a different procedure. Since corners are rarely straight, you need to snap a new plumb line on the next wall every time you turn a corner.

Measure from the edge of the last strip into the corner at both the ceiling and the baseboard, Fig. 20-18. Add 1/2 in. (12 mm) to each measurement

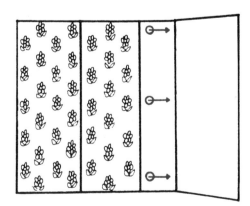

Fig. 20-18. Preparation for hanging a corner. Measure the space. (Sherwin-Williams Co.)

and mark this distance on your next strip. Cut it vertically to that measurement, saving the leftover portion. Paste and hang the first portion of the strip the same way you have hung the others. The only difference is that this strip will wrap onto the next wall about 1/2 in.

Refer to Fig. 20-19. Measure the width of the leftover paper that you have just cut. Measure that same distance from the corner onto the new wall and snap a new plumb line. Hang this cut strip of paper even with your new plumb line. It will overlap the first half of that strip in the corner by 1/2 in. A special vinyl glue may be needed for the overlap area of vinyl wallcoverings.

HANGING DOORS AND WINDOWS

The method of hanging at doors and windows depends on the pattern in the wallcovering. There are two cases to consider:
1. The pattern takes more than 2 ft. to repeat.
2. It takes less than about 2 ft. to repeat.

In the first case, apply the full strip starting at the ceiling just as you did on the rest of the wall. Do not try to fit the pieces, See Fig. 20-20. Only make rough cuts as needed to reduce tension or wrinkles.

Cut out the window or door area with your scissors, leaving 2 in. (50 mm) for closer trimming later. Make some diagonal cuts at the corner so that the wallcovering will be smooth and flat on the wall around the frame. Later, trim it closely with your wallpaper knife just as you did at the ceiling and baseboard.

For the second case, meaning a short pattern repeat, you can cut and fit the pieces around the

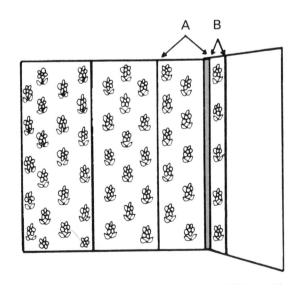

Fig. 20-19. Cut part A of the corner piece 1/2 in. wider than the wall space. Hang part A with the 1/2 in. going around the corner. Snap a plumb line at a distance from the corner equal to the width of the next piece (the remainder). Hang piece B against the plumb line, overlapping A. (Sherwin-Williams Co.)

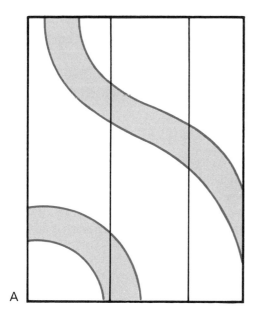

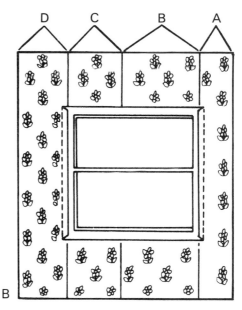

Fig. 20-20. A — If pattern repeat takes more than about 2 ft., then do not stop for windows or doors or you will have trouble matching patterns and butting the seams. Cover over the openings, make rough cuts to release wrinkles, and leave finish cuts until later. B — If pattern repeats in less than about 2 ft., then cut and fit pieces around doors and windows. (Sherwin-Williams Co.)

door or window. Try to produce a 1/2 in. overlap on at least one side. Two overlaps are preferred.

SWITCH PLATES

Remove all of your switch plates before hanging any wallcovering. It is also good to turn off the current at the fuse box as you approach an outlet, particularly if you are handling a mylar or foil wallcovering. Hang right over the outlet. Then with your scissors or wallpaper knife, carefully cut away the paper covering the outlet or switch, Fig. 20-21.

Your room is now completed. Look around to see if you have any partial rolls or strips left over. You can use these for some special decorating touches that will give your room a coordinated look. You can line your drawers or an old chest with the leftover wallcovering. You can cover a wastebasket, a lamp shade, or even books, or you can make placemats and window shades.

PREPASTED WALLCOVERINGS

If you will be hanging a prepasted wallcovering, read the special instructions that come with every roll. Then just cut, match, and trim as with any other wallcovering.

Since the wallcovering is prepasted, all you need is a water tray filled about 2/3 full with lukewarm water, Fig. 20-22.

Turning the pattern side in, loosely roll your first strip from the bottom to the top. Now dip the paper completely into the water for the length of time recommended by the manufacturer.

Fig. 20-21. Cut around electrical openings. Turn electrical power off to avoid shock if a knife or scissors contacts the terminal screws. (Glidden)

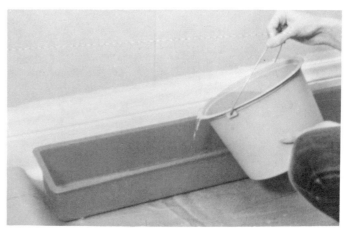

Fig. 20-22. Prepasted wallpaper is available. The paperhanger needs only to moisten to prepare the strip. (Glidden)

Place your water tray right next to the wall and pull the tip of the strip of wallcovering out of the tray as you start to climb the ladder. See Fig. 20-23. Be sure to let the excess water drain back into the tray.

Apply the strip to the wall, flush with your plumb line, leaving a two inch trim allowance at the ceiling and floor. Now smooth the wallcovering along your plumb line. Again, be sure to get out all of the trapped air.

Continue the second strip the same way. Be sure it is lined up so the seams match.

Now rinse the seams, ceiling, and baseboard with clean, cool water. It is extremely important that you always keep your rinse water clean since dry paste on the surface of the wallcovering or ceiling will show up later.

Fig. 20-23. Let paper soak the stated length of time. Grasp the two corners of top edge and steadily lift. Walk up the stepladder unrolling the strip. Hang it as before.
(Sherwin-Williams Co.)

DECORATING CHOICES

Decorating with wallcoverings is one of the least expensive and most dramatic ways of making a room over. New furniture or carpet could cost you hundreds, even thousands of dollars. You can do an entire room of wallcovering and achieve a totally new look for a lot less.

With every room you do, you become more professional. You may choose to do your kitchen in a country print, your bath in a mylar, or your entrance way in coordinated patterns.

Dealer experts will assist you with any questions you have about selecting and hanging wallcoverings or coordinating trim colors. Thousands of wallcovering patterns are available.

PAPERING CEILINGS

Always hang the ceiling before the walls. (However, you have learned about walls first.)

It is easier to hang shorter strips (width-wise in the room), but consider the whole room when deciding which direction to go.

Make a guideline for the ceiling, like that for layout of walls. You need to stretch the chalkline string very tight to snap it upward with enough force.

To prepare a guideline, note that you want an overlap of 1/2 in. (12 mm) on the long edge of the strip and 2 in. (50 mm) on the two ends, Fig. 20-24. To produce the correct overlap, subtract 1/2 in. (12 mm) from the number which is the width of the wallcovering. Measure this distance out from the wall at two or more places on the ceiling and mark with thumbtacks. Attach a chalked line and snap the layout line. Cut the strips 4 in. (100 mm) longer for a 2 in. overlap on each end.

Follow the pasting or applying instructions. Align the first strip with the layout line. It will overlap 1/2 in. on the nearby wall.

Have someone hold the rest of the strip while positioning and smoothing it out. The empty roll tube or a round stick may help to hold the end.

If only the ceiling is being hung, trim the excess with a razor-sharp knife. If the side walls are going to be hung, trim so there is about 1/4 in. (6 mm) overlap down the sidewall.

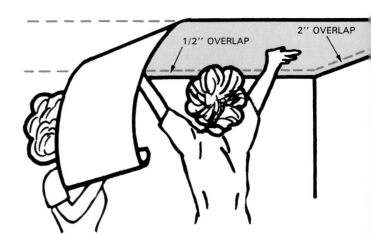

Fig. 20-24. Hanging the ceiling. To avoid getting paste on walls, hang the ceiling first. Note the recommended overlap on ends and sides.

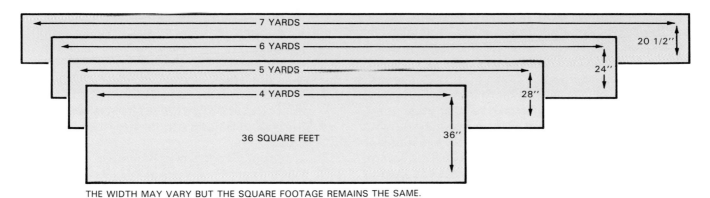

THE WIDTH MAY VARY BUT THE SQUARE FOOTAGE REMAINS THE SAME.

Fig. 20-25. Standard rolls are usually packaged in 2 or 3 roll bolts. Since most walls are 8 ft. high, the greater length helps avoid waste.

ESTIMATING COVERAGE

A single roll of wallcovering contains 36 square feet and is usually packaged in double roll bolts. See Fig. 20-25. For estimating purposes, however, consider each single roll as 30 square feet. That allows for normal waste and matching.

Fig. 20-26 provides an example for a calculation. Measure the distance around your room in feet. Multiply that by the height, floor to ceiling, to get

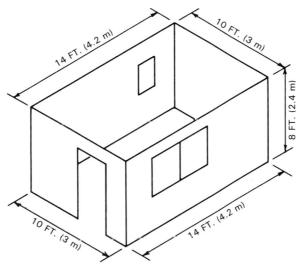

1. Measure the entire distance in FEET around the entire room.	WALLS (AROUND) 10 + 10 + 14 + 14 = 48'
2. Multiply this by the HEIGHT of the walls (in feet).	HEIGHT OF WALL (8') x 8
3. This gives you the SQUARE FOOTAGE of TOTAL wall area.	TOTAL AREA 384 sq. ft.
4. DEDUCT for openings by multiplying the width x the height of each opening and subtracting the sum from the above.	OPENINGS WINDOW 3 x 2 = 6 WINDOW 3 x 6 = 18 DOOR 6½ x 3 = 19½ 43½ − 43½ sq. ft.
5. This gives you the actual wall space to be covered.	ACTUAL AREA 340½ sq. ft.
6. Divide this figure by 30 to find the approximate number of rolls to order.**	ROLLAGE 340½ + 30 = 11.4 or 12 SINGLE ROLLS.

** Keep in mind that there are 36 square feet of wallcovering in a single roll and that by dividing by 30 instead of 36, you are allowing for match and waste on an average room. If the strips must be extra-long, if there are no spaces above doors and windows where shorter pieces can be used, or if the pattern repeat is large, then you must allow for additional rollage.

Fig. 20-26. Calculation for wallcovering amount.

the total area of the room in square feet. Now divide that figure by 30 to get the number of single rolls you'll need. Round off to the next highest number and this should be the number of single rolls needed. Or use a chart to find the number of rolls needed. See Fig. 20-27.

Also consider any windows, doors, or other openings. If a wallcovering is plain or its pattern repeats often, you can cut short pieces to fit instead of wasting a whole strip. So, for every two average size openings in a room, such as regular doors and windows, subtract one single roll. This will be the total number of rolls needed.

For a long pattern do not subtract any rolls. This will avoid running out of paper.

SINGLE ROLLS OF SIDEWALL

Distance around room in feet	8 ft. high	9 ft. high	10 ft. high	12 ft. high	Single Rolls of Ceiling	Single Yards of Border
36	10	12	12	16	4	13
40	12	12	14	16	4	14
44	12	14	16	18	4	16
48	12	14	16	20	6	17
52	14	16	18	22	6	18
56	16	18	20	24	8	20
60	16	18	20	24	8	21
64	18	20	22	26	10	23
68	18	22	24	28	10	24
72	20	22	24	30	12	25

If pattern repeat is less than 2 ft., deduct one single roll approximately 30 sq. ft. for each two openings of ordinary size.

Fig. 20-27. Quick reference chart for estimating wallcoverings. (Imperial)

CLEANING WALLPAPER

For dusty, but not greasy dirt, a good quality dough-type, non-crumbling cleaner will usually give good results. These mixtures are easy to handle and will do a thorough job of cleaning wallpaper or window shades.

Grease spots may be removed by a mixture of Fuller's Earth (a type of tan, brittle clay) and a nonflammable dry cleaning fluid. Make a paste of these two ingredients and apply about 1/8 to 1/4 in. thick. When dry, remove with a brush or soft cloth.

TEST YOUR KNOWLEDGE — CHAPTER 20

1. Because vinyl wall coverings are _____ , they help avoid kinks.
2. Wallcovering rolls bought at one time should have the same _____ number.
3. Before papering, seal walls with a _____ primer.
4. Start the first strip at a corner or _____ .
5. What is "booking"?

6. The most common type of seam is the:
   a. Lapped.
   b. Butt.
   c. Tapered.
   d. Wire edge.
7. If a pattern takes less than 2 ft. to repeat, it is best to leave strips unbroken when covering a wall having a door or window. True or False?
8. A corner overlap should be _____ in.
9. What inexpensive item allows a prepasted wallcovering to be put up quickly?
10. Prepasted wallcoverings are rolled up and placed in the water tray with the pattern side _____ (in, out).
11. Arrange the following jobs in the proper order:
    a. Hanging ceilings.
    b. Painting ceilings.
    c. Hanging walls.
    d. Painting walls.
12. To trim paper while it is in place, guide your knife with:
    a. Skilled wrist control.
    b. A large putty knife.
    c. A carpenter's square.
    d. Knuckle friction on nearby surface.
13. A single roll of wallcovering contains _____ sq. ft.
14. To allow for waste, assume each roll has _____ sq. ft.
15. Most non-greasy dirt can be removed from wallcoverings by using a type of cleaning _____ .
16. Remove grease spots with _____ _____ and nonflammable cleaning fluid.

KNOW THESE TERMS
Wall coverings, plumb line, paste, booking, overlap.

SUGGESTED ACTIVITIES
On sheets of graph paper, draw patterns that represent the straight match, drop match, and random match patterns. You may want to create patterns that repeat after one, two, three, or more cycles. Then fit two or more sheets edge-to-edge. Cut the top and bottom edges even. Note how much waste is produced for each pattern type due to adjusting the pattern.

Visit a local wallcovering supply center. Find out what types of paste are available. Note any special instructions on containers for vinyl coverings. Do any of the adhesives produce hazardous vapors in unventilated areas? Summarize your findings in an essay or report.

CAREERS
Wallpaper hanger, interior designer, materials salesperson.

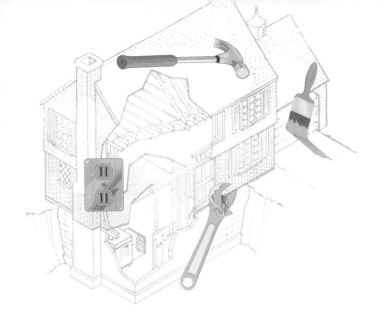

21

PICTURE FRAMING

This chapter tells how to make picture frames with commercial quality. It describes ways to assemble the many parts used.

After studying this chapter, you will be able to:
- State what tools and materials are needed.
- Plan the project.
- Estimate quantities needed.
- Describe how to make miter cuts for frame pieces.
- List some frame clamping devices.
- Explain how glass is cut.
- Choose a type of backing.
- Tell how to drive glazier's points in.
- Tell how to hang a picture frame with cable.

With the right tools and knowledge, the home mechanic can build picture frames with professional results. Excellent frames can be made based on a plan, with a fair amount of time and patience, and with a little practice on scrap lengths of moldings and liners.

GETTING THE MOLDING

The picture framing industry is a competitive industry and locating molding can be difficult. Many professionals will not sell molding stock to home framers and the choice at lumber yards is limited. However, some professionals will sell and even cut the miters.

Mail order suppliers are a good source of picture framing supplies. Usually an additional 25% of molding should be ordered.

Also, the home mechanic can shape many molding pieces with the router and several cutter bits. Selected finishing procedures and materials can provide a large source of picture framing moldings.

TOOLS NEEDED

Tools you need are a hammer, steel tape, nailset, set of drills, miter clamps, a fine toothed miter saw, and a miter box, Fig. 21-1. A miter saw is like a back saw. Materials will include wire blades 1'' to

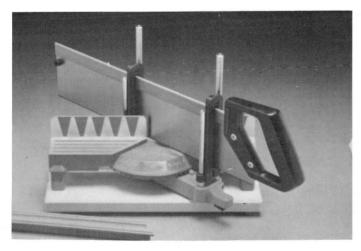

A

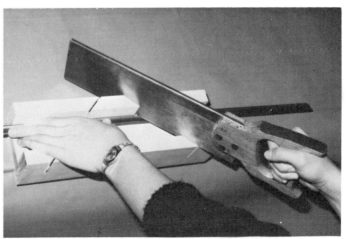

B

Fig. 21-1. A—Miter box with adjustable angle. (Woodcraft Supply Corp.) B—Miter box provides an accurate angle when cutting picture frame molding.

1 1/2'' (25 to 38 mm) in length. Select an adhesive for wood and get fine abrasive paper.

PLANNING THE CUTS AND ESTIMATING MOLDING NEEDED

First determine the size of the frame needed as measured between the rabbets (actual overall size of object being framed). Refer to Figs. 21-2 and 21-3. Add 1/8 in. (3 mm) to each dimension. For example: a picture 8 x 10 in. (203 x 254 mm) needs a frame size between the rabbets of 8 1/8 x 10 1/8 in. (206 x 257 mm). Refer to Fig. 21-3.

Allow enough molding for the waste at the miters and for the saw kerf. Allow the width of the molding for each miter cut. Suppose the selected molding is 1 1/2 in. (38 mm) wide. In this case, allow 1 1/2 in. per cut or a total of 3 in. (76 mm) per piece. Adding up the length of each molding for top and bottom is: 8 1/8 + 3 + 10 1/8 + 3 + 8 1/8 + 3 + 10 1/8 + 3 = 48 1/2 in. (206 + 76 + 257 + 76 + 206 + 76 + 257 + 76 = 1 230 mm). Add 1 in. (25 mm) for the saw kerf making the minimum of molding 49 1/2 in. (1 255 mm). Molding is sold by the foot (cm), so a purchase of 5 ft. (150 cm) will be needed.

Layout and Cutting

All miter cuts are made with the rabbeted edge of the molding toward the operator. Make the miter cut at a 45° angle to the molding length. Now lay your measuring tape or rule along the rabbet, the end carefully lined up with the cut end, Fig. 21-4.

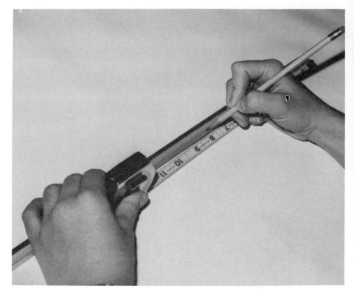

Fig. 21-4. Lay out lengths of picture frame molding on the rabbet side. Back side is up.

Make a pencil mark on the rabbet at desired place. Remember this miter cut is opposite the one already made. Cut each piece in the order that it is used in the frame. Continue until there are four pieces cut.

Before the cutting is started, there are a few precautions to be noted:
1. Secure miter box to work table.
2. Mark guidelines on the bottom of the miter box. This can be done by lightly sawing the kerf at both 45° positions on the bottom of the miter box.
3. Make some practice cuts on wood scraps and assemble to see if the corner makes a 90° angle.
4. Place the back of the molding against the rear fence and cut miter joint.
5. Continue until all pieces are cut.

ASSEMBLING THE FRAME

Many expensive miter clamping devices are available to the home framer, Fig. 21-5. However,

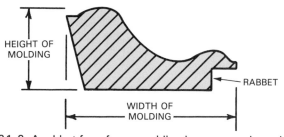

Fig. 21-2. A rabbet for a frame molding is a corner-shaped cut.

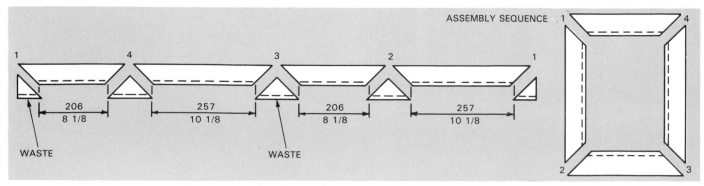

Fig. 21-3. A cutting plan and assembly sequence for picture framing.

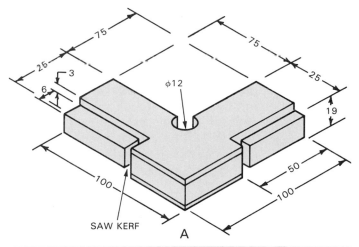

Fig. 21-5. A spring miter clamp holds a picture frame together while gluing. Another useful tool is an alignment jig. (Woodcraft Supply Corp.)

inexpensive and satisfactory clamping devices can be made in the home workshop. Four corner miter blocks with tension applied by strong rubber bands have proved highly reliable. See Fig. 21-6.

Lay out the frame members in the correct sequence. This is to make certain that the frame is not assembled with two sides the same length adjoining. However, some frames are square.

Make a dry-run assembly by clamping the four sides of the frame together with pressure. Check to see that all joints are perfectly aligned. Disassemble and leave frame components in position with respect to each other. Apply a thin coat of polyvinyl glue to both faces of miter joint at all four corners. Reassemble the clamping mechanism. Wipe all excess glue from frame joints with a clean damp cloth. Leave pressure on the joints for approximately 2 hours.

Some framers maintain that wire nails are needed to give the joint additional mechanical strength. Theoretically a well constructed and glued joint is stronger than the surrounding wood. But nails do give security, particularly for the heavier objects such as frames for mirrors and the very large pictures.

If nails are used, they should be long enough to reach nearly 2/3 their length into the second piece of the miter joint. In most cases, nails should be installed only from the top and bottom along the outside edges. Even though the scars of nail holes will be touched up, they are still apparent. However, the top and bottom are the least noticeable edges.

Touch-up

Some repair of nail holes and other blemishes may be needed. Use wax crayons or the commercial

B

Fig. 21-6. A — Corner miter blocks. The inside surface (not shown) can be slightly v-shaped to fit a variety of frames or the surface can be flat. B — Hold the clamp and frame together with strong rubber bands.

putty stix available from the local hardware or building supply store, Fig. 21-7.

MEASURING AND CUTTING GLASS

Carefully measure the length and width of the frame between the rabbets. In the case of the 8 1/8

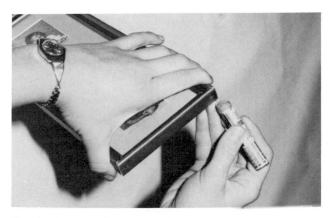

Fig. 21-7. Fill nail holes with a similar color stick putty.

x 10 1/8 in. (206 x 257 mm) frame, subtract the 1/8 in. (3 mm) from each measurement for clearance between glass and frame to arrive at the glass size of 8 x 10 in. (203 x 254 mm).

Mark the cutting lines on the glass with a wax pencil, making certain the layout lines are square.

Figs. 21-8 and 21-9 show steps for cutting glass. Also refer to Chapter 11. Lay a straightedge on the glass. Align it so the wheel of the glass cutter is on the cutting line. (Pieces of masking tape applied to the bottom of the straightedge will keep it from slipping on the glass.)

Helpful hints on cutting glass:
1. Hold the glass cutter perpendicular to the surface of the glass.
2. Keep the cutting wheel well lubricated.
3. Make a continuous even pressure stroke entirely across the glass without stopping. This ensures a clean break.
4. Make certain to score the beginning and finished points over the edge of the glass.
5. Do not delay the break after scoring. Glass tends to heal itself in a day or two. If there is a delay, re-score the glass.

Place the glass on a bench or object with a sharp edge. With the score line up, set it directly above the bench edge. Tap on the underside with the cutter or other object. The glass should break evenly

along the scored line.

Finally, wash the glass with a solution of:
1 pint of alcohol
1 gallon of water
2 tablespoons rottenstone or whiting
1 tablespoon mild liquid dishwashing soap

The alcohol and water dissolves grease and dirt, the rottenstone or whiting will polish the glass, and the detergent is an antistatic agent.

MOUNTING PICTURE INTO FRAME

There are four possible layers in a mounting for artwork: the backing, the image sheet, the matt, and the glass or plastic. They are layered from back to front in the order just given. See Fig. 21-10.

Matting a picture gives the sense of a larger piece of art work, adds difference of color, and gives a sense of a larger frame. Matts may be purchased from most art supply stores or book stores. Matts may be used to hide the white margin around the photo or lithograph image. Make the matt window about 1/8 in. (3 mm) smaller than white border. For the matt edges, allow 1/8 in. on the outside height or width.

Lay the matt face down, then measure and mark the lines for the window. Use the square to guide your pencil.

With the straightedge as a guide, use a utility, x-acto® knife, or matt cutter, Fig. 21-11, to make a bevel cut along the lines. A matt cutter has a vertical edge to follow a straightedge. The other knives require a slight aim toward the straightedge.

Backing

A type of backing material is double-faced corrugated cardboard. Cut backing material identical

Fig. 21-8. Cutting glass with the help of a straightedge. Once you start, keep moving.

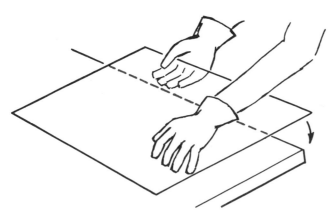

Fig. 21-9. To break glass on the cut line, place the line over a sharp edge. Some workers prefer to tap the underside with a 1/4 in. metal ball. Wear thick gloves.

Fig. 21-10. Possible picture components. You can substitute clear plastic for glass.

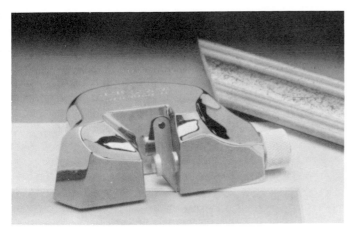

Fig. 21-11. Cut the matt on a bevel with a matt cutting tool or with a hobby knife. Slant a knife to produce about a 45° bevel. (Woodcraft Supply Corp.)

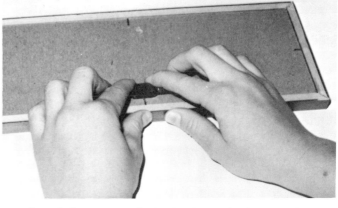

Fig. 21-12. Press a small wire brad into the frame to hold the sandwich in place. Using the side of a nail set, squeeze slowly and evenly.

in size as the glass covering. The backing both stiffens and protects the mount. Backing such as double faced corrugated board will help to absorb impacts. It also serves to pad the artwork from brads or glazier's points that keep the sandwich intact.

Note: For archival work, corrugated board is too high in acid content which might harm the mount. Substitute regular matboard with a much lower acid level, or for best results use a backing of neutral pH board manufactured for this purpose.

Assembly

To assemble the sandwich, proceed as follows:
1. Place the frame face side down on a protected surface.
2. Place the mounting sandwich (glass-object-backing) into rabbeted area.
3. Use glazier points, small brads 1/2 or 5/8 in. (12 or 50 mm), or frame staples. Press into the wood frame at intervals of approximately 4 in. (100 mm). Use one side of the square handle of a nail set to press against the head, while bracing the outside edge with the thumbs, Fig. 21-12.

INSTALLING THE DUST SEAL

Here is a popular method of sealing the sandwich into the frame. Cut a length of kraft paper approximately 1 in. (25 mm) larger in all four directions than the frame. Kraft paper is a tear-resistant paper often colored brown. Lay the kraft paper on the workbench and dampen the side that will face the frame with a sponge. Run a narrow bead of polyvinyl glue along the back edge of the frame. The bead should be sparing but continuous. Place the frame on top of the wet kraft paper. Lift the frame and press the edge so that a complete seal is formed. The paper will shrink taut as it dries. Then, with a sharp knife trim the excess paper along the

edge of frame, Fig. 21-13. Ignore any small wrinkles along the frame edge.

Polyvinyl glue is preferred for the dust seal. Other glues may pull loose under tension.

HANGING THE FRAME

The strongest and best concealed system is the standard screw eye and braided wire combination on the back of the frame. Another strong device is a picture hook, Fig. 21-14, or some nails driven into the wall.

Fig. 21-13. Trim the dust seal with a hobby (x-acto®) knife. Note edges of frame (flat edges under the kraft paper).

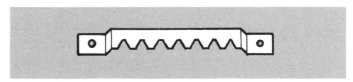

Fig. 21-14. A saw-toothed picture hanger. The notches allow for leveling of the picture frame. It is used for light to moderate weight frames.

For best results, the screw eye should be installed 1/3 of the distance from the top of the frame. See Fig. 21-15. If it is lower than 1/3, the picture tends to tilt out at the top. If higher, the wire may be seen.

With an awl, make starting holes for the screw eye, one on each side. Install the screw eyes. Thread the wire through each eye and wrap the end in a tight spiral close to the eye. Leave enough slack in the wire so the apex (top of v) is one sixth of the distance from the top of the frame (1/4 the distance from top of frame to screw eye level).

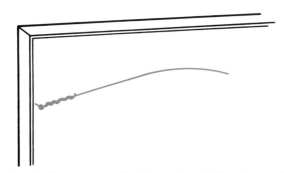

Fig. 21-15. Screw eye and cable method of hanging a picture.

For very heavy frames, install two more screw eyes in the bottom edge of the frame, each one in about one-third the distance from the sides, Fig. 21-16. Fasten one end of the braided wire to a screw eye on the bottom of frame. Thread the other end through the screw eyes on the frame sides and back to the last remaining screw eye on the bottom opposite edge.

On the wall, two hooks are stronger than one. They divide the load and help assure more level pictures.

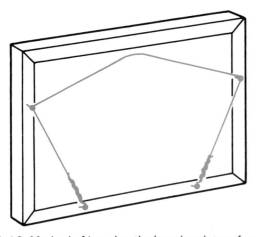

Fig. 21-16. Method of hanging the heavier picture frame. Use two screw eyes on bottom edge of frame to support it.

TEST YOUR KNOWLEDGE — CHAPTER 21

1. When ordering molding, ask for an additional _____ %.
2. A _____ saw is like a back saw.
3. The size of the frame needed is measured between the _____.
4. When estimating molding length needs, allow the _____ of the molding for a right or a left angled cut.
5. Make all miter cuts with the _____ edge of the molding toward you.
6. An inexpensive miter clamp can be made with four corner blocks and:
   a. Wire.　　　　　c. Rubber bands.
   b. Glue.　　　　　d. Kraft paper.
7. The tip of a wire nail should extend _____ of the nail length into the second joint piece.
8. To cut glass straight, the cutter can be rolled against a _____ .
9. Make a glass scoring stroke without _____.
10. Discuss the steps used to break glass on a scored line.
11. Allow _____ in. on the outside height or width of a matt.
12. When cutting the mat window, aim a handheld knife slightly _____ (toward, away from) the straightedge.
13. Arrange the following picture mounting parts in the proper order from front to back:
    a. Matt.　　　　　c. Glass or plastic.
    b. Backing.　　　　d. Image sheet.
14. Glazier points, small brads, or staples can be pushed into the frame with the handle of a _____ .
15. A dust seal that tightens when it dries is made of _____ _____ .
16. When hanging a heavy picture frame with screw eyes, use _____ of them.

KNOW THESE TERMS

Miter box, back saw, miter clamp, matt board, dust seal, straight edge.

SUGGESTED ACTIVITIES

Discuss in class why a frame measurement must be taken on the inside edge of the rabbet. What errors could occur if you measure at other positions?

At a craft supply store, investigate the most recent ways to frame and to hang an artwork piece. Note if any frames are made of plastic or metal. Also note substitutes for glaziers' points. Look at surface fixing fluids for chalk or other smearable colors. When can glass be omitted? Make a report and present it to your class.

CAREERS

Picture framer, gallery proprietor.

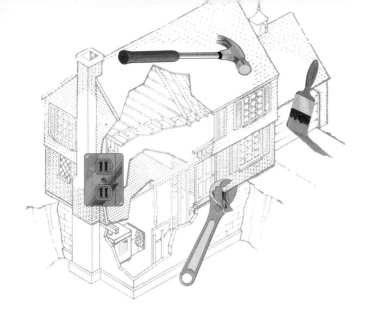

22

UPHOLSTERY

This chapter introduces the tools, materials, and methods used in common upholstery work. It describes overstuffed and spring type chair construction. The chapter includes an estimating chart for fabric amounts needed.

After studying this chapter, you will be able to:
- State the uses of seven tools.
- Describe types of tacks, webbing, springs, and cloth.
- State the purpose of webbing.
- Begin an eight-way tie.
- Estimate fabric needed.
- Recall cleaning procedures.
- Reweb lawn furniture.
- Tell how to repair loose dowel or tenon joints.

Upholstery is usually classified into three categories:
1. Padded construction.
2. Pad and spring combination.
3. Overstuffed.

Parts of the padded and the overstuffed are shown in Fig. 22-1.

Padded construction uses no springs. It uses a solid base or uses webbing to support the padding. When frequent change of outer fabric is necessary, the simple padded method of upholstery is usually preferred. An example is the dining chair.

With pad and spring combination, the seat may have springs while the back is padded. The spring base or back may be made of either the coil or no-sag zigzag type of metal wire spring. Examples of

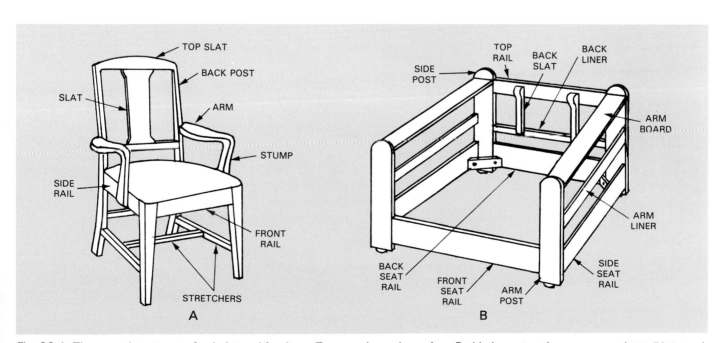

Fig. 22-1. There are three types of upholstered furniture. Two are shown here. A — Padded construction uses no springs. (Universal Seng) B — Overstuffed construction uses springs in seat and back. These frames are usually entirely covered by upholstery.

spring type upholstery are the light chair and the rocker. Springs are sometimes used in a high quality ottoman.

In overstuffed furniture, both seats and backs have springs. Examples are living room chairs and divans. Special interconnected springs may be used under padding and cushions of high quality units.

For overstuffed furniture, padding of cotton or foam products is often 2 in. thick. Some of the latest styles of upholstered furniture use preformed foam shapes of padding.

UPHOLSTERY TOOLS

A complete set of tools is essential to the upholsterer to make the process easier and faster. See Fig. 22-2. Some tools are quite common and still others are highly specialized.

Tack Hammer

The tack hammer is a basic tool needed for the various forms of upholstery tacks. The special shape of the head makes it easy to use in many close places. The double-faced type is recommended. One face is a magnetic face which enables the upholsterer to pick up, hold, and start tacks easily.

Tack Lifter

The tack lifter or tack claw is indispensable for removing the old tacks. The tack lifter has a V-notch on the bevel end. This notch makes it easy to get under the tack head. Then, with lever action, it lifts the tack from the wood frame.

Ripping Chisel

The ripping chisel is similar to the tack lifter but without the notch. It can be used to remove tacks driven tightly into the wood and to help remove an entire panel that may have blind tacks holding it.

Staple Lifter

Today, upholstery manufacturers have found ways to speed up production. They have abandoned the upholstery tack in favor of a staple to hold the fabric and material to the frame. The staple lifter is designed to get under and evenly lift both legs of the staple.

Upholstery Shears

Shears are heavy-duty scissors used to cut coarse fabrics, tying twine, and heavy burlap. The tool is large enough to reduce stress on the hand when cutting a large amount of material.

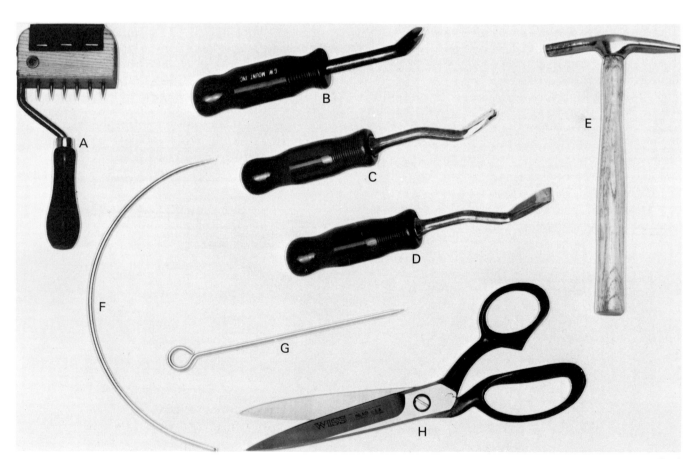

Fig. 22-2. Tools used for upholstery. A—Jute webbing stretcher. B—Tack lifter. C—Staple lifter. D—Ripping chisel. E—Tack hammer. F—Curved needle. G—Pin or skewer. H—Shears. (George W. Mount Co.)

Webbing Stretcher

Webbing stretchers are used to stretch jute webbing on open frames if springs are to be used or if webbing is the only support for padding. Webbing pliers may be used to stretch plastic or rubber in addition to the jute webbing. Stretchers for steel webbing are available.

Needles

An upholstery tool kit includes an assortment of needles. The curved needles range in a variety of sizes from 1 1/2 in. (38 mm) to several inches in circumference.

Straight needles may be single or double pointed with lengths from 4 to 20 in. (10 to 50 cm). Double-pointed needles are used to apply buttons.

Less like a needle is the upholstery pin or skewers, heaving lengths from 2 1/2 in. (62 mm) to 4 in. (100 mm). A pin has a loop for a head. Upholstery pins are convenient for holding fabric covers in place temporarily for tacking or sewing.

UPHOLSTERY MATERIAL

A large variety of materials are used for upholstery of all the different styles: for foundation, stuffing and padding, and for the final covering.

Tacks

These four basic types of tacks are used in upholstery: the upholstery tack, the webbing tack, the gimp tack, and the decorator tack. Some of these are shown in Fig. 22-3.

The upholstery tack has a flat head and a smooth tapered shank. Sizes range from the number 1 ounce to 12 ounces, with the 4, 6, 8, and 12 commonly used. Available tack gauge sizes are listed in Fig. 22-4.

Webbing tacks have barbed shanks which give more holding power to tack webbing. The numbers 12 and 14 ounce sizes are commonly used.

Gimp tacks have a small round head like a half sphere. They have heads about 1/8 in. wide. Gimp tacks range in size from number 2 ounce to number 8 ounce. These are often called No. 2 or No. 8, and so on. The No. 4 and 6 are most commonly used. The gimp tack is usually colored beige, green, rust, black, gold, or tan. These tacks hold the decorative gimp over seams and edges of upholstery material.

Decorator tacks are "metalene" nails. They are fancy sphere-headed tacks used for added decoration on leather or other fabric coverings. The

UPHOLSTERY TACK SIZES AND LENGTH

No.	Length inches	mm
1	3/16	4.76
1 1/2	7/32	5.55
2	1/4	6.32
2 1/2	5/16	7.93
3	3/8	9.52
4	7/16	11.11
6	1/2	12.70
8	9/16	14.28
10	5/8	15.87
12	11/16	17.46
14	3/4	19.05
16	13/16	20.63
18	7/8	22.22
20	15/16	23.40
22	1	25.40
24	1 1/2	28.57

Fig. 22-4. Upholstery tack sizes and lengths.

A

B

Fig. 22-3. Some types of tacks. A—No. 12 upholstery tacks are quite large. B—Gimp tacks are packaged in 1/4 lb. and larger containers.

diameter of the head is about 3/8 in. (10 mm). Decorator tacks are often used where an exposed tack is unavoidable.

Webbing

Three basic types of webbing are found in the catalog of upholstery supplies: jute, steel, and decorative.

Jute webbing, Fig. 22-5, is the most frequently used. It is exceptionally strong, woven of the natural jute fibers, and will stretch very little. It is available in 3, 3 1/2, and 4 in. (76, 88, and 100 mm) widths with the 3 1/2 in. most common. The webbing is interwoven in a crosslap pattern as a base support for the loose coil springs.

Steel webbing is about 3/4 to 1 in. (19 to 25 mm) wide. It is used to support the coil springs on a sofa.

Decorative webbing is usually made of plastic in many different weave patterns and colors. It is used on lawn furniture, folding chairs, and other places where the webbing serves as the complete seat and back.

Fig. 22-5. Jute webbing.

Springs

Upholstery springs are manufactured as single coil, double coil, and zigzag springs, and also bar spring units.

Coil springs are selected for their shape and firmness. A double coil spring is shown in Fig. 22-6. The weight of the spring is governed by the gauge of wire from which they are made. Usually a 9 or 11 gauge is most frequently used and matched to the load the spring is intended to carry.

Since the seat section normally has a greater load, the 9 ga. is used. The back section generally uses the 11 ga. coil springs.

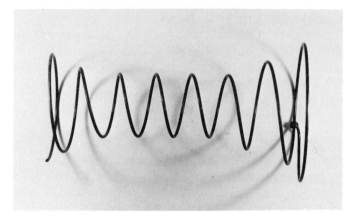

Fig. 22-6. Double coil spring.

Spring length and coil diameter are also factors of selection. They range from 4 to 14 in. (100 to 355 mm) in height and from 3 to 5 in. (76 to 127 mm) in diameter.

Back and cushion coil springs are smaller, made with wire gauge of 12 to 15. Heights range from 4 to 8 in. In back or cushion units, they may be tied together with small helical springs.

Cushion units may have each spring sewn into a small cloth bag and arranged into a series of rows and columns within the unit. The set is called a Marshall spring unit.

Zigzag springs, often called no-sag or sinuous springs, are made of heavy wire (9 or 11 ga). bent into a series of sinuous curves, Fig. 22-7. Two or

Fig. 22-7. No-sag or zigzag spring. (Gregory Lund)

more are usually used from front to back or from side to side. This forms a spring base seat or back. Metal links may distribute the weight from one spring to another.

A bar spring unit or drop-in unit is a bar with multiple single coils attached to it. The bar of each unit is fastened to the frame. These eliminate the use of webbing.

Padding

Padding material may be feathered straw, down, hog hair, cotton felt, or plastic foams. Cotton felt and plastic foams are the most often used padding material today.

Cotton felt is prepared in sheets or layers approximately 1 in. (25 mm) thick and 27 in. (68 cm) wide and in various length rolls. Bolts may be either soft, medium, or firm. Cotton is often used as the only padding for solid base seats. Cotton should always be torn apart instead of cut with shears.

OTHER MATERIALS

There are too many materials to classify them all. The following is a partial list:

1. Plastic foam may be preformed or it is available in sheet thickness of 1/2 to 4 in. (12 to 100 mm). Sheet size is usually 24 in. (60 cm) wide by 30 ft. (9 m) long.

   Preformed cushions are available as replacements for chairs and divans.
2. Burlap in sheet form is used to cover the springs. It is made from jute fibers, a very strong and long-lasting material for the foundation work in the upholstery unit, Fig. 22-8. Usually an 8 to 10 ounce (232 to 290 gram) weight is used. Widths are 30 and 40 in. (76 and 100 cm). Burlap is then covered with the stuffing and padding materials.

3. Muslin is a light cotton cloth, Fig. 22-9. It is used to cover the padding, and helps to hold padding in place while the final covering is being installed. Muslin is supplied in 36 in. (90 cm) wide rolls. It usually has a 64 x 64 count weave.

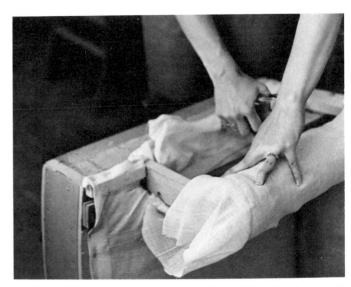

Fig. 22-9. Muslin is used to help hold padding in place. It is a thin cotton cloth that simplifies the job of covering with the final fabric.

4. Welt cord is sewn into the final fabric to form a bead around seats, cushions, or other trim areas. See Fig. 22-10. Welt can be bought in many sizes and is made of jute fibers or twisted cotton. Some furniture makers use a hollow plastic welt to get a variety of seam shapes.
5. Tack strip is made of 3/8 to 1/2 in. (9 to 12 mm) wide cardboard strips, Fig. 22-11. These

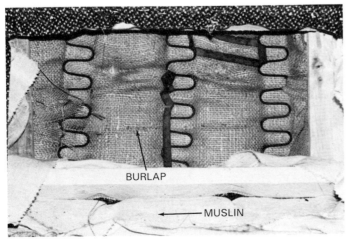

BURLAP

MUSLIN

Fig. 22-8. Burlap is a strong foundation fabric used in upholstery. (The Wrenn House)

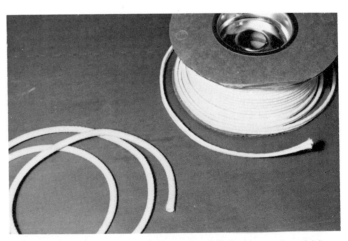

Fig. 22-10. Welt cord placed under fabric is used to hide a seam, provide wear life, or add decoration. Note the double ply cord.

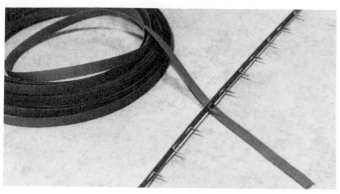

Fig. 22-11. Most tack strips are 1/2 in. (12 mm) cardboard strips. They act as visual guides for placing tacks in straight lines by hand. Strips may be metal and may be available pretacked.

Fig. 22-13. Cambric is a thin dark fabric applied to the bottom of the upholstered unit. In this use, it is often called a dust panel.

strips are used to produce blind tacking on straight and welted seams and on the final cover if it must be blind tacked.

Pretacked tack strip, Fig. 22-12, may be purchased. It is used to blind tack such panels as the back of chairs to help conceal all signs of a tacked edge.

6. Cambric is a very thin, stiff, glazed cotton fabric. See Fig. 22-13. It is usually tacked to the bottom of the chair or couch. It is sometimes referred to as a dust panel. It prevents stuffing particles from sifting through and falling on the floor below. It also keeps house dust from collecting inside.

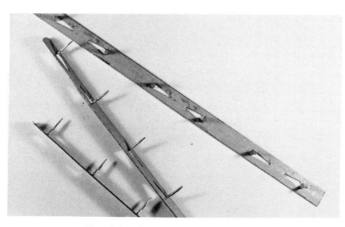

Fig. 22-12. Pretacked tack strip.

The Final Covering

Upholstered furniture is covered with a material of high wearability with many colors, patterns, and weaves. Friezes, tapestries, velours, velvets, prints, and leather texture are several of the materials that are used as the finish cover.

Synthetic products such as bonded vinyl are used as a durable leather substitute. Nylon,

polyester, and polypropylene filaments are used to weave the final fabric. Today the fibers like cotton, linen, wool, and mohair are also much in demand for these final coverings.

REWEBBING AND RETYING SPRINGS

The result or goal of rewebbing is illustrated in Fig. 22-14. The example in the illustration shows how a chair with coil springs is rewebbed.

Rewebbing is a simple job to do. Webbing is expensive. Less expensive webbing will tear sooner, so buy the best. This is recognizable by a red yarn woven in each edge of the jute webbing.

To reweb a chair:
1. Remove all old webbing.
2. Tack new strip at one end with four tacks, fold over first tacks, and tack again using three #12 or #14 webbing tacks.
3. Refer to Fig. 22-15. With webbing stretcher, stretch webbing extra taut across the chair frame (do not break frame) and tack. Cut webbing about 1 1/4 in. (32 mm) longer than the frame, fold a second (or third) time, and tack securely.
4. Repeat until all strips have been replaced from side to side.
5. Repeat the previous steps for those at right angles to the finished set. Interweave the second set through the first set.

Retying Springs

Retie the springs with an upholstery needle and strong twine. Sew the spring base to the intersection of webbing. Another quicker method of fastening the spring to webbing is with the clinch-it tool (an applicator of metal clips).

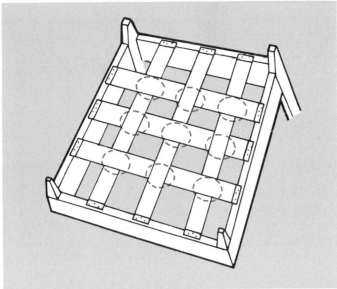

Fig. 22-14. Webbing used if the chair has coil springs. Placement of webbing has been adjusted so springs (circles) can be placed where bands cross. This gives springs better support.

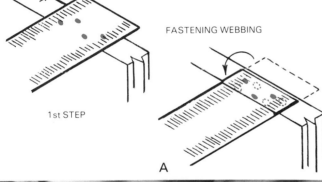

3/4" to 1 1/4"

FASTENING WEBBING

1st STEP

A

B

Fig. 22-15. Rewebbing steps. A—How to tack down the webbing. A fold adds strength. Note that three tacks follow the use of four tacks. B—Stretching jute webbing for second side. Repeat the tack procedure.

The final step is tying at the top. To retie a furniture seat spring at the top to hold it into position permanently, use a pattern called the eight-way tie.

In learning to tie springs, study Fig. 22-16 carefully and try to imagine what happens when the spring is pushed down. Then you will understand why the twine must be placed accurately. The result of good tying is that springs are completely free to move as needed when someone sits down, but they will return to the original (symmetrical) positions when the weight is off.

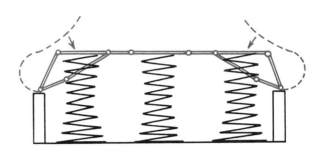

Fig. 22-16. Tying coil springs. Cords pull coils into original positions when chair is not used.

To make an eight-way tie, a tie is placed over each column from front to rear and over rows from side to side, Fig. 22-17. To complete the eight-way tie, a tie is placed in both diagonal directions. See Fig. 22-18. The eight-way tie distributes the weight and serves as an additional safeguard in case a twine breaks.

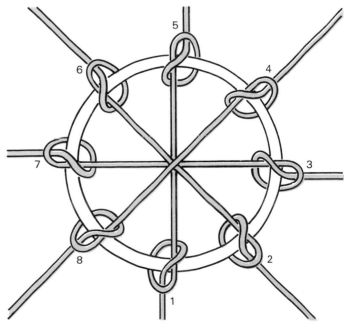

Fig. 22-17. An eight-way tie, looking down on one of the mid-unit springs. Eight knots are made around the circumference of the coil.

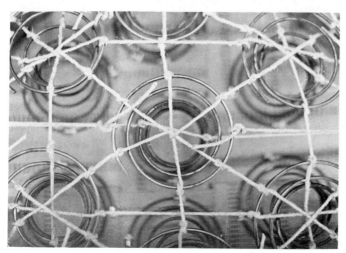

Fig. 22-18. When completed, the tied unit looks something like this. The vertical and horizontal cords were done first. Then the diagonals were tied.

Whenever twines cross, they should be tied with a lock knot. The tension on each twine should be nearly even as they can be made. If one is too loose or too tight, redo it. Otherwise the tight twine will take all the strain and may soon break.

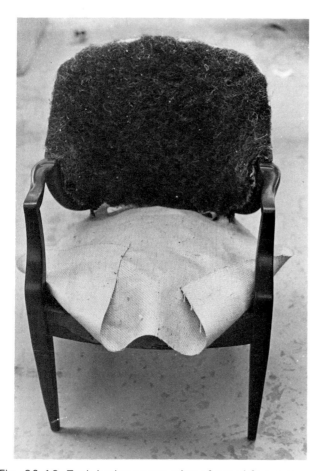

Fig. 22-19. Tack burlap to top edge of wood frame to cover coil springs and keep padding from falling through. Pull by hand as tight as possible. Note the bulge due to springs below.

Cover the Spring

For the first layer covering the springs, use a 10 ounce burlap fabric. See Fig. 22-19. Use No. 8 to 10 tacks and tack burlap to the top edge of spring frame. Start at the back and stretch burlap from back to front. Next stretch and tack the burlap from side to side. Any arm or back support may need a slot cut. Fold over the waste edge and tack a second time.

OTHER OPERATIONS AND PRODUCTS

Some upholstery work depends to a great extent on personal preference. The quantity or arrangement of padding, the fabric weight for the final covering, or the addition of buttons can be chosen for their effects. A description of uses follows.

Stuffing and Padding

All of the operations in upholstery have just one purpose. That is to provide comfortable furniture. Stuffing and padding are the materials between the spring foundation and the final covering, Fig. 22-20. They have several purposes:

1. To cover the springs and level the space between the springs.
2. To give additional resilience to the unit.
3. To give the final shape and contour to the upholstered unit.

Fig. 22-20. Cotton felt and foam padding are used to cover the coarse filling materials just before the final covering.

The padding of fine cotton will give the surface smoothness necessary for the final covering. Some steps involving the final covering are shown in Fig. 22-21.

Tying Buttons

A final step is to add buttons if desired. To tie buttons, use nylon tufting twine. First, thread it through the eyelet of the button. Then thread both ends through the eye of a double-pointed straight needle. Pull the needle through the covering to the inside.

A

B

Fig. 22-21. A—When upholstery coverings must be attached without clear access to the reverse side, use the curved needle. B—Fastening loose edges to frame with staples. (Duo-Fast Corp.)

With thread in place, remove the needle and separate the twine ends. Pull to desired tension while checking the depth of button. Refer to Fig. 22-22. Tie the ends over a wad of cotton.

ESTIMATING THE AMOUNT OF FABRIC

Probably the most precise method of determining how much fabric will be needed to cover a specific piece, is to remove all the present covering. Lay out two parallel chalk marks on the work floor with a width of 54 in. (137 cm). Between

Fig. 22-22. To attach button strings, thread the two ends through the front at one time using a double-pointed needle. Then tie them off using cotton wads for tension.

these lines, lay out all the fabric pieces. Measure the distance in yards. This will be the needed amount.

The reason is as follows. Upholstery fabrics are woven and sold in widths of 54 in. (137 cm). When all pieces are fit together between 54 in. lines, the resulting length corresponds to the probable cut length.

A second method is to measure the fabric while still on the chair, Fig. 22-23. Measure each panel into its rectangular dimensions and transfer these dimensions to the 54 in. width.

Fig. 22-23. To estimate fabric for the chair, measure each piece from side to side and also from front to back or top to bottom. Place each rectangle measure in proper relation to the 54 in. (140 cm) standard roll width.

213

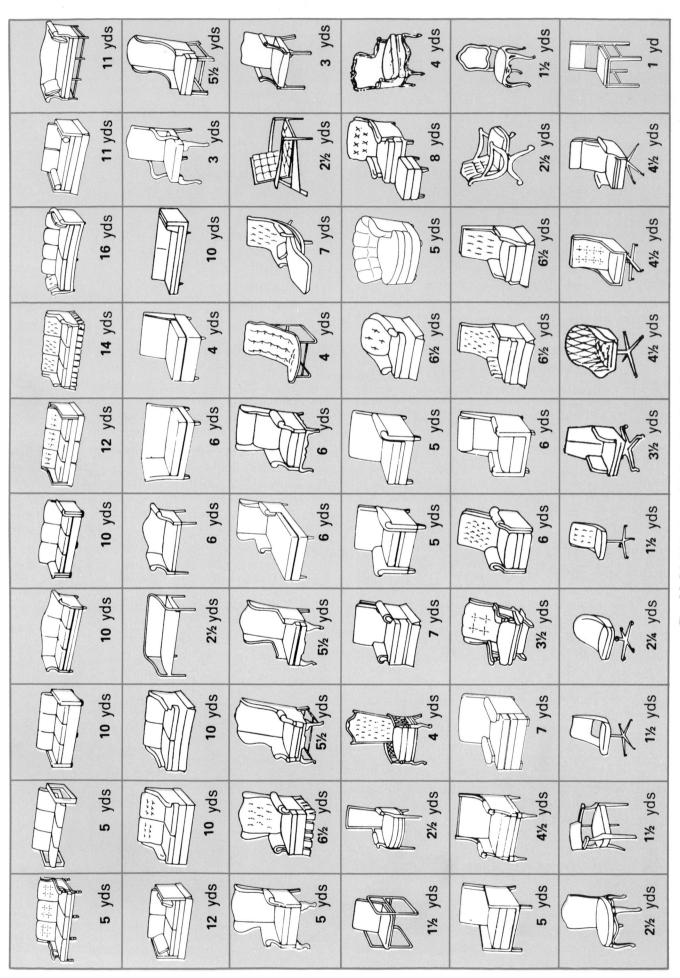

Fig. 22-24. Upholstery fabric estimating table.

A third method is to use the accompanying chart of fabric yardage. Locate the upholstery unit which is similar to the one to be reupholstered and use its estimate, Fig. 22-24.

SUGGESTED CLEANING PROCEDURES

To remove any soil from upholstery, a good understanding is necessary of the type and nature of the many fabrics used in upholstery. However, here are general procedures for some common cleaning problems.

Ordinary Dirt

Most dirt can be removed by washing with warm water and mild soap. Apply water to a large area and allow to soak for a few minutes. Brisk rubbing with a cloth should then remove dirt and soil. This procedure may be repeated in case of stubborn or embedded dirt. A soft bristled brush may be used after the soap has been applied.

If still extremely difficult to remove, a powdered cleanser may be used. These should be used more cautiously. Avoid contact with the wood or metal parts of the furniture or with any soft fabric which may be a part of the furniture.

Removing Chewing Gum

Chewing gum may be removed by careful scraping and by the application of kerosene or naphtha.

Fig. 22-25. A lawn chair often has torn webbing as shown. Webbed lawn chairs can be restored with little cost and time.

Before scraping, use ice to harden the gum. Do not wait too long after discovery of chewing gum to attempt removal.

Tars, Asphalt, and Creosote

These products will stain the vinyl fabrics if allowed to remain in contact. Wipe off as quickly as possible. Clean the area with a cloth dampened with kerosene and naphtha.

Paint

Paint should be removed immediately. Do not use paint remover or a liquid type brush cleaner. Use a clean white cloth dampened with kerosene, painters' naphtha, or turpentine, if the paint is an oil base product. Use water dampened cloth if paint is a latex base product. Try to keep these fluids from contact with soft fabrics or with the wooden areas of furniture.

Nail Polish or Nail Polish Remover

These substances will cause permanent harm to vinyl coverings, and wood or metal parts on prolonged contact. Fast and careful wiping or immediate blotting after contact will minimize the staining. Spreading of the liquid while removing should be avoided.

Ballpoint Pen Ink

Ballpoint pen ink may sometimes be removed if rubbed immediately with a damp cloth using water and soap or rubbing alcohol.

REWEBBING LAWN FURNITURE

Lightweight folding lawn furniture sometimes has torn webbing, Fig. 22-25. The webbing is easily reconditioned. Almost any hardware, variety store, or lumber yard will stock replacement plastic webbing strips for lawn furniture. In just a few minutes, the rewebbing can be completed.

Make a mental note of how the webbing pieces were interwoven and then proceed according to this plan:

1. Remove old webbing by removing holding screws or metal clamps, Fig. 22-26.
2. Measure length of replacement webbing (usually on each unit two different lengths are used). Refer to Fig. 22-27.
3. Cut new pieces.
4. Decide to start with either the side to side pieces or the front-back-top pieces. Prepare to duplicate the folding pattern and mounting holes of the original pieces.
5. Fold the end to reinforce the holding hole and work screw into it, Fig. 22-28.
6. Mount on the frame. Finish all strips in that direction.

Fig. 22-26. Start by removing the metal clip or screws holding the webbing to the tubular frame.

Fig. 22-27. Use the old webbing to get the measurement of the new. To match, unfold both ends of the pattern piece.

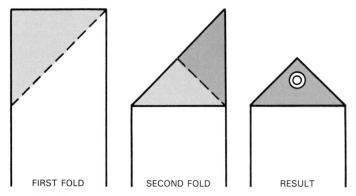

FIRST FOLD   SECOND FOLD   RESULT

Fig. 22-28. Fold to reinforce the webbing end. Extra thickness helps hold the fastening screw.

7. For the second length pieces, interweave them into the existing strips (over-under-over), Fig. 22-29.

8. With the number two strip, weave (under-over-under, etc).

The result is shown in Fig. 22-30.

CHAIR FRAME REPAIR

The simplest chairs, small tables, and other furniture are made by the leg-rail method with joints

Fig. 22-29. Weave each cross web in a basket-weave pattern.

Fig. 22-30. The completed unit is ready for use with little cost in materials and in a small amount of time.

that are either mortise-and-tenon or doweled and glued in place. Through use, the stress put on the legs becomes too much for the wood or glue joint and it loosens.

With a little time and care, the unit can be refinished. Often the upholstered chair will need some work on the frame before the reupholstering begins.

If all the joints seem to be loose, disassemble the entire chair. With the putty knife or other sharp object, scrape all the old glue from the joint. Inspect the mortise-and-tenon or dowel joint for fractured or broken parts.

Replace dowels or repair with dowels or wedges. It is best to insert wooden dowels with a leather mallet. Instead of wood dowels, or in addition to wood dowels, you can use metal pins.

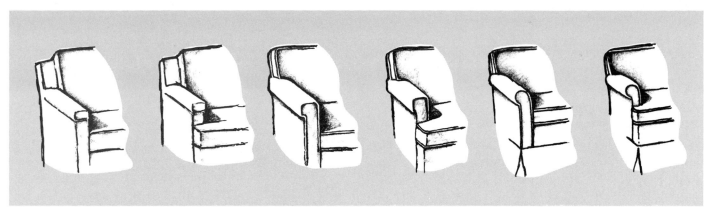

Fig. 22-31. Example of what appearance changes might be produced with slight modification of the chair frame.

You may choose to cut off a bad area instead of repairing it. A slightly different design may be possible and this sometimes is more modern. See Fig. 22-31. Many completely new parts may be made with a moderate amount of skill, experience, and equipment.

Reglue the frame. Select a good strong wood glue, one that gives a fairly long period of working time.

It takes several minutes to apply the glue. Assemble the parts, get the clamping mechanism in place, and apply pressure.

Application of pressure to the glue joints may be the success or failure of the whole project. Most chairs are not perfectly square, but are usually wider at the front than at the back. Bar clamps, Fig. 22-32, are difficult to use in this case. A band clamp is ideal, Fig. 22-33. However, the average home mechanic does not have a band clamp. A rope tourniquet may be devised to apply enough pressure.

Metal fasteners described in Chapter 6 of this text might be considered for minor reinforcing of certain chair components. Corner braces and flat angle fasteners may be used to stabilize face surfaces where edges join at 90 degrees.

When metal reinforcements are used, they should only be placed where they will be out of sight. Flat and/or angle plates may be set into shallow strip areas or ''gains'' to conceal them. See Fig. 22-34. Use a wood filler to cover the area.

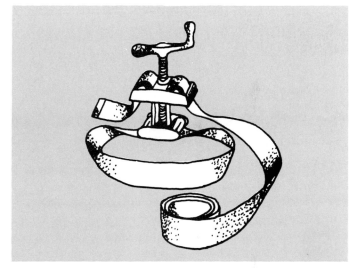

Fig. 22-33. Many applications require clamping round or irregular shaped sections, such as chair frames. This is a difficult problem. The prestretched 2 in. canvas band is a good tool for these unusual shapes. (The Woodworker's Store)

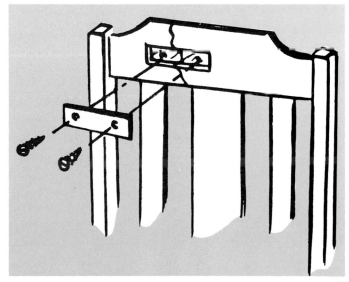

Fig. 22-34. Repair cracked wood with a mending plate. Cut a gain in the wood to conceal it. Use wood filler to blend the area. (Stanley Hardware)

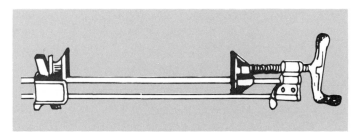

Fig. 22-32. Steel bar clamps will work for in-line clamping problems. (The Woodworker's Store)

TEST YOUR KNOWLEDGE — CHAPTER 22

1. Pick the letters for the three categories of upholstery:
   a. Stuffed.
   b. Padded.
   c. Overstuffed.
   d. Spring.
   e. Webbed.
2. The ripping chisel is used to remove _____ as well as remove panels that are held with blind tacks.
3. Barbed shanks are found on _____ tacks.
4. Common coil spring sizes are 9 ga. for the seat and _____ ga. for the back.
5. Cotton padding should be _____ instead of cut with shears.
6. Often the sheet layer next to and contacting a spring consists of _____ .
7. To tack a webbing strip securely, _____ the strip.
8. How can springs be attached to webbing?
9. Twine helps return _____ to a standard position.
10. Final coverings are attached with tacks, heavy thread, or _____ .
11. The strings for buttons are tied:
    a. To the top of springs.
    b. To webbing.
    c. Using cotton.
    d. a and c above.
    e. b and c above.
12. If you remove coverings to measure the quantity needed, you can lay them out to fit a roll width of _____ in. (cm).
13. To remove chewing gum from cloth, first apply _____ .
14. Oil base paint should be removed from furniture or cloth with:
    a. Paint remover.
    b. Lighter fluid.
    c. Kerosene.
    d. Painters' naphtha.
    e. a and c.
    f. c and d.
15. Remove ballpoint pen ink with _____ .
16. Save the old webbing from lawn chairs to:
    a. Use again.
    b. Form loops for strong support.
    c. Measure its length.
    d. Repair the torn areas.
17. Lawn chair webbing ends must be folded _____ (two times, once).
18. Wood dowels in furniture joints may be replaced with _____ _____ .
19. A band clamp or a rope _____ will provide enough pressure to set a glue joint.
20. A _____ clamp can only be used if the clamped parts are in a straight line.

KNOW THESE TERMS

Overstuffed, webbing frame, staple lifter, tack remover, ripping chisel, stretcher, gimp, double coil, welt, zigzag.

SUGGESTED ACTIVITIES

Examine a small piece of furniture such as a stool or ottoman. Decide how the piece can be reupholstered. Make a list of all steps from wood refinishing to possible slipcovers needed if the piece were in bad condition. If the piece does in fact need repairs, evaluate how long it may take to reupholster it. As time permits, and with guidance from your instructor, carry out the needed steps.

Learn how much weight tacked webbing can support. Tack one strip to a three foot frame as directed in this chapter. (Use four tacks plus three.) Make three samples: one with no fold on the strip end, one with a single fold, and one with two folds. Pile weights on the strip just until it pulls loose, if it loosens at all. Note how much weight was used. Is the weight of any person enough to harm chair webbing? Make a report to your class.

CAREERS

Upholstering, furniture salesperson, interior designer.

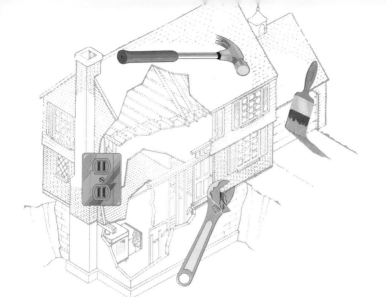

23

POTABLE WATER SYSTEM

This chapter describes the types of pipes, faucets, valves, tanks, and fittings used in a home water supply system. It tells how to repair faucets and other parts of the system. The chapter tells how to join pipes and fittings.

After studying this chapter, you will be able to:
■ Choose kinds of pipe and fittings for a job.
■ Calculate lengths of pipes with fitting allowances.
■ Tell how to solder copper pipe.
■ Tell how to join plastic pipe and fittings.
■ Recognize types of faucets with and without washers.
■ List faucet repairs a home mechanic can do.
■ Give the cause of water hammer.
■ Repair minor leaks.
■ Discuss how to maintain a water softener.

Potable (pronounced like "notable") water enters the house through the water meter and main cutoff valve. Potable water is any water treated and made pure for human consumption.

Some towns also have a non-potable supply of water, usually for lawn sprinkling. This supply is not suitable for human consumption and must be kept separated from the house supply.

The cold potable water to the fixtures and water heater is by pipes of iron, copper, or plastic. These pipes usually decrease in size from 3/4 in. (19 mm) for the main trunk line to 1/2, 3/8, or 1/4 in. (12, 9, or 6 mm) for the branch lines. Fig. 23-1 shows typical branch uses.

Municipal water supplies are moved through a system by a force rated in pounds per square inch in the line. Good joints and strong pipes are required

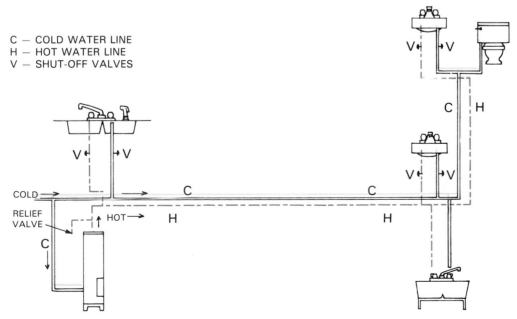

C — COLD WATER LINE
H — HOT WATER LINE
V — SHUT-OFF VALVES

Fig. 23-1. Parts of a typical water supply system. When connecting a new fixture or replacing an old fixture, remember that the hot water line should be on the left, the cold on the right.

to prevent leaks. The domestic supply usually has pressures of from 40 to 80 PSI (275 to 550 kPa).

Shutoff valves are required at several places to allow temporary interruptions and local repair. The main cutoff valve will shut off the water pressure to the entire house. Individual fixtures may have cutoff valves nearby that only affect one fixture. Repairs can be made without disrupting all of the service fixtures.

WATER DISTRIBUTION

While some kinds of pipe will serve for both potable water and drain water, usually the fittings are designed differently. Since potable water is under pressure, the inside walls of pipes and fittings do not need the smooth surface that is required for drainage systems. Removal of waste water is dependent upon gravity flow to carry it away.

IRON SUPPLY LINES

Usually galvanized pipe is joined by threaded fittings, Fig. 23-2. Since the fittings at each end of the pipe are threaded in opposite directions, a length of pipe cannot be removed by unscrewing once it is installed. It must be cut by a hacksaw and each piece must be removed individually.

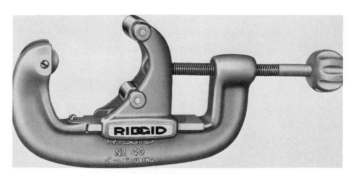

Fig. 23-3. Iron and copper pipe and tubing cutter. (Ridge Tool Co.)

Fig. 23-4. Pipe reamer.

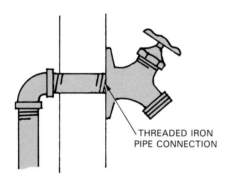

THREADED IRON PIPE CONNECTION

Fig. 23-2. Example of threaded pipe.

Fig. 23-5. Pipe wrench. (Ridge Tool Co.)

The iron should be cut squarely, usually with a special pipe cutting tool, Fig. 23-3. Remove any burrs with a pipe reamer, Fig. 23-4, or round file. A pipe thread cutting die is used to cut threads on the ends of each piece of pipe. The threads are tapered to provide a watertight fit when installed. A leakproof compound or tape is applied to the thread before screwing the fitting onto the pipe. A special pipe wrench is needed to tighten the fitting and pipe together, Fig. 23-5. Two wrenches are often used.

Fittings for galvanized pipes include the T-fitting for branching the system, nipples, couplings, unions, 90° elbows, 45° elbows, and 90° street elbows. Elbows are used to change pipe direction.

The reducing tee and reducing coupling or bushing will allow a change of size in the supply line. The union is used where a length of pipe may have to be disconnected at some future date. Other fittings, like a plug or cap for blocking the flow, and the coupling, which joins two lengths of pipe, are among the many other fittings available in piping systems.

Galvanized-iron pipe is not generally used where the water supply has a high count of minerals like calcium. Iron will attract the minerals, making deposits on the inside. The minerals speed up corrosion of the pipe. The deposits become caked, eventually clogging the pipe opening. This will reduce and even stop the water flow.

Pipe Plan

Prepare a project diagram before shopping for materials. This will show the length of piping required, plus all the fittings, such as nipples, couplings, tees, elbows, and unions that are needed. Refer to Fig. 23-6. To find the length of each piping piece:

1. Sketch the pipe layout.
2. Take the center-to-center distance for pipe to be installed (Dimension A).
3. Deduct dimension (B) and add amount of pipe that enters fitting, using the table in Fig. 23-7. (Note that it is necessary to double this distance if pipe goes into a fitting at each end).
4. List these distances on the sketch.

PIPE SIZE	LENGTH INSIDE THE FITTING
12mm 1/2 inch	12 mm 1/2 inch
19mm 3/4 inch	12mm 1/2 inch
25mm 1 inch	16mm 5/8 inch
32mm 1 1/4 inch	16mm 5/8 inch
38mm 1 1/2 inch	16mm 5/8 inch
50mm 2 inch	19mm 3/4 inch

Fig. 23-7. Distance that pipe is screwed into standard fitting.

Strength	Letter Designation	Uses
Thick wall	Type K	Underground application
Medium wall	Type L	Above ground service
Thin wall	Type M	Above ground, protected service

Fig. 23-8. Copper pipe designations and uses.

Copper pipe and copper tubing are cut in similar fashion. Use a pipe cutter as done for iron pipe.

The differences between copper pipe and tubing are the following. Tubing is soft and can be bent easily. It can be routed around objects. Copper pipe is rigid. Fittings for copper pipe are attached by soldering. Copper tubing can be joined by soldering also but most often is joined by flare fittings or compression fittings.

A flaring tool is shown in Fig. 23-9. Flare and compression fittings allow the tubing to be easily disconnected by unscrewing the threaded fitting, Fig. 23-10.

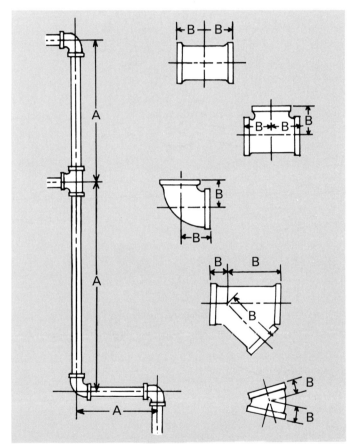

Fig. 23-6. Calculating lengths of pipe sections. For each pipe piece, first take the center-to-center distance labeled A. Then deduct dimension B and add amount of pipe that enters the fitting.

COPPER PIPE AND TUBING

Copper pipe is relatively thin-walled and easily crimped and damaged. However, copper piping is not susceptible to the calcium clogging as is iron. Therefore, copper is better in a house piping system.

The thickness of the walls of copper pipe can vary. Usage may depend on thickness, Fig. 23-8.

Fig. 23-9. Flaring tool for copper tubing. (Ridge Tool Co.)

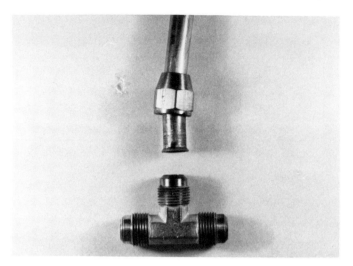

Fig. 23-10. The flared fitting. It is used on soft copper pipe.

When soldering copper joints, Fig. 23-11, the pipe and fitting must be dry, clean, and free from cutting burrs. Clean the end of the pipe and the inside of the fitting with steel wool until the bright copper color is exposed.

Apply soldering flux to the two surfaces. As the pipe is joined to the fitting, turn in a little to spread the flux. Heat the fitting but not the pipe with propane torch. Heat from the fitting will transfer on to the pipe and solder.

When the fitting is hot enough, hold wire solder against the lip of the fitting at the joint. Solder will flow into the gap by capillary action, even though it may have to rise vertically. When the solder forms a complete ring around the fitting, wipe off the excess with cloth for a smooth bead.

When two or three pipes are joined at the same fitting, for example installation of a tee for a branch line, they should all be soldered at the same time. If one end is already soldered, it can be wrapped with a damp cloth to protect it from heat while the other end is being heated. Always inspect to see if any damage has been done to the solder joint when completed.

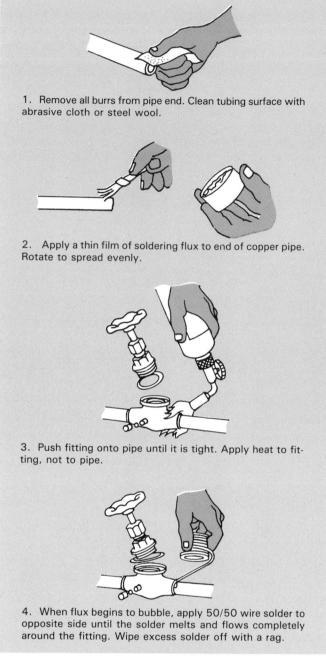

1. Remove all burrs from pipe end. Clean tubing surface with abrasive cloth or steel wool.

2. Apply a thin film of soldering flux to end of copper pipe. Rotate to spread evenly.

3. Push fitting onto pipe until it is tight. Apply heat to fitting, not to pipe.

4. When flux begins to bubble, apply 50/50 wire solder to opposite side until the solder melts and flows completely around the fitting. Wipe excess solder off with a rag.

Fig. 23-11. Making a soldered joint between copper tubing and a brass or copper fitting.

PLASTIC PIPE

Plastic plays an important role in the plumbing industry. Its use is increasing rapidly because of the relatively low material cost and ease of installation.

Plastic pipe for potable supplies is primarily made of polyvinyl-chloride (PVC). PVC pipe is not recommended for hot water distribution. Chlorinated-polyvinyl-chloride (CPVC) is recommended for hot water as well as cold water distribution. CPVC is normally rated at 180° F and 100 psi. PVC is also rated at 100 psi.

Polybutylene (PB) is a heat resistant flexible plastic recently introduced to the plumbing field. PB comes as a flexible pipe for cold and hot water supply. It is available in 1, 3/4, 1/2, and 1/4 in. (25, 19, 12, and 6 mm) inside diameters. Flexible pipe may be cut with a sharp knife and joined with special grip type adaptors or by solvent welding. Flexible pipe is used primarily as connection pieces between fixtures and supply lines.

Plastic piping offers the home mechanic an energy

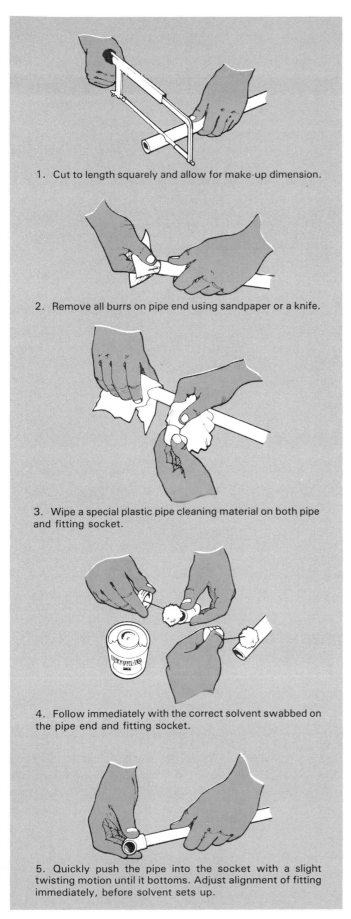

1. Cut to length squarely and allow for make-up dimension.

2. Remove all burrs on pipe end using sandpaper or a knife.

3. Wipe a special plastic pipe cleaning material on both pipe and fitting socket.

4. Follow immediately with the correct solvent swabbed on the pipe end and fitting socket.

5. Quickly push the pipe into the socket with a slight twisting motion until it bottoms. Adjust alignment of fitting immediately, before solvent sets up.

Fig. 23-12. Making a solvent welded joint with plastic pipe. (Genova)

saving piping system. Plastic pipe and fittings retard heat loss in the water supply line better than the metallic plumbing. Once hot, water stays hot longer within this self-insulating system.

Plastic pipe has an additional benefit: it does not corrode. With no build-up of corrosion, pipe bores stay full-sized. An older plastic system will have the same good flow it had when new.

Transition fittings are a part of the plastic pipe system. They allow the addition or repair of metallic systems with plastic. Specially designed transition unions for hot water have two faces that meet across a rubber gasket. Because of the different rates of expansion between plastic and metal, this special rubber gasket prevents breaks. The transition union also lets a connection be taken apart at any time.

Solvent welding is a method of joining plastic. It is simple, fast, and economical. It is based on the concept of solvents: dissolving the plastic surfaces of pipe and letting them intermingle with each other. Two items become one piece, forming a watertight joint which is also permanent.

Solvents used for the plastics must be compatible with the type of plastic used. Plastic pipe manufacturers recommend the two step welding process: clean the pipe, then use solvent.

Clean the pipe with a cleaner containing tetrahydro furan (THF) and methylethyl ketone (MEK). See Fig. 23-12. The cleaner's purpose is to remove any dirt, grease, oil, or other residue which may weaken the joint. (Wear splashproof goggles when handling MEK.) Cleaning materials are sold under various trade names by plastic plumbing manufacturers.

When surfaces are clean, next swab immediately with the recommended solvent for plastic type. Liberally coat the pipe and sparingly coat the fitting socket. Push the two together quickly with a slight twisting motion. Make alignments of fitting immediately. Solvent sets up in about 15 seconds. At 24 hours old, the solvent welded joint will be stronger than the pipe wall.

The chief cause of poor, leaky joints in plastic pipe is generally too little solvent. Also, if water comes into contact with the solvent before it sets, this may cause a joint failure.

Not all plastic types can be solvent welded. Therefore, the split ring compression connection is used.

VALVES

Globe valves and gate valves are the most common type of valves used in household plumbing systems. Other types use electrical solenoids to control water flow and temperature.

A globe valve controls the flow of water by

seating a washer on the end of the valve stem against a valve seat. See Fig. 23-13. This blocks the passage through the valve. An ordinary faucet works in this manner also.

Gate valves control the flow of water by blocking the entire width of the pipe, Fig. 23-14. A tapered extension at the end of the valve stem moves downward across the diameter of the pipe when the valve handle is turned clockwise. This type of valve allows the water to flow straight through without restriction when the valve is all the way open. Shutoff valves are constructed in this manner.

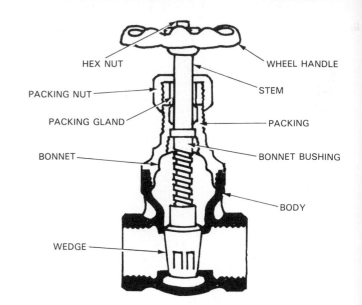

Fig. 23-14. Typical gate valve. Gate wedge slides against machined faces of valve seat instead of rotating.

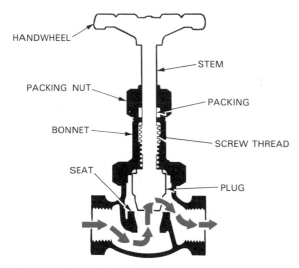

Fig. 23-13. Typical globe valve. (William Powell Co.)

REPAIRING WASHER TYPE FAUCET

See Fig. 23-15. Ordinary faucets leak for one of two reasons:

1. The washer at the valve seat no longer fits the seat.
2. The packing around the faucet spindle is worn.

Dripping indicates a worn washer, or seat, or both. Leaking around the handle when the valve is open indicates worn or damaged packing.

Some later model faucets use a rubber O-ring seal instead of the fiber packing, Fig. 23-16. Most hardware, plumbing stores, or house supply stores keep a wide variety of sizes and shapes of faucet washers, seats, and other parts.

To install a new rubber or plastic washer, first turn off the supply. Then remove the handle. Some handle screws are hidden under a snap-in-place cap which usually is labeled hot or cold.

Remove the decorative bonnet, if the faucet has one, which covers the packing nut located over the spindle nut, Fig. 23-17. With the appropriate size wrench, box end or open end, remove the spindle assembly.

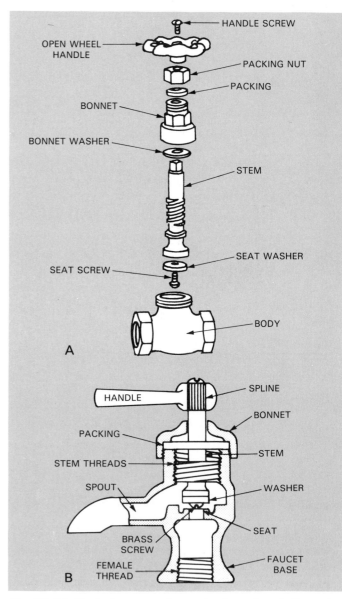

Fig. 23-15. Typical compression seal valves. A — In-line valve body. B — Outdoor faucet spout.

224

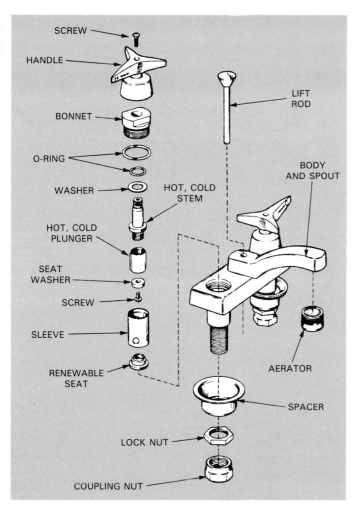

Fig. 23-16. Typical O-ring valve seat.

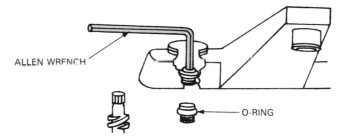

Fig. 23-18. Remove the metal valve seat with a hex key wrench and replace it.

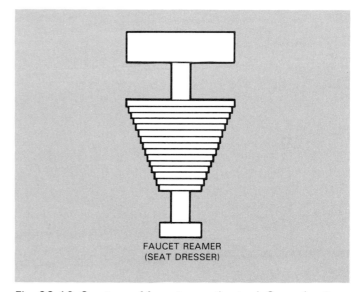

Fig. 23-19. One type of faucet reseating tool. Several cutters are available.

Fig. 23-17. Decorative bonnets. (Kohler)

Located on the lower end of the assembly is the faucet seat washer. The washer is fastened by a machine screw. The washer screw may be removed with a screwdriver. Replace the washer and inspect the metal seat for scars or pitted areas that might allow seapage of water.

The metal seat may need replacing. If so, it will unscrew and a replacement can be installed, Fig. 23-18. Reassemble.

Many outdoor faucets have a washer and seat.

A special tool can be used to smooth a rough seat. See Fig. 23-19.

REPAIRING WASHERLESS FAUCETS

Today most faucets look and work differently from those with washers. See Fig. 23-20. They are less apt to give trouble, but if they do, they are easy to repair. Most manufacturers of faucets design for easy replacement of wearing parts. If working parts are hidden by the handle, remove the Phillips screw and lift the handle off. Handle and bonnet are usually designed in one piece. There is rarely a packing unit: a single spindle or stem nut holds the entire assembly together. Instead of the washer-seat assembly, a nylon disk rotates to stop the flow of water.

Unscrew the spindle nut with a wrench and lift out the assembly. Should the disk or a diaphragm cartridge stay in the faucet, take a small screwdriver and lift it out. The plumbing supply store will have a stack of replacement cartridges. Replace the cartridge assembly and handle. Test the faucet.

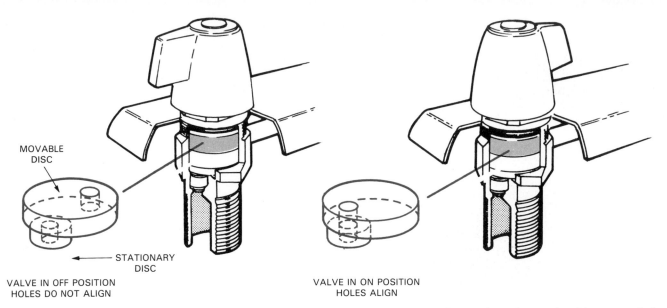

MOVABLE DISC

STATIONARY DISC

VALVE IN OFF POSITION
HOLES DO NOT ALIGN

VALVE IN ON POSITION
HOLES ALIGN

Fig. 23-20. There are many types of washerless faucets. One type is shown. Two valves, hot and cold, are needed. (Delta Faucet Co.)

SINGLE LEVER FAUCETS

Often the only service a single handle faucet needs is cleaning a strainer or aerator. Refer to Fig. 23-21. When water flow gets sluggish, one of these probably has begun to fill with particles of calcium, sand, or other sediment.

If the faucet has a swivel spout, the O-ring may get worn and seep around the neck. Replace the O-ring.

Keep the neck locking nut tight at all times. This could be the source of the leaking.

Some single lever faucets have a long, thin tube assembly called a cam valve. Refer again to Fig. 23-21, which identifies a cam kit. Replace the cam valve if single lever faucet does not operate properly. Repair of the cam valve is not recommended.

Before attempting repair of the single lever faucet, check the manufacturers' assembly drawings of the faucet. Many manufacturers have slightly different operating mechanisms for this valve. Usually total replacement of the cam assembly is necessary and recommended.

REPLACING SINGLE LEVER FAUCET BODY

To replace the single lever faucet for sinks, lavatories, tubs, and showers:
1. Turn off water supply to fixture.
2. Disconnect water supply line from beneath the fixture at the faucet. One joint type is shown in Fig. 23-22.
3. Remove the faucet by dislodging the jam nuts from the faucet body beneath the fixture.
4. Measure the distance between the center of fixture holes, generally 4, 6 or 8 in. (100, 150, or 200 mm).
5. Purchase the replacement according to measurement above.

6. Place new faucet in fixture holes.
7. Bed faucet in plumbers' putty to prevent water from leaking under the faucet and dripping under the fixture.
8. Tighten jam nuts to hold faucet in place.
9. Remove any plumbers' putty which squeezes out from under the faucet.
10. Connect supply lines to faucet.
11. Turn water on.

SHOWER HEAD REPAIR

Parts of a typical shower head are shown in Fig. 23-23. Most shower heads cause little if any trouble. Much of the problems can be fixed with an adjustment. Some problems and their cures are as follows:
1. The spray pattern gets out of adjustment: a locking nut located in the center of the face may work loose. Simply tighten this nut or screw.
2. There may be leaking around neck and head. Tighten head assembly on neck.
3. If the head is equipped with a swivel and the clamp ring works loose frequently, tighten by hand.

A modern shower head saves hot water by adding air to the flow through a Venturi tube. The air inlet tube flange must be kept free of any mineral buildup. If parts are not aluminum, clean them with a 20% solution of vinegar. Otherwise use a commercial mineral remover.

WATER HAMMER

A hammering sound in the faucet supply lines is caused when automatic washer solenoid valves or other faucets are turned off suddenly. Water moving swiftly through the pipes while the valve is

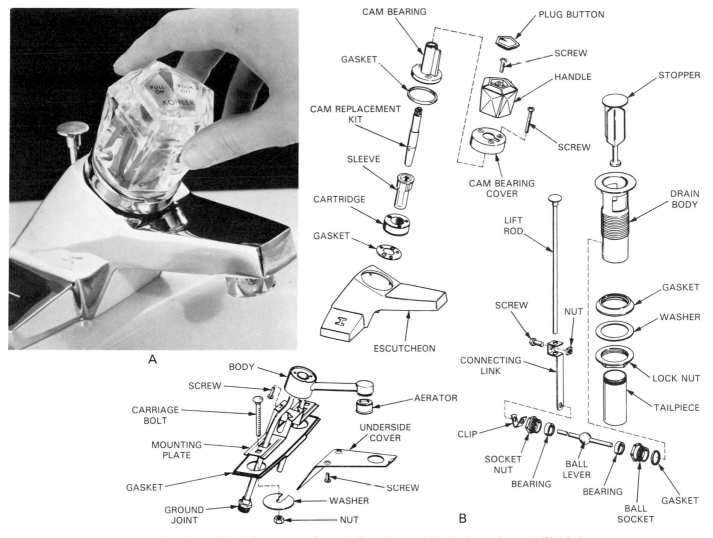

Fig. 23-21. A — Single-lever type faucet. B — Parts of single-lever faucet. (Kohler)

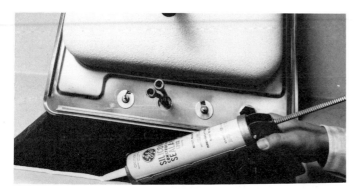

Fig. 23-22. Single-lever faucet supply lines. Part of a sink basin assembly is shown. Note the type of flange on the pipe ends. The outer diameter of a flange is threaded to receive a nut for a compression type of fitting. (General Electric Co.)

open comes to an abrupt halt as the valve is closed. The inertia of many pounds of water is stopped which causes a force within the supply system. Vibration from the pipe to surrounding members increases the noise.

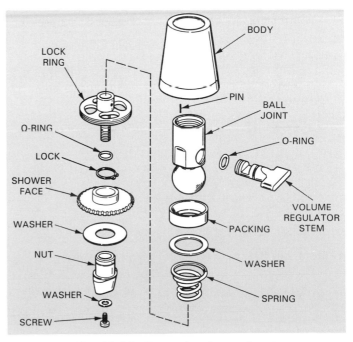

Fig. 23-23. Parts of a shower head.

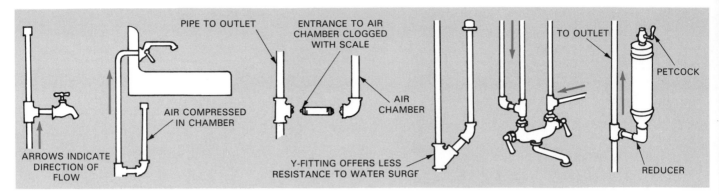

PIPE TO OUTLET

ENTRANCE TO AIR
CHAMBER CLOGGED
WITH SCALE

TO OUTLET

PETCOCK

AIR COMPRESSED
IN CHAMBER

AIR
CHAMBER

ARROWS INDICATE
DIRECTION OF
FLOW

Y-FITTING OFFERS LESS
RESISTANCE TO WATER SURGE

REDUCER

Fig. 23-24. Simple types of air chambers and methods of installing them. An air chamber helps prevent noise from a problem called water hammer.

The problem is lack of or improperly operating air chambers. The air chamber, Fig. 23-24, lets the rushing water bounce gently against a cushion of air when a valve is closed. This absorbs the force and takes the strain off the pipes.

Commercial air chambers are available. However, they are very simple to make with basic plumbing parts. You need to make a capped vertical column of pipe approximately 24 inches high. Attach it to a tee inserted in the supply line near the fixture. It is best placed near the end of a supply line.

TEMPORARY REPAIR OF LEAKY PIPE

Sometimes a pipe will have a leak far from a joint. This type of leak can be stopped until proper repairs are made. See Fig. 23-25. Use a clamp which surrounds the pipe and holds a pad over the leak. Depending on the size of the leak, you can make a clamp with rubber sheet and hose clamps, or you can purchase a unit.

WATER SOFTENER MAINTENANCE

Homes with wells may have a water softener. The softener removes iron and other minerals from the water. For units more than about 10 years old, manual treatment with salt is needed. A common procedure is to pour 10 lb. of salt into the top of the softener every 3 months. After 1/2 hour, reverse the water flow to remove the salt and impurities. Check the manufacturer's directions for amounts, methods, and waiting periods.

Softeners less than 10 years old have systems which add salt automatically. The system does this at night. A separate container of dry salt is attached to the softener. Refill this as specified.

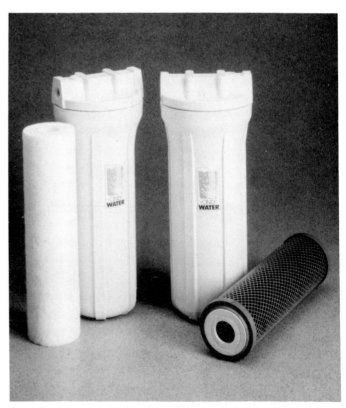

A sediment filter both cleans water and helps reduce rust stains. To replace the filter cartridge, first close water supply valve on inlet side. Open faucet to relieve pressure. Shell will not unscrew unless pressure is relieved. Replace cartridge. (The Coleman Co., Inc.)

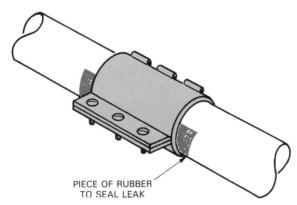

PIECE OF RUBBER
TO SEAL LEAK

Fig. 23-25. To stop a leak from a pipe, clamp a rubber pad to the hole. Proper repairs can be made later.

TEST YOUR KNOWLEDGE — CHAPTER 23

1. Threads on iron pipe are tapered to provide a _____ fit.
2. A leakproof compound or _____ is applied to iron pipe threads to seal them.
3. A _____ coupling joins pipe of two different sizes.
4. To solder a fitting to copper pipe or tubing, directly heat the:
   a. Tubing.
   b. Fitting.
   c. Solder.
   d. Flux.
5. Plastic pipe designated _____ is not recommended for hot water use.
   a. PB.
   b. PVC.
   c. CPVC.
   d. a and c.
6. Metal pipe is joined to plastic pipe with a _____ union.
7. To bond plastic fittings and pipe, after applying solvent, use a _____ motion.
8. The main cause of poor joints in plastic pipe is _____ (too much, too little) solvent.
9. Plastic pipes which cannot be solvent welded to fittings are joined with split ring _____ connections.
10. Faucets of the washer type which leak around the handle may have damaged _____ .
11. Faucet spindle packing is held tightly in place with a packing _____ .
12. One type of washerless faucet controls water flow with a nylon _____ .
13. Replace instead of repair the _____ _____ in a single lever faucet.
14. To reduce noise from water hammer, install a (an) _____ _____ .
15. To stop a pipe leak until proper repairs can be made, use a _____ and rubber pad.
16. A water softener is cleaned of impurities with _____ .

KNOW THESE TERMS

Faucet, valves, fixture, supply, tee, elbow, flare, hacksaw, bonnet.

SUGGESTED ACTIVITIES

Visit a local hardware store. Make a list of the types of replacement faucet parts available. Also note the prices. Determine which assemblies are more expensive to repair with spare parts than to replace them. Report your findings to your class.

With your instructor's guidance, practice making joints of pipes to fittings. Do this for plastic pipe and for copper pipe. For plastic pipe, test a sample joint many times while it sets. Make a note of the time taken for the joint to set. For copper pipe, make joints in vertical as well as horizontal positions. If possible, test all copper and plastic joints with compressed air. Immerse the pipes in water to see if there are any leaks or weak areas.

CAREERS

Plumber, mechanical engineer, mechanical materials salesperson (retail and wholesale).

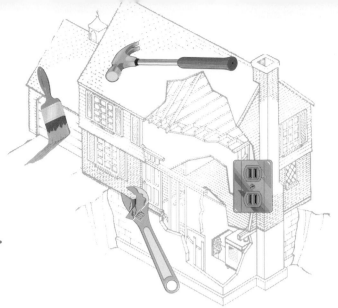

24

WASTE DISPOSAL SYSTEMS

This chapter introduces the types of pipe and fixtures used in waste water systems. It discusses some of the methods needed to maintain or install valves, pipe fittings, traps, and vents. The chapter tells how to unclog pipes and traps and how to clean the surfaces of fixtures.

After studying this chapter, you will be able to:
■ Define terms used for drain, waste, and vent systems.
■ Explain the purpose and operation of traps and vents.
■ Specify the pipe slopes needed for waste flow.
■ List the parts of several toilet flush systems.
■ Tell how to fix common toilet problems and leaks.
■ List some uses for augers and plungers.
■ Solve problems with garbage disposals.
■ Tell how to install a sink and faucet.

Outgoing used water may be handled either by a city or privately. City-wide sewage treatment is much more efficient than private disposal. Municipal-operated sewage collection and treatment systems are necessary to return pure clean water to the original source.

The private sewage disposal system consists of a septic tank and a disposal field, which serves a single-family residence. The septic tank, Fig. 24-1, breaks down the sewage into liquids and solids by bacterial action. Solids settle to the bottom of the tank and must be cleaned out every few years. The effluent is drained off and distributed throughout a system of underground tiles. In the tile field, the liquid is absorbed into the surrounding ground, Fig. 24-2. In time these lateral fields become clogged by solids in the effluent water and they must be enlarged or replaced.

The hydrogen digester is a better, but more expensive system than the septic tank. It works much like the municipal treatment plant, but on a smaller

scale. The containment tank has an aerator inside which pumps air to the bottom of the tank. The air aids the bacterial action. The effluent is returned to the earth by a lateral pipe field.

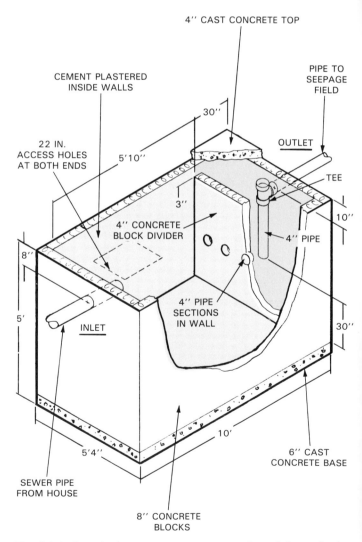

Fig. 24-1. A typical two-compartment septic tank for a single family residence. (Genova)

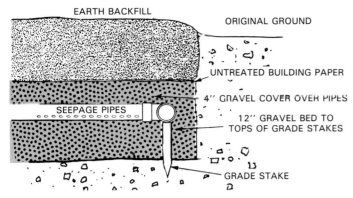

Fig. 24-2. Detail of the lateral field drain line buried in a bed of porous material. The material allows rapid dispersion of waste water. (Genova)

WASTE PIPING

Waste piping materials are much the same as those found in supply lines: iron, copper, and plastic. Drain-waste-vent (DWV) piping is usually 1 1/2, 2, 3, 4, and 6 in. (38, 50, 76, 100, and 152 mm) in size. See Fig. 24-3.

The smaller sizes are used to connect sinks and lavatories where small amounts of water must be carried away. As the collection system continues, the branches increase in size until the trunk line is 6 in. The 6 in. pipe passes from the house to the

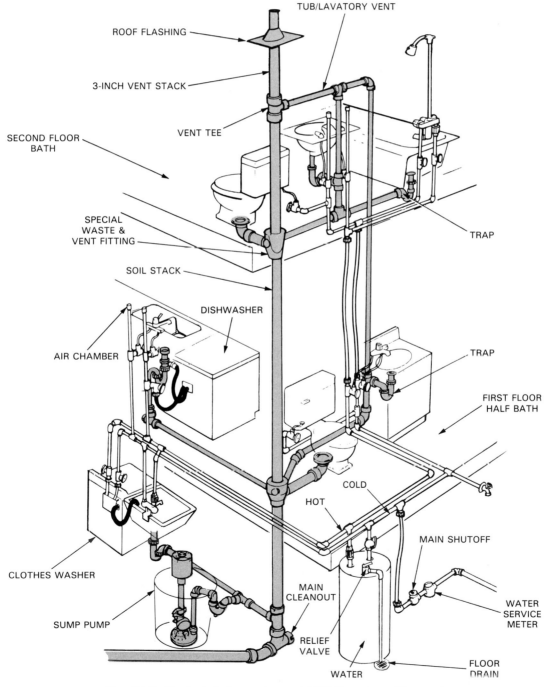

Fig. 24-3. Typical drain-waste-vent (DWV) system. (Genova)

main sewer or septic tank. (Appendix, Plumbing Symbols)

Most older homes have cast iron DWV pipes. Modern houses may have combinations of cast iron and copper, cast iron and plastic, or plastic alone. All piping consists of pipes, and also fittings to join them in a line, at angles, or in branch lines. Joining systems for DWV piping are similar to those discussed for joining supply line piping.

An exception is cast iron piping. Cast iron drainage lines may be joined in different manners:
1. By the oakum molten lead method, Fig. 24-4.
2. Joined with the neoprene rubber sleeve and stainless steel clamp method.

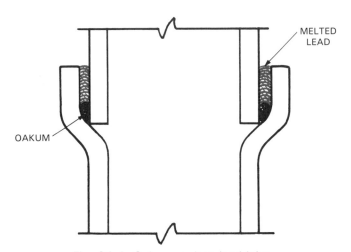

Fig. 24-4. Oakum molten lead joint.

PLUMBING CODES

Government units like cities, counties, states, or even nations make and enforce laws which specify the minimum standards for drainage and waste systems. The purpose of these regulations is to provide health and safety for the people who occupy the structure or live near the waste system. Before the home mechanic undertakes any plumbing installation or modification, Fig. 24-5, check the local code.

Cross Connection

A cross connection is a path between potable water and drainage water. This can make drinking water unfit for human consumption. Good design can avoid a cross connection, Fig. 24-6. Most manufacturers of plumbing fixtures and fittings design them for safety.

A faucet in a bathtub, sink, or tank that would be submerged if the basin should overflow is a cross connection. Should a sink bowl become filled with backed up drain water, the contaminated water could be drawn into the water supply. This may occur during repairs with the pressure turned off and

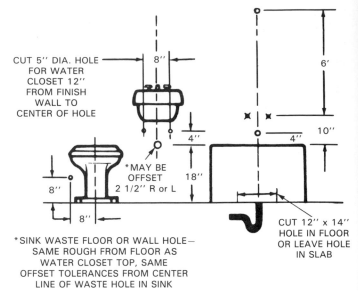

CUT 5'' DIA. HOLE FOR WATER CLOSET 12'' FROM FINISH WALL TO CENTER OF HOLE

8''

6'

4''

4''   10''

*MAY BE OFFSET 2 1/2'' R or L

18''

8''

8''

CUT 12'' x 14'' HOLE IN FLOOR OR LEAVE HOLE IN SLAB

*SINK WASTE FLOOR OR WALL HOLE—SAME ROUGH FROM FLOOR AS WATER CLOSET TOP, SAME OFFSET TOLERANCES FROM CENTER LINE OF WASTE HOLE IN SINK

Fig. 24-5. Dimensions needed for rough-in of bathroom fixtures.

Fig. 24-6. Notice the position of the faucet above the sink rim. No cross connection (siphon) is possible to cause contamination. (AquaLine)

faucets opened. If vacuum is created, it can cause siphonage through a faucet.

THE DRAIN, WASTE, AND VENT SYSTEM

Drain water is not under pressure like potable water is. Since drain water is not under pressure, the DWV piping must slope slightly toward the main drain. Water is moved only by gravity force.

Generally it is recommended that drain lines slope 1 to 2 percent of horizontal run. Most DWV pipe fittings are designed with slightly less than ''square'' (90) turns to help maintain this slope, as on the right in Fig. 24-7.

The first drainpipe which leads waste away from the fixture is called a waste pipe. Toilets require a larger outflow pipe because of the great flow of water (3.5 to 5 gallons, 13 to 19 liters) and because solids must be carried along without clogging. Because of this toilet drainage, those pipes are not called waste pipes, but are called soil pipes.

Stacks

Fixture waste pipes and toilets usually empty into what is called a main stack or soil stack. A main stack is a vertical pipe open above the roof. At its lower end a stack leads into the building drain. Waste water flows to the bottom of the stack and into the building drain.

If the stack serves a toilet, it is called a main stack. Every house has at least one main stack which measures 3 or 4 in. (76 or 100 mm) in diameter. If a stack does not serve a toilet, it is called a secondary stack or waste stack. The waste stack usually measures 1 1/2 or 2 in. (38 or 50 mm) in diameter.

Many houses have no need for secondary stacks. All waste and soil pipes join in a single stack. A vent stack is joined at this point, made of 3 or 4 in. pipes. The vent stack continues through the roof.

Building Drain

After waste water is collected from all fixtures, it leaves the building through one 3 or 4 in. diameter pipe running horizontal. The building drain leads out under the crawl space or basement floor. Most pass under the footing and end approximately 5 ft. (1.5 m) away from the foundation.

At this point, the building drain becomes the house sewer line. It may be increased in size to 6 in. (150 mm). All this is located undergound.

The house sewer line slopes to the city sewer or private septic system.

Traps

The DWV system contains some subsystems not described before. One is the trap. A trap is a water-filled, U-shaped pipe that will allow water and wastes to pass through, but prevents gases and vermin inside the DWV system from slipping backward into the house. Every appliance and every fixture must have a trap. Without traps, the house will soon smell like the inside of a sewer.

Toilets contain built-in traps because their intricate bowl passages are trap-shaped. See Fig. 24-8. The water in the bowl is part of a toilet's trap

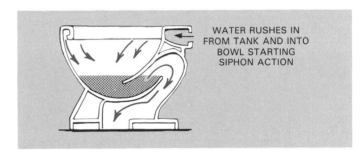

WATER RUSHES IN FROM TANK AND INTO BOWL STARTING SIPHON ACTION

Fig. 24-8. How a toilet trap works. (Genova)

seal. However, when a toilet finishes flushing, the trap's siphon action often depletes most of its trap-sealing water. For this reason, the toilet tank fill mechanism is designed to replace the trap-sealing water as the tank refills.

Other fixtures and appliances use separate traps. Traps for sinks and lavatories are either P-shaped, Fig. 24-9, or S-shaped, Fig. 24-10. Both P and S types contain the U-shaped trap section. These traps are hidden underneath fixtures.

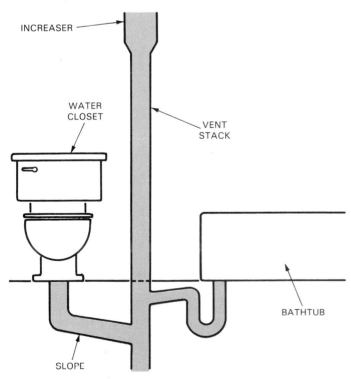

INCREASER

WATER CLOSET

VENT STACK

BATHTUB

SLOPE

Fig. 24-7. Any horizontal run will have a slight slope toward the main stack.

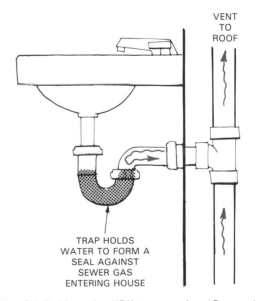

VENT TO ROOF

TRAP HOLDS WATER TO FORM A SEAL AGAINST SEWER GAS ENTERING HOUSE

Fig. 24-9. How the "P" trap works. (Genova)

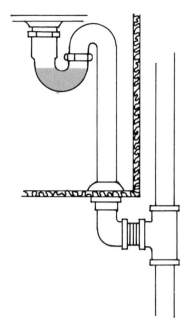

Fig. 24-10. How the "S" trap works. (Genova)

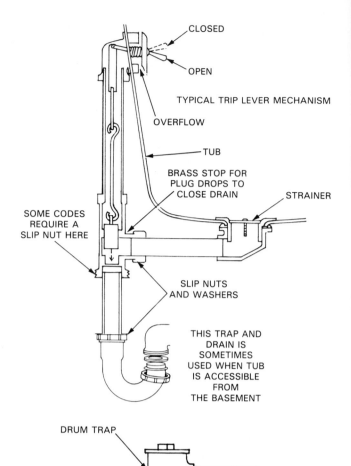

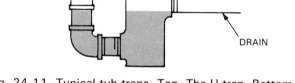

Fig. 24-11. Typical tub traps. Top. The U trap. Bottom. The drum trap. (Genova)

One end of the trap connects to a tailpiece coming out of the fixture drain. The trap must be at least as large as the tailpiece. The other end slips into the DWV system waste pipe. Slip-nut connections with soft ring-type gaskets make slip joints tight for both water and gas.

Tub and shower traps may be drum-type or large P-traps. They are located in or beneath the floor under the fixture, Fig. 24-11.

Wherever a trap is located, access must be provided for cleaning if it clogs. Toilet and sink-lavatory traps can be cleaned from above through the fixture drain. Often, both tub and shower traps are accessible for cleaning through the drain. Some are not. These are designed for cleaning from above through a hole in the floor or from below in the basement or crawlspaces.

The best P- and S- traps are built with a cleanout opening at the lowest point of the dip, Fig. 24-12. Removal of the cleanout plug allows draining and direct access for cleaning.

Vents

The need for traps involves another plumbing necessity, venting. Water rushing along by gravity through a pipe creates a suction or vacuum at the high end of the pipe above it. Refer to Fig. 24-13. This is called siphon action.

Siphon action is powerful enough to pull all the water out of a trap and leave it nearly dry. For example, this happens in a toilet bowl after a flush. But, since other fixtures and appliances are not designed to replace siphoned water as a toilet is, some means of preventing trap siphoning must be built into the system. This is achieved by venting

Fig. 24-12. Some P and S traps have a cleanout at the lowest point of trap for easy removal of clogged material. (Genova)

the system to outside air.

Venting also reduces gas buildup. Gases generated by the bacterial action in sewage are allowed to escape through the vent stack safely.

Venting also prevents any pressure in the DWV system from building to the point where it could

With no vent, trap water siphons off.

This leaves too little water in the trap to stop sewer gases.

With vent, air rushes in to prevent siphoning of trap. The gas seal remains.

Fig. 24-13. How the vent works. (Genova)

force past a trap's water seal. Every trap in a plumbing system should be vented.

Reventing

If the waste pipe from a fixture is short enough or large enough, a fixture's trap can be both drained and vented through the same pipe. This is called wet-venting. All fixtures are wet-vented for a short distance. The length of a wet-vent is limited by plumbing codes and what will work in use.

If the stack is not located near the fixture, the wet-vented distance may be too long. An alternate venting procedure must be provided. This may be in the form of an additional stack closer to the fixture or a branch vent called a revent, Fig. 24-14.

A revent is a vent-only pipe leading upward from the fixture waste pipe. It is bent as needed to connect into a stack above the point where the highest fixture waste pipe enters it. The branch vent stack connection may or may not be connected into the same stack the fixture drains into. It does not mat-

ter. The trap is vented.

Stacks and vents are usually made from the same size pipe as is used for draining the fixture. Sometimes a size or two smaller vent pipe is permitted. No vent pipe or waste pipe is smaller than 1 1/4 in. (30 mm). More recently, 1 1/2 in. (38 mm) is the smallest size used.

TOILET MAINTENANCE

Most toilet problems involve the flushing mechanism or a clogged drain pipe. Occasionally, a toilet tank or bowl will leak because of a bad seal between the base and drain. Leaks may be due to a cracked tank or bowl.

A flushing mechanism looks complicated, but its operation is fairly simple. To understand descriptions of the process for repairing toilets, it is necessary to become familiar with the names of the

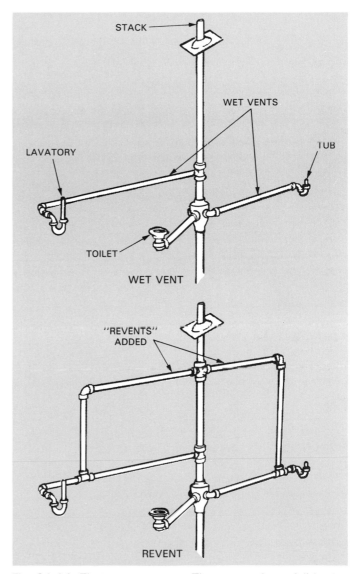

Fig. 24-14. The revent system. The trap seal can fail in the simpler wet-vent system.

parts and what they do. The following will be discussed:

1. Toilet operation.
2. Continuously running water.
3. Tank valve replacement.
4. Obstructions.
5. Leaking bowls.

Operation of the Toilet

The main components of a toilet are the tank, the bowl, and the flush system. The tank contains 3.5 to 5 gal. (1.3 to 2 liters) of flush water and the bowl contains the trap. The flushing and metering mechanism, Fig. 24-15, controls water flow.

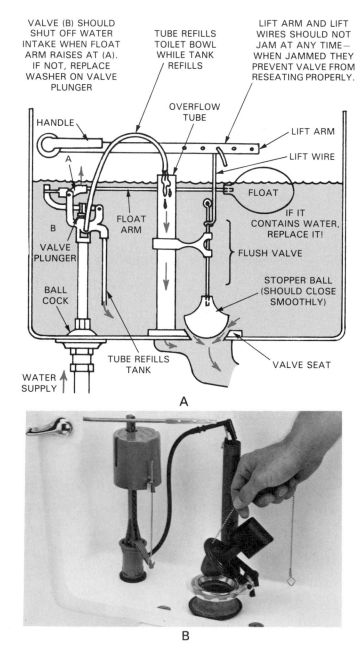

VALVE (B) SHOULD SHUT OFF WATER INTAKE WHEN FLOAT ARM RAISES AT (A). IF NOT, REPLACE WASHER ON VALVE PLUNGER

TUBE REFILLS TOILET BOWL WHILE TANK REFILLS

LIFT ARM AND LIFT WIRES SHOULD NOT JAM AT ANY TIME — WHEN JAMMED THEY PREVENT VALVE FROM RESEATING PROPERLY.

HANDLE

OVERFLOW TUBE

LIFT ARM

LIFT WIRE

A

FLOAT

FLOAT ARM

IF IT CONTAINS WATER, REPLACE IT!

B

VALVE PLUNGER

FLUSH VALVE

BALL COCK

STOPPER BALL (SHOULD CLOSE SMOOTHLY)

TUBE REFILLS TANK

WATER SUPPLY

VALVE SEAT

A

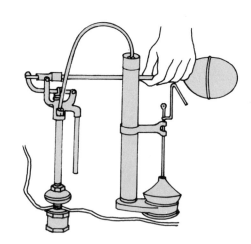

B

Fig. 24-15. Parts of toilet mechanisms. A—Traditional style. B—Recent style saves water. Fillable basket on flush valve acts as counterweight. (Fluidmaster, Inc.)

The toilet flushes when water enters the bowl through the flush valve in the bottom of the tank. See Fig. 24-16. In many older toilets, this valve is opened when the tank ball, which serves as a stopper, is lifted by a lift wire attached to the flush lever.

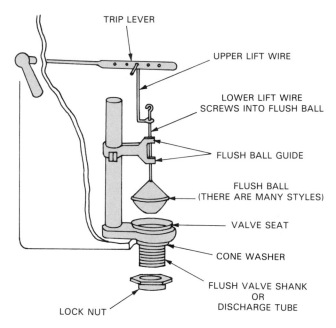

TRIP LEVER

UPPER LIFT WIRE

LOWER LIFT WIRE SCREWS INTO FLUSH BALL

FLUSH BALL GUIDE

FLUSH BALL (THERE ARE MANY STYLES)

VALVE SEAT

CONE WASHER

FLUSH VALVE SHANK OR DISCHARGE TUBE

LOCK NUT

Fig. 24-16. Typical flush valve with lift wire system. (Rockwell)

The tank then fills through a float valve, inlet assembly, and refill tube. See Fig. 24-17. Water flows from the refill tube into the tank and also into an overflow pipe to seal the trap.

Tank water is kept from flowing out by the tank ball that closes the flush valve. As water rises in the tank, it carries the float ball on its surface. When the water is about 3/4 in. (20 mm) below the top of the overflow pipe, the float arm reaches the proper angle to close the inlet valve. The water stops flowing into the tank.

Fig. 24-17. Lever type of toilet tank float valve. (Rockwell)

Continuously Running Water

There are several reasons which might cause water to flow freely into the tank and bowl:

1. The float ball may not rise far enough to shut off the flow completely. To correct, adjust the volume control screw located near the float valve. Slight bending of the float arm downward may be needed. Check for calcium build-up on float valve.

2. Tank valve may not seal to thoroughly stop the flow into bowl. Check condition of tank valve, either flap type or ball type. The guide arm or lift wires may be bent. Trip lever may be bent.

Either the flush valve or the inlet valve may be replaced without much difficulty.

The local plumbing supply dealer will have replacement kits of both balls for easy installation by the home mechanic.

Replacing Tank Valve Systems

There are many designs of the two valve units in a toilet tank. Recent flush and water metering parts may be made of plastic. The installation procedure for a recent style is shown in Fig. 24-18. New parts fit the original mounting surfaces. Follow the manufacturer's directions.

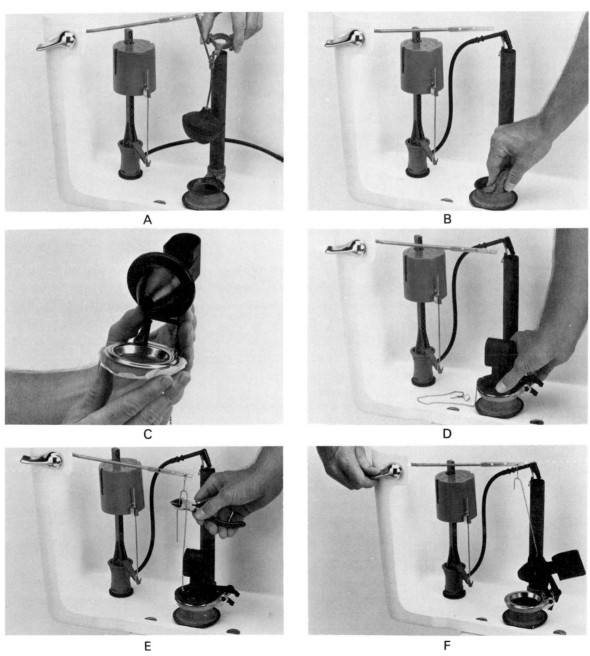

Fig. 24-18. Installation steps for recent style of flush system. A — Removing the original flush valve. Original float and lever arm of supply valve has been replaced. B — Remove corrosion on the flush valve seat with scouring pad. Rinse and dry the surface. C — To install flush valve, peel off protective paper and press unit onto old flange. Before removing paper, test the fit in the tank for any parts getting in the way. D — Press stainless steel seal onto old drain seat. E — Connect the stainless steel ball type of chain to the trip lever. Trim excess chain. F — Turn on tank water and test the operation. (Fluidmaster, Inc.)

Dislodging an Obstruction from the Toilet

When the narrow drain in a toilet bowl becomes clogged, water entering the bowl from the tank is unable to flow out, and will rise and overflow the sides. At the first indication that the drain passage is clogged, hurry to lift the tank cover and raise the float ball lever while pushing the flush valve downward. This shuts off the flow of water to the bowl. Next shut off the supply of water to the tank.

There are several ways to clear the blockage. Try the simplest first. A plunger with an extended rim for toilets should be pressed down over the drain opening and worked up and down several times, Fig. 24-19. This should force most minor obstructions on to the soil drain.

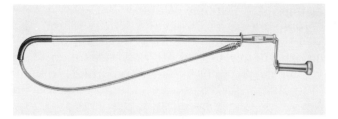

Fig. 24-20. A closet auger. (Ridge Tool Co.)

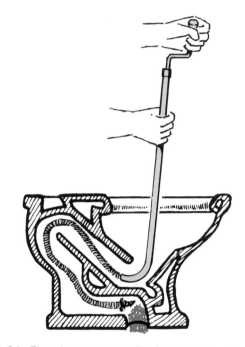

Fig. 24-21. The closet auger will often catch on the clogged material. The auger will then pull the material out. Sometimes the object will be released to go down the drain.
(Ridge Tool Co.)

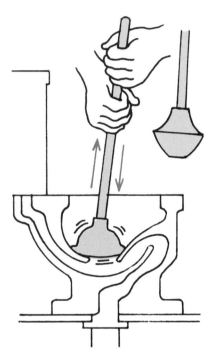

Fig. 24-19. The plunger method of freeing a drain clog. (Rockwell)

The closet auger may be employed for the removal of the more difficult obstructions. See Fig. 24-20. The auger consists of a coil of wire inside a hollow tube and an auger handle attached to the other end. The handle rotates the wire as it is punched into the clogged area. A power auger may be used. Continued turning will snag the obstruction. Then the clog may be pushed or pulled free, Fig. 24-21.

Do not use a caustic drain cleaner to clear a clogged toilet drain. It will not clear the obstruction. It will, however, damage the vitreous china bowl.

Stopping Leaking Bowls

When the seal between the toilet and the floor flange fails, water will begin to leak from around the base of the stool bowl. Water may first be noticed on the ceiling directly below the stool location. In such a case, the water closet assembly must be removed and a new sealing ring must be installed, Fig. 24-22.

Fig. 24-22. To connect the water closet to the closet bend, a flange is mounted at the floor. A wax ring is placed between the flange and water closet to complete the seal.

First, shut off the water supply to the tank. Drain the tank and disconnect the water supply line. Loosen the nuts on the hold-down bolts. Often the nuts are under caps on both sides of the base of the bowl. (A little penetrating oil will help free the nuts if they are frozen.)

Lift the bowl free from the floor and tip it onto its side. Scrape free the old wax ring from both the bowl base and the stool flange mounted to the floor. Mount new wax ring to bowl base and reseal to the mounting flange. Secure bowl with nuts. Replace caps and make supply connection. Turn the water supply on.

DISLODGING OBJECTS FROM OTHER FIXTURES

When a sink, lavatory, bathtub, or shower drains slowly or not at all, the usual cause is an accumulation of hair, grease, or other debris lodged somewhere near the drain. The usual location of clogged drains is the trap. Because of standing water in the natural low area, sediment collects here and eventually solidifies into a clogged drain.

First try clearing it with the plunger, Fig. 24-23. The best type for this job is the one with a wide flat face that gives it good contact with the nearly flat fixture bottom. It probably will be necessary to hold a wet rag over the overflow vent, or the force created by the plunger will be deflected through it rather than to the clogged area. Run about one inch of water into the bottom of fixture before using the plunger. This will help prevent the plunger pressure

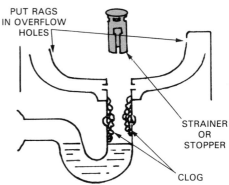

Fig. 24-24. Before using the plunger, remove the lift stopper. (Rockwell)

a larger pipe to be carried away freely. The upward thrust of the suction cup will tend to move the obstruction backward into the fixture for removal.

If the plunger has not proved successful after a few minutes, try a liquid chemical drain cleaner. Chemical drain cleaners are heavier than water. When poured into the clogged drain, a cleaner will settle to the point of obstruction and begin to chemically break down the obstruction. After a few minutes of chemical action, again try the plunger.

If the stoppage persists, use the sink auger, a somewhat smaller version of the closet auger. Rotate it into the clogged drain to cut away the obstruction.

If none of these methods have proved successful, remove the cleanout plug at the bottom of the trap. Not all traps have cleanout plugs. The trap itself may have to be removed, Fig. 24-25.

Cover the trap nuts with a protective material before using a wrench, or use a fiber strap wrench, Fig. 24-26, to prevent scarring of the plastic or chrome plated metal surface.

CLOGGED MAIN DRAIN

Sometimes a fixture overflows because the house drain or main drain is clogged. When this happens,

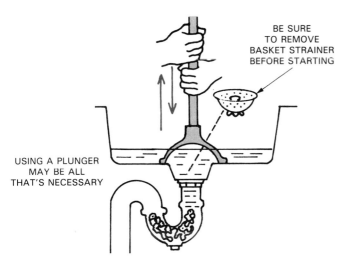

BE SURE TO REMOVE BASKET STRAINER BEFORE STARTING

USING A PLUNGER MAY BE ALL THAT'S NECESSARY

Fig. 24-23. Use of the plunger. (Rockwell)

bypassing the clogged drain. Also remove the lift stopper if the model of fixture has one, Fig. 24-24.

When all is ready, push the plunger downward and pull it up firmly in a rhythmical manner. The force downward will tend to force the obstruction on through the narrow neck of the waste pipe into

Fig. 24-25. The difficult clog may require removal of the trap. (Rockwell)

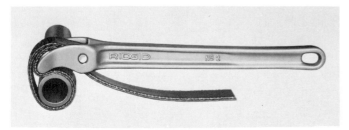

Fig. 24-26. A strap wrench. (Ridge Tool Co.)

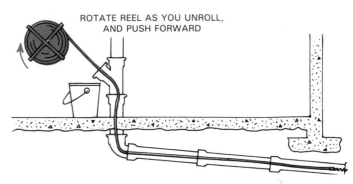

ROTATE REEL AS YOU UNROLL, AND PUSH FORWARD

Fig. 24-28. Use a drain probe to dislodge obstruction from distant area of building drain.

usually you will notice more than one fixture with an obstruction. Main drains clog mainly because of an accumulation of tree roots entering and growing within the drain, Fig. 24-27. The home mechanic will probably want and need to get professional help with this problem. The professional has an electric-powered auger with razor blades at the end of a flexible auger rod. Sometimes a long type of coiled probe will work. See Fig. 24-28.

The root cutter will cut through the tangle. Then the roots can be removed from the drain. Rootcutting power augers can be rented.

GARBAGE DISPOSAL MAINTENANCE

Many houses have garbage disposals located in or near the kitchen sink. The garbage disposal is designed to grind table scraps and kitchen waste into fine bits that may be washed away.

Two major problems occur with the disposal: the drain becomes clogged or the blade jams.

If the discharge drain is clogged, the problem is usually that not enough water was allowed to flow during the time of operation. Usually the rubber plunger placed over the disposal opening will dislodge the clog. It is important to allow enough water flow to wash away the debris.

The other problem is mechanical or electrical. A bone or pit may be caught between the grinding blade and the housing, which in turn causes the electrical protection switch to ''break.''

First, get a soft wood stick about 24 inches long. Place it into the disposal top and gently pry in a

reverse direction, Fig. 24-29. Remove the stuck object. Then, after sufficient time delay for temperature drop, press the red plastic reset button located on the outside bottom to reset the starting mechanism. Turn garbage disposal on and continue. Note: Before attempting to dislodge the grinding mechanism be sure that the electrical power is turned off.

Fig. 24-29. To dislodge a stuck garbage grinder, use a wood rod. Force the grinding blades in the reverse direction. Be sure electric power is shut off at the breaker box.

INSTALLING A NEW KITCHEN SINK

Installation of a kitchen sink is not a difficult job. Measure the correct cutout size by placing the sink upside down in the desired location on the countertop. Next mark a pencil line around the entire outside edge. Remove the sink and make a second pencil mark 3/8 in. (9 mm) smaller on all four sides and all corners, Fig. 24-30. With a sabre saw or keyhole

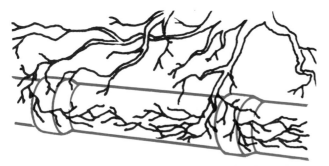

Fig. 24-27. Roots penetrate drains and can lead to solid plugs in the pipe.

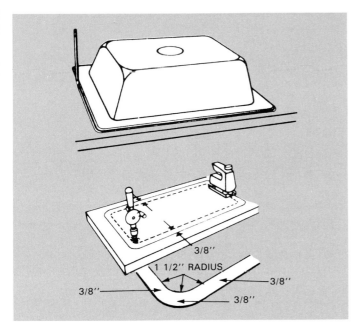

Fig. 24-30. Layout and cutting procedure for hole in counter-top. (Rockwell)

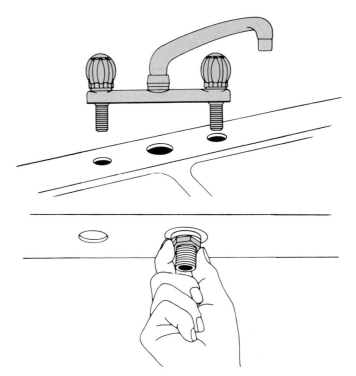

Fig. 24-32. Set faucet in mounting holes and fit locking nuts. (Rockwell)

saw, cut on the inside line, being careful to round corners. Check the dimensions, Fig. 24-31. If the rim does not fit evenly on the countertop, enlarge the cut out opening with the saw.

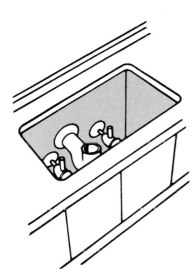

Fig. 24-31. Check opening for proper fit. (Rockwell)

Mount faucet, Fig. 24-32, drain fittings, Fig. 24-33, and accessories before installing sink in counter top. Follow the manufacturers' instructions. Use a good caulk under the faucet base and top flange of the drain, Fig. 24-34. After measuring, connect the water supply line vertical tubes (water riser tubes) to the faucet. The riser tubes run between the faucet flanges and the shutoff valves. They may be solid or may be flexible pipe.

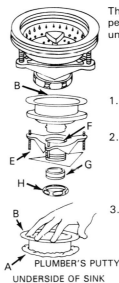
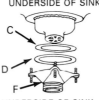

The sink strainer can easily be installed by one person since all connectors can be handled from underneath.

1. Loosen the three screws (E), twist the retainer (F), and remove from the assembly.

2. Insert the body (B) through opening in sink (A) making certain that sufficient putty is used between the body (B) and sink (A) to seal properly.

3. Place the friction ring (D) and washer (C) in position on the retainer (F). From the underside of the sink, attach the retainer to the body by turning it until engaged.

4. Tighten the three screws (E) snugly, making certain that the body, retainer, and washers are lined up properly in the sink opening. Tighten the screws (E) until strainer is water-tight.

5. Insert sleeve (G) into retainer (F). Attach tailpiece or tube to retainer with coupling nut (H).

6. Remove excess putty with soft cloth.

Fig. 24-33. Install the sink strainer assembly. (Rockwell)

PLUMBER'S PUTTY
UNDERSIDE OF SINK
UNDERSIDE OF SINK

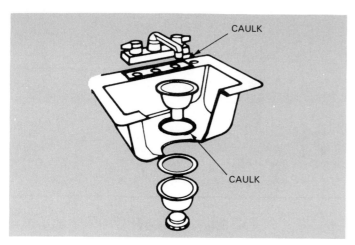

Fig. 24-34. Mount each fitting in a bed of caulk to prevent leakage. (Rockwell)

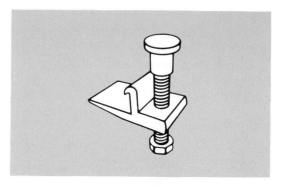

Fig. 24-36. Sink rim locating screw assembly.

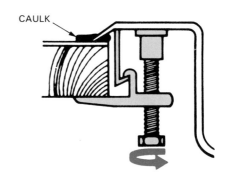

Fig. 24-37. Caulk the rim seat. (Rockwell)

Connecting riser tubes is easier to do at this time than after the sink is in place because of the cramped work space underneath. A dishwasher branch tailpiece may be added to the drain at this point, Fig. 24-35.

Assemble rim fasteners by turning screws through the aluminum lugs, Fig. 24-36. Attach nylon caps (if furnished by manufacturer) to the ends of the screws.

Caulk around rim of sink, Fig. 24-37. Apply a bead of caulk around the entire perimeter of the rim between the channel and edge. Set the sink into the countertop opening and position it squarely. Next, equally space the fasteners.

Tighten screws from the underside of the sink between the edge of sink and countertop. See Fig. 24-38. Fasteners are designed for countertop thicknesses from 5/8 to 3/4 in. (16 to 19 mm) plus the plastic top.

Now wipe the excess caulking from the counter top. Check to see that the sink rim fits tightly around all four sides.

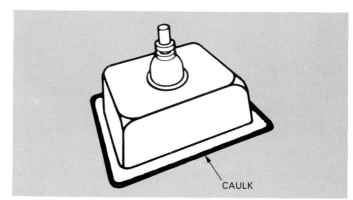

Fig. 24-38. Mounting detail for sink.

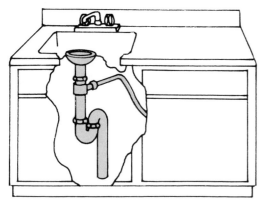

NOTE: A dishwasher branch tailpiece can often be connected to a garbage disposal.

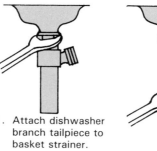

1. Attach dishwasher branch tailpiece to basket strainer.

2. Attach J bend of trap to dishwasher branch tailpiece.

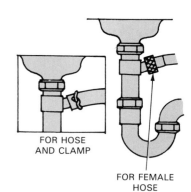

FOR HOSE AND CLAMP

FOR FEMALE HOSE

3. Connect line from dishwasher to branch inlet. Installation is complete.

Fig. 24-35. Dishwasher branch tailpiece. (Rockwell)

Connect faucet supply and drain fittings, Fig. 24-39. Connect drain outlet pipe and water supply fittings. Then connect water supply line and valves. Check for possible water leaks at all connections around drain flange, faucets, and sink rim. Tighten any connection which leaks.

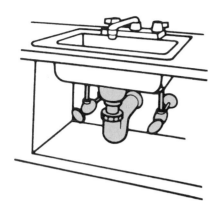

Fig. 24-39. Make the final water connections. (Rockwell)

CLEANING THE SINK

Sinks made of porcelain or stainless steel require very little care. To clean the sink, use a mild cleaning material such as dish cleaning detergent. Any stubborn spots can be readily removed by simple scouring with a non-abrasive cleaner, Fig. 24-40. Use any well known brand of scouring powder with a wet sponge or cloth. Rinse sink thoroughly after cleaning. Water marks are not harmful to the sink surface. To avoid them, simply wipe the sink dry after using.

Some chemicals, such as chlorine products are corrosive to sink surfaces.

Fig. 24-40. To remove stains from enameled surface of plumbing fixtures, choose a non-abrasive cleanser and rub with pad and water. Then rinse.

As a result, it is important to rinse the sink thoroughly after the surface has been exposed to chlorinated cleansing agents and/or chlorinated bleaching agents. Similarly, do not allow these agents to remain in or on the sink for extended lengths of time.

Stainless steel, by its very nature, should not rust. Any rust stains which may appear on the sink surface are usually the result of iron being deposited on the surfaces by other items. Such stains may be readily removed by simple scouring or rubbing. Do not, under any circumstances use steel wool pads to clean the stainless sink. This will scratch all smooth or patterned finishes. Likewise, do not allow rusty utensils to remain in your sink for extended lengths of time.

SUMP PUMPS

A sump pump is used to remove water that seeps into a basement through the foundation. A pit called a sump is built into the floor to collect the water. The floor slopes toward the sump. Modern sump structures are plastic barrels with slotted lids, as shown in Fig. 24-41.

The sump pump has a motor-driven impeller which is located as close to the bottom of the sump

Fig. 24-41. This sump is made of injection molded plastic.

as possible. See Fig. 24-42. The motor is turned on by a float switch when the float rises in the sump.

Some common problems with a sump pump

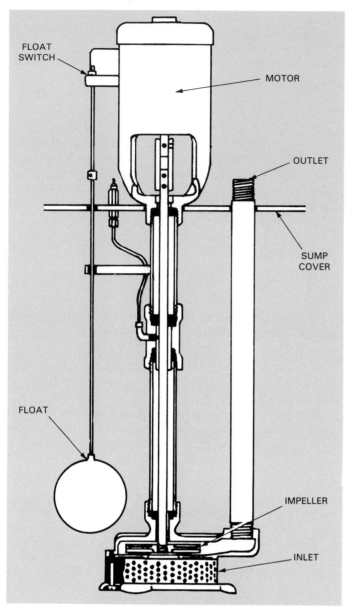

Fig. 24-42. Cutaway view of sump pump which pumps basement water up to the storm sewer near street level. Reverse water flow is often stopped by check valves.

system are:
1. A waterlogged float.
2. Motor will not run.
3. Circuit breaker is tripped when motor is on.
4. Outlet pipe leaks or pipeline freezes outside.
5. Pump takes more than 1 hour to remove two gallons of water.

If float is not working properly, check its weight. If it is full of water, replace it. The float cannot be repaired.

If motor does not come on when needed, check the float switch. Move the switch by hand to check if it will turn on the motor. Check the fuse or circuit breaker at the main service panel.

If the problem is not in the switch or fuse, check if impeller shaft is stuck or drags. Turn off all power

at the service panel. Carefully lift the pump unit from the sump. Avoid bending electrical cables. Remove the filter from the pedestal. Turn impeller blades with a stick or screwdriver. If blades do not turn easily, the supports and perhaps the shaft bushings are corroded. Repairs are best done by a professional.

If motor hums and trips the circuit breaker, the starting circuit in the motor is weak or disconnected. Repairs at a shop are required.

If the outlet pipe leaks, tighten all clamps or look for holes due to corrosion. Metal-to-metal threaded joints may be improved with teflon tape. Plastic pipe may require new hose clamps or may need some clamps added.

To prevent a freezing pipeline, make sure there is enough slope on the outdoor pipe. You may need to place a support under the pipe to keep snow or ice on outer surface from pulling the pipe down. Keep the pipe from flexing and keep from traffic areas to avoid pipe cracks in cold weather.

If the sump pump takes too long to empty the sump, the filter is probably plugged. After turning the breaker off, lift the pump unit out. Remove two or three bolts holding bottom plate. Inspect any related parts at this time. Arrange new filter in the direction stated by the manufacturer. Put unit back in the sump, being careful with electrical cables and switch levers.

TEST YOUR KNOWLEDGE — CHAPTER 24

1. An abbreviation of drain-waste-vent piping is ''_____'' piping.
2. Most older homes have _____ _____ DWV pipes.
3. Contaminated drinking water due to a faucet siphon is called a _____ _____ .
4. Drain lines should slope _____ percent of the horizontal run.
   a. 3 to 4.
   b. 6 to 7.
   c. 9 to 10.
   d. 1 to 2.
5. A main _____ is a vertical pipe open above the roof.
6. Every trap in a plumbing system should be _____ .
7. A vent system often connected as a vertical loop is called a _____ .
8. No vent or waste pipe should be smaller than _____ in.
9. Bending the toilet tank float arm _____ (downward, upward) can help stop continuously flowing water.
10. A _____ drain cleaner will damage a toilet bowl.

11. Seal a toilet base to the waste drain flange with
    a _____ ring.
    a. Rubber.
    b. Wax.
    c. Oakum.
    d. Nylon.
    e. Teflon.
12. The first step in releasing a clogged sink drain
    is to use:
    a. A drain cleaning chemical.
    b. A sink auger.
    c. A plunger.
    d. The trap cleanout plug.
13. To cut tree roots from the inside of a main ser-
    vice drain, use a power _____ .
14. To help prevent clogging of a garbage disposal,
    make sure enough _____ flows through
    it.
15. With electrical power off, loosen a garbage
    disposal blade by pushing in the reverse direc-
    tion with a _____ .
16. Cut a hole for a sink _____ in. (mm) smaller
    on each side than the lip of the basin.
17. When installing a sink and faucet unit, apply
    a good _____ to mating surfaces of all
    fixture pieces.
18. Sink rim fasteners fit countertop thicknesses
    from _____ to _____ in. (mm).
19. Do not use _____ _____ pads to clean
    a stainless steel sink basin.
20. If a sump pump takes too long to pump water,
    one cause is a plugged _____.

KNOW THESE TERMS

Traps, air chamber, soil stack, sump pump, septic system, bacteria, flush ball, float value, closet
auger, plumbers putty.

SUGGESTED ACTIVITIES

Make a model of a drain trap using clear plastic
hose or pipe if possible. Keep the model in the proper scale when you form the types of bends needed.
This means keeping the proper relation between
bend sharpness and the diameter of the pipe you
use. Make an unvented trap by putting the outlet
end in a full bucket of water. Pour water into the
inlet end and note if the trap fails. Next add a T fitting to provide a vent between trap and bucket.
Again note if the trap works or not. Repeat for
various arrangements of bend sharpness and P or
U or S bends. Discuss the results in class.

Visit a local hardware store to discover what
types of waste plumbing parts are available.
Especially note types of toilet tank valves and floats.
Compare prices if two or more types exist. Which
types are easier to repair or replace? Which types
are resistant to corrosion, clogging, or jamming? Do
any of the tank systems conserve water? Tell your
class about your discoveries.

CAREERS

Pipe fitter, plumber, environmental inspector,
waste water engineer.

25

CENTRAL CLEANING SYSTEMS

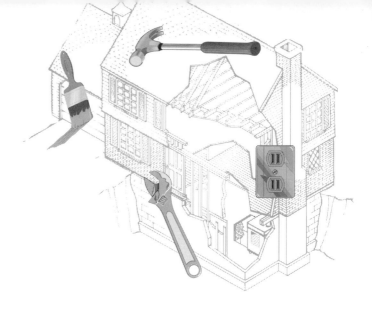

This chapter presents typical equipment and pipe installation steps for central cleaning systems. It includes troubleshooting steps.

After studying this chapter, you will be able to:
■ Plan the location of a central vacuum motor unit.
■ Explain a special air direction for "wye" pipe fittings.
■ Describe the operation of a CCU.
■ List steps for removing clogged objects and starting stalled units.

A central cleaning system is shown in Fig. 25-1. When the homemaker is ready to clean, attach the wand to the hose, add the proper cleaning tool, connect the hose to the wall or floor inlet, and the central cleaning system is ready automatically. When the hose is removed, the power will shut off.

TYPICAL COMPONENTS

The central cleaning system consists of a motor unit, a piping system, a cleaning head, and power and control circuits.

The motor unit, Fig. 25-2, has a heavy duty motor containing its own bypass cooling system. The motor unit also has controls activated by the low voltage switches at each inlet. The low voltage circuit is a remote control system for turning the main motor on or off.

Part of the motor unit is a cannister located in the lower portion that collects the debris pulled in. The

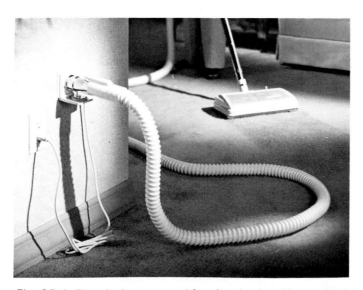

Fig. 25-1. Electrical power cord for cleaning head is wrapped within the hose. Central cleaning system has remote power unit in a location near center of house. It is important there are no leaks at any of the termination covers.
(NuTone Housing Group)

Fig. 25-2. The heart of the central cleaning system is the vacuum motor and collection cannister.
(NuTone Housing Group)

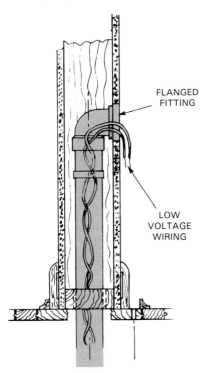

Fig. 25-3. For new construction, the inlet is usually placed within one of the walls. It is spaced about 18 in. (45 cm) from the floor. (NuTone Housing Group)

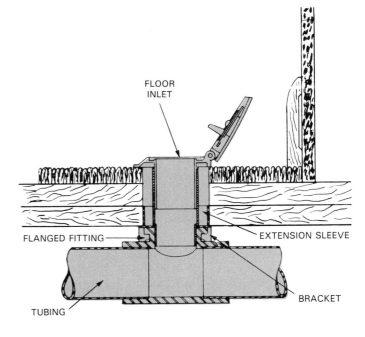

Fig. 25-4. For installation in an older home, the floor inlet is most convenient. (NuTone Housing Group)

cannister has a disposal bag liner for easy and convenient disposal of the collected debris. Replace the bag by removing the metal shroud held closed by the metal snaps.

The inlets, located either in the wall, Fig. 25-3, or floor, Fig. 25-4, are spaced strategically throughout the house for easy access to all cleaning areas. These inlets are connected to the main power unit by plastic piping which is run through the walls. A trunk line run either overhead or under the floor serves all branch lines. See Fig. 25-5. A

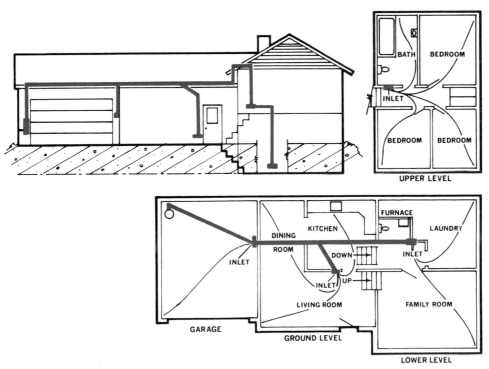

Fig. 25-5. Put inlets in a central location of each room. Plan on a hose length of 20 to 25 ft. (6 to 7.5 m). (NuTone Housing Group.)

low voltage switch is located inside the inlet to turn the motor on or off when the hose is inserted or removed.

The hose is generally constructed of a coiled spring wire covered with soft vinyl for flexibility and interwoven with nylon cord for strength and durability.

Cleaning tools are designed to do all possible vacuuming chores. These tools are usually made of soft vinyl for long life. The attachment wands are chrome-plated metal or are plastic and are held together by a friction fit.

INSTALLING A CENTRAL CLEANING SYSTEM

When planning for the installation of the central cleaning system, sketch the floor plan and elevation view of the house. Locate the power unit in an accessible area, but out of the main traffic patterns. Do not locate the power unit in high temperature areas such as attic spaces or furnace rooms. Garage areas or laundry rooms are excellent locations. The discharge air from the power unit is exhausted to the outside.

Inlets are located centrally to cover the maximum area with the flexible hose. Usually several rooms may be serviced from a single inlet. Some manufacturers have an optional power head that requires a source of 120 volts AC (VAC). When locating the inlet, an electrical outlet should be within six feet for use of the optional current-carrying hose. Be careful not to locate these inlets where they eventually might be blocked by swinging doors or furniture.

Tubing

Refer to Fig. 25-6. Tubing for the installation should consist of a main trunk line running from the farthest wall inlet to the power unit location, with branch lines running to each additional inlet. Generally, an installation will require three or four inlets to cover the entire house. An additional inlet might be located in the garage.

Most manufacturers of central cleaning systems use a 2 in. (5 cm) outside diameter polyvinyl chloride plastic tube. Like other plastic pipe, it is easily cut and welded with solvents to form an airtight, noiseless, and economical tubing system.

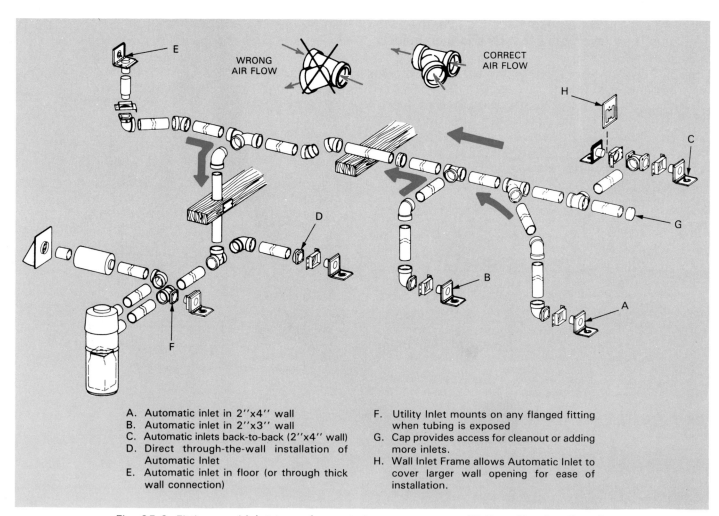

A. Automatic inlet in 2″x4″ wall
B. Automatic inlet in 2″x3″ wall
C. Automatic inlets back-to-back (2″x4″ wall)
D. Direct through-the-wall installation of Automatic Inlet
E. Automatic inlet in floor (or through thick wall connection)
F. Utility Inlet mounts on any flanged fitting when tubing is exposed
G. Cap provides access for cleanout or adding more inlets.
H. Wall Inlet Frame allows Automatic Inlet to cover larger wall opening for ease of installation.

Fig. 25-6. Fittings and joint types for central vacuum system. (NuTone Housing Group)

TROUBLESHOOTING

If a lack of vacuum occurs, any of the following causes could be responsible:

1. Disposable bag filled to capacity. Remove and install replacement. Check secondary filter for possible dirt and dust accumulation. Wash to clean if necessary.
2. Inlet cover not properly sealed. This reduces available suction. Check all covers.
3. Obstruction in the hose. A blockage in the hose can be determined by inserting the hose into any inlet, making sure power unit is running. Too little or no suction can mean a hose blockage. Check each additional inlet for normal suction. Little suction will confirm that hose is blocked. If normal suction is felt at all inlets but one, the blockage is probably located in the tubing system leading to the original inlet.
4. Obstruction in the tubing system inside the walls. If good suction is present at all but one or two inlets, a wall tube is blocked. Insert the spiral cleaning hose end into inlet. With power unit running, place the palm of the hand over the opposite end of the hose. When suction is felt to increase, hold the hand over the hose end for a few more seconds and then quickly remove the hand. This procedure repeated several times should clear the obstruction.

   If the blockage is not cleared, try to move the obstacle with a blunt object like a garden hose. Do not push with more than about five lbs. pressure or you may make it tighter.

   Try a plumbing snake if needed. Otherwise call for professional help.
5. Motor does not run. If the power unit does not start, check the following areas:
   A. Check other wall inlets. Make sure all other inlets are closed so each switch is in proper position. There may be a defective switch in that particular inlet.
   B. Check the overload protection button located in an accessible area. (Check operator's manual.) Press to reset system.
   C. Check the house fuses or circuit breakers for blown fuses or tripped circuit breaker.

If the power unit fails to stop when the hose is removed, an electrical short has occurred somewhere in the system. Make a complete check of all inlets and motor wiring connections. For safety, turn system off by removing fuse, or tripping circuit breaker at house distribution panel. Also, the fuse may be the only way to turn it off until you have time to repair it.

TEST YOUR KNOWLEDGE — CHAPTER 25

1. For the system shown in this chapter, if you remove the hose at a cleaning terminal, the main vacuum motor will turn off. True or False?
2. Plastic pipe for a central cleaning system usually has a _____ in. outside diameter.
3. Explain how a ''wye'' pipe fitting should be installed for the proper air flow direction.
4. Push an obstruction through the pipe in a wall using a smaller pipe such as a _____ _____.
5. If the power unit fails to stop when the hose is removed, a _____ has occurred somewhere in the system.

KNOW THESE TERMS

Vacuum, terminal, outlet, inlet, canister, trunk line, flexible hose.

SUGGESTED ACTIVITY

Sketch the floor plan of your house. With a colored pencil, sketch the layout of a central cleaning system. Show all inlets, motor unit, and power outlets.

CAREERS

Cleaning systems installer, cleaning systems designer, mechanical engineer, salesperson.

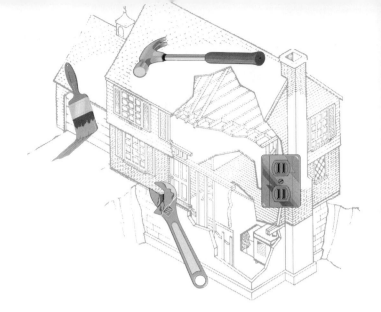

26

ELECTRICAL DISTRIBUTION SYSTEM

This chapter presents some background theory of electricity and provides steps for wiring. It introduces types of cable, circuit breakers, switches, outlets, and low voltage devices. The chapter tells how to extend a branch circuit both inside and on the outside of a wall.

After studying this chapter, you will be able to:
■ Read a watt-hour meter.
■ Calculate current, voltage, and resistance.
■ Choose wiring sizes.
■ Sketch common circuits with duplex outlets.
■ Determine the safety of a circuit.
■ Use a neon test light.
■ Know when to use a fish wire.
■ Attach a wire to a screw terminal properly.

Local and national codes prescribe the sizes and types of electrical conductors and list other specifications for electrical installations. They can also suggest which repairs and installations a homeowner can perform, and which ones require a licensed electrician. By starting with minor electrical repairs, the homeowner may gain enough experience and knowledge to install new circuits and fixtures, to the extent allowed by the code.

Before starting, get the permission of the electrical inspector. Always remember that it is important to know or to ask if the home mechanic is not qualified to perform certain electrical jobs.

Electrical energy can kill. Your safety depends upon awareness of the dangers of working with electricity. Far more important is that others using the electrical energy of the house depend upon the proper use of electrical theories and proper installation of electrical devices.

SOURCES OF ELECTRICITY

Electrical energy is obtained by turning a coil of conducting wire within a strong magnetic field,

thereby inducing an electrical current within the conductor. This current is carried through miles of conducting lines to the populated areas for industrial, commercial, and residential uses.

The force needed to turn the generator is provided by burning coal, oil, or gas, by hydro-dams, or by atomic fission reaction.

Electric power conductors enter the house through an electrical pipe and cap called a service entrance, Fig. 26-1. The power passes through a meter where the amount used by the house is

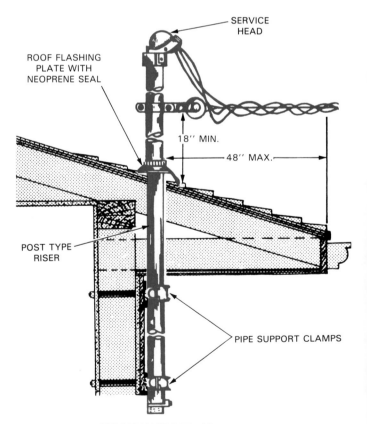

SERVICE HEAD

ROOF FLASHING PLATE WITH NEOPRENE SEAL

18'' MIN.

48'' MAX.

POST TYPE RISER

PIPE SUPPORT CLAMPS

SERVICE MAST FITTINGS

Fig. 26-1. Electric service entrance.

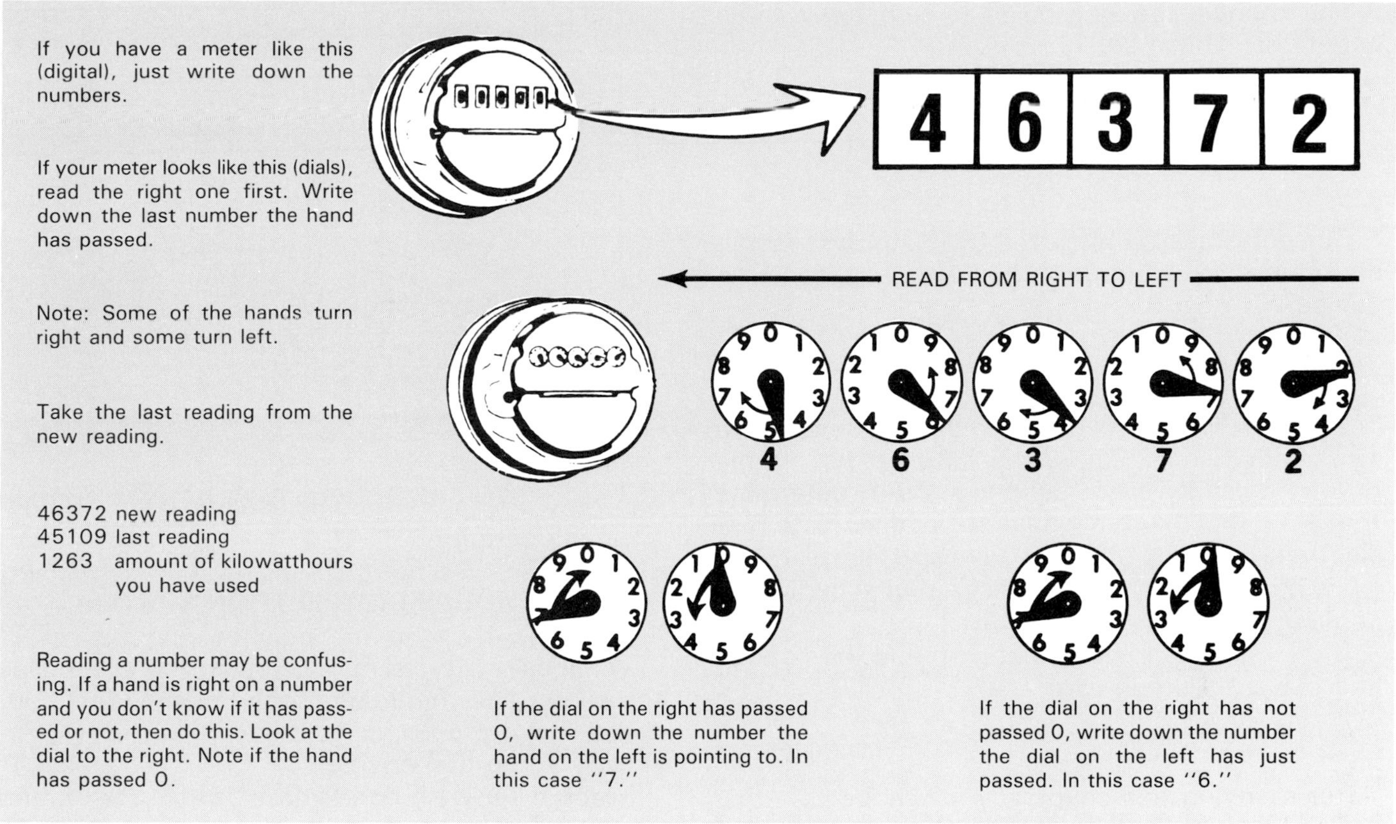

If you have a meter like this (digital), just write down the numbers.

If your meter looks like this (dials), read the right one first. Write down the last number the hand has passed.

Note: Some of the hands turn right and some turn left.

Take the last reading from the new reading.

46372 new reading
45109 last reading
1263 amount of kilowatthours you have used

Reading a number may be confusing. If a hand is right on a number and you don't know if it has passed or not, then do this. Look at the dial to the right. Note if the hand has passed 0.

4 6 3 7 2

READ FROM RIGHT TO LEFT

4   6   3   7   2

If the dial on the right has passed 0, write down the number the hand on the left is pointing to. In this case "7."

If the dial on the right has not passed 0, write down the number the dial on the left has just passed. In this case "6."

Fig. 26-2. Learn to read the watt-hour meter. (University of Missouri Extension Service)

measured. The utility company will then charge for the amount used.

HOW TO READ THE METER

The electric meter has four or five dials, Fig. 26-2. If it has four dials, the extreme left dial is numbered zero through nine, reading counterclockwise. Adjacent to the right, the second dial is numbered zero through nine clockwise. If it has five dials, the left reads clockwise.

Each has a needle as an indicator. When the needle is pointed toward a number, but is located between two numbers, always take the lower number. The indicator needle must have reached the number before it can be read as positive.

ELECTRICAL ENERGY

There is a mathematical relationship between three electrical quantities: voltage, current, and resistance. These are measured in volts, amperes (amps), and ohms. See Fig. 26-3. The respective symbols are V, A, and Ω.

Before understanding the diagram, first learn what is represents:

1. Pressure, the force that propels the energy through the entire system, is referred to as volts (V) or voltage. The most frequently used

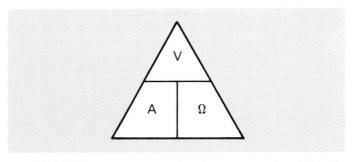

Fig. 26-3. Voltage, current, and resistance are related. Divide upper symbols by lower symbols to get third symbol value. Two symbols on the same level are multiplied to get the third.

voltages for a house are 120 and 240 volts. Most appliances operate on 120 volts, while electric ranges, clothes dryers, or electric heating furnaces use 240 volts.

2. The rate at which electricity is delivered to a house or an appliance is measured in amperes (A).

3. The limiting factor or opposition to flow of current is the resistance or Ohms (Ω).

A limit to the current flow may be due to the size of wire which it must flow through. Just as pipe carries water, the larger the pipe the more water it can deliver to a given point. A larger diameter wire can conduct more amperes of electrical energy.

The triangle drawing helps to remember three equations. These are:

1. $V = A \times \Omega$
2. $A = \dfrac{V}{\Omega}$
3. $\Omega = \dfrac{V}{A}$

Current is easily computed by using the triangle memory device. Suppose 120 V is supplied to a device with 60 Ω.

$$A = \frac{V}{\Omega} \quad \text{OR} \quad A = \frac{120}{60} = 2 \text{ amperes}$$

The current value is useful to determine the wire size needed. For 2 amps, checking against a table of wire capacity sizes, as in Fig. 26-4, determine that a number 14 size would be needed. Note that electrical codes do not allow wire sizes smaller than 14 to be used for ordinary house circuits. (Individual appliance leads may be smaller.)

If the resistance were unknown and the voltage and current were known:

$$\Omega = \frac{V}{A} \quad \text{OR} \quad \Omega = \frac{120}{2} = 60 \; \Omega$$

If the voltage were unknown and the resistance and amperage were known:

$$V = A \times \Omega \quad \text{OR} \quad V = 2 \times 60 = 120 \text{ volts}$$

Watt

The rate at which electrical energy is consumed or used is called electrical power. The unit of measurement of electrical power is the watt, and the international system of measurement uses the capital "W" to represent power. In electrical circuits, the power is equal to the current multiplied by the voltage.

$$W = A \times V \quad \text{or} \quad W = 2 \times 120 = 240 \text{ watts.}$$

Therefore, one watt of power is the result of one ampere of current driven by one volt of force through a circuit.

Watt-Hour

If a circuit with one volt pressure causes a one ampere current to flow for one hour, it is referred to as one watt-hour. A watt-hour is a small unit of measurement. The user will probably be more familiar with the term kilowatt-hour (kWh) which means 1000 watt-hours are used after running one hour. The energy is used at the rate of 1000 watts.

The four-dial meter located close to the service entrance is read in kilowatt-hours. The electric utility company bills in units of kilowatt-hours.

A light bulb in a table lamp may be rated as 100 watts. To keep this bulb lighted for one hour will require 0.1 kilowatt-hours of electrical energy, or

Copper Wire Wire Size	Amperes Capacity	
14	15	
12	20	Solid Wire
10	30	
8	40	
6	55	
4	70	
2	95	
1	110	Stranded Wire
1/0	125	
2/0	145	
3/0	165	

Note: for long runs wire sizes must be increased.

Fig. 26-4. Current capacity for wire sizes.

one kilowatt-hour would be used in 10 hr. of continuous operation.

THE HOUSE DISTRIBUTION SYSTEM

The local utility, in many communities, supplies the wiring and the hookup only for the watt-hour meter. Beyond that point, it becomes the responsibility of the homeowner.

In most new houses in the United States and Canada, the meter is located on the exterior wall generally close to the service head. Power may be brought overhead or underground to the house. (Never attempt to make any changes or work on the electric power system beyond the watt-hour meter. These wires have no fuse protection and are dangerous).

Fig. 26-5. Electrical power is distributed by branch lines from the main electrical panel. Note how large the aluminum incoming lines are. Aluminum wire is only allowed with special fixture alloys.

Electric wires leading from the watt-hour meter usually enter the house directly at or near the meter. These wires, numbering usually three, go directly into the distribution panel, Fig. 26-5.

The distribution provides a location to:
1. Branch all individual circuit lines.
2. Provide individual and master shut-off.

The three-wire electrical services are capable of delivering a total of 100 amperes to household circuits. Larger units with capacities of 150-250 amperes are required for installation of electric heating and cooling, electric ranges, and clothes washers and dryers. Old services may consist of only two wires and one or two 15 or 20-ampere circuits for a total of a 30 or 40-ampere service.

The current in the service cables passes through either cartridge fuses or a main circuit breaker. In the fuse type service, pulling the main unit disconnects and removes the cartridge fuses. This cuts off power to the entire system. In the circuit breaker protected system, simply tripping the main circuit breaker cuts off the power to the house.

Electrical cables from the service enter the distribution panel through a large knockout usually located on top. Some older style connection arrangements are shown in Fig. 26-6. Learn about both old and new systems.

Grounding and Power Wire Colors

The service line cable contains three wires. Two wires are black insulated, and one is a bare copper wire. Each black is connected to one of the two main breaker input terminals. The bare copper ground wire is connected to a neutral bus bar. The neutral bar has a lead attached to a cold water pipe, Fig. 26-7. A second ground wire is attached to a ground rod driven into the ground outside the house.

Simple branch circuits to the rest of the house have a black wire, a white wire, and a bare wire. The bare and the white are connected to the neutral bar of the service box. The black is connected to any convenient fuse or breaker terminal that is an output. With things working correctly, current goes through the hot service entrance wires and the fuses or circuit breaker to the individual circuits.

Circuit Breakers

The amount of current in a circuit is limited by the amperage capacity of the circuit fuse or circuit breaker, Fig. 26-8. If a short-circuit or overload occurs, the protective device will cut off the power. This prevents fires due to wiring overheating from excessive current flow. A 15 ampere circuit breaker, for example, will trip if a frying pan and toaster are on the same circuit at the same time.

Color Codes

Electrical conductors are available in a variety of different types for specific purposes. Within the cable are from two to four insulated wires. One with white insulation is always neutral. The black insulated wire is the hot wire. A second hot, if applicable is color coded with red insulation. The fourth wire is either bare or green and is the grounding wire. According to the National Electrical Code, a ground wire is required in all residential installations. (Appendix, Electrical Symbols commonly used on blueprints).

TYPES OF CONDUCTORS

Each use of electrical wiring around the house requires a prescribed type of conducting cable or tubing. Four types of conductor systems are NM, UF,

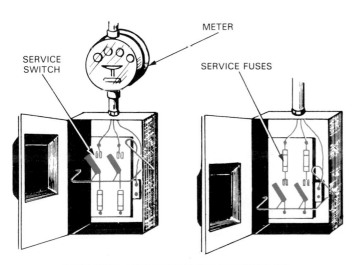

BASIC RULE—EQUIPMENT IS NOT PERMITTED ON SUPPLY SIDE OF SERVICE DISCONNECT

Fig. 26 6. Watt-hour meter connections.

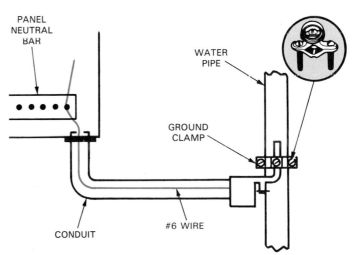

Fig. 26-7. A common practice is to ground the electrical system to a cold water pipe. A second grounding rod in earth is required.

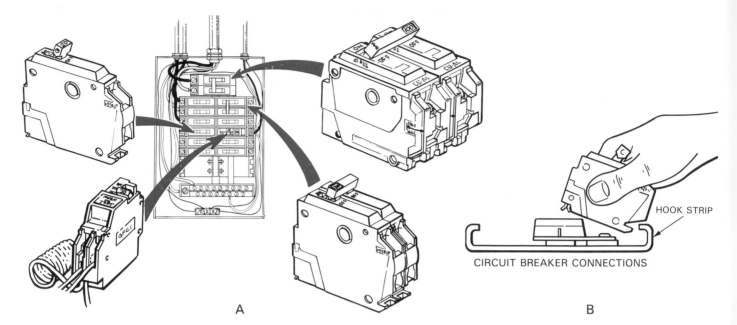

A

B

Fig. 26-8. A—A circuit breaker is a switch in line with the black wire. It opens automatically when a set overload flows through it. Each circuit requires one breaker. B—Inserting or removing a breaker. (General Electric Co.)

armored, and conduit.

Type NM is sheathed in a heavy protective plastic or fiber casing for dry indoor installations, as shown at the top in Fig. 26-9.

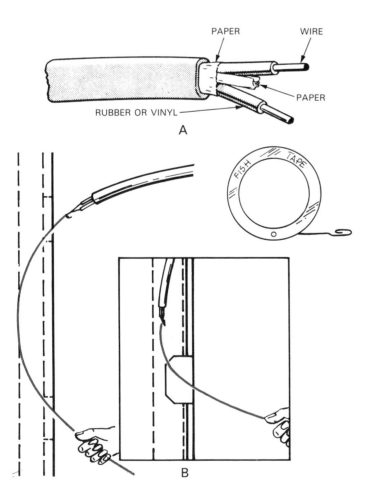

A

B

Fig. 26-9. A — Electrical conductor for indoor use. B — Install using a fish tape. (General Electric Co.)

Type UF electrical cable is used for outdoor and underground installations. An impervious plastic case protects the insulated wires from moisture and decay, Fig. 26-10. This cable can be buried directly in the soil without any additional protection.

Armored cable has a flexible spiral wound steel casing enclosing the insulated conductors, Fig. 26-11. Some codes may require that armor cable be used in certain installations instead of type NM. The steel casing protects the wires against mechanical injury to exposed installations. Armored cable is recommended for dry indoor use. It is sometimes referred to as BX cable, a trade name.

Conduit is a fourth method of cable installation. See Fig. 26-12. It consists of a steel or plastic tube through which the conductors are pulled. Used in locations where an unprotected cable might be damaged, it is required for all exposed and unprotected conductors. Conduit may be cast directly in new concrete. The conducting wires are later pulled.

Only conduit can be placed in an accessible area. All other plastic or armored types must be enclosed to prevent their use as supports for hanging objects.

Cables are usually designated according to their type, size and number of wires they contain. For example: type NM 12-3 with ground.

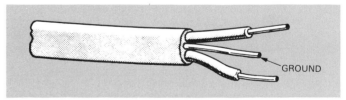

Fig. 26-10. Electrical conductor for direct burial.

254

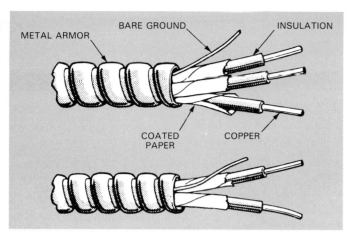

Fig. 26-11. Metallic armored cable. Bare ground is usually aluminum.

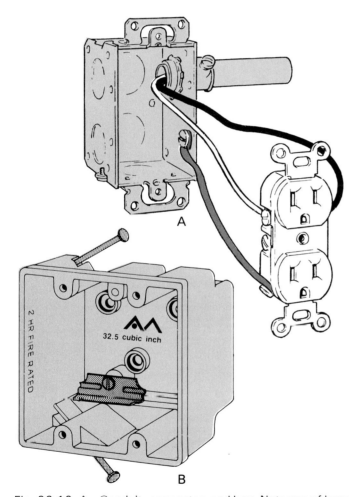

Fig. 26-12. A—Conduit, connector, and box. Note use of bare ground wire. B—Molded fiberglass box.
(Allied Moulded Products)

CIRCUIT LOADS

The circuit load, or capacity to handle several electrical appliances, depends on:
1. Size of wire.

2. Length of the conductors.
3. Capacity of the fuse or circuit breaker.

To determine the power requirement, add all appliances to be supplied by the circuit. A 1000 watt toaster and a 1200 watt frying pan should require a circuit capable of supplying more than 2200 watts.

$$A = \frac{W}{V} \qquad A = \frac{2200}{120} \qquad A = 18.3$$

18.3 amperes of current would be required to operate these appliances. A 20 ampere circuit with number 12 wire can safely supply 2400 watts of power without causing the circuit breaker to trip.

Special circuits must be matched to the ratings of the unit they serve. A kitchen range which is rated at 12,000 watts will require 240 volts capable of carrying 50 amperes. Motor driven appliances such as dishwashers, clothes washers and dryers, and refrigerators must be calculated on the surge requirements. Their circuits must be capable of carrying the current necessary to start the motor. Special circuit breakers or fuses are supplied to delay when they will trip. This compensates for the surge.

SWITCHES

Switches for residential uses are designed to operate at an amperage and voltage common to household energy levels. The common single pole switch is designed for 15A 125V or 7 1/2A 250V meaning that the switch may be used to control loads not over 15 ampere if the voltage is not over 125 volts. Other switches are available for larger amperages and higher voltages. The principle of a switch is explained with the schematic drawing in Fig. 26-13.

SOURCE

Fig. 26-13. Simple schematic drawing of a switch operating a light.

WIRING SWITCHES

How a switch, outlet, or fixture is wired depends upon its location in relation to the power source wires that lead from the main service panel.

According to the National Electrical Code, the white is always neutral and the black is hot. Bare copper or green is the ground. The switch always controls the hot or black wire, Fig. 26-14. The switch is used to break into the hot wire. When a

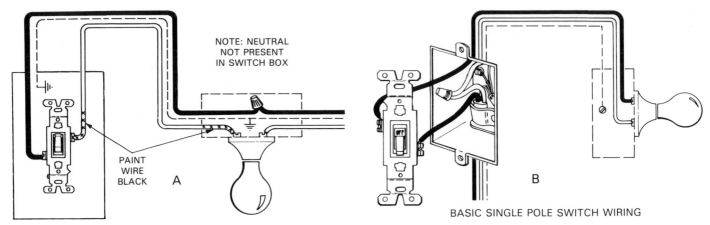

Fig. 26-14. Single load single control. A — Source is in lamp mount box. B — Source is in switch box. (General Electric Co.)

white wire is used on a switch, its end insulation is painted black.

Switches are available in a variety of styles:

1. Silent switches for noiseless operation.
2. Lighted toggle for night location, Fig. 26-15.
3. Dimmer switches for variable control of incandescent lights, Fig. 26-16.
4. Three and four-way switches, Fig. 26-17. Three-way switches are connected to each other by three conductor cables so that each one can override the other, Fig. 26-18.

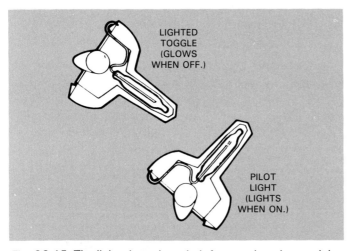

Fig. 26-15. The lighted toggle switch for easy location at night.

Switches may be connected by wrapping the conductor wires around the head of the terminal screws, Fig. 26-19. Put one black wire under one terminal screw and the other black wire under the second terminal screw. The third (green or bare) wire is a ground. Connect it to the metal box enclosing the switch. Some new switches have quick connection terminals which allow the 1/2 in. (12 mm) of bare wire to be pushed into openings on the back of the switch, Fig. 26-20.

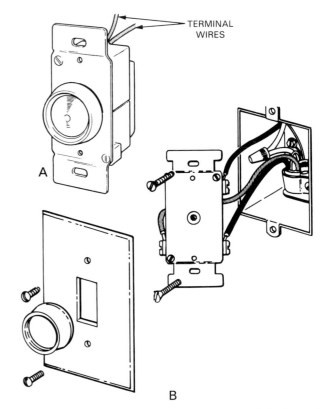

Fig. 26-16. Dimmer switch, a variable control for incandescent lights. A — Typical switch has two pigtail wires. B — Screw terminal type. Follow manufacturer's directions. (General Electric Co.)

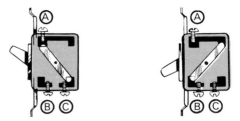

Fig. 26-17. What happens inside a three-way switch when toggle lever is thrown from one position to another. The current enters by way of the common terminal "A", and leaves by either "B" or "C" depending on lever position.

256

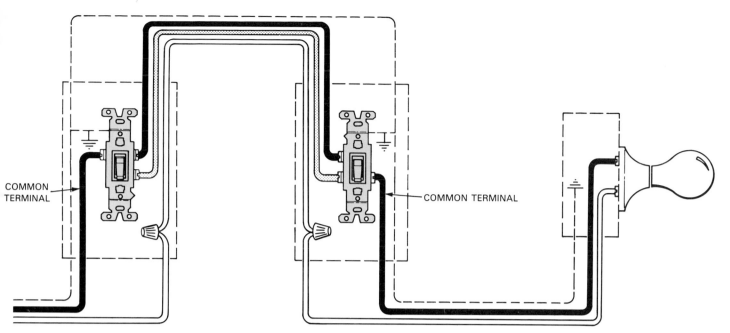

Fig. 26-18. A light controlled from two points. Two three-way switches are needed. (General Electric Co.)

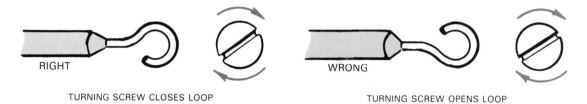

Fig. 26 19. Always insert the loop of wire so that tightening the screw closes the loop.

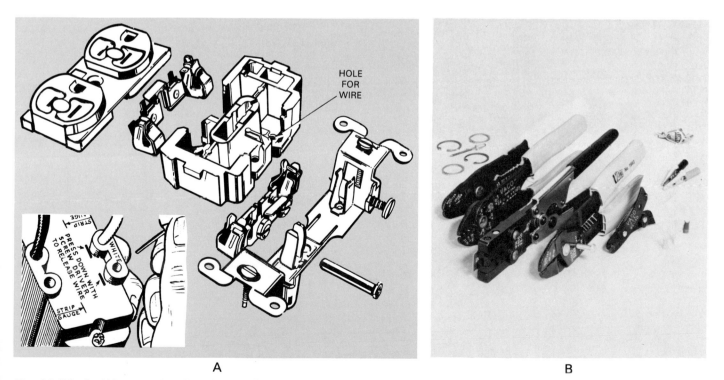

Fig. 26-20. A—Wires can be placed in small holes in back (arrow) instead of on terminal screws. Strip the wire about 1/2 in. (12 mm), push it into small hole, and tighten the proper screw. (General Electric Co.) B—Smallest tool shown is a wire stripper for most home uses. (Vaco Products Co.)

DUPLEX OUTLETS (RECEPTACLES)

Modern duplex outlets or receptacles are designed for grounded wiring systems. They are used with plugs having a third grounding terminal. Connections are made similar to those described for the switch. However, there are some differences.

1. An outlet requires connecting one black wire and one white (neutral) wire. A light colored screw holds the neutral wire and a dark screw, the black wire.
2. There will also be a green hex screw on the outlet housing for connection of the bare or green insulated ground wire.

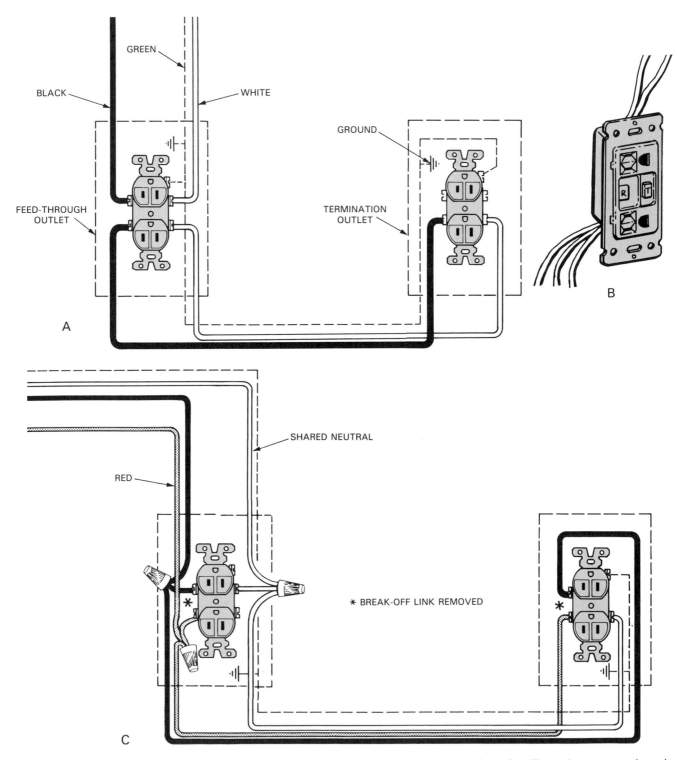

Fig. 26-21. A, B—Standard or Ground Fault type duplex outlet is convenient when a branch will continue to another place. C—Separate circuits with a shared neutral make good use of stated breaker current rating. Use only with double-gang breaker. (General Electric Co.)

3. The duplex receptacle has two sets of terminal connections. This lets the home mechanic continue the branch line for more duplex outlets or other electrical hook-ups, Fig. 26-21. Special outlets are manufactured for special uses. See Fig. 26-22. One example is a 60 A 240 V receptacle for a range connection. Many different power requirements have different receptacles to avoid confusion and possible damage to the appliance by mismatching power to appliance.

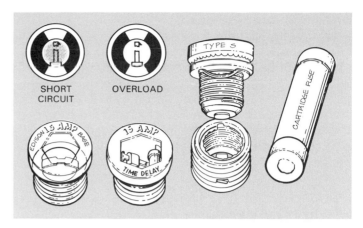

Fig. 26-23. Be sure to turn off the power cutoff devices in the distribution panel.

HEAVY DUTY POWER OUTLETS

Rated Load	3 Wire Polarized 3 Pole 3 Wire	3 Wire Grounding 2 Pole 3 Wire		4 Wire Grounding 3 Pole 4 Wire
30 AMP	125-250V (NEMA #10-30R)	125V (NEMA #5-30R)	250V (NEMA #6-30R)	Grounding (NEMA #14-30R)
50 AMP	125-250V (NEMA #10-50R)	125V (NEMA #5-50R)	250V (NEMA #6-50R)	Grounding (NEMA #14-50R)
60 AMP	—	—	—	Grounding (NEMA #14-60R)

Fig. 26-22. Special outlets for heavy-duty power.

REPLACING DUPLEX OUTLET OR SWITCH

Purchase the same type of receptacle or switch with the same requirements and voltage ratings. One single pole switch can be replaced with one dimmer control.

Replace as follows:
1. Disconnect circuit power by tripping breaker or removing fuse, Fig. 26-23.
2. Double-check by trying the circuit or by testing the unit with a test probe, Fig. 26-24.
3. Remove the cover plate by unscrewing the short exposed screws.
4. The switch or receptacle is fastened to the box by two long screws, one at the top and one at the bottom. Remove these and pull the receptacle or switch from the metal or plastic box.
5. Make a mental or written note of the location of all wires. A switch, if it is a drop-leg, will have one black wire and one white wire painted black under each terminal. If the power is passed through the switch box, both switch terminals will have black wires under them. With power passed through the box, the white wires will be joined and then capped with tape

or a wire nut in the back of the box. The ground wire will be connected to a grounding point on the box.
6. Disconnect all wires. With screwdriver loosen the terminal screw and remove wire. If wires are connected by the quick push-in connection, remove by placing a small screwdriver blade into the slot above the wire and the back of unit and push in. Refer again to Fig. 26-20. At the same time, pull outward on the wire, freeing the connection.
7. Make new connection. Tighten down all screws.
8. Relocate unit into box. Plumb for alignment. For switches, the ON designation should be at the top. For duplex receptacles the grounding prong opening should be on the top.
9. Replace cover plate.
10. Reset the breaker or replace the fuse.

INSTALLING NEW ELECTRICAL BOXES

According to electrical codes, all switches, duplex outlets, fixture wiring, and connections should be

Fig. 26-24. Testing for ''hot'' circuits.

housed in electrical boxes.

In new construction, boxes can be nailed to the studs or crosspieces. Where there are existing walls, holes must be cut through the gypsum board. With lath and plaster, much of it must be removed to get access to the line where the cable will run.

Switch boxes are generally located 48 in. above the floor. Outlet boxes are usually placed 12 in. (30 cm) above the floor. Kitchen outlets are placed about 5 in. (15 cm) above the countertop. Other locations may be arranged for convenience. Boxes for special wiring may also be installed, for instance, telephone wall jacks, television antennas, and furnace thermostats. Electrical boxes provide a sound foundation for the attached units as well as providing a means of securing the electrical cable and giving space for making electrical connections.

When installing boxes in existing locations:
1. Mark the location by outlining the box on wall.
2. With drill or auger bit, bore two holes in diagonal corners. Cut out with a compass saw.
3. Before box is installed in opening, fish the electrical cable through wall and cut the opening, Fig. 26-25. If wall is lath and plaster, much

of it must be removed to get a wire through. A surface-mounted system is easier and is discussed in this chapter.
4. Knock out cable plug for insertion of wire.
5. Insert electrical cable from backside of box. Allow about 6 in. to protrude through box. Tighten the cable clamp.
6. Install box into wall opening and fasten to wall stud, or clamp to gypsum board. This cannot be done with lath and plaster walls.

Ceiling Boxes

Ceiling boxes, sometimes referred to as octagon boxes because of their shape are generally used to support lighting fixtures, Fig. 26-26. Because of the weight of lighting fixtures, these ceiling boxes must be supported by hangers mounted between two ceiling joists.

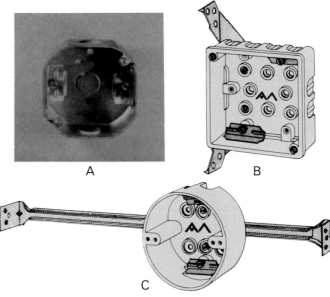

Fig. 26-26. Light fixtures and other connections are enclosed in junction box. A—Octagon or J box. B, C—Junction (hanger) boxes with mounting brackets. (Allied Moulded Products)

CEILING FIXTURES

Ceiling fixtures are made with different brackets for mounting on the ceiling boxes, Fig. 26-27. Some are fastened directly to the octagon box with two machine screws run into the threaded ears of the box. Others may be fastened to a secondary metal mounting bar which is fastened to the octagon box. The bar often has a series of different thread holes for a variety of fixture sizes.

Some fixtures are fastened to a threaded stud extending down from the center of the mounting bar, Fig. 26-28. This method is usually used for the very heavy fixture which has to be held in position while the electrical connections are being made.

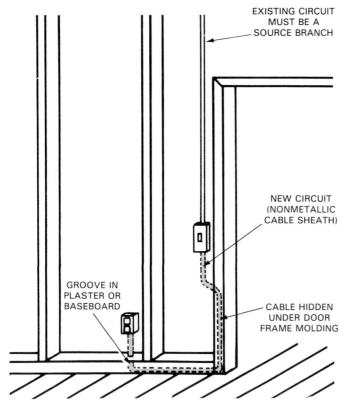

Fig. 26-25. Method of installing a new outlet by feeding from a wall switch if a source branch of power is present in the wall switch box. 1. Remove door trim and baseboard and find wire location in open space behind trim or cut channel behind baseboard in drywall or plaster. Rout a channel in the back of the baseboard. 2. Work wire between studs to outlet opening. 3. Mount box. 4. Replace trim. Any telephone wires may be hidden behind trim while laying other wiring.

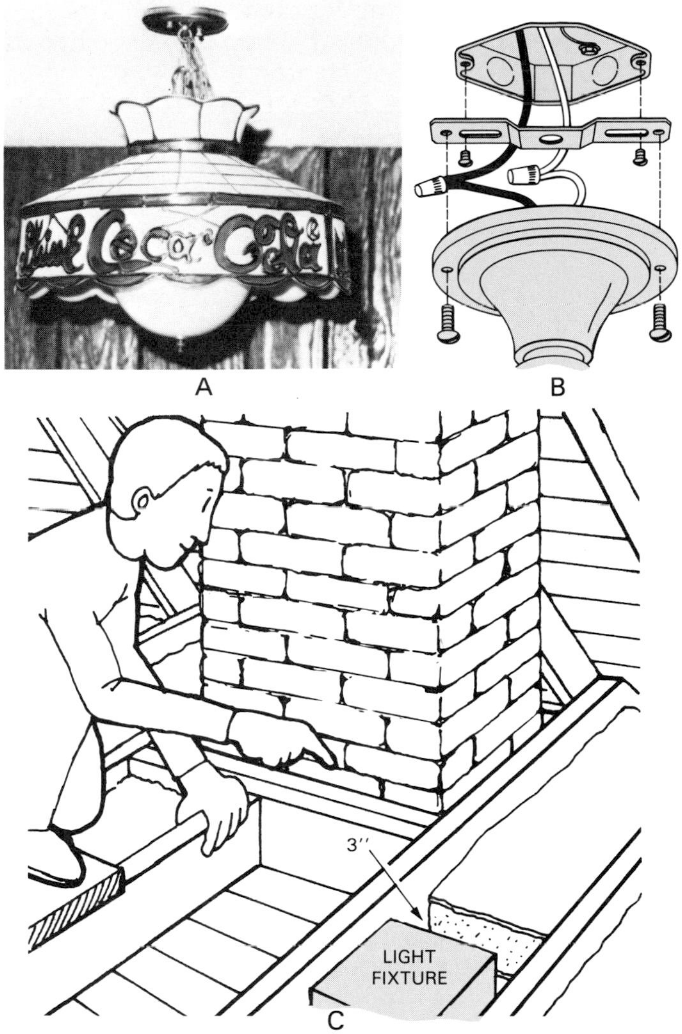

Fig. 26-27. A — Ceiling fixtures are fastened into a junction box which is mounted to the ceiling framework. B — The mounting bar has a slotted opening for several sizes. C — The National Electrical Code requires that insulation be kept 3 in. away from light fixtures. (U.S. HUD Dept.)

SURFACE-MOUNTED WIRING

Recent progress in the design of circuit hardware has led to quick methods of wiring. Refer to Fig. 26-29. Shown is a completed surface or "on-wall" wiring project.

The system is useful for structures with much masonry work that is in the way of a wiring run. A surface mount avoids much work. Tracks can be painted any color, and can be covered with wallpaper.

Installation consists of about four steps. Some manufacturers have a sequence number on each of about 15 parts for easy purchase. The number also aids in installation.

First, select a nearby source of power such as an existing wall outlet, Fig. 26-30, and turn off the power to that outlet. It is best to use surface mounted wiring only with a grounded system.

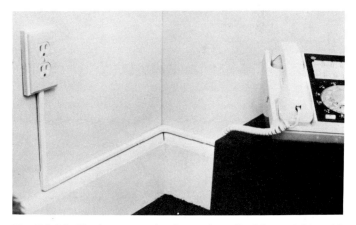

Fig. 26-29. The home mechanic can install wiring quickly with a surface-mount system. This avoids cutting into walls and ceilings. (Wiremold Co.)

Fig. 26-28. The pipe stud mount for heavy light fixtures.

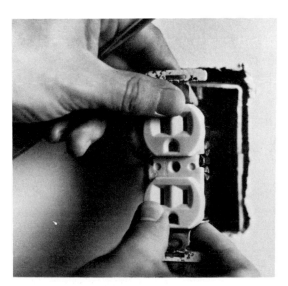

Fig. 26-30. Select a source of power, usually a wall outlet. Use only with a grounded system. (Wiremold Co.)

Next measure and cut the channel. Lay out all pieces and elbows. Allow for fastening hardware. Use a hacksaw as shown in Fig. 26-31.

Choose three (or more) wires by matching the colors of the existing wires at the source outlet. These will be pulled through the channels, Fig. 26-32. The wires can be pulled through or placed inside a track before snapping the track in place. At least three colors are used: white, black, and either green or bare. The green or bare is used as a grounded wire.

Connect each green or bare wire to a convenient screw on a box or ear. Connect each white or black as was arranged at the source. All wires on screws are wrapped in the direction the screw tightens. This assures tight connections.

A

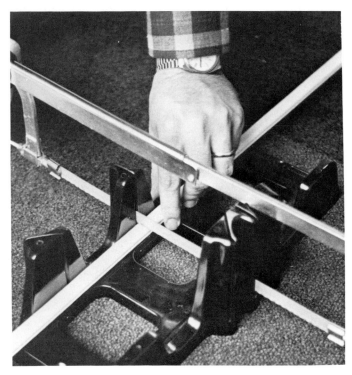

Fig. 26-31. Measure and cut channel. (Wiremold Co.)

Install the cover plates on the source and end receptacles. Test the system, Fig. 26-33.

LOW VOLTAGE CIRCUITS

Heating and cooling thermostat controls and door chimes are usually powered by lower voltage supplies than for the remainder of the house. Each low voltage circuit is equipped with a transformer to reduce the voltage from the 120V household voltage to either 12 or 24V. See Fig. 26-34. A transformer providing a low voltage is referred to as a step-down transformer.

The step-down transformer consists of two coils of wire and a metal core. The primary coil has many

B

Fig. 26-32. A — Install wiring before or after snapping channel into wall clips. B — Attach black wire to dark screw, white to light color screw, and green to ground screw. (Wiremold Co.)

windings of the conductor and the primary voltage of 120 V is induced into it. The secondary coil has only a few wire windings, and the output voltage is proportional to the ratio of secondary windings to the primary windings.

The reduced voltage will not give the home mechanic a shock so long as all work is completed

Fig. 26-33. Connect wiring to new receptacle and test the light. (Wiremold Co.)

on the low voltage circuit. You do not need to shut the circuit off.

Door Chime Failure

First locate the step-down transformer, usually placed in some out of the way place like the attic

or basement. It is most frequently located close to the distribution panel.

Check the low voltage side for presence of power (use voltage tester). A wire may be loose or broken at the terminal screws. If wiring is intact, check the switch button at all doors. Remove push-button switch from door jamb and touch the two lead wires together. If chime sounds, the switch is faulty. Check all push-button switches at other doors.

Thirdly, check chime itself, Fig. 26-35. Most chimes operate on the concept of a solenoid, which when driven by electric current will strike the chime. The solenoid plunger is retracted by a spring. Any restriction of this movement or a damaged solenoid coil will prevent proper chime operation.

Thermostat Controls

The primary control in any heating, cooling, or humidity control system is the thermostat, Fig. 26-36. While there are several types, most thermostat controls are based on the principle of

Fig. 26-35. Parts of a door chime. Clean out any dust on plunger cores.

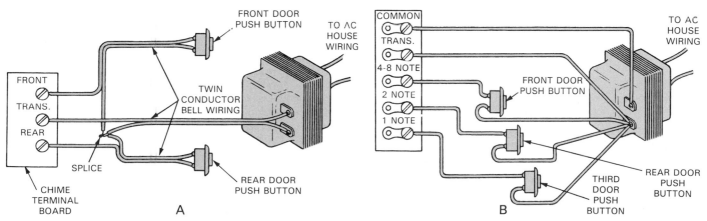

Fig. 26-34. A — Wiring for two-note (NuTone) chime. B — Wiring for eight note chime. Purpose of transformer is to provide low voltage for chimes, thermostats, or automatic door latches.

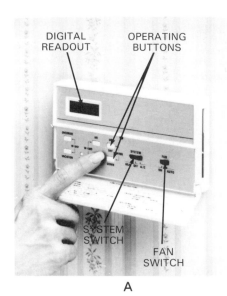

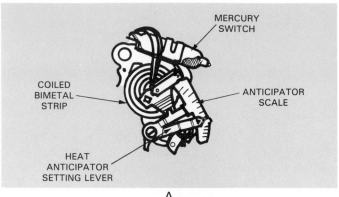

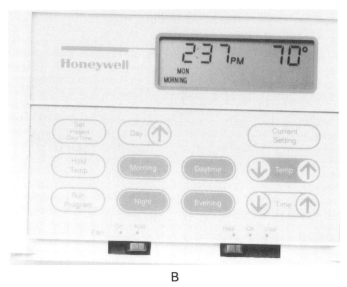

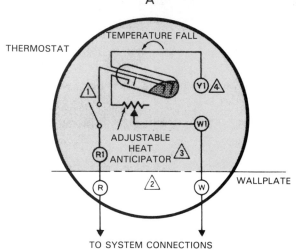

Fig. 26-36. A—Thermostat. (Johnson Controls, Inc., Penn Div.) B—Programmable thermostat for heating and cooling. It can be set for a weekend or longer period. (Honeywell Inc.)

HEATING ONLY THERMOSTAT

△1 Model with positive off switch opens the thermostat circuit when set point dial is moved to the off position.

△2 Make system wiring connections to terminals on wallplate.

△3 R1, W1 terminals on thermostat are directly connected to R, W terminals on wallplate when thermostat is mounted on wallplate.

△4 R1, Y1 terminals are thermostat connection points for air conditioning system.

B

Fig. 26-37. A—A heat-sensing bimetal strip in coil form is the heart of a thermostat. B—Operation of thermostat switch. Tilting of glass vial lets drop of mercury make a contact. "Heat anticipator" helps avoid overshooting desired temperature setting; a resistor adds a little heat to the bimetal strip. (Honeywell)

unequal expansion or contraction of metal if exposed to temperature changes. Different metals, when heated or cooled, expand and contract at different rates. Therefore, if two different metals are joined together into a bimetal strip, this strip or arm, will bend with temperature changes. See Fig. 26-37. This movement is used to open or close an electric circuit which turns on the appropriate unit.

Placement of a thermostat within the home is critical to its operation. A central location is generally sought. Avoid drafty locations. Locations which have variable temperature changes due to lighting, heat, kitchen cooking, bathroom heat, fireplace heat, or north and south walls should be avoided.

The thermostat operates also on a low voltage circuit. The step-down transformer is usually located at or near the furnace location.

Checking Thermostat Mounting

The wall thermostat is usually factory-calibrated and needs no further attention. However, the home mechanic may on occasion find a discrepancy in the thermostat setting and the thermometer reading. Most thermostats have built-in thermometers. In this case, the wall mount may not be level. Refer to Fig. 26-38.

To correct the situation, remove the thermostat cover and locate the level line or plumb line. With a spirit level, make this minor adjustment:

1. Place spirit level on thermostat.
2. Loosen screws of mounting plate, Fig. 26-39,

and rotate until spirit level gives correct reading.

3. Tighten mounting screws and replace cover.

After making adjustment, observe for several hours or days to see if both setting and thermometer are synchronized.

Calibration of the Thermostat

If it appears that the thermostat is out of calibration, make sure that it is level and is not subject to radiant heat from the sun, radiators, or appliances.

Remove thermostat cover ring so the mercury switch may be observed. After a 5 or 10 minute off period (with thermostat setting below room temperature), slowly raise the setting until the switch just makes contact. If thermostat pointer and setting indicator read the same the instant the switch makes contact, no recalibration is necessary.

If calibration is needed, proceed as follows:

1. Turn the setting a few degrees above room temperature and remove cover.
2. Refer to Fig. 26-40. Slip the calibration wrench onto the hex nut under the bimetal strip coil

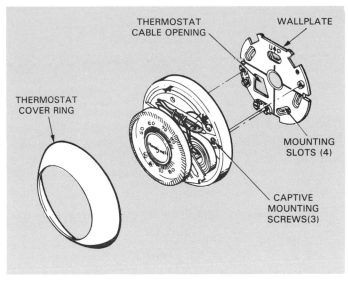

Fig. 26-39. Typical wall-mounted thermostat. (Honeywell)

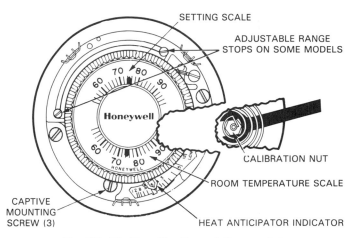

Fig. 26-40. Recalibration of thermostat.

and hold the dial firmly, turn the hex nut until the mercury breaks contact.

3. Turn the dial to a low setting so that the thermostat loses the heat it has gained from the heat of the home mechanic's hands and its own operation. Wait at least 5 minutes.
4. Slowly turn the dial until the pointer reads the same.
5. Firmly hold the dial from turning. Carefully turn the hex nut until the mercury drop slips to the heating-contact end of the glass vial.
6. Recheck calibration, select the desired temperature, and replace cover.

MISCELLANEOUS WIRING

There are many circuits in the home not used for electrical power, but for communication or controlling. Devices include telephones, intercoms, stereo equipment, computer terminals, video cable items,

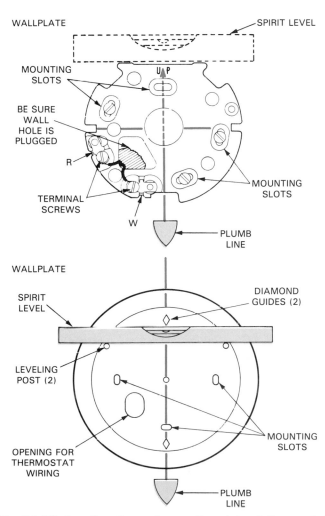

Fig. 26-38. Leveling the wall mounting plate of thermostat. (Honeywell)

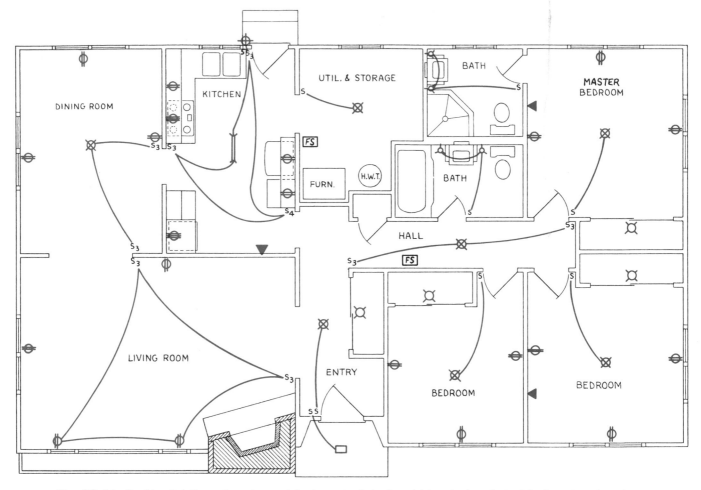

Fig. 26-41. Residential floor plan shows telephone jack (colored triangles) and electrical system locations.

and burglar alarms.

A common wiring project for the home mechanic is adding one or more telephone jacks. If the home is new construction, a great number of jacks should be added before walls are finished. Plan three or more for each floor as a minimum requirement, Fig. 26-41. For other wiring like stereo and burglar alarm circuits, create your own designs or use plans provided by the manufacturer.

If the home is not new construction, more work is needed to install wires or cables. One or more fish tapes will allow you to pull cables through most walls, ceilings, and through bends. Look at one procedure for fishing a cable from 4 or 5 feet away, shown in Fig. 26-42.

Most of the length of a telephone wire run does not need to be inside a wall or ceiling. Since the wires are so thin, they can be easily concealed. See Fig. 26-43. Wires can be run parallel to existing edges of siding, gutters, downspouts, or door frames. Wires can easily be run under baseboards as was suggested for power wiring in Fig. 26-25. Rout a groove in the back side of the molding to fit the wire.

Several termination systems can be used at the same time. If your house has a network interface with screw terminals for individual loop ends of

wire, split off most of the branches there. You may use the screw terminals throughout, or you may convert the screw type to the modular type. Refer to Fig. 26-44 If the closest branch point is at a modular jack, plug in a junction box and wire from this box, or buy a molded joining block in the shape of a ''Y'' or ''T'' to match two cables to a third.

Burglar Alarm

The home mechanic can maintain some parts of a home security system. Parts such as door and window switches, floor mat switches, and alarm horns can be checked for correct operation. Refer to Fig. 26-45.

Most trouble with window and door switches is caused by loose connections. Check all terminal screws and tighten. Look for torn metal strips on windows if these are used. An ohmmeter may be used to check switches and metal strips, but only if the manufacturer's literature gives these instructions. The meter voltage could damage the main control box.

If the floor mat switch can be entirely unplugged from the main control circuit, test it using an ohmmeter. Some weight on the mat should cause the meter to read zero ohms. Most often, you should replace a faulty mat instead of attempting repairs.

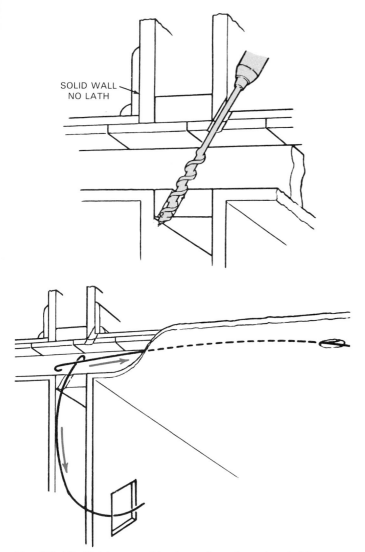

Fig. 26-42. Fishing a cable through a sharp bend. The procedure is good for both power wire and telephone wire.

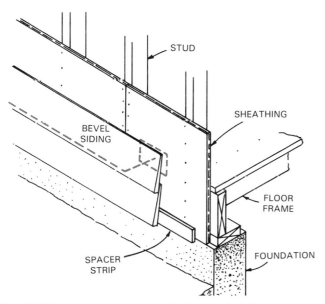

Fig. 26-43. How to conceal telephone wire. Bore under lap siding and into room. Place and paint wire to hide it. Staple a vertical run at a downspout.

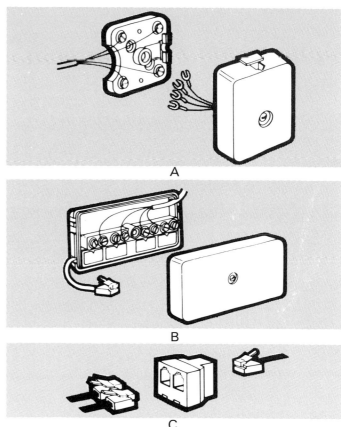

Fig. 26-44. Hardware for converting to other termination systems. A — Converting the old style to modular. B — Converting modular to the old style. C — Joining three modular cables together. (Gemini Industries, Inc.)

To check an alarm horn, disconnect it from the circuit. Apply 12 volts DC from a car battery to the horn terminals. The horn should sound. If it does not, hit it with a hammer or other object to loosen any rust inside. Replace the unit if it is still faulty.

The home mechanic can install some parts in an existing security circuit. Follow the manufactturer's directions. Installation of the main control box is best left to a professional.

TEST YOUR KNOWLEDGE — CHAPTER 26

1. Electrical power enters the house through a _____ entrance.
2. When the needle of a watt-hour meter is pointed near a number, but between two numbers, take the _____ (lower, higher) number.
3. The resistance of a device using 20 amps from a 120 V source is:
   a. 2400 Ω
   b. 0.17 Ω
   c. 140 Ω
   d. 6 Ω

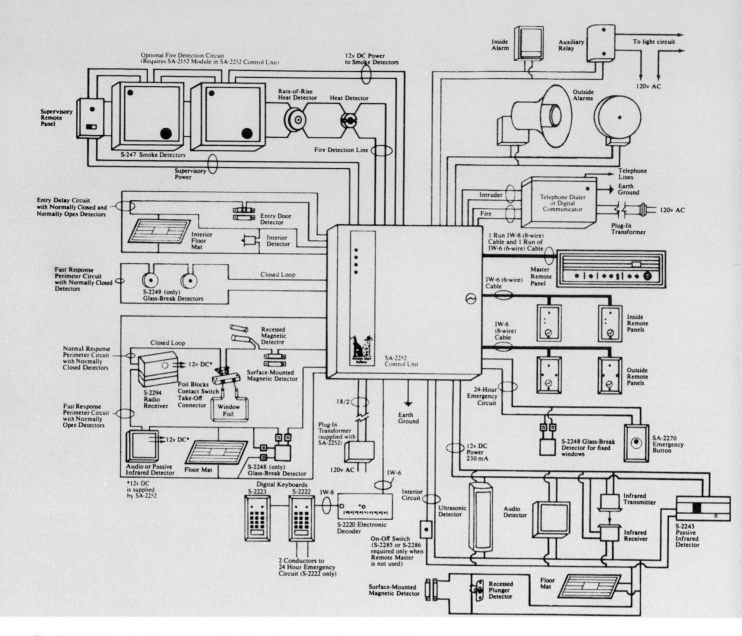

Fig. 26-45. Many devices are available for a home security system. This diagram suggests the circuits needed for these devices. The home mechanic can test wiring, switches, horns, and lamps. (NuTone Div., Scovill Inc.)

4. Use #10 gauge copper wire for a 40 amp current. True or False?
5. Which wires must be connected to the neutral bar of the service box?
6. Of the types of cable runs, only _____ can be placed in an accessible area.
7. Wrap wire around a screw as follows:
   a. Make 1/2 turn clockwise.
   b. Make 1/2 turn counterclockwise.
   c. Make 2/3 turn counterclockwise.
   d. Make 2/3 turn clockwise.
8. The two terminals of a switch can be connected to two white wires. True or False?
9. When using an outlet or two with separate circuits, the source should be only from a _____ _____ _____ .
10. Keep attic insulation _____ in. away from light fixtures.

KNOW THESE TERMS

Circuit, watt-hour, voltage, meter, neutral, color code, conduit, ampere, conductor, schematic, duplex, thermostat, ohm, distribution panel.

SUGGESTED ACTIVITIES

Investigate how you would add a branch circuit starting from a wall switch in your house. Does the switch box have proper source and ground wires? Sketch the circuit that is needed.

Find out about an outlet with a ground fault circuit interrupter (GFCI) at a local store. What kind of circuit do you need to wire it?

CAREERS

Electrician, electrical engineer, electrical supply retailer (wholesale), electrical contractor.

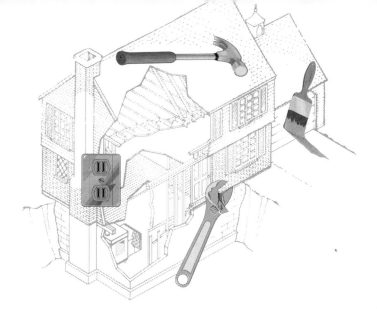

27

APPLIANCE MAINTENANCE, ELECTRICAL AND MECHANICAL

This chapter discusses some of the most common problems with electrical appliances. Some diagnosis and repair steps are given.

After studying this chapter, you should be able to:
- Decide if a problem is electrical or mechanical.
- Recognize when a belt is too loose or tight.
- Repair a dishwasher door seal.
- Design a labeling system for wires before you remove them.
- Recognize poor refrigerator performance due to dirty coils.
- Find and read an appliance data plate.
- Repair lamps and electrical cords.
- Clean the commutator of a motor.
- Use soldering equipment.
- List some parts of a VOM and some steps to use this type of meter.

Home appliances are generally grouped into two categories: major appliances and small appliances. The usual major appliances are the refrigerator, dishwasher, garbage disposal, and the laundry appliances.

Small appliances are highly portable, lightweight devices to aid the homemaker with routine tasks. Such small appliances are: food mixers, can openers, fans, toasters, and many others.

MAJOR APPLIANCES

All failures of appliances are in two areas: electrical or mechanical. Electrical problems are either in the circuit conducting the energy to the device or the internal circuitry of the device. Mechanical failures involve moving parts, power transfer units, or other mechanisms. Mechanical parts often need little more than regular lubrication.

Dishwasher Maintenance

Refer to Fig. 27-1. The most common complaint with dishwashers is that they do not clean each dish equally well. Also, the unit does not clean any of them as well as it once did.

Before the service person is called to remedy this, study the appliance's operating manual to be sure the instructions have been followed concerning the precleaning, loading, and detergent specifications.

Next check the water temperature. Water flowing into the dishwasher should be between 140-160 °F (60-70 °C). Check the setting on the hot water heater.

Dishwashers need some periodic maintenance such as cleaning out the drain strainer. If a residue of coarse food particles is left on dishes following the cycle, a clogged strainer is the most likely cause. Remove strainer and rinse under the top of sink.

Water leaking from around the seal of the loading door is a very common complaint with dishwashers, especially the older models. The problem is a deteriorating rubber seal or gasket around the door. On most appliances, this is simple to replace. Buy a replacement gasket from the local appliance dealer of the appropriate brand and install it. Look for the retaining devices and remove the leaky gasket. Reinsert the new gasket by reversing the removal steps.

If the machine will not start, check the circuit breaker first. If circuit breaker immediately trips following resetting, professional servicing may be required.

Faulty timer switches are often the cause of dishwasher failure. This switch controls the length of the various wash cycles. Dishwasher symptoms from faulty timers are:
1. Machine will not turn on.
2. Machine will not go through all cycles.
3. Machine continues to operate on one cycle.

269

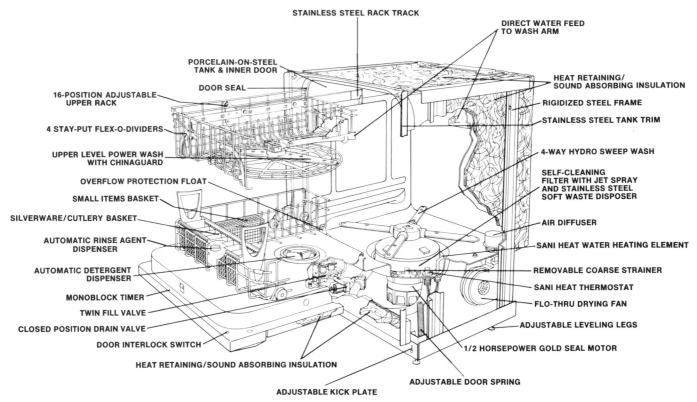

STAINLESS STEEL RACK TRACK

DIRECT WATER FEED
TO WASH ARM

PORCELAIN-ON-STEEL
TANK & INNER DOOR

HEAT RETAINING/
SOUND ABSORBING INSULATION

DOOR SEAL

16-POSITION ADJUSTABLE
UPPER RACK

RIGIDIZED STEEL FRAME

STAINLESS STEEL TANK TRIM

4 STAY-PUT FLEX-O-DIVIDERS

4-WAY HYDRO SWEEP WASH

UPPER LEVEL POWER WASH
WITH CHINAGUARD

SELF-CLEANING
FILTER WITH JET SPRAY
AND STAINLESS STEEL
SOFT WASTE DISPOSER

OVERFLOW PROTECTION FLOAT

SMALL ITEMS BASKET

AIR DIFFUSER

SILVERWARE/CUTLERY BASKET

SANI HEAT WATER HEATING ELEMENT

AUTOMATIC RINSE AGENT
DISPENSER

REMOVABLE COARSE STRAINER

AUTOMATIC DETERGENT
DISPENSER

SANI HEAT THERMOSTAT

MONOBLOCK TIMER

FLO-THRU DRYING FAN

TWIN FILL VALVE

ADJUSTABLE LEVELING LEGS

CLOSED POSITION DRAIN VALVE

DOOR INTERLOCK SWITCH

1/2 HORSEPOWER GOLD SEAL MOTOR

HEAT RETAINING/SOUND ABSORBING INSULATION

ADJUSTABLE DOOR SPRING

ADJUSTABLE KICK PLATE

Fig. 27-1. Parts of the dishwasher. (Hobart)

All symptoms occur without tripping the circuit breaker or blowing a fuse. The first step is to clean all electrical terminals. Turn off all power. If cleaning does not help, you may need to replace the timer

Timer replacement is a fairly simple job. First obtain the manufacturer's data located somewhere on the inside frame or on the door. A data plate will list the make, model, and serial number. Obtain the replacement switch from your local manufacturer's representative.

The timer has numerous wires running from it. Reconnecting them properly will be easy if the home mechanic draws a diagram or labels each wire before removing the switch. Install the new switch carefully.

Other problems often occur in structural or power units. See Fig. 27-2. Usually, these problems should be referred to a professional.

Clothes Washer

Common problems with clothes washers involve timers, devices to spin tubs, hoses, and drain mechanisms. Problems can be similar to those of the dishwasher. Repair or replace a timer in the same way as for dishwashers.

The clothes washer tub spins to remove water from the damp clothes. If the drum fails to spin, or revolves slowly, tighten the V-belt which drives the spinning tub. To check belt tension, push belt in-

ward with finger. It should go in about 1/2 in.

Usually the motor is mounted on a pivot. Loosen the one or more locking bolts. Some models have a separate idler pulley which is moveable for adjusting the belt tension.

Tub does not fill properly with water. The inlet hoses, hot and cold, are connected to the plumbing shutoff valves. Check to see if shutoff valves are fully turned on. If this does not correct the problem, shut off the valves and disconnect the appliance rubber water hoses. Located just inside the brass connecting ring in some hoses is a fine mesh filter screen. Often this becomes clogged with sediment. Remove these filters, clean, and replace. Check for a missing rubber compression gasket. Reconnect water hoses and open the shutoff valves.

If water will not drain from tub, check the drain hose for an obstruction. Also check plumbing drain for obstruction. If water does not drain because tub does not spin, check for broken drive belt.

If problem cannot be isolated to the above problems, professional help is needed.

Refrigerators and Freezers

The most common refrigeration units are the refrigerator with freezer compartments, refrigerator with combined freezer, compact refrigerator, and separate freezer. When purchasing a new refrigerator unit, it is important to check the energy guide number, Fig. 27-3. The higher the number the

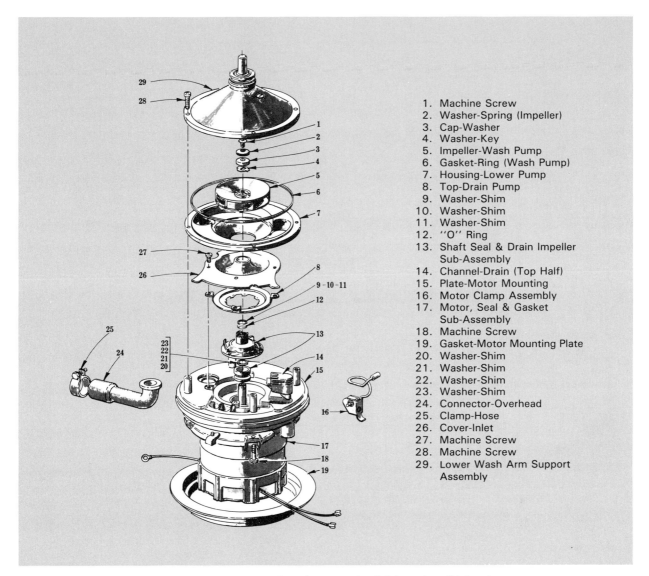

1. Machine Screw
2. Washer-Spring (Impeller)
3. Cap-Washer
4. Washer-Key
5. Impeller-Wash Pump
6. Gasket-Ring (Wash Pump)
7. Housing-Lower Pump
8. Top-Drain Pump
9. Washer-Shim
10. Washer-Shim
11. Washer-Shim
12. "O" Ring
13. Shaft Seal & Drain Impeller Sub-Assembly
14. Channel-Drain (Top Half)
15. Plate-Motor Mounting
16. Motor Clamp Assembly
17. Motor, Seal & Gasket Sub-Assembly
18. Machine Screw
19. Gasket-Motor Mounting Plate
20. Washer-Shim
21. Washer-Shim
22. Washer-Shim
23. Washer-Shim
24. Connector-Overhead
25. Clamp-Hose
26. Cover-Inlet
27. Machine Screw
28. Machine Screw
29. Lower Wash Arm Support Assembly

Fig. 27-2. Typical wash and pump unit of dishwasher. (Hobart)

greater the cost of electrical energy required to operate this unit. The guide number is generally located on the unit front. The energy guide is a bar graph rating the device from 40 to 90. (Appendix, Calculation of yearly energy cost for appliances.)

With any appliance, look for the model number. This helps you get repair parts.

Refrigerator-freezers are also rated by the amount of electricity they consume. (Appendix.) The manufacturer generally indicates the number of kilowatt hours used per month. The various models require different amounts of energy depending on size and style. The amount of electricity required may be reduced by disconnecting the frostless system.

Refrigerator Maintenance

Refrigerators are nearly maintenance-free. If the compression motor fails to start, check the circuit breaker. Allow time for any overload device to cool.

If compression motor runs, but refrigerator does not maintain its cool temperature, the compressor may be bad or the system has lost its refrigerant. In either case, the repair will require specialized equipment and the expertise of a professional technician.

Frequent cleaning of the condensing coils located in the rear side of the unit is about all that is necessary. Each six months, the refrigerator should be moved forward and cleaned with a vacuum cleaner. With a brush attachment, gently remove dust and lint from the condensing coils. Also clean dirt and lint from motor-compressor area for better cooling.

Also provide a good air circulation passageway:
1. From lower front intake area under refrigerator.
2. Through the space between wall and refrigerator unit.
3. Out over the top. This is imperative for heat transfer from condensing coils.

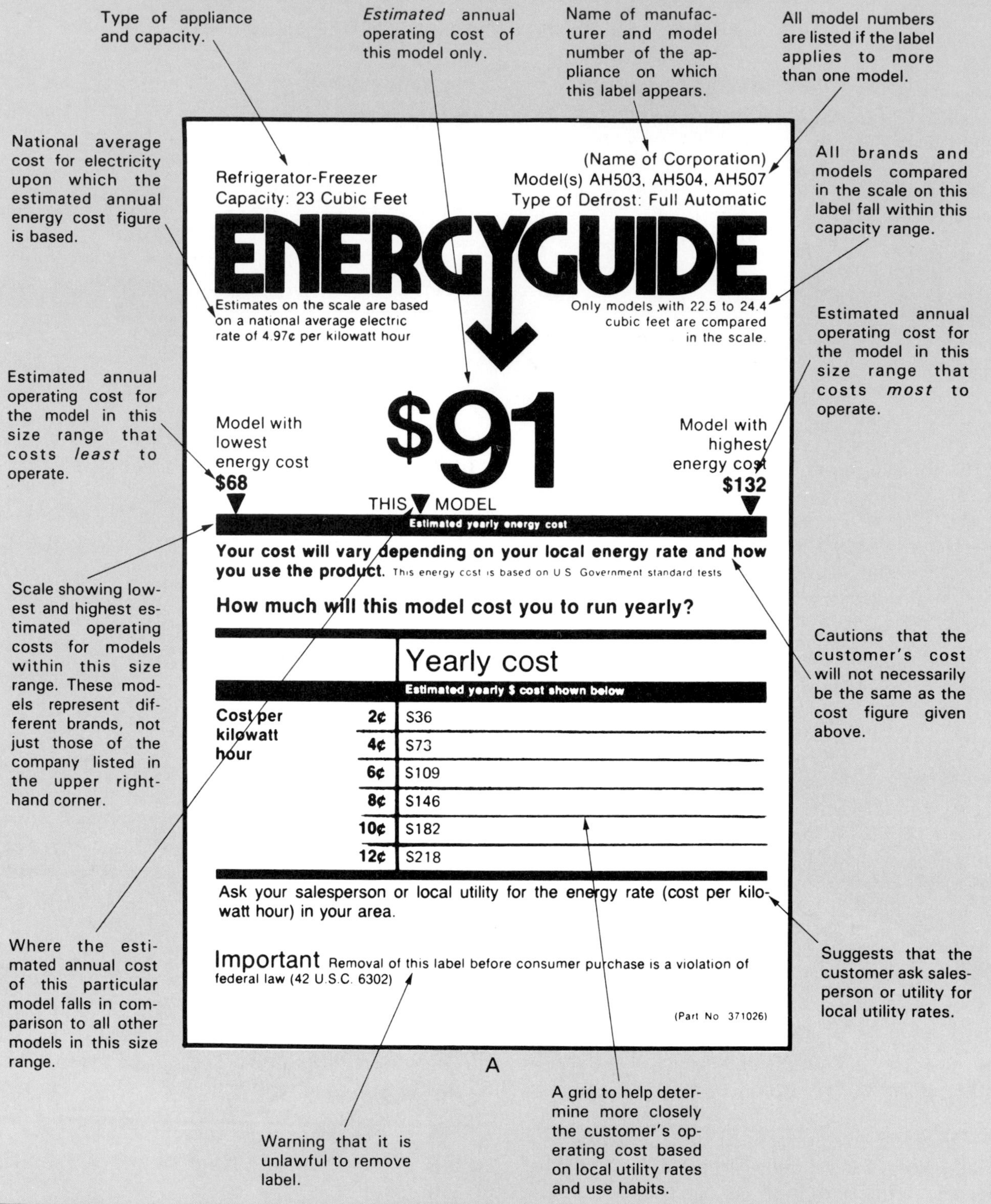

Type of appliance and capacity.

Estimated annual operating cost of this model only.

Name of manufacturer and model number of the appliance on which this label appears.

All model numbers are listed if the label applies to more than one model.

National average cost for electricity upon which the estimated annual energy cost figure is based.

Estimated annual operating cost for the model in this size range that costs *least* to operate.

Scale showing lowest and highest estimated operating costs for models within this size range. These models represent different brands, not just those of the company listed in the upper right-hand corner.

Where the estimated annual cost of this particular model falls in comparison to all other models in this size range.

All brands and models compared in the scale on this label fall within this capacity range.

Estimated annual operating cost for the model in this size range that costs *most* to operate.

Cautions that the customer's cost will not necessarily be the same as the cost figure given above.

Suggests that the customer ask salesperson or utility for local utility rates.

A grid to help determine more closely the customer's operating cost based on local utility rates and use habits.

Warning that it is unlawful to remove label.

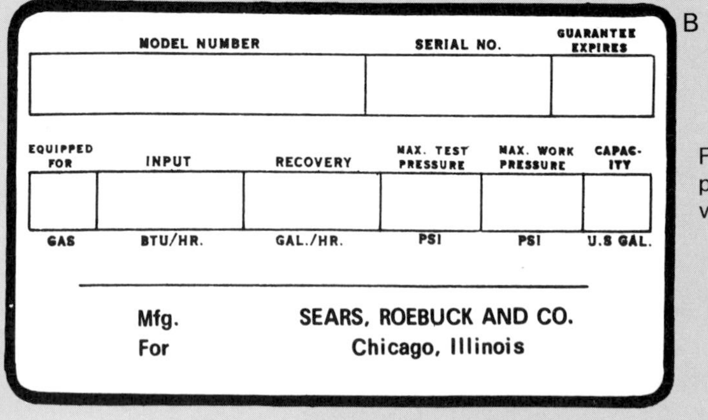

Label A

Refrigerator-Freezer
Capacity: 23 Cubic Feet

(Name of Corporation)
Model(s) AH503, AH504, AH507
Type of Defrost: Full Automatic

ENERGYGUIDE

Estimates on the scale are based on a national average electric rate of 4.97¢ per kilowatt hour

Only models with 22.5 to 24.4 cubic feet are compared in the scale.

$91

Model with lowest energy cost
$68

Model with highest energy cost
$132

THIS MODEL

Estimated yearly energy cost

Your cost will vary depending on your local energy rate and how you use the product. This energy cost is based on U.S. Government standard tests

How much will this model cost you to run yearly?

		Yearly cost
		Estimated yearly $ cost shown below
Cost per kilowatt hour	2¢	$36
	4¢	$73
	6¢	$109
	8¢	$146
	10¢	$182
	12¢	$218

Ask your salesperson or local utility for the energy rate (cost per kilowatt hour) in your area.

Important Removal of this label before consumer purchase is a violation of federal law (42 U.S.C. 6302)

(Part No 371026)

A

B

MODEL NUMBER	SERIAL NO.	GUARANTEE EXPIRES

EQUIPPED FOR	INPUT	RECOVERY	MAX. TEST PRESSURE	MAX. WORK PRESSURE	CAPAC-ITY
GAS	BTU/HR.	GAL./HR.	PSI	PSI	U.S GAL.

Mfg.
For

SEARS, ROEBUCK AND CO.
Chicago, Illinois

Fig. 27-3. Information labels. A—Energy guide numbers compare the efficiency of electrical appliances. B—Data plate. You will often need to know the model number. To replace a damaged data plate, you must return the original.
(Sears, Roebuck and Co.)

A refrigerator should be capable of maintaining a 37 °F (3 °C) temperature in the center of the unit. The freezer section should provide a reliable 0 °F (-20 °C) temperature, although there may be slightly warmer areas around the door. You may rent a special thermometer from the local refrigerator dealer. Adjust the temperature using the controls within the refrigerator unit.

Electric Ranges

The modern electric range is available in a variety of styles: free standing, slide-in units, deep-in units, and built-in cooktop units. Aside from the daily cleaning of exposed surfaces and heating elements, electric cooking ranges need little maintenance. On rare occasions, a heating element will need replacing, a relatively simple procedure.

Obtain the model and serial number from the manufacturer's identification plate located on the rear side or under the top. Buy a replacement element from the local dealer.

Different manufacturers have different means of making the electrical connections. Some are removed by simply uplugging the friction fit connection while others may be connected by two terminal screws. Some ranges have chrome retaining or trim rings which must be removed and put back after the new element is in place.

Ceramic top ranges have a solid section top which is tilted up to work on the heating element.

Oven heating elements are no more difficult to replace. Most electric heating elements for ovens have two or three retaining clips to hold the element

in position. Normally a short sheet metal screw will hold each retainer.

SMALL APPLIANCES

These electrical devices are numerous and just as varied in their uses. Many small appliances are discarded because they no longer operate well. Sometimes they can be reconditioned with very little or no cost.

Small appliances can be classified into two groups: those which create a rotating motion and those that heat. Small kitchen appliances of the rotating type are: can openers, blenders, mixers, and knife sharpeners. Those that heat are: toasters, coffee makers, electric frying pans, griddles, and electric waffle makers.

Many small appliances are manufactured so inexpensively that repair is impossible and replacement by a new device is the most economical means of repair. However, many others can be brought back into service. Here are a few of the common problems of small appliances.

The Electrical Cord

Because of the constant flexing, twisting, and doubling, the electrical cord will frequently fail and need replacement. If the appliance, during operation, starts and stops without visible cause, quite possibly there is a poor connection or a broken conductor within the rubber insulation covering.

A damaged power cord is dangerous and should be repaired or replaced. Refer to Fig. 27-4. A new

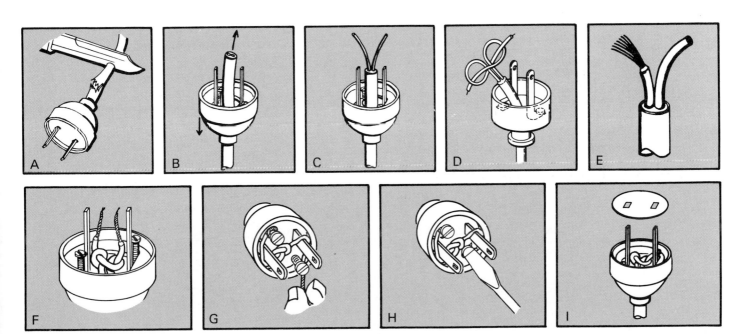

Fig. 27-4. Repairing appliance cord. A — Cut off damaged part. B — Slip plug back on cord. C — Clip lengthwise and separate the wire ends. D — Tie Underwriter's knot. (D — General Electric Co.) E — Remove 1/2 in. of insulation. Do not cut small strands. F — Twist strands together. Pull knot down. G — Wrap wires around screws clockwise. H — Tighten screws. Insulation is up to the screw but not under it. I — Replace insulating disk. (U.S. Dept. of Agriculture)

plug can be put on. Stress on the wires inside the plug body is decreased by tying the ends into an Underwriter's knot. As with all wires on screw terminals, wrap the wire clockwise around the screw so that the wire tightens when screw is tightened.

There are other types of cord plugs which save time in repairs. One type requiring no tools is shown in Fig. 27-5. Sharp points make a connection when they pierce each wire lead.

If the damaged area is near the middle of the power cord, there is no need to cut the cord at the break to make two shorter cords. The cord can be spliced. A strong splice can be made if you follow a hint suggested in Fig. 27-6. As shown, cut the two leads of a length of cord at an offset. One lead is white and one is black. Cut the leads of the other length of cord in a similar way to match. Twist the two stranded white leads together. Then twist the two black leads together. Solder each joint. Wrap each joint with electrical tape run at an angle to the wire. Finally wrap the combined joint area with electrical tape, again at an angle. This wrap should extend about 1 in. onto each side of the outermost cover of the cord.

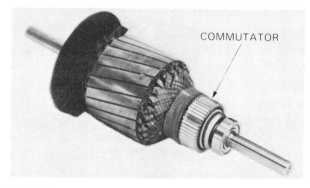

Fig. 27-5. Quick attachment plug is available. The section between prongs is removable when prongs are squeezed. The action also forces sharp points through wire strands to make connection. (Leviton)

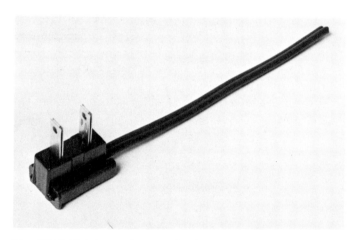

Fig. 27-6. Spliced wires should be offset to reduce the chance of a short circuit. The method also makes splice less bulky. Solder each splice.

Motors and Gears

Aside from the power cord failures, the internal power unit is probably the next most frequent trouble spot. For motor driven appliances, the motor or gearing mechanism is about the only thing to cause trouble.

Most small appliance motors are of the ac-dc type. They have commutators and carbon brushes. See Fig. 27-7. The commutator is a group of copper or brass bars at the end of the armature coils on the main shaft. Carbon brushes make the electrical contact with the commutator.

After considerable use, the commutator will take on a carbon glaze from the brushes and from dirt and grease. This glaze will begin to act as an insulator that stops the flow of electric current. This causes poor operation of the device. Careful cleaning of the commutator with a special electrical contact cleaner or very fine abrasive paper will usually remove this glaze.

Motor electrical brushes wear shorter with time. Most should be 1/2 to 3/4 in. long. If the motor has the removable type of brush, (some of the very small appliance motors do not), they may be replaced with new ones.

The power transfer assembly gearing mechanism or direction-change devices may wear out or slip out of place. Two groups of gear assemblies are used:

1. The enclosed gear box, usually made of a diecast metal with metal gears turning in a thick, white lubricant.
2. The open gear mechanism.

In the open gear unit, the gears are made of nylon or other durable plastic. The open gear type is usually used on the less expensive small appliances. Sometimes the only step needed is to tighten the case which holds the gears steady.

Replacement parts for most appliances are not readily available in the local hardware or appliance store. However, in the owner's manual there is

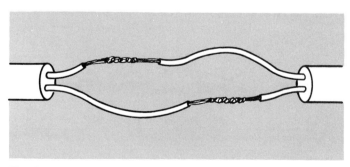

Fig. 27-7. Steps in commutator maintenance. 1. Look for black glazed coating on commutator. 2. Use a contact cleaner to dissolve the glaze. 3. Remove thicker glaze with fine abrasive cloth.

often a list of service centers for that manufacturer's appliance. The home mechanic with the model and serial numbers and identification numbers of the replacement parts, should have no problem getting any of the service parts.

Heating Device Repairs

The heating types of small appliances are much more difficult to repair. The heating element is often cast directly into the appliance housing. Examples include frying pans or griddles. For others, a solder-less sleeve can be used to splice a heating element.

The electrical power cords sometimes become frayed and dangerous. When repairing or replacing these cords always make certain the type of power cord used is able to withstand the high temperatures.

Many heating appliances have variable temperature controls. These fail from time to time. Use a voltmeter or test light to check if power is present at the output sleeves of the control. If not, replace the control. If power is present, the heating element is bad.

Some electrical controls are not replaceable. Again check with a service center for help.

Rewiring Lamps

To save work, make a few simple tests first. If a lamp flickers or will not go on, be sure the bulb is good and check that it is tightly seated in the lamp socket. Check to see if the plug is firmly in the outlet. If none of these is the cause of failure, then the problem must be internal.

Unplug the lamp and check the cord for frayed wire, bare wires, or loose connections at the plug end. If the cord is not the problem, next check the socket and socket/switch, Fig. 27-8. If it is necessary to install a new socket/switch, observe the old one before disconnecting the wires, Fig. 27-9. Then connect the new switch in the same manner.

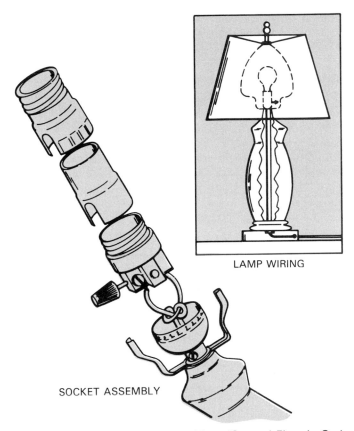

Fig. 27-9. Lamp socket and wiring. (General Electric Co.)

To completely rewire a lamp follow this procedure:

1. First disconnect the lamp from power source.
2. With a sharp knife, pry off the protective felt pad covering on the base to give access to the wiring.
3. Use a wrench to loosen the nut that secures the long electrician pipe running through the lamp. Some lamps may have lead weights in the base.
4. Pull the electrician pipe out from the top of the lamp.
5. Unscrew the socket from the pipe by turning it counterclockwise. (Note: If the socket is also the socket/switch, a setscrew on the side may have to be loosened.)

Fig. 27-8. The socket and switch is easily removed from lamp. Remove the snap-fit base to expose terminal screws. (Leviton)

6. Remove the outer shell of the socket by pressing at the base and pulling it straight up. Slide off the cardboard insulating sleeve to expose the socket terminal screws.
7. Unscrew the two terminal screws and slip out the wires.
8. Tie an Underwriter's knot in the new wires.
9. Fit the new wires under the terminal screws and tighten.
10. Feed the new wire through the pipe and screw the socket onto the pipe threads.
11. Reassemble to the lamp base and place the nut on base end of pipe.
12. Reglue the felt pad onto base.

Some lamps have a harp which must be removed before dismantling. The lamp harp is the hardware that supports the shade. To remove, press the two arms together near the socket base and lift out.

To prevent fraying of the stranded wire of the lamp cord, some home mechanics tin the ends. Frayed ends will cause electrical shorts. Tinning the wire tip will hold all the strands of copper wire together by flowing solder through the wire ends.

To tin the ends, dip wire into paste flux. Apply sufficient heat with soldering gun to melt solder wire held on the opposite side. Just a very little bit is necessary. Do not heat wire enough to melt the insulation covering the wires.

Replacing Vacuum Cleaner Belt

The most common problem with a vacuum cleaner is a worn or broken belt. A belt usually drives the rug agitator in the power head. Fig. 27-10 shows how to replace the belt in a typical upright vacuum cleaner.

First unplug the power. Then turn the cleaner over. Remove the bottom plate by pushing the latches toward the outside of cleaner. Remove the belt from the motor shaft end. Lift out the rug agitator held in slots at the two ends. Remove the old belt and place new belt in center groove of agitator.

Replace the agitator. There is a raised metal plate on one end of the agitator roll. Make sure this end is placed in the groove on the side of the cleaner body. Place the belt on the motor shaft pulley. The innermost half of the belt loop should align with molded marks on bottom of cleaner base. This assures that the roll turns in the proper direction. Replace the bottom cover plate and push latches into position. Test the unit for correct operation.

A related repair is best done at the same time as the belt is replaced. The brushes on the agitator roll may be worn too short. Often the spiral brush strip is removable, Fig. 27-11. With agitator removed, use pliers to pull the brush strip out.

Replace both brush strips at the same time. Push them into the channels as far as possible. Assemble the unit as stated for belt repair.

Checking Appliance Grounding

The most valuable test you can do is to check if an appliance is safely grounded. The device should have no short circuits that can energize an outer

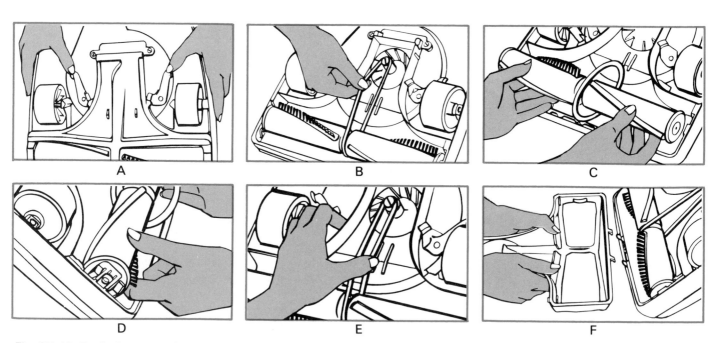

Fig. 27-10. Replacing worn cleaner belt. A — After unplugging the power, remove bottom plate by pushing latches to outside of cleaner. B — Remove worn belt from pulley. C — Lift out agitator, remove old belt, and place new belt in groove of agitator. D — Replace agitator. There is a raised metal plate on one end of agitator roll. Put this in groove on side of cleaner. E — Place belt on pulley. Side of belt nearer cleaner should be in line with marks on cleaner base. F — Replace bottom plate. (Hoover Co.)

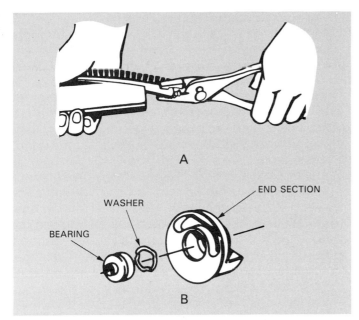

Fig. 27-11. A — Remove vacuum cleaner agitator brushes by pulling them from channels. Slide new brushes in as far as possible. B — If you accidentally displace the bearing, reassemble as shown. (Hoover Co.)

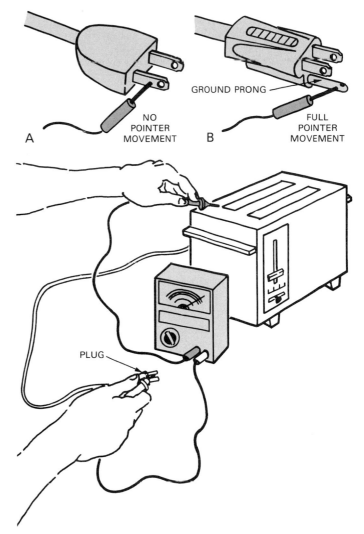

Fig. 27-12. Check toasters, drills, and other appliances for safe grounding. With appliance switch on, take two different resistance readings between the metal housing and several prongs of the plug. A—Desired result is no pointer movement with second probe on flat plug blades. B—Good ground circuit through the round pin shows full meter reading.

metal case. See Fig. 27-12. No connection should ever be found between the flat blades of the power plug and any metal case part.

Set a multimeter to Rx1K on the ohms scale or use a continuity tester. With the appliance switch on, touch one probe to a flat prong on the plug and one probe to metal parts on the device housing. Even the slightest meter movement shows a faulty device. A continuity tester should give no response.

Often the fault cannot be fixed easily if it involves complex parts. Get professional help or discard the unit.

Next, check for proper function of the plug's ground pin if it has one. Check for a continuous path from the round ground pin to the metal parts on the device housing. Set the meter to Rx1 or Rx100. Connect the meter or continuity tester between the ground pin and the metal housing. The meter should read nearly full scale. The continuity tester lamp should go on.

If the ground circuit tests bad, look for a loose ground wire. A green wire from the power cord should be attached somewhere to the wall of the appliance. If it is attached, the problem could be in the power cord. Check the power cord for continuity and replace if it is not continuous.

TEST YOUR KNOWLEDGE — CHAPTER 27

1. Water flowing into a dishwasher should be between _____ and _____ °F (°C).
2. Before disconnecting wires from a timer or complex component, _____ each wire.
3. An energy guide label for an appliance gives:
   a. The relative wasted heat for two similar appliances.
   b. Maintenance steps.
   c. The relative cost to run two similar appliances.
   d. The duty cycle the appliance maintains.
4. The heating element of a ceramic top electric range is reached by _____ the top surface.
5. What kind of knot adds strength to an electric cord connection in a plug?
6. What part of a small appliance motor needs service most often?
7. A brush inside an electric motor should be about _____ in long.
8. Parts for small appliances are usually obtained through a _____ _____.

9. A _____ _____ sometimes holds a lamp socket and switch onto the electrician pipe in the base.
    a. Retaining ring.
    b. Setscrew.
    c. Spring.
    d. Nut and washer.
10. To prevent fraying of stranded wire, _____ the ends.
11. Which half of a vacuum cleaner belt loop must align with the marks on the cleaner base? (innermost, outermost)
12. When removing insulation from a stranded wire, do not _____ any of the small strands.
13. With proper appliance belt tension, you can push the belt inward about _____ in.

KNOW THESE TERMS

Energy guide number, commutator, condensing coils, underwriters knot.

SUGGESTED ACTIVITIES

Compare energy guide numbers for several appliances of the same kind at one or more retail outlets. Collect literature on these units and ask the salesperson for information or an explanation of an extremely high or of an extremely low number. Also make a calculation to see how long you need to pay off an investment in a more expensive, but more efficient unit. Make a chart if you check three or more appliance ratings. Give a report in class.

Ask your instructor how to use a VOM (volt ohm meter). Check ac and dc voltages, resistance, and current in circuits having known values. Make a list of do's and don'ts when using the various settings of the meter. Ask your instructor what the red meter numbers mean.

CAREERS

Appliance repair person, appliance salesperson, mechanical/electrical engineer, retail appliance store owner.

A typical small appliance is a food processer. (NuTone)

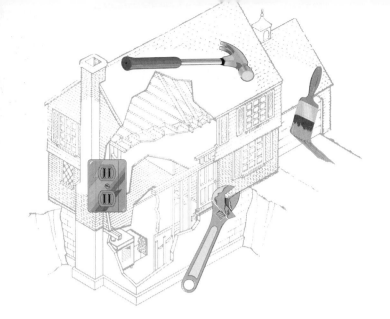

HEATING

This chapter tells how heat is transferred and shows how several furnace designs transfer heat. The chapter shows the components of oil, gas, wood, and electric furnaces and lists steps for adjusting gas burners and for maintaining other burners. Solar hot water heater maintenance is included.

After studying this chapter, you will be able to:
■ Bleed air from a radiator.
■ Adjust the primary air ratio for a gas burner.
■ Replace air and fuel filters and clean the electric ignition for an oil burner.
■ State the requirements for wood stove clearances.
■ Reduce corrosive oxides in solar collectors.

All heating and air conditioning systems treat air to maintain a comfortable level of temperature and humidity. Houses were once heated by the fireplace or by potbellied stoves. Doors and windows were opened for ventilation or the house was of such loose construction that ventilation was not a major concern.

Today, it is more important to maintain an even temperature in a house and the correct moisture content in the air. Both affect the health and comfort of people.

It is important that the home mechanic recognize a few basic facts about heat. Heat is constantly moving, always seeking the areas of lesser temperatures. Heat moves by one of three ways: conduction, convection, and radiation.

CONDUCTION

Heat will always leave an object that is warm for an object with a lower temperature. When heat passes through the walls, roof, and floors of a house, it moves by conduction, Fig. 28-1. Conduction of heat through a material is by molecular "bucket brigade," jumping from molecule to molecule. Materials that have widely spaced molecules are poorer conductors of heat than those with closely spaced molecules.

CONVECTION

Air tends to expand when heated. The expansion makes it less dense than before. Therefore, warm air is lighter than colder air and will rise above the cooler air. Warm air always rises to the ceiling of a room while the cold air drifts down, Fig. 28-2.

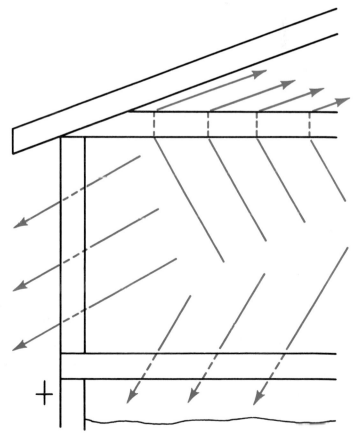

Fig. 28-1. Heat transfer by conduction.

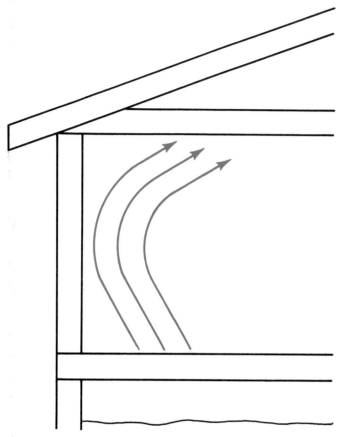

Fig. 28-2. Heat transfer by convection.

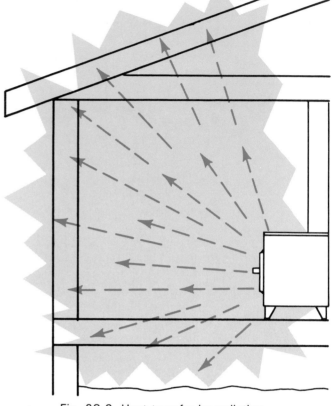

Fig. 28-3. Heat transfer by radiation.

The current formed by warm air's tendency to rise is called a convection current. Convection currents can rapidly disperse heat.

RADIATION

All materials are constantly radiating energy in all directions because of the continual vibration of molecules at their surface. See Fig. 28-3. The traveling or transfer of heat from one object directly out into the air is known as radiation. Note that all forms of heat held in matter are due to the vibration of molecules. Faster vibration means a higher temperature.

The three ways of transferring heat are the basis of all of our home heating and cooling systems.

TYPES OF HOME HEATING FURNACES

There are many types of furnaces. These include the gravity warm-air furnace, the electric baseboard, the forced warm-air, the hot water system, and the electric wall grid.

The Gravity Warm-Air

The furnace of this type uses the convection method of heat transfer. The fact that warm air rises and cold air settles will distribute the heated air from the furnace into the room, Fig. 28-4.

In operation, the air in the furnace's air jacket becomes heated from its close contact with the outer wall of the combustion chamber or fire box. It then rises through ducts and passes through registers into various rooms. As it does, it replaces colder air which drifts downward through the cold air ducts. From the ducts, cold air moves into the lower part of the air jacket where it is heated, and the cycle begins again.

Besides the central heating gravity warm-air furnace, the convection principle is used in floor furnaces and wall furnaces. In these smaller furnaces, heated air rises and circulates into the room space. Cool air is drawn along the floor and into the furnace for reheating.

Electric baseboard heating or hot water baseboard heat is transferred to the room by convection currents. Air is heated within the baseboard unit and rises through openings in the top. Cool air is brought in through vents located in the underside. For this reason, the home mechanic should avoid placing obstructions to air flow next to baseboard heating devices.

Forced Warm-Air

This furnace system is an improvement over the gravity type because a blower forces air to circulate between furnace and registers. Forced air is a type of convection which is better than natural convection. Besides making warm air distribution more even, this system minimizes the difference between warm air entering and cold air leaving rooms.

With a forced warm-air system, it is possible to send heat just to rooms that require it. To make this possible, the house is divided into zones, each with its own thermostat to call for heat. Individual blower arrangements or damper control devices direct the heat where it is needed.

There are four basic designs of forced warm-air furnaces: the upflow highboy, the downflow, the upflow lowboy, and the horizontal. The one type of downflow furnace is least used.

The selection depends on room height and structural access in the planned location.

The upflow highboy discharges warm air from the top and takes return air from the lower side or back, Fig. 28-5. This is best used with a full basement.

The downflow, Fig. 28-6, is designed to take return air in through the top and discharge warm

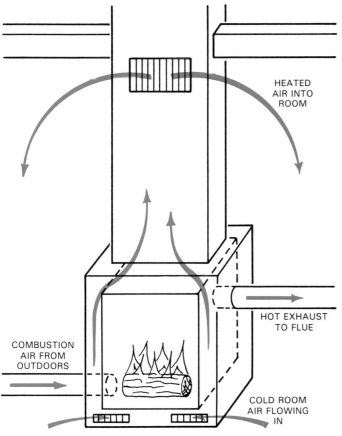

Fig. 28-4. Operation of gravity flow furnace.

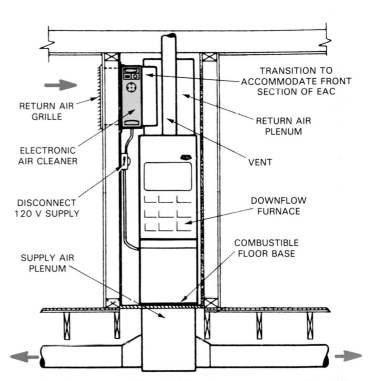

Fig. 28-6. The downflow highboy furnace system. (Bryant)

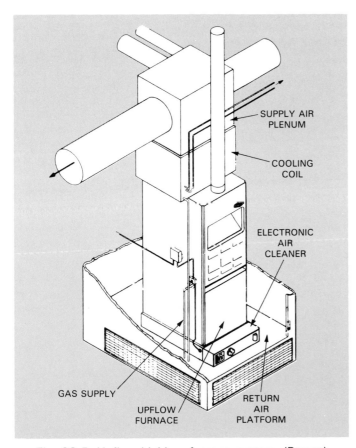

Fig. 28-5. Upflow highboy furnace system. (Bryant)

air from the bottom. This is used on a main floor.

The upflow lowboy is designed for a compact area. This furnace has both warm air and return air duct systems coming through the top. See Fig. 28-7. It is excellent for areas with poor access to floor joist spaces.

The horizontal furnace takes return air in one end and discharges warm air through the opposite end, Fig. 28-8. This design is good for crawl space

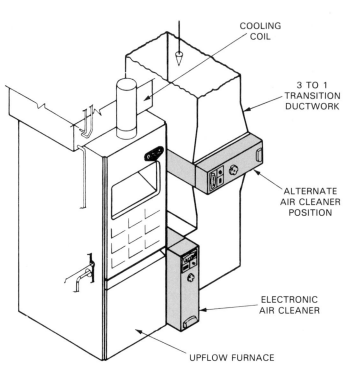

Fig. 28-7. The upflow lowboy furnace system. It is a popular system for full basement installation. (Bryant)

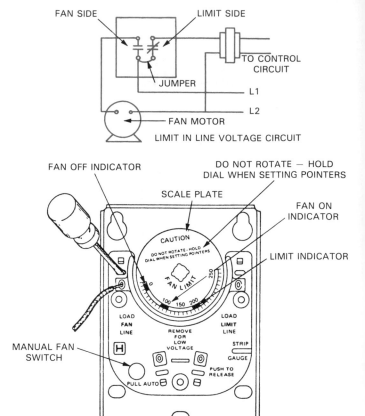

Fig. 28-9. Combination fan and limit control. Wiring schematic is above. Use manual fan switch to move air for summer cooling or summer air conditioning. (Honeywell)

or attic installations.

Each furnace equipped with a blower must also have a combination fan and limit control device, Fig. 28-9. The purpose of the control is to switch on the fan when the heat exchanger reaches a predetermined temperature. Later the thermostat turns off the burner unit. The fan continues to run until the internal temperature of the furnace is reduced to a second predetermined temperature.

A second function of the load limit control is to shut down the burner should the unit temperature exceed a preset critical temperature. Another safety device is called a "spill switch," Fig. 28-10. It shuts off the furnace if an object blocks the flue.

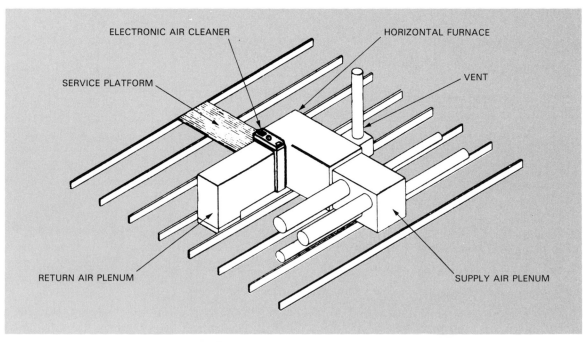

Fig. 28-8. The horizontal furnace system. (Bryant)

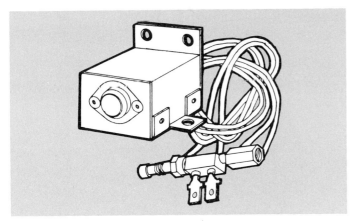

Fig. 28-10. A spill switch fits in the draft control or draft diverter. It protects against chimney blockage which might spill carbon monoxide fumes back into the house. The switch detects hot flue gases and shuts off water heater or furnace. A draft diverter is shown in Fig. 30-1. (deflect-o corp.)

Fig. 28-11. Changing air filters.

All models are equipped with a fan to distribute warm air. The fan can be used to move air for summer air exchange or air conditioning. A manual fan switch will keep the fan on all the time. You can set the fan limit pointer to room temperature for fully controlled operation. Set the fan-off position about 10 °F lower than the limit pointer.

Air Filtering

Most forced warm-air furnaces have an air filter to clean the circulating air, usually a loose packed pad of fiberglass or other nonflammable substance. Airborne dust particles are trapped and kept from returning to the living space. Filters are available in two types:
1. Permanent filters which may be periodically cleaned by washing. They are then returned to the furnace.
2. Disposable filters which are removed, thrown away, and replaced by a new clean filter, Fig. 28-11.

Filters should be either cleaned or replaced every three months. Infrequent cleaning or replacement may result in laboring of the fan motor. Fuel will be wasted trying to keep the house warm.

Hot-Water System

Hot water can be used to operate several types of heating systems: radiators, baseboard units, and floor radiant systems. One advantage of water heating is the large surface area exposed to the room air compared to a forced warm-air heat exchanger. However, hot water systems do not have the advantage of a fan. Thus hot water systems are less efficient than forced air systems.

The most expensive system is the floor tubing system.

The most even distribution of heat for a low cost installation is the baseboard system because of its continuous exchange around the outside walls.

Radiant floor heating is a system of copper lines coiled through the concrete floor. The lines transfer heat from the hot water to the concrete which in turn radiates heat energy to the room air above. Radiant floor heating is a very quiet and uniform distribution system.

There are two types of hot water systems: gravity and forced hot water systems. The gravity system relies on natural convection of water currents to move hot water from the boiler through the supply lines to the transfer units. When the water passes through the transfer unit, it cools and flows back to the boiler through a second set of pipes. It is important that the boiler be at a lower location than the transfer units. The rate of flow is relatively slow and the maximum temperature of the water does not exceed 180 °F (82 °C). Gravity systems which have an open expansion tank usually located in the attic are called open systems. Gravity systems which have a closed expansion tank usually located next to the boiler are called closed systems.

Hydronic systems are forced hot water systems using a circulation pump to increase the rate of water flow in a system under pressure. Since these must be closed systems, the temperature of the circulating water may be close to the boiling point 212 °F. The result is greater efficiency. The high temperature allows the furnace, distribution system, and heat transfer units to be smaller than for the gravity system.

Periodically air must be bled from the water system, Fig. 28-12. There is usually a valve on each radiator unit. With boiler off, open the valve until only water comes out.

Electric Heating

There are two ways electricity is used for heat: resistance heating and the heat pump run by electric motor. Resistance heating systems are simpler to install than air, water, or heat pump systems because the heating units are supplied by electrical conductors rather than by ducts or pipes. Baseboard units, for example, are attached along outside walls in place of baseboards and heat the surrounding areas. Heavy resistance type heating elements within the unit generate the heat which is transferred to the air by a large number of fins.

Wiring for electrical heating can be installed in the ceiling or walls during the construction of the house. Surface-mounted heating panels are used as a retrofit type of installation.

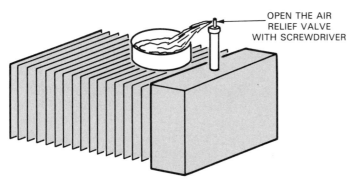

Fig. 28-12. Air relief valve for hydronic baseboard heater or standing radiator. With boiler off, open valve with screwdriver, wrench, or key. Bleed air away until water comes out.

SOURCES OF HEAT ENERGY

More basic than the air movement system is the production of heat energy. Sources include gas, oil, wood, electricity, heat pumps, and solar collectors.

Gas Burners

Gas burners are probably the simplest, mechanically, of all sources of heat energy. Refer to Fig. 28-13. Very little difference exists between burners for natural gas and for manufactured gas.

Gas is piped into the house to either a single or multijet burner head, where it mixes with air. Gas is ignited by a pilot light or electronic igniter. The pilot flame may need adjustment, Fig. 28-14. A flame spreader broadens the flame so that each flame heats an 8 x 2 in. section of the plenum chamber.

A pipe feeds gas to the burner under pressure. This pressure is regulated very carefully.

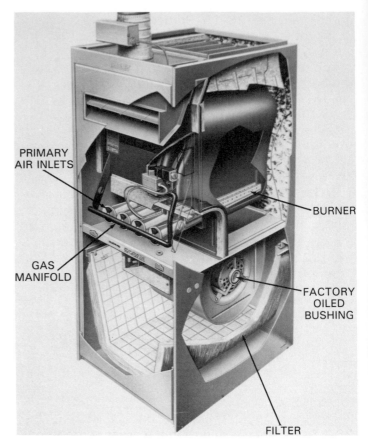

Fig. 28-13. Gas-fired, forced-air furnace. Note four primary air inlets. (Lennox)

FLAME TYPES	POSSIBLE CAUSES	FLAME TYPES	POSSIBLE CAUSES
LIGHT BLUE / YELLOW / LAZY YELLOW FLAME	1 DIRTY LINT SCREEN OR PRIMARY AIR OPENING 2 STARVING DUE TO EXCESSIVE INPUT TO MAIN BURNER 3 ORIFICE TOO LARGE	NOISY LIFTING BLOWING FLAME	HIGH GAS PRESSURE
WAVING BLUE FLAME	1 EXCESSIVE DRAFT AT PILOT LOCATION 2 RECIRCULATING PRODUCTS OF COMBUSTION	HARD SHARP FLAME	1 CHARACTERISTIC OF MANUFACTURED BUTANE AIR AND PROPANE AIR 2 ORIFICE TOO SMALL
SMALL BLUE FLAME	1 ADJUSTING SCREW CLOSED OFF 2 LOW GAS SUPPLY PRESSURE 3 CLOGGED PILOT BURNER ORIFICE 4 IMPROPER ORIFICE (TOO SMALL) 5 CLOGGED PILOT LINE FILTER	NORMAL FLAME 3/8 TO 1/2	PROPER INSTALLATION

Fig. 28-14. Pilot flame conditions. (Honeywell)

To prevent gas from flowing when the pilot light is out, heat from the pilot light controls an electrical valve in the gas line. When the pilot goes out, the valve closes and shuts off the gas flow. There are also manual controls which will shut the gas off.

Gas burners require air to be mixed with the gas before entering the burner jets. This air is called primary air, Fig. 28-15. Primary air constitutes approximately one-half of the total required for combustion.

Too much primary air causes the flame to lift off the burner surfaces. Too little primary air causes a yellow flame.

Air that is supplied to the burner at the time of combustion is called secondary air. To be certain that enough secondary air is provided, most units operate on an excess of secondary air. An excess of about 50% is considered good practice.

To produce a good flame, it is essential to maintain the proper ratio between primary and secondary air. To adjust the air setting, allow 5 min. for the burners to heat up. Open the air shutter, Fig. 28-16, until the flame lifts off the burner (a sign of too much air) then close it slowly until the flame returns to the burner. There should be no yellow flame.

Some furnaces are so efficient (97%) that the flue pipe can be made of plastic. They may have more than one heat exchanger. Less heat goes up the flue, so the gases are cooler.

Oil Burners

The function of the oil-burning furnace, Fig. 28-17, is to mix oil and air in the proper proportions for efficient combustion. The burner may provide heat to a boiler or to a warm-air system. Furnaces

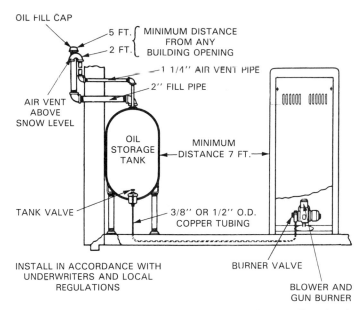

Fig. 28-17. Oil-burning furnace. (Webster Electric Co., Inc.)

have units for storing oil, delivering it to the burner, and blowing in air. They have combustion controls and use several types of combustion chambers.

Fuel oil is fed to the burner by one of two different methods. Oil is pumped from the storage tank to the burner by an electric powered pump or oil is fed to the burner by gravity. If the storage tank can be located a sufficient height above the burner, then gravitational forces will deliver the fuel to the burner.

Oil burners are divided into two different types: the pot burner and the gun type. For the pot burner, oil flows or is pumped into the base of the pot where it is allowed to vaporize. Oil mixes with air in controlled amounts, releasing heat. This method requires a constant pilot flame.

The injector nozzle or gun type, Fig. 28-18, is more widely used than the pot burner. Fuel oil is usually pumped to the gun and nozzle, and converted to a fine spray mist. Oil mixed with air is forced into the combustion chamber and ignited.

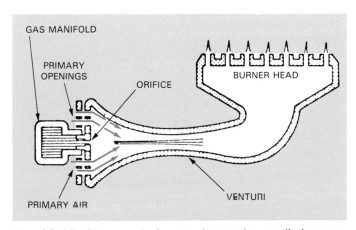

Fig. 28-15. Primary air for gas burner is supplied at gas manifold end. (Carrier)

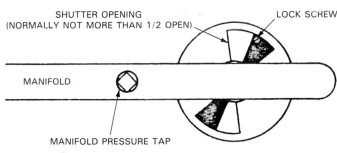

Fig. 28-16. Primary air adjustment on end of venturi tube.

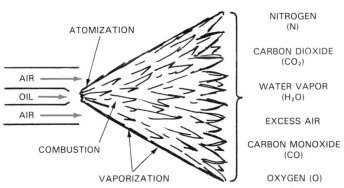

Fig. 28-18. Oil nozzle and air channel for oil burner. Blower forces air into a stream surrounding oil nozzle.

Electrical sparks generated by a transformer ignite the fuel-air mixture. The ignition process is intermittent and stops after the burner is in operation.

Maintenance of oil burning furnaces is generally limited to:

1. Periodic cleaning of the fuel filter.
2. Periodic cleaning of the electric ignition system, Fig. 28-19.
3. Replacement of air filters in the burner for a forced-air system.
4. Check fan motor for lubrication schedule and check V-belt drive for fan. Many newer models have sealed motor and fan bearings and are direct drive, eliminating these maintenance problems.

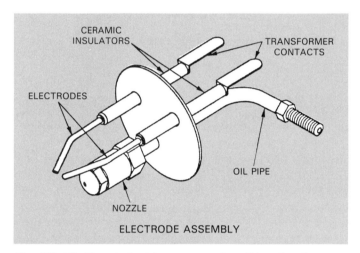

Fig. 28-19. Electric ignition system for oil-burning furnace. (Carrier)

Fig. 28-20. Electric furnace. Label the wires before replacing heating elements. (Amana)

Electric Furnaces

Electrical heating systems may use direct resistance conversion of electrical energy to heat energy or use mechanical conversion through a heat pump. The electric furnace operates in much the same manner as any forced air system except with a bank of resistance heating coils in place of fuel burners in the furnace. The home mechanic can replace heating elements, Fig. 28-20.

Heat Pump

The heat pump, Fig. 28-21, is a very effective type of electric heating system. It extracts heat from outdoor air (or water) and transfers it indoors in the winter. In summer it reverses the cycle and becomes a cooling unit by absorbing heat indoors and disposing of it to the outdoors. As a heater, the heat pump can produce as much heat as six times the electrical energy supplied to it.

The basic components of a heat pump are: the compressor, the condensing coil, the evaporating coil, and the reversing valve. To operate the heat pump, the thermostat needs only to be set for the desired temperature and it will maintain that desired setting the entire year. The heat pump will automatically reverse itself to cool or heat depending upon outside temperature.

Heat pump maintenance mainly involves the air filter as for any forced air furnace. Due to the higher technology involved in the heat pump, specialized test equipment and knowledge is required.

The home mechanic should inspect the unit as follows:

1. Check for physical obstruction around the outside coil.
2. Check the breaker panel for tripped breakers.
3. Check thermostat for correct setting.
4. Check filtering system for obstruction. If a problem persists, call the local professional service.

Wood Heating

With the increased cost of nonrenewable energies, there is a return to the use of wood as the main source of heat. In those regions with low cost wood, fireplaces, wood stoves, and wood furnaces are becoming popular. They may be used as a primary source of heat energy or as a supplemental heat source. (Appendix)

The homeowner can choose among many types of wood stoves. Types include cast iron or plate steel models. Both materials are good and retain roughly the same amount of heat per pound of unit.

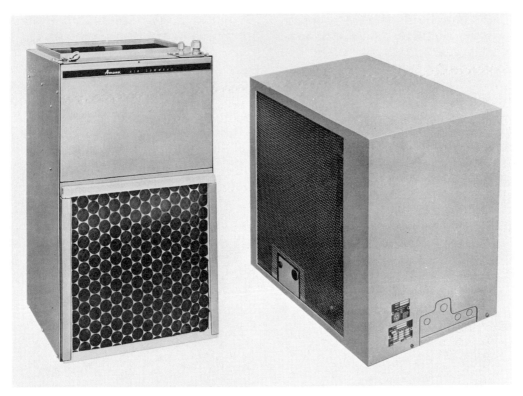

Fig. 28-21. Heat pump unit and fan unit. (Amana)

Both cost about the same. Generally the thicker the metal in the stove, the longer it will last. A thick frame also holds more heat. Any well-made stove will have good clean castings, smooth welds, and exhibit quality work.

Most good steel stoves or wood-burning fireplace inserts, Fig. 28-22, have firebrick liners. Firebrick liners have two advantages:

1. They provide a shield, preventing an early burn-out of the steel fire box.
2. Firebrick provides thermal mass (approximately 500 lbs.).

A good firebrick lined stove may give off stored heat for as long as four hours after the fire has burnt out.

Today wood stoves are designed and manufactured to be almost airtight. This permits controlled combustion of the wood, even maintaining burning overnight.

The rate of combustion and the amount of heat delivered is regulated by damper controls. Some stoves and furnaces have thermostats to open or close damper controls. These units use mechanical or electrical devices to set dampers automatically. Many are designed and fitted with blowers to help control combustion through forced or injected air for combustion. Still other models have air baffle systems that allow some exhaust gases back into the fire box. This recirculation of air radiates more into the room, burns up volatile gases, and keeps heat from going up the chimney.

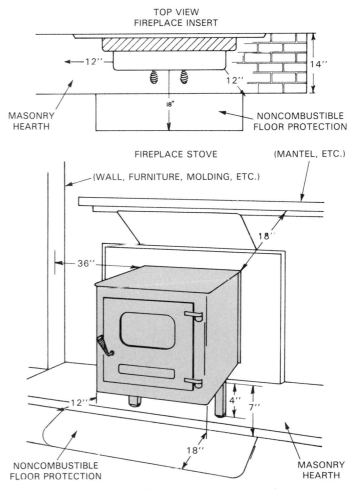

Fig. 28-22. Fireplace insert. (Hayes)

It is essential to install and operate a wood-burning stove correctly so there is no fire danger. Refer to Fig. 28-23. When purchasing the stove check if the model is listed by a national testing laboratory (example: Underwriter's Laboratory, U.L.). Follow recommended installation procedures. Before installing any wood-burning unit, have your plans checked by the local building codes inspector. Also, many insurance companies require filing installation plans with their office.

Always complete the installation according to the standards provided by the National Fire Protection Association.

The home mechanic may plan to add a prefabricated chimney for a woodburning stove. These chimneys consist of double-walled metal or of masonry-lined walls. Prefabricated chimneys are most often needed in houses without chimneys.

Follow the manufacturer's recommended procedures very carefully. Pay acute attention to the distances of all combustible materials from the chimney.

Following is a list of recommended procedures for installing the wood-burning stove:

1. The sides of an unprotected stove should be at least 36 in. (91 cm) from any combustible material.
2. Floor protection of 28 ga. metal is recommended.
3. Extend floor protection 18 in. (45 cm) in front

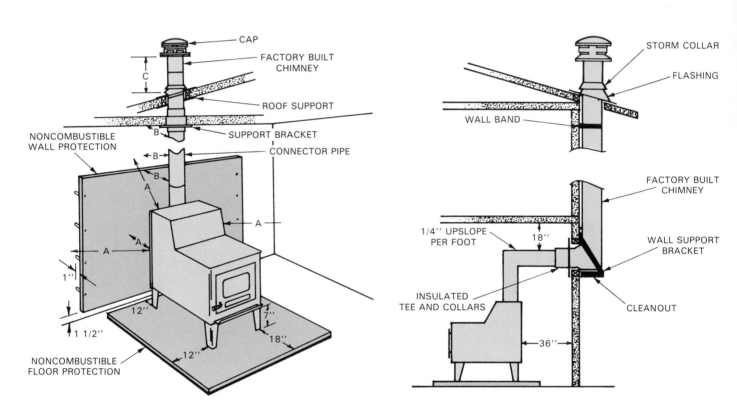

STOVE INSTALLATION CLEARANCES

STOVE SYSTEM COMPONENT	COMBUSTIBLE MATERIAL	1/4'' ASBESTOS MILLBOARD SPACED OUT 1'' noncombustible spacers	MASONRY/ CONCRETE WALL	4'' BRICK VENEER
FIREBOX: (Radiant) Floor—Front —Side/Rear Side/Rear (A)	18'' 12'' 36''	☐ ☐ 18''	☐ ☐ 6''	☐ ☐ 18''
SINGLE WALL Connector Pipe (B)	18''	12''	6''	8''
INSULATED Connector Pipe	2''	2''	2''	2''
Chimney: (C) Three feet above adjacent roof and two feet above any roof ridge within 10 feet.				
Damper: Where a damper is not an integral part of your stove model, one must be installed in the connector pipe.				

Fig. 28-23. Measurements for wood-burning stove installation clearances. (Hayes)

and 12 in. (31 cm) on both sides and rear of stove.

4. A stove pipe should be used only to connect the stove to the chimney and never instead of a chimney.

5. The chimney should be 3 ft. (1m) higher than the roof and 2 ft. (0.6 m) higher than any portion of the roof within 10 ft. (3 m) to prevent any downdrafts.

Solar Heat

There are many possible arrangements of solar heating systems. Water heating, space heating, and collector types are shown in Figs. 28-24 through 28-26. The economy of a system depends upon two basic factors: available sunshine and the ability to use collected energy effectively. (Appendix, A Word about Solar Energy.) The continued increase in fuel prices is turning the home mechanic's attention to solar energy for home space heating and domestic hot water heating.

Much of the technology and skill learned through plumbing is employed in solar technology. The home mechanic will be able to maintain or even install future systems.

The home mechanic will need a checklist to insure prolonged and efficient operation of the collection/storage system. Following are some items needing periodic attention:

1. Collector surface cleaning. From time to time, use a mild detergent to remove dust, industrial pollutants, insects, and bird droppings.

2. Condensation within the collector surface can cause oxidation and promote electrolytical attack between dissimilar metals. Clean all white oxide powder from aluminum parts. The oxide speeds up hole formation.

3. Collector fittings may suffer from movement due to large temperature differences and due to building settlement. Keep snow weight to a minimum.

4. Some sealants for collector frames are not stable to ultra-violet radiation, causing deterioration. Consult the manufacturer and the hardware dealer when getting sealants for repair.

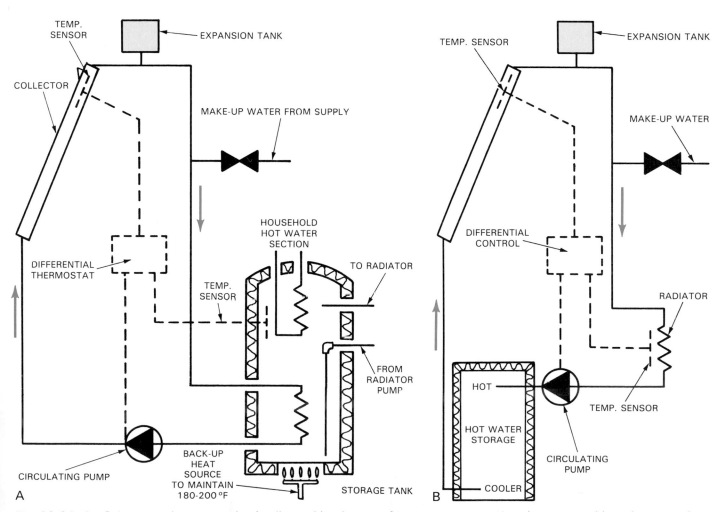

Fig. 28-24. A—Solar space heater supply. As directed by the manufacturer, pour an anti-scale compound into the expansion tank at regular intervals. System can be heat source for household hot water. B—Solar heat directly to space heater. Keep pump motors ventilated against heat buildup.

Fig. 28-25. Solar collector. (Libby-Owens-Ford)

5. In direct-circulation water systems, such as for swimming pool heaters, there is a large turnover of water. In some hard water areas, severe scaling or furring-up of the pipes may occur. In soft water areas, corrosion is more likely.
6. In installations which use anti-freeze fluid, degradation into organic acids is possible.
7. Circulating pump failures.
8. Any number of plumbing control valve failures.
9. Electrical control failures.
10. Thermal insulation covering on pipes will likely deteriorate over a period of time.

TEST YOUR KNOWLEDGE — CHAPTER 28

1. Name the three methods of heat transfer.
2. Convection relies on the property that hot air _____ .
3. The type of furnace often installed in a crawl space or attic is the _____ furnace.
4. To use a fan for summer air conditioning, set the fan limit control to room temperature, and the off limit to _____ °F below this.
5. Clean or replace furnace filters every _____

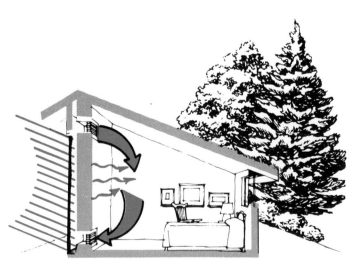

Fig. 28-26. Maintain window glass, sealing strips, and brickwork as you would for standard wall structures. Shown is a convection system called a Trombe wall. (Iowa Energy Policy Council)

months.
6. A pilot flame should be steady and yellow. True or False?
7. A burner flame with proper air:
   a. Is yellow and begins just at the burner.
   b. Is blue and begins just at the burner.
   c. Is yellow and lifts off of the burner.
   d. Is blue and lifts off of the burner.
8. An oil burner may need new air filters in two areas and also a _____ filter.
9. Keep a wood burning stove _____ in. from side and rear room walls.
10. Never use a _____ _____ instead of a standard chimney for a wood stove.
11. Clean any white _____ powder from aluminum solar framework to reduce pitting.
12. In winter, prevent _____ buildup on solar panels.

KNOW THESE TERMS

Conduction, convection, radiation, upflow, downflow, filter, burner, heat pump.

SUGGESTED ACTIVITIES

Your instructor may plan a laboratory day to investigate how gas flames behave. Obtain a gas burner unit from a furnace or use a Bunsen burner. If possible work under a fume hood. Discover the effects of high and low gas flow using standard chemistry lab gas source 'spigots'. Learn about high and low primary air flow by adjusting the pie-shaped sectors on the furnace burner. With the Bunsen burner, adjust primary air by threading the outer cylinder to cover more or less of the bottom inlet holes or by covering the holes with aluminum foil which may then be poked to create holes. During the tests, note the flame color, height, and position above the burner. Summarize your results in a report listing your initial theory or expectations, your test steps, and your results compared with your theory.

Visit a supplier or installer of solar water heaters, space heaters, or swimming pool heaters. Get brochures on some types of equipment. Also get information on passive solar systems, such as thermal storage walls, heat storage pits, and solar-powered air movement and ventilation systems. Note any maintenance steps suggested for water systems and for passive solar systems. Try to get efficiency ratings for some types of equipment. Make a report to your class.

CAREERS

Heating specialists, heating installer, heating systems designer, mechanical engineer, environmental control specialists.

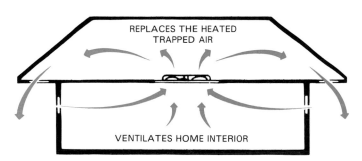

29

HOME COOLING

This chapter introduces types of air conditioning equipment and cooling fans. It discusses routine maintenance steps for these devices.

After studying this chapter, you will be able to:
- Specify the size of fans and vents needed.
- Tell how to install a ceiling or wall-mounted fan.
- Plan the cooling capacity needed for each building size.
- State some of the principles of air conditioners.
- List some do's and don'ts for air conditioner operation.

Many methods have been developed to help keep the summer's heat out of the home. Many specially designed houses keep the sun's rays from entering the house. Wraparound porches found on many older homes shade the south-facing windows. A carefully planned floor arrangement allows air currents to flow with the prevailing breezes. Plantings of deciduous trees shade the entire house from the sun. Light colored exterior paint and roofing materials reflect solar radiation and minimize the absorption of heat by the house. Insulation is important to the maintenance of cool temperature.

ATTIC FANS

Attic fans cool the home by forced ventilation of the structure. By removing the upper level warm air and replacing it with cool air, cooler air will flow in at the floor level. A second function of the attic fan is to cool the attic, Fig. 29-1, reducing the heat conduction downward from the attic. Hot attic air leaves through roof vents and is replaced by cooler, but uncomfortable, house air.

Attic fans are rated by their size and the number of cubic feet of air they will remove in one minute (CFM). Most home attic fans are either 30 x 30 in. (76 x 76 cm) or 36 x 36 in. (91 x 91 cm). The CFM will vary greatly between manufacturers of these units. The CFM is dependent upon two factors: the pitch of the blade, and the speed of the blade in revolutions per minute (rpm).

Increased speed of the fan blades will proportionally increase the CFM. However, the noise level of the fan will also increase. For home operation quietness is important.

An attic fan should be able to change the total volume of air in the house once every minute. See Fig. 29-2. In the southern warmer parts of the country, once every 1 1/2 minutes is recommended.

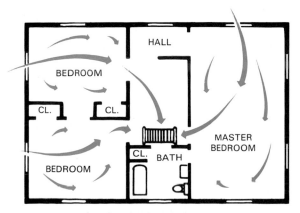

Fig. 29-1. Attic fans create a cooling effect by removing hot air near the ceiling.

Fig. 29-2. Locate fan for maximum circulation of air from each room.

Manufacturers of attic fans will provide the CFM of the model. It is listed on the identification plate of every model. To find the number of cubic feet of air in all rooms, halls, and stairways to be ventilated, multiply the length times the width times the height and sum all spaces.

Fan Opening

It is necessary to provide adequate unobstructed openings to the outside through attic windows, grilles, gable louvers, or roof vents, Fig. 29-3. This reduces back pressure in the attic that lowers the efficiency of the fan. The minimum ratio of unobstructed opening to fan capacity is 1 1/2 square feet to each 1000 CFM.

INSTALLING ATTIC FANS

Some basic carpentry skills are needed to prepare the ceiling opening. Select a centrally located area, for example, a hallway. Follow any specific installation instruction supplied by the manufacturer. See Fig. 29-4. The fan must be mounted so that it does

Fig. 29-3. Provide a sufficient vent opening in the attic to keep average attic temperature below 90°F.

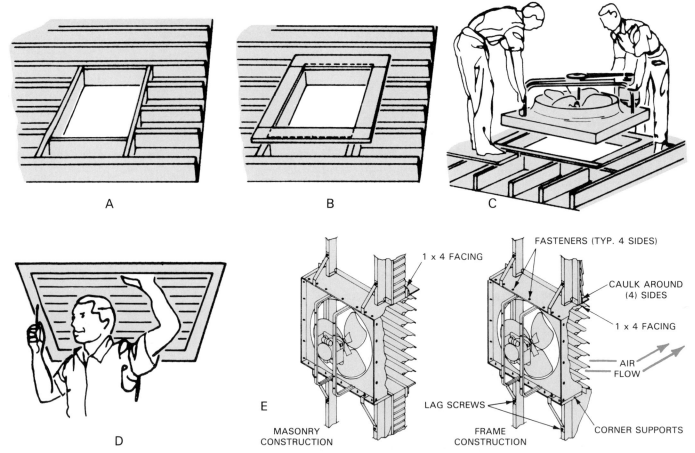

Fig. 29-4. Installing attic fan. A — Make opening in hallway ceiling or ceiling in other central area. Frame in the opening. B — Make a flange at edge of hole with 1'' boards. C — Install and wire the fan, switch, and/or timer. The switch should be in a convenient place in the hall. D — Install shutter in ceiling and trim it for appearance. (Williamson) E — For special cases, such as 24 in. spacing of ceiling joists or wall studs, no cutting of framework is required. Note how studs continue through. (Sears, Roebuck and Co.)

Fig. 29-5. Ceiling fan sends hot ceiling air down where it can be used in winter. (Hunter Fan Company)

Fig. 29-7. Window air conditioner unit.

not cause vibration of the ceiling or adjoining walls.

Another type of fan is the ceiling fan, Fig. 29-5. Ceiling fans serve to move air upward and move the hot upper level of room air out.

AIR CONDITIONING

Air conditioning systems are of two general types:

1. Central air conditioning, which cools the entire house, Fig. 29-6.
2. Window units, which cool individual rooms, Fig. 29-7.

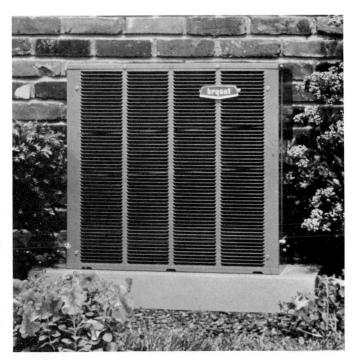

Fig. 29-6. Condensing coil section of central air conditioning unit. (Bryant)

A window air conditioner's basic function is to provide comfort by cooling, dehumidifying, filtering, or cleaning and circulating air through the room. These units can be mounted on the window sill or installed in a wall. The wall installation involves placing a metal sleeve in the wall. Most models draw some outside air in through the cooling coils, while most of the air to be cooled is taken from the room.

The operation of a typical window air conditioner is shown in Fig. 29-8. Warm air passes over the cooling coil giving up its heat. The heat in moist air is also absorbed. The conditioned air is then circulated by a fan or blower into the room. The heat from the warm room air is absorbed by the cold liquid refrigerant flowing through the evaporator. The vaporized refrigerant then carries the heat to the compressor pump. The pump compresses the vapor and increases the temperature to a point higher than that of the outdoor air. In the condenser, the hot, high pressure refrigerant vapor liquifies and gives up the heat to the outdoor air. The high pressure liquid refrigerant then passes through a restrictor which reduces its pressure and temperature. The cold, low pressure liquid refrigerant then re-enters the evaporator and the entire refrigerant cycle is repeated.

Technical Information

Here is some basic information about the window air conditioner:

1. BTU, British thermal unit, the amount of energy required to raise the temperature of one pound of water one degree Fahrenheit.

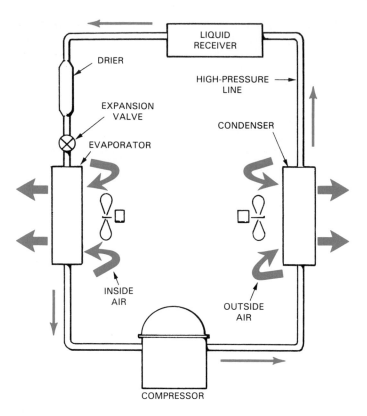

LIQUID
RECEIVER

DRIER

HIGH-PRESSURE
LINE

EXPANSION
VALVE

CONDENSER

EVAPORATOR

INSIDE
AIR

OUTSIDE
AIR

COMPRESSOR

Fig. 29-8. Schematic diagram of compression cooling system. Some units can be used as heat pumps by turning two valves to reverse the refrigerant flow.

1 BTU = 1054 joule
1 BTU = 252 calories

One calorie of heat raises the temperature of one gram of water one degree Celsius.

2. Tonnage is another rating used for room units. It refers to a unit's cooling capacity. One ton of cooling equals the cooling effect of melting one ton of ice in one hour. A general rule of thumb is that the average air conditioner will provide 12,000 BTU of cooling an hour for every ton of rating.

3. A horsepower rating is still applied to some models. It is not considered an accurate rating. The horsepower mentioned is that of the compressor motor. Many other components affect the cooling capacity of a unit. A one horsepower air conditioner may vary from 8000 BTU to over 10,000 BTU.

4. The Seasonal Energy Efficiency Rating (SEER), is a relatively new rating which rates the energy conversion to cooling on a scale of 0-10. Currently the best energy-converting models rate from 7 1/2 to 9 on the SEER scale. The SEER is established by:

SEER = BTU output ÷ wattage input.

That is, dividing the cooling effect of the unit by the power required.

Estimating the Size Required

To cool a particular space by a window unit, several things must be kept in mind:

1. The climate condition of the local region.
2. Insulation ability of the surrounding walls, ceiling, and floors.
3. Space to be cooled.
4. Air circulation requirements of the space.

As a general rule of thumb, figure 1 ton of cooling capacity (12,000 BTU) for every 500 square feet of floor space. See Fig. 29-9. (Figure square feet of space by multiplying the length of the room by the width of the room.)

INSTALLING A WINDOW UNIT

Many small 120 volt models simply slip through the window opening with an installation kit that adjusts to the window width. Furnished with the kit is a gasket, panel, and wintertight seals. Instructions and procedures make installation easy.

Installation of the larger capacity, heavier units requires additional preparation of the window sill to support this increased weight. The local dealer will assist in the installation of these models.

Through-the-wall installation avoids blocking the window. These installations require some basic carpentry skills. The particular model will usually have dimension and mounting information in the package. The home mechanic will normally need to

GENERAL SIZE/SPACE REQUIREMENT

BTU's	AREA	
	Ft²	m²
3600	150	14
4800	200	19
6000	250	22
7200	300	29
8400	350	32
9600	400	39
Require 1 15/20 volts		
10800	450	41
12000	500	48
13200	550	51
14400	600	58
15600	650	61
16800	700	68
18000	750	71
20400	800	77
21600	850	80
22800	900	86
24000	950	90
25200	1000	96
26400	1050	100
27600	1100	105
28800	1150	110
30000	1200	115
31200	1250	120
32400	1300	125
33600	1350	130
34800	1400	135
36000	1450	140
Require 230/240 volts		

Fig. 29-9. Air conditioner BTU requirements for amount of floor area.

purchase a special metal mounting sleeve for this type of installation.

The power supply for a room air conditioner is dependent upon size. It is good practice to provide a separate circuit for the air conditioner. All units come equipped with grounding type plugs on a service cord. Do not remove this ground prong. Provide a circuit which will give the necessary ground. Do not use an extension cord with an air conditioner.

General care and maintenance of the air conditioner is relatively simple. Air filters need periodic cleaning, depending on use. Remove and wash in warm water, dry, and install. Wash front air diffuser grille with soft cloth and warm water and a mild soap. Keep insect spray away from air conditioner. Some contain solvents that may soften the plastic or corrode metal parts.

CENTRAL AIR CONDITIONING

Central air conditioning cools the whole house at one time. Lower operating costs, more efficient cooling, and quieter operation are major advantages of the central system although central systems are usually more expensive to purchase and install. These costs are usually modified when a unit is combined with the heating system. Often a split system is installed with the upflow type of forced air heating system.

The basic mechanical operation of the central air conditioning system is the same as the window unit. The split system, which is most common, simply places the compressor and condenser coils outside the house, Fig. 29-10. The evaporator or cooling coils are set within the air distribution system of the forced air system and connected by the high pressure and low pressure refrigerant lines. In the upflow system, the cooling coils are located above the furnace. The downflow system has the cooling coil located underneath the furnace. This downflow system is often used for homes built with slab construction or homes without a basement. In another system, a horizontal evaporator can be installed at the air-discharge outlet of a horizontal furnace. This is ideal for the attic or crawl space installation.

Maintenance of the central air conditioner by the home mechanic is very limited. The manufacturers of these units have developed a system which is nearly maintenance-free. Aside from the replacement of the furnace air filter as described in a previous chapter, check for tripped breakers. For ammonia units having a chiller in the outdoor section, check the drive belts. There should be no more than 1/2 in. of play.

The homeowner has a unit free of major maintenance. In winter, keep the outdoor condensing unit covered. Each spring, before the cooling season begins, check the compressor-condenser unit for shrub growth, debris, leaves, and other particles which may have accumulated around or have worked their way into the housing area, Figs. 29-11 and 29-12. This debris will obstruct the airflow through the condensing coil, thereby reducing the unit's efficiency.

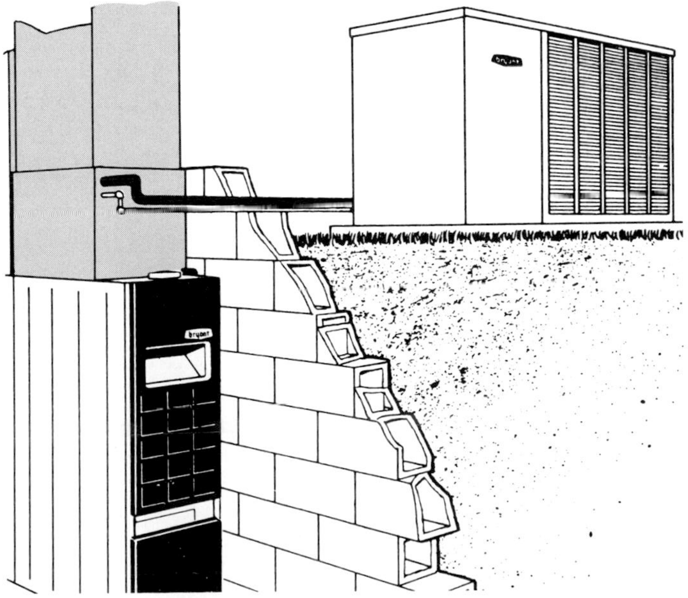

SOLID STATE REFRIGERATOR MODULE

A solid state refrigerator module is an electric cooling board with no moving parts, Fig. 29-13. Picnic coolers using these modules are available. The coolers operate from a car or truck battery. Some

Fig. 29-10. In the most common residential cooling system, the evaporating coil is inside the furnace plenum chamber. The furnace fan moves air over the evaporator coil. This cools the air sent to parts of the house

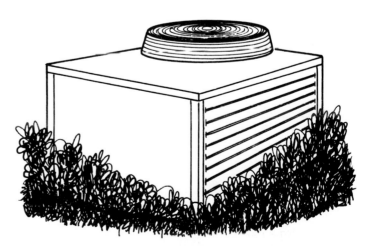

Fig. 29-11. Trim the surrounding shrubs to increase airflow through the condensing coil.

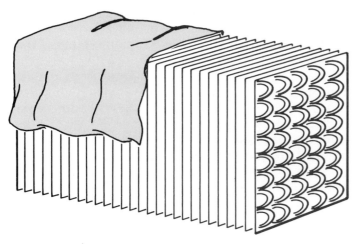

Fig. 29-12. When working in areas next to any air conditioning coil, cover the sharp fins with a cloth to prevent cutting yourself. Wear gloves. When vacuuming or dusting the coil, avoid bending the fins since this reduces air flow.

manufacturers provide home cooling units.

Maintenance involves cleaning all exchanger fins and keeping electrical switch contacts shiny. Due to high electrical current, switch contacts must be kept polished. Rotate the switch knobs frequently to wear off any corrosion.

Warning: Never re-start an air conditioning compressor until at least three minutes have passed. Otherwise, high liquid pressure can stall the compressor motor. This could damage it.

TEST YOUR KNOWLEDGE — CHAPTER 29

1. The attic vent for a fan should have _____ square feet for each 1000 CFM of airflow.
2. List two purposes of an attic fan.
3. Studs or joists do not need to be cut for a fan mounting if their spacing is:
   a. 20 in.
   b. 24 in.
   c. 18 in.
   d. 16 in.

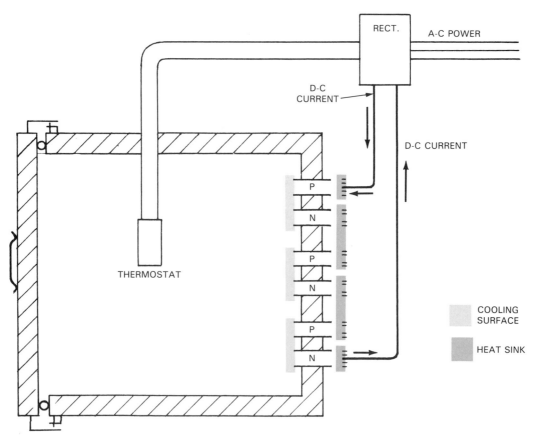

Fig. 29-13. Thermoelectric module cooling device. A dc current is the only requirement. Symbols ''P'' and ''N'' refer to special semiconductor materials. All electrical contacts must be kept extremely clean.

4. One ton of cooling capacity equals the movement of _____ BTU per hour.
5. Plan about 1 1/2 ton of cooling for every _____ sq. ft. of floor space.
6. Do not use an _____ _____ for electricity to an air conditioner.
7. In winter, _____ the outdoor condensing unit of the air conditioner.
8. A heat pump is like an air conditioner with the refrigerant flow _____ .
9. Before restarting an air conditioner, wait at least _____ min.
10. To keep electrical switch contacts for solid state cooling units polished, _____ the control knob frequently.

KNOW THESE TERMS

CFM, BTU, SEER, joule, calorie, evaporator, compressor, Celsius, Fahrenheit, HVAC.

SUGGESTED ACTIVITIES

The Automotive Service class in your school may have equipment for recharging auto air conditioners. If so, your instructor may plan a visit to this class to teach about air conditioning test instruments and repair tools. Perhaps your instructor will identify the tools which are identical to those used for home air conditioning repair.

Some ceiling fans have a variable speed control. Often this control is the same type as a lamp dimmer control. Find information on these at the hardware store or home improvement center. Get literature that shows how to wire a ceiling fan.

CAREERS

Refrigeration service person, HVAC systems installer, environmental inspector, mechanical engineer, HVAC systems control specialists, mechanical contractor.

Water-cooled condensing unit designed for central comfort cooling installation.

30

DOMESTIC WATER HEATING

This chapter discusses water heating by gas, oil, electricity, and solar. It gives hints for avoiding burnt heating elements and wasted energy.

After studying this chapter, you will be able to:
■ Test the flue draft.
■ Avoid heating elements boiling dry.
■ Remove sediment from heater tanks.
■ Make good pipe seals with teflon tape.

Proper maintenance of the house hot water system is important for conservation of water and energy. One of the most common problems with all water heating systems is leaking. Pipes can be repaired whereas tanks are usually not repaired. Hot water tanks have an average life expectancy of 10 years, depending on the mineral content of the water source.

The hot water tank is always completely filled with water. Its temperature is controlled by a thermostat, usually set between 120 and 180 °F. Cold water enters through a dip tube and flows to the bottom of the tank. See Fig. 30-1. The hot water is removed from the upper portion of the tank.

THE OIL-FIRED WATER HEATER

The oil-fired water heater has an oil burner with a combustion chamber located beneath the water storage compartment. The fuel oil used is thin and clear. The hot burning gases from the firebox move upward around the water compartment where heat is transferred to the water by conduction. The hazardous gases are vented through the flue and into a second chimney to a point above the roof. Maintain the oil burner gun as you would a furnace gun.

GAS-FIRED WATER HEATER

Water heaters are fired by both natural and manufactured gases with only slight modification.

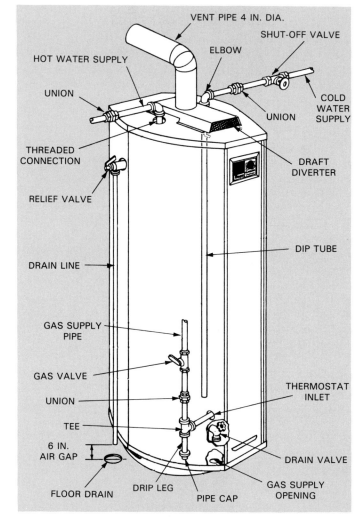

Fig. 30-1. Parts of a gas hot water heater. Dip tube keeps cold water separate from hot water. (Sears, Roebuck and Co.)

The gas burner is positioned below the water compartment, Fig. 30-2. Heat from the burning is vented upward through the center of the water compartment and transferred by conduction to the water. The centrally located vent contains a spiral baffle to aid transfer of heat, Fig. 30-3.

The hazardous gases are vented directly outside through a draft diverter and chimney. The draft diverter was shown in Fig. 30-1. Test the draft flow with a match, Fig. 30-4. Room air should be flowing into the funnel by natural convection.

To save energy, keep the thermostat below 120 °F, or below 140 °F for a dishwasher. Greater heat can shorten the life of glass-lined heaters.

ELECTRIC WATER HEATER

The typical electric water heater has two electrically powered heating elements, one located near the bottom of the tank and the second about midway between top and bottom of tank, Fig. 30-5.

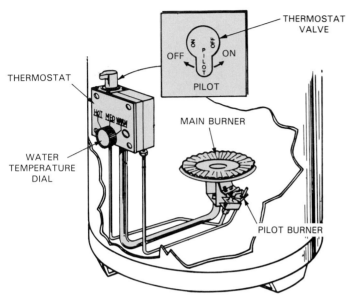

Fig. 30-2. Gas burner is below tank of gas water heater. Homeowner can make burner adjustments and can control pilot light. (Sears, Roebuck and Co.)

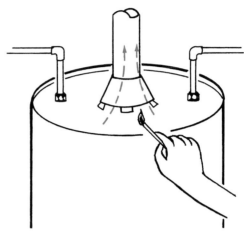

Fig. 30-4. Testing gas heater draft with a match. Proper structure provides strong upward convection. One style of draft diverter is shown.

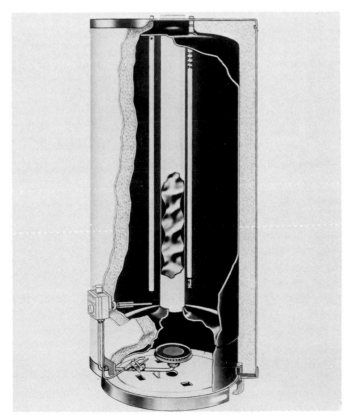

Fig. 30-3. Cutaway of a gas-fired water heater shows spiral baffle for heat transfer. (A.O. Smith)

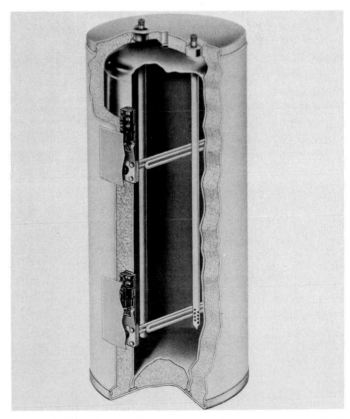

Fig. 30-5. Electric water heater has two heating elements. Each element has its own control. (A.O. Smith)

These heating elements are independently controlled by thermostats. The home mechanic may need to replace the heating elements, Fig. 30-6. Follow these steps:

1. Disconnect power by tripping the breaker or pulling the fuse.
2. Remove power wires by loosening terminal screws on exposed end of heating element.
3. Shut off water supply to water heater.
4. Drain water from tank.
5. Unscrew heating element. Note gasket locations.
6. Insert replacement. This may be purchased from the local home maintenance supplier after getting model number from the data plate.
7. Reconnect the electrical wires under terminal screws of new element.
8. Open water supply valve. Fill tank completely to avoid burning out the elements.
9. Reset the circuit breaker.

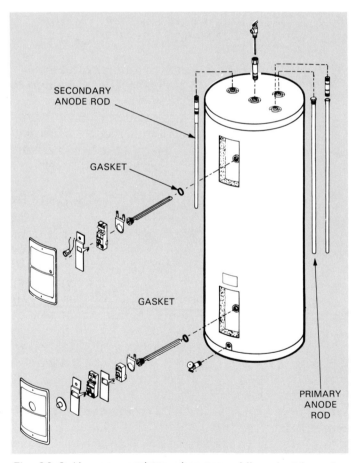

Fig. 30-6. Use new gaskets when assembling electric water heater. (Sears, Roebuck and Co.)

SOLAR-ASSISTED WATER HEATING

The basic home solar hot water system is a closed system, Fig. 30-7. Closed systems are the most

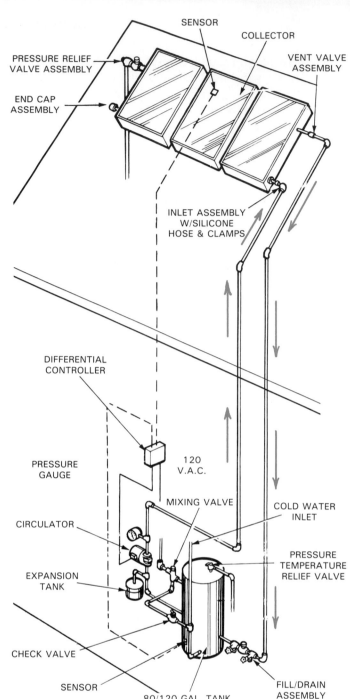

Fig. 30-7. Solar-assisted domestic hot water system keeps heating fluid separate from drinking water. (Exxon Solar Systems)

Fig. 30-8. Solar hot water collector is black to absorb heat. (Lennox)

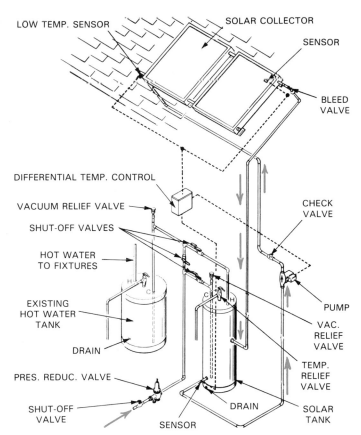

LOW TEMP. SENSOR SOLAR COLLECTOR
SENSOR
BLEED VALVE
DIFFERENTIAL TEMP. CONTROL
VACUUM RELIEF VALVE
CHECK VALVE
SHUT-OFF VALVES
HOT WATER TO FIXTURES
EXISTING HOT WATER TANK
DRAIN
PUMP
VAC. RELIEF VALVE
PRES. REDUC. VALVE
SHUT-OFF VALVE
DRAIN
SOLAR TANK
SENSOR
TEMP. RELIEF VALVE

Fig. 30-9. Solar pre-heat system. Valves allow choice of flow pattern. (Exxon Solar Systems)

dependable of solar hot water systems for climates with freezing conditions.

In the closed system, a special solar heating fluid is pumped through the solar collectors, Fig. 30-8, to be heated by the sun. The fluid is then circulated through the heat exchanger in the storage tank. The heating fluid transfers the heat to the water inside

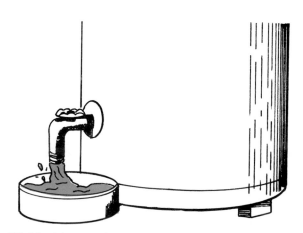

Fig. 30-10. After turning the pressure off, remove sediment from the water heater with the drain valve. Sediment slows heat flow from the heat source and can waste energy. Also clean any carbon from the underside of tank plate to improve heat flow.

the storage tank. It is then returned to the solar collector to absorb more heat and repeat the cycle.

Keep all tubing insulation very dry. Replace or tape any insulation burned by the sun.

Be sure the temperature is limited to no more than 140°F. On hot days you could be scalded.

Usually a supplemental heating source is combined with the solar water heater. This is normally an electric heating element. Maintain as stated for electric water heaters.

THE SOLAR PRE-HEATED WATER SYSTEM

Instead of using a special fluid in a separate loop, the pre-heat system runs the incoming water supply through the solar collector to raise the water temperature. See Fig. 30-9. The preheated water then goes into a storage tank. From the storage tank, water then goes into the hot water heater for its final temperature rise and use by the home.

Wiggle any snap-fit electrical connections to bite through corrosion.

FEATURES COMMON TO ALL HOT WATER SYSTEMS

1. The drain valve is found in all systems.
2. A relief valve is a safety feature designed to relieve any excessive pressure buildup.

The drain valve is used to remove sediment from the tank, Fig. 30-10. Sediment reduces the efficiency of a water heater. Turn off the water pressure to avoid splattering of hot water on yourself.

INSTALLING A REPLACEMENT WATER HEATER

To remove the old water heater, turn off both water supply and energy supply valves and/or switches. The location of the gas shut-off valve is sometimes recorded on a label near the data plate, Fig. 30-11. Disconnect the fuel supply, gas line, air line, electric wire, etc, and vent pipes. Disconnect the hot and cold water lines.

Empty the tank using a garden hose attached to the drain valve. Run it to a disposal point (basement drain).

Uncrate the new replacement. The home mechanic may have to install a relief valve and drain valve. Use pipe joint compound or teflon tape to seal the threaded joint against leaks. Dispose of the old tank. Set the new heater in place. If it has a different height, make the necessary adjustments in the water supply pipes to connect hot and cold water lines. Refer to the chapter on potable water. Install the draft diverter (gas) or draft regulator (oil) normally supplied with the new heater. Connect flue-pipe and fuel line or electric wires.

Fill the water heater before lighting the burner or

Model No. _____

Installed by _____

_____

_____

Installation Date _____

Location of gas shut-off valve _____

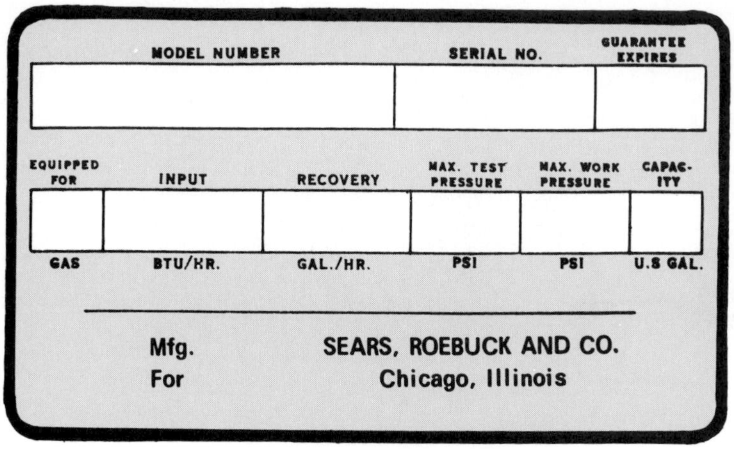

MODEL NUMBER		SERIAL NO.	GUARANTEE EXPIRES

EQUIPPED FOR	INPUT	RECOVERY	MAX. TEST PRESSURE	MAX. WORK PRESSURE	CAPAC- ITY
GAS	BTU/HR.	GAL./HR.	PSI	PSI	U.S GAL.

| Mfg. | SEARS, ROEBUCK AND CO. |
| For | Chicago, Illinois |

Fig. 30-11. Installation record helps plan a maintenance schedule. This record is for a gas water heater. Before working on heater, shut off gas valve. (Sears, Roebuck and Co.)

resetting breaker. Set the thermostat to about 120°F.

TEST YOUR KNOWLEDGE — CHAPTER 30

1. Cold water enters a water heater through:
   a. A venturi tube.
   b. A dip tube.
   c. A relief valve.
   d. A diffuser.
   e. An anode rod.
2. To save energy, keep the water heater thermostat below 120°F, or below _____ for a dishwasher.
3. Why must you fill the tank completely if the unit is an electric water heater?
4. To remove sediment from a water heater tank, use a _____ _____ .
5. Seal any threaded pipe joints with pipe joint compound or _____ _____ .

KNOW THESE TERMS

Mineral content, sediment, efficiency, draft flow, glass lined, vent.

SUGGESTED ACTIVITIES

Some gas water heaters do not have a temperature setting dial labeled in degrees. The dial may list HOT, MED, or WARM. If you have one of these units, find out from the manufacturer or from a local heating service what these labels mean. Also look for information in the owner's manual or data plate. Make labels to place at the pointer positions for future reference.

Find out and give reasons for some of the following facts:
1. A rod called a sacrificial anode is used in a water heater.
2. Metal normally feels cold to the hand. If a water heater housing feels like it is at room temperature, is the unit losing heat or not? Is a cold surface losing heat? What should you do to stop most of the heat loss? Will the saving cover the cost?

CAREERS

Thermal engineer, water heating system installer, water heating system designer, service person, plumbing appliance salesperson.

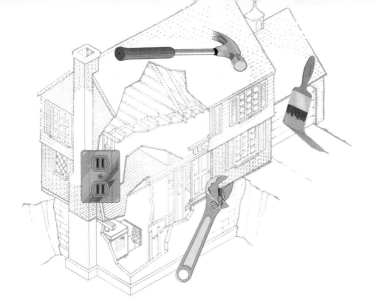

31

HOME ENVIRONMENTAL CONSIDERATIONS

This chapter introduces four of the many styles of humidifiers. It describes two humidifying methods. The chapter discusses the operation of electronic air cleaners and presents efficient non-electronic filters.

After studying this chapter, you will be able to:
■ Define relative humidity.
■ Describe a bypass type of humidifier.
■ Describe how a dehumidifier can ice up.
■ Specify a location for an electronic air filter.
■ Suggest sizes found for common air pollutant particles.
■ Tell how an electronic air cleaner works.
■ Tell how to clean an electronic grid cell.

During the colder winter months, the atmospheric air becomes drier. The air may be as dry as 3% relative humidity. Relative humidity is the amount of moisture in the air as compared with the greatest amount that the air could contain at the same temperature. Relative humidity is expressed in a percentage.

People feel cooler or warmer in proportion to the rate of evaporation of moisture from the body. To keep comfortably warm with a 20% relative humidity, we must maintain air temperatures between 75 and 80°F. If enough moisture is added to the air, the comfort zone may be lowered to 68 to 70°F. For comfortable air in wintertime, the relative humidity should be between 30 and 50%. This range helps keep wood furniture in good condition. The home mechanic may purchase a hygrometer which indicates the percentage of moisture in the air within the house, Fig. 31-1.

The home owner should consider the addition of safety warning devices. A home should have early warning systems for fire/smoke detection, radon detection, and carbon monoxide detecting. Several devices are available from building supply, or hardware retailers.

HUMIDIFIERS

The best device used to maintain a proper home humidity level is a power humidifier. An automatic humidistat permits setting of the desired humidity level, Fig. 31-2. Most humidifiers are installed and operate in conjunction with the forced air furnace. See Fig. 31-3.

Types of Humidifiers

Power humidifiers operate on two basic principles: evaporation and atomization.

Evaporation occurs when air moves over water and picks up moisture. Warm air is better for

Fig. 31-1. Wall type hygrometer shows the percent relative humidity. A — Air openings. (Abboon Cal, Inc.)

Fig. 31-2. This humidistat is combined with a thermostat.

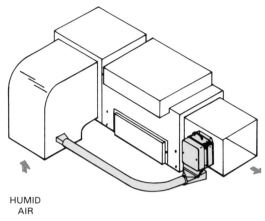

HUMID
AIR

Fig. 31-3. This humidifier, installed with a horizontal furnace, bypasses the furnace and fan. It operates on the pressure difference between furnace air outlet and inlet. (Bryant)

evaporation. Several powered evaporators are available. One is shown in Fig. 31-4. There is the stationary evaporator pad type and the dip system.

In the stationary pad type, Fig. 31-5, water is allowed to drain down over a fiber or metal pad. A motor-driven fan draws warm air from the supply duct, passes it through the evaporator pad, and returns humidified air back into the supply duct.

The dip and dry system, Fig. 31-6, depends on motor power to dip evaporative disks in water and then expose the wet surfaces to moving warm air.

The atomizer type is independent of the movement of warm air. It is usually installed in the cold air return of forced air furnaces. Other atomizer models can be installed almost anywhere that water and electrical connections are available. The atomizer type mechanically breaks up water into fine particles which the surrounding air can absorb.

Maintenance of humidifiers usually centers on the evaporator pads or disks. These periodically need replacement. Mineral deposits left by evaporating water must be removed to avoid reduced airflow. Bacteria must be periodically removed. Some models use excess water to flush away the mineral deposits. In either case, these pads need to be changed at the beginning of each winter season.

Some humidifiers have a granular surface on the top water distributor tray. Do not scrape this off. It spreads water evenly onto the evaporator panel.

DEHUMIDIFIERS

In some areas during the warmer seasons of the year, unwanted high relative humidity may exist. This condition may be due to other factors aside from atmospheric conditions. Wet towels, drying clothes, showers, cooking, floor scrubbing, and other household chores often add moisture to

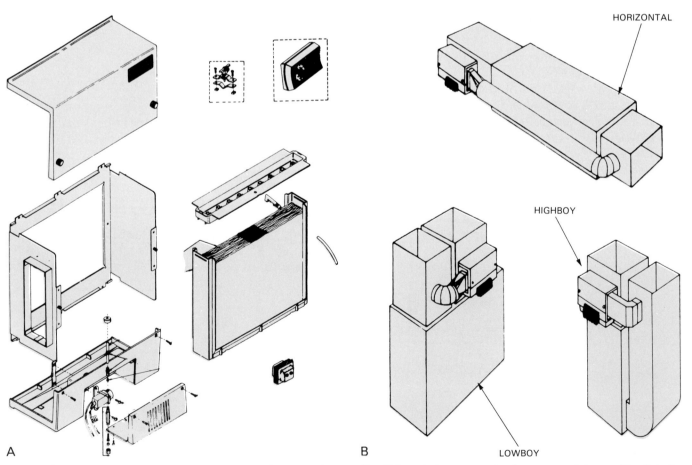

HORIZONTAL

HIGHBOY

LOWBOY

Fig. 31-4. A—This humidifier mounts on a furnace plenum. B—This unit bypasses the furnace and fan. (Aprilaire)

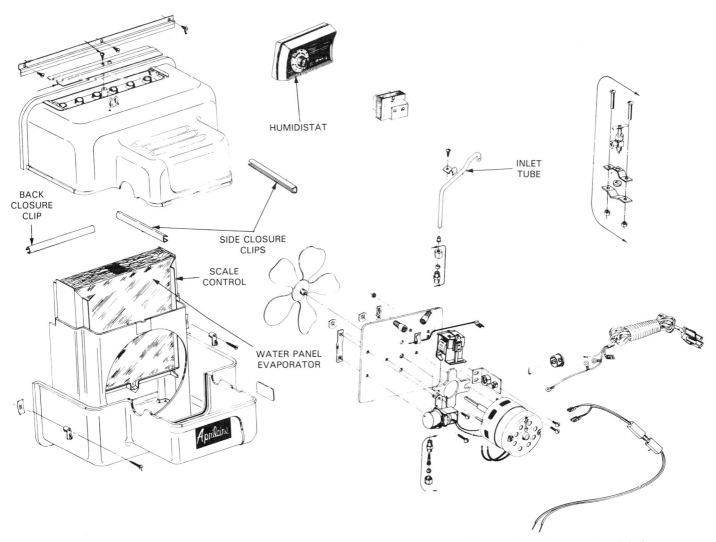

HUMIDISTAT

INLET TUBE

BACK CLOSURE CLIP

SIDE CLOSURE CLIPS

SCALE CONTROL

WATER PANEL EVAPORATOR

Aprilaire

Fig. 31-5. Remove side closure clips to replace the evaporator panel. Discard the old panel. (Aprilaire)

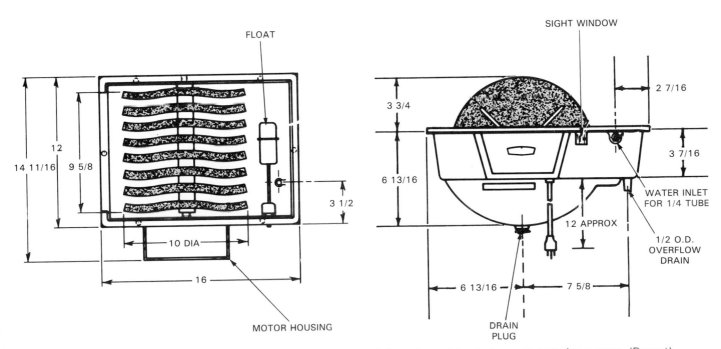

FLOAT

SIGHT WINDOW

2 7/16

3 3/4

3 7/16

12

14 11/16   9 5/8

6 13/16

WATER INLET FOR 1/4 TUBE

3 1/2

1/2 O.D. OVERFLOW DRAIN

10 DIA

12 APPROX

16

6 13/16   7 5/8

MOTOR HOUSING

DRAIN PLUG

Fig. 31-6. The power disc humidifier. Remove the mineral deposits and bacteria once or twice a year. (Bryant)

the home.

Two common units that reduce humidity in the home are:

1. Attic fans which replace the warm moist air with cooler, drier air from the outside.
2. Mechanical dehumidifiers which use a refrigerated surface (sometimes called the drying coil), a condenser, air circulating fan, a humidistat, and a cabinet to house these components.

Moisture-laden air is drawn over the refrigerated coils (evaporator) by the fan. As the warm moist air hits the cold surface, the moisture condenses and drips off into a collection container or is carried to a drain. The home which has mechanical air conditioning has a secondary benefit since the air conditioner also acts as a dehumidifier.

Common maintenance required by a dehumidifier unit is the occasional removal of dust and dirt from the evaporator coil, the condenser, and the fan unit. Other requirements involve oiling or special operating instructions. See Fig. 31-7. Most other problems should be left to the professional service person.

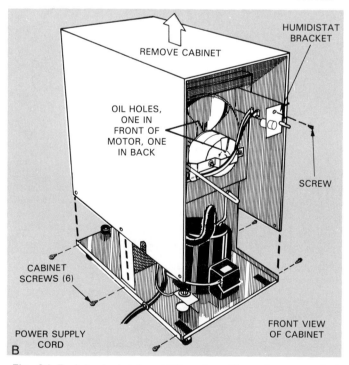

Fig. 31-7. A typical dehumidifier. A — Some have a switch operated by the drip pan. The unit will not turn on unless the pan is in place. B — Oil may be needed at the ends of the fan motor shaft. (Sears, Roebuck and Co., Kenmore Div.)

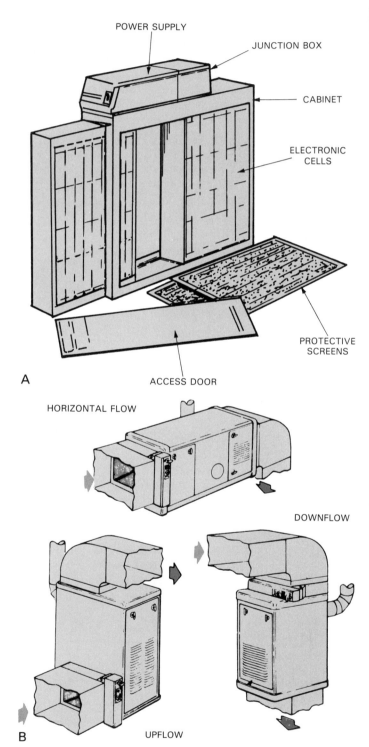

Fig. 31-8. A—An electronic air cleaner. (Honeywell, Inc.) B—Use one of these locations for the electronic air cleaner in the furnace system. (Tennessee Plastics, Inc.)

306

ELECTRONIC AIR CLEANERS

An electronic air cleaner is an investment in healthful comfort. Electronic air cleaners are efficient replacements for ordinary furnace or air conditioner filters. They are placed where older filters were. See Fig. 31-8.

Any air cleaner is effective only on the air that is circulated through it. So, it is unrealistic to expect complete removal of all contaminants. However, the efficiency of an electronic air cleaner increases as the use increases. These cleaners remove a very high percentage of the pollutants from the circulated air.

There is pollution in air everywhere, even in the air we normally consider to be fresh outdoor air, Fig. 31-9. If the entry of this air into the home is minimized by keeping doors and windows closed as much as possible, it reduces pollution further.

Operation of the electronic air cleaner is based on the principles of static electric charges. Unlike charges attract each other. Dirt particles in incoming air are given a positive (+) charge while several metal grids are given a negative (−) charge. Any airborne particle with a positive charge is drawn to the grids. The pollutants are held by this attraction,

Fig. 31-11. Some electronic air cleaner cells can be cleaned in a dishwasher or laundry tub. (Honeywell Inc.)

COMMON POLLUTANTS
Particle Sizes in Microns (1 micron = 1/25,400 inches)

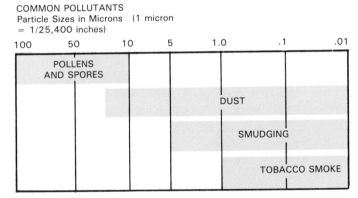

Fig. 31-9. Common pollutants in the home can be invisible. (American Society of Heating, Refrigeration, and Air Conditioning Engineers)

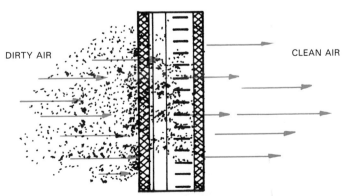

Fig. 31-10. Operation of an electronic air cleaner. (Tennessee Plastics, Inc.)

leaving the air clean, Fig. 31-10.

Occasionally, the home mechanic will need to remove the collected pollutants. Follow the manufacturer's cleaning procedure. Generally the steps are:

1. Disconnect power and wait a few minutes for the charge to dissipate.
2. Tap the metal grid gently allowing the particles to drop to the bottom and collect in a collection tray. Or clean with water, as suggested in Fig. 31-11.
3. Remove the collection tray and properly dispose of the pollutants.
4. Replace tray into cleaner.
5. Return power to cleaner.

Most electronic air cleaners have a signaling device to warn the homeowner at cleaning time.

TEST YOUR KNOWLEDGE — CHAPTER 31

1. What is relative humidity?
2. For comfortable air in wintertime, the relative humidity should be between _____ and _____%.
3. The humidity level is kept constant with a:
   a. Hygrometer.
   b. Psychrometer.
   c. Humidistat.
   d. Thermostat.

4. Power humidifiers operate on two principles: evaporation and _____ .
5. Change humidifier pads at the beginning of each _____ season.
6. If there is a _____ surface on a humidifier water distributor tray, do not scrape it off.
7. Units that are used to reduce humidity include the _____ _____ and the mechanical dehumidfier.
8. In a dehumidifier, water condenses on the:
   a. Condenser.
   b. Regenerator.
   c. Evaporator.
   d. Evaporator pad.
9. The principle of an electronic air cleaner is that unlike charges _____ (repel, attract).
10. Name the first step in cleaning a grid cell in an electronic air cleaner.

KNOW THESE TERMS

Humidity, electronic air cleaner, pollutants, dehumidifier.

SUGGESTED ACTIVITIES

List some advantages of a bypass humidifier system. List some disadvantages. To help you, compare the operation with a disk type humidifier and a fan-and-pad type. What type would you use in your home if you do not already have one?

A dehumidifier can ice up at room temperatures less than 65 °F. What part will ice up? Will the unit remove any more water vapor? How does the unit's location cause ice formation? What are the seasonal effects? Propose some steps to avoid the ice problem.

CAREERS

Home environmental systems designer, mechanical engineer, environmental specialist, home environmental systems installer.

Today's homeowners are concerned with indoor air quality. This air cleaner removes 98 percent of the particles as small as .03 microns in a single pass. It is installed in the return air duct. (Emerson Electric Co.)

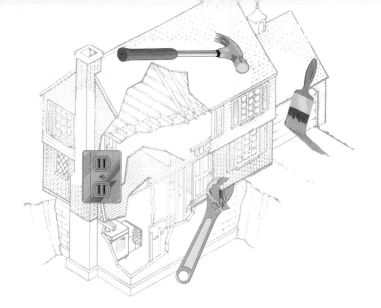

32

INSULATION

This chapter describes four types of insulation and explains an insulating property called the R-value. The chapter defines a vapor barrier and shows what direction it should face. The chapter suggests ways to install insulation and weatherstripping.

After studying this chapter, you will be able to:
■ List some types of insulation.
■ Recall approximate R-values for blanket or batt insulation.
■ Identify an uninsulated area in a house.
■ Tell how wire mesh is used when insulating.
■ State when staples are convenient.
■ Describe some steps for insulating a garage, attic, or crawl space.
■ Tell where a door area should be insulated and weatherstripped.
■ List some places to caulk.

With increased energy cost, the home mechanic has changed some attitudes toward the heating, cooling, and lighting of the house. Also, new house designers are beginning to change their house designs. Today, houses in general are being designed to conserve energy by:
1. Reducing their size.
2. Lowering ceiling heights.
3. Decreasing window sizes (unless solar designed).
4. Increasing the amount of insulation material used.

Houses under construction are the simplest to insulate because insulation is installed before the wall spaces and exposed floor are covered over. Refer to Fig. 32-1. Attic and crawl spaces are usually easy to enter in older homes as well as those under construction. Attic and crawl spaces may be insulated

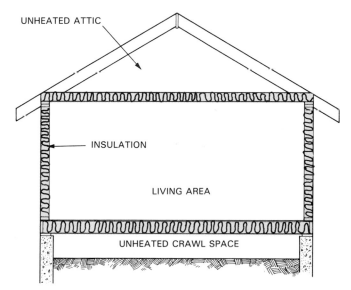

Fig. 32-1. Insulation is only required for surfaces forming the living space. The walls of an unheated crawl space do not need insulation.

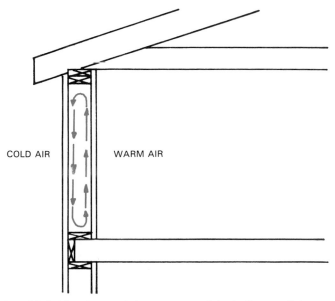

Fig. 32-2. The thermosiphon pattern of the hollow wall. Insulation reduces the air current pattern.

without special equipment. Doors benefit from weatherstripping since air will flow readily through poor seals.

HOW INSULATION WORKS

Insulation is the creation of a dead air space between the warm air inside the structure and the colder air outside. Without insulation, heat is transferred to the air between the interior and exterior walls. This air circulates by the thermosiphon effect, Fig. 32-2. The air transfers its heat to the exterior siding where the heat is conducted to the outside air. Any insulating material that traps the air and prevents this thermosiphon current will reduce the loss of heat.

MEASUREMENT OF INSULATION VALUES

The resistance of a material to the transfer of heat depends on its composition and physical characteristics. The specific resistance (R) of any material, however, varies directly with its thickness. For example, a 2 in. (5 cm) thickness of a material will provide twice the resistance to heat flow as a 1 in. (2.5 cm) thickness of the same material. Conversely, the amount of heat that will be conducted by that material decreases with increasing thickness. A 2 in. thickness of a material will transfer only half as much as a 1 in. thickness.

A total R-value can be found for layers of many materials. For this, the R-values are added together. R (total) = $R_1 + R_2 + R_3$.

The amount of heat a material will conduct through one sq. ft. (0.092 m²) of surface area per unit of thickness is called conductance C. Resistance is equal to 1 divided by conductance.

R = 1/C

Some manufacturers list the R-value of their products. Testing laboratories have established R-values for many building materials. See Fig. 32-3 for a list of common construction materials and their R-values.

TYPES OF INSULATION

Insulation is available to the home mechanic in several different forms: batts, board, blankets, foam loose-fills, foams, and reflective. Some of these are shown in Fig. 32-4. Special shapes for special purposes are available for home insulation projects.

Batts

Batts are placed between studs or joists in 15 and 23 in. (38 and 58 cm) widths. They are either faced or unfaced, Fig. 32-5. Faced insulation batts provide a vapor barrier. Faced batts have tabs to mount the insulation on the framing parts.

TABLE OF R-VALUES

Material	Thickness	R Value
Air Film and Spaces:		
Air space, bounded by ordinary materials	1.9 (3/4 or more)	.91
Air space, bounded by aluminum foil	1.9 (3/4 or more)	2.17
Exterior surface resistance	– – – – –	.17
Interior surface resistance	– – – – –	.68
Masonry:		
Sand and gravel concrete block	20 (8)	1.11
	30 (12)	1.28
Lightweight concrete block	20 (8)	2.00
	30 (12)	2.13
Face brick	10 (4)	.44
Concrete cast in place	20 (8)	.64
Building Materials — General		
Wood sheathing or subfloor	1.9 (3/4)	1.00
Fiber board insulating sheathing	1.9 (3/4)	2.10
Plywood	1.5 (5/8)	.79
	1.2 (1/2)	.63
	0.9 (3/8)	.47
Bevel lapped siding	1.2x20 (1/2x8)	.81
	1.9x25 (3/4x10)	1.05
Vertical tongue and groove board	1.9 (3/4)	1.00
Drop Siding	1.9 (3/4)	.94
Asbestos board	0.6 (1/4)	.13
0.9cm (3/8'') gypsum lath and 0.9cm (3/8'') plaster	1.9 (3/4)	.42
Gypsum board (sheet rock)	0.9 (3/8)	.32
Interior plywood panel	0.6 (1/4)	.31
Building paper	– – – – –	.06
Vapor barrier	– – – – –	.00
Wood shingles	– – – – –	.87
Asphalt shingles	– – – – –	.44
Linoleum	– – – – –	.08
Carpet with fiber pad	– – – – –	2.08
Hardwood floor	– – – – –	.71
Insulation Materials (mineral wool, glass wool, wood wool):		
Blanket or batts	2.5 (1)	3.70
	8.8 (3 1/2)	11.00
	15.2 (6)	19.00
Loose fill	2.5 (1)	3.33
Rigid insulation board (sheathing)	1.9 (3/4)	2.10
Windows and Doors:		
Single Window	– – – – –	approx. 1.00
Double Window	– – – – –	approx. 2.00
Exterior Window	– – – – –	approx. 2.00

Fig. 32-3. Table of R-values. Note the large R-value for blanket and batt insulation.

Boards

Rigid boards of brown fiber also double as sheathing or other construction members. Rigid boards may either be glued or nailed in place. However, do not expect these boards to supply any

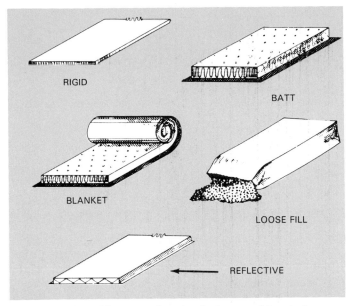

Fig. 32-4. There are four basic forms of insulation.

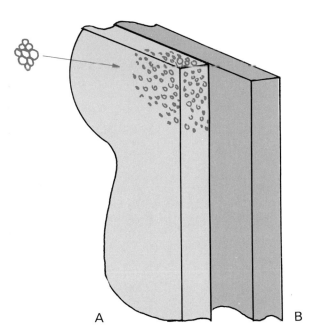

Fig. 32-6. This rigid board insulation is made of a material often called styrofoam. A—Bead board is distinguished by its pattern of isolated "beads." B—Foam board is distinguished by its uniform "open cell" structure. Some foam sheets may have foil backs for radiant reflection.

Fig. 32-5. Laying unfaced insulation on top of attic floor above original insulation. With no insulation under attic floor, use faced insulation with foil side down. (Owens-Corning Fiberglass)

structural strength. Boards usually are available in 4 × 8 ft. (1 200 × 2 400 mm) sheets. Boards also consist of styrofoam, Fig. 32-6.

Blankets

Blankets are similar to batts in nature but come in much larger sizes. Blankets with widths of 4, 6, or 8 ft. (1 200, 1 800 or 2 400 mm) are not uncommon. Rolls can be up to 50 ft. (15 m) in length. Wide blankets are used in commercial buildings rather than houses.

Loose Fill

Fiberglass, cellulose, mineral fill, or plastic beads are the most common loose fill materials. They are used in attic spaces or other horizontal installations. Hollow masonry walls are filled with loose insulation.

Foams

Foam-in-place insulation is finding use in the home, Fig. 32-7. Foams have long been used as insulating materials for refrigerators and freezers. These materials are usually plastic and require special equipment for their installation, Fig. 32-8.

Vapor Barriers

Moisture from everyday activities inside the house passes through uninsulated walls and condenses on the cold exterior walls. There it causes the paint to blister and peel. If there is insulation between the walls but no vapor barrier, the insulation will become saturated, Fig. 32-9. Wet insulation loses its effectiveness as an insulation. Wet insulation is a good conductor of heat energy.

To contain the moisture within the house, a vapor barrier of moisture-resistant material is needed. It is placed over the insulation between the studs and gypsum board of the walls and ceiling, and between joists over any crawl space or unconditioned space.

A 6 mil (0.006 in.) thick film of polyethylene plastic is an excellent vapor barrier. Fiberglass rolls or blankets are usually faced with an asphalt-coated kraft paper and covered with an aluminum foil. Wide blankets are covered with a vinyl plastic film.

Fig. 32-7. Foam-in-place insulation is used both in new construction and to retro-fit a home. (Thermco)

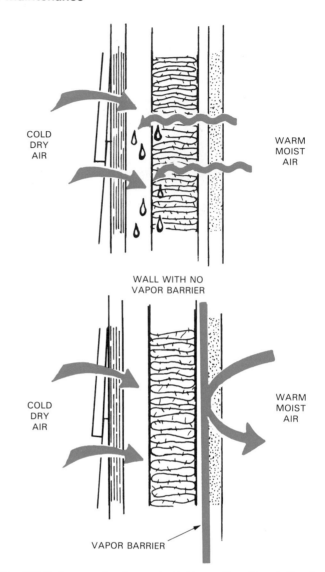

WALL WITH NO VAPOR BARRIER

COLD DRY AIR

WARM MOIST AIR

VAPOR BARRIER

Fig. 32-9. A vapor barrier protects the wall and insulation from condensation.

Fig. 32-8. Insulating an older home with pumped foam. The foam fills in around wiring and plumbing. Plugs hide the holes. (Thermco)

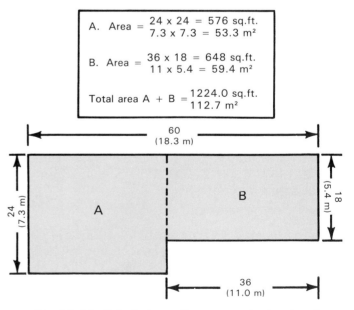

A. Area = $\dfrac{24 \times 24 = 576 \text{ sq.ft.}}{7.3 \times 7.3 = 53.3 \text{ m}^2}$

B. Area = $\dfrac{36 \times 18 = 648 \text{ sq.ft.}}{11 \times 5.4 = 59.4 \text{ m}^2}$

Total area A + B = $\dfrac{1224.0 \text{ sq.ft.}}{112.7 \text{ m}^2}$

60 (18.3 m)

24 (7.3 m)

A

B

18 (5.4 m)

36 (11.0 m)

Fig. 32-10. Calculating ceiling area to be insulated.

Aluminum foils also help to reflect radiant heat energy back into the warm interior of the house.

Although the attic is a home's number one source of winter heat loss and summer heat gain, and sidewalls rank as number two, they are not the areas that should be insulated first.

A substantial amount of energy also is lost through crawl spaces, basement walls, and garage ceilings and walls.

With fuel prices soaring, the home mechanic is beginning to realize that anything which can conserve energy and keep fuel bills down is worth the time, effort, and cost. Adding insulation to crawl spaces, basement walls, or garage ceilings and walls that are underinsulated or contain no insulation at all is relatively easy.

FIRST STEP: MEASURE

Once you have determined the specific areas of your home that need insulating, the first step is to measure how much insulation you will need. A sketch may help.

Measure the length and width of the area to be insulated and multiply these two dimensions to determine the area of material required. See Fig. 32-10. After the area has been calculated, the next step is to determine how wide the insulation should be.

Since insulation usually is installed between structural framing members, such as joists or studs, the space between these members almost always measures a constant 22 1/2 in. (57 cm) or 14 1/2 in. (35 cm), depending on local building codes and the age of the house. Therefore, your insulation project will require a material that is either 23 to 24 in. or 15 to 16 in. wide.

Fig. 32-12. To convert an attic into a living space, install batts between rafters and between collar beams. Vapor barrier should face down. (Owens-Corning Fiberglass)

NEXT STEP

Having found the required area and width, you now should determine whether a vapor barrier is needed and decide the insulation thickness or R-value to use. Refer to the next chapter. The higher a material's R-value, the greater its insulating power.

If the area to be insulated already has some insulation, then unfaced insulation (no vapor barrier) should be used. If there is no existing insulation, a material with a vapor barrier should be installed. Building material dealers carry an ample supply of both faced and unfaced material.

For deciding on the proper R-value, the home mechanic should check with their local utility, building supply dealer, or insulation contractor, or follow the recommendation of the U.S. Department of Energy.

Each of these sources is prepared to offer valuable advice in selecting the right R-value for the climate and area of the home to be insulated. Also refer to the next chapter of this book.

INSTALLING THE INSULATION

It does not matter which area is insulated first. If there is an unheated attic area or attached garage, one of these may be the starting area.

For an unfloored, unfinished attic, begin laying insulation batts at outer edge of the attic, working toward the center, Fig. 32-11. The vapor barriers if used should be face down toward the warm-in-winter side of the attic floor. For converting an attic to living space, install batt insulation between rafters and collar beams, Fig. 32-12. Again, the vapor barrier should face the warm-in-winter side.

Fig. 32-11. Vapor barrier should be face down, toward the warm-in-winter surface of the attic floor. (Owens-Corning Fiberglass)

Take care not to seal off any soffit vents or airflow paths. See Fig. 32-13. A barrier of some kind must be present to avoid pushing insulation down too far. If there is none, use cardboard shields. To finish, apply gypsum board, paneling, or other such material directy over the insulation. Do not leave insulation exposed.

To insulate between heated and unheated spaces, wedge insulation between wall studs. The vapor barrier should be nearer to the warm-in-winter side of the wall. To insulate floors above unheated crawl spaces, install wire mesh or crisscross wire over floor joist to keep insulation permanently in place.

Also insulate all attic heating ducts, Fig. 32-14. Air conditioning ducts require insulation with a vapor barrier on the outside.

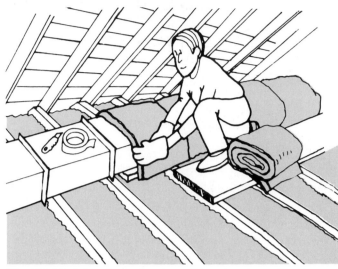

Fig. 32-14. It is wise to insulate all heating ducts in unheated attic. Use duct insulation, 2 in. thick if possible. For air conditioning ducts, insulation must have vapor barrier on the outside. (HUD)

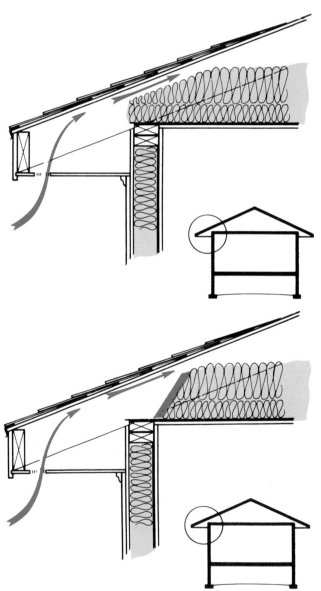

Fig. 32-13. Top. Insulation for ceiling. Keep at least a 2 in. gap above insulation for ventilation. (Illinois Dept. of Energy and Natural Resources). Bottom. Hold back loose fill with cardboard pieces.

Fig. 32-15. Install framework of furring strips or studs to masonry walls. (Owens-Corning Fiberglass)

Insulating Basement Walls

The first step in basement wall insulation is to install a framework of furring strips to the concrete or masonry walls, Fig. 32-15. Space them either on 16 in. (40 cm) or 24 in. (60 cm) centers. Install insulation between furring strips or studs. Staple the flange on the facing of the insulation to the framing members, Fig. 32-16. The facing is the vapor barrier. Follow with cut pieces of insulation to fit among spaces at band joists between subfloor and sill plate, Fig. 32-17. Finally, cover insulation with desired wall finish, Fig. 32-18. Do not leave insulation exposed.

Insulating Garage Walls

Wedge batt or board insulation materials between wall studs or use loose fill behind gypsum. The

Fig. 32-16. Faced insulation batts have reinforced tabs at each edge for fastening insulation to studs. (Owens-Corning Fiberglass)

Fig. 32-19. If the garage is below a living space, the living space floor is often cold. Install insulation with an R-value of 8. Hold with staples until adding a final support. (Owens-Corning Fiberglass)

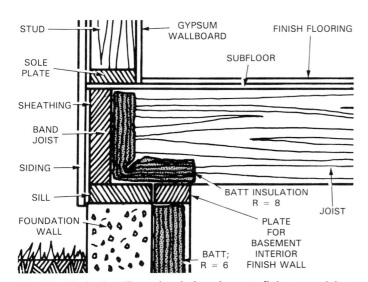

Fig. 32-17. At the sill, cut insulation pieces to fit between joists to reduce heat loss. (Owens-Corning Fiberglass)

Fig. 32-18. Finish the basement wall with gypsum board or paneling. Do not leave insulation exposed. (Owens-Corning Fiberglass)

vapor barrier can be polyethylene film. The vapor barrier should be nearer to the warm-in-winter side of wall. Always finish the insulation job by filling in the cracks and small spaces around doors and window frames.

Insulating closed walls in a home is usually a job for a professional contractor, since the stud cavities are not accessible. But exterior walls that have been left unfinished, as is often the case in an attached unheated garage, can be insulated easily with faced insulation. Faced insulation should be installed in the stud cavities with the vapor barriers facing the warm-in-winter side of the wall. The insulation should not be left exposed. Plywood, particle board, or paneling can be used as a covering.

Insulate Garage Ceilings

Floors above such garages can be cold in winter. They also can be hot in summer and cause high fuel bills all year. To avoid this, the garage ceiling (bottom side of this floor) should be insulated. See Figs. 32-19 and 32-20.

To do the job, place insulation batts between the ceiling joists with the vapor barrier facing up, against the surface. Use staples to hold the insulation in place temporarily. Finishing can be done with a covering such as gypsum board or a wire mesh, which will secure the insulation, Fig. 32-21.

Crawl Spaces

Crawl spaces are frequently a source of uncomfortable drafts and energy waste. There are two types of crawl spaces, heated and unheated. Applying insulation is slightly different for each.

Unheated crawl spaces are insulated by slipping insulation batts between the floor joists with the vapor barrier facing up toward the warm-in-winter side. The insulation will remain in place temporarily. Begin at one end of wall and install wire mesh

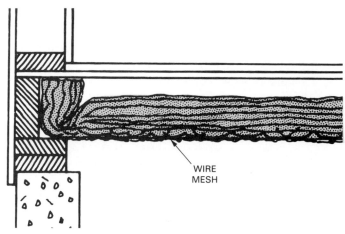

Fig. 32-20. In the garage, be sure insulation fits snugly against band joist and overlaps the bottom plate. Note wire mesh for support. (Owens-Corning Fiberglass)

Fig. 32-21. To keep material in place, install wire mesh over the joists. (Owens-Corning Fiberglass)

perpendicular to the floor joists to hold the insulation in place permanently. Be sure the insulation fits snugly up against the band joist and overlaps the bottom plate.

To insulate heated crawl spaces, begin by measuring and cutting small pieces of insulation to fit snugly against the band joist. These and other pieces are shown in Fig. 32-22. Using longer furring strips, nail vertical lengths of insulation batt to the sill. Or adhesive can be used at the sill. Make sure the insulation is long enough to cascade down the wall and extend 2 ft. along the ground in the crawl space.

You may need to insulate two walls that run at right angles to joists, and two walls running parallel.

On walls that run parallel to joists, it is not necessary to use separate header strips. Simply use longer pieces of insulation nailed with furring strips directly to the band joists.

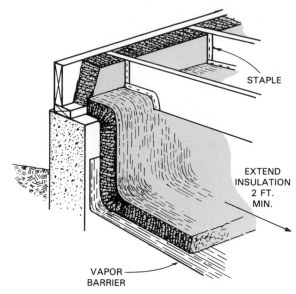

Fig. 32-22. Insulation for a heated crawl space. Fasten insulation at sill with adhesive or use furring strips. Install vapor barrier last to avoid walking on it. Finish fastening using adhesive.

After the insulation has been installed, lay a 0.006 in. thick polyethylene film under the insulation and the entire floor area. Adhesive can be used to hold the insulation to the masonry wall. Use old boards or rocks to help hold the insulation in place on the ground.

ADDITIONAL TIPS FOR HOME INSULATION

1. Do Not Cover Lights. Keep insulation a minimum of 3 in. (7 cm) from recessed light fixtures. Recessed lights can build up heat. While this heat usually is not enough to ignite surrounding materials, the heat trapped could damage the fixture.

2. Eave Vents Must Be Open. Eave vents in attics should not be covered with insulation. Their purpose is to provide adequate ventilation the whole year. In the summer, the vents allow cool outside air to enter the attic, reducing the temperature and making the house cooler. In the winter, moisture vapor escapes through the vents, preventing ceiling or attic floor damage.

3. Repair Tears. Even with adequate ventilation, a vapor barrier still is needed and it must be in good shape to do its job. Too often, when insulation is being installed, the vapor barrier is accidentally torn. Even small tears can reduce the vapor barrier's effectiveness, so be sure to repair it with a heavy duty tape.

4. Level Loose Fill. Loose fill insulation is an alternative to any of the other types of insulation. To level the fill that is put in an attic, use a screed as shown in Fig. 32-23.

Fig. 32-23. Pour loose fill insulation to the top of joists. Level it with a board, rake, or a paddle of your own design. (HUD)

Fig. 32-24. Use scraps to fill cracks and small openings around doors and windows. (Owens-Corning Fiberglass)

Fig. 32-25. Caulk around areas where pipes penetrate outside walls.

FINAL STUFFING AND WEATHERSTRIPPING

Leaks occur through cracks, around doors and windows. As a part of the house insulation job, the home mechanic should include door and window stud insulation, weatherstripping, and caulking.

Doors and Windows

Doors and windows that are insulated and sealed will reduce air infiltration as well as insulate against exterior temperatures. See Fig. 32-24. The quality of seal between the door and door opening is important. Check carefully the threshold seal.

If insulated doors cannot be used, then two doors are an alternative. Use a storm and a standard door.

Weatherstripping is a must. All doors and windows should be weatherstripped with metal or rubber strips, or vinyl cord. Better quality products add little to finished cost but they are preferred due to their superior durability. The better strips retain their ability to reduce air infiltration for a longer time.

Reflective Barriers

Materials developers and manufacturers have completed research on the heat loss/gain values of a reflective surface. The mirrored surface of aluminized membranes, vapor barriers, and insulation have the characteristics of reversing the waves that carry energy through material. This helps to conserve thermal energy. The reflective films have no thermal resistive value. They serve to reflect the waves back into the room in the case of heat conservation or reflect incoming rays outward in the case of cool space maintenance. Installation of reflective materials, in the attic below the rafters and above the insulation, has proven values relating to the heating/cooling of the structure.

CAULKING AND SEALING

At specified locations, caulking is a must. Of the many types of caulks and sealants available, the preferred types are a polysulfide, polyurethane, or silicone material, Fig. 32-25. These types may more than pay for their high initial cost by eliminating additional expense at a later date due to the need for recaulking.

Required caulking locations are:
1. Between drip caps and siding around doors and windows.
2. At joints between window and door frames and siding.
3. Between window sills and siding.
4. At corners formed by siding.
5. At sills where wood structures meet the foundation. Another material for this is a soft strip between foundation and sill called a sill sealer. It is placed during new construction.

6. Around outside water faucets, electrical outlets, or other breaks in outside house surface.
7. Where pipes and wires penetrate the ceiling below an unheated attic.
8. Between porches and main body of the house.
9. Where chimney masonry meets siding.
10. Where the wall meets the eave at the gable ends of a heated attic.

TEST YOUR KNOWLEDGE — CHAPTER 32

1. Air inside of walls circulates by the _____ effect.
   a. Venturi. c. Wall surface.
   b. Whirlpool. d. Thermosiphon.
2. A 2 in. thickness of material will transfer _____ (half, twice) the heat as a 1 in. thickness.
3. Faced insulation has _____ on the edges to mount it to studs.
4. A vapor barrier on an insulation strip should be nearer to the:
   a. Warm-in-winter side.
   b. Warm-in-summer side.
   c. Outer or inner side or both sides.
   d. Air space, if any is left over after filling with insulation.
5. A material's resistance to heat flow is given as its _____ .
6. For an attic cathedral ceiling, vapor barrier faces _____ (up, down).
7. Air conditioning ducts require insulation with a vapor barrier on the _____ (inside, outside).
8. Insulation in a heated crawl space should extend _____ ft. horizontally onto its floor.
9. Insulation in a garage ceiling is held in place with _____ _____ .
10. Keep insulation at least _____ in. from all light fixtures.
11. Use heavy tape to repair a _____ in a vapor barrier.
12. Doors need insulation at stud structures and need _____ on the edges of the door.
13. Two doors can be used instead of a/an _____ door.
14. Weatherstripping consists of metal or rubber strips, or _____ _____ .
15. To prevent cuts in garage or other insulation, do not leave it _____ .
16. If no sill sealer was used, you should _____ the joint between foundation and sill.

KNOW THESE TERMS

R-value, vapor barrier, insulation, reflective barriers.

SUGGESTED ACTIVITIES

What will happen if the vapor barrier is nearer to the cold-in-winter side of the wall or ceiling? Give some reasons for your answer. Try not to look up the answer in a book. Make a sketch of your idea. Discuss in class the reasons you have devised.

Refer to the chapter on energy saving and the energy audit. Find out the R-values required for insulation in ceilings, walls, and floors for your climate. Then use the chart in Fig. 32-3 to determine the thickness in inches of blanket or batt insulation which will provide each R-value. Collect your results in a chart.

CAREERS

General contractor, materials salesperson, insulation installer.

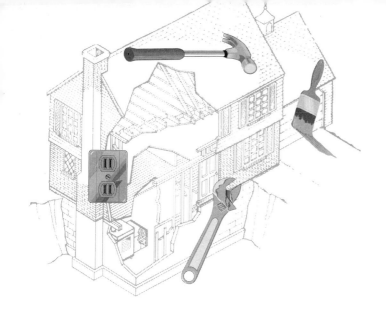

HOME ENERGY SAVING

This chapter lists ideas to save energy with many appliances and with house structures. It suggests using a form to calculate cost versus payback for possible retrofit jobs. The chapter tells how to add components to windows to save energy.

After studying this chapter, you will be able to:
- List some better ways to use water utilities.
- List some better ways to use appliances.
- List problems with lamps, fireplaces, and attic fans.
- Tell how to begin a sample calculation for a home energy audit.
- Describe a material used for an inside storm window.
- Describe a material used for a solar screen.
- Use a spline to mount sheets in window frames.

Being comfortable in winter means keeping warm by using heat energy. Being cool in the summer requires energy to power the air conditioner. Heating water for showers, the laundry, and dishwasher requires energy.

Most homes can use much less energy without sacrificing comfort. The home mechanic can conserve energy and lessen the portion of the family's budget required for it.

Most energy saving improvements cost money. However, the energy they save usually is greater than the expense.

The typical home loses 25% of its heat through the ceiling, roof, or attic. Another 25% of the heat produced by the furnace is lost through the windows and doors. See Fig. 33-1. Walls, joints, and cracks lose 15%. If the house has a fireplace, approximately 13% goes up the flue. About 10% may be lost due to air infiltration around electrical outlets or switches located in the exterior walls.

Fortunately, there are plenty of things which may be done to reduce the amount of energy lost from the older home. The home energy audit can be done by the home mechanic. The audit provides a self-study of the energy demand and losses with ideas for correcting the waste of energy. By understanding and following the suggestions, home maintenance steps may reduce the energy requirement and save as much as 25% of the out-of-the-pocket expenditure for energy. Most are simple enough for the home mechanic to do with minimal cost.

HOUSEHOLD ENERGY SAVING IDEAS

Energy can be saved for the following partial list of home systems: the water heater, furnace, refrigerator, stove, dishwasher, shower, laundry, fireplace, and the weatherstripping materials.

Domestic Water Heating

A family of four uses about 65 gallons of hot water each day. If the hot water heater is electric, it now costs about $250 to $350 a year. If the heater is gas fired, the annual bill is more likely to be $150 a year.

Naturally, using cold water rather than hot water whenever possible will bring the cost of hot water down. A brief inspection of the water heater may save energy. See Fig. 33-2. If the tank is warm to the touch, it needs additional insulation. The local building supply dealer has in stock a fiberglass blanket to wrap the heater. The cost is about $25 and will save enough in energy cost to return the investment in about a year.

Check the temperature setting of the hot water heater, Fig. 33-3. Most thermostats are set for 140°F or higher. By turning the thermostat down to 110-120°F, a saving of about $20 a year may be gained on natural gas, even more for electricity. If this change in temperature to a lower setting produces spotty dishes in the automatic dishwasher, lengthen the rinse cycle for the dishwasher.

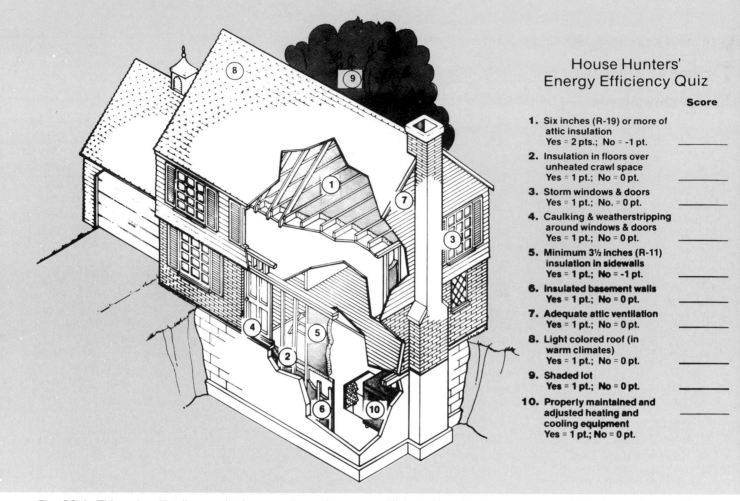

House Hunters' Energy Efficiency Quiz

Score

1. **Six inches (R-19) or more of attic insulation**
   Yes = 2 pts.; No = -1 pt. _____

2. **Insulation in floors over unheated crawl space**
   Yes = 1 pt.; No = 0 pt. _____

3. **Storm windows & doors**
   Yes = 1 pt.; No = 0 pt. _____

4. **Caulking & weatherstripping around windows & doors**
   Yes = 1 pt.; No = 0 pt. _____

5. **Minimum 3½ inches (R-11) insulation in sidewalls**
   Yes = 1 pt.; No = -1 pt. _____

6. **Insulated basement walls**
   Yes = 1 pt.; No = 0 pt. _____

7. **Adequate attic ventilation**
   Yes = 1 pt.; No = 0 pt. _____

8. **Light colored roof (in warm climates)**
   Yes = 1 pt.; No = 0 pt. _____

9. **Shaded lot**
   Yes = 1 pt.; No = 0 pt. _____

10. **Properly maintained and adjusted heating and cooling equipment**
    Yes = 1 pt.; No = 0 pt. _____

Fig. 33-1. This quiz will tell you whether your home is energy efficient. You should get a score of 7 points or better. (Owens-Corning Fiberglass)   A home energy audit form helps locate areas that waste energy.

Fig. 33-2. If the water heater feels warmer even than room temperature, it is losing heat. This is because metal should normally feel cold.

Fig. 33-3. The water heater thermostat rarely needs to be set on "hot".

Most families only need hot water for about four hours a day. The home mechanic may want to buy a timer that will automatically turn the hot water heater on only during the hours you regularly need it, saving up to 35% on operating costs.

Furnace

The furnace is the single most costly appliance. Having your furnace serviced once a year could cut your current fuel consumption by 10%. Oil furnaces, especially, can waste 13% of the fuel if they are not kept clean. Changing filters alone will save fuel.

Of course, the best furnace fuel-saving adjustment is still the thermostat. Settings of 68 °F in winter and 78 °F in summer operation are well within the comfort zone. Every degree the house is artificially held above or below outdoor temperature adds to the fuel bill. A 10 °F nighttime setback is one way to achieve 10-25% savings on heating bills while the family is asleep. If it is difficult to remember to adjust the thermostat, the heating service centers have automatic clock thermostats. Computer controlled thermostats for residential use, Fig. 33-4, are available.

Refrigerator

Refrigerators include the kitchen or food freezers. Many variations among models and brands are found. The least efficient uses more than twice as much energy as the most efficient. A manual defrost refrigerator saves energy over the automatic defrost, if the unit is defrosted once a month. If the refrigerator is not defrosted regularly however, ice buildup will make it inefficient. The savings over the best frost-free models will be small. But regardless of the model, don't make it work doubly hard by

placing it next to a stove, oven, dishwasher, or in a continually sunny window.

The recommended temperatures are 38 °F to 40 °F for the fresh food compartment; 5 °F to 10 °F for the food freezer section. Some refrigerators for outdoor use have heating elements in the walls or doors to prevent sweating on the outside. In most climates you can keep these heating elements off. You may need the heaters only in fall and spring.

Also try a little restraint when opening the refrigerator door. Plan the number of openings and only for short periods of time. Each cubic foot of cool air shows up on the energy bill.

The Stove and Oven

Stoves and ovens require as much as 1/2 the energy needed by a furnace, especially for larger families. If choosing a gas stove, be sure to avoid models with pilot lights. They burn one third of all gas used in residential cooking for no purpose and unnecessarily warm the kitchen in summer.

Self-cleaning ovens tend to be very well insulated. Therefore they save energy (as long as the self-cleaning feature is not used often). Microwave ovens save energy compared to conventional ovens. (There is some debate over their health impact.) Regardless of which type oven you use, 20% of the heat is lost each time the oven door is opened to look at the contents, so keep the number of openings down.

The Dishwasher

On the average, the dishwasher will use 14 gallons of hot water for each load regardless of the number of dishes loaded into it. Full loads will naturally save on the hot water bill.

The "rinse hold" feature on some models uses 3 to 7 gallons of hot water each time it is used. Savings of up to 10% of the total dishwashing energy cost can be gained by letting the dishes air dry.

Some models have air-power and overnight dry settings. If there is not an automatic air-dry setting, turn the control knob to "off" after the final rinse. Prop open the door slightly to speed the drying. In the winter months, this will add much-needed moisture to the home.

Showers

Showers take about 25 gallons of water for the first five minutes. By contrast, the average bath takes about 30 gallons to fill the tub. Assuming that half cold and half hot water is used, a saving of 2.5 gallons of hot water can be experienced by substituting the shower for the bath.

Consider installing a flow restrictor in the pipe leading to the shower head. Or use a device like that shown in Fig. 33-5A which restricts the flow at the shower head, but maintains a good spray.

Fig. 33-4. Computer-controlled thermostat saves energy. It makes heat pump operation more efficient. (Honeywell Inc.)

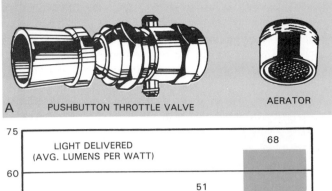

PUSHBUTTON THROTTLE VALVE | AERATOR

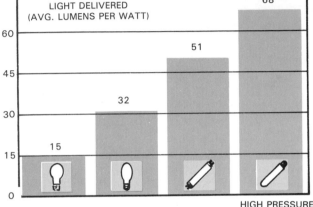

B INCANDESCENT   MERCURY   FLUORESCENT   HIGH PRESSURE SODIUM

Fig. 33-5. Ways to save energy in the form of heat. A—To save hot water, this shower head restricts water flow. Then it mixes air with the water to recreate the original jet action. Often, 50% less hot water is used. (Whedon Products, Inc.) B—Compare efficiency of light sources. (Commonwealth Edison)

A restrictor can reduce the flow of water in the shower from 5 gallons per minute to 2 gallons per minute, but still give a good spray. This can save over $55 per year for the electric water heater.

Water lost at leaking faucets may add up quickly. In a year, the faucet can waste 1000 gallons of water. If heated water is leaking, it can waste 25 to 30 gallons of oil or 3,000 cubic feet of gas.

Clothes Dryer and Washer

It takes about 35 gallons of water to do a full load of wash. How much of that 35 gallons is hot water depends on which button is selected for the wash. Changing the rinse water to cold, which does not affect the results, will save a considerable amount of hot water over the year.

On machines that have variable water levels, the utility bill also may be cut by using less water per load. For those models that do not have the small load adjustment, try to arrange full loads to get the most out of the wash water.

It costs 25 to 30 cents an hour to operate the clothes dryer. At that rate, consider drying the clothes outside when weather is good. However, for convenience and to avoid clothesline clutter, most people use the clothes dryer. Before using the dryer, clean the lint screen. Otherwise the dryer will use more energy just to move air through.

When purchasing these appliances, be sure to compare their energy efficiencies. By federal regulations, manufacturers of these appliances must provide an Energy Guide label for each model.

Lighting

Nearly 50% of the energy used for incandescent lighting is spent without giving light. In other words, the incandescent lamp produces about as much heat as light. See Fig. 33-5B.

Fluorescent lighting tubes deliver three to four times as much light per kilowatt-hour of electricity as incandescent bulbs do. Enormous amounts of energy could be saved by switching from filament to fluorescent lights whenever practical. If there is an objection to the color and flicker associated with commercial fluorescent lights, substitute warm or warm white fluorescent tubes at only a slight energy penalty. The flicker occurs at the cool blue end of the light spectrum, but not at the warm red end.

There are many ways to save energy in lighting:
1. Solid state dimmers add atmosphere and save energy by cutting light intensity. (Do not add dimmer controls to fluorescent fixtures.)
2. Lighting a specific work area is more efficient than lighting an entire room from overhead.
3. The lower the wattage of a light bulb, the less energy used. Hallway and closet lights can be 40 watt bulbs and still do the job.

Fireplaces

Be aware that the traditional fireplace is a heat robber. Over 13% of the household heat can be lost through the chimney if you leave the damper open when the fireplace is not in use. Even with the damper closed, there may be a gap where the warm house air will escape.

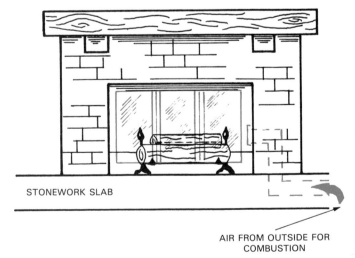

STONEWORK SLAB

AIR FROM OUTSIDE FOR COMBUSTION

Fig. 33-6. An energy-efficient fireplace has closed glass door front and tubes to bring outside air into the firebox to support combustion.

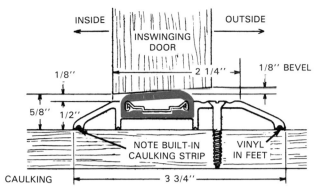

Fig. 33-7. The threshold seal helps prevent energy loss below door. (Macklanburg Duncan)

One way to stop the heat loss is to cover the chimney with a cap or place a fiberglass pad under the damper. However, remember to remove before starting a fire.

The building supply dealer has a large assortment of glass door units to place over the fireplace opening. Glass doors with their vents give better control of the draft for burning. Also, a new fireplace should be designed to use outside air for combustion, Fig. 33-6.

Air Infiltration

You should plan to caulk and weatherstrip around windows and doors when air infiltration is considered, Fig. 33-7. Also, energy studies of houses show that much of the costly heat loss comes through other places as well. A large percentage of air slips through underneath the baseboard, through wall outlets, through holes where plumbing lines, electrical lines, and telephone lines enter the house. Loss can occur through holes around exhaust fans, around dryer vents, and around sink and bathtub drainpipes where they exit from the house. If the home has a ceiling attic fan, it must be sealed carefully to prevent winter air from leaking in.

No matter how the house is heated or cooled, the load can be reduced by as much as 20 to 30 percent through investing in insulation. Insulation should be brought up to standard for the given geographic region, according to a recently developed computer model, Fig. 33-8. For example: the home mechanic living in Kansas City, Missouri, would need to have R-30 for the ceiling, R-19 for the walls, and R-19 in the floor area to be energy efficient.

Weatherstripping, which costs $12 to $75 per door, will cut door edge heat loss by one half, Fig. 33-9. Sliding glass doors, even double-glazed ones, are big heat losers. Use drapes at sliding glass doors to help retain the heat. Special thermo-lined drapes are especially well suited to retain heat energy.

Windows, single-glazed ones especially, are responsible for about 25% of the total heat loss in a house. Most of this heat loss occurs after the sun

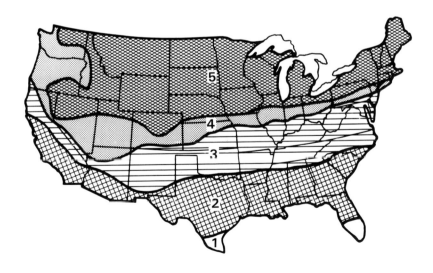

| | Winter Heating Plus Summer Cooling | | |
Zone	Ceiling Insulation R-Value	Wall Insulation R-Value	Floor Insulation R-Value
1	R-19	R-11	R-11
2	R-30	R-19	R-11
3	R-38	R-19	R-13
4	R-38	R-19	R-19
5	R-49	R-19	R-25

Fig. 33-8. Zones of recommended R-values of the United States.   (CertainTeed Corporation)

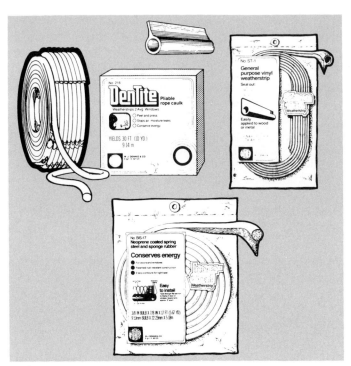

Fig. 33-9. Several types of weatherstrip are available. (Dennis)

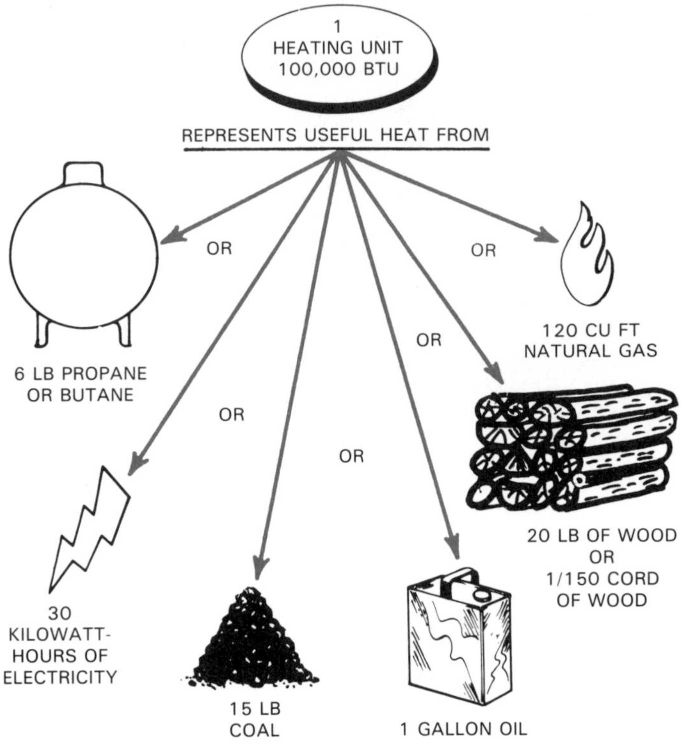

Fig. 33-10. Each of these amounts of fuel or energy is equal to one heating unit. (U.S. Dept. of Energy)

goes down. Light-colored, lined draperies during the day and tightly closed shades at night can reduce heat loss by up to 38%.

HOME ENERGY AUDIT

The home mechanic can conduct an evaluation without detailed knowledge of science and without big numbers. Any energy evaluation requires four basic steps:
1. Inspection of the building to determine the nature of the construction.
2. Calculation of heat loss from the structure.
3. Evaluation of the structure and its heat loss to determine what additional energy conservation measures should be taken.
4. Installation of the weatherization materials.

Working with BTUs means doing calculations with large numbers. It is easy to make errors with large numbers. Project RetroTech, a home weatherization program by the Department of Energy, uses the concept of heating units to simplify the calculations, (Appendix). The heating unit, Fig. 33-10, is used when listing approximately that number of gallons of heating oil or other fuel to provide the heat loss per year through the particular season of a typical structure.

To allow for climatic differences between areas, heating engineers use degree days (DD), Fig. 33-11. A degree day represents a 24 hour period in which the average outside temperature is 1 °F below a base temperature of 65 °F. In the same way, 2 DD means the average temperature was 2 °F below

65 °F for 24 hours. Many northern areas will have over 7000 degree days in a single heating season. The project RetroTech program uses the district heating factor, which for an area having 4000 degree days will be 1; for 5000 DD, 1.25; and for 6000 DD, 1.5. The map shows the district heating factors for various areas. Simply look up the approximate factor for specific regions. Use this multiplier in figuring all heat losses of that region.

Some principles affecting the annual heat loss by conduction through any component of a building are suggested in Fig. 33-12.

The form in the Appendix shows how to calculate the heating units required:

Heating Units Required = area (sq. ft.) x district heating factor ÷ total R's. R is the measure of the resistance of a material to the transfer of heat.

To conduct the home energy audit inspection, follow the ten steps listed below:
1. Involve the entire family.
2. Take overall building dimension (length, width, and height).
3. Measure window (height, width).
4. Measure doors (height, width).
5. Check conditions of exterior (look for cracks, lack of paint, caulking).
6. Check all insulation R-values, Fig. 33-13.
7. Check ceiling and roof, Fig. 33-14.
8. Check floor insulation, Fig. 33-15.
9. Inspect foundation for cracks.
10. Check for infiltration, feel for drafts.

Record all information on the job book. A sample job book is given in the Appendix.

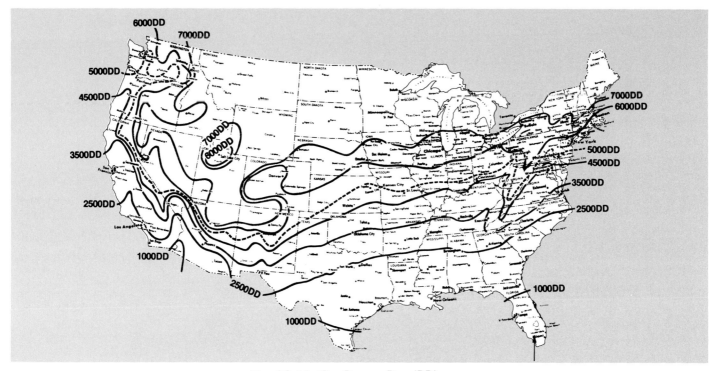

Fig. 33-11. The Degree Day (DD) map.

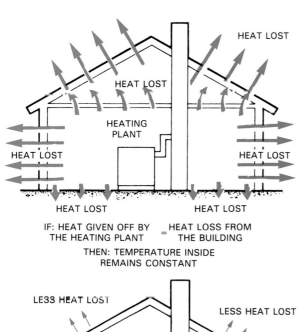

HEAT LOST

HEAT LOST

HEATING PLANT

HEAT LOST

HEAT LOST

HEAT LOST

HEAT LOST

HEAT LOST

IF: HEAT GIVEN OFF BY = HEAT LOSS FROM
THE HEATING PLANT   THE BUILDING

THEN: TEMPERATURE INSIDE
REMAINS CONSTANT

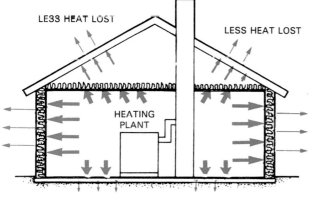

LESS HEAT LOST

LESS HEAT LOST

HEATING PLANT

LESS HEAT ESCAPING
MEANS LESS HEAT AND
LESS FUEL NEEDED TO
STAY COMFORTABLE INSIDE

Fig. 33-12. Introduction to the principles of heat loss. (U.S. Dept. of Energy)

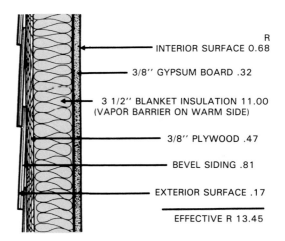

R
INTERIOR SURFACE 0.68

3/8'' GYPSUM BOARD .32

3 1/2'' BLANKET INSULATION 11.00
(VAPOR BARRIER ON WARM SIDE)

3/8'' PLYWOOD .47

BEVEL SIDING .81

EXTERIOR SURFACE .17

EFFECTIVE R 13.45

Fig. 33-13. R-values for wall cross section. R-values can be added. (U.S. Dept. of Energy)

Calculation of Heat Losses

Heat losses are calculated as the number of BTUs lost through one square foot of surface area for each hour. With the home weatherization job book, the heat loss is calculated in potential heating units. These are converted to potential savings to the household budget.

Evaluation of the Data

During the evaluation, the home mechanic will identify the areas of the house where the greatest potential savings may be obtained. Locate one or more areas of energy loss: loss at ceilings, walls, floors, windows, and doors. Next rank the loss areas in order of their amounts and the cost of home weatherization materials and labor. Costs should be

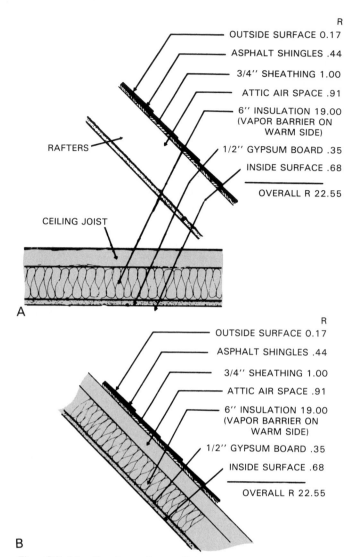

Fig. 33-14. R-values for ceiling and roof construction A — Roof and ceiling cross section. B — Roof cross section. (U.S. Dept. of Energy)

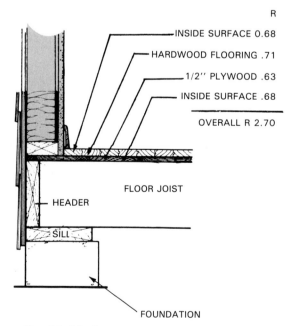

Fig. 33-15. R-values for floor cross section. (U.S. Dept. of Energy)

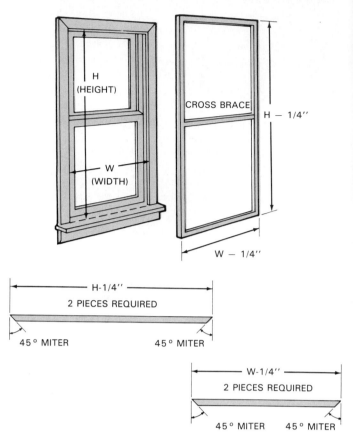

Fig. 33-16. Frame to support plastic film for the inside storm window. Subtract 1/4 in. from the height and width of window to be covered. (Reynolds Metals)

amortized over (spread out over) the expected life of the weatherization measure or the expected life of the house, whichever is least. Compare the amortized cost with the potential energy cost savings to decide which weatherization project is most needed.

INSTALLATION OF MATERIALS

Some projects involve adding inexpensive hardware or adding insulation. Window hardware is the most simple. See the previous chapter for steps on placing insulation.

Building Storm Windows and Solar Screens

Inside storm windows help keep heat and fuel dollars inside. Light frame storm windows are designed to help reduce heat loss through the window area. They are easy to make and install. These storm windows will not interfere with draperies, curtains, shades, or blinds. They will hardly be noticed until the saving on the energy bill is noted.

The Inside Storm Window

Measure the inside of the window. See Fig. 33-16. First measure the width (W) of the window, then measure the height (H) from windowsill to top. Next subtract 1/4 in. (6 mm) from the overall width and height measurements. This subtraction allows

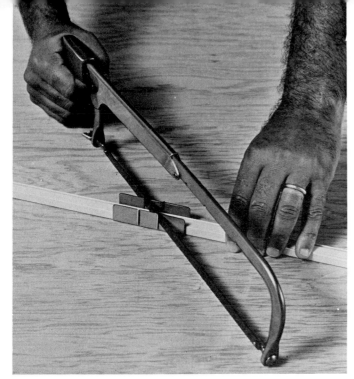

Fig. 33-17. Cutting aluminum frame. (Reynolds Metals)

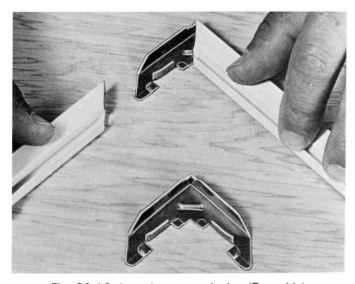

Fig. 33-18. Inserting corner locks. (Reynolds)

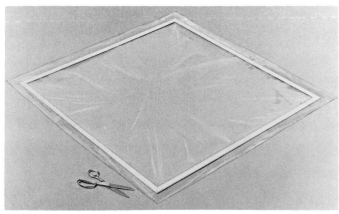

Fig. 33-19. Cut plastic film a little larger than the frame. (Reynolds)

enough space for the foam tape insulation that goes around the frame. The foam tape gives the storm window a snug fit.

Follow this procedure:

1. Use a miter box and hacksaw. Cut the sections to correspond to the sizes measured, Fig. 33-17. For frames longer than 3 ft. (1m) you may need to prepare a center brace.
2. Smooth the cut edges with a fine-tooth metal file. This will make it easier to insert corner locks.
3. Four corner locks are required for each frame. See Fig. 33-18. Insert lock ends into ends of frame section.
4. Use a rubber mallet to tap the lock in place.
5. Cut the window film (mylar plastic sheet) 1 in. (2.5 cm) larger all around than the frame, Fig. 33-19. Place frame with groove side up on flat surface and lay film across the frame. Begin at one corner. Lightly press the spline into the groove and proceed to the next corner.
6. Using spline roller, carefully roll spline into place. See Fig. 33-20. It will lock in firmly. Repeat the process on the opposite side from the first. Hold film tight as the spline is locked in place. Note: To avoid bowing the frame, do not pull film too tight.
7. Carefully trim excess film close to outside edge of spline, Fig. 33-21.
8. Before installing window, add a foam tape strip along all edges, Fig. 33-22. Beginning at one corner, press the adhesive side of self-

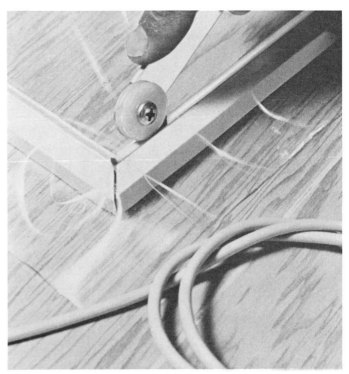

Fig. 33-20. Fasten film with plastic spline.

327

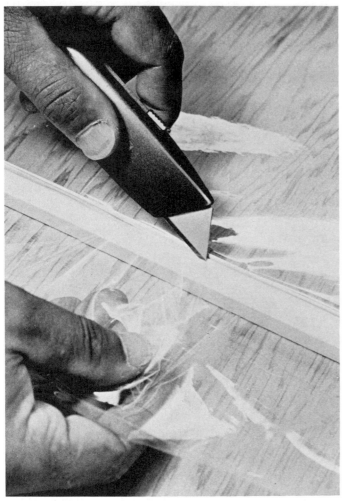

Fig. 33-21. Trim excess plastic film at the spline edge.

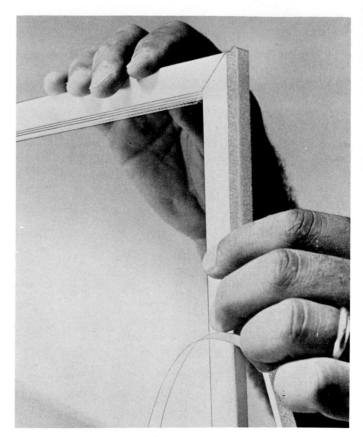

Fig. 33-22. Apply foam tape to window frame. To get proper fit, avoid stretching tape. (Reynolds)

adhesive tape along the outer edge of the window frame.

9. Install window by simply inserting unit in window opening. It is suggested to allow no more than 4 in. (10 cm) of air space between window and storm window. More space could encourage a thermosiphon effect with loss of heat. The panel should fit easily, creating snug, tight seal.

Solar Screens

With or without air conditioning, solar screens can mean a cooler home. Having a lattice woven of 1/64 in. fiberglass ribbons, a solar screen provides a shade barrier for a window. It helps keep out the hot summer rays and still lets light and fresh air in.

Follow this procedure:

1. To determine the correct size for the solar screen, take measurements of the exterior window frame, Fig. 33-23. Measure the width (W) and height (H) of the outside wood frame. Subtract 1/8 in. (3 mm) on top and sides.
2. Construct frame with identical procedure as for inside storm window.

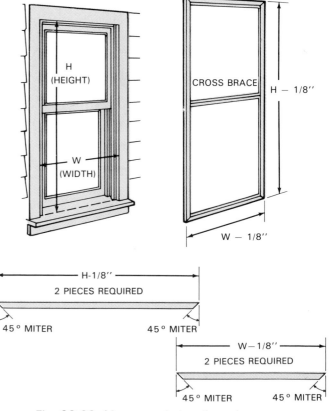

Fig. 33-23. Measure window for solar screen. (Reynolds Metals)

3. Before using a spline mounting of the solar screen, install loop latches, Fig. 33-24. Install these latches on bottom of frame, in from either side about 4 in. (10 cm).

4. Cut a section of solar screen 1 in. larger all around the frame, Fig. 33-25. Place frame with groove side up on a flat surface and lay screen across the frame. Beginning in one corner, lightly press the spline into the groove.

5. Using spline roller, carefully roll spline into place, Fig. 33-26. It will lock in place. Be careful to pull the solar screen taut. To avoid bowing the frame, do not pull the screen too tight when rolling spline into groove.

6. Carefully trim excess screen close to outside edge of spline, Fig. 33-27. The screen is now ready to install.

7. Install screen hangers. See Fig. 33-28. Use low-profile nails provided, or use screws. Hangers should be approximately 1/4 in. (6 mm) from the top of the window frame.

8. Slide the solar screen frame into the channels until it is flush with the top of the window frame, Fig. 33-29. Install ball-head screws in windowsill to line up with loop latches.

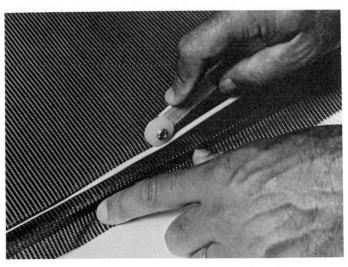
Fig. 33-26. Lock screen in place with spline.

Fig. 33-27. Trim excess screen.

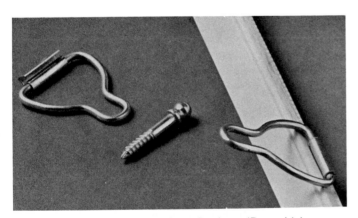
Fig. 33-24. Attach loop latches. (Reynolds)

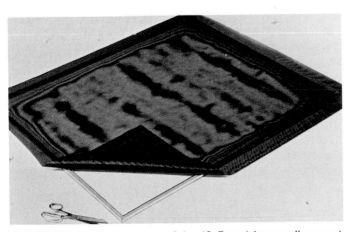
Fig. 33-25. Cut solar screen 1 in. (2.5 cm) larger all around frame.

Fig. 33-28. Upper frame hanger attached to window. (Reynolds)

Fig. 33-29. Install solar screen frame in both hangers. "Catch clips" at the bottom of screen hold screen securely. (Reynolds Metals)

Solar Overhang

The sun is helpful in winter, but provides too much heat in summer. An overhang may be built above a window to let in the sun in winter, but not in summer.

The sun angle is less in the winter and the sunlight can enter under the overhang. In summer, the sun is higher and the rays are blocked by the overhang. Be sure the overhang roof is insulated.

TEST YOUR KNOWLEDGE — CHAPTER 33

1. If a water heater tank feels like it is at room temperature, does it need insulation?
2. What should you do if a lowered water heater temperature produces spotty dishes in the dishwasher?
3. An air conditioner or _____ should not be put near a stove or sunny window.
4. To save hot water in the dishwasher, avoid using the:
   a. Overnight dryer.
   b. Air-power setting.
   c. Unit with a full load.
   d. Rinse-hold feature.
5. Keep the _____ screen of the automatic clothes dryer clean.
6. Which lamp type is more efficient, the filament or the fluorescent?
7. Design a new fireplace to use _____ air for combustion.
8. How many degree days result from an average temperature of 63 °F for 48 hours?
9. If the heat produced by the furnace equals the heat loss from the house, the inside temperature will _____ (fall, rise, remain constant).
10. From the Appendix of this book, you should have learned that home energy audit calculations are done using booklets like that developed by "Project _____ ."
11. An inexpensive inside storm window can be made from _____ (glass, mylar plastic, polyethylene, plexiglass).
12. Leave 1/4 or 1/8 in. gap around homemade screens or storm windows for a _____ strip.
13. What holds a plastic sheet or a woven screen into a frame?
    a. Adhesive.
    b. Clips.
    c. Splines.
    d. Staples.
14. If storm window sheet is spaced more than 4 in. from the original glass, this can encourage a _____ effect.
15. A solar _____ for a window consists of a lattice of 1/64 in. fiberglass ribbons that lets air through.
16. A roof overhang helps block out the _____ (winter, summer) sun.

KNOW THESE TERMS

Energy audit, fluorescent, air infiltration, weatherstripping, heat loss, heat gain, solar.

SUGGESTED ACTIVITIES

Examine the home energy audit form in the Appendix of this book. Work out one of the easy pages in the form. Begin with the page involving single-glass windows. After calculating the potential heating savings, convert the result to a money value by using the Cost Per Heating Unit (on the opening pages). Is the cost to add extra window sheets more or less than the potential money savings? (Work out one line of the last page chart.) If the priority result stated on the form is more than 3, the job is not worth the expense.

Find out from the hardware store what clear plastic sheet materials are available for inside storm windows. Is polyethylene one of the clear materials? One brand of clear film is called Flex-O-Glass. It is very tough to tear. If possible, get sample strips of some materials. List those you think will not tear when using a spline mounting in a frame. Compare your results in class.

CAREERS

Audit specialist, housing engineer.

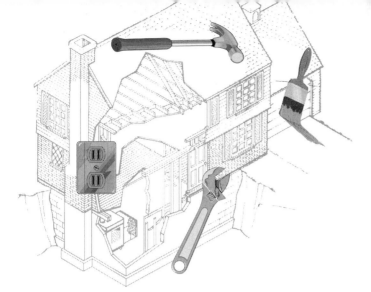

DEVELOPING A CAREER PATH

The study of home maintenance is an effort to understand the technology of the house. This chapter explores the idea that careers are possible as a result of understanding the technology of house maintenance. This chapter identifies the types of careers that are related to home maintenance and repair. It also describes methods of preparing and planning for those careers.

After studying this chapter, you will be able to:

■ List careers that are related to home repair and maintenance.
■ Define the term career.
■ Tell how technology has changed career opportunities.
■ Prepare and plan for selecting a career.

A career path is the activity or activities that lead an individual to a position where they have money to support their needs. It is natural to want the money to support and satisfy the basic needs, such as shelter, clothing, and food.

Technology has made it easier to make a home cheaper and with less effort to run. Today, technology and technology education is an important component of developing such a home. As a result, today there are career paths in design and creation of a home (architectural and engineering ideas), executing and developing (contracting and business), and servicing and maintaining (skills, trades, and professions).

A house can be viewed as a road map that consists of many career paths. Each path contains a level of skills required to complete its tasks. Careers can be classified as unskilled, skilled, technical, managerial, and professional. Unskilled careers require little or no education or training, and usually have the lowest salaries. The skilled careers require advanced knowledge and learning, and usually have salaries greater than the unskilled careers. Technical careers generally require a considerable amount of technology and technical training, and usually have salaries greater than the skilled careers. Managerial careers demand several years of experience in the business, and some management training. Professional careers require formal education. College degrees are usually required. Some professional careers require professional certification.

Today and as we move into the 21st century, the home is moving into a new age of technology—an age of home automation. This means a computer may control inside and outside lights, heating, cooling, sprinkler systems, locking or unlocking doors, security systems, and a number of appliances. Home automation is opening a new set of careers.

CAREER PATHS

Career paths have changed and will likely continue to change in the future. The tasks and elements of a career match the change of technology. Today, many careers change as technology changes. More and more people need to know that mathematics, social sciences, industrial sciences, which include computer, electrical, mechanical, and graphic sciences.

Technology has changed what most people want. It has changed the way people get their basic needs. A home today is not just walls, floors, roofs, doors, windows, paint, paper, and carpet. A home today is made up of new appliances, materials, and systems. These new items are created to make living simple. A number of those new ideas, materials, and products are discussed in other chapters of this text. These items have made new career paths in manufacturing, sales, installation, service, repair, and maintenance.

There is a Careers section at the end of a number of chapters in this text. This section lists careers that relate to the topics in that chapter. To find more information on one of these careers, refer to the *Dictionary of Occupational Titles* from the U.S. Department of Labor Employment and Training Administration or the *Occupations Outlook Handbook* from the U.S. Department of Labor Bureau of Labor Statistics. These books can be found in a school or public library.

SELECTING A CAREER PATH

Selecting a career path is done because of some level of information about job, proper skill level, prior experience, basic knowledge of job, or an interest in the job. Career seekers must first understand their skills. Then they must be able to put these skills down on a resume and express them in an interview. Knowing your skills is a large part of writing a resume and interviewing. Also, knowing the type of job wanted, where work is wanted, and in what kind of place is an important part of a career search. Think about what is wanted. Why is a career search being done? Use the following questions to access the career strengths. Apply the findings to the career goals of a resume.

- What skills do I have that are a necessary component of the career?
- What are the specific job skills I have and should sell to the employer?
- What type of transferable skills and abilities do I have that can be utilized in this career (managerial, organizational, analytical)?
- What special skills do I have that would make me stand out among other candidates (computer literacy, bilingual)?
- What past accomplishments can I offer the future employer that will benefit the employer?
- What interpersonal strengths can I bring to the career (leadership, customer relations)?

Knowing your skills is an important part of setting a realistic match between a career seeker and a career. The career search usually takes the following set of logical steps:

1. Preparing a resume and cover letter.
2. The interview.
3. Employment and trial period.

Preparing a Resume and Cover Letter

The purpose of the resume and cover letter is to receive an interview. The goal is to make the employer interested in meeting and learning more about the applicant. The resume and cover letter are sent together to the employer.

The conventional resume is a short one-page document that allows the career seeker the opportunity to summarize their qualifications that make them ideal for the position. See Fig. 34-1. The

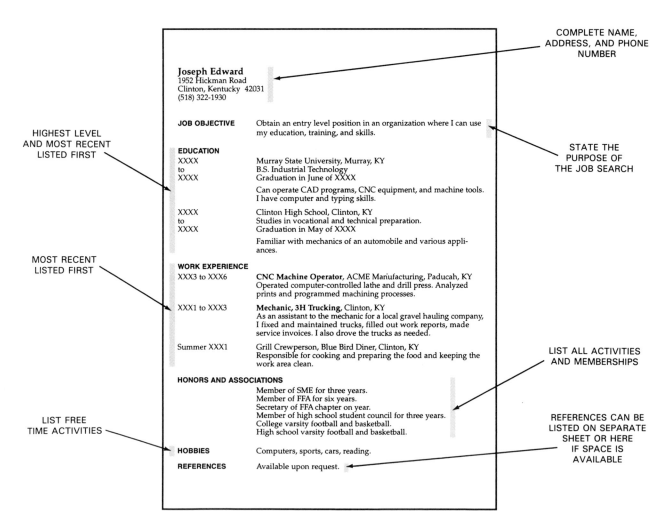

Fig. 34-1. A well-written resume will help make a good impression on employers.

resume is the first chance to show the applicant's skills. It gives the employer a chance to note those skills. A resume that is well written will add to the importance of these skills. Present work history and education in a clear manner. Give the employer enough information to think the applicant will help the company. Extra information can ruin a resume.

Remember a resume is more than an outline of what the applicant has done—it is a sample of writing skills. A resume must show that the applicant is right for the position, and show their ability to organize and present ideas. Proofread the finished resume, and then have someone proofread it. This will help eliminate poor grammar and misspelled words. A clean resume shows concern for quality and attention to detail.

A cover letter is also known as a letter of application. When used with a resume, the cover letter is an introduction to the employer. It is used to capture the interest of the employer. A cover letter should make the employer want to review the resume.

A cover letter should be directed to the appropriate person. See Fig. 34-2. Use the complete title and address of the employer. If at all possible, address a particular person by name.

In the first paragraph, state why the letter is being written. List the position or type of career that is being sought. Then state where the applicant heard about the job opening. Also, include career goals in this paragraph.

The body of the cover letter is usually two or three paragraphs long. Explain the interest in working for the employer. Explain the reason for desiring this type of career. Be sure to point out past related work or education. Do not repeat the entire resume. Make clear the skills that apply to the position. Remember, the employer also views the cover letter as an example of the applicant's writing skills.

Use the closing paragraph to tell the employer you have also sent a resume. Use this paragraph to express thanks for the employer's time. Include an appropriate closing that asks for an interview. Always tell the employer when or where they can contact the applicant. Make sure to sign the cover letter.

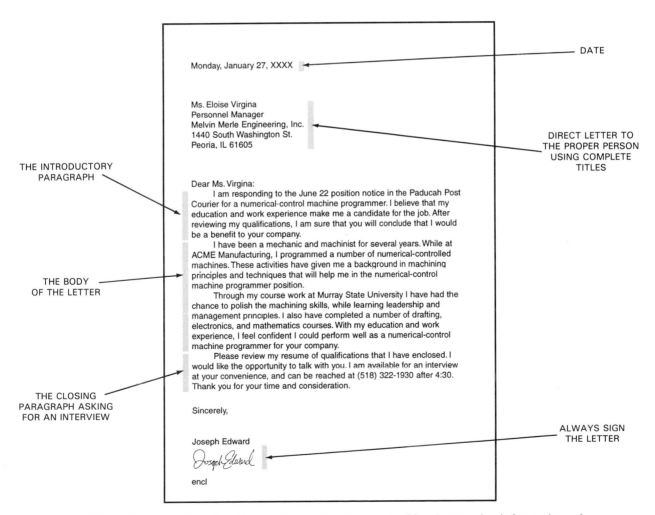

Fig. 34-2. A cover letter should attract attention to your qualifications and ask for an interview.

The overall look of the package counts. Create a nice looking package. With a personal computer, printer, and desktop program a clean package can be created. Also, there are businesses that create and print resumes and cover letters. cover letters.

The Interview

During an interview, an applicant is usually asked to fill out an application. See Fig. 34-3. Remember, this is another writing example. The applicant should take some time and fill in all required information. Be as neat and as organized as possible.

Good interviewing skills can be obtained by practicing. Practicing an interview can be done, but can be somewhat difficult. However, preparing for the interview can be a good replacement. The applicant should research the interviewing company, the job, and its requirements. To an interviewer, this shows drive and leads to more conversation during the interview. This can make an employer remember the applicant. Preparing builds confidence that can help the applicant to relax during the interview. Confident and relaxed applicants will have better interviews. If made a career offer, the applicant can make a more informed decision about the career and its future. The following is a list of items that can be done to help prepare for an interview:

- Read magazine and newspaper articles that deal with the company.
- Obtain company literature such as financial reports, annual reports, and newsletters.
- Practice talking about yourself, your past accomplishments, and career objectives.
- Talk to friends, teachers, or colleagues who have gone through a career search.

There are certain questions that are usually asked during an interview. The following questions are some of the most asked of an applicant during an interview:

- Tell me about yourself. Who are you?
- How did you hear about the job opening?
- What attracted you to our organization?
- Do you plan to further your education?
- Where do you see yourself in ten years?
- What are your lifetime goals?
- What do you know about the position?
- What skills, experiences, and training do you have that qualify you for the job?
- What motivates you?
- Can you meet deadines?
- What awards or honors have you received?
- Are you associated with any civic groups or clubs?
- Are you a member of any professional associations?
- What hobbies do you enjoy?
- Have you ever traveled? Where have you been?
- Are you willing to travel with this position?
- Can you furnish personal references?
- What are your salary requirements?

An interview is not just the interviewer talking and asking questions. It should be a meeting between the interviewer and the applicant. An informed applicant will ask questions. The following are some questions an applicant should ask of the employer:

- What are the duties of the job?
- What skills are needed for this position?
- What type of benefit package is offered with this job?
- Is there a trial period of employment?
- How often are performance reviews given?
- Is there any financial assistance for further education?
- What are the organization's growth projections for the next year?
- Does the organization have plans for expansion?
- Is there a profit sharing or retirement plan?
- What are the daily hours?

Melvin Merle Engineering, Inc.
1440 South Washington Street
Peoria, Illinois 61605

Employment Application

Name _____

Address _____

Telephone _____

How long have you lived at present address? ____ If hired can you furnish proof of age? ___

Employment Record for 5 Years Starting with Last Job

Employed by _____ From/To _____
Address _____ Telephone _____
Salary _____ Job Description _____
Reason for leaving _____

Employed by _____ From/To _____
Address _____ Telephone _____
Salary _____ Job Description _____
Reason for leaving _____

Employed by _____ From/To _____
Address _____ Telephone _____
Salary _____ Job Description _____
Reason for leaving _____

Use back of sheet if more space is required.

Type of work applying for: _____
Expected starting salary: _____
References _____
_____

Important information for the applicant from Melvin Merle Engineering, Inc. EMPLOYMENT-AT-WILL. Your employment is for an indefinite period. It is at the will of either you or Melvin Merle Engineering, Inc. to end the employment relationship at any time. No one, except the Board of Directors, has the authority to offer or promise, express or imply, an employment contract. Provisions may be modified at such times as Melvin Merle Engineering, Inc. determines there are changes that need to be made. This application does not constitute a contract, express or implied, nor does it constitute an offer of an employment contract. EQUAL OPPORTUNITY/AFFIRMATIVE ACTION EMPLOYER. Melvin Merle Engineering, Inc. is an Equal Opportunity/Affirmative Action Employer. It is the continuing policy of Melvin Merle Engineering, Inc. to recruit and employ the best qualified individuals without regard to race, color, religion, creed, national origin, age, handicap, veteran status, or sex. Equal employment opportunity applies to all personnel actions such as recruiting, hiring, compensation, benefits, promotions, opportunities for training, transfers, and terminations. No preference is given to the hiring of relatives or friends of current employees, although referrals are welcome.

Signature _____ Date _____

Fig. 34-3. Complete application form(s) accurately and neatly.

- What is your vacation policy?
- Are there any paid vacations?
- How much authority will I have over decisions?
- What is the possibility of advancement in the organization from this position?
- Is there much turnover in this job area?
- Will I have the opportunity to work on special projects?
- What is the salary range for this position?

Answering and reviewing these questions will give an applicant a better view about interviews. The materials just studied point out how interviews can be alike. However, each interview is different. The applicant should learn from each interview, and take that knowledge to the next one.

Employment and Trial Period

Once a career choice has been made and a job taken, the new worker is usually employed under a trial period. It is common during this trial period for the worker to be closely supervised. A new employee should expect random reviews and comments about their work during this period. At the end of the trial period, the new worker is usually given an overall review of the work done during the trial period. Review the company's policy handbook for more information on this matter.

Growing in a Career

There are many items that help people grow and become successful in their career. A few of these items include job safety, work ethic, and leadership. A person should be aware that these items can help their career growth. Lack of attention can hurt their career.

Job safety includes more than your safety. A worker must be aware of their coworkers. Before doing any job, think about the result of your action. Follow all safety rules. If something does not seem right, ask a supervisor. Asking questions and being aware of safety rules may stop injuries or save a life.

Work ethic is the attitude a worker brings to work. It includes such items as not being late, being happy on the job, and be willing to stay late. Other work ethic items relate to coworkers. What a worker does must not stop, hurt, or change the way a coworker does their job. A worker should respect the rights and abilities of their coworkers.

Many people think leadership is about the job position they hold. Leadership includes working hard, being positive, seeing a problem—not being one, solving a problem, checking for details, being truthful, and being fair. No matter what the job is, these leadership items should be used.

TEST YOUR KNOWLEDGE — CHAPTER 34

1. _____ _____ is the activity or activities that lead an individual to a position of financial and economic stability.
2. _____ careers require little or no education or training, and usually have the lowest salaries.
3. _____ careers require advanced knowledge and learning, and usually have salaries greater than the unskilled careers.
4. _____ careers generally require considerable amounts of technology an technical training, and usually have salaries greater than the skilled careers.
5. _____ careers require formal education as described by a collegiate degree, equivalent education, and certain professional certification.
6. The purpose of a resume and cover letter is to receive a(n) _____.
7. _____ can be a perfect substitute of practicing interviewing skills.
8. _____ _____ is the attitude a worker brings to work.

KNOW THESE TERMS

Career path, resume, cover letter, interview, trial period, job safety, work ethic, leadership.

SUGGESTED ACTIVITIES

Research and prepare a resume. Write a cover letter to accompany your resume. Review job notices (trade magazines, newspapers, etc.) and complete a background search on an organization that has listed a career position you wish to obtain. Answer the questions that an interviewer may ask you—use the questions listed in this chapter. Prepare specific questions you will ask the interviewer—do not use the questions listed in this chapter.

APPENDIX A

METRICS FOR THE HOME MECHANIC

The metric system is an international language of measurement. Its symbols are identical in all languages. Just as the English language is governed by rules of spelling, punctuation, and pronunciation, so is the language of measurement. SI stands for Le Systeme International d'Unites — the International System of Units. All units are based on multiples of 10.

BASIC TERMINOLOGY

In SI, there are seven base units of measurement and two supplementary units. The seven units are the meter, kilogram, second, ampere, degree kelvin, candela, and mole. The other two are the radian and the steradian. There are 17 derived units: newton, hertz, pascal, joule, watt, coulomb, volt, ohm, farad, weber, henry, tesla, lumen, lux, siemens, gray, and becquerel.

In SI, powers of ten provide multiples and submultiples of units. The prefix used with each unit denotes the multiple or submultiple. Once the meaning of the set of prefixes has been learned, the relationship between values is clear.

Any of the prefixes can be used to designate multiples and submultiples of any SI base unit or of SI units with special names. Prefixes are not used alone.

Each unit and prefix has a symbol. Generally, these symbols are letters or combinations of letters of the alphabet. They generally use at least the first letter of the unit name. They are not abbreviations and should not be treated as such.

Following are some rules of usage. Some conversion charts are given afterwards.

Spelling

For the terms meter, liter, kilometer, the "er" spelling is used in this book. The "re" spelling is used in many other countries.

Punctuation

A. The Decimal Point: When writing numbers less than one, a zero must be written before the decimal point (because of the possibility that the decimal point will be obliterated or overlooked). Avoid using fractions to express numbers less than one.
Examples: The oral expression "point seven five" should be written 0.75.

B. The Dot As A Multiplier Symbol: The dot, when raised above the line, is used to show that two quantities are multiplied together.

C. Grouping of Numbers:
1. Separate digits into groups of three, counting from the decimal point. The comma should not be used. Instead, a space is left to avoid confusion, since many countries use a comma for the decimal marker.
2. In numbers of four digits, the space is not recommended, unless four digit numbers are grouped in a column with numbers of five digits or more.
Examples:
For 4,720,525 write 4 720 525
For 0.52875 write 0.528 75
For 6875 write either 6875 or 6 875

D. Spacing:
1. When writing symbols or names for units having prefixes (e.g., kilopascal or milligram), no space is left between letters making up the symbol, or the name.
Examples: kPa, mg
2. When writing a symbol after a number to which it refers, a space must be left between the number and the symbol.
Examples: Correct—455 kHz, 22 mg
Incorrect—455kHz, 22mg

E. Superscripts
When writing symbols for such units as square metres or cubic centimetres the correct method is to write the symbol for the unit, followed by the superscript ^{2} or ^{3} respectively.
Example: For 14 square meters, write 14 m^2
The degree sign is also a superscript. The sign $^\circ$ typed by raising the lower case letter "o" is used in designating angles and temperatures measures in °C (degree Celsius).

F. The Letter "Ell" Liter: On most typewriters there is no difference between the lower case "ell" and the figure "one". Since the former is the recognized symbol for liter which is an everyday metric unit it is preferable to spell the word in full or to use a capital "L." However, it is in order to use ml for milliliter, since there is then no longer any confusion.

Examples:
Correct — 1 liter = 1L = 1000 ml
Incorrect — 1 Liter = 1l = 1000 mL

G. Usage and Format:
Avoid mixing units, symbols, and words.
Example: Correct - 12.75 m
meter per second
m/s
Incorrect - 12 m 750 mm
meter/s

Rules for the Use of Prefixes

A. A prefix is combined with the unit name and the combination is written as one word:
Examples: millimeter, microgram, megawatt, picofarad

B. Avoid mixing prefixes within a text or drawing.
Example: Correct - The plate is 10 mm thick and 1000 mm wide
Incorrect - The plate is 10 mm thick and 1 m wide

C. Choose prefixes that give numerical values of 0.1 through 1000 except when it results in mixing of prefixes in text or drawings.
Example: 1.2×10^4 N can be written 12 kN
0.003 94 m can be written 3.94 mm
1401 Pa can be written 1.401 kPa
3.1×10^{-8}s can be written 31 ns

D. Avoid using prefixes in a denominator.
Example: Correct - km/s
Incorrect - m/ms
Exception: The exception to the rule is the prefix k in kg (kilogram) which is a base SI unit.

Prefixes of SI Units

Name	Symbol	Amount	Multiple
exa	E	1 000 000 000 000 000 000	10^{18}
peta	P	1 000 000 000 000 000	10^{15}
tera	T	1 000 000 000 000	10^{12}
giga	G	1 000 000 000	10^{9}
mega	M	1 000 000	10^{6}
kilo	k	1 000	10^{3}
hecto	h*	100	10^{2}
deka	da*	10	10
deci	d*	0.1	10^{-1}
centi	c*	0.01	10^{-2}
milli	m	0.001	10^{-3}
micro	μ	0.000 001	10^{-6}
nano	n	0.000 000 001	10^{-9}
pico	p	0.000 000 000 001	10^{-12}
femto	f	0.000 000 000 000 001	10^{-15}
atto	a	0.000 000 000 000 000 001	10^{-18}

*avoid these whenever possible

COMMON METRIC EQUIVALENTS AND CONVERSIONS

APPROXIMATE Common Equivalents		ACCURATE Conversion to Parts Per Million	
1 inch	= 25 millimeters	inches × 25.4*	= millimeters
1 foot	= 0.3 meter	feet × 0.3048*	= meters
1 yard	= 0.9 meter	yards × 0.9144*	= meters
1 mile	= 1.6 kilometers	miles × 1.609 34	= kilometers
1 square inch	= 6.5 square centimeters	sq inches × 6.4516*	= square centimeters
1 square foot	= 0.09 square meter	sq feet × 0.092 903 0	= square meters
1 square yard	= 0.8 square meter	sq yards × 0.836 127	= square meters
1 acre	= 0.4 hectare†	acres × 0.404 686	= hectares
1 cubic inch	= 16 cubic centimeters	cu inches × 16.3871	= cubic centimeters
1 cubic foot	= 0.03 cubic meter	cu feet × 0.028 316 8	= cubic meters
1 cubic yard	= 0.8 cubic meter	cu yards × 0.764 555	= cubic meters
1 quart (lq)	= 1 liter†	quarts (lq) × 0.946 353	= liters
1 gallon	= 0.004 cubic meter	gallons × 0.003 785 41	= cubic meters
1 ounce (avdp)	= 28 grams	oz (avdp) × 28.349 5	= grams
1 pound (avdp)	= 0.45 kilogram	lbs (avdp) × 0.453 592	= kilograms
1 horsepower	= 0.75 kilowatt	hp × 0.745 700	= kilowatts

APPROXIMATE Common Equivalents		ACCURATE Conversion to Parts Per Million	
1 millimeter	= 0.04 inch	millimeters × 0.039 370 1	= inches
1 meter	= 3.3 feet	meters × 3.280 84	= feet
1 meter	= 1.1 yards	meters × 1.093 61	= yards
1 kilometer	= 0.6 mile	kilometers × 0.621 371	= miles
1 square centimeter	= 0.16 square inch	sq centimeters × 0.155 000	= square inches
1 square meter	= 11 square feet	sq meters × 10.7639	= square feet
1 square meter	= 1.2 square yards	sq meters × 1.195 99	= square yards
1 hectare†	= 2.5 acres	hectares × 2.471 05	= acres
1 cubic centimeter	= 0.06 cubic inch	cu centimeters × 0.061 023 7	= cubic inches
1 cubic meter	= 35 cubic feet	cu meters × 35.3147	= cubic feet
1 cubic meter	= 1.3 cubic yards	cu meters × 1.307 95	= cubic yards
1 liter†	= 1 quart (lq)	liters × 1.056 69	= quarts (lq)
1 cubic meter	= 250 gallons	cu meters × 264.172	= gallons
1 gram	= 0.035 ounces (avdp)	grams × 0.035 274 0	= ounces (avdp)
1 kilogram	= 2.2 pounds (avdp)	kilograms × 2.204 62	= pounds (avdp)
1 kilowatt	= 1.3 hrosepower	kilowatts × 1.341 02	= horsepower

†Common term not used in SI.   *Exact.

INCHES INTO MILLIMETERS

Decimals

Inches	Millimeters	Inches	Millimeters
0.001	0.0254	0.460	11.68
0.002	0.0508	0.470	11.94
0.003	0.0762	0.480	12.19
0.004	0.1016	0.490	12.45
0.005	0.1270	0.500	12.70
0.006	0.1524	0.510	12.95
0.007	0.1778	0.520	13.21
0.008	0.2032	0.530	13.46
0.009	0.2286	0.540	13.72
0.010	0.254	0.550	13.97
0.020	0.508	0.560	14.22
0.030	0.762	0.570	14.48
0.040	1.016	0.580	14.73
0.050	1.270	0.590	14.99
0.060	1.524	0.600	15.24
0.070	1.778	0.610	15.49
0.080	2.032	0.620	15.75
0.090	2.286	0.630	16.00
0.100	2.540	0.640	16.26
0.110	2.794	0.650	16.51
0.120	3.048	0.660	16.76
0.130	3.302	0.670	17.02
0.140	3.56	0.680	17.27
0.150	3.81	0.690	17.53
0.160	4.06	0.700	17.78
0.170	4.32	0.710	18.03
0.180	4.57	0.720	18.29
0.190	4.83	0.730	18.54
0.200	5.08	0.740	18.80
0.210	5.33	0.750	19.05
0.220	5.59	0.760	19.30
0.230	5.84	0.770	19.56
0.240	6.10	0.780	19.81
0.250	6.35	0.790	20.07
0.260	6.60	0.800	20.32
0.270	6.86	0.810	20.57
0.280	7.11	0.820	20.83
0.290	7.37	0.830	21.08
0.300	7.62	0.840	21.34
0.310	7.87	0.850	21.59
0.320	8.13	0.860	21.84
0.330	8.38	0.870	22.10
0.340	8.64	0.880	22.35
0.350	8.89	0.890	22.61
0.360	9.14	0.900	22.86
0.370	9.40	0.910	23.11
0.380	9.65	0.920	23.37
0.390	9.91	0.930	23.62
0.400	10.16	0.940	23.88
0.410	10.41	0.950	24.13
0.420	10.67	0.960	24.38
0.430	10.92	0.970	24.64
0.440	11.18	0.980	24.89
0.450	11.43	0.990	25.15
		1.000	25.40

Fractions

Inches	Millimeters	Inches	Millimeters	Inches	Millimeters	Inches	Millimeters	Inches	Millimeters	Inches	Millimeters
1/64	0.3969	53/64	21.0344	2 1/32	51.5939	3 31/32	100.806	5 21/32	143.669	8 11/16	220.663
1/32	0.7937	27/32	21.4312	2 1/16	52.3876	4	101.600	5 11/16	144.463	8 3/4	222.250
3/64	1.1906	55/64	21.8281	2 3/32	53.1814	4 1/32	102.394	5 23/32	145.257	8 13/16	223.838
1/16	1.5875	7/8	22.2250	2 1/8	53.9751	4 1/16	103.188	5 3/4	146.050	8 7/8	225.425
5/64	1.9844	57/64	22.6219	2 5/32	54.7688	4 3/32	103.981	5 25/32	146.844	8 15/16	227.013
3/32	2.3812	29/32	23.0187	2 3/16	55.5626	4 1/8	104.775	5 13/16	147.638	9	228.600
7/64	2.7781	59/64	23.4156	2 7/32	56.3564	4 5/32	105.569	5 27/32	148.432	9 1/16	230.188
1/8	3.1750	15/16	23.8125	2 1/4	57.1501	4 3/16	106.363	5 7/8	149.225	9 1/8	231.775
9/64	3.5719	61/64	24.2094	2 9/32	57.9439	4 7/32	107.156	5 29/32	150.019	9 3/16	233.363
5/32	3.9687	31/32	24.6062	2 5/16	58.7376	4 1/4	107.950	5 15/16	150.813	9 1/4	234.950
11/64	4.3656	63/64	25.0031	2 11/32	59.5314	4 9/32	108.744	5 31/32	151.607	9 5/16	236.538
3/16	4.7625	1	25.4001	2 3/8	60.3251	4 5/16	109.538	6	152.400	9 3/8	238.125
13/64	5.1594	1 1/32	26.1938	2 13/32	61.1189	4 11/32	110.331	6 1/16	153.988	9 7/16	239.713
7/32	5.5562	1 1/16	26.9876	2 7/16	61.9126	4 3/8	111.125	6 1/8	155.575	9 1/2	241.300
15/64	5.9531	1 3/32	27.7813	2 15/32	62.7064	4 13/32	111.919	6 3/16	157.163	9 9/16	242.888
1/4	6.3500	1 1/8	28.5751	2 1/2	63.5001	4 7/16	112.713	6 1/4	158.750	9 5/8	244.475
17/64	6.7469	1 5/32	29.3688	2 17/32	64.2939	4 15/32	113.506	6 5/16	160.338	9 11/16	246.063
9/32	7.1437	1 3/16	30.1626	2 9/16	65.0876	4 1/2	114.300	6 3/8	161.925	9 3/4	247.650
19/64	7.5406	1 7/32	30.9563	2 19/32	65.8814	4 17/32	115.094	6 7/16	163.513	9 13/16	249.238
5/16	7.9375	1 1/4	31.7501	2 5/8	66.6751	4 9/16	115.888	6 1/2	165.100	9 7/8	250.825
21/64	8.3344	1 9/32	32.5438	2 21/32	67.4689	4 19/32	116.681	6 9/16	166.688	9 15/16	252.413
11/32	8.7312	1 5/16	33.3376	2 11/16	68.2626	4 5/8	117.475	6 5/8	168.275	10	254.001
23/64	9.1281	1 11/32	34.1313	2 23/32	69.0564	4 21/32	118.269	6 11/16	169.863	10 1/16	255.588
3/8	9.5250	1 3/8	34.9251	2 3/4	69.8501	4 11/16	119.063	6 3/4	171.450	10 1/8	257.176
25/64	9.9219	1 13/32	35.7188	2 25/32	70.6439	4 23/32	119.856	6 13/16	173.038	10 3/16	258.763
13/32	10.3187	1 7/16	36.5126	2 13/16	71.4376	4 3/4	120.650	6 7/8	174.625	10 1/4	260.351
27/64	10.7156	1 15/32	37.3063	2 27/32	72.2314	4 25/32	121.444	6 15/16	176.213	10 5/16	261.938
7/16	11.1125	1 1/2	38.1001	2 7/8	73.0251	4 13/16	122.238	7	177.800	10 3/8	263.526
29/64	11.5094	1 17/32	38.8938	2 29/32	73.8189	4 27/32	123.031	7 1/16	179.388	10 7/16	265.113
15/32	11.9062	1 9/16	39.6876	2 15/16	74.6126	4 7/8	123.825	7 1/8	180.975	10 1/2	266.701
31/64	12.3031	1 19/32	40.4813	2 31/32	75.4064	4 29/32	124.619	7 3/16	182.563	10 9/16	268.288
1/2	12.7000	1 5/8	41.2751	3	76.2002	4 15/16	125.413	7 1/4	184.150	10 5/8	269.876
33/64	13.0969	1 21/32	42.0688	3 1/32	76.9939	4 31/32	126.206	7 5/16	185.738	10 11/16	271.463
17/32	13.4937	1 11/16	42.8626	3 1/16	77.7877	5	127.000	7 3/8	187.325	10 3/4	273.051
35/64	13.8906	1 23/32	43.6563	3 3/32	78.5814	5 1/32	127.794	7 7/16	188.913	10 13/16	274.638
9/16	14.2875	1 3/4	44.4501	3 1/8	79.3752	5 1/16	128.588	7 1/2	190.500	10 7/8	276.226
37/64	14.6844	1 25/32	45.2438	3 5/32	80.1689	5 3/32	129.382	7 9/16	192.088	10 15/16	277.813
19/32	15.0812	1 13/16	46.0376	3 3/16	80.9627	5 1/8	130.175	7 5/8	193.675	11	279.401
39/64	15.4781	1 27/32	46.8313	3 7/32	81.7564	5 5/32	130.969	7 11/16	195.263	11 1/16	280.988
5/8	15.8750	1 7/8	47.6251	3 1/4	82.5502	5 3/16	131.763	7 3/4	196.850	11 1/8	282.576
41/64	16.2719	1 29/32	48.4188	3 9/32	83.3439	5 7/32	132.557	7 13/16	198.438	11 3/16	284.163
21/32	16.6687	1 15/16	49.2126	3 5/16	84.1377	5 1/4	133.350	7 7/8	200.025	11 1/4	285.751
43/64	17.0656	1 31/32	50.0063	3 11/32	84.9314	5 9/32	134.144	7 15/16	201.613	11 5/16	287.338
11/16	17.4625	2	50.8001	3 3/8	85.7252	5 5/16	134.938	8	203.200	11 3/8	288.926
45/64	17.8594			3 13/32	86.5189	5 11/32	135.732	8 1/16	204.788	11 7/16	290.513
23/32	18.2562			3 7/16	87.3127	5 3/8	136.525	8 1/8	206.375	11 1/2	292.101
47/64	18.6531			3 15/32	88.1064	5 13/32	137.319	8 3/16	207.963	11 9/16	293.688
3/4	19.0500			3 1/2	88.9002	5 7/16	138.113	8 1/4	209.550	11 5/8	295.276
49/64	19.4469			3 17/32	89.6939	5 15/32	138.907	8 5/16	211.138	11 11/16	296.863
25/32	19.8437			3 9/16	90.4877	5 1/2	139.700	8 3/8	212.725	11 3/4	298.451
51/64	20.2406			3 19/32	91.2814	5 17/32	140.494	8 7/16	214.313	11 13/16	300.038
13/16	20.6375			3 5/8	92.0752	5 9/16	141.288	8 1/2	215.900	11 7/8	301.626
				3 21/32	92.8689	5 19/32	142.082	8 9/16	217.488	11 15/16	303.213
				3 11/16	93.6627	5 5/8	142.875	8 5/8	219.075	12	304.801
				3 23/32	94.4564						
				3 3/4	95.2502						
				3 25/32	96.0439						
				3 13/16	96.8377						
				3 27/32	97.6314						
				3 7/8	98.4252						
				3 29/32	99.2189						
				3 15/16	100.013						

AREA EQUIVALENTS

1 sq. in.		= .0065 sq. meters (m²)
1 sq. ft.	= 144 sq. in.	= .093 sq. meters (m²)
1 sq. yd.	= 9 sq. ft.	= .836 sq. meters (m²)
1 sq. yd.	= 1296 sq. in.	

VOLUME EQUIVALENTS

1 cu. in.		= .016 liters = 16.39 cm³
1 cu. ft.	= 1728 cu. in. = 7.481 gal.	= 28.317 liters = .0283 m³ = 28 317.00 cm³
1 cu. yd.	= 27 cu. ft. = 46,656 cu. in.	
1 gal.	= .1337 cu. ft. = 231 cu. in.	= 3.79 liters = 3 785 cm³
1 cm³	= .155 cu. in.	
1 liter	= 61.03 cu. in. = .2642 gal.	= 1 000 cm³

PRESSURE EQUIVALENTS

1 psia	= 0.068 atmosphere = 144 lb./sq. ft. = 2.036 in. of water = 2.307 ft. of water = 27.7 in. of water	= .0703 kg/cm² = .703 meters water = 70.3 cm water = 51.7 mm Hg. = 6.9 kPa
1 oz./sq. in.	= .128 in. of mercury = 1.73 in. of water	
1 in. of mercury	= .0334 atmosphere = .491 psi = 1.13 ft. of water = 70.73 psf	= .0345 kg/cm² = 25.4 mm Hg. = .3453 m water
1 ft. of water	= .0295 atmosphere = .434 psi = 62.43 lb./sq. ft. = .03 atmosphere = .883 in. of mercury (Hg.)	= .03 kg/cm² = 22.42 mm Hg. = .305 m water
1 atmosphere	= 29.92 in. of mercury = 33.94 ft. of water = 14.696 psi = 2116.35 psf	= 1.03 kg/cm² = 760 mm Hg. = 10.33 m water

1 psf	= .007 psi = 4.725 x 10⁻⁴ atmosphere = .01414 in. Hg. = .016 ft. water	= .488 g/cm² = .359 mm Hg. = .0049 m water
1 kilogram/sq. cm	= 14.22 psi = 2048.17 psf = .967 atmosphere = 28.96 in. Hg = 32.8083 ft. water	= 10 meters of water
1 meter of water	= 1.42 psi = 204.8 psf = .097 atmosphere = 2.896 in. Hg. = 3.28 ft. water	= 73.55 mm Hg. = .10 kg/cm²
1 mm Hg.	= .019 psi = 2.78 psf = .001316 atmosphere = .039 in. Hg. = .0446 ft. water	= .00136 kg/cm² = .0136 m water = .133 kPa

WEIGHT EQUIVALENTS

AVOIRDUPOIS

1 ounce	= 437 grains	= 28.35 grams = .028 kilogram
1 pound (lb.)	= 7000 grains	= .4536 kilograms = 453.6 grams
1 pound	= 16 ounces	= 453.6 grams
1 grain	= .000143 pounds	= .06480 grams
1 ton	= 2000 pounds	= 907.2 kilograms
1 gram	= 15.43 grains = .03527 ounces = .002205 pounds	= .001 kilogram
1 kilogram	= 2.2 pounds	

SPECIFIC WEIGHTS (DENSITY)

1 lb./cu. in.	= 1728 lb./cu. ft.	= 27.68 g/cm³ = 2.768 × 10⁷ g/m³
1 lb./cu. ft.	= 5.787 x 10⁻⁴ lb./cu. in.	= .016 g/cm³
1 gm/cm³	= 62.43 lb./cu. ft.	
1 kg/m³	= .06243 lb./cu. ft.	

VELOCITY EQUIVALENTS

1 mi./hr.	= 1.47 ft./sec. = .87 knots	= 1.61 km/hr. = .45 meters/sec.
1 ft./sec.	= .68 mi./hr. = 60 ft./min. = .59 knots	= 1.1 km/hr. = .305 meters/sec.
1 meter/sec.	= 3.28 ft./sec. = 2.24 mi./hr = 1.94 knots	= 3.6 km/hr.
1 km/hr.	= .91 ft./sec. = .62 mi./hr. = .54 knots	= .28 meters/sec.

FLOW EQUIVALENTS

1 cu. ft. per min.	= 7.481 gal./min. = 449 gal./hr.	= 28 317 cm³/min. = 28.32 liters/min. (l/min.) = 1700 l/hr.
1 cu. ft. per hour	= .0167 cu. ft./min. = .1247 gal./min. = 7.481 gal./hr.	= .472 l/min. = 28.317 l/hr. = 472 cm³/min.
1 gal. per min.	= .1337 cu. ft./min. = 8.002 cu. ft./hr.	= 3.79 l/min. = 3785 cm³/min.
1 liter per min.	= .0353 cu. ft./min. = 2.118 cu. ft./hr. = .2642 gal./min. = 15.852 gal./hr	= 1000 cm³/min.

LIQUID MEASURE EQUIVALENTS

Liquid Measure	U.S.	Metric
1 pint	= 16 ounces	= .473 liters
1 quart	= 2 pints = 32 ounces	= .946 liters
1 gallon	= 4 quarts = 8 pints = 231 cubic inches = 8.34 pounds of water	= 3.785 liters
1 cubic foot	= 7.48 gallons	
1.136 quart		= 1 liter

CONVERSION TABLE FOR WOODWORK

Customary (English)	METRIC				
	Actual	Accurate Woodworkers' Language	Tool Sizes	Lumber Sizes	
				Thickness	Width
1/32 in	0.8 mm	1 mm bare			
1/16 in	1.6 mm	1.5 mm			
1/8 in	3.2 mm	3 mm full	3 mm		
3/16 in	4.8 mm	5 mm bare	5 mm		
1/4 in	6.4 mm	6.5 mm	6 mm		
5/16 in	7.9 mm	8 mm bare	8 mm		
3/8 in	9.5 mm	9.5 mm	10 mm		
7/16 in	11.1 mm	11 mm full	11 mm		
1/2 in	12.7 mm	12.5 mm full	13 mm	12 mm	
9/16 in	14.3 mm	14.5 mm bare	14 mm		
5/8 in	15.9 mm	16 mm bare	16 mm	16 mm	
11/16 in	17.5 mm	17.5 mm	17 mm		
3/4 in	19.1 mm	19 mm full	19 mm	19 mm	
13/16 in	20.6 mm	20.5 mm	21 mm		
7/8 in	22.2 mm	22 mm full	22 mm	22 mm	
15/16 in	23.8 mm	24 mm bare	24 mm		
1 in	25.4 mm	25.5 mm	25 mm	25 mm	
1 1/4 in	31.8 mm	32 mm bare	32 mm	32 mm	
1 3/8 in	34.9 mm	35 mm bare	36 mm	36 mm	
1 1/2 in	38.1 mm	38 mm full	38 mm	38 mm	
1 3/4 in	44.5 mm	44.5 mm	44 mm	44 mm	
2 in	50.8 mm	51 mm bare	50 mm	50 mm	50 mm
2 1/2 in	63.5 mm	63.5 mm	63 mm	63 mm	
3 in	76.2 mm	76 mm full		75 mm	75 mm
4 in	101.6 mm	101.5 mm		100 mm	100 mm
5 in	127.0 mm	127 mm			125 mm
6 in	152.4 mm	152.5 mm			150 mm
7 in	177.8 mm	178 mm bare			
8 in	203.2 mm	203 mm full			200 mm
9 in	228.6 mm	228.5 mm			
10 in	254.0 mm	254 mm			250 mm
11 in	279.4 mm	279.5 mm			
12 in	304.8 mm	305 mm bare			300 mm
18 in	457.2 mm	457 mm full	460 mm		
24 in	609.6 mm	609.5 mm			
36 in	914.4 mm	914.5 mm			
48 in—4'	1219.2 mm	1220 mm			
96 in—8'	2438.4 mm	2440 mm			

Panel Stock Sizes
1220 mm width
2440 mm length

Present Length, ft	6	8	10	12	14	16	18	20
Replacement Length, m	1.8	2.4	3.0	3.6	4.2	4.8	5.5	6.0

AMERICAN			METRIC		
Nominal Dia.	Threads/Inch		Nominal Dia., mm	Pitch in mm	
	UNC	UNF		Coarse	Fine
0	—	80			
			1.6	0.35	0.2
			1.7	0.35	0.2, 0.25
			1.8	0.35	0.2
1	64	72			
2	56	64	2.0	0.4	0.25, 0.35
			2.2	0.45	0.25
			2.3	0.4	0.25, 0.35
			2.5	0.45	0.35
3	48	56	2.6	0.45	0.25, 0.35
4	40	48			
5	40	44	3.0	0.5	0.35
6	32	40	3.5	0.6	0.35, 0.5
8	32	36	4.0	0.7	0.5
10	24	32	4.5	0.75	0.5
12	24	28	5.0	0.8	0.5, 0.75
1/4	20	28	6.0	1.0	0.5, 0.75
			7.0	1.0	0.5, 0.75
5/16	18	24			
			8.0	1.25	0.5, 0.75, 1
3/8	16	24	9.0	1.25	0.75, 1
			10.0	1.5	1.25, 1, 0.75
7/16	14	20	11.0	1.5	1, 0.75, 1.25
1/2	13	20	12.0	1.75	1, 1.25, 1.5
			14.0	2.0	1.25, 1.5
9/16	12	18			
5/8	11	18			
			16.0	2.0	1, 1.25, 1.5
3/4	10	16	18.0	2.5	1, 1.5, 2
			20.0	2.5	2, 1.5
7/8	9	14	22.0	2.5	2, 1.5, 1
1	8	12	24.0	3.0	2, 1.5, 1
1 1/16	—	12	27.0	3.0	2, 1.5, 1
1 1/8	7	12	28.0	—	2, 1.5, 1
1 1/4	7	12	30.0	3.5	3, 2, 1.5
1 3/8	6	12	32.0	—	2, 1.5, 1
			33.0	3.5	3, 2, 1.5
			34.0	—	2, 1.5, 1
			35.0	—	1.5, 1, 2
1 1/2	6	12	36.0	4.0	3, 2, 1.5
			37.0	—	1.5
			38.0	—	1.5, 2
			39.0	4.0	3, 2, 1.5

UNC—Unified National Coarse. UNF—Unified National Fine.

THREAD CONVERSION CHART
(McMaster and Carr)

PLYWOOD GRADES

Classification of Species

Group 1	Group 2	Group 3	Group 4	Group 5
Apitong	Cedar, Port	Alder, Red	Aspen	Basswood
Beech,	Orford	Birch, Paper	Bigtooth	Poplar,
American	Cypress	Cedar, Alaska	Quaking	Balsam
Birch	Douglas	Fir,	Cativo	
Sweet	Fir 2[a]	Subalpine	Cedar	
Yellow	Fir	Hemlock,	Incense	
Douglas	Balsam	Eastern	Western	
Fir 1[a]	California	Maple	Red	
Kapur	Red	Bigleaf	Cottonwood	
Keruing	Grand	Pine	Eastern	
Larch,	Noble	Jack	Black	
Western	Pacific	Lodgepole	(Western	
Maple, Sugar	Silver	Ponderosa	Poplar)	
Pine	White	Spruce	Pine	
Caribbean	Hemlock,	Redwood	Eastern	
Ocote	Western	Spruce	White	
Pine, South.	Lauan	Engelmann	Sugar	
Loblolly	Almon	White		
Longleaf	Bagtikan			
Shortleaf	Mayapis			
Slash	Red			
Tanoak	Tangile			
	White			
	Maple, Black			
	Mengkulang			
	Meranti,			
	Red[b]			
	Mersawa			
	Pine			
	Pond			
	Red			
	Virginia			
	Western			
	White			
	Spruce			
	Black			
	Red			
	Sitka			
	Sweetgum			
	Tamarack			
	Yellow-			
	Poplar			

(a) Douglas Fir from trees grown in the states of Washington, Oregon, California, Idaho, Montana, Wyoming, and the Canadian Provinces of Alberta and British Columbia shall be classed as Douglas Fir No. 1. Douglas Fir from trees grown in the states of Nevada, Utah, Colorado, Arizona and New Mexico shall be classed as Douglas Fir No. 2.

(b) Red Meranti shall be limited to species having a specific gravity of 0.41 or more based on green volume and oven dry weight.

Span Ratings

APA RATED SHEATHING, APA RATED STURD-I-FLOOR and APA RATED SIDING panels carry numbers in their trademarks called Span Ratings. These denote the maximum recommended center-to-center spacing in inches of supports over which the panels should be placed in construction applications.

The Span Rating in the trademark on APA RATED SHEATHING panels appears as two numbers separated by a slash, such as 32/16, 48/24, etc. The left-hand number denotes the maximum recommended spacing of supports when the panel is used for roof sheathing with the **long dimension of the panel across three or more supports.** The right hand number indicates the maximum recommended spacing of supports when the panel is used for subflooring with the **long dimension of the panel across three or more supports.** A panel marked 32/16, for example, may be used for roof sheathing over supports 32 inches on center or for subflooring over supports 16 inches on center.

The Span Ratings in the trademarks on APA RATED STURD-I-FLOOR and RATED SIDING panels appear as a single number. APA RATED STURD-I-FLOOR panels are designed specifically for residential or other light-frame single-floor (combined subfloor-underlayment) applications and are manufactured with Span Ratings of 16, 20, 24, and 48 inches. These ratings, like those for APA RATED SHEATHING, are based on application of the panel with the **long dimension across three or more supports.**

APA RATED SIDINGS are manufactured with Span Ratings of 16 and 24 inches and may be used direct to studs or over nonstructural wall sheathing (Sturd-I-Wall construction), or over nailable panel or lumber sheathing (double-wall construction). Panels with a Span Rating of 16 inches may be applied vertically direct to studs spaced 16 inches on center. Panels bearing a Span Rating of 24 inches may be used vertically direct to studs spaced 24 inches on center.[2] All RATED SIDING panels may be applied horizontally direct to studs 16 or 24 inches on center provided horizontal joints are blocked. When used over nailable structural panel or lumber sheathing, the RATED SIDING Span Rating refers to the maximum recommended spacing of vertical rows of nails rather than to stud spacing.

Guide to APA Performance-Rated Panels[1][2]

APA RATED SHEATHING

TYPICAL TRADEMARK	
APA	Specially designed for subflooring and wall and roof sheathing. Also good for a broad range of other construction and industrial applications. Can be manufactured as conventional veneered plywood, as a composite, or as a nonveneer panel. For special engineered applications, veneered panels conforming to PS 1 may be required. EXPOSURE DURABILITY CLASSIFICATIONS: Exterior, Exposure 1, Exposure 2. COMMON THICKNESSES: 5/16, 3/8, 7/16, 15/32, 1/2, 19/32, 5/8, 23/32, 3/4.
RATED SHEATHING	
32/16 15/32 INCH	
SIZED FOR SPACING	
EXPOSURE 1	
000	
NER-QA397 PRP-108	

APA STRUCTURAL I RATED SHEATHING[3]

TYPICAL TRADEMARK	
APA	Unsanded grade for use where shear and cross-panel strength properties are of maximum importance, such as panelized roofs and diaphragms. Can be manufactured as conventional veneered plywood, as a composite, or as a nonveneer panel. For special engineered applications, veneered panels conforming to PS 1 may be required. EXPOSURE DURABILITY CLASSIFICATIONS: Exterior, Exposure 1. COMMON THICKNESSES: 5/16, 3/8, 7/16, 15/32, 1/2, 19/32, 5/8, 23/32, 3/4.
RATED SHEATHING	
32/16 15/32 INCH	
SIZED FOR SPACING	
EXPOSURE 1	
000	
STRUCTURAL I RATED	
DIAPHRAGMS · SHEAR WALLS	
PANELIZED ROOFS	
NER-QA397 PRP-108	

APA RATED STURD-I-FLOOR

Specially designed as combination subfloor-underlayment. Provides smooth surface for application of carpet and pad and possesses high concentrated and impact load resistance. Can be manufactured as conventional veneered plywood, as a composite, or as a nonveneer panel. 1-1/8" plywood panels marked PS 1 may be used for heavy timber roof construction. Available square edge or tongue-and-groove. EXPOSURE DURABILITY CLASSIFICATIONS: Exterior, Exposure 1, Exposure 2. COMMON THICKNESSES: 19/32, 5/8, 23/32, 3/4, 1-1/8.

APA RATED STURD-I-FLOOR 48 oc (2-4-1)

For combination subfloor-underlayment on 32-and 48-inch spans and for heavy timber roof construction. Manufactured only as conventional veneered plywood. Available square edge or tongue-and-groove. EXPOSURE DURABILITY CLASSIFICATIONS: Exposure 1. THICKNESS: 1-1/8.

(1) Specific grades, thicknesses and exposure durability classifications may be in limited supply in some areas. Check with your supplier before specifying.

(2) Specify Performance-Rated Panels by thickness and Span Rating. Span Ratings are based on panel strength and stiffness. Since these properties are a function of panel composition and configuration as well as thickness, the same Span Rating may appear on panels of different thickness. Conversely, panels of the same thickness may be marked with different Span Ratings.

(3) All plies in Structural I panels are special improved grades and limited to Group 1 species.

Guide to APA Sanded & Touch-Sanded Panels[1][2][3]

APA A-A

TYPICAL TRADEMARK

A-A · G-1 · EXPOSURE1-APA · 000 · PS1-83

Use where appearance of both sides is important for interior applications such as built-ins, cabinets, furniture, partitions; and exterior applications such as fences, signs, boats, shipping containers, tanks, ducts, etc. Smooth surfaces suitable for painting. EXPOSURE DURABILITY CLASSIFICATION: Interior, Exposure 1, Exterior. COMMON THICKNESSES: 1/4, 11/32, 3/8, 15/32, 1/2, 19/32, 5/8, 23/32, 3/4.

APA A-B

TYPICAL TRADEMARK

A-B · G-1 · EXPOSURE1-APA · 000 · PS1-83

For use where appearance of one side is less important but where two solid surfaces are necessary. EXPOSURE DURABILITY CLASSIFICATION: Interior; Exposure 1, Exterior. COMMON THICKNESSES: 1/4, 11/32, 3/8, 15/32, 1/2, 19/32, 5/8, 23/32, 3/4.

APA A-C

For use where appearance of only one side is important in exterior applications, such as soffits, fences, structural uses, boxcar and truck linings, farm buildings, tanks, trays, commercial refrigerators, etc. EXPOSURE DURABILITY CLASSIFICATION: Exterior. COMMON THICKNESSES: 1/4, 11/32, 3/8, 15/32, 1/2, 19/32, 5/8, 23/32, 3/4.

APA A-D

For use where appearance of only one side is important in interior applications, such as paneling, built-ins, shelving, partitions, flow racks, etc. EXPOSURE DURABILITY CLASSIFICATION: Interior, Exposure 1. COMMON THICKNESSES: 1/4, 11/32, 3/8, 15/32, 1/2, 19/32, 5/8, 23/32, 3/4.

APA B-B

TYPICAL TRADEMARK

B-B · G-2 · EXPOSURE1-APA · 000 · PS1-83

Utility panels with two solid sides. EXPOSURE DURABILITY CLASSIFICATION: Interior, Exposure 1, Exterior. COMMON THICKNESSES: 1/4, 11/32, 3/8, 15/32, 1/2, 19/32, 5/8, 23/32, 3/4.

APA B-C

Utility panel for farm service and work buildings, boxcar and truck linings, containers, tanks, agricultural equipment, as a base for exterior coatings and other exterior uses or applications subject to high or continuous moisture. EXPOSURE DURABILITY CLASSIFICATION: Exterior. COMMON THICKNESSES: 1/4, 11/32, 3/8, 15/32, 1/2, 19/32, 5/8, 23/32, 3/4.

APA B-D

Utility panel for backing, sides of built-ins, industry shelving, slip sheets, separator boards, bins and other interior or protected applications. EXPOSURE DURABILITY CLASSIFICATION: Interior, Exposure 1. COMMON THICKNESSES: 1/4, 11/32, 3/8, 15/32, 1/2, 19/32, 5/8, 23/32, 3/4.

APA UNDERLAYMENT

For application over structural subfloor. Provides smooth surface for application of carpet and possesses high concentrated and impact load resistance. EXPOSURE DURABILITY CLASSIFICATION: Interior, Exposure 1. COMMON THICKNESSES[4]: 3/8, 1/2, 19/32, 5/8, 23/32, 3/4.

APA C-C PLUGGED

TYPICAL TRADEMARK

APA
C-C PLUGGED
GROUP 2
EXTERIOR
000
PS 1-83

For use as an underlayment over structural subfloor, refrigerated or controlled atmosphere storage rooms, pallet fruit bins, tanks, boxcar and truck floors and linings, open soffits, and other similar applications where continuous or severe moisture may be present. Provides smooth surface for application of carpet and pad and possesses high concentrated and impact load resistance. EXPOSURE DURABILITY CLASSIFICATION: Exterior. COMMON THICKNESSES[4]: 11/32, 3/8, 1/2, 19/32, 5/8, 23/32, 3/4.

APA C-D PLUGGED

TYPICAL TRADEMARK

APA
C-D PLUGGED
GROUP 2
EXPOSURE 1
000
PS 1-83

For built-ins, cable reels, separator boards and other interior or protected applications. Not a substitute for Underlayment or APA Rated Sturd-I-Floor as it lacks their puncture resistance. EXPOSURE DURABILITY CLASSIFICATION: Interior, Exposure 1. COMMON THICKNESSES: 3/8, 1/2, 19/32, 5/8, 23/32, 3/4.

(1) Specific grades and thicknesses may be in limited supply in some areas. check with our supplier before specifying.
(2) Exterior sanded panels, C-C Plugged, C-D Plugged and Underlayment grades can also be manufactured in Structural I (all plies limited to Group 1 species).
(3) Some manufacturers also produce panels with premium N-grade veneer on one or both faces. Available only by special order. Check with the manufacturer.

Guide to APA Specialty Panels[1]

APA RATED SIDING

TYPICAL TRADEMARK

APA
RATED SIDING
303-18-S/W
16 OC   11/32 INCH
GROUP 1
SIZED FOR SPACING
EXTERIOR
000
PS 1-83   FHA-UM-64
NER-QA397   PRP-108

Proprietary plywood products for exterior siding, fencing, etc. Special surface treatment such as V-groove, channel groove, striated, brushed, rough-sawn and texture-embossed (MDO). Stud spacing (Span Rating) and face grade classification indicated in trademark. TYPE: Exterior. COMMON THICKNESSES: 11/32, 3/8, 15/32, 1/2, 19/32, 5/8.

APA TEXTURE 1-11

TYPICAL TRADEMARK

APA
RATED SIDING
303-18-S/W
16 OC   19/32 INCH
GROUP 1
SIZED FOR SPACING
EXTERIOR
T1-11   000
PS 1-83   FHA UM 64
NER-QA397   PRP-108

Special 303 Siding panel with grooves 1/4" deep, 3/8" wide, spaced 4" or 8" o c. Other spacings may be available on special order. Edges shiplapped. Available unsanded, textured and MDO. TYPE: Exterior. THICKNESSES: 19/32 and 5/8 only.

APA DECORATIVE

TYPICAL TRADEMARK

APA
DECORATIVE
GROUP 2
INTERIOR
000
PS 1-83

Rough-sawn, brushed, grooved, or striated faces. For paneling, interior accent walls, built-ins, counter facing, exhibit displays. Can also be made by some manufacturers in Exterior for exterior siding, gable ends, fences and other exterior applications. Use recommendations for Exterior panels vary with the particular product. Check with the manufacturer. EXPOSURE DURABILITY CLASSIFICATION: Interior, Exposure 1, Exterior. COMMON THICKNESSES: 5/16, 3/8, 1/2, 5/8.

APA HIGH DENSITY OVERLAY (HDO)[2]

TYPICAL TRADEMARK

HDO · A-A · G-1 · EXT-APA · 000 · PS1-83

Has a hard semi-opaque resin-fiber overlay both sides. Abrasion resistant. For concrete forms, cabinets, countertops, signs, tanks. Also available with skid-resistant screen-grid surface. EXPOSURE DURABILITY CLASSIFICATION: Exterior. COMMON THICKNESSES: 3/8, 1/2, 5/8, 3/4.

APA MEDIUM DENSITY OVERLAY (MDO)[2]

TYPICAL TRADEMARK

APA
M. D. OVERLAY
GROUP 1
EXTERIOR
000
PS 1-83

Smooth, opaque, resin-fiber overlay one or both sides. Ideal base for paint, both indoors and outdoors. Also available as a 303 Siding. EXPOSURE DURABILITY CLASSIFICATION: Exterior. COMMON THICKNESSES: 11/32, 3/8, 1/2, 5/8, 3/4.

APA MARINE

TYPICAL TRADEMARK

MARINE · A-A · EXT-APA · 000 · PS1-83

Ideal for boat hulls. Made only with Douglas fir or western larch. Subject to special limitations on core gaps and face repairs. Also available with HDO or MDO faces. EXPOSURE DURABILITY CLASSIFICATION: Exterior. COMMON THICKNESSES: 1/4, 3/8, 1/2, 5/8, 3/4.

APA B-B PLYFORM CLASS I

TYPICAL TRADEMARK

APA
PLYFORM
B-B CLASS I
EXTERIOR
000
PS 1-83

Concrete form grades with high reuse factor. Sanded both sides and mill-oiled unless otherwise specified. Special restrictions on species. Also available in HDO for very smooth concrete finish, in Structural I (all plies limited to Group 1 species), and with special overlays. EXPOSURE DURABILITY CLASSIFICATION: Exterior. COMMON THICKNESSES: 19/32, 5/8, 23/32, 3/4.

APA PLYRON

TYPICAL TRADEMARK

PLYRON · EXPOSURE1-APA · 000

Hardboard face on both sides. Faces tempered, untempered, smooth or screened. For countertops, shelving, cabinet doors, flooring. EXPOSURE DURABILITY CLASSIFICATION: Interior, Exposure 1, Exterior. COMMON THICKNESSES: 1/2, 5/8, 3/4.

(1) Specific grades and thicknesses may be in limited supply in some areas. Check with your supplier before specifying.

(2) Can also be manufactured in Structural I (all plies limited to Group 1 species).

APPENDIX C

PLUMBING SYMBOLS

PIPING SYMBOLS:

VENT

COLD WATER

HOT WATER

HOT WATER RETURN

GAS ———— G ———— G ————

SOIL, WASTE OR LEADER
(ABOVE GRADE)

SOIL, WASTE OR LEADER
(BELOW GRADE)

FIXTURE SYMBOLS:

BATHS

WATER CLOSET (WITH TANK)

WATER CLOSET (FLUSH VALVE)

SHOWER

LAVATORY

DW — DISHWASHER

SS — SERVICE SINK

HWT — HOT WATER TANK

HWT

HWH — HOT WATER HEATER

DF — DRINKING FOUNTAIN

M — METER

HB — HOSE BIB

C O / CO — CLEANOUTS

FD — FLOOR DRAIN

RD — ROOF DRAIN

OTHER FITTINGS

FITTING OR VALVE	TYPE OF CONNECTION		
	SCREWED	BELL AND SPIGOT	SOLDERED OR CEMENTED
ELBOW – 90 DEG.			
ELBOW – 45 DEG.			
ELBOW – TURNED UP			
ELBOW – TURNED DOWN			
ELBOW – LONG RADIUS			
ELBOW WITH SIDE INLET – OUTLET DOWN			
ELBOW WITH SIDE INLET – OUTLET UP			
REDUCING ELBOW			
SANITARY T			
T			
T – OUTLET UP			

FITTING OR VALVE	TYPE OF CONNECTION		
	SCREWED	BELL AND SPIGOT	SOLDERED OR CEMENTED
T – OUTLET DOWN			
CROSS			
REDUCER – CONCENTRIC			
REDUCER – OFFSET			
CONNECTOR			
Y OR WYE			
VALVE – GATE			
VALVE – GLOBE			
UNION			
BUSHING			
INCREASER			

344

PLUMBING ABBREVIATIONS

A.F.D.	area floor drain	FIXT.	fixture	LDR.	leader
B.W.V.	backwater valve	F.D.	floor drain	O.D.	outside diameter
CODP.	deck plate cleanout	F.H.	fire hose	(R)	roughing only
C.W.	cold water	F.E.	fire extinguisher unit	R.D.	roof drain
C.W.R.	cold water return	H.W.	hot water	S.C.	sill cock
DEG.	degree	H.W.C.	hot water circulating line	S.S.	service sink
D.F.	drinking fountain	H.W.R.	hot water return	TOIL.	toilet
D.H.W.	domestic hot water	H.W.S.	hot water supply	UR.	urinal
DR.	drain	H.W.P..	hot water pump	V.	vent
D.W.	dishwasher	I.D.	inside diameter	W.C.	water closet
F.	fahrenheit	LAV.	lavatory	W.H.	wall hydrant
FDR.	feeder				

APPENDIX D

ELECTRICAL SYMBOLS COMMONLY USED
ON BLUEPRINTS

GRAPHICAL ELECTRICAL SYMBOLS FOR RESIDENTIAL WIRING PLANS

General Outlets

Lighting Outlet

Ceiling Lighting Outlet for recessed fixture (Outline shows shape of fixture.)

Continuous Wireway for Fluorescent Lighting on ceiling, in coves, cornices, etc. (Extend rectangle to show length of installation.)

Lighting Outlet with Lamp Holder

Lighting Outlet with Lamp Holder and Pull Switch

Fan Outlet

Junction Box

Drop-Cord Equipped Outlet

Clock Outlet

To indicate wall installation of above outlets, place circle near wall and connect with line as shown for clock outlet.

Convenience Outlets

Duplex Convenience Outlet

Triplex Convenience Outlet (Substitute other numbers for other variations in number of plug positions.)

Duplex Convenience Outlet — Split Wired

Duplex Convenience Outlet for Grounding-Type Plugs

Weatherproof Convenience Outlet

Multi-Outlet Assembly (Extend arrows to limits of installation. Use appropriate symbol to indicate type of outlet. Also indicate spacing of outlets as X inches.)

Combination Switch and Convenience Outlet

Combination Radio and Convenience Outlet

Floor Outlet

Range Outlet

Special-Purpose Outlet. Use subscript letters to indicate function. DW-Dishwasher, CD-Clothes Dryer, etc.

Switch Outlets

S Single-Pole Switch

S_3 Three-Way Switch

S_4 Four-Way Switch

S_D Automatic Door Switch

S_P Switch and Pilot Light

S_{WP} Weatherproof Switch

S_2 Double-Pole Switch

Low-Voltage and Remote-Control Switching Systems

S Switch for Low-Voltage Relay Systems

MS Master Switch for Low-Voltage Relay Systems

O_R Relay—Equipped Lighting Outlet

Low-Voltage Relay System Wiring

Auxiliary Systems

Push Button

Buzzer

Bell

Combination Bell-Buzzer

CH Chime

Annunciator

D Electric Door Opener

M Maid's Signal Plug

Interconnection Box

T Bell-Ringing Transformer

Outside Telephone

Interconnecting Telephone

R Radio Outlet

TV Television Outlet

FS Automatic Fire Alarm Device

Miscellaneous

Service Panel

Distribution Panel

Switch Leg Indication. Connects outlets with control points.

$O_{a,b}$ Special Outlets. Any standard symbol given above may be used with the addition of subscript letters to designate some special variation of standard equipment for a particular architectural plan. When so used, the variation should be explained in the Key of Symbols and, if necessary, in the specifications.

APPENDIX E

CALCULATION OF YEARLY ENERGY COST
FOR APPLIANCES

How to Calculate the Yearly Energy Cost at Various Utility Rates.

The yearly energy cost figures given for Appliances are based upon the national average utility rates for 1980 of 4.97¢/KWH for electricity and 36.7¢/Therm or .38¢/Cu.Ft. for gas. To calculate the annual cost of operation at various utility rates, use these formulas.

1. The yearly energy cost for electric water heaters, freezers, refrigerators, refrigerator-freezers plus dishwashers and washers that use electricity to heat the water should be calculated as follows:

   Yearly Cost of Operation = Cost/KWH x Yearly KWH Consumption of Product

2. The annual cost of operation for dishwashers and washers that use natural gas to heat the water should be calculated as follows:

   Yearly Cost of Operation = Cost/KWH x Yearly KWH Consumption of Product + Cost/Therm or Cost/Cu.Ft. x Yearly Therm or Cu. Ft. Consumption to Heat Water

3. The annual cost of operation for room air conditioners should be calculated as follows:

   Yearly Cost of Operation = Cost/KWH x $\frac{\text{Rated Watts}}{1000}$ x Hours of Cooling

How To Use the ENERGYGUIDE Label (Example)

First, answer five questions

1. **Are the appliances comparable in size and features?** _Yes_

2. **What is the price of the energy-efficient model?** _$545_ (model with lower yearly energy cost or higher energy efficiency rating)
   What is the price of the standard model? _$485_ (model with higher yearly energy cost or lower energy efficiency rating)

3. **How often will you use the product?** _all the time._

4. **What is your local energy rate?**
   _6_ ¢/kWh
   _____ ¢/therm

How much will each model cost you to run yearly, based on your local energy rate? (determine from energy label on product)

Standard model _$85_

Energy-efficient model _$62_

5. **How long do you expect to keep the appliance?** _10 years_

Then figure out whether you are better off buying the more energy-efficient appliance

First, calculate the price difference:

Cost of energy-efficient model	$ _545_
minus cost of standard model	_-485_
Price difference	$ _60_

Second, estimate your annual energy-cost savings with the more energy-efficient model:

Annual energy cost of standard model	$ _85_
minus annual energy cost of energy-efficient model	_-62_
Annual energy-cost savings	$ _23_

Third, calculate your energy-cost savings over the life of the appliance:

Annual energy-cost savings	$ _23_
multiplied by years you expect to keep the appliance	_x 10 yrs_
	$ _230_
minus price difference	_-60_
Energy-cost savings over life of appliance	$ _170_

Finally, figure out how soon you can expect to recover your investment:

Price difference	$ _60_
divided by annual energy-cost savings	_÷23_
Years to recover investment	_2.6 yrs._

THE INFORMATION IN THIS GUIDE IS BASED UPON PRODUCTS AND ENERGY FIGURES AVAILABLE AS OF MAY 19, 1980

Electrical power (in watts) used by electric household appliances.

Appliance	Average Wattage	Appliance	Average Wattage
Hair dryer	381	Microwave oven	1,450
Shaver	15	Range with oven	12,000
Radio	71	Toaster	1,146
Television		Waste disposal	445
b&w solid state	45	Refrigerator/Freezer	
color solid state	145	manual defrost, 10-15 cu. ft.	1,300
Clock	2	automatic defrost, 16-18 cu. ft.	1,700
Sewing machine	75	Clothes dryer	4,856
Vacuum cleaner	630	Automatic washer	512
Blender	300	Room air conditioner	860
Broiler	1,140	Attic fan	370
Coffee maker	894	Window fan	200
Dishwasher	1,201	Portable heater	1,322
Hot plate	1,200		

APPENDIX F

THREE IDEAS ABOUT WOOD AS A FUEL

Measuring in cords; troubleshooting stoves; keeping wood stored and dry.
(With thanks to Better 'n Ben's)

Four cords of dry, seasoned hardwood are enough to keep the average woodstove going full time throughout the average heating season in the average home. In almost every home, those four cords of wood will reduce the need for other sources of heat by over 60%. In many homes the wood will produce *all* the heat required.

How and where to get those four cords, is a challenge that faces every woodburner every year.

LESS THAN IT LOOKS

A standard cord is a stack of 4-foot logs piled 4 feet high and 8 feet long. Simple multiplication tells you that the volume of wood in a cord is therefore 128 cubic feet. Wrong. Once you subtract the air space, you've really only got about 80 cubic feet of usable fuel. And that depends on how tightly the pile is stacked.

Beware of the so called "face cord" — it's not a full cord and should not command a full cord price. A face cord is typically four feet high and eight feet long, but the logs are usually a lot less than four footers.

What should you pay for firewood? That depends on where you live, what kind of wood you're buying, and frankly, what the market will bear. Green (recently felled) wood is generally cheaper than dry, seasoned wood. Delivery is expensive, so you'll save if you have a truck or trailer to haul the load home yourself. You'll also save if you buy bigger and longer hunks of wood, then cut it and split it yourself.

In descending order of heat content, here are the best woods for your stove: apple, beech, elm, hickory, locust, white oak, white ash, birch, cherry, sugar maple, red oak, and walnut.

WHAT IF IT SMOKES?

If your chimney isn't drawing well, any stove you connect to it may smoke. When this is the case, there are a number of things to check.

Make sure the chimney damper plate is *wired* in the wide open position. Be certain there are no obstructions lodged in the chimney. Or maybe your chimney just needs a good cleaning. If you have an ash dump in the floor of your fireplace, cover it with aluminum foil and then with sand to seal off any air leaks. If you use stove pipe, seal all the joints with furnace cement to eliminate leaks.

Believe it or not, some houses are actually ''too tight'' to allow a proper draft for a woodstove. Open a window just a bit and see if that helps.

NEEDS MORE SEASONING

Although green wood normally takes 12 to 18 months to dry out enough to burn efficiently, there is a way to compress that time to as little as three months. First of all, split the wood while it's still green. It'll split more easily then anyway, and the air can get to it better. Then stack it in an exposed location and cover it with plastic. The sun's heat, magnified by the plastic, will greatly accelerate the drying process. Be sure to leave the ends of the logs uncovered to maximize air circulation.

The ideal piece of fuelwood should be as long as the stove can accommodate, but only 3 to 5 inches in diameter. Bigger logs don't burn as readily and smaller ones burn up too fast.

Even if you don't use the plastic cover technique, try to keep at least a couple weeks' worth of wood under cover somewhere. If you don't, you're sure to get a spell of wet weather, and you'll be putting too much water into your stove. Insects and other creatures would like nothing better than to call your woodpile their home, so don't put the wood against the house. But don't put it too far away either, or you'll regret it when the snow gets up to your knees.

If you have the space, you might consider building yourself a good sized wood box that'll hold at least a day's supply of wood indoors near the stove. That way, your trip to the woodpile can be planned as a regular chore each day.

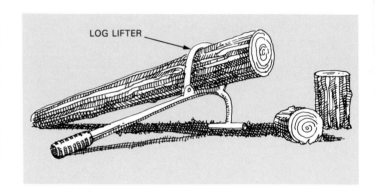

LOG LIFTER

APPENDIX G

SOLAR ENERGY

The home mechanic with limited knowledge, skills, and materials can utilize to a certain extent the energy of the sun through active and passive solar principles. Any solar heating system has three essential jobs to do:

1. It must collect the sun's energy.
2. It must store the sun's warmth.
3. It must distribute the heat as needed.

Additionally, most solar applications have some provisions for summer cooling. Some systems include controls to regulate losses and gains.

In an active solar installation, collectors, heat ex-changers, thermostats, and other mechanical equipment do the work. Passive systems do not need most of this gear. Many passive systems use a natural heat flow principle called the thermosiphon. Hot air rises while cooler air falls. The circulation of the air distributes the heat.

THREE PASSIVE SOLAR METHODS

Three passive solar methods include direct gain, indirect gain, and the attached sunspace/green-house. These methods are explained in the follow-

GENERALIZED PASSIVE SOLAR SYSTEM TYPES

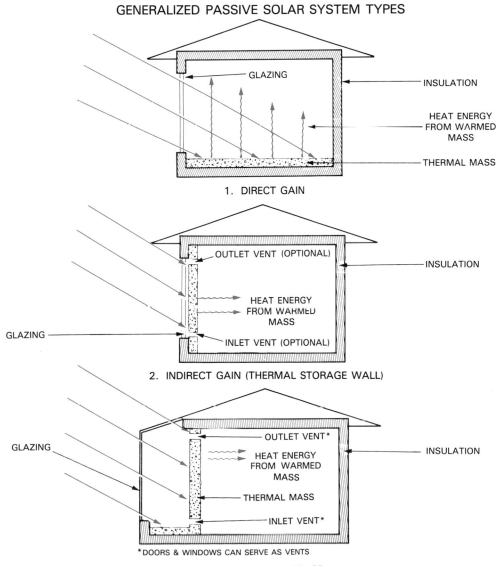

1. DIRECT GAIN

2. INDIRECT GAIN (THERMAL STORAGE WALL)

*DOORS & WINDOWS CAN SERVE AS VENTS

3. ATTACHED SUNSPACE

ing paragraphs:

1. Direct gain is the simplest and least costly method of passive solar heating. Large south facing windows simply let the winter sun's radiant energy in to heat the house and its contents directly.

2. Indirect gain is a very effective method of passive solar heating which keeps the bright sunlight out of the living areas. For more privacy and a more constant interior temperature, a thermal mass (heat storage) wall—made of concrete or brick, or filled with water—may be placed directly behind the glass areas. This is called a Trombe wall. During evening hours, a steady stream of radiant heat from the Trombe wall will warm the house. Vents in the thermal wall will bring heat into the house early in the day.

3. The attached sunspace/greenhouse is a combination of direct and indirect gain heating methods. Illustrated in Figure 3, this is simply an indirect gain system with a lot of space between the storage mass wall and the glass. The sunny space can be used for a greenhouse, for additional living space, or simply to provide heat to the main portion of the house.

INSULATION IS IMPORTANT

All walls, foundations, and ceilings or roofs must be insulated. Use of caulking around doors, windows, and foundation is necessary. High quality, weatherstripped and insulated doors and windows should be used. Since doors and windows account for the greatest amount of heat loss from a home, storm doors and windows should be added.

VENTILATION IS IMPORTANT

A passive solar home is usually very "tight." This means that all cracks and potential air leaks have been plugged with caulking, weatherstripping, or insulation. With tight construction, it becomes necessary to provide controlled ventilation in the winter in order to bring in fresh air. Also, in a passive solar home, properly designed ventilation will greatly reduce summer cooling requirements.

OVERHEATING COULD BE A PROBLEM

It is possible that during the winter, passive solar homes, using direct gain systems, might experience mid-day overheating. This problem is caused by using either too large a glass collection area or an insufficient amount of thermal storage mass. It is important that the thermal storage mass be placed in a location where it will be struck by the sun's radiant energy. Covering up thermal mass with carpet is sure to cause overheating.

ACTIVE SOLAR HEATING SYSTEMS

Active solar heating systems are very different from passive systems. Passive systems depend upon natural radiation and convection to distribute the solar heat. Active systems depend on several mechanisms or parts to move and distribute the heat. And, whereas passive structures are usually part of the architecture of the building, active systems are separate from the supporting structure of the building.

PARTS OF AN ACTIVE SOLAR SYSTEM

The active solar energy heating system is designed to do the following:

1. Collect and trap solar rays.
2. Pick up heat from the collector and move it to where it can be used.
3. Store heat for later use when the sun is not shining.

The various mechanisms which provide all these functions include solar collectors, piping or ductwork, fans, pumps, motors, heat exchangers, and storage bins or storage tanks. See Figs.

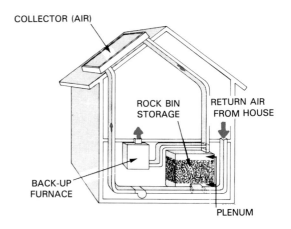

Diagram of an active solar collector using air to transfer heat. (HUD)

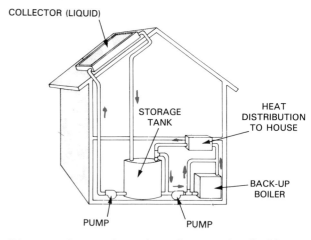

Diagram of an active solar collector using liquid to transfer heat.

APPENDIX H

RESIDENTIAL ENERGY AUDIT FORM
(PROJECT RETROTECH)

Description of Building

Sketch all views and put dimensions on each part shown, for example, length of walls, width and length of windows, etc. Label all single glass windows S and double glass and doors D. Complete all items in the job book labeled "Fill in at Job Site."

FILL IN AT JOB SITE

These grids are provided as guides for lines. Drawings need not be done to scale.

Front View

Left Side View

Plan View

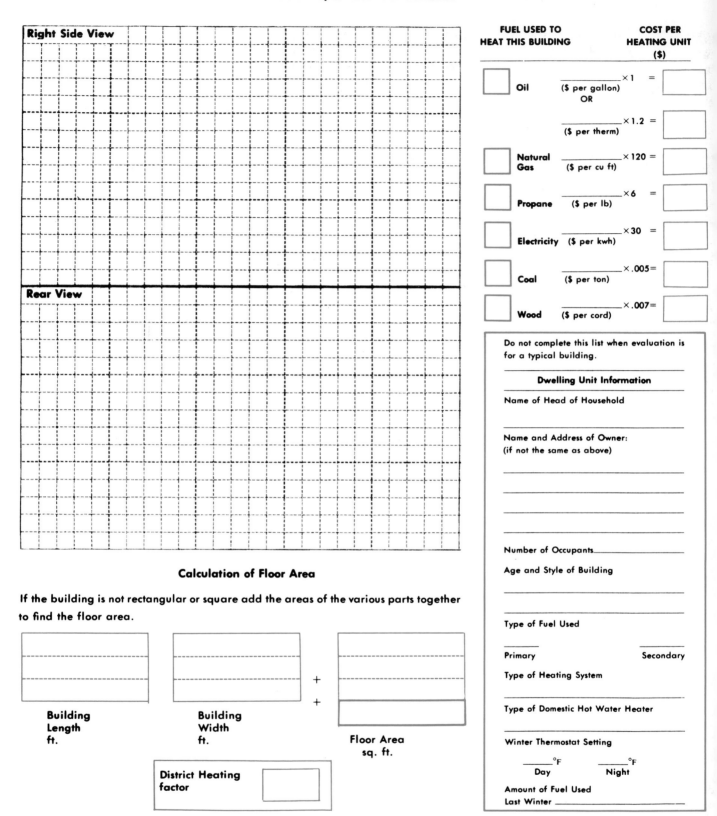

Right Side View

Rear View

Calculation of Floor Area

If the building is not rectangular or square add the areas of the various parts together to find the floor area.

Building Length ft.

Building Width ft.

+

+

Floor Area sq. ft.

District Heating factor

FUEL USED TO HEAT THIS BUILDING		COST PER HEATING UNIT ($)
Oil	_____ ×1 = ($ per gallon)	
	OR	
	_____ ×1.2 = ($ per therm)	
Natural Gas	_____ ×120 = ($ per cu ft)	
Propane	_____ ×6 = ($ per lb)	
Electricity	_____ ×30 = ($ per kwh)	
Coal	_____ ×.005 = ($ per ton)	
Wood	_____ ×.007 = ($ per cord)	

Do not complete this list when evaluation is for a typical building.

Dwelling Unit Information

Name of Head of Household

Name and Address of Owner:
(if not the same as above)

Number of Occupants _____

Age and Style of Building

Type of Fuel Used

Primary   Secondary

Type of Heating System

Type of Domestic Hot Water Heater

Winter Thermostat Setting

_____°F   _____°F
Day   Night

Amount of Fuel Used
Last Winter _____

Heat Losses by Conduction Through Ceilings

Area of Ceiling
(Take area of upstairs ceiling in a two-story house)

Ceiling area will normally be the same as floor area (from building description sheet)

Always include the materials in the roof deck in addition to the materials in the actual ceiling, as even if the attic is ventilated the roof deck adds some protection. Include the attic as an air space with R = .91.

Material	Thickness (inches)	R Value
inside surface	—	0.68
Outside Surface	–	0.17
Total R value		

FILL IN AT JOB SITE

If the Job Book is for a sample house complete both sections 1 and 2 below. For a specific house complete the section which describes the actual ceiling.

(1) Heat losses through uninsulated ceilings

If the Job Book is being completed for a sample house it is necessary to determine the potential heat savings for those examples **without** insulation. If the sample house has some insulation, subtract its R value from the total above and calculate the heating units required without insulation as below.

[ ] × [ ] ÷ [ ] = [ ]

Ceiling area sq. ft. District heating factor Total R value Heating units required

(2) Heat losses through partially insulated ceilings

If ceilings are partially insulated, e.g. to no more than R-10, further savings can be made by adding insulation. However, the primary savings have already been made and the investment in **extra** insulation may not be as worthwhile as some other measures. Evaluate the savings by the calculations below, using R=10 for a sample building or actual R value for an individual case to determine what priority should be assigned to this measure.

[ ] × [ ] ÷ [ ] = [ ]

Ceiling area sq. ft. District heating factor Total R value Heating units required

(Use R=10 for sample houses)

The appropriate amount of insulation for a ceiling depends on climate, fuel prices and insulation costs. Check the current DOE recommendation on maximum appropriate R value for your area. This indicates the maximum amount of insulation which will be cost effective for your climate. Any less amount of insulation than this will **save less total fuel** but will **save more per dollar spent.**

[ ] × [ ] ÷ [ ] = [ ]

Ceiling area sq. ft. District heating factor Appropriate R value Potential heating units

Subtract the potential heating units from those now required for uninsulated or partially uninsulated ceilings and enter here:

Potential savings

1. | Conduction through Uninsulated ceilings | |

Potential savings

2. | Conduction through Partially insulated ceilings | |

Heat Losses by Conduction Through Floors

Do not complete this page for concrete slab floors. Heat loss due to them is usually small but cannot be evaluated by this method.

Floor Exposure Factor

Select the appropriate factor from the descriptions below:

Building on posts or pillars with no perimeter protection	1.0
Building on posts or rocks with some protection against wind blowing under building	.8
Tight skirt or foundation wall around perimeter	.5
Tight foundation wall with equivalent of R4 or better insulation on inside or outside of wall	.3

R value of floor

A typical uninsulated, uncarpeted wood floor will have an R value of about 3. Carpet and pad will increase the R value to 5.

FILL IN AT JOB SITE

Potential Savings on Heat Loss through Floors

	×		×		÷		=	
Floor area (from building description) sq ft		Floor exposure factor		District heating factor		Floor R value from above		Heating Units Required

1. Reducing below floor drafts

Unless vigorous underfloor ventilation is needed to remove moisture rising from the ground, a floor should be protected from drafts, so that it has a floor exposure factor of only 0.5. If the floor in this building has an exposure factor over 0.5., cutting out drafts below the floor could reduce the heat loss to:

		0.5	×		÷		=	
Floor area from above sq. ft.		Floor exposure factor		District heating factor		Floor R value from above		Potential heating units

2. Adding Insulation

EITHER (a) The perimeter wall of the crawl space or basement can be insulated (with R=4 or better) down to grade level or just below, to cut both drafts and conduction losses, reducing the floor exposure factor to 0.3. The heat loss with an insulated perimeter would be approximately:

	×	0.3	×		÷		=	
Floor area from above sq. ft.		Floor exposure factor		District heating factor		Floor R value from above		Potential heating units

OR (b) Where perimeter walls cannot be insulated because the insulation would become wet (if water seeps through the basement walls or if water rises above the level of the insulation or if underfloor ventilation is needed) the whole floor may be insulated instead of the perimeter. This is usually more expensive than perimeter insulation but can give extra savings. Insulating this floor with a minimum of 3½" fiberglass between the joists will increase the R value to 15. More insulation will increase the R value further still. The potential heating units will be:

	×		×		÷		=	
Floor area from above sq. ft.		Floor exposure factor (Use 0.5 if drafts can be eliminated. 0.8 if underfloor ventilation is needed)		District heating factor		Floor R value (minimum of 15		Potential heating units with whole floor insulation

Subtract the potential heating units for any of the three possible floor treatments which are feasible from the heating units now required and enter in the boxes below.

1	2a	2b
Potential heating savings by reducing drafts	Potential heating savings by perimeter insulation	Potential heating savings by whole floor insulation

Heat Losses by Conduction Through Uninsulated Walls

(Partially insulated frame walls cannot normally be further insulated.)

R Value of Outside Walls

Uninsulated frame walls usually have a total **R value around 3.0** no matter what type of interior finish or siding treatment is present. If the wall is of different construction list all materials in the wall in the table at right, starting from inside and including air spaces within the wall. Insert R value for each component from Table 1.

FILL IN AT JOB SITE

Material	Thickness (inches)	R Value
Interior surface	–	0.68
Outside surface	–	0.17
Total R value		

$$\boxed{} \times \boxed{} = \boxed{}$$

Total perimeter of outside wall ft.	Total height of outside wall ft.	Gross wall area sq. ft.

$$\boxed{} - \boxed{} = \boxed{}$$

Gross wall area sq. ft.	Total area of all windows and doors from sketches on pages 2 and 3	Net wall area sq. ft.

$$\boxed{} \times \boxed{} \div \boxed{} = \boxed{}$$

Net wall area	District heating factor	**Total R Value**	**Heating units required**

Potential Savings by Insulation

Fully insulated frame walls should have an R value of 15. If this were so for this building, the wall heat loss would be:

$$\boxed{} \times \boxed{} \div \boxed{15} = \boxed{}$$

New wall area (from box above)	District heating factor	R value	Potential heating units

Subtract the potential heating units from those now required and enter here ⟶

Potential Heating Savings

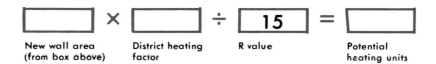

Type of Heat Loss	Potential Heating Savings
Conduction Through Uninsulated Walls	

Heat Losses by Conduction and Infiltration Through Single-Glass Windows

Area of Single Glass Windows:
(Assuming R = 1 for single glass)

Width	×	Height	×	Number	=	Area

Total sq. ft.

If this Job Book covers a **sample house** determine the potential heat savings for **single glass.**

$$\boxed{} \times \boxed{} = \boxed{}$$

Total sq. ft.   **District heating factor**   **Heating units required**

Potential Saving by Adding Storm Windows

Adding storm windows will cut the conduction heat loss by half and will probably save half again by reducing infiltration. i.e. cut heat loss to 25%. Calculate the potential heating units below.

$$\boxed{} \times .25 = \boxed{}$$

Heating units now required with single glass

Potential Heating Units

Subtract the potential heating units from those now required and enter here

Potential Heating Savings

Type of Heat Loss	
Conduction and Infiltration Through Single Glass Windows	

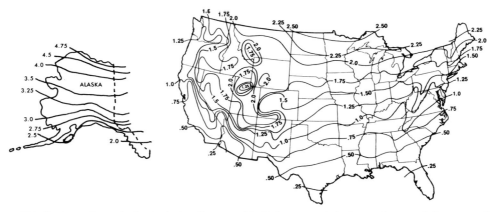

Table 1: Insulation Value of Common Materials

This list is not intended to include all types of building materials, but only materials commonly used in residences. If necessary, select the material most similar, and the resulting values will not substantially affect the calculation.

MATERIAL	THICKNESS (Inches)	R VALUE
Air Film and Spaces:		
Air space, bounded by ordinary materials	¾ or more	.91
Air space, bounded by aluminum foil	¾ or more	2.17
Exterior surface resistance	—	.17
Interior surface resistance	—	.68
Masonry:		
Sand and gravel concrete block	8	1.11
	12	1.28
Lightweight concrete block	8	2.00
	12	2.13
Face brick	4	.44
Concrete cast in place	8	.64
Building Materials — General:		
Wood sheathing or subfloor	¾	1.00
Fiber board insulating sheathing	¾	2.10
Plywood	⅝	.79
	½	.63
	⅜	.47
Bevel-lapped siding	½ × 8	.81
	¾ × 10	1.05
Vertical tongue and groove board	¾	1.00
Drop siding	¾	.94
Asbestos board	¼	.13
⅜" gypsum lath and ⅜" plaster	¾	.42
Gypsum board (sheet rock)	⅜	.32
Interior plywood panel	¼	.31
Building paper	—	.06
Vapor barrier	—	.00
Wood shingles	—	.87
Asphalt shingles	—	.44
Linoleum	—	.08
Carpet with fiber pad	—	2.08
Hardwood floor	—	.71
Insulation Materials (mineral wool, glass wool, wood wool):		
Blanket or batts	1	3.70
	3½	11.00
	6	19.00
Loose fill	1	3.33
Rigid insulation board (sheathing)	¾	2.10
Windows and Doors:		
Single window	—	approx. 1.00
Double window	—	approx. 2.00
Exterior door	—	approx. 2.00

Summary Table for Priority Rating of Weatherization Measures

Fill out the Summary Table at the right by entering the fuel cost per Heating unit from p. 3 in Column 4, and the Potential Heating Savings from pp. 4-8 in Column 5. Enter the estimated material cost for the required changes in Column 1, the appropriate Installation factor in Column 2 and the expected life of each Weatherization measure in Column 4. From these figures determine the Total Cost and Lifetime Savings from each measure, and then in Column 8 calculate the Benefit : Cost Ratio. Finally, in column 9, rank the weatherization measures in order of cost effectiveness.

Source of Heat Loss	Weatherization Measure Required to Minimize Heat Loss	Unit Cost of Material ($/ft²)	Quantity of Material (sq. ft.)	1 Total Material Cost Unit Cost ×Quantity) ($)
General Waste of Heat	See separate Job Order Sheet	—	—	—
Uninsulated Ceilings (from p. 4)	Insulate to Local Standard of R =			
Partially Insulated Ceilings (from p. 4)	Insulate to Local Standard of R =			
Exposed Floors (from block 1 page 5)	Reduce Exposure factor to 0.5			
*Uninsulated Perimeter (from block 2a page 5)	Insulate perimeter with R=4 or better			
*Uninsulated floors (from block 2b page 5)	Insulate floor with R=11 or better			
Uninsulated Walls (from p. 6)	Insulate Wall to R=15			
Single Glass Windows (from p. 7)	Add Glass Storm Windows			
	Other:			

*Only one of these alternate measures is usually applied to a specific building. See Weatherization Manual for details.

Recommended Weatherization Priority List

Enter the various sources of heat loss and appropriate weatherization measures from the Summary Table above in priority order in the list at right. This is the order of importance of weatherization measures in a building of the type examined regardless of size or age. A copy of this list should be included in the local Building Check and Job Order Sheet for this type of building.

2 Labor Cost to Install (If appropriate)	3 Total Cost (Col 1 + Col 2) ($)	4 Expected Life of Weatherization Measure (years) OR Expected Life of Bldg., which-ever is least	5 Potential Heat Savings from bottom of pages 4-8 (Heating Units/ year)	6 Fuel Cost per Heating Unit (from page 3) ($/HU)	7 Lifetime Savings due to Weatherization Measure (Col 4 × Col 5 × Col 6) ($)	8 Benefit: Cost Ratio (Col 7 ÷ Col 3)	9 Order of Cost Effec-tive-ness
—	Usually Small	—	Usually Substantial	—	—	Usually Favorable	1

RECOMMENDED WEATHERIZATION PRIORITY LIST

for _____ in _____ by Job Book Reference No. _____
(building/type)   area/address

Priority	Source of Heat Loss	Weatherization Measure Required	Approximate Allowable Unit Cost of Materials	If list is for a Typical Building check if item is included on Job Order Sheet or note reason for omission
1	General Heat Waste	See Job Sheet	—	
2				
3				
4				
5				
6				
7				
8				
9				

FRACTIONAL AND DECIMAL EQUIVALENTS

$\frac{1}{64}$	.015625
$\frac{1}{32}$	.03125
$\frac{3}{64}$	.046875
$\frac{1}{16}$	.0625
$\frac{5}{64}$	.078125
$\frac{3}{32}$	.09375
$\frac{7}{64}$	.109375
⅛	.125
$\frac{9}{64}$	.140625
$\frac{5}{32}$	.15625
$\frac{11}{64}$	.171875
$\frac{3}{16}$	.1875
$\frac{13}{64}$	.203125
$\frac{7}{32}$	.21875
$\frac{15}{64}$	.234375
¼	.25
$\frac{17}{64}$	.265625
$\frac{9}{32}$	.28125
$\frac{19}{64}$	.296875
$\frac{5}{16}$	.3125
$\frac{21}{64}$	.328125
$\frac{11}{32}$	.34375
$\frac{23}{64}$	.359375
⅜	.375
$\frac{25}{64}$	.390625
$\frac{13}{32}$	.40625
$\frac{27}{64}$	.421875
$\frac{7}{16}$	.4375
$\frac{29}{64}$	.453125
$\frac{15}{32}$	.46875
$\frac{31}{64}$	.484375
½	.5

$\frac{33}{64}$	.515625
$\frac{17}{32}$	.53125
$\frac{35}{64}$	.546875
$\frac{9}{16}$	.5625
$\frac{37}{64}$	.578125
$\frac{19}{32}$	.59375
$\frac{39}{64}$	.609375
⅝	.625
$\frac{41}{64}$	.640625
$\frac{21}{32}$	.65625
$\frac{43}{64}$	.671875
$\frac{11}{16}$	.6875
$\frac{45}{64}$	.703125
$\frac{23}{32}$	.71875
$\frac{47}{64}$	.734375
¾	.75
$\frac{49}{64}$	.765625
$\frac{25}{32}$	.78125
$\frac{51}{64}$	.796875
$\frac{13}{16}$	.8125
$\frac{53}{64}$	.828125
$\frac{27}{32}$	.84375
$\frac{55}{64}$	.859375
⅞	.875
$\frac{57}{64}$	.890625
$\frac{29}{32}$	.90625
$\frac{59}{64}$	.921875
$\frac{15}{16}$	.9375
$\frac{61}{64}$	.953125
$\frac{31}{32}$	.96875
$\frac{63}{64}$	.984375
1	1.

Recreation Pavilion Plan 116

This is a perfect ongoing summer project for those who want outdoor elegance and a chance to move special occasions outdoors.

With various options and additions you will find this idea attractive and versatile.

First, set out foundation and grade beams on *level* 26' square as shown in drawing. Set support posts on footings to correct height and place beams for upper deck. When level, apply 2x8 diagonal decking to beams of upper deck. Finish exposed edge with 2x8 fascia. Apply diagonal decking to lower deck in the opposite direction.

Now you are ready to begin the pavilion frame. Start by placing 4x4 uprights and temporarily brace to floor. Fasten all uprights to deck with

metal brackets as shown in drawing. Now place 4x6 side beams on top of uprights and securely bolt as indicated.

Keeping temporary bracing in place, lift ridge beam into place and bolt securely to upright and corner as indicated. (You will need help with this.) With ledgers in place set double 2x6 rafters and toenail securely. Continue with other rafters and 2x2 sunscreen. Once roof framing is nailed securely, remove temporary bracing and finish pavilion with lath work as shown in drawing.

Fabricate steps and brace well to 4x4 blocking on lower deck. Options from here on are icing on the cake.

For corner seating arrangement, laminate

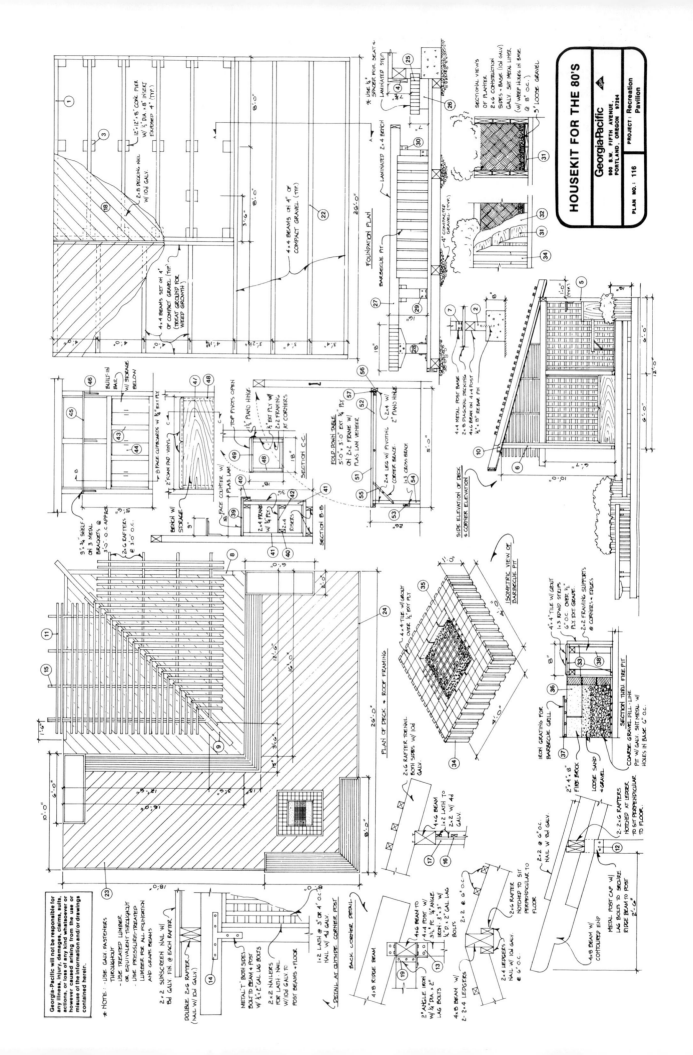

2x4s as indicated with waterproof glue and galvanized nails. Assemble cross braces and 4x4 supports and bolt to deck as indicated. Securely toenail 2x4 seating to cross braces and finish with fascia.

One finishing touch that adds warmth and comfort to your new outdoor environment is our tiled barbecue pit.

Fabricate double line box as shown in detail and cover top with 4x4 tiles of your choice. Line base with sheet metal and sides of the box with fire brick. Fill the pit with coarse gravel and sand to within 4" of top.

The tilt-down table adds a functional touch to your recreation pavilion. It consists of a simple 3/4" piece of plywood in a 2x2 frame with 2x4 legs and metal pivoting cross brace. Cover table and edges with plastic veneer.

The built-in bar/storage bench and planters are easily completed by following the simple details in the drawing.

Materials List

Part	Description	Quantity Required
1	4×6 beams: approx. 16'	8
2	4×4 posts: approx. 6" (foundations)	19
3	12×12×8 concrete piers (+8" rebar inset)	19
4	2×8 facing: approx. 16'	2
5	4×4 posts: 6'7" (roof support)	5
6	4×4 posts: 10' (roof support)	1
7	metal post base (for 4×4s)	6
8	4×6 roof beams: 15'	2
9	4×8 ridge beam: 22'6" (or 2 2×8s glued & nailed)	1
10	2×4 ledgers: 17'	2
11	2×2 sunscreen	282 lin. ft. (approx.)
12	metal H bracket (for 4×4 post)	1
13	4"×4"×¼" angle iron (with 2⁹/₁₆" dia. holes both flanges)	2
14	metal T bracket (6 holes predrilled ⁹/₁₆" dia.)	8
15	2×6 rafters	86 lin. ft.
16	1×2 lath: approx. 6'	104
17	2×2 nailers: approx. 6'	16
18	2×8 diagonal decking	256 sq. ft.
19	2×2 angle iron: 5½"	1
22	4×4 pressure-treated lumber grade beams	166 lin. ft.
23	2×8 diagonal decking	420 sq. ft.
24	2×6 fascia	52 lin. ft.
25	2×4 (laminated steps)	280 lin. ft. (+ ¼" spacers)
26	4×4 blocking (stairs)	20 lin. ft.
27	2×4 (laminated seating)	160 lin. ft. (+ ¼" spacers)
28	4×4: approx. 14" (seat supports)	4
29	3½" 4×4 angle brackets + lag bolts (4 per bracket)	8
30	2"×6"×18" cross supports (seats)	8

Part	Description	Quantity Required
31	2×6 pressure-treated lumber	136 lin. ft.
32	6 mil polyethylene liner or equivalent (planters)	100 sq. ft. (approx.)
33	½" exterior grade plywood: 4'×8'	2
34	1×3 redwood strips	128 lin. ft.
35	4×4 tile (+ grout)	80 (approx.)
36	2"×4"×8" fire brick	48 (approx.)
37	32"×16" iron grill	1
38	2×2 framing (barbecue pit)	28 lin. ft. (approx.)
39	½" exterior grade plywood: 18"×6'	1
40	2×4 cross framing: approx. 6' (bar)	6
41	2×4 framing (bar)	24 lin. ft.
42	½" plywood: approx. 15"×6' (shelving)	2
43	½" plywood: 2"×29" & 4"×29"	2 each
44	½" plywood: 10"×29" (doors & hardware)	6
45	¾" plywood: 9"×6' (shelf)	1
46	8"×8" brackets—angle supports (shelf)	3
47	½" exterior grade plywood: 4'×8' (storage seat)	2 (approx.)
48	2×2 framing (storage seat)	21 lin. ft.
49	2" foam: 18"×3' (seats)	2
50	1½" piano hinge	6 ft.
51	¾" plywood: 3'×58½" (table top)	1
52	2×2 framing	16 lin. ft.
53	1×3 cross bracing: 3'	1
54	2×4 logo: 26½"	2
55	metal pivoting corner braces	2
56	2×4 ledger: 3'	1
57	2" piano hinge: 3'	1
58	3'×58½" plastic veneer	1
59	2¼"×13' plastic trim	1

Note: Use pressure-treated lumber and plywood designated for exterior use throughout.

Chair/Hassock Plan 115

There's no need to feel that furniture making is beyond the average person's capabilities. Here is a simple, enjoyable project to prove it.

For outdoor use select a good grade of lumber, plywood designated for exterior use, and waterproof, washable vinyl fabric or equivalent.

Begin this project by cutting structural members to exact size, making sure that all cuts are perfectly square. Join 2x10 base pieces to uprights. Locate position for hardwood dowels in 2x10, then drill and set dowels with waterproof glue. Hole size should be such that dowels need only to be tapped in *lightly* with a mallet. Hardwood dowels 5/16" in diameter by 2" in length should do nicely.

Once dowels are set in 2x10, locate position for dowels on edge of upright for arm support. Drill holes and set dowels again with glue. Clamp joint and allow to set.

For 2x10 to 2x10 joint at back lower corner, use 1/2" diameter by 3" lag bolts. Locate position for predrilled holes on 2x10 side piece. Drill 1/2" diameter hole and countersink 1" diameter to a depth of 3/8". When holes are drilled in the side pieces, locate position in the end grain of back 2x10. Drill 3/8" holes in end grain to a depth of 1-1/2". Now bolt together with lag bolts and washers; joint may be glued for extra strength. Proceed with other dowel joints in a similar fashion to that first

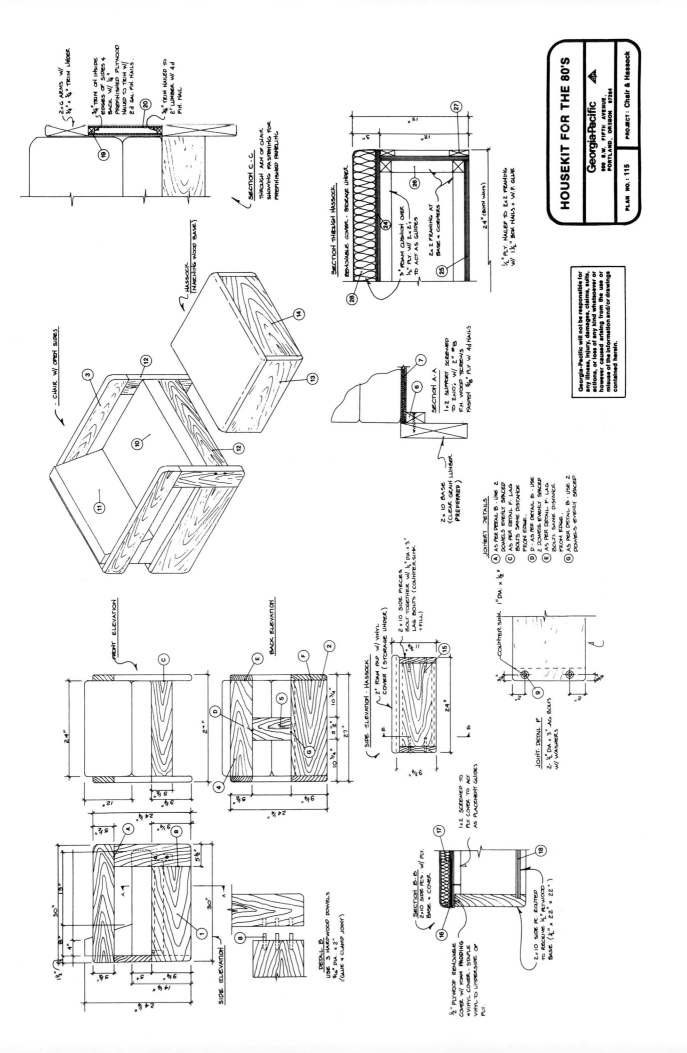

HOUSEKIT FOR THE 80'S

Georgia-Pacific

900 S.W. FIFTH AVENUE,
PORTLAND, OREGON 97204

PLAN NO.: 115

PROJECT: Chair & Hassock

Georgia-Pacific will not be responsible for any illness, injury, damage, claims, suits, actions, or loss of any kind whatsoever or however caused arising from the use or misuse of the information and/or drawings contained herein.

described. Start with front cross piece, back vertical support, back rest, and finally the arms. When all joints are assembled, glued, and set, you are ready to attach support members for plywood base. For this, cut 1x2s to appropriate lengths and fasten inside to 2x10 base and front piece recessed to a depth of 5/8".

Fasten 1x2 with 2-1/2" #8 woodscrews, using predrilled pilot holes. Set screws 4" o.c. With 1x2 supports in place, cut and set 5/8" plywood seats. Nail into place with 2" finishing nails.

Foam may be purchased in standard sizes and covered with fabric.

The hassock is assembled with joints similar to those already described. Pad and cover hassock as indicated, choosing fabric matched to your chair cushions. Chair and hassock may be stained and finished as desired.

Materials List

Part	Description	Quantity Required
Open Sides Chair		
1	2×10 lumber: 24½" (base)	2
2	2×10 lumber: 24" (base)	1
3	2×6 lumber: 30" (arms)	2
4	2×6 lumber: 24" (back)	1
5	2×6 lumber: 9½" (back support)	1
6	1×2 lumber (seat support)	9 lin. ft.
7	⅝" plywood: 24"×24" (seat)	1
8	5/16" dia. × 2" wood dowel	14
9	½" dia. × 3" lag bolts	12
10	5" foam pad: 24"×24" (seat)	1
11	24"×8"×12" foam bolster (back-sloped)	1
12	2×6 lumber (front arm supports & face)	approx. 6'
Hassock		
13	2×10 lumber: 24"	2
14	2×10 lumber: 21"	2
15	½" dia. × 3" lag bolts	8
16	½" plywood: 24"×24"	1
17	2" foam pad: 24"×24"	1
18	½" plywood: 22"×22"	1

Garden Window Plan 114

Here is a project that gives more light to any room and allows the plant fancier to enjoy a lovely garden from the comfort of indoors.

Start by choosing an appropriate wall location, avoiding northern exposure. Living room, kitchen, dining room — it's up to you.

Mark out a rough opening through the wall 6' wide by 6'8" high. For a load-bearing wall, check with an architect or engineer to ensure that the header is of sufficient size. When sizing your opening, be sure to allow enough room to install header and side supports.

This step will also allow you the option of a sliding glass door. (Check manufacturer's data to be sure.)

It will be best to avoid cutting your opening until exterior framing is complete and just before you are ready to set your glazing.

Start by positioning a 4" slab on the outside of wall and pour with anchor bolts inset as indicated. After concrete is sufficiently set, you can begin the framework for your garden window. Remove exterior siding to outer edge of garden window frame, marking its location. Place the base plate and bolt it securely to slab. Be sure to cut grooves for weepholes on the bottom of base plate. (Pressure-treated lumber for the base plate is essential.) Next, bolt double 2x4 ledger to header at appropriate height. Begin carefully fitting 2x4 framing with re-

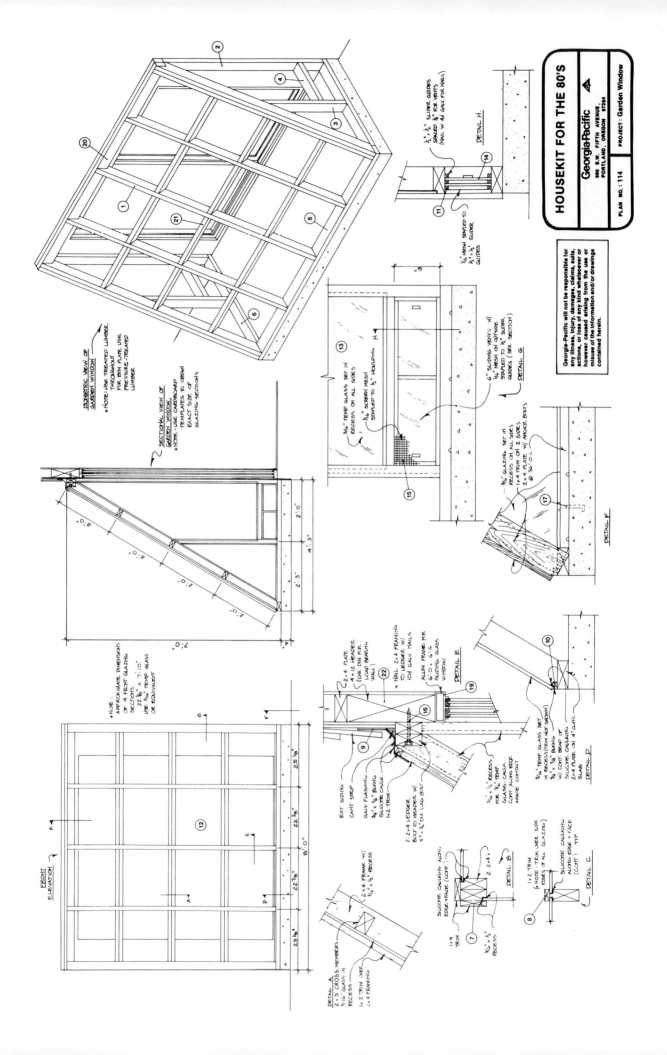

HOUSEKIT FOR THE 80'S

Georgia-Pacific
900 S.W. FIFTH AVENUE
PORTLAND, OREGON 97204

PROJECT: Garden Window

PLAN NO: 114

cessed edges as shown in drawing. When the main 2x4 frame members are properly cut and positioned parallel to one another, nail securely to base plate and ledger.

Proceed with secondary framing on sides, with exception of the headers above side vents. Before this header can be placed, you must install moulding for sliding glass vents. When this is completed, place header in position and nail securely to 2x4 studs.

With framing complete, securely support ceiling above wall opening and cut through wall at marked-out location.

You are now ready to begin the installation of the glazing. Four major strips of 3/16" tempered glass and four custom side pieces of the same material are all that is required. For each separate piece, make a cardboard template that you are confident will comfortably fit into position between the recesses that you have cut in your framing members. When you have eight templates, take them to your local glass store and request your materials.

To set the glazing, use silicone caulking at all edges as indicated and cover the edges with trim as shown in details.

With all glass and trim in place, set and nail galvanized flashing under exterior sheathing, extending the flashing out over the front of the garden window as indicated. Again caulk seam under flashing. You may paint, stain, or finish framing and trim as desired.

With a little care and precision, you should find this project a rewarding and attractive addition to any room. Remember that optional sliding glass door will give you added thermal control of your green space in areas with excessive heating and cooling seasons.

Materials List

Part	Description	Quantity Required
1	2×4 lumber: approx. 8' (main framing)	7
2	2×4 lumber: approx. 7' (side studs)	2
3	2×4 lumber: approx. 4' (stud)	2
4	2×4 lumber: 2' (vent header)	2
5	2×4 pressure-treated lumber: 8' (base plate)	2
6	2×4 pressure-treated lumber: approx. 4' (base plate)	2
7	1×4 lumber trim: approx. 8'	4
8	1×2 lumber trim: approx. 8'	5
9	8"×8' galvanized flashing	1
10	¾" blocking	16 lin. ft. (approx.)
11	½" blocking	12 lin. ft. (approx.)
12	3/16" tempered glass: 22⅜"×7'10" (glazing)	4 (check with template)
13	side pieces (glazing cut from template—see drawing)	4

Part	Description	Quantity Required
14	3/16" glazing: 6"×10½" (sliding vents)	4
15	1/16" mesh	2 sq. ft. (approx.)
16	½" dia.×5" lag bolts	4
17	½" dia.×5" anchor bolts	6
18	silicone caulking	enough for 120 lin. ft. of bead (approx.)
19	6'×6'6" aluminum sliding glass door (optional)	1
20	8'×2"×4" ledger	2
21	2"×3"×2' (approx.) (cross bracing)	12
22	4×12: approx. 8' (header)	1

Note: Refer to drawing for pressure-treated lumber requirements. All exposed parts should be painted or stained.

Outdoor Deck Plan 113

Ever feel your backyard isn't providing the enjoyment it should? Here is a project ideally suited for people ready to take that next step in backyard living.

This attractive split-level deck allows you to begin the work in your garage, proceeding at your own leisure with fabrication of modular wooden floor panels.

As a general policy use pressure-treated lumber throughout, including all foundation supports and any member that comes in contact with cement or ground.

For level backyards measure the distance from the finished floor line to level ground (see section BB). Then calculate the height of support columns so that the level deck will take you to ground level with four or more steps, a maximum of 7-1/2″ each. This deck is well-suited to houses with a 30″ or more drop from floor to ground level.

Once deck-to-ground height has been established, you may fabricate 27 4x4 panels (see detail 8 & 9) consisting of 2x6s nailed to 2x4 runners. Once all panels are completed, it is time to begin the foundation work.

On level compacted ground set concrete piers according to foundation plan layout, making sure all organic material is removed from the area. Once piers are in place and level, it is time to cut and place the 6x6 column supports.

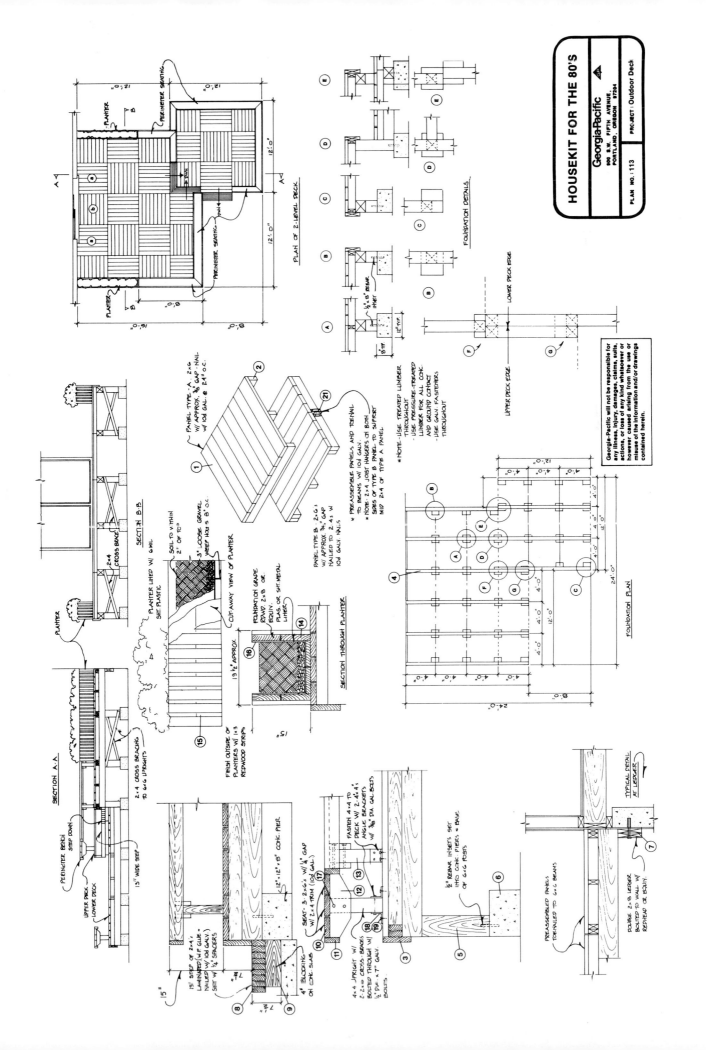

HOUSEKIT FOR THE 80'S

Georgia-Pacific
900 S.W. FIFTH AVENUE,
PORTLAND, OREGON 97204

PROJECT: Outdoor Deck

PLAN NO.: 113

PLAN OF 2-LEVEL DECK

FOUNDATION DETAILS

FOUNDATION PLAN

SECTION B-B

SECTION A-A

SECTION THROUGH PLANTER.

CUT-AWAY VIEW OF PLANTER

TYPICAL DETAIL AT LEDGER.

Start with outside edge of upper deck and proceed back toward the house. Cut columns to appropriate height and bore base for 1/2" rebar (see pier detail), making sure the tops of all columns come out level. After the last row of columns, install ledger as shown in detail.

Now cut 6x6 beams and set them on top of the columns; securely toenail 6x6s to columns. Secure cross bracing as in section BB and then proceed in a similar fashion with foundation for the lower deck.

With this work done, begin to lay your prefabricated floor panels. Note the two types of panels, A & B. Set B panels so that double 2x4s span between 6x6 beams. Panels are placed in basketweave pattern and securely toenailed to 6x6 beams.

Once floor is completed, apply 2x8 fascia around all edges as shown in drawing. Now proceed with the steps. The steps are formed by laminating 2x4s face to face with waterproof glue, nailing at 6" o.c. Set on 4x4 risers and toenail to steps and deck.

Seating is formed with 2x6s nailed to beveled 2x8 blocks bolted securely to 4x4 uprights (see detail). Proceed as shown in drawing, bolting seat to deck with 4" angle iron.

Planters add an attractive finishing touch to the deck and eliminate the need for railing. Be sure to choose pressure-treated 2x8s or equivalent for planters, and line as indicated to protect from soil.

Materials List

Part	Description	Quantity Required
1	2×6 lumber: 4' (A & B panels)	216
2	2×4 lumber: 4' (A & B panels)	117
3	2×8 fascia	88 lin. ft. (approx.)
4	6×6 lumber beams	136 lin. ft. (approx.)
5	6×6 lumber supports (calculate according to slope and level of ground)	varies
6	12×12×8 concrete piers (+ ½"×8" rebar insets)	35
7	2×8 ledger (or equivalent)	24 lin. ft.
8	2×4 lumber (steps)	108 lin. ft. (+ ¼" spacers)
9	4×4 lumber blocking	12 lin. ft.
10	2×6 lumber (seat)	84 lin. ft.
11	2×4 trim lumber	56 lin. ft.
12	2×8 cross brace (seat supports)	20 lin. ft.
13	4×4 support post (seat)	10 lin. ft.
14	2×8 pressure-treated lumber (planter)	108 lin. ft. (approx.)
15	1×3 redwood strips (planter)	324 lin. ft. (approx.)
16	planter liner (galvanized sheet metal or 6 mil plastic sheet)	68 sq. ft. (approx.)
17	½" dia. × 7" galvanized hex head bolts	10
18	4"×4"×¼" angle irons (seat)	10
19	⅜" dia. × 2" galvanized lag bolts	40
20	10d & 6d galvanized nails	varies
21	2×4 metal joist hangers (floor panels)	26

Note: Refer to drawing for pressure-treated lumber requirements.

Patio Cart Plan 112

Here is a functional addition to your backyard living environment. Its well-designed compartment layout and complete mobility offer the type of convenience you will enjoy for outdoor living.

For this project select a good grade of lumber and exterior grade plywood; the finish is up to you. Start with your plywood sides (part 1). When cut to size, lay out position of 2x3 slider supports and 2x3 base frame. Fasten plywood to face of 2x3s with 6d nails and waterproof glue. Position 1x2 shelf supports and join in a similar fashion.

Now is the time to cut your back pieces. Brace main side members in correct position and fasten (parts 3 & 4) back pieces to side members

with wood screws into end grain of 2x3s. Waterproof glue is also a must. Join two main sides on the open front with 2x4 stops and 2x3 braces. For these joints use 2-1/2" woodscrews and, again, waterproof glue. If you have dimensioned properly, you can now place your fixed shelves and top piece. Glue and nail as indicated.

Next, fabricate your two swing-out shelving units. Set shelves, top piece, and base-nail and glue as indicated.

After fastening back piece to swing-out shelving unit, you can now hang these on your main component with a 1-1/2" continuous hinge as indicated. Remember to wet screws with glue to give the hinge added strength.

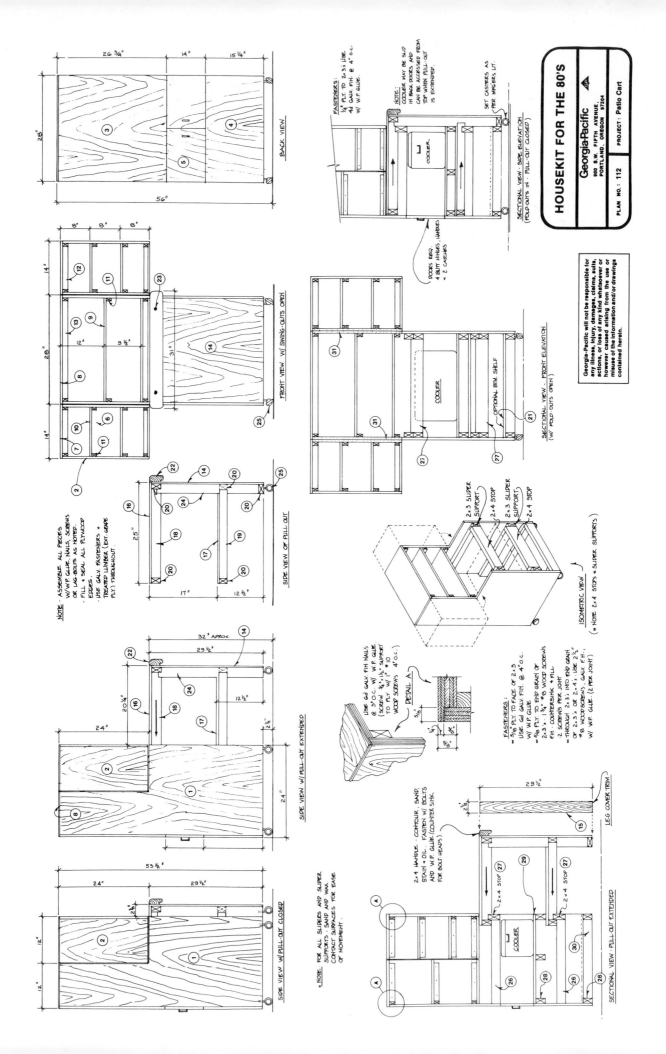

HOUSEKIT FOR THE 80'S

Georgia-Pacific
900 S.W. FIFTH AVENUE,
PORTLAND, OREGON 97204

PLAN NO.: 112   PROJECT: Patio Cart

With these in place, begin pull-out component. Start by cutting the plywood top and 2x3 framing members. Assemble top and shelf and join together with lags and cross members.

With all framing in place, fasten the plywood front piece and bolt the handle to front. At this point you may wish to apply plastic veneer of your choice to the pull-out countertop. Make sure you have allowed room for clearance underneath the swing-out shelving unit.

When your pull-out component is complete with all joints nailed and glued, lift the 2x3 back cross braces over the 2x4 stops and push the slide-out component into place. The best way to avoid sticking is by sanding and waxing the slider support.

You may wish to face the side edge of the leg of the pull-out with matching plywood to give your unit a finished look.

After setting the back doors with butt hinges, handles, and stops, you are now ready to finish your patio cart. Set the six Sheppard's casters as indicated, and for that final touch, stain and finish to taste. (Remember to fill all exposed plywood edges.)

After this one, you deserve a party—so invite the whole gang and show off your handiwork.

Materials List

Part	Description	Quantity Required
1	⅝" exterior grade plywood: 23⅜"×53"	2
2	⅝" exterior grade plywood: 11¾"×23¾"	4
3	⅝" exterior grade plywood: 28"×26½"	1
4	⅝" exterior grade plywood: 28"×15¼"	1
5	⅝" exterior grade plywood: 14"×14"	2
6	⅝" exterior grade plywood: 14"×23¾"	2
7	⅝" exterior grade plywood: 12"×14"	2
8	⅝" exterior grade plywood: 12"×28"	1
9	½" exterior grade plywood: 11⅜"×26¾"	2
10	½" exterior grade plywood: 12¾"×11¾"	6
11	11"×¾"×1½" #3 common lumber	22
12	11"×¾"×1½" #3 common lumber	4
13	25"×¾"×1½" #3 common lumber	1
14	¼" exterior grade plywood: 26¾"×29½"	1
15	⅝" exterior grade plywood: 2⅞"×29½"	1
16	⅝" exterior grade plywood: 25"×26¾"	1
17	⅝" exterior grade plywood: 21¾"×26¾"	1
18	21¾"×1½"×2⅝" #3 common lumber	2
19	21¾"×1½"×2⅝" #3 common lumber	2
20	26¾"×1½"×2⅝" #3 common lumber	5
21	⅝" exterior grade plywood: 26¾"×23⅜" (optional)	1
22	31"×1½"×3½" #1 common lumber	1
23	2½"×⅜" dia. lag bolts (galvanized + fill)	2
24	27⅝"×1½"×2⅝" #3 common lumber	2
25	Sheppard's casters (approx. 2½" height)	6
26	23⅜"×1½"×2⅝" #3 common lumber	2
27	23¾"×1½"×3½" #3 common lumber	2
28	23¾"×1½"×2⅝" #3 common lumber	5
29	⅝" exterior grade plywood: 26¾"×23⅜"	1
30	⅝" exterior grade plywood: 23⅜"×1½"	2
31	1¼"×24" piano hinge (+ screws)	2

Fasteners:

⅝" plywood to face of 2×3; use 6d galvanized finish nails 4" o.c. with waterproof glue

⅝" plywood to end grain of 2×3s; use 1¾" #8 wood screws; F.H. (countersink & fill, 2 screws per joint) through 2×3s into end grain of 2×3s or 2×4s; use 2½" #8 wood screws; galvanized F.H. with waterproof glue (2 per joint)

Note: All exposed parts should be painted or stained.

INDEX

Index